**A Stanley Gibbons
Thematic Catalogue**

COLLECT
SHIPS
ON STAMPS

Peter Bolton

Second Edition 1993

**Stanley Gibbons Ltd
London and Ringwood**

By Appointment to Her Majesty The Queen
Stanley Gibbons Ltd., London
Philatelists

Published by **Stanley Gibbons Publications**
Editorial, Sales Offices and Distribution Centre:
5 Parkside, Christchurch Road, Ringwood,
Hants BH24 3SH

Second Edition – December 1993

© Stanley Gibbons Ltd. 1993

ISBN: 0-85259-362-7

Item No. 2889 (93)

Printed in Great Britain by BPCC Wheatons, Exeter, Devon.

Down to the Sea in Ships

The geographers have calculated that over 70% of the Earth's surface is covered by water. In such a circumstance it is not surprising that the history of water transport mirrors that of mankind itself. Ships and boats have also played an important part in the development of national and international communications. It is certainly fitting that they should have been amongst the first objects to be shown on stamp designs once the formal portraits of the classic era had been abandoned.

Over the years many different sorts of craft have been shown on stamps, stretching from the pedalo to the *Queen Elizabeth 2* and from the Greek galley to the nuclear submarine. One of the attractions of collecting ships on stamps is to search for the identity of the vessel depicted. Three thousand different identified vessels are included in the 13,000 stamps listed in this new edition.

Peter Bolton and his helpers from the Ship Stamp Society have been very busy in the four and a half years since the first edition in assembling notes of errors, omissions and new listings to be included in this catalogue. In addition to the 2,000 plus new stamps included it has also been possible to improve the index section so that each of the 3,000 thousand odd entries for individually-named ships now contains a cross-reference to the ship type depicted . This is particularly useful for those names which, over the years, have been popular choices for sailors and ship owners. This feature is, of course, in addition to the second section of the index which provides entries by ship type under forty main headings.

Collecting ships and other watercraft on stamps has always been one of the most popular topics in the thematic field and it is hoped that this much-expanded second edition of *Collect Ships on Stamps* will persuade even more collectors to up anchor and put to sea!

David J. Aggersberg

About This Book

This catalogue is a listing of stamps depicting ships and boats issued by countries throughout the world. It is based on the Stanley Gibbons *Stamps of the World Simplified Catalogue* published annually in three volumes. This second edition contains over 13,000 stamps which depict over 3,000 different named ships. It has been updated to include all ship and boat stamps that have appeared in *Gibbons Stamp Monthly* Catalogue Supplements up to and including the September 1993 issue.

What is Included

All issues, including overprints and surcharges, depicting ships and boats as listed in the *Stamps of the World Catalogue*. Miniature sheets are included where they contain designs different from those in the basic set.

What is Excluded

All stamp variations of watermark and perforation outside the scope of *Stamps of the World*. The list also omits designs showing symbolic or stylised ships or those where only a small part of the vessel is visible. Stamps listed as Appendix entries in *Stamps of the World* are treated in a similar manner in this catalogue.

Countries Section

This section lists in alphabetical order, with prices, the various countries and territories which have issued ship and boat stamps. Within each country the stamps are listed in chronological order with the year of issue and catalogue number taken from the *Stamps of the World Catalogue*.

Each vessel is identified by its name, if known, its type and, in appropriate instances, the name of a famous person connected with it.

For sailing ships the descriptions of naval vessels are based on their rate and those for merchantmen on the principal rig types:

Barque—three or more masts. Fore and aft sails on the mizzen-mast, square-rigged on the remainder.

Barquentine—three or more masts. Square-rigged on the foremast, fore and aft sails on the remainder.

Brig—two masts. Both square-rigged, but the mainmast also carries a fore-and-aft spanker sail.

Brigantine—two masts. Square-rigged on the foremast, fore and aft on the mainmast with square-rigged topsails above.

Full-rigged Ship—three or more masts. All square-rigged with the mizzen mast also carrying a fore and aft spanker sail.

Schooner—two or more masts. Rigged fore and aft. Some vessels of this type carried square-rigged topsails and are known as topsail schooners.

Index Section

This is divided into two parts with entries under name or by type. Each entry gives, in alphabetical order, country names and catalogue numbers of those stamps depicting that particular ship or type. Many ships have experienced changes of name or function, but the entries refer to the name and ship type depicted on the stamps concerned.

Acknowledgments

As well as the new issues which have appeared since the first edition a considerable number of vessels on previously listed stamps have now been identified. Members of the Ship Stamp Society throughout the world have contributed much information as have the American and Italian bulletins, as well as various postal administrations. Their help is gratefully acknowledged.

Once again it is David Aggersberg, Stanley Gibbons Catalogue Editor, Pam Basley and all their staff who have made possible the transformation of this information into the present catalogue and I am much indebted to them for all their help and guidance.

Peter Bolton

Useful Books

There are many hundreds of books devoted to all aspects of shipping and it would be quite impossible to list all the different reference works, but the following have been of particular assistance in the editing of this catalogue.

British Warships and Auxiliaries (annual edition), M. Critchley. Maritime Books.

British Warships since 1945 (five volumes), M. Critchley or J. Worth (volume 4). Maritime Books.

Dictionary of Ship Types, A. Dudszus and E. Henriot. Conway Maritime Press.

Dreadnought, R. Hough. Michael Joseph.

Frigates, Sloops and Patrol Vessels of the Royal Navy 1900 to date, M. Cocker. Westmoreland Gazette.

Janes Merchant Ships. Janes Publishing.

Janes Fighting Ships. Janes Publishing.

Stamps and Ships, J. Watson. Faber.

Ships of the Royal Navy (revised edition), J. Colledge. Greenhill Books.

Ships on Stamps (various parts), E. Argyle. Picton Publishing.

The Last of the Windjammers (two volumes), B. Lubbock. Brown, Son & Fergusson.

The Author

Although having a general interest in all types of shipping Peter Bolton specialises in collecting stamps of the merchant sailing ships from the mid-19th century onwards with a particular interest in present day cadet ships.

Since retiring he has also been able to devote more time to his other hobbies of travel and photography in connection with these Tall Ships.

The Ship Stamp Society

The aims of the Society, which now has members in over twenty-three countries, are the advancement and study of ship stamps. The monthly illustrated magazine, *Log Book*, provides a medium for collectors to discuss their interests and to exchange and acquire material.

Local meetings are organised and a full week-end, at a venue of nautical interest, is held each Spring for the Annual General Meeting and a programme of visits and social events.

Membership details can be obtained from Mr T. Broadley, 10 Heyes Drive, Lymm, Cheshire WA13 0PB.

Ship Stamp Society

Member of B.T.A – Affiliated to I.F.M.P.

The Ship Stamp Society was formed in 1970. Its objects are the general study and advancement of ship stamps in all their classifications and the provision of a medium for collectors to discuss their various interests and to acquire stamps.

The society has a worldwide membership and prides itself on being the foremost society of its kind, catering specially for collectors of Ships on Stamps.

Every ship has its own name, features, purpose and history – and there are many types in which to specialise such as Cable ships, Passenger ships, Naval ships, Merchant ships, Wrecks, Sailing ships, Dhows and Ferries.

The Annual General Meeting is usually held in a place of maritime interest and the Merseyside Branch meets monthly.

The Annual subscription (due August) for U.K. members is £10 and for those Overseas £9. All members receive the Society monthly magazine *LOG BOOK*, a 24pp. illustrated publication full of detailed information about Ships on Stamps and other relevant subjects.

The Society publishes a Ship Stamp Encyclopedia which lists all NAMED ships that appear on stamps up to 1989. A Supplement, updating information and including all new issues, is published annually. These listings give known information about the ships together with a brief history. The latest Supplement has many illustrations of the stamps listed.

For U.K. members there is an Exchange Packet, for those who wish to purchase and sell stamps Postal Auctions are also held from time to time.

We cater for beginners and the specialist alike who collect Ships on Stamps.

If you would like more information and a free copy of *Log Book* please write to the Hon Secretary:-

T. Broadley
10 Heyes Drive
LYMM
Cheshire. WA13 0PB
Tel: 0925 75 2760

Full details will be sent by return post.

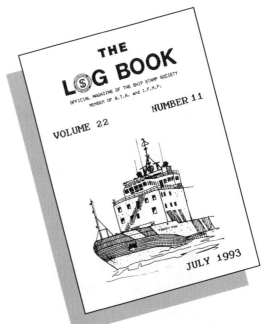

Countries Section

Arrangement

The various countries and territories are listed in the same order as in *Stamps of the World*. Those few which are not in alphabetical order are covered by cross-references. Each entry includes the geographical location and details of the currencies used. The dates quoted against these currencies are those on which they were first used for stamps in this catalogue.

Illustrations

These are three-quarters of actual size. One design from each issue is depicted, but only those overprints and surcharges required for identification are included.

Listings

These are divided into years by dates and into individual issues by the illustrations.

For philatelic details the *Stamps of the World*, or the 22 volume standard catalogue, should be consulted.

A † against the catalogue number indicates an issue where unlisted stamps in the set depict designs other than ships.

Miniature sheets are indicated by a **MS** prefix.

Prices

Those in the left hand column are for unused stamps and those in the right hand column for used.

Issues where all the designs depict ships are priced as sets only; single stamps and those from "broken" sets are priced individually.

Our prices are for stamps in fine average condition, and in issues where condition varies we may ask more for the superb and less for the sub-standard.

The prices of unused stamps are for lightly hinged examples for those issued before 1946, thereafter for unmounted mint.

Prices for used stamps refer to postally used examples, though for certain issues they may be for cancelled-to-order.

The minimum price quoted is 10p which represents a handling charge rather than a basis for valuing common stamps.

The prices quoted are generally for the cheapest variety of stamps but it is worth noting that differences of watermark, perforation, or other details, outside the scope of this catalogue, may often increase the value of the stamp.

All prices are subject to change without prior notice and we give no guarantee to supply all stamps priced. Prices quoted for albums, publications, etc. advertised in this catalogue are also subject to change without prior notice.

Guarantee

All stamps supplied by us are guaranteed originals in the following terms:

If not as described, and returned by the purchaser in the original transaction, we undertake to refund the price paid to us. If any stamp is certified as genuine by the Expert Committee of the Royal Philatelic Society, London, or by B.P.A. Expertising Ltd., the purchaser shall not be entitled to make any claim against us for any error, omission or mistake in such certificate.

Consumers' statutory rights are not affected by the above guarantee.

ABU DHABI

Arabian Peninsula
1000 fils = 1 dinar

1969

53†	60f Marine drilling platform	2.50	85
54†	125f Oil tanker	4.00	1.50

1971

77†	60f *Baniyas* (patrol boat)	2.50	80

ADEN

Arabian Peninsula
1937 16 annas = 1 rupee
1951 100 cents = 1 shilling

1937

1	½a Dhow		
2	9p Dhow		
3	1a Dhow		
4	2a Dhow		
5	2½a Dhow		
6	3a Dhow		
7	3½a Dhow		
8	8a Dhow		
9	1r Dhow		
10	2r Dhow		
11	5r Dhow		
12	10r Dhow		
	Set of 12	£325	£225

1939

18†	1a *Canton* (liner) at anchor	20	25
19†	1½a *Al Nasr* (dhow)	45	60
21†	2½a Fishing boats, Mukalla	30	30
22†	3a H.M.S. *Volage* (frigate) and H.M.S. *Cruizer* (sloop) Aden, 1839	50	25
23†	8a Fishing boats, Mukalla	35	40
23a†	14a H.M.S. *Volage* and H.M.S. *Cruizer*, Aden, 1839	2.25	1.00
24†	1r *Al Nasr* (dhow)	1.50	1.50
25†	2r *Canton* (liner) at anchor	4.50	1.75
27†	10r H.M.S. *Volage* and H.M.S. *Cruizer*, Aden, 1839	24.00	11.00

1949

As No. 115 of Antigua, but surch

33†	3a on 30c Paddle-steamer	1.50	1.00

1951

Nos. 18, 21/25 and 27 surch

36†	5c on 1a *Canton* (liner) at anchor	15	40
38†	15c on 2½a Fishing boats, Mukalla	20	1.00
39†	20c on 3a H.M.S. *Volage* and H.M.S. *Cruizer*, Aden, 1839	25	40
40†	30c on 8a Fishing boats, Mukalla	25	55
41†	50c on 8a Fishing boats, Mukalla	25	35
42†	70c on 14a H.M.S. *Volage* and H.M.S. *Cruizer*, Aden, 1839	75	1.00
43†	1s on 1r *Al Nasr* (dhow)	35	30
44†	2s on 2r *Canton* (liner) at anchor	4.00	2.50
46†	10s on 10r H.M.S. *Volage* and H.M.S. *Cruizer*, Aden, 1839	22.00	9.00

1953

81†	35c Dhow	1.00	1.50
62†	1s Dhow building (brown and violet)	30	10
63†	1s Dhow building (black and violet)	55	10
71†	20s European ships, Aden, 1572 (brown and lilac)	6.50	10.00
72†	20s European ships, Aden, 1572 (black and lilac)	32.00	13.00

1954

As No. 62 but inscr "Royal Visit 1954"

73	1s Dhow building	30	30

ADEN PROTECTORATE STATES

Arabian Peninsula
1946 16 annas = 1 rupee
1955 100 cents = 1 shilling
1966 100 fils = 1 dinar

Kathiri State of Seiyun

1946

As No. 115 of Antigua, but surch

17†	3a on 30c Paddle-steamer	40	65

1966

92†	10f Fishing boat, Antibes	1.25	15

Qu'aiti State in Hadhramaut

1949

As No. 115 of Antigua, but surch

17	3a on 30c Paddle-steamer	55	50

1955

38†	2s Dhow building	2.50	60

1963

As No. 38 but with portrait of Sultan Awadh bin Saleh el Qu'aiti

50†	2s Dhow building	2.25	1.00

1966

No. 50 surch **SOUTH ARABIA** *in English and Arabic*

62†	100f on 2s Dhow building	55	75

AEGEAN ISLANDS

Mediterranean
100 centesimi = 1 lira

1929

18†	10c Galley of Knights of St. John	15	15

1930

No. 18 optd **XXI Congresso Idrologico**

27†	10c Galley of Knights of St. John	1.10	2.75

1931
No. 18 *optd* **1931 CONGRESSO EUCARISTICO ITALIANO**
57† 10c Galley of Knights of St. John 60 1.40

1934
Nos. 436/7 *of Italy optd* **ISOLE ITALIANE DELL'EGEO**
169† 50c Naval launch.................... 23.00 42.00
170† 75c Naval launch.................... 23.00 42.00

1938
No. 513 *of Italy optd* **ISOLE ITALIANE DELL'EGEO**
193† 1li25 Roman galley 75 90

1943
No. 18 *surch* **CENT. 10 PRO ASSISTENZA EGEO**
215† 10c + 10c Galley of Knights of St. John 25 30

1944
No. 18 *surch* **L 3 PRO SINISTRATI DI GUERRA** *and symbol*
225† 10c + 3li Galley of Knights of St. John 45 1.40

AFGHANISTAN
Central Asia
100 poul (pul) = 1 afghani (rupee)

1986

1137 4a 11th-century ship
1138 5a Roman galley
1139 6a English royal kogge
1140 7a Early dhow
1141 8a Nao
1142 9a Ancient Egyptian ship
1143 11a Medieval galeasse
　　　　　　　　　　　　　　Set of 7 3.75 90
MS1144 50a Early dhow 2.25 75

1987

1170 42a Freighter 1.25 15

AITUTAKI
South Pacific
100 cents = 1 dollar

1974

114† 1c H.M.S. *Bounty* and Bligh 25 10
115† 1c H.M.S. *Bounty*..................... 25 10
116† 5c H.M.S. *Bounty* and Bligh 55 15
118† 8c H.M.S. *Resolution* and Cook 85 20

　　　Designs as Nos. 114/18, but inscr "AIR MAIL"
123† 10c H.M.S. *Bounty* and Bligh............ 55 15
124† 10c H.M.S. *Bounty* 55 15
125† 25c H.M.S. *Bounty* and Bligh 70 25
127† 30c H.M.S. *Resolution* and Cook 70 25

1976

191† 35c Sailing yachts 40 20

No. 191 *optd* **ROYAL VISIT JULY 1976**
196† 35c Sailing yachts 40 25

1977

225† 25c H.M.S. *Bounty* 50 45

1978

249† 50c Figurehead of H.M.S. *Resolution*
　　(Cook) 75 40

1979

267† 75c H.M.S. *Resolution* and H.M.S.
　　Adventure (Cook) 1.75 95

1984

504† 60c H.M.S. *Bounty* 1.50 1.60
505† 96c H.M.S. *Bounty* 1.75 1.75

1989

596† 55c H.M.S. *Bounty* at Spithead 1.00 1.00
599† 95c H.M.S. *Bounty* and outrigger off
　　Aitutaki 1.75 1.75
MS601† $4.20 H.M.S. *Bounty* and launch
　　(Bligh cast adrift) 5.50 6.50

1992

632 30c Vaka Motu (canoe type)
633 50c Hamatafua (canoe type)
634 95c Alia Kalia Ndrua (canoe type)
635 $1.75 Hokule'a (Hawaiian canoe type)
636 $1.95 Tuamotu Pahi (canoe type)
　　　　　　　　　　　　Set of 5 3.25 3.50

Nos. 632/6 *overprinted* **ROYAL VISIT**
637 30c Vaka Motu (canoe type)
638 50c Hamatafua (canoe type)
639 95c Alia Kalia Ndrua (canoe type)
640 $1.75 Hokule'a (Hawaiian canoe type)
641 $1.95 Tuamotu Pahi (canoe type)
　　　　　　　　　　　　Set of 5 3.25 3.50

647† $1.25 Ship's boat and *Santa Maria*
　　(Columbus) 80 85
649† $1.95 *Santa Maria* (Columbus) 1.25 1.40

AJMAN
Arabian Peninsula
1965 100 naye paise = 1 rupee
1967 100 dirhams = 1 riyal

1965

32† 1r Sailing yacht 55 30
35† 3r Sailing yacht 1.60 1.10

No. 35 *optd* **PAN ARAB GAMES CAIRO 1965**
49† 3r Sailing yacht 1.60 1.60

1967

139† 5d *Brasil* (liner)........................ 10 10
140† 15d *Yankee* (sail training and cruise ship) 20 10
148† 10r *Brasil* (liner) 4.75 1.00

ALAND ISLANDS

Northern Europe
100 penni = 1 markka

1984

1†	10p Local fishing boat	10	10
2†	20p Local fishing boat	10	10
3†	50p Local fishing boat	10	10
5†	1m10 Local fishing boat	35	10
6†	1m20 Local fishing boat	35	10
7a†	1m30 Local fishing boat	50	10

16†	2m *Pommern* (barque) and modern car ferries	2.75	2.75

1988

30	1m80 Mail sailing boat, Eckero	55	55

32	1m80 *Albanus* (Baltic galeass)		
33	2m40 *Ingrid* (schooner)		
34	11m *Pamir* (barque)		
	Set of 3	6.00	6.00

1992

54	1 klass (2m10) *Herzogin Cecilie* (cadet barque)	55	55

55†	2m10 Rowing boat, Ranno lighthouse	55	55

COLLECT RAILWAYS ON STAMPS
Second revised edition of this Stanley Gibbons thematic catalogue. Now available at £9.50 (p. + p. £3) from: Stanley Gibbons Publications, 5 Parkside, Christchurch Road, Ringwood, Hants BH24 3SH.

ALBANIA

South-east Europe
1957 leks
1965 100 qint = 1 lek

1957

600	2lek50 *Aurora* (Russian cruiser)		
601	5lek *Aurora* (Russian cruiser)		
602	8lek *Aurora* (Russian cruiser)		
	Set of 3	5.50	3.75

1964

848†	7lek Olympic yacht	1.25	80

1965

964	10q *Teuta* (freighter)		
965	20q Punt		
966	30q 19th-century sailing ship		
967	40q 18th-century brig		
968	50q *Vlora* (freighter)		
969	1lek Illyrian galliots		
	Set of 6	6.50	2.00

1967

1126†	65q Fishing boat, Saranda	2.00	50

1968

1257†	25q Sailor and naval craft	75	15

1972

1533†	80q *Tirana* (freighter)	80	15

1975

1752†	15q Ferry carrying men and horse	20	10
1753†	20q Barque	20	10

1977

1875†	25q Fishing boat	30	10

1980

2059†	2lek40 *Tirana* (freighter)	1.75	1.25

1989

2424	30q Galley		
2425	80q Kogge		
2426	90q Schooner		
2427	1lek30 Container ship		
	Set of 4	1.40	80

1991

2489†	1lek20 Rowing boat	25	15

1992

2504†	90q *Santa Maria* (Columbus)	15	10
2505†	1lek80 *Vitoria* (Magellan)	35	20

2535†	60q Columbus's ships	10	10

ALDERNEY
See under Guernsey

ALGERIA
North Africa
1930 100 centimes = 1 franc
1964 100 centimes = 1 dinar

1930

106	10f *Provence* (sailing ship) in Bay of Algiers	12.00	13.00

1939

159	20c *Extavia* (freighter)		
160	40c *Extavia* (freighter)		
161	90c *Extavia* (freighter)		
162	1f25 *Extavia* (freighter)		
163	2f25 *Extavia* (freighter)		
	Set of 5	6.00	5.25

1949

288	10f + 15f *Richelieu* (French battleship)		
289	18f + 22f *Arromanches* (French aircraft carrier)		
	Set of 2	9.25	10.00

1957
No. 1322 of France optd **ALGERIE**

371	12f + 3f 18th-century felucca	1.00	1.00

1970

550	30c Freighter	40	15

1981

807	60c 17th-century galley		
808	1d60 17th-century xebec		
	Set of 2	1.90	70

1989

999†	2d50, Rowing boat, Algiers, 1830	60	35
1001†	5d Sailing ships, Algiers, 1830	1.50	70

1990

1036†	3d30 Trawler	1.25	35

1992
As No. 1001, *but different face value*

1078†	30c Sailing ships, Algiers, 1830	10	10

ANDORRA
Pyrenees Mountains between France and Spain

French Post Offices
100 centimes = 1 franc

1992

F459	2f50 *Santa Maria*, *Pinta* and *Nina* (Columbus)		
F460	3f40 *Santa Maria*, *Pinta* and *Nina* (Columbus)		
	Set of 2	1.40	1.40

Spanish Post Offices
100 centimos = 1 peseta

1992

227†	27p *Santa Maria* (Columbus)	30	30

ANGOLA
South-west Africa
1913 100 centavos = 1 escudo
1949 100 centavos = 1 angolar
1954 100 centavos = 1 escudo
1977 100 lweis = 1 kwanza

1913
Surch **REPUBLICA ANGOLA** *and value in figures*

(a) On Nos. 1, 2, 5 *and* 7 *of Portuguese Colonies*

181†	¼c on 2½r Departure of Vasco da Gama's fleet	40	30
182†	½c on 5r Vasco da Gama's fleet at Calicut	40	30
185†	5c on 50r *Sao Gabriel* (flagship)	40	30
187†	10c on 100r *Sao Gabriel*	75	50

(b) On Nos. 104, 105, 108 *and* 110 *of Macao*

189†	¼c on ¼a Departure of Vasco da Gama's fleet	70	60
190†	½c on 1a Vasco da Gama's fleet at Calicut	70	60
193†	5c on 8a *Sao Gabriel* (flagship)	50	45
195†	10c on 16a *Sao Gabriel*	95	60

(c) On Nos. 58, 59, 62 *and* 64 *of Timor*

197†	¼c on ¼a Departure of Vasco da Gama's fleet	70	60
198†	½c on 1a Vasco da Gama's fleet at Calicut	70	60
201†	5c on 8a *Sao Gabriel* (flagship)	50	45
203†	10c on 16a *Sao Gabriel*	90	60

1949

450	1a *Tentativa Feliz* (19th-century sailing ship)		
451	4a *Tentativa Feliz* (19th-century sailing ship)		
	Set of 2	13.00	1.50

1967

658	1e *Don Carlos I* (Portuguese cruiser)		
659	2e50 *Mindelo* (Portuguese sail/steam corvette)		
	Set of 2	85	35

1968

676†	2e50 Cabral's fleet	50	10

1969

678	2e50 *Loge* (Portuguese gunboat)	45	15

1970

696†	1e50 Mailships *Infante Dom Henrique* and *Principe Perfeito*	35	10

1972

704	1e 16th-century galleon	30	10

705	50c Sailing yachts	20	10

1985

846† 11k Oil rig 80 50

1990

921† 9k Oil tanker 50 30

1991

950† 35k Yachts, Lobito Bay 55 30

958† 6k Sailing dinghies 10 10

963 5k Galleon
964 15k Caravel
965 20k Caravel
966 50k Galleon
                    Set of 4 1.25 75

1992

998† 65k Fishing canoe 15 10
1001† 120k Fishing canoes 30 25

MS1002 500k Santa Maria (Columbus) 1.25 1.00

ANGUILLA
West Indies
100 cents = 1 dollar

1967
No. 138 of St. Kitts-Nevis optd **INDEPENDENT ANGUILLA** and
bar
10† 20c Boat building 90.00 12.00

1968

32 10c Yachts
33 15c Boat on the beach
34 25c Warspite (schooner)
35 40c Atlantic Star (schooner)
                    Set of 4 90 40

1969

51† 40c Punt on salt pond 25 10

1970

84† 1c Boat building 10 30

1971

112 10c Magnanime and Aimable (ships of the
     line)
113 15c H.M.S. Duke, Glorieux and H.M.S.
     Agamemnon (ships of the line)
114 25c H.M.S. Formidable, H.M.S. Namur
     and Ville de Paris (ships of the line)
115 40c H.M.S. Canada (ship of the line)
116 50c H.M.S. St. Albans and wreck of
     Hector (ships of the line)
                    Set of 5 5.25 5.25
Nos. 112/16 were issued in horizontal se-tenant strips to form a
composite design of a sea battle.

1972

133† 4c Ferry at Blowing Point 15 20
140† 40c Boat building 1.50 1.50

145 25c Malcolm Miller (cadet ship)
146 40c Malcolm Miller (cadet ship)
                    Set of 2 2.10 3.25

1973

159 1c Santa Maria (Columbus)
160 20c Santa Maria, Pinta and Nina
161 40c Santa Maria
162 70c. Columbus's fleet at sea
163 $1.20 Columbus's fleet at anchor
                    Set of 5 5.00 5.00

1974

195† 1c Island rowing boat 10 10

1975

213† $1 Boston Tea Party ships 50 40

1976
Nos. 133 and 140 optd or surch **NEW CONSTITUTION 1976**
226† 3c on 40c Boat building 30 40
227† 4c Ferry at Blowing Point 30 40
228† 5c on 40c Boat building 20 30
235† 40c Boat building 45 70

255 1c Les Desius (French frigate) and La
     Vaillante (French brig) approaching
     Anguilla, 1796
256 3c Margaret (sloop) leaving Anguilla to
     fetch help, 1796
257 15c H.M.S. Lapwing (frigate) engaging Le
     Desius and Le Vaillante, 1796
258 25c La Vaillante aground, 1796
259 $1 H.M.S. Lapwing (frigate), 1796
260 $1.50 Le Desius burning and H.M.S.
     Lapwing, 1796
                    Set of 6 6.25 6.00

1977

269† 25c H.M.S. Minerva (frigate) 15 10
270† 40c Launch from Royal Yacht Britannia . . 20 15

283†	22c Lobster fishing boat...............	35	45
284†	35c Island dinghies....................	40	45

Nos. 269/70 *optd* **ROYAL VISIT TO WEST INDIES**

298†	25c H.M.S. *Minerva* (frigate)	20	15
299†	40c Launch from Royal Yacht *Britannia* ..	25	25

1978

Nos. 283/4 *optd* **VALLEY SECONDARY SCHOOL 1953-1978**

325†	22c Lobster fishing boat...............	20	15
326†	35c Island dinghies....................	30	20

1980

Nos. 283/4 *optd* **SEPARATION 1980**

432†	22c Lobster fishing boat...............	25	40
434†	35c Island dinghies....................	30	45

1981

449	22c Ships in Nelson's Dockyard	
450	35c H.M.S. *Agamemnon*, *Captain*, *Vanguard*, *Elephant* and *Victory* (ships commanded by Nelson)	
451	50c H.M.S. *Victory* (Nelson)	
452	$3 Battle of Trafalgar	

	Set of 4	3.00	3.25

1982

486†	5c Ferries at Blowing Point.............	15	20
487†	10c Island dinghies....................	15	20
489†	20c Launching boat, Sandy Point........	30	20

517†	75c Scout yacht	1.25	90

No. 487 *optd* **COMMONWEALTH GAMES 1982**

530†	10c Island dinghies....................	15	15

1983

No. 487 *optd* **150th ANNIVERSARY ABOLITION OF SLAVERY ACT**

573†	10c Island dinghies....................	10	10

1984

Nos. 486/7 *optd* **U.P.U. CONGRESS HAMBURG 1984** *or surch also*

625	5c Ferries at Blowing Point	15	10
626	20c on 10c Island dinghies	20	15

1985

No. 486 *optd* **GIRL GUIDES 75TH ANNIVERSARY 1910-1985**

676	5c Ferries at Blowing Point	20	10

690	10c *Danmark* (Danish full-rigged cadet ship)		
691	20c *Eagle* (U.S. coastguard cadet barque)		
692	60c *Amerigo Vespucci* (cadet ship)		
693	75c *Sir Winston Churchill* (cadet schooner)		
694	$2 *Nippon Maru* (cadet ship)		
695	$2.50 *Gorch Fock* (German cadet barque)		
	Set of 6	8.00	8.00

No. 487 *optd* **80TH ANNIVERSARY ROTARY 1985**

697	10c Island dinghies	10	10

1986

704†	$4 Mississippi riverboat	3.50	3.50

734	10c Trading sloop		
735	45c *Lady Rodney* (cargo liner)		
736	80c *West Derby* (19th-century sailing ship)		
737	$3 *Warspite* (sloop)		
	Set of 4	5.50	5.50
MS738	$6 Island dinghies	7.00	8.00

741†	35c *Santa Maria* (Columbus)...........	75	75

1987

753†	80c Previous sailing ferry and new motor ferry, Blowing Point	35	40

1988

798†	45c Sailboard	45	40

1992

883†	$5 Sailing dinghies racing	2.25	2.40

890	20c Sailing dinghies racing	
891	35c Sailing dinghies (on poster)	
892	45c Sailing dinghies on beach	
893	80c *Blue Bird* (sailing dinghy)	
894	80c Construction drawings of *Blue Bird* (sailing dinghy)	
895	$1 Sailing dinghies (on poster)	
	Set of 6	1.50	1.75
MS896	$6 Sailing dinghies racing and drawn up on beach	2.50	2.75

902†	80c Columbus's fleet and ship's boat	35	40
904†	$2 Columbus's fleet at sea	85	90
905†	$3 *Pinta*	1.25	1.40
MS906†	$6 *Santa Maria*	2.50	2.75

ANTIGUA

West Indies
1932 12 pence = 1 shilling
20 shillings = 1 pound
1951 100 cents = 1 dollar

1932

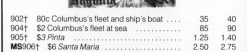

87†	6d H.M.S. *Victory* (Nelson)	11.00	12.00
88†	1s H.M.S. *Victory* (Nelson)	14.00	25.00
89†	2s6d H.M.S. *Victory* (Nelson)	42.00	50.00
90†	5s Sir Thomas Warner's *Concepcion*, 1632	85.00	£120

1949

115†	3d Paddle-steamer	80	75

1962

142	3c *Solent I* (paddle-steamer)	
143	10c *Solent I* (paddle-steamer)	
144	12c *Solent I* (paddle-steamer)	
145	50c *Solent I* (paddle-steamer)	
	Set of 4	1.25	70

1967

208†	4c *Susan Constant* (17th-century settlers' ship)	10	10
210†	25c *Susan Constant*	20	10

1968

218†	25c Yachts	25	10

221	2c Ships in old harbour St. Johns, 1768		
222	15c Ships in old harbour St. Johns, 1829		
223	25c Freighter and chart of new harbour		
224	35c New harbour		
225	$1 Ships in old harbour, 1768		
	Set of 5	1.60	65

1969

230†	4c *Gothic* (liner)	10	10
231†	15c *Gothic* (liner)	15	10

1970

269	½c War canoe		
270	1c *Nina* (Columbus)		
271	2c Sir Thomas Warner's *Concepcion*		
325	3c Viscount Hood and H.M.S. *Barfleur* (ship of the line)		
326	4c Sir George Rodney and H.M.S. *Formidable* (ship of the line)		
274	5c Nelson and H.M.S. *Boreas* (frigate)		
275	6c William IV and H.M.S. *Pegasus* (frigate)		
329	10c Blackbeard and pirate ketch		
330	15c Collingwood and H.M.S. *Pelican* (frigate)		
278	20c Nelson and H.M.S. *Victory*		
279	25c *Solent I* (paddle-steamer)		
280	35c George V and H.M.S. *Canada* (screw corvette)		
281	50c H.M.S. *Renown* (battle cruiser)		
282	75c *Federal Maple* (freighter)		
283	$1 *Sol Quest* (yacht)		
333	$2.50 H.M.S. *London* (destroyer)		
285	$5 *Pathfinder* (tug)		
	Set of 17	32.00	27.00

1972

345†	35c Yachts	15	10
346†	50c Yachts	20	15
348†	$1 Liner	30	35

1974

387†	1c *Orinoco* (mail paddle-steamer)	10	10
388†	2c Hydrofoil	10	10

1975

No. 282 surch

425†	$10 on 75c *Federal Maple* (freighter)	7.50	11.00

427	5c Carib war canoe		
428	15c Ship of the line, 1770		
429	35c H.M.S. *Boreas* (frigate), 1787, and Nelson		
430	50c Yachts		
431	$1 Yachts		
	Set of 5	4.00	1.75

440†	20c Galleon, 1775	45	10

1976

492†	$1 *Montgomery* (American brig)	1.50	55
493†	$5 *Ranger* (privateer sloop)	3.75	3.50

504†	1c Sailing dinghies	10	10
506†	20c Game-fishing boat	15	10

524†	$2 *Freelance* (yacht)	3.00	3.25

1977

540†	$2 Scout raft	1.75	1.75

1978

576	10c Yacht regatta		
577	50c Fishing and work boat race		
578	90c Yacht race		
579	$2 Power boat race		
	Set of 4	2.50	1.75
MS580	$2.50 Guadeloupe–Antigua yacht race	1.90	2.50

1979

623†	50c H.M.S. *Endeavour* (Cook)	65	65
MS626†	$2.50 H.M.S. *Resolution* (Cook)	2.25	2.50

1981

715†	90c Sailing dinghy	65	65

1984

830	45c *Booker Vanguard* (freighter)		
831	50c *Canberra* (liner)		
832	60c Sailing boats		
833	$4 *Fairwind* (cargo liner)		
	Set of 4	8.50	8.00
MS834	$5 18th-century English man-o-war	4.50	4.75

1985

911†	$1 Statue of Liberty and cadet ship	60	60
MS913†	$5 Liner and New York skyline	6.00	3.75

944†	$3 Sailboard	1.60	1.75

967†	$4 Royal Yacht *Britannia*	4.75	3.75

1986

1009	30c Tug		
1010	60c Game-fishing boat		
1011	$1 Yacht		
1012	$4 Lugger		
	Set of 4	3.50	3.75
MS1013	$5 Boat building	3.00	4.00

1987

1072	30c *Canada I* (yacht), 1981		
1073	60c *Gretel II* (yacht), 1970		
1074	$1 *Sceptre* (yacht), 1958		
1075	$3 *Vigilant* (yacht), 1893		
	Set of 4	3.50	3.50
MS1076	$5 *Australia II* defeating *Liberty* (yachts), 1983	4.00	4.50

1100†	10c *Spirit of Australia* (powerboat), 1978	25	15
1102†	30c U.S.S. *Triton* (submarine), 1960	45	25
1104†	60c U.S.S. *New Jersey* (battleship), 1942	70	45
1106†	90c *United States* (liner), 1952	1.00	65
1109†	$3 *Queen Elizabeth 2* (liner), 1969	2.50	2.00

1988

1172†	10c Fleet of Columbus, 1493	15	10
1173†	30c Fleet of Columbus off Indian village	20	15
1174†	45c *Santa Mariagalante* (Columbus), 1493	25	25
1175†	60c Painos Indian canoe, 1493	30	30
1177†	$1 Fleet of Columbus and ship's boat, 1493	50	50
1178†	$3 Fleet of Columbus at anchor, 1493 . .	1.40	1.50
1179†	$4 Fleet of Columbus at sea, 1493	1.75	2.00

1190	30c Two yachts rounding buoy		
1191	60c Three yachts		
1192	$1 British yacht under way		
1193	$3 Three yachts		
	Set of 4	2.50	2.75
MS1194	$5 Two yachts	2.75	3.25

1989

1281	25c *Festivale* (liner)		
1282	45c *Southward* (liner)		
1283	50c *Sagafjord* (liner)		
1284	60c *Daphne* (liner)		
1285	75c *Cunard Countess* (liner)		
1286	90c *Song of America* (liner)		
1287	$3 *Island Princess* (liner)		
1288	$4 *Galileo* (liner)		
	Set of 8	4.00	4.50
MS1289	Two sheets (a) $6 *Norway* (liner); (b) $6 *Oceanic* (liner)		
	Price for 2 sheets	5.25	5.50

1990

1382†	50c *Britannia* (mail paddle-steamer), 1840	20	25

1991

1483†	$5 Landing ship and landing craft, North Africa, 1942	2.25	2.40
MS1484†	Two sheets (a) $6 American battleships sinking, Pearl Harbor, 1941 (other sheet shows air attack on Germany)		
	Price for 2 sheets	5.25	5.50

1503	10c Phoenician galley (Hanno), 450 B.C.		
1504	15c Greek warship (Pytheas), 325 B.C.		
1505	45c Viking ship (Eric the Red), 985		
1506	60c Viking ship (Leif Eriksson), 1000		
1507	$1 Dhow (Scylax), 518		
1508	$2 Venetian merchant ship (Polo) 1259		
1509	$4 Pharonic galley (Queen Hatsheput), 1493 B.C.		
1510	$5 Irish coracle (St. Brendan), 500		
	Set of 8	5.50	5.75

MS1524†	Three sheets (c) $6 Sailing dinghies, Trinquetaille (other sheets show different Van Gogh paintings)		
	Price for 3 sheets	7.00	7.25

1585†	$1 *Nimitz* class aircraft carrier and *Ticonderoga* class cruiser	45	50
1586†	$1 Tourist launch, Pearl Harbor	45	50
1591†	$1 American warships burning, Pearl Harbor, 1941	45	50
1592†	$1 American battleships in flames, Pearl Harbor,1941	45	50
1593†	$1 U.S.S. *Nevada* (battleship), Pearl Harbor, 1941	45	50

1992

1605†	30c Yachts, Nelson's Dockyard	15	20

1611†	30c Yacht	15	20

ARGENTINE REPUBLIC

South America
1892 100 centavos = 1 peso
1985 100 centavos = 1 austral
1992 100 centavos = 1 peso

1892

219	2c Columbus's fleet		
220	5c Columbus's fleet		
	Set of 2	32.00	9.50

1902

290	5c Ships in Port Rosario	7.00	2.00

1933

635	3c Harbour scene, La Plata	75	25

1939

670 5c *Presidente Sarmiento* (cadet ship) 35 10

1944

735 5c Liner, warship and yacht 15 10

1947

791 5c Ship in the Antarctic
792 20c Ship in the Antarctic
           Set of 2 1.25 30

795 5c *Presidente Sarmiento* (cadet ship) 30 10

1948

MS808a 45c 18th-century shipping, Buenos
Aires; 85c Sailing ship, 1767
MS808b 1p20 Sailing ship, 1798
    Price for 2 sheets 15.00 13.00
Nos. **MS**808a/b each contain a total of four designs.

1951

829† 25c President Peron (liner) 45 10

1953

855 50c *Uruguay* (sail/steam gunboat) 60 10

1954

868† 50c Tug and liner, Buenos Aires
     (33 × 22 *mm*) 45 10
869† 50c Tug and liner, Buenos Aires
     (32 × 21 *mm*) 55 10

1957

900† 40c *Hercules* (sail frigate) 30 10
902† 60c *Zefiro* and *Nancy* (sail warships) at
     Battle of Montevideo (air) 50 10

1958

916† 40c + 20c River ferry 45 20

933† 80c Paddle-steamer, Buenos Aires, 1858 30 10

1960

990 1p Galleon
991 5p Galleon
992 1p80 Galleon (air)
993 10p70 Galleon
           Set of 4 1.75 60

1961

1007 2p *America* at Battle of San Nicolas,
     1810 . . . . 30 10

1963

1093 4p *La Argentina* (sail frigate) 45 10

1964

1116† 11p + 5p Sailing yacht 65 65

1965

1127† 4p *General San Martin* (ice-breaker) 1.40 30

1146 8p *Mimosa* (sail merchantman) 35 10

1966

1161† 8p River boats, San Fernando 40 10

1967

1200 20p *Invincible* (schooner) 95 15

1211 20p *General Brown* (cadet ship) 95 15

1968

1224 20p *Libertad* (full-rigged cadet ship) 95 15

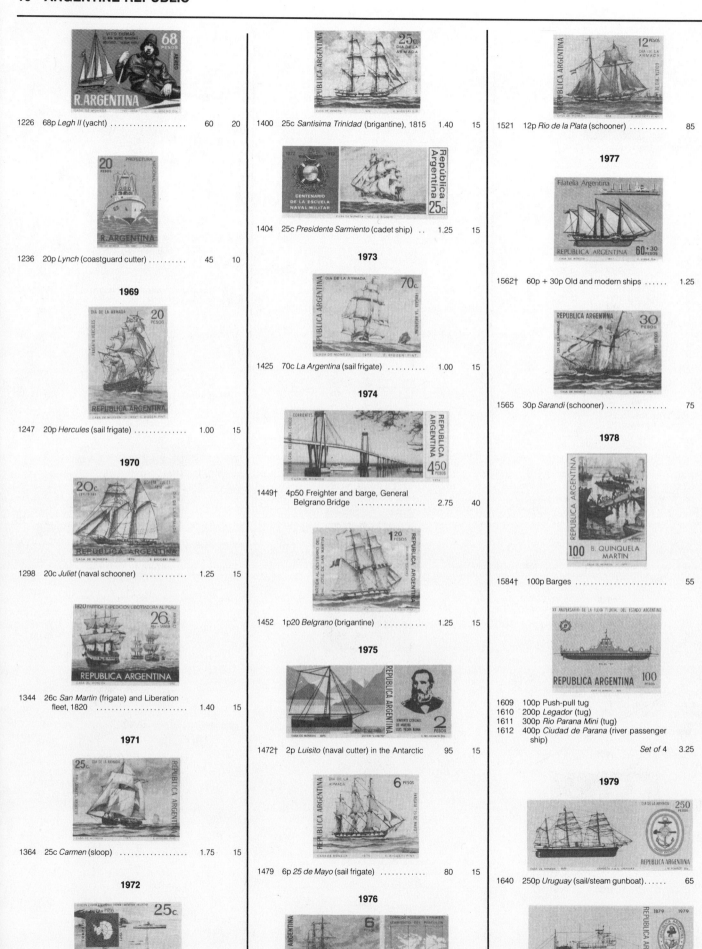

| 1226 | 68p *Legh II* (yacht) | 60 | 20 |

1236 20p *Lynch* (coastguard cutter) 45 10

1969

1247 20p *Hercules* (sail frigate) 1.00 15

1970

1298 20c *Juliet* (naval schooner) 1.25 15

1344 26c *San Martin* (frigate) and Liberation
fleet, 1820 .... 1.40 15

1971

1364 25c *Carmen* (sloop) 1.75 15

1972

1397 25c *Libertad* (liner) 75 15

1400 25c *Santisima Trinidad* (brigantine), 1815 1.40 15

1404 25c *Presidente Sarmiento* (cadet ship) .. 1.25 15

1973

1425 70c *La Argentina* (sail frigate) 1.00 15

1974

1449† 4p50 Freighter and barge, General
Belgrano Bridge 2.75 40

1452 1p20 *Belgrano* (brigantine) 1.25 15

1975

1472† 2p *Luisito* (naval cutter) in the Antarctic 95 15

1479 6p *25 de Mayo* (sail frigate) 80 15

1976

1514 6p *Heroina* (sail frigate), 1820 .... 75 15

1521 12p *Rio de la Plata* (schooner) 85 15

1977

1562† 60p + 30p Old and modern ships 1.25 1.00

1565 30p *Sarandi* (schooner) 75 15

1978

1584† 100p Barges 55 15

1609 100p Push-pull tug
1610 200p *Legador* (tug)
1611 300p *Rio Parana Mini* (tug)
1612 400p *Ciudad de Parana* (river passenger
ship)
Set of 4 3.25 90

1979

1640 250p *Uruguay* (sail/steam gunboat)...... 65 20

1642 250p *Comodoro Rivadavia* (hydrographic
survey ship) 65 20

1646	400p + 400p *Magdalena* (caravel)		
1647	500p + 500p Three-masted sailing ship		
1648	600p + 600p *Descubierta* (corvette)		
1649	1500p + 1500p *Fortuna* (yacht)		
	Set of 4	27.00	22.00

1662	1000p Oil rig	3.00	65

MS1663 250p + 250p Paddle-steamer (on Buenos Aires stamp No. P4); 1000p + 1000p Columbus's fleet (on No. 220) 12.00 12.00
No. MS1663 also contains two other designs

1980

1675	500p *La Argentina* (sail frigate)	90	30

1676	500p *Villarino* (transport), 1880	90	30

1981

1702†	2000p *Almirante Irizar* (ice-breaker)	2.75	95

1719	1300p 15th-century caravel	55	20

No. 1719 *optd* **CURSO SUPERIOR DE ORGANIZACION DE SERVICIOS FILATELICOS–UPAE BUENOS AIRES–1981**

1724	1300p 15th-century caravel	40	20

1982

1770	3000p + 1500p Fishing boat	75	30

1984

1866†	5p + 2p50 *Nina* (Columbus)	1.00	30
1867†	5p + 2p50 *Pinta* (Columbus)	1.00	30
1868†	5p + 2p50 *Santa Maria* (Columbus)	1.00	30

1891†	20p *Parana* (sail/steam corvette)	90	30

1987

2075†	50c Yachts	30	15

1988

2134†	1a+1a *La Poste* (yacht)	35	30

1989

2143†	5a Tugs and sailing barge	10	10

2167†	150a *Weser* (immigrant steamer), 1889	65	35

2187	300a Battle of Vuelta de Obligado, 1845	1.10	65

1990

2188	200a Container ship and yacht		
2189	200a Container ship (blue hull) and full-rigged sailing ship		
2190	200a Full-rigged ship and container ship (green hull)		
2191	200a Container ship (green hull)		
	Set of 4	40	20

2215†	3000a Sailing packet and despatch boat	90	60
2216†	3000a *Rio Carcarana* (cargo liner)	90	60

MS2218 2000a+1000a *Descubierta* (Spanish corvette), 1789; 2000a + 1000a *Atrevida* (Spanish corvette, 1789 (sheet also contains two other designs) 3.25 2.25

1991

2258	4000a *Vitoria* (Magellan)		
2259	4000a Caravel (Juan Diaz de Solis)		
	Set of 2	1.40	85

1992

2301†	38c *General Belgrano* (cruiser)	65	40

2308† 38c Early 19th-century Argentine warships 65 40

2315† 38c *Santa Maria* (Columbus) 65 40

OFFICIAL STAMPS

1985
No. 868 optd **S. OFICIAL**
O879 50c Tug and liner, Buenos Aires 20 10

ARMENIA

Western Asia
100 kopeks -1 rouble

1923

Unissued stamp surcharged
231† 50000 on 1000r Peasant in a punt 80 80

ARUBA

West Indies
100 cents = 1 gulden

1990

87† 45c + 20c Sailboards 70 70

1992

115† 40c Caravel (Columbus) 30 30

ASCENSION

South Atlantic
1924 12 pence = 1 shilling
20 shillings = 1 pound
1971 100 pence = 1 pound

1924

10 ½d *London* (East Indiaman)
11 1d *London* (East Indiaman)
12 1½d *London* (East Indiaman)
13 2d *London* (East Indiaman)
14 3d *London* (East Indiaman)
15 4d *London* (East Indiaman)
15d 5d *London* (East Indiaman)
16 6d *London* (East Indiaman)
17 8d *London* (East Indiaman)
18 1s *London* (East Indiaman)
19 2s *London* (East Indiaman)
20 3s *London* (East Indiaman)
Set of 12 £250 £375

1949
As No. 115 of Antigua
53 4d Paddle-steamer 5.50 1.10

1969

121 4d Crest of H.M.S. *Rattlesnake* (screw corvette)
122 9d Crest of H.M.S. *Weston* (sloop)
123 1s9d Crest of H.M.S. *Undaunted* (destroyer)
124 2s3d Crest of H.M.S. *Eagle* (aircraft carrier)
Set of 4 3.50 75

1970

130 4d Crest of H.M.S. *Penelope* (frigate)
131 9d Crest of H.M.S. *Carlisle* (cruiser)
132 1s6d Crest of H.M.S. *Amphion* (submarine)
133 2s6d Crest of H.M.S. *Magpie* (sloop)
Set of 4 7.50 2.75

1971

140† 3½p 18th-century ship and Harrison's chronometer 1.25 55

149 2p Crest of H.M.S. *Phoenix* (sloop)
150 4p Crest of H.M.S. *Milford* (sloop)
151 9p Crest of H.M.S. *Pelican* (sloop)
152 15p Crest of H.M.S. *Oberon* (submarine)
Set of 4 6.50 2.40

1972

154 1½p Crest of H.M.S. *Lowestoft* (frigate)
155 3p Crest of H.M.S. *Auckland* (sloop)
156 6p Crest of H.M.S. *Nigeria* (cruiser)
157 17½p Crest of H.M.S. *Bermuda* (cruiser)
Set of 4 4.25 4.50

160† 4p *Quest* (Shackleton) 1.10 70
161† 7½p *Quest* (Shackleton) 1.25 75

1973

166 2p Crest of H.M.S. *Birmingham* (destroyer)
167 4p Crest of H.M.S. *Cardiff* (destroyer)
168 9p Crest of H.M.S. *Penzance* (sloop)
169 13p Crest of H.M.S. *Rochester* (sloop)
Set of 4 12.50 4.25

1975

195† 2p H.M.S. *Peruvian* and H.M.S. *Zenobia*, (sloops), 1815 .... 35 25

1976

Ascension Island

217† 25p *Southampton Castle* (liner) 50 45

1979

242† 3p H.M.S. *Resolution* (Cook) 45 25

249† 3p Cable ship 15 10
250† 8p *Anglia* (cable ship) 25 20
252† 15p *Seine* (cable ship) 35 35

256† 12p *London* (East Indiaman) (on stamp
No. 20) 35 25

1980

264 8p 17th-century sailing ship
265 12p 19th-century sailing ship
266 15p *Garth Castle* (mail steamer)
267 50p *St. Helena* (mail ship), 1980
Set of 4 1.75 1.50

274† 10p H.M.S. *Tortoise*, (storeship), 1830 .. 45 40

1982

317† 40p H.M.S. *Beagle* (Darwin) 1.10 95

1984

360† 15p *Southampton Castle* (liner) 35 35
362† 70p *Dane* (screw steamer) 1.50 1.50

1985

384† 70p Crest and gun from H.M.S. *Hood*
(battle cruiser) 2.50 2.25

1986

403† 15p *St. Helena* (mail ship) (on stamp
No. 267) 50 50

409 1p H.M.S. *Ganymede* (frigate), *c* 1811
410 2p H.M.S. *Kangaroo* (sloop), *c* 1811
411 4p H.M.S. *Trinculo* (sloop), *c* 1811
412 5p H.M.S. *Daring* (brig), *c* 1811
413 9p H.M.S. *Thais* (sloop), *c* 1811
414 20p H.M.S. *Pheasant* (sloop), *c* 1819
415 15p H.M.S. *Myrmidon* (frigate), 1819
416 18p H.M.S. *Atholl* (frigate), 1825
417 18p H.M.S. *Medina* (frigate), 1830
418 25p H.M.S. *Saracen* (sloop), 1840
419 30p H.M.S. *Hydra* (paddle-sloop), *c* 1845
420 50p H.M.S. *Sealark* (brig), 1849
421 70p H.M.S. *Rattlesnake* (screw corvette),
1868
422 £1 H.M.S. *Penelope* (armoured corvette),
1889
423 £2 H.M.S. *Monarch* (battleship), 1897
Set of 15 15.00 17.00

1987

431† £1 U.S.S. *Randolph* (aircraft carrier),
1962 .... 2.25 2.25

1988

461 9p H.M.S. *Resolution* (ship of the line),
1667
462 18p H.M.S. *Resolution* (Cook), 1772
463 25p H.M.S. *Resolution* (battleship), 1892
464 65p H.M.S. *Resolution* (battleship), 1916
Set of 4 4.50 2.75

Nos. 461/4 optd **SYDPEX 88 30.7.88–7.8.88**
465 9p H.M.S. *Resolution* (ship of the line),
1667
466 18p H.M.S. *Resolution* (Cook), 1772
467 25p H.M.S. *Resolution* (battleship), 1892
468 65p H.M.S. *Resolution* (battleship), 1916
Set of 4 2.40 2.40

475† 18p *Alert IV* (cable ship) 50 50
477† 65p *Good Hope Castle* (cargo liner) on
fire, 1973 .... 1.50 1.50

1989

498† 15p *Queen Elizabeth 2* (liner) and U.S.S.
John F. Kennedy (aircraft carrier), New
York 30 35
502† 15p U.S.S. *Yorktown* (cruiser) *Tourville*
(French destroyer), H.M.S. *Cleopatra*
and H.M.S. *Sirius* (frigates), New York 30 35
503† 15p *Jean de Vienne* (French destroyer),
New York 30 35

1990

531† 9p *Garth Castle* (mail steamer), 1910 .... 50 35
532† 18p. *St. Helena I* (mail ship), Falklands,
1982 .... 75 55
533† 25p Floating out of *St. Helena II* (mail
ship), 1989 .... 95 75
MS535 £1 *St. Helena II* 3.00 3.75

1991

Nos. 418, 420 *and* 422 overprinted **BRITISH FOR 175 YEARS**
536 25p. H.M.S. *Saracen* (sloop), 1840
537 50p H.M.S. *Sealark* (brig), 1849
538 £1 H.M.S. *Penelope* (armoured corvette),
1889
Set of 3 5.00 5.00

1992

574 9p *Eye of the Wind* (cadet brig)
575 18p *Soren Larsen* (cadet brigantine)
576 25p *Santa Maria, Pinta* and *Nina*
(Columbus)
577 70p *Santa Maria*
Set of 4 3.25 3.25

AUSTRALIA

Oceania
1932 12 pence = 1 shilling
20 shillings = 1 pound
1966 100 cents = 1 dollar

1932

141 2d *Orford* (liner)
142 3d *Orford* (liner)
143 5s *Orford* (liner)
Set of 3 £375 £180

1953

270† 2s H.M.S. *Calcutta* (transport) at Hobart, 1804 .... 2.00 2.50

1963

353 5d Freighter 10 10

355† 4s Tasman and *Heemskerk* 4.50 55
356† 5s Dampier and *Roebuck* 6.00 75
358† 10s Flinders and *Investigator* 42.00 4.25
359† £1 Bass and whale boat 48.00 12.00
360† £2 Admiral King and survey cutter
      Mermaid 85.00 75.00

1966

398† 40c Tasman and *Heemskerk* 12.00 10
399† 50c Dampier and *Roebuck* 15.00 10
401† $1 Flinders and *Investigator* 3.75 15
402† $2 Bass and whale boat 10.00 30
403† $4 Admiral King and survey cutter
      Mermaid 9.50 5.50

408 4c Dirk Hartog's *Eendracht*, 1616 .... 10 10

1969

438 5c *Walumba* (tug) 15 10

1970

459† 5c H.M.S. *Endeavour* and Captain Cook ... 50 10
460† 5c H.M.S. *Endeavour* and sextant 50 10
461† 5c H.M.S. *Endeavour* at Botany Bay 50 10
463† 5c H.M.S. *Endeavour* and raising Union
      Flag 50 10
464† 30c H.M.S. *Endeavour*, Cook and sextant 1.75 2.75

1971

485† 20c Surfboat, junk and sampans 65 90

1972

529† 80c *Gem* (paddle-steamer) 60 1.00

1974

567† $5 *St. Leonards* (ferry) 5.50 2.25

703 20c Sailing ship in Sydney Cove, 1788 .... 15 15

1979

704 20c *Canberra* (river paddle-steamer) 20 20
705 35c *Lady Denman* (river vessel) ....
706 50c *Murray River Queen* (river paddle-
      steamer)
707 55c *Curl Curl* (hydrofoil)
      Set of 4 2.40 3.00

726† 50c Game fishing launch 40 90

WHEN YOU BUY AN ALBUM LOOK
FOR THE NAME "STANLEY GIBBONS"
It means Quality combined with Value for Money.

1981

833 24c Ocean racing yacht
834 35c "Sharpie" yacht
835 55c 12 metre yacht
836 60c "Sabot" yacht
      Set of 4 2.40 2.25

1982

864 27c *Orford* (liner) (on stamp No. 143) 35 30

1983

879 27c H.M.S. *Sirius* (frigate), 1788
880 27c H.M.S. *Supply* (brig), 1788
      Set of 2 80 1.00

886 27c Royal Yacht *Britannia* 45 30

1984

911 30c *Cutty Sark* (clipper)
912 45c *Orient* (clipper)
913 75c *Sobraon* (clipper)
914 85c *Thermopylae* (clipper)
      Set of 4 3.25 3.50

1985

973† 33c Dirk Hartog's *Eendracht*, 1616 ...... 45 35

1986

1000† 33c H.M.S. *Buffalo* (storeship), 1836 .... 70 90

1021† 33c Captain Arthur Phillip and ship of
1788 .... 80 50

1036† 36c *Australia II* (yacht) and *Black
Knight* (tender) 65 55

1987

1046 36c Aerial view of Americas Cup yacht
1047 55c Two yachts tacking
1048 90c Two yachts turning
1049 $1 Two yachts under full sail
Set of 4 3.50 4.25

1059 36c H.M.S. *Sirius* (frigate), 1787
1060 36c Ship's boat, 1787
1061 36c Ship of the line on stocks, 1787
1062 36c H.M.S. *Sirius* and *Supply* (brig) in
River Thames
1063 36c First Fleet in English Channel, 1787
Set of 5 3.25 3.75

1064 36c Ship's boat off Tenerife, 1787
1065 36c Ship's boat off Tenerife, 1787
1066 $1 First Fleet off Tenerife, 1787
Set of 3 2.00 2.75

1077† 37c First Fleet off Rio de Janeiro, 1787 70 85
1078† 37c Brazilian fishing boat, 1787 .... 70 85
1081† 37c Brazilian fishing boats and First
Fleet, 1782 .... 70 85

1091† 37c First Fleet loading livestock, Cape
of Good Hope, 1787 .... 50 50
1092† $1 Cape fishing boat and First Fleet 1.25 1.25

1988

1105† 37c Arrival of First Fleet, 1788 .... 70 80
1106† 37c Aborigine canoe 70 80
1107† 37c First Fleet in cove 70 80
1108† 37c Ship's boat 70 80

1140† 37c *Portland* (brig) on stocks, 1800 .... 60 60

1145† 37c Sailing clipper 75 1.00

1989

1174† 10c Sailboards 10 15

1203† 39c Immigrant ship, 1830s 40 40

1990

1245† $1.10 Troopships 1.25 1.25

1991

1303 $1.05 H.M.S. *Discovery* (Vancouver),
1701 .... 1.25 1.25

1992

1333 45c *Young Endeavour* (cadet brigantine)
1334 45c *Britannia* (yacht)
1335 $1.05 *Akarana* (cutter)
1336 $1.20 *John Louis* (pearling lugger)
Set of 4 3.25 3.50

1341† $1.05 H.M.A.S. *Australia* (cruiser) and
American aircraft carrier, Coral Sea,
1942 .... 1.25 1.40

1365 45c Yachts under Sydney Harbour
Bridge (face value at left)
1366 45c Yachts under Sydney Harbour
Bridge (face value at right)
Set of 2 1.10 1.10

1993

1387 45c H.M.A.S. *Sydney* (cruiser, launched
1934)
1388 85c H.M.A.S. *Bathurst* (minesweeper)
1389 $1.05 H.M.A.S. *Arunta* (destroyer)
1390 $1.20 *Centaur* (hospital ship) and tug
Set of 4 2.75 3.00

OFFICIAL STAMPS

Nos. 142 and 144 optd **O.S.**
O134† 2d *Orford* (liner) 5.00 2.00
O135† 3d *Orford* (liner) 15.00 7.00

AUSTRALIAN ANTARCTIC TERRITORY

Antarctica
100 cents = 1 dollar

1966

| 10† | 4c Ship and iceberg | 70 | 80 |

1972

| 22† | 35c H.M.S. *Resolution* (Cook) | 9.00 | 6.00 |

1979

37	1c *Aurora*		
38	2c *Penola* (Rymill)		
39	5c *Thala Dan* (Antarctic supply ship)		
40	10c H.M.S. *Challenger* (survey ship)		
41	15c *Morning* (whaling ship) (bow view) (incorrectly inscribed "S.Y.Nimrod")		
42	15c *Nimrod* (stern view) (Shackleton)		
43	20c *Discovery II* (polar supply vessel)		
44	22c *Terra Nova* (Scott)		
45	25c *Endurance* (Shackleton)		
46	30c *Fram* (Amundsen)		
47	35c *Nella Dan* (Antarctic supply ship)		
48	40c *Kista Dan* (polar supply ship)		
49	45c *L'Astrolabe* (D'Urville)		
50	50c *Norvegia* (research ship)		
51	55c *Discovery* (Scott)		
52	$1 H.M.S. *Resolution* (Cook)		
	Set of 16	11.00	13.00

1988

| 79† | 37c *Nella Dan* (supply ship) | 80 | 60 |

1991

| 89† | $1.20 *Aurora Australis* (research ship) | 1.75 | 2.00 |

AUSTRIA

Central Europe
1915 100 heller = 1 krone
1925 100 groschen = 1 schilling

1915

| 245† | 20 + 3h *Viribus Unitas* (battleship) | 35 | 1.25 |

1935

| 773† | 1s Danube river steamer | 20 | 70 |
| 777† | 10s Yachts on Attersee | 38.00 | 60.00 |

1937

805	12g *Maria Anna* (Danube paddle-steamer)		
806	24g *Helios* (Danube paddle-steamer)		
807	64g *Oesterreich* (Danube paddle-steamer)		
	Set of 3	1.40	90

1945

| 932† | 12g Yacht, Schafberg | 10 | 10 |

1954

| 1267 | 1s + 25g 18th-century river boat | 4.75 | 4.75 |

1957

| 1312† | 2s50 Danube river steamer, Linz | 45 | 10 |

1961

| 1364 | 3s Canal barge | 1.10 | 40 |

1962

| 1381 | 1s50 Danube barge | 40 | 20 |

1971

| 1625† | 4s Danube barge, Linz | 75 | 45 |

1973

| 1666 | 2s50 *Admiral Tegetthoff* (polar vessel) | 80 | 15 |

| 1687† | 10s Yachts on Neusiedlersee | 80 | 10 |

1979

1831	1s50 *Franz I* (Danube paddle-steamer)		
1832	2s50 *Linz* (Danube pusher tug)		
1833	3s *Theodor Korner* (Danube passenger vessel)		
	Set of 3	1.10	60

1987

| 2133 | 4s Passenger ferry, Achensee | 65 | 20 |

1989

| 2196 | 6s Model salt barge from Viechtau | 75 | 30 |

2198   5s *Gisela* (paddle-steamer), Traunsee .. 70 25

1990

2236   9s *Telegraph* (1880) and *Anton Chekhov* (1978) (river vessels) 1.40 60

1992

2296   7s Caravel (Columbus) (woodcut) 1.00 50

2297   7s Rhine dredger 1.00 50

AZORES

Atlantic Ocean
1898 1000 reis = 1 milreis
1912 100 centavos = 1 escudo

1898

As Nos. 378/9 and 384 of Portugal, but inscr "ACORES"
171†   2½r Departure of Vasco da Gama's fleet 70 55
172†   5r Vasco da Gama's fleet at Calicut 1.00 60
175†   50r *Sao Gabriel* (flagship) 3.00 1.75
177†   100r *Sao Gabriel* 6.50 3.00

1911

Nos. 171/2, 175 and 177 optd **REPUBLICA** *or surch also*
218†   2½r Departure of Vasco da Gama's fleet 20 20
219†   15r on 5r Vasco da Gama's fleet at Calicut 20 20
221†   50r *Sao Gabriel* (flagship) 70 40
224†   100r *Sao Gabriel* 45 40

1985

466   40e *Jeque* (small sailing boat)
467   60e *Bote* (small sailing boat)
                    Set of 2 2.10 90

1989

496   80e Rowing boat 65 30

499†   87e 15th-century Portuguese caravel 70 30

1990

511†   120e Building a motor launch 1.10 55

1991

522†   35e *Helena* (schooner) 30 15
524†   80e *Cruzeiro do Canal* (ferry), 1987 .... 65 30

1992

526   85e *Santa Maria* (Columbus) off the Azores 80 40

527   38e *Insulano* (steamer), 1868
528   65e *Carvalho Araujo* (freighter), 1930
529   85e *Funchal* (ferry), 1961
530   120e *Terceirense* (freighter), 1948
                    Set of 4 2.50 1.25

BAHAMAS

West Indies
1948 12 pence = 1 shilling
20 shillings = 1 pound
1966 100 cents = 1 dollar

1948

183†   3d Fishing fleet 40 85
185†   6d Tuna fishing 1.25 80
188†   1s Racing yacht 60 40
190†   3s Boat building 6.50 8.50
191†   5s Liners at anchor 3.75 4.50

1949

As No. 115 of Antigua
197†   3d Paddle-steamer 80 1.00

1954

As Nos. 183, 185, 188 and 190/1 but with portrait of Queen Elizabeth II and without commemorative inscription
205†   3d Fishing fleet 30 40
208†   6d Liners at anchor 30 10
211†   1s Yacht racing 40 10
213†   2s6d Boat building 3.50 2.00
214†   5s Tuna fishing..................... 16.00 75

1964

Nos. 205, 208, 211 and 213/14 overprinted **NEW CONSTITUTION 1964**
232†   3d Fishing fleet 50 30
235†   6d Liners at anchor 30 30
238†   1s Yacht racing 45 15
240†   2s6d Boat building 2.00 2.50
241†   5s Tuna fishing..................... 4.50 3.25

No. 211 surcharged with Olympic rings and value
245   8d on 1s Yacht racing 10 10

1965

248†   1d Yacht regatta 25 20
252†   4d *Queen Elizabeth* (liner) 55 1.25
254†   8d Yachts 50 30
259†   5s Launch with underwater camera 2.25 1.00
261†   £1 *Santa Maria* (Columbus) 9.50 6.00

No. 254 surcharged
264   9d on 8d Yachts....................... 15 10

1966

Nos. 248, 252, 254, 259 and 261 surcharged in decimal currency
274†   2c on 1d Yacht regatta 10 10
277†   5c on 4d *Queen Elizabeth* (liner) 15 50
279†   10c on 8d Yachts 30 50
285† $1 on 5s Launch with underwater camera 1.25 1.50
287† $3 on £1 *Santa Maria* (Columbus) 5.00 4.00

1967

296†   2c Yacht regatta 15 15
299†   5c *Oceanic* (liner) 60 50
301†   10c Yachts 30 50
309† $3 *Santa Maria* (Columbus) 3.75 2.00

1968

316†   11c Yachts 1.00 30

319†   5c Racing yacht 25 15
322† $1 Racing yacht 1.75 3.00

1969

333†	3c Game fishing boats	35	10
335†	12c "Sunfish" sailing boats	50	15

1970

349†	12c *Canberra* (liner)	90	25

1971

367†	10c Bahamian sponge boat	40	30
469†	40c Bahamian sponge boat	1.75	75

1972

385	18c Olympic yacht	60	70

393	11c Galleon		
394	18c Galleon		
	Set of 2	30	35

1976

480†	25c Racing yachts	30	35

1977

499†	21c Scout yacht	75	25

1979

543†	40c 19th-century mail boat	65	70

1980

557†	1c Columbus's fleet	20	60
563†	16c Wrecking in the 1800s...........	30	40
564†	18c Blockade running during American Civil War	40	70
570†	$2 *Queen Elizabeth 2* (liner)	3.00	3.25

1983

644†	$1 Liner at anchor	1.40	1.40

Nos. 563/4 surcharged

647†	35c on 16c Wrecking in the 1800s	70	60
648†	80c on 18c Blockade running during American Civil War	1.50	1.40

649†	31c Liner and customs officers	1.50	45

1984

675	5c *Trent I* (paddle-steamer)		
676	31c *Orinoco II* (mail ship), 1886		
677	35c *Maxim Gorky, Oronsay, Oceanic, Flavia, Emerald Seas* and *Bahama Star* (liners) in Nassau harbour		
678	50c *Oropesa* (container ship)		
	Set of 4	1.90	2.10

1986

746†	5c Columbus's fleet and blockade running during American Civil War (on stamps Nos. 557 and 564)	20	15

1987

782†	10c Yachts, Great Isaac................	75	30
783†	40c Yachts, Bird Rock	2.25	1.25
784†	45c Fishing boats, Castle Island	2.25	1.25

786	10c Pirate ship (Anne Bonney)		
787	40c Pirate ship (Blackbeard)		
788	45c Pirate ship attacking merchantman (Edward England)		
789	50c British ship of the line (Woodes Rogers)		
	Set of 4	6.00	4.00

804†	40c *Norway* (liner) and catamaran	75	75
805†	40c Cruise liner and speedboat	75	75
806†	40c Game fishing boat and cruising yachts	75	75
807†	40c Game fishing boat and cruising yachts	75	75
808†	40c Fishing boat and schooner..........	75	75

1988

836†	40c Cruise liners, Freeport Harbour	60	55
838†	$1 *Yarmouth Castle* (freighter) on fire	1.40	1.40

1989

845†	40c Medieval merchantman, lateen-rigged caravel and caravel of Columbus	1.25	85
MS848†	$1.50 Caravel under construction	1.75	1.90

1990

870	10c Launching caravel			
871	40c Caravels in harbour			
872	45c Caravel at sea			
873	50c Lucayan canoe			
		Set of 4	4.00	3.25
MS874	$1.50 Columbus's fleet		3.25	4.00

1991

909†	40c Columbus's fleet in storm		80	80
MS912†	$1.50 *Pinta* (Columbus)		3.25	3.75

1992

933†	15c Columbus's fleet		30	20
934†	40c *Santa Maria* (Columbus)		70	70
935†	55c Lucayan canoes		90	90

MS943†	$2 Yachts	3.00	3.50

MS946	$2 *Santa Maria* (Columbus) and rowing boat	2.25	2.40

1993

MS961†	60c Submarine (sheet also contains three other 60c designs showing aircraft)	2.75	3.00

BAHRAIN

Arabian Peninsula
1955 16 annas = 1 rupee
1000 fils = 1 dinar

1955

Nos. 509/10 of Great Britain surcharged **BAHRAIN** *and new value*

94†	2r on 2s6d H.M.S. *Victory*	5.50	1.25
95†	5r on 5s Yacht and Thames sailing barge	11.00	2.75

1966

145†	50f *True Vels* and other freighters in dock	55	10
146†	75f *True Vels* and other freighters in dock	10	10
150†	1d Dhow	11.00	3.50

151	10f Freighter			
152	20f Freighter			
153	40f Freighter			
154	200f Freighter			
		Set of 4	7.25	3.25

1972

184†	30f Dhow	1.60	30
185†	60f Dhow	2.50	60

1974

211†	120f Tankers	2.50	1.50
212†	150f Tankers	3.25	2.00

1977

249a†	80f Dhow	1.60	1.10

252	40f Tankers			
253	80f Tankers			
		Set of 2	2.40	1.10

1979

258	100f Dhow (Boom type)			
259	100f Dhow (Baghla type)			
260	100f Dhow (Shu'ai type)			
261	100f Dhow (Ghanja type)			
262	100f Dhow (Kotia type)			
263	100f Dhow (Sambuk type)			
264	100f Dhow (Jaliboot type)			
265	100f Dhow (Zarook type)			
		Set of 8	9.00	8.00

1984

324	15f Dhows, Manama			
325	50f Dhows, Manama			
326	100f Dhows, Manama			
		Set of 3	2.75	1.40

1992

460†	200f Pearling dhows	60	30

1993

466†	80f Patrol boat	25	10
467†	150f Missile corvette	50	30

BANGLADESH

Indian sub-continent
100 paisa = 1 taka

1973

34†	5t Fishing boat	4.50	1.25

1974

As No. 34 but showing Bengali letter instead of "TA" in front of "5"

51†	5t Fishing boat	3.00	70

1976

As No. 51, but redrawn smaller (32 × 20 mm)

74†	5t Fishing boat	2.75	1.00

82† 5t Pilgrim Fathers' *Mayflower* 80 50

1978

129† 25p Local jute boat 15 10

1980

156 1t Early mail boat
157 10t *Sirdhana* (liner)
                            Set of 2 1.40 95

1983

200† 3t Racing canoes 20 30

218† 5t 15th-century sailing ship 1.50 75

220† 5p Local mail rowing boat 10 10

1987

288† 5t Paddle-steamer 30 35

1989

318a† 4t Freighter loading at Chittagong 10 10

1990

349† 10t 15th-century sailing ship (on stamp
     No. 218) 1.00 65

362† 2t Canoes racing 25 10

1992

446† 4t Canoes racing 10 10

OFFICIAL STAMPS

1973
No. 34 overprinted **SERVICE**
O10† 5t Fishing boat 4.00 4.50

1974
No. 51 overprinted **SERVICE**
O13† 5t Fishing boat 5.00 4.00

1976
No. 74 overprinted **SERVICE**
O23† 5t Fishing boat 30 50

1981
No. 129 overprinted **SERVICE**
O28† 25p Local jute boat 80 80

1983
Nos. 220 and 318a overprinted **SERVICE**
O35† 5p Local mail rowing boat 5 5
O44† 4t Freighter loading at Chittagong 10 10

BARBADOS
West Indies
1906 12 pence = 1 shilling
20 shillings = 1 pound
1950 100 cents = 1 dollar

1906

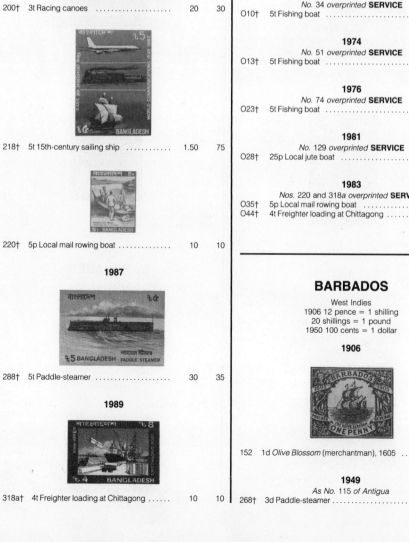

152 1d *Olive Blossom* (merchantman), 1605 . . 10.00 25

1949
As No. 115 of Antigua
268† 3d Paddle-steamer 40 35

1950

273† 3c *W.L. Eunica* (schooner) 15 60
276† 8c *Frances W. Smith* (schooner) 55 60
280† 60c *W. L. Edricia* (schooner) 6.00 5.50

1953
*As Nos. 273, 276 and 280, and new design, all showing portrait of
Queen Elizabeth II*
291† 3c *W. L. Eunica* (schooner) 15 30
293† 5c Schooner and Harbour Police rowing
     boat 20 30
295† 8c *Frances W. Smith* (schooner) 70 30
299† 60c *W. L. Edricia* (schooner) 7.00 2.00

1967

365† 35c *BP I* (police launch) 20 10

1969

394† 25c Sea Scouts' rowing boat and H.Q
     ship 35 10

1971

429 1c "Sailfish" craft 10 10

1972

441† 10c *Stanley Angwin* (cable ship) 15 10

1974

480 15c Sail fishing boat
481 35c Rowing boat
482 50c Motor fishing boat
483 $1 *Calamar* (fishing boat)
                            Set of 4 2.00 1.90

504† $1 Sailing ship 55 80

1975

506† 8c Royal Yacht *Britannia* 20 15
507† 25c Royal Yacht *Britannia* 50 25

538† 4c 17th-century sailing ship 35 10

1976

569† 5c Coastguard launches 1.25 1.75

1979

613 12c Early mail steamer
614 25c *Queen Elizabeth 2* (liner)
615 50c *Ra II* (raft)
616 $1 Early mail steamer (*different*)
          Set of 4 2.40 2.25

1981

681† $1 Harbour scene 70 75

1982

701 20c Lighter
702 35c Rowing boat
703 55c Speightstown schooner
704 $2.50 Inter-colonial schooner
          Set of 4 2.75 2.75

1983

726† 20c Convoy of freighters 60 10

741† $2.50 18th-century warship, Carlisle Bay 3.75 4.50

1984

752† 75c *Philosopher* (full-rigged ship), 1857 1.10 70
753† $1 *Sea Princess* (liner) 1.25 95

1986

816† $2.50 *Lady Nelson* (cargo liner) 2.00 1.90

MS821† $2 *Queen Elizabeth 2* (liner).......... 4.50 4.50

1988

866† $2 Olympic yachts 1.50 1.50

870† 65c *Author* (container ship) 90 45
871† $2 *Titanic* (liner) sinking, 1912 .... 2.00 2.00

ALBUM LISTS

Write for our latest list of albums and accessories.
This will be sent on request.

1989

907† 50c Yacht 80 75

1991

952† 5c Fishing launch 15 10
954† 75c Fishing launch and rowing boat 80 80
955† $2.50 Game fishing launch 2.25 2.75

1992

986† $2 *Festivale* (liner) 1.10 1.25

BARBUDA

West Indies
100 cents = 1 dollar

1968

30† 75c Yachts 45 45

1969

37 75c Sea Scouts' rowing boat 70 85

1971

95† 25c Yachts 10 30

1973

Nos. 269/85 of Antigua overprinted **BARBUDA**

116	½c War canoe		
104	1c *Nina* (Columbus)		
105	2c Sir Thomas Warner's *Concepcion*		
117	3c Viscount Hood and H.M.S. *Barfleur*		
106	4c Sir George Rodney and H.M.S. *Formidable*		
107	5c Nelson and H.M.S. *Boreas*		
108	6c William IV and H.M.S. *Pegasus*		
109	10c Blackbeard and pirate ketch		
118	15c Collingwood and H.M.S. *Pelican*		
111	25c *Solent I* (paddle-steamer)		
112	35c George V and H.M.S. *Canada* (screw corvette)		
113	50c H.M.S. *Renown* (battle cruiser)		
114	75c *Federal Maple* (freighter)		
119	$1 *Sol Quest* (yacht)		
115	$2.50 H.M.S. *London* (destroyer)		
121	$5 *Pathfinder* (tug)		
	Set of 17	20.00	16.00

1974

Nos. 387/8 of Antigua overprinted

(a) with **BARBUDA 13 JULY 1922**

150†	1c *Orinoco* (mail paddle-steamer)	10	10
152†	2c Hydrofoil	15	15

(b) with **BARBUDA 15 SEPT. 1874 G.P.U.**

151†	1c *Orinoco* (mail paddle-steamer)	10	10
153†	2c Hydrofoil	15	15

1975

Nos. 427/31 of Antigua overprinted **BARBUDA**

217	5c Carib war canoe		
218	15c Ship of the line, 1770		
219	35c H.M.S. *Boreas*, 1787, and Nelson		
220	50c Yachts		
221	$1 Yachts		
	Set of 5	1.75	1.75

223	35c Battle of the Saints, 1782		
224	50c H.M.S. *Ramillies* (ship of the line), 1782		
225	75c Firing broadside		
226	95c Burning ship		
	Set of 4	8.00	4.25

1977

345†	50c Royal Yacht *Britannia*	25	20

363†	75c *Buchorn* (tug) and barge	50	35
364†	75c German battleship (1914–18 War)	50	35

1978

Nos. 576/80 of Antigua overprinted **BARBUDA**

403	10c Yacht regatta		
404	50c Fishing and work boat race		
405	90c Yacht race		
406	$2 Power boat race		
	Set of 4	1.50	1.25
MS407	$2.50 Guadeloupe—Antigua yacht race	1.25	1.60

1979

Nos. 623 and **MS**626 of Antigua overprinted **BARBUDA**

475†	50c H.M.S. *Endeavour* (Cook)	50	45
MS478†	$2.50 H.M.S. *Resolution* (Cook)	1.25	1.50

1981

No. 715 of Antigua overprinted **BARBUDA**

600	90c Sailing dinghy	1.40	45

1984

Nos. 830/4 of Antigua overprinted **BARBUDA MAIL**

721	45c *Booker Vanguard* (freighter)		
722	50c *Canberra* (liner)		
723	60c Sailing boats		
724	$4 *Fairwind* (cargo liner)		
	Set of 4	8.00	3.75
MS725	$5 18th-century English man-o-war	4.25	4.50

1985

Nos. 911 and **MS**913 of Antigua overprinted **BARBUDA MAIL**

791†	$1 Statue of Liberty and cadet ship	55	60
MS793†	$5 Liner and New York skyline	2.75	3.00

1986

No. 944 of Antigua overprinted **BARBUDA MAIL**

840†	$3 Windsurfing	1.50	1.60

No. 967 of Antigua overprinted **BARBUDA MAIL**

844†	$4 Royal Yacht Britannia	2.50	2.10

1987

Nos. 1009/13 of Antigua overprinted **BARBUDA MAIL**

918	30c Tug		
919	60c Game-fishing boat		
920	$1 Yacht		
921	$4 Lugger		
	Set of 4	3.50	3.50
MS922	$5 Boat building	8.00	8.50

Nos. 1072/6 of Antigua overprinted **BARBUDA MAIL**

936	30c *Canada I* (yacht), 1981		
937	60c *Gretel II* (yacht), 1970		
938	$1 *Sceptre* (yacht), 1958		
939	$3 *Vigilant* (yacht), 1893		
	Set of 4	2.75	2.75
MS940	$5 *Australia II* defeating *Liberty* (yachts), 1983	2.75	3.50

Nos. 1100, 1102, 1104, 1106 and 1109 of Antigua overprinted **BARBUDA MAIL**

950†	10c *Spirit of Australia* (powerboat), 1978	35	25
952†	30c U.S.S. *Triton* (submarine), 1960	75	55
954†	60c U.S.S. *New Jersey* (battleship), 1942	1.00	75
956†	90c *United States* (liner), 1952	1.25	1.00
959†	$3 *Queen Elizabeth 2* (liner), 1969	3.00	2.50

1988

Nos. 1172/9 of Antigua overprinted **BARBUDA MAIL**

1043†	10c Fleet of Columbus, 1493	15	15
1044†	30c Fleet of Columbus, 1493	20	20
1045†	45c *Santa Mariagalante* (Columbus), 1493	35	35
1046†	60c Painos Indian canoe, 1493	35	35
1048†	$1 Fleet of Columbus and ship's boat, 1493	65	65
1049†	$3 Fleet of Columbus at anchor, 1493	1.50	1.50
1050†	$4 Fleet of Columbus at sea, 1493	2.00	2.00

Nos. 1190/4 of Antigua overprinted **BARBUDA MAIL**

1066	30c Two yachts rounding buoy		
1067	60c Three yachts		
1068	$1 British yacht under way		
1069	$3 Three yachts		
	Set of 4	2.75	2.75
MS1070	$5 Two yachts	2.50	3.00

1989

Nos. 1281/9 of Antigua overprinted **BARBUDA MAIL**

1126	25c *Festivale* (liner)		
1127	45c *Southward* (liner)		
1128	50s *Sagafjord* (liner)		
1129	60c *Daphne* (liner)		
1130	75c *Cunard Countess* (liner)		
1131	90c *Song of America* (liner)		
1132	$3 *Island Princess* (liner)		
1133	$4 *Galileo* (liner)		
	Set of 8	5.00	5.00
MS1134	Two sheets (a) $6 *Norway* (liner); (b) $6 *Oceanic* (liner)		
	Price for 2 sheets	12.00	13.00

1991

No. 1382 of Antigua overprinted **BARBUDA MAIL**

1244†	50c *Britannia* (mail paddle-steamer), 1840	25	25

Nos. 1483/4 of Antigua overprinted **BARBUDA MAIL**

1283†	$5 Landing ships and landing craft, North Africa, 1942	2.75	2.75
MS1284†	Two sheets (a) $6 American battle-ships sinking, Pearl Harbor, 1941 (other sheet shows air attack on Germany)		
	Price for 2 sheets	7.00	7.50

Nos. 1503/10 of Antigua overprinted **BARBUDA MAIL**

1285	10c Phoenician galley (Hanno), 450 B.C.		
1286	15c Greek warship (Pytheas), 325 B.C.		
1287	45c Viking ship (Eric the Red), 985		
1288	60c Viking ship (Leif Eriksson), 1000		
1289	$1 Dhow (Scylax), 518		
1290	$2 Venetian merchant ship (Polo), 1259		
1291	$4 Pharonic galley (Queen Hatsheput), 1493 B.C.		
1292	$5 Irish coracle (St. Brendan), 500		
	Set of 8	6.25	6.50

1992

No. **MS**1524 of Antigua overprinted **BARBUDA MAIL**

MS1333	Three sheets (c) $6 Sailing dinghies, Trinquetaille (other sheets show different Van Gogh paintings)		
	Price for 3 sheets	7.00	7.25

Nos. 1585/6 and 1591/3 of Antigua overprinted **BARBUDA MAIL**

1364†	$1 *Nimitz* class aircraft carrier and *Ticonderoga* class cruiser	45	50
1365†	$1 Tourist launch, Pearl Harbor	45	50
1370†	$1 American warships burning, Pearl Harbor, 1941	45	50
1371†	$1 American battleships in flames, Pearl Harbor	45	50
1372†	$1 U.S.S. *Nevada* (battleship), Pearl Harbor, 1941	45	50

BASUTOLAND

Southern Africa
12 pence = 1 shilling
20 shillings = 1 pound

1949

As No. 115 of Antigua

39†	3d Paddle-steamer	65	50

BECHUANALAND

Southern Africa
12 pence = 1 shilling
20 shillings = 1 pound

1949

As No. 115 of Antigua

139†	3d Paddle-steamer	70	50

BELARUS

Eastern Europe
100 kopeks = 1 rouble

1992

3	2r Medieval ship	4.00	4.00

BELGIAN CONGO

Central Africa
100 centimes = 1 franc

1894

27†	40c Native canoe	3.00	2.00

29†	10f *Deliverance* (stern wheel paddle-steamer)	70.00	15.00

1909

Nos. 27 and 29 overprinted **CONGO BELGE**

50†	40c Native canoe	1.75	1.75
55b†	10f *Deliverance* (stern wheel paddle-steamer)	70.00	14.00

1910

As Nos. 27 and 29 but inscribed "CONGO BELGE-BELGISCH CONGO"

64†	40c Native canoe (black and green)	1.75	1.50
69†	10f *Deliverance* (stern wheel paddle-steamer)	16.00	13.00

1915

As No. 64 but colour changed

74†	40c Native canoe (black and red)	3.25	1.50

1918

As Nos. 69 and 74, with centres in blue, surcharged with red cross and premium

82†	40c + 40c Native canoe	35	45
86†	10f + 10f *Deliverance* (stern wheel paddle-steamer)	70.00	80.00

1920

89†	2f Native canoes on beach	55	20

1921

No. 64 surcharged

91†	5c on 40c Native canoe	20	20

No. 69 overprinted **1921**

100†	10f *Deliverance* (stern wheel paddle-steamer)	4.00	2.75

1922

No. 74 surch **.25c.** *without bars*

103	25c on 40c Native canoe	2.00	30

No. 74 surcharged **0.25** *with bars*

112	25c on 40c Native canoe	70	30

1925

141	25c + 25c Native canoe	20	20

1931

193†	4f Beached canoes	30	15

1949

293	4f 19th-century full-rigged ship	60	15

1953

319	3f Canoe, Lake Kivu		
320	7f Canoe, Lake Kivu		
	Set of 2	2.50	45

BELGIAN OCCUPATION OF GERMANY

North-west Europe
100 centimes = 1 franc
100 pfennig = 1 mark

1919

No. 191 of Belgium overprinted **ALLEMAGNE DUITSCHLAND**

14	1f Shipping in the Scheldt	23.00	21.00

1920

No. 191 of Belgium surcharged **EUPEN & MALMEDY 1 MK 25**

24	1m25 on 1f Shipping in the Scheldt	22.00	30.00

No. 191 of Belgium overprinted **Eupen**

38	1f Shipping in the Scheldt	22.00	22.00

No. 191 of Belgium overprinted **Malmedy**

55	1f Shipping in the Scheldt	22.00	22.00

BELGIUM

North-west Europe
100 centimes = 1 franc

1915

191†	1f Shipping in the Scheldt	17.00	25

1918

No. 191 surcharged **1F** *and cross*

232†	1f + 1f Shipping in the Scheldt	38.00	38.00

1927

438	25c + 10c Rowing boat		
439	35c + 10c Rowing boat		
440	60c + 10c Rowing boat		
441	1f75 + 25c Rowing boat		
442	5f + 1f Rowing boat		
	Set of 5	5.75	6.00

1929

556†	1f75 + 25c *Aquitania* and *Dinteldyk* (liners)	3.50	3.00

1946

1174	1f35 *Prince Baudouin* (mail steamer)		
1175	2f25 *Marie Henriette* (paddle-steamer)		
1176	3f15 *Diamant* (paddle-steamer)		
	Set of 3	1.25	35

1197†	1f35 + 1f15 *Bobby* (fishing boat)	35	35

1947

1202†	2f25 *Belgica* (Gerlache)	3.50	85

1948

1222†	2f25 Freighter in Antwerp Docks	1.75	35
1224†	3f Freighter in Antwerp Docks	12.00	10

1953

1442†	80c + 20c Fishing boats *Marcel, De Meeuw* and *Jacqueline Denise*	1.00	35
1444†	2f + 50c Fishing boats and *Elisabethville* (liner)	2.00	70

1956

1589†	20c + 5c Medieval ship	10	10
1590†	80c + 20c Medieval ship	60	30
1591†	1f20 + 30c Medieval ship	60	35
1592†	1f50 + 50c Medieval ship	60	30

1957

1611	2f Steamer entering Zeebrugge harbour	70	10

1958

1665†   3f + 1f50 Rowing boat 3.25   1.25

1966

1991   1f + 50c *Erika Dan* (polar vessel)
1992   3f + 1f50 *Belgica* (Gerlache)
1993   6f + 3f *Magga Dan* (Antarctic supply ship)

            Set of 3   1.10   60

MS1994   10f + 5f *Magga Dan* (Antarctic supply ship) 1.25   1.25

1968

2082†   13f + 5f Yachts   45   55

2090†   6f *Mineral Seraing* and *Gand* (ore carriers)   25   15
2091†   10f Canal barges on "lift", Ronquieres ..   35   25

2101   6f Cargo ship in Ghent Canal   25   15

1969

2132†   3f Cargo ship on aqueduct   25   10

1970

2157†   2f50 *Skaustrand* (freighter), Zelzate   30   10

1971

2230   10f *Erika Dan* (polar vessel) 1.00   80

1973

2318†   10f + 5f 18th-century sailing ship from Ostend 2.25   2.50

1975

2384†   6f50 + 2f50 Gondola, Venice   40   50

1981

2650†   6f50 Yacht   25   15

1982

2689†   50f + 14f *Treaty of Rome* (yacht) 2.25   2.25
MS2690†   25f *Treaty of Rome* (yacht) (sheet also contains three other sports designs) 3.50   3.50

1985

2844†   24f Freighter and landing craft 1.10   30

1988

2936   10f *Snipe* (trawler) leaving harbour
2937   10f *Asannat* (trawler) and beach scene

2938   10f Cross-channel ferry and yacht
2939   10f Container ship

          Set of 4   1.60   1.75

1990

3027†   10f Container ship and tug in Berendrecht Lock, Antwerp   40   20

1991

3059†   14f Tourist boat in the Neptune Grottoes, Couvin   70   15

3091†   14f 16th-century sailing ship   65   15

1992

3132†   30f Barque 1.25   40

OFFICIAL STAMPS

1946

As No. 1224 *but additionally inscribed* "B"
O1242†   3f Freighter in Antwerp Docks 23.00   8.25

BELIZE

Central America
100 cents = 1 dollar

1979

481†   10c *Heron H* (mail boat), 1949   15   10
482†   35c Mail canoe, 1920   20   20
485† $2 *Eagle* (mail boat), 1856 ....   1.10   1.75

GIBBONS STAMP MONTHLY

Finest and most informative magazine for all collectors. Obtainable from your newsagent or by postal subscription — details on request.

1981

671   10c British 19th-century sail warship
672   25c *Madagascar* (sail merchantman), 1837
673   35c *Whitby* (brig), 1838
674   50c *China* (sail merchantman), 1850
675   85c *Swiftsure* (sail merchantman), 1850
676   $2 *Windsor Castle* (sail merchantman), 1857
                                    Set of 6   9.50   2.75
MS677 $5 18th–19th-century naval battle 9.00   5.00

1983

755† $2 *Heron H* (mail boat) 2.75   3.00

1985

847†   15c *Hinchinbrook II* (sailing packet) engaging *Grand Turk* (American privateer),1814   55   15
848†   25c *Duke of Marlborough II* (sailing packet)   70   25
849†   75c *Diana* (sailing packet) 1.25   60
850† $1 *Falmouth* packet ship 1.50   1.00
851† $3 *Conway* (mail paddle-steamer) 3.75   3.00

864† $4 Royal Yacht *Britannia* 3.00   3.00

1986

932†   75c U.S.S. *Constitution* (frigate) 1.00   1.00

No. 932 overprinted **STOCKHOLMIA 86** *and emblem*
953†   75c U.S.S. *Constitution* (frigate)   90   90

1987

985   25c *America II* (yacht)
986   75c *Stars and Stripes* (yacht)
987   $1 *Australia II* (yacht), 1983
988   $4 *White Crusader* (yacht)
                                    Set of 4   4.75   4.25

1988

1046†   75c Hospital ship and ambulance launch, 1937   80   65

1991

1115†   50c Yachts and "Jack-o-Lantern"   30   35

1993

1142† $1 Submarine   60   65

BENIN
West Africa
100 centimes = 1 franc

1977

675†   60f Tourist boat, Ganvie stilt village   55   35

1978

727†   60f Pirogue   45   25

1979

750†   20f H.M.S. *Resolution* and H.M.S. *Discovery* (Cook)   60   30

753†   50f Mail canoe   60   40

1980

806†   15f Fishing canoe   15   10

1983

886   125f Oil rig and support vessels   75   20

1984

968   90f 2nd-century Sidon merchant ship
969   125f *Wavertree* (sail merchantman), 1895
                                    Set of 2   1.50   1.10

1985

987†   200f Oil rig 2.00   1.40

1988
No. 987 surcharged **125f**
1087†   125f on 200f Oil rig   ....

1099   125f Dugout canoes
1100   190f Dugout canoe
                                    Set of 2   1.75   1.25

1990

1125   150f Liner   90   55

POSTAGE DUE STAMPS
1978

721†   80f Postman in canoe   65   55

BERMUDA

North Atlantic Ocean
1902 12 pence = 1 shilling
20 shillings = 1 pound
1970 100 cents = 1 dollar

1902

34a ½d Vessel in dry dock and schooner
35 ½d Vessel in dry dock and schooner (black and green)
41 ½d Vessel in dry dock and schooner (green)
32 1d Vessel in dry dock and schooner (brown and red)
42 1d Vessel in dry dock and schooner (red)
37 2d Vessel in dry dock and schooner
38 2½d Vessel in dry dock and schooner (brown and blue)
43 2½d Vessel in dry dock and schooner (blue)
33 3d Vessel in dry dock and schooner
39 4d Vessel in dry dock and schooner
Set of 10 65.00 42.00

1910

76b†	¼d Sailing ship, *c.* 1620	1.00	1.25
77†	½d Sailing ship, *c.* 1620	50	15
79†	1d Sailing ship, *c.* 1620	7.50	30
79b†	1½d Sailing ship, *c.* 1620	3.50	35
80†	2d Sailing ship, *c.* 1620	1.25	1.50
81a†	2½d Sailing ship, *c.* 1620 (green)	1.00	1.50
82†	2½d Sailing ship, *c.* 1620 (blue)	2.50	35
83†	3d Sailing ship, *c.* 1620 (blue)	15.00	26.00
84†	3d Sailing ship, *c.* 1620 (purple on yellow)	80	1.00
85†	4d Sailing ship, *c.* 1620	1.00	1.25
86†	6d Sailing ship, *c.* 1620	80	80
51†	1s Sailing ship, *c.* 1620	2.00	3.75

1918

No. 79 overprinted **WAR TAX**

56	1d Sailing ship, *c.* 1620	35	40

1920

59 ¼d Sailing ship, *c.* 1620
60 ½d Sailing ship, *c.* 1620
65 1d Sailing ship, *c.* 1620
61 2d Sailing ship, *c.* 1620
66 2½d Sailing ship, *c.* 1620
62 3d Sailing ship, *c.* 1620
63 4d Sailing ship, *c.* 1620
67 6d Sailing ship, *c.* 1620
64 1s Sailing ship, *c.* 1620
Set of 9 60.00 £150

1936

98†	½d *Song of the Wind* (yacht)	10	10
101†	2d *Lucie* (yacht)	4.50	2.00
106†	1s6d *Song of the Wind* (yacht)	40	10

1938

110†	1d *J. W. Clise* (schooner) and *Monarch of Bermuda* (liner)	40	20
111b†	1½d *J. W. Clise* (schooner) and *Monarch of Bermuda* (liner)	1.25	35

1940

No. 110a surcharged **HALFPENNY**

122	½d on 1d *J. W. Clise* (schooner) and *Monarch of Bermuda* (liner)	30	45

1949

As No. 115 of Antigua

131†	3d Paddle-steamer	90	75

1953

138†	2d *Victory II* (racing dinghy)	40	40
139†	2½d Sir George Somers's *Sea Venture* (galleon), 1609	1.25	50
142†	4½d *Sea Venture* and inter-island boat	45	1.00
143b†	9d *Sea Venture* and inter-island boat	6.50	2.50

1964

183	3d *Tsotsi in the Bundu* (Finn class yacht)	10	10

1967

208†	3d *Mercury* (cable ship)	10	10
211†	2s6d *Mercury*	25	40

1968

220 3d Olympic yachts
221 1s Olympic yachts
222 1s6d Olympic yachts
223 2s6d Olympic yachts
Set of 4 45 60

1971

275 4c Building *Deliverance* (galleon), 1609
276 15c *Deliverance* and *Patience* (pinnace) at Jamestown
277 18c Wreck of *Sea Venture* (galleon), 1609
278 24c *Deliverance* and *Patience* at sea
Set of 4 5.00 6.00

1975

336†	17c Rowing boats	40	30
337†	20c *Lady Catherine* (American sail merchantman), 1775	45	70

1976

357†	5c *Ready* (bathysphere)	35	10
358†	17c *Panulirus II* and *MicMac* (research vessels)	70	60
359†	20c H.M.S. *Challenger* (survey ship), 1873	75	2.00

361†	5c *Christian Radich* (cadet ship)	60	20
362†	12c *Juan Sebastian de Elcano* (Spanish cadet schooner)	1.00	1.75
363†	17c *Eagle* (U.S. coastguard cadet ship)	1.25	1.75
364†	20c *Sir Winston Churchill* (cadet schooner)	1.40	2.50
365†	40c *Kruzenshtern* (Russian cadet barque)	2.00	3.00

1977

379 5c 17th-century merchant ship
380 15c H.M.S. *Resolution* (ship of the line), 1795
381 17c Pilots rowing out to *Marco Bozzaris* (paddle-steamer)
382 20c Pilot gig and *Harvest Queen* (brig)
383 40c Pilot cutter and *Queen Elizabeth 2* (liner)
Set of 5 3.00 5.00

1979

411†	25c *Blue Heron* (police launch)	50	50

1980

418†	50c *Orduna I* (liner), 1926	45	35
419†	$1 *Delta* (screw steamer), 1856	85	1.00
420†	$2 *Lord Sidmouth* (sailing packet), 1818	1.40	1.75

1981

434† 50c 19th-century onion boat 65 1.10
435† $1 *Devonshire* (privateer) and *Felipe Quinto* (Spanish galleon) 1.50 2.50

1983

461 12c Early dinghy
462 30c Modern dinghy
463 40c Early dinghy (different)
464 $1 Modern dinghy with spinnaker
Set of 4 2.50 4.25

468† $1 U.S.S. *Patoka* (airship tender) 2.00 3.25

1984

472† $1 *Lady Hammond* (packet boat) 2.00 3.25

475† 40c Wreck of the *Sea Venture* (galleon), 1609 . . . . 90 1.00
476† $1 Fleet leaving Plymouth, 1609 . . . . 2.00 3.25

481† $1 Olympic yachts 2.25 2.75

1986

507 3c *Constellation* (schooner), 1943
508 5c *Early Riser* (pilot boat), 1876
509 7c *Madiana* (screw steamer), 1903
510 10c *Curlew* (sail/steamer), 1856
511 12c *Warwick* (sailing ship), 1619
512 15c H.M.S. *Vixen* (gunboat), 1890

512c 18c *Madiana* (screw steamer), 1903
513 20c *San Pedro* (Spanish galleon), 1594
514 25c *Alert* (fishing sloop), 1877
515 40c *North Carolina* (barque), 1880
516 50c *Mark Antonie* (Spanish privateer), 1777
517 60c *Mary Celestia* (Confederate paddle-steamer), 1864
517c 70c *Caesar* (brig), 1818
518 $1 *L'Herminie* (French frigate), 1839
519 $1.50 *Caesar* (brig), 1818
520 $2 *Lord Amherst* (transport), 1778
521 $3 *Minerva* (sailing ship), 1849
522 $5 *Caraquet* (cargo liner), 1923
523 $8 H.M.S. *Pallas* (frigate), 1783
Set of 19 26.00 27.00

532† $1 *Eagle* (cadet ship) (on stamp No. 363) 2.25 2.50
MS533† $1.50 *Queen of Bermuda* (liner) 5.00 4.50

1987

538† $1.50 *Prince David* (liner) 2.50 3.50

549† 15c Rowing boat (flying boat tender) . . . . /5 15

1988

566 18c H.M.S. *Lutine* (frigate), 1799
567 50c *Sentinel* (cable ship)
568 60c *Bermuda* (liner), 1931
569 $2 H.M.S. *Valerian* (sloop), 1926
Set of 4 4.00 4.25

1989

574 18c *Corona* (ferry)
575 50c Rowing boat ferry
576 60c Barge ferry, St. George's
577 $2 *Laconia* (ferry)
Set of 4 3.75 4.00

578† 18c Fishing boat, Morgan's Island 25 25
580† 50c Sailing ship at quay, Front St., Hamilton 70 85
582† 70c Boat-yard, Hamilton 95 1.25
583† $1 Naval dockyard 1.25 2.00

1990

609† 60c Fishing boat, Salt Kettle, 1916 . . . . . . 85 1.25

Nos. 511, 516 *and* 519 *surcharged*
615 30c on 12c *Warwick* (sailing ship), 1619
616 55c on 50 c *Mark Antonie* (Spanish privateer), 1777
617 80c on $1.50 *Caesar* (brig), 1818
Set of 3 1.75 1.90

619† 55c *Westmeath* (cable ship), 1890 . . . . . . 85 1.00
621† $2 *Sir Eric Sharp* (cable ship) 2.75 3.25

1991

No. 619 *overprinted* **BUSH-MAJOR 16 MARCH 1991**
623† 55c *Westmeath* (cable ship), 1890 . . . . . . 1.25 1.50

636† 20c H.M.S. *Argonaut* (cruiser) in floating dock 40 30

1992

640† 20c Sailboards 35 30

651† 25c Wreck of *Sea Venture*, 1609 . . . . 30 35

1993

679† 25c Liner 30 35
682† $2 Liner 2.25 2.40

BHUTAN

Central Asia
100 chetrum = 1 ngultrum

1972

Appendix stamp surcharged

264† 90ch on 2n50 Liner 4.50 6.00

1974

285† 3ch *Hindoostan* (paddle- steamer) and
Iberia (liner) 20 10

1986

678 50ch *Libertad* (Argentine full-rigged cadet
ship)
679 1n *Shalom* (Israeli liner)
680 2n *Leonardo da Vinci* (Italian liner)
681 3n *Mircea* (Rumanian cadet barque)
682 4n *France* (French liner)
683 5n *United States* (American liner)
684 15n *Queen Elizabeth 2* (British liner)
685 20n *Europa* (West German liner)
Set of 8 5.50 5.50
Captions on Nos. 678 and 681 were transposed in error.

1987

687† 20ch *Santa Maria* (Columbus) 30 15
689† 50ch *Santa Maria* (Columbus) 40 15

1988

731† 5n *Natchez* and *Robert E Lee*
(Mississippi paddle-steamers), 1870 70 50
733† 7n U.S.S. *Constitution* (frigate), 1797 .... 80 65

1989

782† 25n Tug 1.40 1.25

798 50ch *La Reale* (Spanish galley), 1680
799 1n *Turtle* (submarine), 1776
800 2n *Charlotte Dundas* (steamship), 1802
801 3n *Great Eastern* (paddle-steamer), 1858
802 4n H.M.S. *Warrior* (armoured ship), 1862
803 5n Mississippi river steamer, 1884
804 6n *Preussen* (full-rigged ship), 1902
805 7n U.S.S. *Arizona* (battleship), 1915
806 10n *Bluenose* (fishing schooner), 1921
807 15n Steam trawler, 1925
808 20n "Liberty" freighter, 1943
809 25n *United States* (liner), 1952
Set of 12 5.00 4.00
MS810 Twelve sheets (a) 25n Chinese junk,
1988; (b) 25n U.S.S. *Constitution* (frigate),
1797; (c) 25n VIIC type U-boat, 1942; (d) 25n
Cutty Sark (clipper), 1869; (e) 25n H.M.S.
Dreadnought (battleship), 1906; (f) 25n U.S.S.
Monitor (ironclad), 1862; (g) 25n Moran
Company tug, 1950; (h) 25n *Normandie*
(liner), 1933; (i) 25n H.M.S. *Resolution* (Cook),
1772; (j) 25n *Titanic* (liner), 1912; (k) 25n
H.M.S. *Victory* (ship of the line), 1805; (l) 25n
Yamato (Japanese battleship), 1944;
Price for 12 sheets 13.00 13.00

1990

865† 20ch Japanese fishing boat 10 10
866† 50ch Japanese raft 10 10
867† 75ch Japanese sailing ship and fishing
boats 10 10
870† 6n Japanese sampans 30 30
871† 7n Japanese hay boat 35 35

918† 4ch Ancient Egyptian ship 10 10
920† 10ch Greek galley 10 10
928† 30n Inflatable dinghy 1.40 1.40
MS929 Fourteen sheets (l) 25n Yacht; (m) 25n
Tug (other sheets show Disney scenes)
Price for 14 sheets 15.00 16.00

1991

MS955 Twelve sheets (j) 30n Fishing punts
Pont de Clichy (other sheets show different
Van Gogh paintings)
Price for 12 sheets 16.00 16.00

1992

977† 15n *Santa Maria* (Columbus) 70 70

Appendix

The following stamps have either been issued in excess of
postal needs, or have not been made available to the public in
reasonable quantities at face value. Miniature sheets, imperforate
stamps etc. are excluded from this section.

1970

Famous Paintings. 3n Sailing dinghy
New U.P.U. Headquarters Building, Berne 3, 10, 20ch, 2n50 (all
show liner)

BOLIVIA

South America
1916 100 centavos = 1 boliviano
1963 100 centavos = 1 peso boliviano

1916

144† 2c Balsa boat, Lake Titicaca 30 15

1930

No. 144 surch **R.S. 21-4 1930** *and value*
225† 0.03c on 2c Balsa boat, Lake Titicaca .. 85 70
227† 25c on 2c Balsa boat, Lake Titicaca 70 50

245† 15c Plane over river boat 50 35
246† 20c Plane over river boat 50 35
248† 50c Plane over river boat 50 15
250† 2b Plane over river boat 50 25

1941

380† 10b Balsa boat on Lake Titicaca 4.00 50
381† 20b Balsa boat on Lake Titicaca 4.50 85

1942

384 5c Balsa boat (on stamp No. 380)
385 10c Balsa boat (on stamp No. 380)
386 20c Balsa boat (on stamp No. 380)
387 40c Balsa boat (on stamp No. 380)
388 90c Balsa boat (on stamp No. 380)
389 1b Balsa boat (on stamp No. 380)
390 10b Balsa boat (on stamp No. 380)
Set of 7 20.00 11.50

1982

1079	14p Naval Base, Puerto Busch	60	20

1987

1141	20c *Nina* (Columbus)			
1142	20c *Santa Maria* and *Pinta* (Columbus)			
		Set of 2	60	30

1992

1244†	50c Columbus's fleet	15	10

1251†	60c Columbus's ships leaving Palos	20	10

1265†	1b20 Rowing boat	40	30

BOTSWANA

Southern Africa
1967 100 cents = 1 rand
1976 100 thebe = 1 pula

1976

240†	35c Fishing punt	70	70

1978

432†	25t "Mokoro" canoe	40	40

1981

477	6t Paddle-steamer (on Bechuanaland stamp No. 139)	30	15

1991

717†	8t Canoe	25	15
720†	2p Canoe	2.25	2.50

BRAZIL

South America
1900 1000 reis = 1 milreis
1942 100 centavos = 1 cruzeiro
1986 100 centavos = 1 cruzado
1990 100 centavos = 1 cruzeiro

1900

226†	100r Discovery of Brazil, 1500	2.50	2.50

1916

286	100r Ship of 1616	7.00	3.75

1920

361†	600r Steamer	1.25	60
342†	1000r Steamer	2.50	10

1935

583†	300r Coutinho's *Gloria*, 1535	1.25	95

1948

774	5cr Ship of 1648 on arms of Paranagua	3.75	95

1953

847	1cr50 *Almirante Saldanha* (cadet ship) ..	70	20

1954

911†	40c Battle of Riachuelo	70	15

1957

969	2cr50 *Almirante Tamandare* (cruiser)		
970	3cr30 *Minas Gerais* (aircraft carrier)		
		Set of 2	1.10	20

1958

972	2cr50 19th-century sail merchantman	60	10

990	2cr50 Modern freighters	55	10

1960

1036	6cr50 Caravel of 1460	30	10

1967

1202	10c *Almirante Tamandare* (cruiser)	30	15

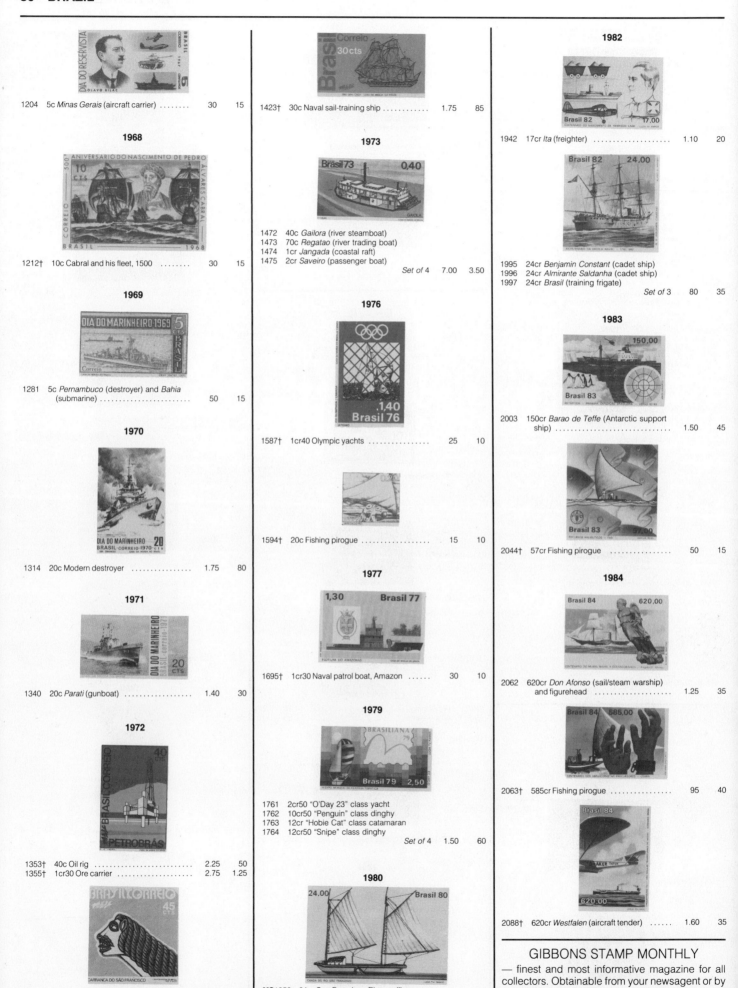

1204   5c *Minas Gerais* (aircraft carrier)   30   15

1968

1212†   10c Cabral and his fleet, 1500   30   15

1969

1281   5c *Pernambuco* (destroyer) and *Bahia* (submarine)   50   15

1970

1314   20c Modern destroyer 1.75   80

1971

1340   20c *Parati* (gunboat) 1.40   30

1972

1353†   40c Oil rig 2.25   50
1355†   1cr30 Ore carrier 2.75   1.25

1371†   45c Figurehead of local river craft   45   15

1423†   30c Naval sail-training ship 1.75   85

1973

1472   40c *Gailora* (river steamboat)
1473   70c *Regatao* (river trading boat)
1474   1cr *Jangada* (coastal raft)
1475   2cr *Saveiro* (passenger boat)
Set of 4   7.00   3.50

1976

1587†   1cr40 Olympic yachts   25   10

1594†   20c Fishing pirogue   15   10

1977

1695†   1cr30 Naval patrol boat, Amazon   30   10

1979

1761   2cr50 "O'Day 23" class yacht
1762   10cr50 "Penguin" class dinghy
1763   12cr "Hobie Cat" class catamaran
1764   12cr50 "Snipe" class dinghy
Set of 4   1.50   60

1980

MS1858   24cr Sao Francisco River sailing canoe 1.00   1.00

1982

1942   17cr *Ita* (freighter) 1.10   20

1995   24cr *Benjamin Constant* (cadet ship)
1996   24cr *Almirante Saldanha* (cadet ship)
1997   24cr *Brasil* (training frigate)
Set of 3   80   35

1983

2003   150cr *Barao de Teffe* (Antarctic support ship) 1.50   45

2044†   57cr Fishing pirogue   50   15

1984

2062   620cr *Don Afonso* (sail/steam warship) and figurehead 1.25   35

2063†   585cr Fishing pirogue   95   40

2088†   620cr *Westfalen* (aircraft tender) 1.60   35

1985

2174 220cr Modern corvette 65 30

2194 500cr *Especuladora* (ferry), 1835
2195 500cr *Segunda* (ferry), 1862
2196 500cr *Terceira* (ferry), 1911
2197 500cr *Urca* (ferry), 1981
　　　　　　　　　　　　　Set of 4 1.25 45

1986

2264† 50c *Minas Gerais* (cruiser), 1930s 20 10

1987

2281† 3cz Sailing canoes 30 15

2290 5cz Caravels, Recife, 1537 .... 20 10

2300 7cz Galleon, 1587 .... 30 15

1988

2309† 50cz Slave ship 10 10

1990

2406 3cz Container ship and barque 10 10

2425 20cz Amazon post launch 35 25

1991

2471† 36cr Yacht 10 10

2498 50cr *Vitoria* (Magellan)
2499 400cr Amazon canoe
　　　　　　　　　　　　　Set of 2 1.25 85

1992

2517 300cr Freighter and container ship 25 20

2528† 500cr Columbus's fleet 30 25

MS2531 500cr Three river boats; 1000cr Two
　　galleys; 2500cr River boat, Vila de Cameta,
　　1784 .... 1.50 1.25

2540† 500cr Canoe 20 15

BRITISH ANTARCTIC TERRITORY

Antarctica
1963 12 pence = 1 shilling
20 shillings = 1 pound
1971 100 pence = 1 pound

1963

1†	½d *Kista Dan* (polar supply ship)	45	1.00
6†	3d *John Biscoe II* (research ship)	1.75	60
8†	6d H.M.S. *Protector* (ice patrol ship)	2.00	1.00
14†	10s *Shackleton* (research ship)	45.00	23.00
15a†	£1 H.M.S. *Endurance* (ice patrol ship), 1956	£150	£120

1971

Nos. 1, 6, 8 and 14 surcharged in decimal currency

24†	½p on ½d *Kista Dan* (polar supply ship) ..	60	1.50
29†	3p on 3d *John Biscoe II* (research ship) ..	2.50	55
31†	5p on 6d H.M.S. *Protector* (ice patrol ship)	4.25	2.50
37†	50p on 10s *Shackleton* (research ship) ..	60.00	35.00

1973

64a†	½p H.M.S. *Resolution* (Cook)	75	80
65†	1p *Vostok* (Bellingshausen)	60	1.00
66†	1½p *Jane* (Weddell)	60	1.00
67†	2p *Tula* (Biscoe)	1.50	80
68†	2½p *L'Astrolabe* (D'Urville)	1.50	80
69†	3p H.M.S. *Erebus* (Ross)	2.25	85
70†	4p *Jason* (Larsen)	55	1.75
71†	5p *Belgica* (Gerlache)	2.25	1.75
72†	6p *Antarctic* (Nordenskjold)	80	1.75
73†	7½p *Scotia* (Bruce)	1.50	2.00
74†	10p *Pourquoi-pas?* (Charcot)	1.75	2.50
75†	15p *Endurance* (Shackleton).............	1.25	1.50
78a†	£1 *Penola* (Rymill)	2.00	3.75

1974

62† 15p *Trepassey* (supply ship) 2.25 2.00

1977

83† 6p Royal Yacht *Britannia* 95 20

1980

93†	3p *Tula* (Biscoe) and Sir John Barrow	20	10
94†	7p *Discovery* (Scott) and Sir Clement Markham	25	25
95†	11p *James Caird* (whale boat) (Shackleton) and Lord Curzon	30	30

1985

139†	7p *Penola* (Rymill), 1935	30	45

1987

156†	24p *Discovery* (Scott), Ross Island, 1902–4	80	1.00

1991

200†	12p H.M.S. *Erebus* and H.M.S. *Terror* (Ross), 1839	45	50
201†	26p Launch of *James Clark Ross* (research vessel)	85	95
202†	31p *James Clark Ross* (research vessel)	95	1.10

Nos. 200/2 additionally inscribed "200th Anniversary M. Faraday 1791–1867"

204†	12p H.M.S. *Erebus* and H.M.S. *Terror* (Ross), 1839	45	50
205†	26p Launch of *James Clark Ross* (research vessel)	85	95
206†	31p *James Clark Ross* (research vessel)	95	1.10

BRITISH GUIANA

South America
100 cents = 1 dollar

1852

9	1c *Sandbach* (sail merchantman)	£8500	£4250
10	4c *Sandbach* (sail merchantman)	£10000	£4500

1853

12	1c *Sandbach* (sail merchantman)	£2250	£800
20	4c *Sandbach* (sail merchantman)	£800	£300

1856

Imperforate

23	1c *Sandbach* (sail merchantman)		
24	4c *Sandbach* (on magenta)	—	£5500
26	4c *Sandbach* (on blue)	—	£32000

1860

29	1c *Sandbach* (red)	£950	£180
40	1c *Sandbach* (brown)	£275	80.00
85	1c *Sandbach* (black)	7.50	2.00
87	2c *Sandbach*	15.00	1.25
90	4c *Sandbach*	65.00	6.00
69	6c *Sandbach*	90.00	38.00
95	8c *Sandbach*	95.00	12.00
100	12c *Sandbach* (lilac).................	£110	15.00
99	12c *Sandbach* (grey)	£110	15.00
64	24c *Sandbach* (oval frame)	£140	50.00
78	24c *Sandbach* (round frame)	£110	9.00
82	48c *Sandbach*	£150	42.00

1876

170	1c *Sandbach*		
171	2c *Sandbach*		
172	4c *Sandbach*		
173	6c *Sandbach*		
174	8c *Sandbach*		
131	12c *Sandbach*		
132	24c *Sandbach*		
133	48c *Sandbach*		
134	96c *Sandbach*		

Set of 9 £550 £250

1878

Overprinted with thick horizontal or horizontal and vertical bars

(a) On Nos. 69 and 173

137	1c on 6c *Sandbach*	
141	1c on 6c *Sandbach*	

(b) On Nos. O1, O3 and O6/10

138	1c *Sandbach* (No. O1)	
139	1c *Sandbach* (No. O6)	
140	2c *Sandbach*	
144	4c *Sandbach*	
145	6c *Sandbach*	
146	8c *Sandbach* (No. O3)	
148	8c *Sandbach* (No. O10)	

Set of 9 £1300 £650

1881

Surcharged with figure. Old value barred out in ink

(a) On Nos. 82 and 134

152	"1" on 48c *Sandbach*	
149	"1" on 96c *Sandbach*	
150	"2" on 96c *Sandbach*	

(b) On No. O4 and unissued stamps overprinted **OFFICIAL**

154	"1" on 12c *Sandbach* (No. O4)	
153	"1" on 48c *Sandbach*	
155	"2" on 12c *Sandbach*	
158	"2" on 24c *Sandbach*	

Set of 7 £650 £500

COLLECT RAILWAYS ON STAMPS

Second revised edition of this Stanley Gibbons thematic catalogue. Now available at £9.50 (p. + p. £3) from: Stanley Gibbons Publications, 5 Parkside, Christchurch Road, Ringwood, Hants BH24 3SH.

1882

164	1c *Sandbach*		
163	2c *Sandbach*		

Set of 2 90.00 75.00
Each stamp is perforated with the word "SPECIMEN".

1888

As Nos. 170, etc, but without value in bottom tablet, surcharged **INLAND REVENUE** *and value*

175	1c *Sandbach*	
176	2c *Sandbach*	
177	3c *Sandbach*	
178	4c *Sandbach*	
179	6c *Sandbach*	
180	8c *Sandbach*	
181	10c *Sandbach*	
182	20c *Sandbach*	
183	40c *Sandbach*	
184	72c *Sandbach*	
185	$1 *Sandbach*	
186	$2 *Sandbach*	
187	$3 *Sandbach*	
188	$4 *Sandbach*	
189	$5 *Sandbach*	

Set of 15 £1200 £1000

1889

No. 176 surcharged with additional **2**

192	"2" on 2c *Sandbach*	55	25

193	1c *Sandbach* (purple and grey)	
213	1c *Sandbach* (green)	
194	2c *Sandbach* (purple and orange)	
234	2c *Sandbach* (purple and red)	
235	2c *Sandbach* (purple and black on red)	
253	2c *Sandbach* (red)	
195	4c *Sandbach* (purple and blue)	
254	4c *Sandbach* (brown and purple)	
255	5c *Sandbach* (blue)	
243	5c *Sandbach* (purple and blue on blue)	
198	6c *Sandbach* (purple and brown)	
236	6c *Sandbach* (black and blue)	
256	6c *Sandbach* (grey and black)	
199	8c *Sandbach* (purple and red)	
215	8c *Sandbach* (purple and black)	
200a	12c *Sandbach* (purple and mauve)	
257	12c *Sandbach* (orange and purple)	
201	24c *Sandbach*	
202	48c *Sandbach* (purple and red)	
247	48c *Sandbach* (grey and brown)	
248	60c *Sandbach*	
203	72c *Sandbach*	
205	96c *Sandbach* (purple and red)	
250	96c *Sandbach* (black and red on yellow)	

Set of 24 £250 £250

1890

Nos. 185/8 surcharged **ONE CENT**

207	1c on $1 *Sandbach*	
208	1c on $2 *Sandbach*	
209	1c on $3 *Sandbach*	
210	1c on $4 *Sandbach*	

Set of 4 4.25 6.00

1905

Design as Nos. 193, etc, overprinted **POSTAGE AND REVENUE**

251	$2.40 *Sandbach*	£160	£275

1913

272	1c *Sandbach*	
260a	2c *Sandbach* (red)	
274	2c *Sandbach* (violet)	
275	4c *Sandbach*	
262	5c *Sandbach*	
263	6c *Sandbach* (grey and black)	
276	6c *Sandbach* (blue)	
264	12c *Sandbach*	

278 24c *Sandbach*
279 48c *Sandbach*
280 60c *Sandbach*
281 72c *Sandbach*
282 96c *Sandbach*

Set of 13 42.00 £100

1918
No. 260a optd **WAR TAX**

271 2c *Sandbach* 15 15

1934

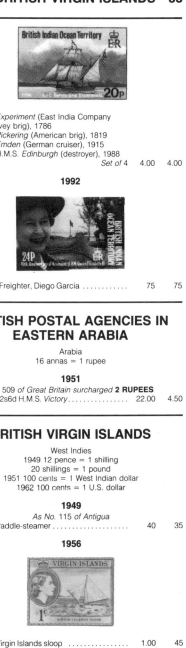

294† 24c Sugar cane in punts 1.75 2.50

1938
As No. 294, but with portrait of King George VI
312a† 24c Sugar cane in punts 1.00 10

1944
As No. 115 of Antigua
325† 6c Paddle-steamer 25 35

1954

344† $2 Gold dredger 11.00 3.25

OFFICIAL STAMPS

1875
Nos. 78, 85, 87, 95 and 100 overprinted **OFFICIAL**
O1 1c *Sandbach* 28.00 11.00
O2 2c *Sandbach* £100 14.00
O3 8c *Sandbach* £250 £100
O4 12c *Sandbach* £1000 £425
O5 24c *Sandbach* £700 £190

1877
Nos. 170/4 overprinted **OFFICIAL**
O6 1c *Sandbach* £150 55.00
O7 2c *Sandbach* 70.00 13.00
O8 4c *Sandbach* 75.00 20.00
O9 6c *Sandbach* £1800 £425
O10 8c *Sandbach* £1600 £350

BRITISH HONDURAS
Central America
100 cents = 1 dollar

1938

157† 25c "Dorey" (local canoe) 90 65

1949

169† 5c H.M.S. *Merlin* (sloop), 1798 . . . . 30 15
170† 10c H.M.S. *Merlin* 30 20
171† 15c H.M.S. *Merlin* 30 15

As No. 115 of Antigua
173† 5c Paddle-steamer 45 15

1973

343† 3c Racing yachts 10 10

BRITISH INDIAN OCEAN TERRITORY
Indian Ocean
1968 100 cents = 1 rupee
1990 100 pence = 1 pound

1968
No. 203 of Seychelles overprinted **B.I.O.T.**
7† 45c Outrigger canoe 20 30

1969

32 45c Outrigger canoe
33 75c Pirogue
34 1r *Nordvaer* (travelling post office)
35 1r50 *Isle of Farquhar* (schooner)

Set of 4 2.50 3.00

1974

56 85c *Nordvaer* (travelling post office)
57 2r50 *Nordvaer*

Set of 2 1.25 2.00

1990

105† 54p *Nordvaer* (travelling post office) (on
stamp No. 34) 2.00 2.00

1991

114† 54p Customs motor boat and inflatable
intercepting yacht 2.50 2.50

115 20p *Experiment* (East India Company
survey brig), 1786
116 24p *Pickering* (American brig), 1819
117 34p *Emden* (German cruiser), 1915
118 54p H.M.S. *Edinburgh* (destroyer), 1988
Set of 4 4.00 4.00

1992

121† 24p Freighter, Diego Garcia 75 75

BRITISH POSTAL AGENCIES IN EASTERN ARABIA
Arabia
16 annas = 1 rupee

1951
No. 509 of Great Britain surcharged **2 RUPEES**
41† 2r on 2s6d H.M.S. *Victory* 22.00 4.50

BRITISH VIRGIN ISLANDS
West Indies
1949 12 pence = 1 shilling
20 shillings = 1 pound
1951 100 cents = 1 West Indian dollar
1962 100 cents = 1 U.S. dollar

1949
As No. 115 of Antigua
127† 3d Paddle-steamer 40 35

1956

150† 1c Virgin Islands sloop 1.00 45
156† 12c *New Idea* (sloop) under
construction 1.25 55

1962
Nos. 150 and 156 surcharged in U.S. currency
163† 2c on 1c Virgin Islands sloop 40 10
168† 10c on 12c *New Idea* (sloop) under
construction 30 10

1964

186† 12c *Youth of Tortola* (inter-island ferry) . . 1.00 80
191† $1.40 Yachts 12.00 5.50

1966

203† 5c *Atrato I* (paddle-steamer), 1866 . . . . . . 20 10
206† 60c Mail packet ship at Road Town,
1866 . . . . 85 60

No. 191 surcharged
208† $1.50 on $1.40 Yachts 2.00 2.00

1967

217† 4c *Mercury* (cable ship) 10 10
219† 50c *Mercury* 30 20

1968

223† 40c Game fishing boat 85 40

1969

237† 10c Yachts, Tortola 20 10

1970

240 ½c Carib canoe
241 1c *Santa Maria* (Columbus)
242 2c *Elizabeth Bonaventure* (Drake)
243 3c Dutch buccaneer, 1660
244 4c *Thetis* (sail merchantman), 1827
245 5c Henry Morgan's ship
246 6c H.M.S. *Boreas* (Nelson) (frigate), 1784
247 8c H.M.S. *Eclair* (schooner), 1804
248 10c H.M.S. *Formidable* (ship of the line),
     1782
249 12c H.M.S. *Nymph* (sloop), 1778
250 15c *Windsor Castle* (sailing packet)
     engaging *Jeune Richard* (French brig),
     1807
251 25c H.M.S. *Astraea* (frigate), 1808
252 50c Wreck of *Rhone* (mail steamer), 1867
253 $1 Tortola sloop
254 $2 H.M.S. *Frobisher* (cruiser)
255 $3 *Booker Viking* (cargo liner)
256 $5 *Sun Arrow* (hydrofoil)
     Set of 17 32.00 32.00

1972

Nos. 244 and 251 overprinted **VISIT OF H.R.H. THE PRINCESS**
MARGARET 1972
269 4c *Thetis* (sail merchantman), 1827
270 25c H.M.S. *Astraea* (frigate), 1808
     Set of 2 40 40

271 ½c Seaman (1800) and H.M.S. *Naiad*
     (frigate)
272 10c Boatswain (1787–1807) and ship
273 30c Captain (1795–1812) and ship
274 60c Admiral (1787–95) and ship
     Set of 4 2.50 1.75

275 15c *Sir Winston Churchill* (cadet
     schooner)
276 25c *Sir Winston Churchill* (cadet
     schooner)
     Set of 2 40 30

1972

277 ½c Game fishing boat and Blue Marlin
278 ½c Game fishing boat and Wahoo
279 15c Game fishing boat and Allison Tuna
280 25c Game fishing boat and White Marlin
281 50c Game fishing boat and Sailfish
282 $1 Game fishing boat and Dolphin
     Set of 6 3.75 3.00

1973

289† 1c Yacht 10 10

1974

307 5c Crest of *Canopus* (French
     minesweeper)
308 18c Crest of U.S.S. *Saginaw*
309 25c Crest of H.M.S. *Rothesay* (frigate)
310 50c Crest of H.M.C.S. *Ottawa* (frigate)
     Set of 4 1.40 1.10

1975

325 5c Figurehead of H.M.S. *Boreas* (frigate)
326 18c Figurehead of *Golden Hind* (Drake)
327 40c Figurehead of H.M.S. *Superb* (ship of
     the line)
328 85c Figurehead of H.M.S. *Formidable*
     (ship of the line)
     Set of 4 2.50 1.25

ALBUM LISTS
Write for our latest list of albums and accessories.
This will be sent on request.

1976

355 8c *Hazard* (Massachusetts brig)
356 22c *Spy* (American privateer)
357 40c *Raleigh* (American frigate)
358 75c *Alliance* (frigate) & H.M.S. *Trepassy*
     (sloop)
     Set of 4 4.50 3.25

1978

375† 5c Wreck of *Rhone* 15 10
376† 8c Wreck of *Rhone* 20 10

1980

449† 75c *Golden Hind* (Drake) 1.75 80

453† 13c Island schooner, Virgin Gorda 20 10

1983

508 15c Traditional boat building—Frame
509 25c Traditional boat building—Planking
510 50c Traditional boat building—Launch
511 $1 Traditional boat building—Maiden
     voyage
     Set of 4 2.75 2.50

1984

528† 50c Wreck of *Rhone* (mail steamer),
     1867 .... 90 95
529† $1 *Booker Viking* (cargo liner) 1.50 1.60
MS530 $1 *Boyne* (mail steamer) 2.75 2.50

533†	20c Sailboards	45	35
534†	20c Sailboard	45	35
535†	30c Olympic yachts	65	50
536†	30c Yacht	65	50

543†	30c Green and yellow sailing dinghies	40	45
544†	30c Blue and red dinghies	40	45
545†	30c White and blue dinghies	40	45
546†	30c Red and yellow dinghies	40	45
547†	30c Blue and white dinghies	40	45

548	10c Sloop		
549	35c Fishing boat		
550	60c Schooner		
551	75c Cargo boat		
	Set of 4	4.00	3.00

1985

556	25c Cruising yachts	45	45

1986

592	35c *Flying Cloud* (sail cruise ship)		
593	50c *Newport Clipper* (liner)		
594	75c *Cunard Countess* (liner)		
595	$1 *Sea Goddess* (liner)		
	Set of 4	9.00	6.00

612†	$1 Loading rum barrels into rowing boat	2.00	2.00

615	35c *Sentinel* (cable ship)		
616	35c *Retriever* (cable ship), 1961		
617	60c *Cable Enterprise* (cable ship), 1964		
618	60c *Mercury* (cable ship), 1962		
619	75c *Recorder* (cable ship), 1955		
620	75c *Pacific Guardian* (cable ship), 1984		
621	$1 *Great Eastern* (cable ship), 1860s		
622	$1 *Cable Venture* (cable ship), 1971		
	Set of 8	9.50	9.50

MS623 Four sheets. (a) 40c *Sentinel*, 40c *Retriever*; (b) 50c *Cable Enterprise*, 50c *Mercury*; (c) 80c *Recorder*, 80c *Pacific Guardian*; (d) $1.50 *Great Eastern*, $1.50 *Cable Venture*

	Set of 4 sheets	11.00	12.00

1987

625	12c Wreck of 18th-century Spanish galleon		
626	35c Wreck of H.M.S. *Astraea* (frigate), 1808		
627	75c Wreck of *Rhone* (mail steamer), 1867		
628	$1.50 Wreck of *Captain Rokos* (freighter), 1929		
	Set of 4	8.00	7.75
MS629	$2.50 Wreck of *Volvart* (brig), 1819	8.50	9.00

662†	10c 18th-century sailing packet	50	30
MS666†	$2.50 Mail steamer, 1880s	5.00	6.00

1988

680†	20c Sailboards	45	40

684†	12c Yacht	50	30
686†	60c Yacht	1.50	1.50
687†	$1 Rowing boat and safety equipment	2.25	2.50

1989

702	12c Yachts at start of race		
703	40c Yacht tacking		
704	75c Yachts at sunset		
705	$1 Yachts rounding buoy		
	Set of 4	4.00	4.00
MS706	$2 Yacht under full sail	3.75	4.00

715†	$1 "Apollo II" capsule and inflatable dinghy	1.75	1.00

1990

MS731†	$2 Royal Yacht *Britannia*	2.25	2.40

757†	40c Yacht	45	50
MS760†	$2 Sailboard	2.25	2.40

1991

793	12c *Vitoria* (Magellan) in Pacific, 1521		
794	50c La Salle's ship on Mississippi, 1682		
795	75c *Matthew* (John Cabot) off Nova Scotia, 1497–98		
796	$1 *Grande Hermine* and *Petite Hermine* (Cartier) on St. Lawrence, 1534		
	Set of 4	2.40	2.50
MS797	$2 *Santa Maria* (Columbus)	2.25	2.50

1992

819†	15c Fleet of Columbus	15	20
825†	$1.50 *Santa Maria* replica at New York World's Fair, 1964	1.75	1.40
MS826†	Two sheets (a) Ships from Second voyage of Columbus at Virgin Gouda, 1493 (other sheet shows map)		
	Price for 2 sheets	4.75	5.00

BRUNEI

South-east Asia
100 cents = 1 dollar

1949

As No. 115 *of Antigua*

97†	15c Paddle-steamer	1.25	90

1969

169	12c Oil rig		
170	40c Oil rig		
171	50c Oil rig		
	Set of 3	1.75	1.60

1971

180†	75c *Pahlawan* (patrol boat)	2.50	4.25

1972

194†	25c Royal barge	75	1.00

1983

337†	50c Fishing canoe	65	65
338†	75c Trawler	90	1.25

1984

343†	50c Liquid gas tanker	55	60

1986

390†	50c *Seteria* (missile boat)	1.50	1.50

1989

464†	60c Loading tanker	70	70

1992

510†	25c Oil tanker	30	30

BUENOS AIRES

South America
8 reales = 1 peso

1858

P13	4r Early steamship	£100	80.00
P17	1(IN)p Early steamship (brown)	£125	80.00
P20	1(IN)p Early steamship (blue)	65.00	50.00
P25	1(TO)p Early steamship (blue)	£150	£100
P1	2p Early steamship	90.00	50.00
P4	3p Early steamship	£450	£250
P7	4p Early steamship	£1500	£900
P10	5p Early steamship	£1500	£900

BULGARIA

South-east Europe
100 stotinki = 1 lev

1947

694	50lev *Rodina* (freighter)	90	35

1948

735†	9lev *Radetski* (river paddle-steamer)	20	10

1950

775†	3lev Shipbuilding	35	10

815†	50lev Freighter	2.00	75

1953

892†	8s Crossing Danube by pontoon, 1877	30	10

1957

1071†	16s *Aurora* (Russian cruiser)	85	10

1962

1298†	2s Yacht, Varna	20	10

1302	1s *Varna* (freighter)		
1303	5s *Komsomols* (tanker)		
1304	20s *Georgi Dimitrov* (liner)		
	Set of 3	2.25	40

1307†	6s Fishing boats, Nesebur	60	10
1308†	8s Danube shipping	80	20

1966

1605†	10s River steamer, 1886	60	10

1619	2s *Radetski* (river paddle-steamer)	20	10

1968

1772†	1s Crossing Danube by pontoon, 1877	25	10

1799†	10s *Die Fregatte* (cruise ship)	55	10

1828	20s Viking ships	1.00	85

1969

1872†	1s Galleon	10	10

1949† 1s Deep sea trawler 20 10

1970

2018† 4s Yachts, Albena 20 10
2019† 8s Yachts, Rousalka 30 10

1972

2138 18s Vikhren (ore carrier) 1.25 20

1973

2215† 2s Shelf I (underwater research vessel) 10 10
2216† 18s NIV 100 (diving bell) 85 35

2282 1s "Finn" class yacht
2283 2s "Flying Dutchman" class yacht
2284 3s "Soling" class yacht
2285 13s "Tempest" class yacht
2286 20s "470" class yacht
2287 40s "Tornado" class yacht
Set of 6 4.50 2.40

1975

2410 13s Ryukyu sailing boat 20 10

COLLECT BUTTERFLIES AND OTHER INSECTS ON STAMPS

A Stanley Gibbons thematic catalogue — available at £12.95 (p. + p. £3) from: Stanley Gibbons Publications, 5 Parkside, Christchurch Road, Ringwood, Hants. BH24 3SH.

2435 1s Egyptian galley
2436 2s Phoenician galley
2437 3s Greek trireme
2438 5s Roman galley
2439 13s Mora (Norman ship), 1066
2440 18s Venetian galley
Set of 6 1.50 75

1977

2597 1s Hansa kogge
2598 2s Santa Maria (Columbus)
2599 3s Golden Hind (Drake)
2600 12s Santa Catherina (carrack)
2601 13s Corona (galleon)
2602 43s Mediterranean galley
Set of 6 1.75 65

1978

2655 23s Kor Karoli (circumnavigating yacht) 55 25

2703 13s Geroi Plevny (ferry), Varna–Ilichovsk 40 10

1980

2864 5s Jesus of Lubeck (Hansa kogge)
2865 8s Roman galley
2866 13s Eagle (galleon)
2867 23s Mayflower (Pilgrim Fathers)
2868 35s Maltese galleon
2869 53s Royal Louis (galleon)
Set of 6 2.40 90

2883† 8s Missile boat and Ropucha (landing ship) 30 10

1981

2935 35s Georgi Dimitrov (liner)
2936 43s Petimata ot RMS (freighter)
2937 53s Khan Asparuch (tanker)
Set of 3 3.75 1.25

1982

3051 13s Aurora (Russian cruiser) 45 10

1984

3135 5s General VI Zaimov (bulk carrier)
3136 13s Mesta (tanker)
3137 25s Veleka (tanker)
3138 32s Geroite na Odesa (ferry)
3139 42s Rozhen (bulk carrier)
Set of 5 3.25 1.25

MS3151 3lev Hamburg kogge 4.50 4.50

3209 13s Sofia (Danube cruise ship) 65 10

1985

MS3218 80s Akademik (research ship) 1.25 1.25

3286 5s 17th-century Dutch fly
3287 12s Sovereign of the Seas (English galleon), 1637
3288 20s Mediterranean polacca
3289 25s Prince Royal (17th-century English warship)
3290 42s Xebec
3291 60s 17th-century English warship
Set of 6 3.00 1.40

1986

3372	5s *King of Prussia* (galleon)		
3373	13s 18th-century East Indiaman		
3374	25s 18th-century xebec		
3375	30s *Sv. Pavel* (Russian ship of the line)		
3376	32s 18th-century topsail schooner		
3377	42s *Pobeda* (Russian ship of the line)		
	Set of 6	2.75	1.25

1988

MS3570	1lev *Ruse* (Danube river boat); 1lev *Al Stamboliiski* (Danube river cruiser)	2.75	1.40

3580†	25s Paddle-steamer	35	15

1990

3664	5s *Santa Maria* (Columbus)		
3665	8s *Sao Gabriel* (Vasco da Gama)		
3666	13s *Vitoria* (Magellan)		
3667	32s *Golden Hind* (Drake)		
3668	42s *Discoverie* (Hudson)		
3669	60s *H.M.S. Endeavour* (Cook)		
	Set of 6	1.25	55

1992

3830†	50s Spanish boats on Amazon (Orellana)	10	10
3831†	1lev *Vitoria* (Magellan)	10	10
3833†	2lev *Golden Hind* (Drake)	15	15
MS3835	4lev *Santa Maria* (Columbus)	40	35

3837†	1lev *Santa Maria* (Columbus)	10	10
3838†	2lev *Santa Maria* (Columbus)	10	10

3870	30s *Bulgaria* (freighter)		
3871	50s *Kastor* (tanker)		
3872	1lev *Geroite na Sebastopol* (ferry)		
3873	2lev *Aleko Konstantinov* (tanker)		
3874	2lev *Bulgaria* (tanker)		
3875	3lev *Varna* (container ship)		
	Set of 6	45	30

BURKINA FASO

West Africa
100 centimes = 1 franc

1986

853	250f Columbus before King of Portugal and *Nina*		
854	300f Columbus using astrolabe and *Santa Maria*		
855	400f Columbus in prison and *Santa Maria*		
856	450f Landing on San Salvador and *Pinta* (air)		
	Set of 4	7.50	4.25
MS857	1000f Fleet leaving Palos	6.00	4.75

1990

988†	120f Mail steamer	70	45
MS989	500f Early mail steamer	2.50	1.60

1992

1034†	50f *Santa Maria* (Columbus)	25	20
1035†	150f Columbus's fleet	75	55

BURMA

South-east Asia
1938 12 pies = 1 anna
16 annas = 1 rupee
1953 100 pyas = 1 kyat

1938

25†	2a6p Royal barge (red)	1.25	55
29†	8a Sailing craft on River Irrawaddy (green)	2.00	30

1940

No. 25 surcharged **COMMEMORATION POSTAGE STAMP 6TH MAY 1840 ONE ANNA 1A**

34	1a on 2a6p Royal barge	1.75	60

1945

Nos. 25 and 29 overprinted **MILY ADMN**

42†	2a6p Royal barge	40	60
46†	8a Sailing craft on River Irrawaddy	10	40

1946

As Nos. 25 and 29, but colours changed

57†	2a6p Royal barge (blue)	10	1.00
59†	8a Sailing craft on River Irrawaddy (mauve)	1.75	80

1947

ကြားဖြတ်
အစိုးရ။

Nos. 57 and 59 overprinted

74†	2a6p Royal barge	90	65
78†	8a Sailing craft on River Irrawaddy	90	60

OFFICIAL STAMPS

1939

Nos. 25 and 29 overprinted **SERVICE**

O21†	2a6p Royal barge	12.00	3.50
O23†	8a Sailing craft on River Irrawaddy	20.00	3.25

1946

Nos. 57 and 59 overprinted **SERVICE**

O34†	2a6p Royal barge	45	1.75
O36†	8a Sailing craft on River Irrawaddy	15	1.25

1947

Nos. O34 and O36 overprinted as on Nos. 74 and 78

O47†	2a6p Royal barge	4.00	2.25
O49†	8a Sailing craft on River Irrawaddy	2.50	1.50

BURUNDI

Central Africa
100 centimes = 1 franc

1970

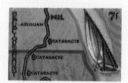

534†	7f Red Sea felucca	80	25
535†	14f Red Sea felucca	80	30

Nos. 534 and 535 each cover 18 different designs forming a map of the Nile.

1971

723†	31f + 1f Gondolas, Venice	1.10	35

1974

978†	14f Modern mail boat	80	50
979†	14f Modern mail boat	80	50
986†	31f Modern mail boat (air)	1.50	70
987†	31f Modern mail boat	1.50	70

Nos. 978/9 and 986/7 each form a composite design

1977

1278†	5f *Aurora* (Russian cruiser) and Russian 5r stamp	15	10
1279†	5f *Aurora* and 10r stamp	15	10
1280†	5f *Aurora* and 30k stamp	15	10
1281†	5f *Aurora* and 40r stamp	15	10

1294†	1f Tanker unloading	10	10

1979

1347†	27f *Hohenzollern* (on German East Africa stamp No. 21)	65	65
1350†	60f Modern mail boat (on stamps Nos. 978/9)	1.75	1.75

1984

1436†	10f *Hohenzollern* (on German East Africa stamp No. 21)	40	40
1439†	65f Modern mail boat (on stamps Nos. 978/9)	1.50	1.50

1992

1535	200f Columbus's fleet		
1536	400f Columbus's fleet		
	Set of 2	6.00	5.25

CAICOS ISLANDS

West Indies
100 cents = 1 dollar

1983

18†	35c Boat building, North Caicos	55	60
21†	$1.10 *Pinta* (Columbus)	2.00	1.75

1984

No. 21 overprinted **UNIVERSAL POSTAL UNION 1874-1984**

56†	$1.10 *Pinta* (Columbus)	1.75	1.50

59†	70c Fleet of Columbus	1.75	1.10
MS61†	$2 Fleet of Columbus	2.75	3.00

CAMBODIA

South-east Asia
100 cents = 1 riel

1960

98	2r Freighter		
99	5r Freighter		
100	20r Freighter		
	Set of 3	2.25	2.25

CAMEROUN

West Africa
1900 100 pfenning = 1 mark
1915 12 pence = 1 shilling
20 shillings = 1 pound
1915 100 centimes = 1 franc

GERMAN COLONY

1900

K 7	3pf *Hohenzollern* (German Imperial yacht)	
K 8	5pf *Hohenzollern*	
K 9	10pf *Hohenzollern*	
K10	20pf *Hohenzollern*	
K11	25pf *Hohenzollern*	
K12	30pf *Hohenzollern*	
K13	40pf *Hohenzollern*	
K14	50pf *Hohenzollern*	
K15	80pf *Hohenzollern*	
K16	1m *Hohenzollern*	
K17	2m *Hohenzollern*	
K18	3m *Hohenzollern*	
K19	5m *Hohenzollern*	
	Set of 13	£190 £650

BRITISH OCCUPATION

1915

Nos. K7/19 surcharged **C.E.F.** and value in English currency

1	½d on 3pf *Hohenzollern* (German Imperial yacht)	
2	½d on 5pf *Hohenzollern*	
3	1d on 10pf *Hohenzollern*	
4	2d on 20pf *Hohenzollern*	
5	2½d on 25pf *Hohenzollern*	
6	3d on 30pf *Hohenzollern*	
7	4d on 40pf *Hohenzollern*	
8	6d on 50pf *Hohenzollern*	
9	8d on 80pf *Hohenzollern*	
10	1s on 1m *Hohenzollern*	
11	2s on 2m *Hohenzollern*	
12	3s on 3m *Hohenzollern*	
13	5s on 5m *Hohenzollern*	
	Set of 13	£475 £650

FRENCH ADMINISTRATION

1915

Nos. 56/62 of Gabon overprinted **Corps Expeditionnaire Franco-Anglais CAMEROUN**

7†	25c Fishing boats, Libreville	35.00	16.00
8†	30c Fishing boats, Libreville	£100	85.00
9†	35c Fishing boats, Libreville	35.00	16.00
10†	40c Fishing boats, Libreville	£100	95.00
11†	45c Fishing boats, Libreville	£100	95.00
12†	50c Fishing boats, Libreville	£100	£100
13†	75c Fishing boats, Libreville	£150	£100

1931

109†	1f50 *Leconte de Lisle* (liner)	3.00	2.25

1937

110†	20c Liner	90	1.25
111†	30c Sailing ships	75	1.00

1941

190m†	50f Freighters in harbour	85	90

1953

262†	200f Freighters, Douala	6.00	3.50

1954

264	15f Landing craft, Normandy, 1944	2.25	2.50

1961

No. 262 surcharged **REPUBLIQUE FEDERALE 10/-**

296a†	10s on 200f Freighters, Douala	15.00	15.00

1965

383†	18f *De Grasse* (cruiser)	1.10	60

402† 50f Racing pirogues, Edea 1.60 50

1966

434† 60f *Vigilant* (gunboat) 1.10 40

1968

494† 60f Tug and freighters, Douala 1.40 60

505 30f Tanker, Port Gentil 55 35

1971

601† 20f Pirogue 30 25

606† 30f *Villalba* (deep sea trawler) 35 25
608† 70f Fishing boats, Douala 1.00 35
609† 150f Shrimp boats, Douala 2.25 1.00

614† 50f *Hohenzollern* (German Imperial
        yacht) (on stamp No. K19) 55 30

620 250f Pirogue 4.00 3.00

1972

639† 100f Gondolas, Venice 90 45
640† 200f Gondolas, Venice 2.25 90

644† 40f Pirogue, River Wouri 35 25

1973

679† 45f Pirogue (on stamp No. 620) 35 20

704† 50f Pirogue on beach 50 30

1975

745 40f Local fishing boats
746 45f Local fishing boats
                          Set of 2 1.25 50

757† 100f Lafayette and French warship, 1776 90 55

1977

803 70f *Hohenzollern* (German Imperial yacht)
        (on stamp No. K16) 55 35

1978

835 100f Capt. Cook and Siege of Quebec
836 250f H.M.S. *Adventure* and H.M.S.
        Resolution (Cook)
                          Set of 2 2.50 1.50

1979

855 100f *Hohenzollern* (German Imperial
        yacht) (on stamp No. K9) 55 40

1981

913 60f *Cam Iroko* (freighter) 65 30

1983

966 500f Container ship 3.00 2.00

CANADA

North America
100 cents = 1 dollar

1908

195† 20c *Grande Hermine* and *Petite Hermine*
        (Cartier), 1534 .... £100 60.00

1928

284† 50c *Bluenose* (fishing schooner) £100 30.00

1933

331 5c *Royal William* (paddle-steamer) 6.00 1.75

1934

334　2c Full-rigged ship .... 75　1.00

1935

340†　13c *Britannia* (Royal racing yacht), 1935　5.50　2.50

1937

371†　6c *Distributor* (stern paddle-steamer) ....　6.50　30

1942

386†　20c Launching H.M.C.S. *La Malbaie* (corvette) ....　12.00　15
388†　$1 H.M.S. *Cossack* (destroyer) ....　55.00　3.50

1946

406†　$1 *Abegweit* (train ferry) ....　30.00　1.50

1949

412　4c Cabot's *Matthew*, 1497 ....　10　10

1951

437†　5c *City of Toronto* and *Prince George* (paddle-steamers) ....　65　1.50

1953

477†　10c Eskimo in kayak ....　15　10

1957

491†　5c Canadian canoe ....　25　10

1963

537　5c Frobisher's barque *Gabriel*, 1575 ......　20　10

1966

571　5c 17th-century French warship ....　15　10

1967

606†　6c Bulk carrier (red) ....　80　10
607†　6c Bulk carrier (black) ....　30　10
609†　7c Bulk carrier ....　30　10

1968

624　5c *Nonsuch* (ketch), 1668 ....　20　10

1972

724†　8c Alogonkian canoes ....　40　10

1975

818　8c *Wm. D. Lawrence* (full-rigged ship)
819　8c *Neptune* (steamer)
820　8c *Beaver* (paddle-steamer)
821　8c *Quadra* (steamer)
　　　　　　　　　　　　　Set of 4　2.75　2.00

1976

851　10c *Northcote* (paddle-steamer)
852　10c *Passport* (paddle-steamer)
853　10c *Chicora* (paddle-steamer)
854　10c *Athabasca* (steamer)
　　　　　　　　　　　　　Set of 4　1.10　1.40

1977

893†　12c *Arctic* (survey ship) ....　15　10

902　12c "Pinky" (fishing boat)
903　12c *Malahat* (five-masted schooner)
904　12c "Tern" schooner
905　12c Mackinaw boat
　　　　　　　　　　　　　Set of 4　55　70

1978

925†　14c Sculpture of Inuitumiak ....　15　15

931　14c *Chief Justice Robinson* (paddle-steamer)
932　14c *St. Roch* (steamer)
933　14c *Northern Light* (steamer)
934　14c *Labrador* (steamer)
　　　　　　　　　　　　　Set of 4　1.25　1.60

1982

1041†　60c *Bluenose* (fishing schooner) (on stamp No. 284) ....　50　75

1984

1118　32c Cartier's *Grande Hermine*, 1534　....　35　30

1119	32c *Eagle* (U.S. Coastguard cadet ship)	35	30

1122	32c Freighter in St. Lawrence seaway ..	45	30

1128†	32c 18th-century scow, Louisbourg	85	85
1130†	32c 19th-century three-masted ship, Ile Verte	85	85
1131†	32c Early paddle-steamer, Gibraltar Point	85	85

1986

1209†	34c Viking ships	35	55
1210†	34c *Matthew* (Cabot), 1497	35	55
1211†	34c Henry Hudson cast adrift in rowing boat, 1611	35	55

1222	34c *Accommodation* (paddle-steamer)	50	50

1987

1232†	34c Indian canoe, Lake Superior	75	45

1244†	36c *Great Eastern* (cable ship)	50	35

1245	36c *Segwun* (lake steamer)		
1246	36c *Princess Marguerite* (coastal steamer)		
	Set of 2	2.50	3.00

1247†	36c Figurehead from wreck of *Hamilton*, 1813	45	45
1248†	36c Wrecked hull of *San Juan*, 1565	45	45

1988

1286†	37c H.M.S. *Discovery* (Vancouver), 1795	50	40
1287†	37c Expedition portaging canoes, 1808	50	40

1313	37c Voyageurs' canoe	35	40

1314	37c *Bluenose* (yacht)	35	40

1989

1315	38c Chipewyan canoe		
1316	38c Haida canoe		
1317	38c Inuit kayak		
1318	38c Micmac canoe		
	Set of 4	1.75	1.75

1349†	38c North Atlantic convoy, 1939	40	45

1990

Designs as Nos. 1315/18

1377	39c Fishing dory		
1378	39c Logging pointer		
1379	39c York boat		
1380	39c North canoe		
	Set of 4	1.75	2.00

1991

Designs as Nos. 1315/18

1428	40c Verchere rowboat		
1429	40c Touring kayak		
1430	40c Sailing dinghy		
1431	40c Cedar strip canoe		
	Set of 4	2.25	2.40

1433†	40c Canoe on Athabasca River	70	70
1435†	40c Inflatable dinghy on Jacques-Cartier River	70	70

1444†	40c Lifeboat and oil rig	70	70

1445†	40c Voyageurs' canoe	60	60
1448†	40c Pirate ship	60	60

1992

1487†	42c Fishing boat, Ville-Marie	50	55
1488†	42c Container ship, Montreal	50	55
1489†	48c Crows nest of *Grande Hermine* (Cartier)	55	60

Design as No. 1433, but horizontal

1494†	42c Tug with raft of logs, Ottawa River	50	55

MS1503†	42c Freighters and fishing boats, Hurst Island, British Columbia; 42c Fishing dory, Newfoundland; 42c Trawlers and schooner, Nova Scotia (sheet also contains nine other designs)	6.00	7.00

1506†	42c Captain William Jackman and wreck of *Sea Clipper*, 1867	40	45

Designs as No. 1349

1522†	42c Freighter, Newfoundland, 1942	40	45
1523†	42c Landing craft, Dieppe, 1942	40	45
1524†	42c Freighter being torpedoed, 1942 ..	40	45

OFFICIAL STAMPS

1949

No. 406 overprinted **O.H.M.S.**

O9†	$1 *Abegweit* (train ferry)	50.00	45.00

1951

No. 406 overprinted **G**

O28†	$1 *Abegweit* (train ferry)	50.00	42.00

1953

No. 477 overprinted **G**

O45† 10c Eskimo in kayak 30 10

SPECIAL DELIVERY

1927

S5 20c *Ile de France* (liner) 8.00 7.50

CANAL ZONE

Central America
1917 100 centesimos = 1 balboa
1924 100 cents = 1 dollar

1915

Nos. 178/82 of Panama overprinted **CANAL ZONE**

59†	12c *Panama* (cargo liner) at Culebra Cut	13.50	4.75
60†	15c *Panama* (cargo liner) at Culebra Cut	40.00	23.00
61†	24c *Cristobal* (cargo liner) in Gatun Lock	38.00	9.00
62†	50c Freighters in Balboa docks	£250	£150
63†	1b *Nereus* (U.S. Navy collier) in Pedro Miguel Lock	£130	50.00

1924

No. 698 of U.S.A. overprinted **CANAL ZONE**

94† 20c Sailing ship, Golden Gate, San
Francisco 6.00 3.25

1931

126	4c Steamer in Panama Canal	
127	5c Steamer in Panama Canal	
128	6c Steamer in Panama Canal	
129	10c Steamer in Panama Canal	
130	15c Steamer in Panama Canal	
131	20c Steamer in Panama Canal	
132	30c Steamer in Panama Canal	
133	40c Steamer in Panama Canal	
134	$1 Steamer in Panama Canal	

Set of 9 17.00 5.25

1939

152†	5c *Andrea F. Luckenbach* (freighter)	1.40	95
154†	7c U.S.S. *Houston* (cruiser)	2.75	1.40
158†	12c *Santa Clara* (liner)	7.00	5.50
160†	15c *Panama* (liner)	15.00	12.50
162†	20c *Duchessa D'Aosta* and *President Polk* (liners)	15.00	8.00
145†	15c Freighter and fishing boat, Fort Amador (air)	3.25	1.10
146†	25c Fishing boat, Cristobal Harbour	16.00	11.00
147†	30c U.S.S. *Chester* (cruiser)	12.00	8.00

1949

196†	6c Raft on River Chagres	1.25	50
198†	18c *Panama* (paddle-steamer) *c* 1848 ..	2.75	2.00

1958

214 4c *Ancon II* (liner), 1939 .... 55 20

1976

249 13c *Cascadas* (dredger) 60 20

OFFICIAL STAMPS

1941

Nos. 127/34 overprinted **Official Panama Canal**

O167	5c Steamer in Panama Canal	
O168	6c Steamer in Panama Canal	
O169	10c Steamer in Panama Canal	
O170	15c Steamer in Panama Canal	
O171	20c Steamer in Panama Canal	
O172	30c Steamer in Panama Canal	
O173	40c Steamer in Panama Canal	
O174	$1 Steamer in Panama Canal	

Set of 8 90.00 32.00

CAPE JUBY

North-west Africa
100 centimos = 1 peseta

1929

Nos. 506 and 508 of Spain overprinted **CABO JUBY**

38†	15c Caravel	20	15
40†	25c Caravel	20	15

1948

No. 317 of Spanish Morocco overprinted **CABO JUBY**

164† 10p *Arango* (freighter) at quay 2.25 3.00

CAPE VERDE ISLANDS

Atlantic Ocean
100 centavos = 1 escudo

1913

Surcharged **REPUBLICA CABO VERDE** *and new value*

(a) On Nos. 1/2, 5 and 7 of Portuguese Colonies

147†	½c on 2½r Departure of Vasco da Gama's fleet	50	30
148†	½c on 5r Vasco da Gama's fleet at Calicut	50	30
151†	5c on 50r *Sao Gabriel* (flagship)	70	60
153†	10c on 100r *Sao Gabriel*	70	70

(b) On Nos. 104/5, 108 and 110 of Macao

155†	½c on ½a Departure of Vasco da Gama's fleet	50	40
156†	½c on 1a Vasco da Gama's fleet at Calicut	50	40
159†	5c on 8a *Sao Gabriel* (flagship)	2.50	1.90
161†	10c on 16a *Sao Gabriel*	80	70

(c) On Nos. 58/9, 62 and 64 of Timor

163†	½c on ½a Departure of Vasco da Gama's fleet	50	40
164†	½c on 1a Vasco da Gama's fleet at Calicut	50	40
167†	5c on 8a *Sao Gabriel* (flagship)	2.50	1.90
169†	10c on 16a *Sao Gabriel*	80	70

1921

No. 153 surcharged

253† 4c on 10c on 100r *Sao Gabriel* (flagship) 70 70

1952

348†	30c Caravel	10	10
350†	1e Caravel	10	10

1967

403 1e *Mandovy* (Portuguese gunboat)
404 1e50 *Augusto Castilho* (Portuguese minesweeper)

Set of 2 1.00 50

1968

409† 50c *Mauretania II* (liner), 1939 .... 10 10

1972

425 5e Galleons at Cape Verde 50 15

1978

463 1e *Cabo Verde* (freighter) 30 10

1980

470 4e Sailing ships, Mindelo, 1880 .... 30 15

492	3e *Arca Verdel* (freighter)	
493	5e50 *Ilha do Maio* (freighter)	
494	7e50 *Ilha do Komo* (freighter)	
495	9e *Boa Vista* (freighter)	
496	12e *Santo Antao* (freighter)	
497	30e *Santiago* (freighter)	

Set of 6 3.00 1.50

1982

532 12e *Morrissey Ernestina* (schooner) 1.00 30

533 10e50 Freighters under construction, San
Vicente shipyard 75 30

1987

586† 12e Fishing boats, Santiago 30 15

588 12e *Carvalho* (schooner)
589 16e *Nauta* (cutter)
590 50e *Maria Sony* (schooner)
Set of 3 2.25 80
MS591 60e × 2 *Madalan* (brigantine) 1.40 1.40

1991

670 10e Fishing boat
671 24e Fishing boat
672 25e Fishing boat
673 50e Fishing boats
Set of 4 2.25 1.40

685 10e Fishing boats
686 20e Fishing boats
687 29e Fishing boats
688 47e Fishing boats
Set of 4 1.90 1.10

1992

696 40e Columbus's fleet off Cape Verde
Islands
697 40e Caravel
Set of 2 2.00 1.10

CAROLINE ISLANDS

Pacific Ocean
100 pfennig = 1 mark

1901

As Nos. K7/19 of *Cameroun*, but inscribed "KAROLINEN"
13 3pf *Hohenzollern* (German Imperial yacht) 65 1.25
14 5pf *Hohenzollern* 65 1.40
15 10pf *Hohenzollern* 65 3.00
16 20pf *Hohenzollern* 1.00 7.00

17 25pf *Hohenzollern* 1.25 13.00
18 30pf *Hohenzollern* 1.25 13.00
19 40pf *Hohenzollern* 1.25 13.00
20 50pf *Hohenzollern* 1.50 17.00
21 80pf *Hohenzollern* 2.25 23.00
22 1m *Hohenzollern* 3.00 55.00
23 2m *Hohenzollern* 6.00 7.00
24 3m *Hohenzollern* 8.00 £140
29b 5m *Hohenzollern* 16.00

CASTELROSSO

Mediterranean
100 centesimi = 1 lira

ITALIAN OCCUPATION

1932

No. 333 of Italy overprinted **CASTELROSSO**
30† 10c Fishing boats, Nice 6.50 12.00

CAYES OF BELIZE

Central America
100 cents = 1 dollar

Appendix

The following stamps have either been issued in excess of postal needs, or have not been made available to the public in reasonable quantities at face value. Miniature sheets, imperforate stamps etc, are excluded from this section.

1984

Marine Life. Map and Views. 75c Spanish Galleon, $5 Game fishing boat
Lloyd's List. 25c *Queen Elizabeth 2*, $1 Loss of the *Fishburn*
90th Anniv of "Caye Service" Local Stamps. 75c Steam yacht

1985

Shipwrecks. $1 *Santa Yaga*, $1 *Comet*, $1 *Yeldham*, $1 *Oxford*

CAYMAN ISLANDS

West Indies
1935 12 pence = 1 shilling
20 shillings = 1 pound
1969 100 cents = 1 Jamaican dollar

1935

101† ½d Cat boat 1.00 40
104† 2d Cat boat 1.75 80
108† 1s Cat boat 4.00 4.50

1938

120† 2½d *Rembro* (schooner) (blue) 15 20
120a† 2½d *Rembro* (orange) 1.50 40
125† 5s *Rembro* 27.00 15.00

1949

As No. 115 of *Antigua*
132† 3d Paddle-steamer 60 20

1950

135† ½d Cat boat 15 60
145† 2s *Ziroma* (schooner) 7.50 6.00
146† 5s Boat building 9.00 7.00

1953

As Nos. 135 and 145/6, but with portrait of Queen Elizabeth II
148† ½d Cat boat 60 50
159 2s *Ziroma* (schooner) 7.50 6.00
160 5s Boat building 8.50 4.00

1962

166† 1d Cat boat 20 20
172† 6d *Lydia E. Wilson* (schooner) 3.00 30
176† 1s9d Sailing dinghy 7.50 85

1966

203 1s Cayman schooner
204 1s9d Cayman schooner
Set of 2 50 30

1967

205† 4d Speed boat 20 10
207† 1s Game fishing boat 20 15
208† 1s9d Sailing yachts 30 35

1969

229† 8d Motor vessels at berth 30 10

No. 229 surcharged
244† 7c on 8d Motor vessels at berth 10 10

1970

As No. 229, but face value in decimal currency
279† 7c Motor vessels at berth 30 10

1972

320 6c Cayman schooner (on currency note) 15 10

1974

360† 8c Cayman schooner 10 10

1976

410   20c Olympic yachts
411   50c Olympic yachts
　　　　　　　　　　　　Set of 2   60   60

1977

427†   8c Prince Charles and sailing ship   10   20

1978

441†   3c *Southward* (liner)
442†   5c *Renaissance* (liner)
443†   30c Freighter in new harbour
444†   50c *Daphne* (liner)
　　　　　　　　　　　　Set of 4   1.75   85

1980

501†   10c Cat boat   15   10

1982

556†   50c Catamaran   85   85

1984

586   5c *Song of Norway* (liner)
587   10c Cat boats in George Town harbour
588   25c Wreck of *Ridgefield* (freighter)
589   50c *Goldfield* (schooner)
　　　　　　　　　　　　Set of 4   2.10   1.75
MS590 $1 *Goldfield* (schooner) (different) 2.10   2.25

　　No. 589 overprinted **U.P.U. CONGRESS HAMBURG 1984**
591   50c *Goldfield* (schooner) 1.00   1.25

597†   5c Schooner   15   20
600†   25c Yachts   55   55
601†   25c Power boat   55   55

1985

609   5c Wreck of freighter
610   25c Wreck of sailing ship
611   35c Wreck of trawler
612   40c Submerged wreck
　　　　　　　　　　　　Set of 4   4.50   4.00

1987

648†   15c Catamaran and sailboard   60   40
649†   25c Diving launch   75   55

1988

673† $1 Yacht 1.40   1.50

1989

678†   25c *Orinoco* (mail steamer)   65   65
680† $1 Cayman schooner (on stamp No. 203)   2.00   2.00

682†   50c H.M.S. *Providence* (sloop), 1793 ....   1.75   1.75
683†   50c H.M.S. *Assistant* (transport), 1793 ..   1.75   1.75
684†   50c Ship's boats 1.75   1.75

693†   50c H.M.S. *Mutine* (survey ship), 1914 ..   1.75   1.75
694† $1 H.M.S. *Vidal* (survey ship), 1956 ......   2.75   3.00

1991

730†   50c *Song of America* (liner) at George
　　　　Town   70   75
731†   60c Rowing boat, The Bluff, Cayman
　　　　Brac   85   90
735† $2 *Nieuw Amsterdam* (1983) and
　　　　Holiday (liners) 2.75   3.00

CENTRAL AFRICAN EMPIRE

Central Africa
100 centimes = 1 franc

1977

Nos. 395 and 432 of Central African Republic overprinted
EMPIRE CENTRAFRICAIN
491†   100f Dugout canoe   90   90
464†   200f Dr. Schweitzer in dugout canoe 1.75   1.75

1978

558†   60f Paddle-steamer   40   20

578†   60f H.M.S. *Endeavour* (Cook) 1.00   35
581†   350f Masked paddlers in canoe 2.25   1.00

609†   150f *Aurora* (Russian cruiser)   90   50
MS612†   500f *Aurora* (Russian cruiser) 2.75   2.75

CENTRAL AFRICAN REPUBLIC

Central Africa
100 centimes = 1 franc

1968

163   30f Tanker, Port Gentil, Gabon   70   30

177   10f *Ville de Bangui* (river vessel), 1958
178   30f *J. B. Gouandjia* (river vessel), 1968
179   50f *Lamblin* (river vessel), 1944
180   100f *Pie X* (river vessel), 1894 (air)
181   130f *Ballay* (river vessel), 1891
　　　　　　　　　　　　Set of 5   4.50   2.25

1975

395	200f Dr Schweitzer in dugout canoe	1.75	1.00

400†	150f River tug	1.00	65

1976

404	30f *Jean Bedel Bokassa* (river vessel)		
405	40f *Jean Bedel Bokassa*		
	Set of 2	1.00	55

432	100f Dugout canoe	80	50

1981

779	40f C. V. Rietschoten and ship		
780	50f M. Pajot and ship		
781	60f L. Jaworski and ship		
782	80f M. Birch and ship		
783	100f O. Kersauson and ship (air)		
784	200f Sir Francis Chichester and *Gipsy Moth IV*		
	Set of 6	3.50	2.00
MS785	500f A. Colas and ship	3.25	2.25

1982

835†	300f *Savannah* (nuclear-powered freighter)	2.50	1.50

1983

949	300f Olympic yacht	1.00	1.00

1984

1012	65f *Le Pericles* (mail-ship)		
1013	120f *Pereire* (steamer)		
1014	250f *Admella* (passenger steamer)		
1015	400f *Royal William* (paddle-steamer)		
1016	500f *Great Britain* (steam/sail)		
	Set of 5	7.00	4.75

1060	90f Piccard's *Trieste* (bathyscaphe)	65	30

1985

Nos. 1014/15 overprinted

1083†	250f *Admella* (overprinted **ARGENTINA '85 BUENOS AIRES**)	90	80
1085†	400f *Royal William* (overprinted **ITALIA '85 ROME**)	1.40	1.25

1092	5f Yachts, Stockholm	10	10

1111†	400f Mississippi stern-wheeler	2.50	1.75

1986

1179†	240f Landing of Columbus	2.00	1.25
1181†	400f Fleet of Columbus (air)	3.00	2.00
1182†	500f Fleet of Columbus	3.50	2.25

Appendix

The following stamps have either been issued in excess of postal needs, or have not been made available to the public in reasonable quantities at face value. Miniature sheets, imperforate stamps, etc, are excluded from this section.

1981

Navigators. 1500f *Riguidel* and ship

CEYLON

Indian Ocean
100 cents = 1 rupee

1949

410	5c Liner		
411	15c Liner		
412	25c Barque		
	Set of 3	3.25	1.40

1951

426†	50c Outrigger canoe	30	10

1956

438†	3c Ancient sailing craft	15	10

1958

As No. 426 but inscriptions changed

459†	50c Outrigger canoe	30	10

CHAD

Central Africa
100 centimes = 1 franc

1931

As No. 109 of Cameroun

61†	1f50 *Leconte de Lisle* (liner)	2.75	2.75

1959

62†	15f Fishing canoe	45	35

1964

109†	30f Canoe building	45	25

1969

222† 100f H. Barth in canoe, 1851 .... 1.40 65

251† 1f Olympic yacht 20 20

1972

369 40f Sailing ship, Venice
370 45f Gondolas, Venice
371 140f Gondolas, Grand Canal, Venice
　　　　　　　　　　　　　　Set of 3　2.75　1.40

1974

410† 30f Mail canoe 35 25

1976

MS447† 400f De Grasse and Battle of Virginia
　　　　Capes, 1781 .... 3.25 1.60

480† 120f 19th-century French sail warship .. 2.50 90

COLLECT FUNGI ON STAMPS

A Stanley Gibbons thematic catalogue — available at £5 (p. + p. £3) from: Stanley Gibbons Publications, 5 Parkside, Christchurch Road, Ringwood, Hants. BH24 3SH.

1977

485† 200f Harbour ferry, New York 1.60 55
MS486 500f Harbour ferry, New York 3.00 1.40

495† 100f Lafayette and French ships, 1777 1.10 50

1979

MS577† 500f Olympic yachts 2.50 1.10

578 65f Reed canoe
579 100f Sailing canoe
580 200f *Curacao* (paddle-steamer)
581 300f *Calypso* (liner)
　　　　　　　　　　　　Set of 4　3.50　1.25
MS582 500f *Normandie* (liner) 2.50 1.10

1981

Nos. 578/9 surcharged **POSTES 1981 60F**
594† 60f on 65f Reed canoe 30 20
595† 60f on 100f Sailing canoe 30 20

1983

654† 300f Paddle-tugs, London, 1837 .... 1.50 1.25

1984

730 50f Freighter
731 60f Freighter
732 70f Freighter
733 125f Freighter (air)
734 250f Freighter
　　　　　　　　　　　　Set of 5　3.00　2.00

741† 200f Sailing boat on Lake Chad 1.25 65

749 90f British East Indiaman
750 125f *Vera Cruz* (steamer)
751 200f *Carlisle Castle* (sail merchantman)
752 300f *Britannia* (steamer), 1887
　　　　　　　　　　　　Set of 4　4.25　2.75

1985

784† 350f Piccard's *Trieste* (bathyscaphe) 2.00 1.40

809† 250f Modern liner 2.50 1.25

1987

No. 734 surcharged **170**
826† 170f on 250f Freighter 90 75

POSTAGE DUE STAMPS

1930

D77† 1f Pirogue on Lake Chad 1.75 2.00
D78† 2f Pirogue on Lake Chad 3.00 3.25
D79† 3f Pirogue on Lake Chad 21.00 22.00

CHAMBA

Indian sub-continent
12 pies = 1 anna
16 annas = 1 rupee

1938

No. 256 of India overprinted **CHAMBA STATE**
91† 6a *Strathnaver* (liner) 7.50 22.00

CHILE
South America
1910 100 centavos = 1 peso
1960 100 centesimos = 1 escudo
1975 100 centavos = 1 peso

1910

123†	10c *Lautaro* and *Esmeralda* (sail frigates) in battle	1.25	25
124†	12c Capture of *Maria Isabel* (sail frigate)	2.75	90

1936

257†	10c Fishing boats	15	10
263†	1p *Orduna* (liner), Valparaiso	1.25	35

1938

274†	1p *Calbuco* (fishing boat)	15	10
275†	1p80 Lake steamer	60	20
338h†	2p Freighter, Valparaiso	15	10

1940

279	80c + 2p20 *Abtao* (armed steamer)		
280	3p60 + 6p40 *Abtao*		
	Set of 2	3.75	2.75

1942

404c†	60c Fishing boat	20	10

1948

378	40c *Esmeralda* (sail corvette) at Battle of Iquique, 1879	35	10

ALBUM LISTS
Write for our latest list of albums and accessories.
This will be sent on request.

1959

476†	40p Yacht	20	10

1965

561†	40c Fishing boats, Angelmo	30	10

1966

572	10c *Chile* and *Peru* (paddle-steamers)		
573	70c *Chile* and *Peru* (air)		
	Set of 2	50	20

1967

578†	20c *Yelcho* (coastguard vessel), 1917	30	10

1968

600†	30c Galleon and *Alonso de Erckla* (ferry)	30	10

1970

640	40c Schooner, 1820		
641	2e Schooner, 1820 (air)		
	Set of 2	50	20

1971

660	52c *Lago Maihue* (freighter)		
661	5e *Lago Maihue* (air)		
	Set of 2	40	20

662	5e O'Higgins and fleet, 1821		
663	1e O'Higgins and fleet, 1821 (air)		
	Set of 2	50	20

676	35c Magellan and caravel	20	10

1972

697	1e15 *Esmeralda* (barquentine)	40	15

1973

707	20e Destroyer	30	10

1974

736†	200e Galleon, 1574	60	20

1975

745†	150e Wreck of *Teotopoulis*	25	15
746†	150e *Cap Christiansen* (lifeboat)	25	15

749	500e *Baquedano* (sail/steam corvette)		
750	500e *Lautaro* (sail frigate)		
751	500e *Chacabuco* (cruiser)		
752	500e *Esmeralda* (cadet barquentine)		
753	800e *Baquedano*		
754	800e *Lautaro*		
755	800e *Chacabuco*		
756	800e *Esmeralda*		
757	1000e *Baquedano*		
758	1000e *Lautaro*		
759	1000e *Chacabuco*		
760	1000e *Esmeralda*		
	Set of 12	6.50	2.00

769 1p Lord Cochrane and fleet, 1820
770 1p Battle of Valdiva, 1820
771 1p Capture of *Esmeralda* (sail frigate), 1820
772 1p *Cochrane* (cruiser), 1874
773 1p *Cochrane* (destroyer), 1962
Set of 5   2.50   90

1977

790 2p Schooner 20 10

1978

799 10p Freighter loading timber 55 15

As No. 799, but inscribed "CORREOS" and Chilean flag added
800 20p Freighter 1.50 20

807 20p Chilean fleet, 1778 .... 1.50 80

1979

817 3p50 Battle of Iquique, 1879
818 3p50 Battle of Punta Gruesa, 1879
819 3p50 Battle of Angamos, 1879
Set of 3   1.75   75

838 3p50 *Micalvi* (freighter), Puerto Williams 50 15

1981

875 3p50 Rowing boats, Arturo Prat Base 75 20

1982

917 20p Trawler 1.50 70

933 7p *Copiapo* (steamer), 1872 .... 85 25

1984

977† 9p Freighter, Valparaiso 55 20

1986

1053 40p *Santiaguillo* (caravel), 1536 .... 85 30

1060 35p *Ancud* (schooner) 80 45
1061 35p *Aguila* (brigantine) 80 45
1062 35p *Esmeralda* (sail corvette) 80 45
1063 35p *O'Higgins* (sail frigate) 80 45

1987

1093† 15p Wrecked sailing ship 20 10

1096 100p Rowing boat, Arturo Prat Base
1097 100p Rowing boats, Arturo Prat Base
Set of 2   2.00   1.25

1110 60p *Almirante Latorre* (battleship), 1920
1111 60p *O'Higgins* (cruiser)
Set of 2   1.40   70

1134 50p Battle of Iquique, 1879 .... 80 30

1142 45p *Capitan Luis Alcazar* (Antarctic supply ship) 90 30

1988

1158† 50p *Esmeralda* (cadet barquentine) 55 20

1181† 50p *Angamos* (transport) 55 20

1989

1197† 100p Battle of Casma, 1839, and Roberto Simpson 65 40
1198† 100p Battle of Casma, 1839, and seaman 65 40

No. 1093 surcharged **$25**
1203 25p on 15p Wrecked sailing ship 10 10

1215† 100p *Santa Maria, Pinta* and *Nina* (Columbus) 70 40

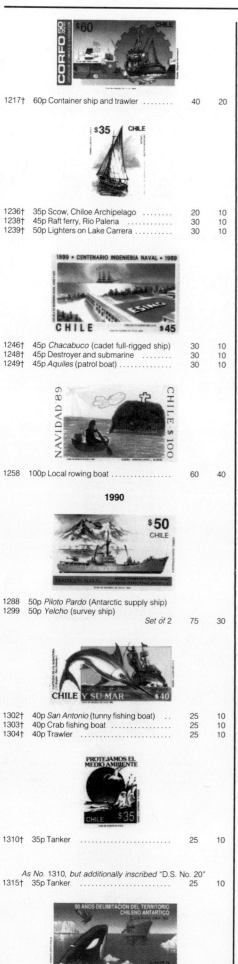

1217† 60p Container ship and trawler 40 20

1236† 35p Scow, Chiloe Archipelago 20 10
1238† 45p Raft ferry, Rio Palena 30 10
1239† 50p Lighters on Lake Carrera 30 10

1246† 45p Chacabuco (cadet full-rigged ship) 30 10
1248† 45p Destroyer and submarine 30 10
1249† 45p Aquiles (patrol boat) 30 10

1258 100p Local rowing boat 60 40

1990

1288 50p Piloto Pardo (Antarctic supply ship)
1299 50p Yelcho (survey ship)
　　　　　　　　　　　Set of 2 75 30

1302† 40p San Antonio (tunny fishing boat) .. 25 10
1303† 40p Crab fishing boat 25 10
1304† 40p Trawler 25 10

1310† 35p Tanker 25 10

As No. 1310, but additionally inscribed "D.S No. 20"
1315† 35p Tanker 25 10

1337† 250p Antarctic supply ship 1.40 65

1991
As No. 1238, but additionally inscribed "D.S No. 20"
1346 45p Raft ferry, Rio Palena 20 10

1373† 50p Yelcho (coastguard vessel), 1916 25 10
1375† 50p Endurance (Shackleton) 25 10

1379 45p Maipo (container ship) 20 10

1409 50p Columbus's fleet
1410 150p Columbus's fleet
　　　　　　　　　　　Set of 2 90 50

1992
No. 1238 surcharged $60
1420 60p on 45p Raft ferry, Rio Palena 20 15

As No. 1310, but face value changed
1424† 60p Tanker 20 15

As No. 1424, but additionally inscribed "D.S. No. 20"
1429† 60p Tanker 20 15

1452† 200p Liner and launch, Easter Island .. 65 50

1456† 150p Submarine 50 35

1472† 250p Santa Maria (Columbus) 85 60

OFFICIAL STAMPS
1939
No. 274 overprinted **Servicio del ESTADO**
O280† 1p Calbuco (fishing boat) 3.25 2.00

1941
Nos. 274/5 and 338h overprinted **OFICIAL**
O339† 1p Calbuco (fishing boat) 1.60 80
O288† 1p80 Lake steamer 5.75 3.75
O442† 2p Freighter, Valparaiso 1.60 25

CHINA
Eastern Asia
100 cents = 1 dollar (yuan)

Chinese Republic

1913

309† ½c Junk 15 10
310† 1c Junk 60 10
311† 1½c Junk 60 60
312† 2c Junk 75 10
313† 3c Junk 75 10
292† 4c Junk (red) 1.10 10
314† 4c Junk (grey) 6.00 20
315† 4c Junk (olive) 85 10
316† 5c Junk 1.50 10
294† 6c Junk (grey) 1.50 45
317† 6c Junk (red) 1.75 10
318† 6c Junk (brown) 15.00 2.00
319† 7c Junk 3.25 1.75
320† 8c Junk 3.25 40
321† 10c Junk 2.25 10

1920
Nos. 292, 294 and 312/13 surcharged in Chinese with English figures at the bottom
349 1c on 2c Junk
361 2c on 3c Junk
350 3c on 4c Junk
351 5c on 6c Junk
　　　　　　　　Set of 4 11.00 6.25

1925
Nos. 312/15 surcharged in Chinese with English figures at the top
366 1c on 2c Junk
367 1c on 3c Junk
369 1c on 4c Junk (olive)
370 1c on 4c Junk (grey)
　　　　　　　　Set of 4 3.50 35

1936

449† 5c Freighters and junks 65 10

1947

985† $100 Momus (liner) 10 75
988† $400 Junk 10 75
989† $500 Junk 10 75

1948

1001 $5000 Junk (on stamp No. 989) (red)
1002 $5000 Junk (on stamp No. 984) (green)
　　　　　　　　Set of 2 55 2.40

1044 $20000 Hai Tien (freighter) and Eton
　　　　　(steamer), 1872
1045 $30000 Hai Tien and Eton
1046 $40000 Kiang Ya (freighter)
1047 $60000 Kiang Ya
　　　　　　　　Set of 4 60 3.50

1949

Revenue stamps surcharged

1122	50c on $20 Liner			
1137	$1 on $15 Liner			
1127	$2 on $50 Liner			
1144	$3 on $50 Liner			
1138	$5 on $500 Liner			
1129	$10 on $30 Liner			
1140	$15 on $20 Liner			
1141	$25 on $20 Liner			
1145	$50 on $50 Liner			
1147	$50 on $300 Liner			
1130	$80 on $50 Liner			
1146	$100 on $50 Liner			
1124	$200 on $50 Liner			
1142	$200 on $500 Liner			
1125	$300 on $50 Liner			
1143	$500 on $15 Liner			
1134	$500 on $30 Liner			
1135	$1,000 on $50 Liner			
1150	$1,000 on $100 Liner			
1126	$1,500 on $50 Liner			
1151	$2,000 on $300 Liner			
		Set of 21	12.00	32.00

Surcharged as Nos. 1122/51 but key pattern inverted at top and bottom

1183	$50 on $10 Liner			
1184	$100 on $10 Liner			
1185	$500 on $10 Liner			
1186	$1,000 on $10 Liner			
1187	$5,000 on $20 Liner			
1188	$10,000 on $20 Liner			
1189	$50,000 on $20 Liner			
1190	$100,000 on $20 Liner			
1191	$500,000 on $20 Liner			
1192	$2,000,000 on $20 Liner			
1193	$5,000,000 on $20 Liner			
		Set of 11	£900	£325

Revenue stamps overprinted for type of service

1232	$10 Liner (B)			
1233	$30 Liner (A)			
1234	$50 Liner (C)			
1235	$100 Liner (D)			
1236	$200 Liner (A)			
1237	$500 Liner (A)			
		Set of 6	£120	85.00

Overprint translation: (A) Domestic Letter fee: (B) Express Letter Fee: (C) Registered Letter Fee: (D) Air Mail Fee

Revenue stamps surcharged

1312	1c on $20 Liner			
1284	1c on $5,000 Liner			
1285	4c on $100 Liner			
1286	4c on $3,000 Liner			
1313	10c on $20 Liner			
1287	10c on $50 Liner			
1288	10c on $1,000 Liner			
1289	20c on $1,000 Liner			
1290	50c on $30 Liner			
1291	50c on $50 Liner			
1292	$1 on $50 Liner			
		Set of 11	75.00	55.00

On Nos. 1312/13 the Key pattern is inverted at top and bottom

Manchuria

KIRIN AND HEILUNGKIANG

1927

Nos. 309/21 of Chinese Republic overprinted

1†	½c Junk		25	25
2†	1c Junk		40	10
3†	1½c Junk		75	75

4†	2c Junk		65	40
5†	3c Junk		80	60
6†	4c Junk (olive)		75	10
7†	5c Junk		95	30
8†	6c Junk (red)		1.00	50
9†	7c Junk		2.00	2.00
10†	8c Junk		2.25	1.50
11†	10c Junk		2.25	10

PORT ARTHUR AND DARIEN

1949

NE57	S10 Liner		11.00	15.00

No. 57 surcharged

NE67	$100 on $10 Liner		£250	£250
NE70	$500 on $10 Liner		£425	£425

Sinkiang

1915

限新省貼用

Nos. 309/21 of Chinese Republic overprinted

47†	½c Junk		25	25
48†	1c Junk		55	10
49†	1½c Junk		1.00	1.75
50†	2c Junk		75	40
4†	3c Junk		75	10
5†	4c Junk (red)		85	45
52†	4c Junk (grey)		3.75	1.75
53†	4c Junk (olive)		1.25	75
6†	5c Junk		85	40
7†	6c Junk (grey)		70	50
55†	6c Junk (red)		2.00	1.00
56†	6c Junk (brown)		14.00	13.00
8†	7c Junk		1.50	1.50
9†	8c Junk		2.00	1.25
10†	10c Junk		2.25	25

1932

空航

Nos. 6 and 10 overprinted

83†	5c Junk		£150	£100
84†	10c Junk		£150	£100

Szechwan

1933

限四川貼用

Nos. 310 and 316 of Chinese Republic overprinted

1†	1c Junk		1.50	45
2†	5c Junk		3.00	10

Yunnan

1926

限滇省貼用

Nos 309/21 of Chinese Republic overprinted

1†	½c Junk		20	30
2†	1c Junk		60	10
3†	1½c Junk		70	1.00
4†	2c Junk		1.00	40
5†	3c Junk		1.00	40
6†	4c Junk (olive)		1.00	10
7†	5c Junk		1.00	35
8†	6c Junk (red)		2.25	1.00
9†	7c Junk		2.50	2.25
10†	8c Junk		2.25	1.50
11†	10c Junk		2.25	10

Chinese People's Republic

1949 100 cents = 1 yuan
1955 100 fen = 1 yuan

1952

1563†	$800 Destroyers		30	10

1955

1677†	8f Freighter		35	10

1956

1691†	4f Rowing boats, Summer Palace, Peking		50	10

1957

1730†	52f Collier		10.00	50

1733†	8f Yellow River ferry		2.50	40

1960

1894†	10f Sampan		6.50	2.00

1965	8f *Yue Jin* (freighter)		3.75	1.00

1972

2485   8f *Fenglei* (freighter)
2486   8f *Taching No 30* (tanker)
2487   8f *Chang Seng* (cargo-liner)
2488   8f *Hsien-feng* (dredger)

                   Set of 4   5.50   2.75

1976

2638†   8f Canal vessels 1.40   65
2644†   8f Freighters in shipyard 1.40   65

1977

2709†   60f Oil rigs 45   15

1978

2751†   8f Tanker 40   20
2752†   20f *Exploration* (drilling ship) and oil rig   40   30

2753†   8f Sampans 80   45

1979

2871†   8f Sampan 50   15

2891†   8f Submarine 25   10

1980

2975†   2f Freighter 85   50

2983†   60f Ancient junk 5.50   3.75

3009†   60f Guilin ferry 2.00   85

1983

3279†   70f Sailboard 1.00   45

1984

3317†   20f Freighter in lock 25   15

1986

3427†   20f Freighter 30   15

1987

3509†   10f Submarine 30   15

1988

3570†   8f Bulk carrier loading coal 30   15

1989

3617†   1y30 Sampan 45   10

1991

3744†   20f Pleasure boat on Lake Nanhu 30   15

Taiwan
100 cents = 1 yuan

1957

265   40c *Hai Min* (freighter) and *Kiang Foo* (river vessel)
266   80c *Hai Min* and *Kiang Foo*
267    $2.80 *Hai Min* and *Kiang Foo*

                   Set of 3   2.40   65

1960

348    $1.60 *Yu-Khi* (postal launch) 85   20

1962

461   80c Liner
462    $3.60 *Hai Min* (freighter)

                   Set of 2   2.50   60

1964

512 $2 Ancient ship and modern freighter
513 $3.60 Ancient ship and modern freighter
　　　　　　　　　　　　　　　Set of 2　1.00　30

518 80c *Tai Ho, Tai Choa* and *Tai Tsang*
　　　(destroyers)
519 $6 *Tai Ho, Tai Choa* and *Tai Tsang*
　　　(destroyers)
　　　　　　　　　　　　　　　Set of 2　2.75　40

1966

581† $2.50 Dragon boat race .... 7.50　10

1967

601 $5 Freighter .... 1.50　15

1970

782† $2.50 Dragon boat race .... 2.75　60

1971

850 $4 *Hai King* (freighter)
851 $7 Liner
　　　　　　　　　　　　　　　Set of 2　1.40　65

COLLECT CHESS ON STAMPS
A Stanley Gibbons thematic catalogue — available at £5 (p. + p. £3) from: Stanley Gibbons Publications, 5 Parkside, Christchurch Road, Ringwood, Hants. BH24 3SH.

1972

878† $1 Three Ming ceremonial barges ...... 10　10
880† $1 Two Ming ceremonial barges .... 10　10
885† $8 Ming ceremonial barges .... 5.00　30

907† $2.50 Container ship .... 20　10

1973

923† $1 Bamboo model of sampan .... 45　10

1974

994† $5 Taiwan canoes, Lanya .... 50　15

1027† $4.50 Tanker under construction
　　　　Kaohsiung .... 35　25

1976

1099† $8 Mail ship .... 50　15

As No. 1027 *but face value changed*
1122g† $7 Tanker under construction,
　　　　Kaohsiung .... 35　10

1977
As No. 1122g, *but face value in double-lined figures*
1151† $7 Tanker under construction,
　　　　Kaohsiung .... 35　10

1979

1243† $10 Rowing boat .... 75　30

1980

1324† $2 Shipyard, Kaohsiung .... 40　10

1981

1397† $3 Container ship unloading .... 30　10

1984

1553 $2 *Ming Comfort* (container ship)
1554 $18 *Prosperity* (tanker)
　　　　　　　　　　　　　　　Set of 2　1.40　75

1985

1602† $2 Ching ivory model of dragon boat .. 60　10

1987

1764† $3 Sampan .... 55　10

1988

1802† $3 Police launch .... 40　10

1989

1843† $7.50 Freighter .... 75　15

1990

1899 $3 Freighter 35 10

1900 $3 Gas tanker in harbour
1901 $16 Gas tanker
Set of 2 1.00 25

1991

1963 $16 Container ship 1.00 30

CHRISTMAS ISLAND

Indian Ocean
100 cents = 1 dollar

1963

17† 12c *Islander* (freighter) 40 30
18† 20c *Triadic* (freighter) 1.00 35

1972

37 1c *Eagle* (merchant sailing ship), 1714
38 2c H.M.S. *Redpole* (gunboat), 1890
39 3c *Hoi Houw* (freighter), 1959
40 4c *Pigot* (sailing ship), 1771
41 5c *Valetta* (cargo-liner), 1968
42 6c H.M.S. *Flying Fish* (survey ship), 1887
43 7c *Asia* (sail merchantman), 1805
44 8c *Islander* (freighter), 1929–60
45 9c H.M.S. *Imperieuse* (armoured cruiser), 1888
46 10c "Cyclops" class coast defence turret ship, 1871 (inscr H.M.S. *Egeria* in error)
47 20c *Thomas* (galleon) , 1615
48 25c Royal Navy sail sloop, 1864,(inscr "H.M.S. GORDON" in error)
49 30c *Cygnet* (flute), 1688
50 35c *Triadic* (freighter), 1958
51 50c H.M.S. *Amethyst* (frigate), 1857
52 $1 *Royal Mary* (warship), 1643
Set of 16 13.00 11.50

1977

69† 3c H.M.S. *Flying Fish* (survey ship), 1887 30 30
77† 20c Ocean yacht 50 40

1981

143† 60c *Consolidated Venture* (bulk carrier) loading phosphate 70 55

1983

171 27c Mirror dinghy
172 35c Ocean yachts
173 50c Cargo ship and fishing launch
174 75c Sailing dinghies
Set of 4 1.75 1.75

1986

214† 60c *Consolidated Venture* (bulk carrier) loading phosphate 1.00 1.25
215† 90c Yachts 1.50 1.75

1987

227 36c H.M.S. *Flying Fish* (survey ship), 1887
228 90c H.M.S. *Egeria* (survey ship), 1887
Set of 2 2.40 3.00

1988

As Nos. 1105/8 of Australia, but inscribed "CHRISTMAS ISLAND"
246† 37c Arrival of First Fleet, 1788 .... 1.25 1.25
247† 37c Aborigine canoe 1.25 1.25
248† 37c First Fleet in cove 1.25 1.25
249† 37c Ship's boat 1.25 1.25

253† 95c H.M.S. *Imperieuse* (armoured cruiser), 1888 .... 90 95

1989

270† $1.10 H.M.S. *Challenger* (survey ship), 1872 .... 1.50 1.50

1990

295† 40c Passenger barge 35 40
296† 50c Kolek (outrigger canoe) 55 55

1991

316† 43c *Islander* (phosphate freighter) 60 60

324† $1.20 *Fregata Andrews* (police launch) towing rescued launch 1.75 1.75

340† $1 Rowing boat 1.10 1.25

1992

344† $1.05 Launch and *Islander* (freighter), 1942 .... 1.40 1.40
345† $1.20 Departure of *Islander*, 1942 ...... 1.60 1.60

362 45c Torpedoing of *Eidsvold* (freighter), 1942
363 80c *Eidsvold* sinking
364 $1.05 *Nissa Maru* (freighter) under attack, 1942
365 $1.20 *Nissa Maru* beached
Set of 4 2.75 3.00

CISKEI
Southern Africa
100 cents = 1 rand

1985

81 12c *Antelope* (sail troopship)
82 25c *Pilot* (sail troopship)
83 30c *Salisbury* (sail troopship)
84 50c *Olive Branch* (sail troopship)
Set of 4 1.25 1.25

COCOS (KEELING) ISLANDS
Indian Ocean

1963 12 pence = 1 shilling
20 shillings = 1 pound
1969 100 cents = 1 dollar

1963

5† 2s Jukong (Cocos sailing boat) 11.00 3.25

1976

20 1c *Dragon* (galleon), 1609
21 2c H.M.S. *Juno* (frigate), 1857
22 5c H.M.S. *Beagle* (Darwin), 1836
23 10c H.M.A.S. *Sydney* (cruiser), 1914
24 15c *Emden* (German cruiser), 1914
25 20c *Ayesha* (schooner), 1907
26 25c *Islander* (freighter), 1927
27 30c *Cheshire* (cargo liner), 1951
28 35c Jukong (Cocos sailing boat)
29 40c *Scotia* (cable ship), 1900
30 50c *Orontes* (liner), 1929
31 $1 *Gothic* (liner acting as Royal Yacht), 1954
Set of 12 9.00 8.50

1979

33† 50c Jukong (Cocos sailing boat) 35 50

48† 25c Jukongs (Cocos sailing boats) 25 35

1980

58† 22c *Eye of the Wind* (cadet brigantine) 20 15
60† 35c *Golden Hind* (Drake) 20 15
61† 60c *Eye of the Wind* 35 30

1981

77† 60c H.M.S. *Beagle* (Darwin), 1832 ...... 70 35

1984

112† 55c Jukongs (Cocos sailing boat) 60 50
113† 70c *Morea* (liner) 70 55
MS114 $1 Jukong (Cocos sailing canoe) 90 1.25

116† 65c *Hector* (Keeling), 1609 .... 1.50 90

MS121† $2 Jukongs 2.75 2.50

1985

126† 30c Jukong building 65 25

129 33c *Scotia* (cable ship)
130 65c *Anglia* (cable ship)
131 80c *Patrol* (cable ship)
Set of 3 4.25 1.75

1986

154† $1 H.M.S. *Beagle* (Darwin), 1836 .... 1.75 2.00

1987

158 36c Jukong (Cocos sailing boat)
159 36c Ocean racing yachts
160 36c *Sarimanok* (replica of early dhow)
161 36c *Ayesha* (schooner)
Set of 4 4.00 4.00

170† 65c Jukong building 1.50 1.50

1988
As Nos. 1105/8 *of Australia, but inscribed* "COCOS (KEELING) ISLANDS"
175† 37c Arrival of First Fleet, 1788 .... 1.25 1.25
176† 37c Aborigine canoe 1.25 1.25
177† 37c First Fleet in cove 1.25 1.25
178| 37c Ship's boat 1.25 1.25

189† 90c Jukong (Cocos sailing boat) (on stamp No. 5) 1.60 1.60

1989

211 35c Jukong (Cocos sailing boat)
212 80c Jukong (Cocos sailing boat)
213 $1.10 Jukong (Cocos sailing boat)
Set of 3 2.25 2.40

214 40c H.M.A.S. *Sydney* (cruiser), 1914
215 70c *Emden* (German cruiser), 1914
216 $1 *Emden's* steam launch
217 $1.10 H.M.A.S. *Sydney* (1914) and crest
Set of 4 5.50 5.50

1990

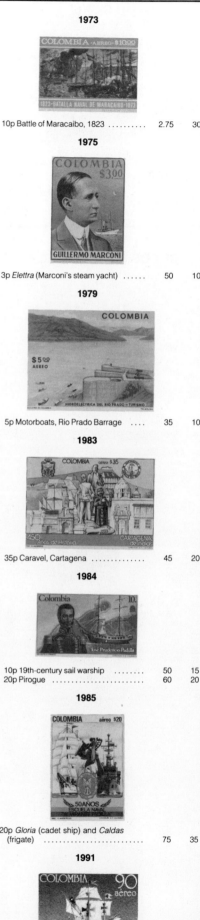

223 45c *Hector* (Keeling), 1609
224 75c H.M.S. *Beagle* (Darwin), 1836
225 $1 H.M.S. *Samarang* (Belcher), 1846
226 $1.30 H.M.S. *Juno* (frigate) (Fremantle),
     1857
                              Set of 4   5.50   5.50

1992

269 $1.05 *Santa Maria* (Columbus) 1.50   1.50

COLOMBIA

South America
100 centavos = 1 peso

1903

225† 5c *Cartagena* (gunboat) (blue) 1.25   1.40
226† 5c *Cartagena* (brown) 2.75   2.75

1932

Overprinted **CORREO AEREO**
422† 1p Galleon 7.25   4.50
423† 2p Galleon 26.00   14.50
424† 3p Galleon 45.00   45.00
425† 5p Galleon 65.00   65.00

1954

801† 2p Schooner, Cartagena 3.25   25

1955

844† 20c *City of Manizales* (freighter) 55   15
847† 50c *City of Manizales* (air) 75   15

857† 23c *Santa Maria, Pinta and Nina*
      (Columbus) 1.25   30

1956

873† 4c Fishing boats, Cartagena 25   10

1959

No. 873 surcharged
955 2c on 4c Fishing boats, Cartagena 10   10

No. 801 overprinted **UNIFICADO** *within outline of aeroplane*
985† 2p Schooner, Cartagena 1.75   20

990† 10c River steamer 25   15

1961

1085† 35c Paddle steamer, Barranquilla 45   10

1965

1153† 10p *Manuel Mejia* (freighter) 1.50   25

1966

1171 5c 16th-century galleon
1172 15c Riohacha brigantine, 1850
1173 20c Uraba schooner
1174 40c Steamer and barge, Magdalena,
      1900
1175 50c Modern freighter
                              Set of 5   2.00   70

1971

1290† 1p30 Yachts 40   30

1972

1311 1p20 *Almirante Padilla* (frigate), 1952 75   15

1973

1341 10p Battle of Maracaibo, 1823 .... 2.75   30

1975

1380 3p *Elettra* (Marconi's steam yacht) 50   10

1979

1484† 5p Motorboats, Rio Prado Barrage 35   10

1983

1697† 35p Caravel, Cartagena 45   20

1984

1705† 10p 19th-century sail warship 50   15
1708† 20p Pirogue 60   20

1985

1723 20p *Gloria* (cadet ship) and *Caldas*
      (frigate) 75   35

1991

1910 90p *Santa Maria* (Columbus)
1911 190p *Santa Maria*
                              Set of 2   80   40

1992

1935† 230p *Santa Maria* (Columbus) 50 20

COMORO ISLANDS
Indian Ocean
100 centimes = 1 franc

1950

1†	10c Local sailing craft	....	15	25
2†	50c Local sailing craft	....	15	25
3†	1f Local sailing craft	....	15	25

1954
As No. 264 of Cameroun
17 15f Landing craft, Normandy, 1944 .... 19.00 20.00

1964

42	15f Pirogue		
43	30f Felucca		
44	50f Pirogue		
45	85f Schooner		
	Set of 4	11.50	8.25

1970

91	5f Feluccas		
92	10f Feluccas		
93	40f Feluccas		
	Set of 3	2.50	2.00

1974

159† 90f Fishing boat, Mamutzu 2.25 1.50

1976

194† 35f Viking longship 30 15

1978

309† 35f Shipwreck 45 15

1980

419† 60f Pirogue 45 15

1981

476†	75f Scout pirogue	60	20
477†	250f Scout felucca	1.60	55

1983

510	150f Type "470" Olympic yacht		
511	200f "Flying Dutchman" Olympic yacht		
512	300f Type "470" Olympic yacht		
513	400f "Finn" class Olympic yacht		
	Set of 4	4.00	3.50
MS514	500f "Soling" class yachts	2.25	2.50

1984

542	100f *William Fawcett* (paddle-steamer)	
543	150f *Lightning* (clipper)	
544	200f *Rapido* (barque)	
545	350f *Sindia* (barque)	
	Set of 4	4.50 3.50

1985
No. MS514 overprinted **OLYMPHILEX '85 LAUSANNE**
MS554 500f "Soling" class yachts 2.00 2.50

555† 200f Fishing boats at quay 1.50 85

559† 300f Mississippi paddle-steamer 1.75 1.25

578	25f Galleon	
579	75f Galleon	
580	125f Galleon	
581	500f Galleon	
	Set of 4	5.00 4.00

1988

653†	75f *Santa Maria* (Columbus)	45	30
654†	125f *Pinta*	75	50
655†	150f *Nina*	90	60
657†	375f Wreck of *Santa Maria* (air)	2.00	1.50
658†	450f Columbus's fleet preparing for fourth voyage	2.50	2.00

694†	750f *Stars and Stripes* (yacht)	3.50	3.00
695†	1000f *New Zealand* (yacht)	4.50	4.00

1989
Nos. 511 and 555 surcharged **150F**

729†	150f on 200f Flying Dutchman class yacht	85	50
730†	150f on 200f Fishing boats at quay	85	50

Appendix
The following stamps have either been issued in excess of postal needs, or have not been made available to the public in reasonable quantities at face value. Miniature sheets, imperforate staps etc., are excluded from this section.

1975
No. 159 surcharged **ETAT COMORIEN.** 100f on 90f Fishing boat, Mamutzu.

CONGO (BRAZZAVILLE)

Central Africa
100 centimes = 1 franc

1962

21	50f *Yang-tse* (freighter) loading timber	....	1.00	50

1968

As No. 163 of Central African Republic

158	30f Tanker, Port Gentil, Gabon	....	60	25

1969

169	50f Freighter, Pointe Noire	....	1.40	1.00

1973

355†	260f Oil rig	....	3.75	1.50

359†	50f Fishing boat	....	75	35

375†	30f Oil rig	....	55	20
377†	100f Oil rig	....	1.75	85

1974

437†	30f Yachts, Argenteuil (Monet)	....	35	25

1975

463†	40f Pirogue	....	65	30

467†	40f Pirogue	....	65	30
469†	90f Pirogue	....	1.40	80

1976

504	5f *Alphonse Fondere* (river steamer)			
505	10f *Hamburg* (paddle-steamer), 1839			
506	15f *Gomer* (paddle-steamer), 1831			
507	20f *Great Eastern* (paddle-steamer), 1858			
508	30f *Alphonse Fondere*			
509	40f *Hamburg*			
510	50f *Gomer*			
511	60f *Great Eastern* (screw steamer)			
512	95f *J.M. White II* (river steamer), 1878			
		Set of 9	4.25	3.00

1977

552	35f Pirogue racing			
553	60f Pirogue racing			
		Set of 2	1.25	75

MS588†	500f *Mauretania I* (liner)	....	3.00	1.40

1978

633†	200f Roman sailing ship, Alexandria	....	1.25	55

1979

662†	250f Hawaiian canoes	....	2.00	70
663†	350f H.M.S *Resolution* (Cook) and			
	H.M.S. *Adventure*	....	2.75	1.10

1983

908	100f Sailboard			
909	200f Sailboard			
910	300f Sailboard			
911	400f Sailboard			
		Set of 4	4.00	4.00

1984

958†	100f Pusher tug	....	80	55
959†	150f Pusher tug	....	1.25	65
960†	300f Buoying boat	....	2.50	1.75
961†	500f *Saint* (freighter)	....	3.75	3.25

966†	20f Fishing pirogue	....	20	10

974	100f Sailboards			
975	150f "Soling" class yachts			
976	200f "470" class yachts			
977	500f "Flying Dutchman" class yachts			
		Set of 4	6.50	5.50

978	60f Log raft and boats			
979	100f Log raft and boats			
		Set of 2	1.25	75

1988

1117 240f Pirogues 1.00 90

1131† 35f Local fishing canoes 20 10

1990

1180† 150f Yachts racing 80 60
1181† 200f Yachts racing 95 80
1183† 350f Yachts in Barcelona harbour (air) 1.75 1.50

1991

1215† 75f Canoe 55 20

1225† 55f Santa Maria (Columbus) 45 20
1226† 75f Nina 70 30
1227† 150f Pinta 1.25 30

1992

1301† 120f Stern trawler 60 30

POSTAGE DUE STAMPS

1961

D23† 2f Pirogue 10 15
D24† 2f River steamer, 1932 .... 10 15

CONGO (KINSHASA)

Central Africa
1963 100 centimes = 1 franc
1967 100 sengi = 1 (li)kuta
100 (ma)kuta = 1 zaire

1963

460 2f Pirogue
461 4f Pirogue
462 7f Pirogue
463 20f Pirogue

Set of 4 1.75 1.25

Nos. 460/3 overprinted 10 DECEMBRE 1948 10 DECEMBRE 1963 15e anniversaire DROITS DE L'HOMME
507 2f Pirogue
508 4f Pirogue
509 7f Pirogue
510 20f Pirogue

Set of 4 45 45

1969

697† 8k Unloading freighter 55 25

COOK ISLANDS

South Pacific
1920 12 pence = 1 shilling
20 shillings = 1 pound
1967 100 cents = 1 dollar

1920

82† 1d Schooner 5.00 1.50
84† 4d Local sailing canoe 3.50 13.00

1932

106† ½d Captain Cook and ship 40 1.25
108† 2d Double Maori canoe 35 30
109† 2½d Schooner 30 1.50
111† 6d Monowai (liner) 75 2.25

1935

As Nos. 109 and 111 but colours changed, overprinted SILVER JUBILEE OF KING GEORGE V. 1910 – 1935.
114† 2½d Schooner 75 1.00
115† 6d Monowai (liner) 3.25 4.50

1938

145† 3s Canoe 17.00 15.00

1949

152† 2d Messenger of Peace (missionary schooner) 60 1.50
155† 6d Canoe 1.75 2.00
159† 3s Matua (inter-island freighter) 4.75 8.50

1963

173† 5s Tiare Taporo (schooner) 8.50 3.25

1966

No. 173 overprinted In Memoriam SIR WINSTON CHURCHILL 1874 – 1965
184† 5s Tiare Taporo (schooner) 2.00 1.75

No. 173 overprinted Airmail and aircraft
191† 5s Tiare Taporo (schooner) 1.50 1.50

1967

No. 173 surcharged 50c
217† 50c on 5s Tiare Taporo (schooner) 3.50 1.25

225† 18c (1s9d) Moana Roa (inter-island ship) 1.40 25

1968

269† ½c H.M.S. Endeavour (Cook), Matavai Bay, Tahiti 10 10
270† 1c H.M.S. Resolution and H.M.S. Discovery at Huaheine 15 10
271† 2c H.M.S. Resolution and H.M.S. Discovery, Kamchatka 40 35
272† 4c H.M.S. Resolution in Antarctica 40 35
273† 6c H.M.S. Resolution and H.M.S. Discovery (Cook) (air) 90 65
275† 15c H.M.S. Resolution and H.M.S. Discovery, Hawai 1.50 90

277† 1c Olympic yacht 10 10

1970

329† 30c H.M.S. *Endeavour* (Cook) 2.75 1.75

No. 329 overprinted **FIFTH ANNIVERSARY SELF-GOVERNMENT AUGUST 1970**
333† 30c H.M.S. *Endeavour* 1.25 35

1971

349† 25c Royal Yacht *Britannia* 1.50 2.00

1973

437 ½c Tipairua (canoe type)
438 1c Wa'a Kaulua (canoe type)
439 1½c Tainui (canoe type)
440 5c War canoe
441 10c Pahi (canoe type)
442 15c Amatasi (canoe type)
443 25c Vaka (canoe type)
Set of 7 3.50 1.10

1974

492 $2.50 H.M.S. *Resolution* (Cook) and H.M.S. *Adventure*
493 $7.50 H.M.S. *Adventure*
Set of 2 40.00 20.00

1975

515† 10c *Vitoria* (Del Cano), 1520 .... 75 20
516† 25c Friar Andres de Urdaneta and ship, 1564 .... 1.75 75
517† 30c Miguel Lopez de Legazpi and ship, 1564 .... 1.75 80

528† 25c Motor launch 70 30

1976

541 $1 H.M.S. *Resolution* and Benjamin Franklin
542 $2 H.M.S. *Resolution* and Capt. Cook
Set of 2 14.00 4.00
MS543 $3 H.M.S. *Resolution* with Cook and Franklin 17.00 8.00

Nos. 541/MS543 overprinted **Royal Visit July 1976**
544 $1 H.M.S *Resolution* and Benjamin Franklin
545 $2 H.M.S. *Resolution* and Capt. Cook
Set of 2 9.00 4.00
MS546 $3 H.M.S. *Resolution* with Cook and Franklin 10.00 7.50

1978

584† 50c H.M.S. *Resolution* 1.50 60
585† $1 H.M.S. *Resolution* at Hawaii 2.00 1.00

Nos. 584/5 overprinted **1728 · 250th ANNIVERSARY OF COOK'S BIRTH · 1978**
613† 50c H.M.S. *Resolution* 1.50 75
614† $1 H.M.S. *Resolution* at Hawaii 2.00 1.00

1979

629† 30c H.M.S. *Resolution* (Cook) 70 35
630† 35c H.M.S. *Royal George* (ship of the line) 80 45

637† 35c *Cap Hornier* (full-rigged ship) 40 25
638† 35c River steamer 40 25
639† 35c *Deutschland* (liner) 40 25
640† 35c *United States* (liner) 40 25

1980

Nos. 637/40 overprinted **ZEAPEX STAMP EXHIBITION–AUCKLAND 1980** *and New Zealand 1865 2d stamp*
691† 35c *Cap Hornier* 35 35
692† 35c River steamer 35 35
693† 35c *Deutschland* 35 35
694† 35c *United States* 35 35

1984

999† 48c H.M.S. *Endeavour* careened (Cook) 1.40 1.40
MS1002† 90c H.M.S. *Endeavour* careened (Cook) (sheet also contains three other designs) 6.50 7.00

1986

MS1064† $4 Royal barge on Thames, 1759 .. 3.25 4.25

1069† $1 H.M.S. *Resolution* (Cook) 2.50 2.50
1071† $2 H.M.S. *Resolution* (Cook) 3.75 3.75

1987

No. 999 surcharged
1141† $1.30 on 48c H.M.S. *Endeavour* careened (Cook) 1.40 1.50

Nos. 1069 and 1071 surcharged **HURRICANE RELIEF + 50c**
1172† $1 + 50c H.M.S. *Resolution* (Cook) 1.00 1.10
1174† $2 + 50c H.M.S. *Resolution* 1.75 1.90

1989

1220† 75c U.S.S. *Hornet* (aircraft carrier) at recovery of "Apollo II" capsule, 1969 90 90

1992

1302 $6 Ships of Columbus, 1492 .... 5.75 6.00
MS1303 $10 Ships of Columbus 6.50 6.75

1311† 80c Polynesian sea-going outrigger canoe 55 60

No. 1311 overprinted **ROYAL VISIT**
1315† 80c Polynesian sea-going outrigger canoe 55 60

OFFICIAL STAMPS

No. 542 overprinted **O.H.M.S.**
O29† $2 H.M.S. *Resolution* and Capt. Cook 5.50 3.00

COSTA RICA

Central America
100 centimos = 1 colon

1911

Surcharged **Correos Un centimo** *or* **Correos 5 5 centimos**

94	1c on 10c *Antilles* (liner), 1906		
96	1c on 25c *Antilles*		
97	1c on 50c *Antilles*		
98	1c on 1col *Antilles*		
99	1c on 5col *Antilles*		
100	1c on 10col *Antilles*		
101	5c on 5c *Antilles*		
	Set of 7	4.00	2.75

1923

144†	12c *Santa Maria* (Columbus)	5.50	1.75

1926

No. 144 *surcharged* **10 10** *between bars*

163	10c on 12c *Santa Maria* (Columbus)	1.75	45

1928

No. 144 *surcharged* **LINDBERGH ENERO 1928 10 10** *and aircraft*

169	10c on 12c *Santa Maria* (Columbus)	9.50	7.50

1936

226	5c Fleet of Columbus		
227	10c Fleet of Columbus		
	Set of 2	1.25	30

1947

No. O228 *overprinted* **CORREOS 1947**

431	5c Fleet of Columbus	30	10

435	25c Fleet of Columbus		
436	30c Fleet of Columbus		
437	40c Fleet of Columbus		
438	45c Fleet of Columbus		
439	50c Fleet of Columbus		
440	65c Fleet of Columbus		
	Set of 6	5.50	1.40

1948

No. 437 *surcharged* **HABILITADO PARA C 0.35**

472	35c on 40c Fleet of Columbus	45	30

1952

502	15c 16th-century caravels		
503	20c 16th-century caravels		
504	25c 16th-century caravels		
505	55c 16th-century caravels		
506	2col 16th-century caravels		
	Set of 5	4.00	1.60

1953

Nos. 436/8 *and* 440 *surcharged* **HABILITADO PARA CINCO CENTIMOS 1953**

515a	5c on 30c Fleet of Columbus		
516	5c on 40c Fleet of Columbus		
517	5c on 45c Fleet of Columbus		
518	5c on 65c Fleet of Columbus		
	Set of 4	1.75	1.40

1963

666†	25c *William le Lacheur* (sail merchantman)	30	10

1970

843	1col *Santa Maria* (on stamp No. 144)		
844	2col *Santa Maria* (on stamp No. 144)		
	Set of 2	1.10	55

853†	80c Fishing boats	65	15

1976

1055†	2col 20 Sail merchantman, Boston Tea Party, 1773	70	25

1990

1502†	500col Full-rigged ship (on arms of Costa Rica)	4.75	1.60

OFFICIAL STAMPS

1936

Nos. 226/7 *overprinted* **OFICIAL**

O228	5c Fleet of Columbus		
O229	10c Fleet of Columbus		
	Set of 2	45	20

CRETE

Mediterranean
100 lepta = 1 drachma

1907

31†	1d Warships, Suda Bay, 1898	4.00	3.50

1908

No. 31 *optd in Greek*

52†	1d Warships, Suda Bay, 1898	3.25	1.75

CROATIA

South-east Europe
1943 100 banicas = 1 kuna
1991 100 paras = 1 dinar

1943

85†	1k + 50b Motor torpedo boats	10	15

1991

151	1d70 Medieval ship	10	10

1992

No. 151 *surcharged* **20oo HPT** *and posthorn*

169	20d on 1d70 Medieval ship	20	20

195†	30d 15th-century carrack, Dubrovnik	25	25

As No. 195, *but with new face value and with C.E.P.T. emblem added*

198†	60d 15th-century carrack, Dubrovnik	50	50

CUBA

West Indies
100 centavos = 1 peso

1899

304†	5c *Umbria* (liner)	3.00	45

1936

403†	4c *Rex* (liner)	1.25	20
404†	5c Freighter in harbour	1.25	20
408†	50c Sailing ship and steamer	7.00	3.25
412†	50c Liner, San Severino (air)	7.00	2.00

1937

422	1c Caravel		
423	2c Caravel		
424	5c Caravel		
		Set of 3 2.75	1.00

424o	25c Fleet of Columbus	28.00	18.00

1944

478†	13c Caravels at Pinar del Rio (Columbus)	5.50	1.25
479†	5c Fleet of Columbus (air)	75	35

1951

556	5c *Creole* (paddle-steamer)	1.10	45

1952

585	2c Fleet of Columbus		
586	25c Fleet of Columbus (air)		
		Set of 2 7.50	2.00

1955

728†	10c 19th-century sailing ships, Havana	3.00	65
732†	24c *Umbria* (liner) (on stamp No. 304) (air)	1.90	55

757†	8c *Three Friends* (tug)	1.50	45

1960

922†	2c *Granma* (launch)	90	15

954†	1c Olympic yachts	45	20

1962

1022	10c 18th-century mail ship	2.50	60

1028b†	3c Speed boat	75	15
1028e	3c Racing yacht	75	15

1964

1122	1c *Rio Jibacoa* (freighter)		
1123	2c *Camilo Cienfuegos* (freighter)		
1124	3c *Sierra Maestra* (freighter)		
1125	9c *Bahia de Siguanea* (freighter)		
1126	10c *Oriente* (freighter)		
		Set of 5 4.00	1.25

1965

1193†	13c Merchantman	2.50	65

1196	1c *Sondero* (fishing schooner)		
1197	2c *Omicron* (fishing boat)		
1198	3c *Victoria* (fishing boat)		
1199	9c *Cardenas* (fishing boat)		
1200	10c *Sigma* (fishing boat)		
1201	13c *Lambda* (fishing boat)		
		Set of 6 6.00	1.75

1216†	3c 18th-century mail ship	1.50	20

1249†	13c *Granma* (launch)	1.60	40

1315†	10c *R.D.A.* (tug)	1.00	25
1316†	13c *13 de Marzo* (freighter)	1.60	45

1966

1320†	3c Torpedo-boat	45	10

1340†	2c 18th-century English yacht	40	10

1351†	3c *Houston* (freighter) sinking	40	10

1413†	3c *Havana* (tanker)	40	10

1431† 10c *Granma* (launch) 1.25 35

1967

1460† 13c *Corynthia* (launch) 1.50 50

1971

1823† 30c Weather ship 2.50 80

1846 13c Burning ship, Giron, 1961 .... 1.50 40

1847 13c *Windsor Castle* (sailing packet)
attacked by *Jeune Richard* (French
privateer brig), 1807
1848 30c *Orinoco* (mail paddle-steamer), 1851
Set of 2 4.25 1.40

1972

1906† 30c Fishing boats, Valencia 2.00 70

1978 1c Viking longship
1979 2c Caravel
1980 3c Galley
1981 4c Galleon
1982 5c Clipper
1983 13c Steam packet
1984 30c *Lenin* (atomic ice-breaker)
Set of 7 5.50 1.75

1973

2027† 30c *Kosmonavt Yury Gagarin* (research
ship) 2.50 65

2047 3c Destroyer 60 20

1974

2087 3c *Granma* (launch) (on stamp No. 922) 20 10

1975

2187 1c Fishing boat (Bonito)
2188 2c Fishing boat (Tunny)
2189 3c Fishing boat (Grouper)
2190 8c Fishing boat (Hake)
2191 13c Fishing boat (Prawn)
2192 30c Fishing boat (Lobster)
Set of 6 3.00 1.00

1976

2262† 3c Yacht, Guadalquivir River 30 10

2319 1c *Imias* (freighter)
2320 2c *Commandante Camilo Cienfuegos*
(freighter)
2321 3c *Commandante Pinares* (cargo liner)
2322 5c *Vietnam Heroico* (cargo liner)
2323 13c *Presidente Allende* (ore carrier)
2324 30c *XIII Congreso* (bulk carrier)
Set of 6 4.00 1.25

2333† 1c *Granma* (launch) 10 10

1977

2347† 5c 18th-century sailing ships, Venice .. 20 10

2411† 3c *Aurora* (Russian cruiser) 20 10

2423† 13c *Corynthia* (launch) 45 10

1978

2434† 13c Fishing boats, Guadalquivir River 50 10

2436 13c Patrol boat 70 15

2487 1c *Pargo* (tunny fishing boat)
2488 2c Fish-processing ship
2489 5c Shrimp fishing boat
2490 10c Stern trawler

2491 13c *Mar Carbide* (stern trawler) (air)
2492 30c Refrigeration and processing ship
Set of 6 2.25 90
MS2493 50c Venetian fishing boat 1.50 1.25

1980

2652 1c *Nuestra Sra de Atocha* (galleon),
1620
2653 3c Building *El Rayo* (ship of the line),
1749
2654 7c Building *Santissima Trinidad* (ship of
the line), 1769
2655 10c *Santissima Trinidad* at sea, 1805
2656 13c Building *Colon* and *Congresso*
(steamships), 1851
2657 30c Cardenas and Chullima shipyards
Set of 6 2.50 90

1981

MS2753   1p Sailing packet 2.40   1.90

2762†   1p *Granma* (launch) 2.25   1.00

1982

2791†   4c Lobster fishing boat   30   10

2818†   9c Sailing ships in bay   40   10

MS2822   1p *Louisiane* (steamer) 2.40   1.90

2855   5c *Santa Maria* (Columbus)
2856   20c *Santa Maria* (Columbus)
2857   35c *Pinta* (Columbus)
2858   50c *Nina* (Columbus)

Set of 4   4.25   1.75

MS2864   1p *Almendares* (paddle-steamer) 2.50   1.75

1983

2910   30c Sailing ships in harbour, 1883 . . . . . .   1.25   45

1984

MS3009   1p *Buenos Aires* (mail steamer)   2.50   2.00

3051†   20c Departure of Columbus from Palos   1.00   45
3052†   30c *Santa Maria, Pinta, Nina*
(Columbus) 1.40   65

1985

3085†   5c Carib canoe   20   10
3088†   50c Caribs building canoe 1.90   1.10

MS3119   1p Roman cargo ship 2.50   2.00

1986

3187   5c Tanker   30   15

1987

MS3274   1p Galleon, Coruna, 1525 . . . .   2.50   1.75

3283†   5c Ship's boat, 1492 (on Spain stamp
No. 602)   10   10

1988

MS3345   1p *Furst Menschikoff* (paddle-
steamer) 2.00   1.50

3378†   5c Caravels at Pinar del Rio (on stamp
No. 478)   10   10
3383†   10c Fleet of Columbus (on stamp No.
479)   15   10

1989

MS3407   1p Indian river post boat, 1858 . . . . . .   2.00   1.50

3430†   50c 18th-century sailing packet 1.25   80

3450   1c *El Fenix* (galleon)
3451   3c *Triunfo* (ship of the line)
3452   5c *El Rayo* (ship of the line)
3453   10c *San Carlos* (ship of the line)
3454   30c *San Jose* (ship of the line)
3455   50c *San Genaro* (ship of the line)

Set of 6   2.50   1.50

3456†   5c Dugout canoe   10   10

3483†   20c Fishing boat   35   20
3485†   50c Fishing boats and 18th-century
warship in harbour   90   60

1990

3497† 5c *Almendares* (paddle-steamer) 15 10

3517† 2c German liner 10 10

3535† 30c Research vessel 60 35

3542† 5c Sailboard 15 10

3559† 5c Caravel 15 10

3565† 1c Columbus's fleet (on Argentine
       Republic stamp No. 220) 10 10
3575† 10c Ship's boat, 1493 (on Puerto Rico
       stamp No. 110) 25 10

3586† 5c Sailing dinghies 15 10

**WHEN YOU BUY AN ALBUM LOOK
FOR THE NAME "STANLEY GIBBONS"**
It means Quality combined with Value for Money.

1991

3618† 50c Freighter under attack, 1961 ...... 1.25 55

3645† 20c Sailing dinghy 40 20
3646† 20c Sailing dinghy 40 20

3658† 50c Japanese sampans 1.25 55

3664† 20c *Santa Maria*, *Pinta* and *Nina* 60 20

3689† 50c *Granma* (launch) 1.25 60

1992

3719 5c *Santa Maria* (Columbus)
3720 20c Fleet of Columbus
                                   Set of 2 70 30

3738 10c Sailboards
3739 20c Pedalo
3740 30c Replica caravel
3741 50c Sailboard
                                   Set of 4 2.25 1.25

3747 5c Cabral's ship
3748 10c *Pinta* (Pinzon)
3749 20c Ojeda's ship
3750 30c Vespucci's ship
3751 35c Caravel (Prince Henry the Navigator)
3752 40c Dias's ship
                                   Set of 6 2.75 1.50
MS3753 1p *Santa Maria* (Columbus) 2.25 1.25

3773† 1c Columbus's fleet departing from
       Palos 10 10
3774† 5c Columbus's fleet off Canary Islands 10 10
3775† 5c Columbus addressing crew on *Santa
       Maria* 10 10
3777† 5c Ship's boats 10 10
3779† 10c *Santa Maria* aground, Hispaniola .. 15 10
3780† 10c *Nina* returning to Palos 15 10
3783† 10c Columbus's fleet leaving Cadiz for
       second voyage 15 10
3785† 20c Columbus's fleet leaving for third
       voyage 35 20
3786† 20c Ship's boat 35 20
3787† 20c Columbus's fleet leaving for fourth
       voyage 35 20

1993

3796† 30c Tug 50 30

SPECIAL DELIVERY STAMPS

1936

E413 15c Liner 8.50 2.00

1962

E1023 10c 18th-century sailing packet 5.50 1.25

CURACAO
West Indies
100 cents = 1 gulden

1928

112	6c Liner and freighter		
113	7½c Liner and freighter		
114	10c Liner and freighter		
115	12½c Liner and freighter		
116	15c Liner and freighter		
117	20c Liner and freighter		
118	21c Liner and freighter		
119	25c Liner and freighter		
120	27½c Liner and freighter		
121	30c Liner and freighter		
122	35c Liner and freighter		
	Set of 11	38.00	29.00

1929
No. 113 surcharged **6 ct.**

126	6c on 7½c Liner and freighter	1.10	85

1934

146†	20c *Johannes van Walbeeck* (Dutch galleon), 1634	3.50	2.25
147†	21c *Johannes van Walbeeck*, 1634	12.00	17.00
148†	25c *Johannes van Walbeeck*, 1634	11.00	11.00

CYPRUS
Mediterranean
1949 40 paras = 1 piastre
180 piastres = 1 pound
1955 1000 mils = 1 pound
1983 100 cents = 1 pound

1949
As No. 115 *of Antigua*

169†	2pi Paddle-steamer	1.00	80

1955

180†	30m Yachts, Kyrenia	35	10
182†	40m *Maltese Prince* (freighter)	40	60

1960
Nos. 180 *and* 182 *overprinted in Greek and Turkish*

195†	30m Yachts, Kyrenia	1.25	10
197†	40c *Maltese Prince* (freighter)	2.00	65

1966

286†	15m Minoan wine ship of 700 BC (painting)	15	10

1967

301†	100m Freighters, Famagusta	30	70

1976

449†	50m *Marcel Bayard* (cable ship)	40	10

1977

484†	120m Barges	70	1.25

1982

586†	40m Byzantine dromons, 965	60	10

1983

619†	3c Motor launch	10	10
621†	13c *Sol Olympia* (liner) and *Polys* (tanker)	40	30

1985

652†	5c Speed boat	20	20
655†	13c Sailboards	55	25

1986
No. 655 surcharged **18c**

685†	18c on 13c Sailboards	1.40	60

STANLEY GIBBONS
STAMP COLLECTING SERIES

Introductory booklets on *How to Start, How to Identify Stamps* and *Collecting by Theme.* A series of well illustrated guides at a low price. Write for details.

1987

706	2c Remains of ancient ship		
707	3c *Kyrenia II* (replica of ancient ship) under construction		
708	5c *Kyrenia II* at Paphos, 1986		
709	17c *Kyrenia II* at New York, 1986		
	Set of 4	2.25	1.60

1992

819†	10c Ships of Columbus at Palos	50	50
820†	30c Fleet of Columbus at sea	1.00	1.00

826	50c 7th-century BC Minoan wine ship and modern tanker	1.40	1.50

Turkish Cypriot Posts
1977 1000 mils = 1 pound
1978 100 kurus = 1 lira

1977

50†	100m Motor yachts, Kyrenia	35	65

1978

66†	100k Hydrofoil	10	10

1982

126†	30k Remains of ship from 300 B.C.	50	30

1988

228†	200li *Piyale Pasha* (tug)	1.00	30

1989

264† 100li Freighter unloading at Gazi Maguso 10 15

1991

323† 500li Motor launches, Girne 10 15

1992

MS334 1500li Ships of Columbus (sheet also
contains 3500li value) 1.00 1.10

CYRENAICA

North Africa
100 centesimi = 1 lira

1924

No. 157 of Italy overprinted **CIRENAICA**
13† 30c Ferry boat 60 12.00

1933

103† 5li Roman galley 4.00 35.00
105† 12li Roman galley 4.00 85.00

CZECHOSLOVAKIA

Central Europe
100 haleru = 1 koruna

1936

362† 10k River tug and barge, Bratislava 80 40

1939

No. 362 surcharged **Otvorenie slovenskeho snemu 18.1.1939
300 h** *and arms*
393b 300k on 10k River tug and barge,
Bratislava 75 90

1949

547† 13k Sailing ship 1.75 55

1952

732 1k50 River steamers, Bratislava 30 10

1953

796† 1k20 *Stalingrad* (tug) 3.25 2.00

1959

1130† 60h *Elettra* (Marconi's steam yacht) 30 10

1960

1136 30h *Praha Liben* (dredger)
1137 60h *Kharito Latjev* (tug)
1138 1k *Komarno* (river boat)
1139 1k20 *Lidice* (freighter)
                              Set of 4 3.50 1.75

1166 60h River tug and barge, Bratislava (on
stamp No. 362)
1167 1k River tug and barge, Bratislava (on
stamp No. 362)
                              Set of 2 1.25 20

1962

1318† 60h Sailing dinghy 30 10

1319 30h *Aurora* (Russian cruiser)
1320 60h *Aurora* (Russian cruiser)
                              Set of 2 65 20

1964

1409† 1k80 Sailing dinghies, Cesky Krumlow 90 25

1419† 1k U.S.S. *Intrepid* (aircraft carrier) 75 25

1966

1584† 20h Red Indian canoe 20 10

1967

1694† 2k Freighter in dock, Amsterdam 65 25

1971

1931† 50h Local trading punt 20 10

1972

2053 50h *Jiskra* (freighter)
2054 60h *Mir* (freighter)
2055 80h *Republika* (freighter)
2056 1k *Kosice* (tanker)
2057 1k60 *Dukla* (freighter)
2058 2k *Kladno* (freighter)
                              Set of 6 4.50 1.10

1976

2292	40h 16th-century warship		
2293	60h 17th-century Dutch merchantman		
2294	1k 17th-century ship at anchor		
2295	2k 18th-century galleon		
	Set of 4	2.50	90

1977

| 2372† | 30h *Aurora* (Russian cruiser) | 15 | 10 |

1979

2500	3k Danube ferry, Bratislava, *c.* 1787		
2501	3k60 Danube ferry, Bratislava, *c.* 1815		
	Set of 2	3.50	3.50

1980

2545	3k Danube ferry, Bratislava, *c.* 1810		
2546	4k Danube ferry, Bratislava, *c.* 1820		
	Set of 2	3.25	3.25

1982

2639	3k *Kamzik* (ferry)		
2640	3k60 *TR 100* (tug)		
	Set of 2	2.75	1.25

2642	3k Paddle-steamer, Bratislava, 1818		
2643	4k 19th-century river craft, Bratislava		
	Set of 2	4.00	2.00

1984

| 2754† | 2k River barge | 90 | 30 |

1989

2969	50h *Republika* (freighter)		
2970	1k *Pionyr* (trawler)		
2971	2k *Brno* (tanker)		
2972	3k *Trinec* (container ship)		
2973	4k *Orlik* (container ship)		
2974	5k *Vltava* (tanker)		
	Set of 6	2.25	1.25

1991

| 3053† | 5k *Bohemia* (paddle-steamer) | 75 | 40 |

1992

| 3089 | 22k *Santa Maria* (Columbus) | 1.50 | 1.10 |

DAHOMEY
West Africa
100 centimes = 1 franc

1931
As No. 109 *of Cameroun*

| 99† | 1f50 *Leconte de Lisle* (liner) | 2.75 | 3.00 |

1937
As Nos. 110/11 *of Cameroun*

| 100† | 20c Liner | 35 | 70 |
| 101† | 30c Sailing ship | 35 | 80 |

1941

133†	80c Sailing pirogue on Lake Nokoue	45	55
134†	1f Sailing pirogue on Lake Nokoue	30	45
135†	1f30 Sailing pirogue on Lake Nokoue	50	60

136†	1f40 Sailing pirogue on Lake Nokoue	60	70
137†	1f50 Sailing pirogue on Lake Nokoue	50	70
138†	2f Sailing pirogue on Lake Nokoue	55	90

1960

| 144† | 25f Pirogues, Ganvie | 45 | 25 |

1961
No. 144 *overprinted* **JEUX SPORTIFS D'ABIDJAN 24 AU 31 DECEMBRE 1961**

| 162† | 25f Pirogues, Ganvie | 45 | 30 |

1963

| 172† | 2f Ganvie girl in pirogue | 10 | 10 |
| 183† | 85f Ganvie girl in pirogue | 1.50 | 75 |

1964

| 204 | 25f Sacred boat of Isis, Pharaonic Egypt | 80 | 50 |

1965

| 228† | 25f Freighter, Cotonou Port | 45 | 25 |

1966
No. 229 *surcharged* **ACCORD DE COOPERATION FRANCE – DAHOMEY 5e Anniversaire – 24 Avril 1966 15F**

| 247† | 15f on 100f Freighter, Cotonou Port | 35 | 70 |

1967
No. 183 *surcharged* **30F**

| 280† | 30f on 85f Ganvie girl in pirogue | 40 | 30 |

284	30f *Suzanne* (barque)		
285	45f *Esmeralda* (schooner)		
286	80f *Marie Alice* (schooner)		
287	100f *Antonin* (barque)		
	Set of 4	4.75	2.50

1968

| 341† | 55f Mail pirogue | 60 | 35 |

1970

396   100f Pirogue 1.25   50

405†   40f *La Justice* and *La Concorde* (French
        warships), 1670   85   35

1971

440†   100f *General Mangin* (liner) 1.75   70

1972

479   40f Freighter   65   20

1973

499†   15f Scout pirogue   35   15

1974

No. 499 *surcharged* **100F XIe JAMBOREE PANARABE DE
BATROUN - LIBAN**

547†   100f on 15f Scout pirogue   65   45

POSTAGE DUE STAMPS

1967

D308†   1f Pirogue   10   10

DANISH WEST INDIES

West Indies
100 bit = 1 franc

1905

57†   1f *Ingolf* (training ship) 13.00   27.00
58†   2f *Ingolf* (training ship) 22.00   35.00
59†   5f *Ingolf* (training ship) 45.00   £160

DANZIG

Baltic
1921 100 pfennige = 1 mark
1923 100 pfennige = 1 Danzig gulden

1921

44   5pf Hanse kogge (medieval sailing vessel)
45   10pf Hanse kogge (medieval sailing vessel)
46   25pf Hanse kogge (medieval sailing vessel)
55   40pf Hanse kogge (medieval sailing vessel)
48   80pf Hanse kogge (medieval sailing vessel)
49   1m Hanse kogge (medieval sailing vessel)
50   2m Hanse kogge (medieval sailing vessel)
51   3m Hanse kogge (medieval sailing vessel)
52   5m Hanse kogge (medieval sailing vessel)
53   10m Hanse kogge (medieval sailing vessel)
        Set of 10   11.50   15.00

1924

201†   2g Freighter and tugs, River Mottlau
        (black and purple) 45.00   90.00
206†   2g Freighter and tugs, River Mottlau
        (black and red) 2.00   2.75

1932

No. 201 surcharged **15 15 Luftpost-Ausstellung 1932**
222†   15pf + 15pf on 2g Freighter and tugs,
        River Mottlau (black and purple) 9.00   19.00

1936

242†   25pf Fishing boats, Brosen Beach   85   2.00

245†   15pf + 5pf Tug 2.00   4.50

1938

276   5pf + 5pf *Peter von Danzig* (yacht), 1936
277   10pf + 5pf *Fu Shing* (dredger)
278   15pf + 10pf *Columbus* (liner)

279   25pf + 10pf *Hansestadt Danzig* (liner)
280   40pf + 15pf *Peter von Danzig* (sailing
        ship), 1472
        Set of 5   8.00   16.00

DENMARK

Northern Europe
100 ore = 1 krone

1927

Solid background

246   15ore Caravel
247   20ore Caravel
248   25ore Caravel
249   30ore Caravel
250   35ore Caravel
251   40ore Caravel
        Set of 6   24.00   1.10

1933

As Nos. 246/51, but with lined background
277b   15ore Caravel (red)
277d   15ore Caravel (green)
278a   20ore Caravel (grey)
278b   20ore Caravel (red)
279   25ore Caravel (blue)
279ab   25ore Caravel (brown)
280a   30ore Caravel (orange)
280b   30ore Caravel (blue)
281   35ore Caravel
282   40ore Caravel (green)
282b   40ore Caravel (blue)
        Set of 11   65.00   4.75

1934

Nos. 279 and 280a surcharged
285   "4" on 25ore Caravel (blue)
286   "10" on 30ore Caravel (orange)
        Set of 2   3.75   1.75

1937

306†   5ore *Rita* (King Christian X's yacht),
        1930 . . . .   1.50   15

1940

Nos. 277b, 280b and 282 surcharged
319a†   15ore on 40ore Caravel (green)   90   75
320†   20ore on 15ore Caravel (red) 1.10   10
321†   40ore on 30ore Caravel (blue) 1.00   20

1941

324   10ore *Sv. Pyotr* (Vitus Bering)
325   20ore *Sv. Pyotr* (Vitus Bering)
326   40ore *Sv. Pyotr* (Vitus Bering)
        Set of 3   1.90   45

1947

355†   40ore *Fyn* (train ferry) 1.50   75

1951

378 25ore *Fredericus Quartus* (Danish warship), *c.* 1700
379 50ore *Fredericus Quartus*

Set of 2 3.25 55

383 25ore + 5ore *Jutlandia* (hospital ship) 60 80

1960

426 30ore Sailing ship of 1560 .... 30 10

1962

448 60ore *Selandia* (freighter) 1.75 1.25

1963

453 60ore *Copenhagen* (paddle-steamer) 25 15

1970

517 30ore Figurehead from *Elephanten* 10 10

520 30ore Bronze-age ship
521 50ore Viking shipbuilding
522 60ore *Emanuel* (schooner)
523 90ore *A.P. Moller* (tanker)

Set of 4 1.10 65

1971

534 90ore Yachts 35 40

1974

594† 90ore H.M.S. *Edgar* (ship of the line) and H.M.S. *Dictator* (floating battery), 1808 40 10

1976

618 70ore + 20ore Viking longship
619 90ore + 20ore *Thingvalla* (freighter)
620 100ore + 20ore *Frederik VIII* (liner)
621 130ore + 20ore *Danmark* (cadet full-rigged ship)

Set of 4 2.50 3.00

1978

662† 1k80 Fishing boats 35 20

1980

690† 280ore Fishing boats, Vorupor 50 60

1982

740 1k60 *Argus* (revenue cutter) 60 10

1983

760† 3k50 Yacht 65 40

765† 3k50 Lifeboat 80 50

1984

774† 2k70 Pilot boat 50 15

783† 2k70 Fishing fleet 65 10
784† 3k30 *Bettina* (deep sea fishing boat) 70 60
785† 3k70 *Jonna Tornby* (trawler) 80 30

1985

812 2k80 Rowing boat 55 30

1986

MS817 25ore Ice boat, 1880 (sheet also contains three other designs) 2.25 2.75

825 2k80 Sailing dinghies, Aalberg 65 15

1990

932 4k75 17th-century ships and dockyard, Nyholm 1.00 55

PARCEL POST STAMPS

1914
Nos. 246, 249 and 251 overprinted **POSTFAERGE**
P252† 15ore Caravel 13.50 7.25
P253† 30ore Caravel 11.00 9.00
P254† 40ore Caravel 13.00 6.75

1936
Nos. 277b, 280a/b, 282 and 282b overprinted **POSTFAERGE**
P303a† 15ore Caravel (red) 65 75
P304† 30ore Caravel (blue) 3.50 3.00
P305† 30ore Caravel (orange) 50 50
P306† 40ore Caravel (green) 4.50 4.50
P307† 40ore Caravel (blue) 60 70

DJIBOUTI
East Africa
100 centimes = 1 franc

1894

103† 5f *Pingouin* (French gunboat) £150 95.00

1899
No. 103 *surcharged* **0,75**
111† 0,75 on 5f *Pingouin* (French gunboat) £375 £300

DJIBOUTI REPUBLIC

East Africa
100 centimes = 1 franc

1979

749†	40f Freighter	75	30

1980

799	55f H.M.S. *Endeavour* (Cook)		
800	90f Capt. Cook's ships		
	Set of 2	2.50	1.75

1981

804	100f Tanker	2.50	1.40

818	100f H.M.S. *Victory* (Nelson)		
819	175f H.M.S. *Victory*		
	Set of 2	4.00	2.50

1982

854†	25f Ferry and dhow	50	25

1983

874†	125f Sailboards	2.00	1.00

884†	90f Yacht	1.75	1.25

1984

MS905	250f *Leon Thevenin* (cable ship)	4.00	4.25

1985

957†	80f Oil rig	1.75	1.25

969†	100f Sailboards	1.75	1.10

1986

977	60f *Santa Maria* (Columbus)		
978	90f *Nina* and *Pinta* (Columbus)		
	Set of 2	3.25	2.50

1987

1011†	100f Dhow-building, 1887	1.50	1.00

DOMINICA

West Indies
1923 12 pence = 1 shilling
20 shillings = 1 pound
1949 100 cents = 1 dollar

1923

71	½d British ship of the line	
72	1d British ship of the line (black and violet)	
73	1d British ship of the line (black and red)	
74	1½d British ship of the line (black and red)	
75	1½d British ship of the line (black and brown)	
76	2d British ship of the line	
77	2½d British ship of the line (black and yellow	
78	2½d British ship of the line (black and blue)	
79	3d British ship of the line (black and blue)	
80	3d British ship of the line (black and red on yellow)	
81	4d British ship of the line	
82	6d British ship of the line	
83	1s British ship of the line	
84	2s British ship of the line	
85	2s6d British ship of the line	
86	3s British ship of the line	
87	4s British ship of the line	
90	5s British ship of the line	
91	£1 British ship of the line	
	Set of 19	£250 £350

1949

As No. 115 *of Antigua*

115†	6c Paddle-steamer	30	20

1954

147†	5c Canoe building	8.50	75

1963

164†	3c Sailing canoe	30	20
168†	8c Dugout canoe	10	10
170†	12c Canoes on beach	10	10

1967

206†	10c *Santa Maria* (Columbus)	10	10

1968

Nos. 164, 168 *and* 170 *overprinted* **ASSOCIATED STATEHOOD**

216†	3c Sailing canoe	10	10
220†	8c Dugout canoe	10	10
222†	12c Canoes on beach	10	10

No. 164 *overprinted* **NATIONAL DAY 3 NOVEMBER 1968**

234†	3c Sailing canoe	10	10

1969

261†	24c Freighter and tug	15	10

279†	8c Cargo liner	20	10

1971

328†	10c Boat building	10	10
329†	30c Yacht	20	10
330†	50c Motor yacht and speed boat	35	30

1974

441†	10c *Orinoco* (mail paddle-steamer), 1851, and *Geesthaven* (freighter), 1974	15	10

1975

467	½c *Yare* (cargo liner)		
468	1c *Thames II* (liner), 1890		
469	2c *Lady Nelson* (cargo liner)		
470	20c *Lady Rodney* (cargo liner)		
471	45c *Statesman* (freighter)		
472	50c *Geestcape* (freighter)		
473	$2 *Geeststar* (freighter)		
	Set of 7	6.00	4.50

1976

509†	1c British three-deck warship, 1782	10	10

1977

581†	$3 Sailing dinghies	2.00	1.75

1978

608†	40c Tug and barge (launch of Zeppelin *LZ1*), 1900	50	20

1979

655†	30c Canoe	35	15

667†	10c H.M.S. *Endeavour* (Cook)	45	10
668†	50c H.M.S. *Resolution* (Cook)	1.00	60
669†	60c H.M.S. *Discovery* (Cook)	1.10	70

1982

828†	$3 Canoe	4.25	5.00

1984

890	45c *Atlantic Star* (freighter)		
891	60c *Atlantic* (liner)		
892	90c Carib fishing boat		
893	$4 *Norway* (liner)		
	Set of 4	8.00	8.50
MS894	$5 *Santa Maria* (Columbus)	4.00	4.50

1985

956†	$3 Rowing boat	4.25	5.50

965†	$4 Royal Yacht *Britannia*	4.50	5.00

1986

988†	15c Police rowing boat, New York, 1890	80	40
989†	25c New York Police Dept launch, 1986	1.10	50

WHEN YOU BUY AN ALBUM LOOK
FOR THE NAME "STANLEY GIBBONS"
It means Quality combined with Value for Money.

1987

1052	45c *Reliance* (yacht), 1903		
1053	60c *Freedom* (yacht), 1980		
1054	$1 *Mischief* (yacht), 1881		
1055	$3 *Australia* (yacht), 1977		
	Set of 4	2.40	2.50
MS1056	$5 *Courageous* (yacht), 1977	6.50	7.00

1076†	10c Fleet of Columbus, 1493	35	20
1077†	15c Fleet of Columbus, 1493	40	20
1079†	60c Wreck of *Santa Maria*, 1492	70	40
1080†	90c Fleet of Columbus, 1492	85	70
1083†	$5 Fleet of Columbus, 1493	3.00	3.75
MS1084†	Two sheets. (a) $5 Fleet off Dominica, 1493 (other sheet shows map)		
	Price for 2 sheets	5.00	6.00

1085†	10c H.M.S. *Warrior* (ironclad)	40	40
1087†	25c *Flying Cloud* (clipper)	60	60
1090†	60c *Spray* (yacht), 1895	75	75
1091†	90c *Sea-Land Commerce* (container ship), 1973	1.00	1.00
1094†	$4 *Clermont* (first commercial paddle-steamer), 1807	3.00	3.00

1988

No. **MS**1084 *overprinted* **OLYMPHILEX '88**

MS1128†	Two sheets (a) $5 Fleet of Columbus off Dominica (other sheet shows map)		
	Price for 2 sheets	4.25	4.75

1989

1221†	20c Carib canoe	10	10
1223†	$1 Making dugout canoe	40	45

1228†	$1 French warship of 1720	40	45

1286†	60c U.S.S. *Constitution* (frigate) defeating H.M.S. *Guerriere* (frigate), 1812	35	35
1287†	60c *Alligator* (settlers' ship), Liberia, 1822	35	35

1288† 60c Barge on Erie Canal 35 35
1289† 60c Perry's fleet off Japan, 1853 . . . . . . 35 35
1303† 60c *Gorch Fock* (German cadet barque) 35 35

1990

1381† $3 "Star" class yacht 1.25 1.40

1991

1406 10c Caravel of Gil Eannes, West African
      coast, 1433–34
1407 25c Alfonso Baldaya's ships, West
      African coast, 1436
1408 45c Flagship of Bartolomeu Dias, Cape
      of Good Hope, 1487
1409 60c Da Gama's ships in Indian Ocean,
      1497–99
1410 $1 Vallarte the Dane's caravels off West
      African coast
1411 $2 Aloisio Cadamosto's caravel at Cape
      Verde Islands, 1456–58
1412 $4 Caravel of Diogo Gomes on River
      Gambia, 1457
1413 $5 Diogo Cao's caravel at mouth of
      Congo, 1482–85
                              Set of 8 5.25 5.75
MS1414 Two sheets (a) $6 Bow of *Santa
Maria* (Columbus); (b) $6 Caravel
                        Price for 2 sheets 5.25 5.50

1470† 10c Japanese aircraft leaving carrier
       Akagi before Pearl Harbor 10 10
1471† 15c U.S.S. *Ward* (destroyer) attacking
       Japanese midget submarine 10 10
1472† 45c Japanese aircraft leaving carrier . . 20 25
1474† $1 U.S.S. *Breeze, Medusa* and *Curtiss*
       (destoyers) sinking Japanese midget
       submarine 45 50
1475† $2 U.S.S. *Nevada* (battleship) under
       attack 85 90
1476† $4 U.S.S. *Arizona* (battleship) sinking . . 1.75 1.90
MS1478† Two sheets (a) $6 Japanese torpedo
bomber over American ships, Pearl Harbor
(other sheet shows attack on airfield)
                        Price for 2 sheets 5.25 5.50

DOMINICAN REPUBLIC

West Indies
100 centavos = 1 peso

1899

89† 1c 15th-century sailing boat (purple) 4.50 3.50
90† 1c 15th-century sailing boat (green) 1.00 40

1902

125† 1c Galleon and early steamship 25 25
126† 2c Galleon and early steamship 25 25
127† 5c Galleon and early steamship 25 25
128† 10c Galleon and early steamship 25 25
129† 12c Galleon and early steamship 25 25
130† 20c Galleon and early steamship 25 25

1937

385† 10c Fleet of Columbus 3.75 1.25
392† 1p Fleet of Columbus 12.00 2.75

1940

443† 10c Caravels 1.00 50
447† 50c Caravel 3.25 1.60

1958

747 7c *Rhadames* (freighter) 75 20

756† 17c Olympic yachts 75 40

1959
No. 756 surcharged **ANO GEOFISICO INTERNACIONAL
1957-1958 + 2c** *and globe*
772† 17c + 2c Olympic yachts 1.00 1.00

1974

1199† 7c *Eider* (mail steamer) 40 15

1976

1255 20c *Separacion Dominicana* (schooner) 1.25 30

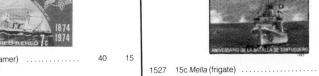

1273† 6c Caravel and map 45 15

1977

1297 20c Battle of Tortuguero, 1844 . . . . 75 30

1978

1316 7c *Duarte* (schooner) 55 15

1982

1509† 7c Rowing boats, San Pedro de Macoris 45 20

1510† 7c *Santa Maria* (Columbus) 75 20
1511† 10c *Santa Maria* (Columbus) 1.00 30

1983

1527 15c *Mella* (frigate) 1.00 30

1543 10c Caravels
1544 21c *Santa Maria* (Columbus) (trophy)
1545 33c *Sotavento* (yacht)
                              Set of 3 2.50 1.40
MS1546 50c *Santa Maria, Nina* and *Pinta*
      (Columbus) 2.50 2.50

1984

1569	10c Coastguard patrol boat	65	15

1985

1617†	35c Racing yachts	75	20

1626†	10c Harbour scene, Haina	30	10

1986

1637	10c *Leonor* (schooner)	45	10

1649†	25c Racing yachts	15	10

1988

1660†	5c Fishing boat	15	10

1989

1737	40c Battle of Tortuguero, 1844	30	15

1990

1777†	50c Yachts	20	10

1781†	50c Amerindian canoe	20	10

DUBAI

Persian Gulf
1963 100 naye paise = 1 rupee
1966 100 dirhams = 1 riyal

1963

26†	1np Dhow	10	10
30†	20np Dhow (air)	60	25

1964

74†	75np *Rigorous* (tug)	70	40
75†	2r *Rigorous*	1.50	70
76†	3r *Rigorous*	2.00	1.10

82†	20np Dhows	25	10
84†	40np Dhows	40	10
85†	1r Tug and launches (air)	85	25
86†	2r Dhow and barge	2.00	65
87†	3r Tug and launches	3.00	1.40
88†	5r Dhow and barge	5.50	2.75

No. 30 overprinted **ANTI TUBERCULOSE**, *in English and Arabic, with Cross of Lorraine*

101†	20np Dhow	3.00	2.50

1966

173†	10np *Tasman* (oil rig)	20	10
175†	30np *Tasman* (oil rig)	40	10
177†	50np *Tasman* (oil rig)	70	15
179†	75np *Tasman* (oil rig)	1.25	35

1967

263†	1r25 *Bayan* (dhow)	1.50	45
264†	3r *Bayan* (dhow)	3.00	1.25
265†	5r *Bayan* (dhow)	5.00	2.50
266†	10r *Bayan* (dhow)	8.00	5.00

1969

318†	25d *Bamora* (freighter), 1914	20	10
320†	60d *Sirdhana* (liner), 1947	55	15
322†	1r25 *Chandpara* (freighter), 1949	90	40
MS324†	1r25 *Bombala* (freighter), 1961	1.00	95

342†	20d *Thames* (tug)	20	10
343†	35d *Majamaa 2* and other tankers	60	15
344†	60d Oil rig	1.25	30
345†	1r Pipe-laying ship	1.75	60

1970

349†	60d *Weather Reporter* (weather ship)	35	15

363†	10d Dhow building	25	10
364†	20d Speedboat	40	15
366†	60d Dhows	75	15

ECUADOR

South America
100 centavos = 1 sucre

1930

477†	10c Freighter	70	15

1936

522† 20c H.M.S. *Beagle* (Darwin) 1.75 25

1948

829†	10c *Santa Maria* (Columbus)	40	10
830†	20c *Santa Maria*	70	10
831†	30c *Santa Maria*	90	15
832†	50c *Santa Maria*	1.25	15
833†	1s *Santa Maria*	1.75	15
834†	5s *Santa Maria*	4.25	55

1956

1044†	10c Manta fishing canoe (blue)	20	10
1044a†	10c Manta fishing canoe (brown)	35	10
1045†	20c Canoe, River Babahoya (brown)	30	10
1045a†	20c Canoe, River Babahoya (pink)	30	10
1045b†	20c Canoe, River Babahoya (green)	35	10
1047†	50c Canoe, River Pital (green)	30	10
1047a†	50c Canoe, River Pital (violet)	35	10
1050b†	1s Raft, San Pablo (black)	50	10
1053†	1s Raft, San Pablo (blue) (air)	50	10
1053a†	1s Raft, San Pablo (orange)	40	10

1975

1582 2s Naval landing ship 45 15

1976

1658 5s Battle of Flamborough Head, 1779 .... 1.75 40

1979

1741 5s Deep sea trawler 90 25

1982

1864 3s50 *Isla Salango* (freighter) 90 25

1985

1949† 10s *Calderon* (gunboat) 50 20

1991

2119 200s Columbus's fleet
2120 500s *Santa Maria* (Columbus)
Set of 2 1.40 75

1992

2131 300s *Calderon* (gunboat)
2132 500s *Atahualpa* (despatch vessel)
Set of 2 75 35

2145† 200s *Santa Maria* (Columbus) 15 10

OFFICIAL STAMPS

1936
No. 522 overprinted **OFICIAL**
O527† 20c H.M.S. *Beagle* (Darwin) 1.10 30

EGYPT

North Africa
1000 milliemes = 100 piastres = 1 pound

1914

73† 1m Nile felucca 15 30

1922

No. 73 overprinted
98† 1m Nile felucca 40 10

1926

138 5m Ancient Egyptian ship, Temple of
Deir-el-Bahari
139 10m Ancient Egyptian ship, Temple of
Deir-el-Bahari
140 15m Ancient Egyptian ship, Temple of
Deir-el-Bahari
Set of 3 3.75 2.10

Nos. 138/40 overprinted **PORT FOUAD**
141† 5m Ancient Egyptian ship, Temple of
Deir-el-Bahari £120 80.00
142† 10m Ancient Egyptian ship, Temple of
Deir-el-Bahari £120 80.00
143† 15m Ancient Egyptian ship, Temple of
Deir-el-Bahari £120 80.00

1948

351 10m Battle of Navarino, 1827 .... 30 25

1956

517 10m Freighter and Suez Canal 40 35

519 10m Sinking ship, Port Said 30 30

1957
No. 519 overprinted **EVACUATION** 22.12.56 *in English and Arabic*
520 10m Sinking ship, Port Said 45 30

As No. 517, but with inscription in English instead of French and also inscribed "PORT SAID" and "REOPENING 1957"
524 100m Freighter and Suez Canal 70 50

530   10m *Sudan* (paddle-steamer) and felucca   30   15

1959

597†   10m *Al Mokattam* (freighter)   40   25
598†   10m Motorised Nile barge   40   25

1961

668   10m *Al Nasser* (destroyer)   15   10

1964

771†   3m Ancient funerary barge (alabaster
         model)   10   10
780†   40m Nile felucca   35   10

1965

850†   10m *Discoverer* (oil rig)   40   20

1966

886†   10m *Salah-el-Deen* being built   35   20

891†   10m *Southern Cross* (liner) and freighter   45   20

1967

937   80m + 20m Gondola, Venice
938   115m + 30m Gondola, Venice
                          Set of 2   2.50   3.25

1969

1035†   20m Merchant ships of 1869 and 1969   50   25

1974

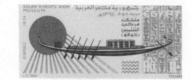

1226   110m Solar boat of Cheops 1.75   1.25

1977

1309   20m Pharaonic ship   35   10

1332   20m Marine gas rig   60   15

1978

1337†   140m Nile feluccas   95   55

1980

1429   70m Tanker   50   20

1983

1518†   3p Pharaonic ship and modern freighter   30   10

1988

1689   5p Container ship   30   10

1991

1832   10p Inflatable dinghy   10   10

1992

1852   70p Pharaonic ship   25   15

OFFICIAL STAMPS

1915

No. 73 overprinted **O.H.H.S.** *in English and Arabic*
O83†   1m Nile felucca 1.00   2.00

1922

No. 73 overprinted **O.H.E.M.S.** *in English and Arabic*
O111†   1m Nile felucca   50   1.75

EGYPTIAN OCCUPATION OF PALESTINE

Western Asia
1000 milliemes = 100 piastres = 1 pound

1964

As Nos. 771 and 780 of Egypt, but additionally inscribed "PALESTINE" in English and Arabic
142†   3m Ancient funerary barge (alabaster
         model)   10   10
150†   40m Nile felucca   40   10

EL SALVADOR

Central America
1896 100 centavos = 1 peso
1912 100 centavos = 1 colon

1896

162†   10c Steamship   20   25
163†   12c Steamship   20   30

GIBBONS STAMP MONTHLY
— finest and most informative magazine for all collectors. Obtainable from your newsagent or by postal subscription — details on request.

1933

810 15c Fleet of Columbus
811 20c Fleet of Columbus
812 25c Fleet of Columbus
813 40c Fleet of Columbus
814 1col Fleet of Columbus

Set of 5 25.00 15.00

1954

1051†	1c Fishing boats	10	10
1061†	7c Fishing boats	20	10
1067†	22c *Fle-Ja-Lis* (coastguard cutter)	80	35
1070†	1col *Fle-Ja-Lis*	90	35
1072†	5c Fishing boats (air)	30	10
1075†	10c *Fle-Ja-Lis*	40	10
1080†	25c *Fle-Ja-Lis*	70	15

1957
No. 1061 surcharged
1123† 6c on 7c Fishing boats 30 15

1962
No. 1070 surcharged
1171† 10c on 1 col *Fle-Ja-Lis* (coastguard cutter) 30 10

1969

1308† 40c Dugout canoe, Jaltepeque estuary 60 25

1970

1327† 50c *Nohaba* (coastguard patrol boat) 1.25 35

1971
No. 1327 overprinted **1951-12 Octubre-1971 XX Aniversario MARINA NACIONAL**
1374 50c *Nohaba* (coastguard patrol boat) 70 30

1979

1632† 1col Freighter 90 45

1983

1799† 1col Canoes on beach 1.10 60

1811† 25c Trawler and rowing boat 55 20

1985

1879 55c Inflatable inshore lifeboat 70 30

1986

1948† 20c Fishing boat 30 15

1990

2120† 1 col *Santa Maria* (Columbus) 30 15
2121† 1 col *Pinta* and *Nina* 30 15

1991

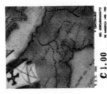

2167† 1 col *Santa Maria* (Columbus) 30 15
2168† 1 col Caravel 30 15
2169† 1 col Caravels 30 15

1992

2182† 4 col 50 Inflatable dinghy 75 45

2207† 1 col Caravel in human eye 30 15
2208† 1 col Caravel and Mexican pyramids .. 30 15
2209† 1 col Caravel and satellite 30 15

2216† 2 col 20 Stern of caravel 60 25

EQUATORIAL GUINEA
West Africa
1968 100 centimos = 1 peseta
1973 100 centimos = 1 ekuele (plural = bikuele)
1985 100 centimos = 1 franc

1979

29† 1e Freighter, Bata 15 10

1984

72 125b Whaling pirogues
73 150b Pirogue on beach

Set of 2 2.50 1.50

1990

148 170f *Santa Maria* (Columbus)
149 300f *Santa Maria*, *Pinta* and *Nina*

Set of 2 2.50 1.50

Appendix
The following have either been issued in excess of postal needs, or have not been made available to the public in reasonable quantities at face value. Miniature sheets, imperforate stamps etc. are excluded from this section.

1972
Olympic Games, Munich. Sailing events at Kiel. 1, 2, 3, 5, 8p

1973
Transatlantic Yacht Race. Postage 1, 2, 3, 5, 8p; Air 15, 50p

1974
Centenary of U.P.U. 2e25 Mail canoe

1975
Historical Ships. Postage 30, 35, 40, 45, 50, 55, 60, 65, 70, 75c; Air 8, 10, 50, 60e

1976
Olympic Games, Montreal. 7e Yacht
Olympic Games, Montreal. Sailing. Postage 70, 80, 90c; Air 30, 60e
Steamships. Postage 80, 85, 90, 95c, 1p; Air 15, 40p
Ship Paintings. Postage 5, 10, 15, 20, 25, 30e; Air 50, 60, 65, 70e

ERITREA
North-east Africa

ITALIAN ADMINISTRATION
100 centesimi = 1 lira

1924
No. 157 of Italy overprinted **ERITREA**
76† 30c Ferry boat 55 11.00

BRITISH ADMINISTRATION
100 cents = 1 shilling

1951
Nos. 509/10 of Great Britain surcharged **B.A.ERITREA** *and value*
E30† 2s50 on 2s6d H.M.S. *Victory* (Nelson) 5.50 9.00
E31† 5s on 5s Yacht and Thames sailing
   barge, Dover 16.00 17.00

ESTONIA
1919 100 penni = 1 Estonian mark
1928 100 senti = 1 kroon

1919

11† 1m Viking longship 30 90
12† 5m Viking longship 1.10 20
33† 15m Viking longship 2.00 40
34† 25m Viking longship 2.75 1.50

1936

127† 2k *Aegna* (cargo liner) 1.25 3.25

ETHIOPIA
East Africa
1947 100 cents = 1 dollar
1976 100 cents = 1 birr

1947

373a† 60c Canoe, Lake Tana 1.50 60
374† 70c Canoe, Lake Tana 1.75 65

1949
No. 374 surcharged **EXPOSITION 1949 +70c** *and two lines of Amharic*
394† 70c + 70c Canoe, Lake Tana 10.00 7.00

1951
No. 394 further overprinted **1951** *and date in Amharic*
420† 70c + 70c Canoe, Lake Tana 7.00 5.00

1952

435† 15c Dhows, Assab 1.00 30
437† 30c Dhows, Assab 1.75 70

1953

444 10c Freighter, Massawa
445 15c Freighter and pilot boat
446 25c Freighter, Massawa
447 30c Freighter and pilot boat
448 50c Freighter, Massawa
   Set of 5 22.00 7.50

1960
No. 373a overprinted **World Refugee Year 1959-1960** *in English and Amharic*
499† 60c Canoe, Lake Tana 65 75

1962

554† 20c Kaleb's Fleet, 520 .... 65 20

1972

808 10c Reed Raft Lake Haik
809 20c Canoes, Lake Abaya
810 30c Punts, Lake Tana
811 60c Dugout canoes, River Baro
   Set of 4 3.50 1.25

1981

1186† 15c Canoes, River Baro 20 10

1983

1263† 1b Liner 1.75 70

1989

1436 15c *Abyot* (container ship)
1437 30c *Wolwol* (container ship)
1438 55c *Queen of Sheba* (freighter)
1439 1b *Abbay Wonz* under construction
   Set of 4 2.00 1.25

FALKLAND ISLANDS
South Atlantic
1933 12 pence = 1 shilling
20 shillings = 1 pound
1971 100 pence = 1 pound

1933

129† 1½d *Bransfield* (whale catcher) 5.50 7.50
130† 2d H.M.S. *Clio* (sloop), Port Louis, 1833 .. 7.00 15.00

1938

155† 6d *Discovery II* (polar supply vessel)
   (black and brown) 4.50 3.50
156† 6d *Discovery II* (polar supply vessel)
   (black) 2.75 4.50
157† 9d *William Scoresby* (research ship) 5.50 50

1949
As No. 115 of Antigua
169† 3d Paddle-steamer 4.50 1.75

1952

173† 1d *Fitzroy* (supply ship) 80 40
178† 6d *John Biscoe I* (research ship) 12.00 1.00
185† £1 Hulk of *Great Britain* (steam/sail) 24.00 30.00

1953
As Nos. 173 and 178 but with portrait of Queen Elizabeth II
188† 1d *Fitzroy* (supply ship) 1.25 60
190† 6d *John Biscoe I* (research ship) 5.50 60

1964

215† 2½d H.M.S. *Glasgow* (cruiser), 1914 .... 6.00 2.25
216† 6d H.M.S. *Kent* (cruiser), 1914 .... 1.00 25
217† 1s H.M.S. *Invincible* (battle cruiser), 1914 .. 2.00 60

1970

258 2d *Great Britain* (steam/sail in 1843)
259 4d *Great Britain* (steam/sail in 1845)
260 9d *Great Britain* (steam/sail in 1876)
261 1s *Great Britain* (sailing ship in 1886)
262 2s *Great Britain* (as a hulk in 1970)
   Set of 5 9.00 3.25

ALBUM LISTS
Write for our latest list of albums and accessories.
This will be sent on request.

1974

301†	5p Packet ship, 1841		35	45
303†	16p *Ile de France* (liner), 1920		60	75

305†	20p H.M.S. *Inflexible* and H.M.S. *Invincible* (battle cruisers), 1914		1.90	1.60

307	2p H.M.S. *Exeter* (cruiser), 1939			
308	6p H.M.N.Z.S. *Achilles* (cruiser), 1939			
309	8p *Admiral Graf Spee* (German pocket battleship)			
310	16p H.M.S. *Ajax* (cruiser), 1939			
		Set of 4	17.00	17.00

1976

324†	20p *Monsunen* (wool freighter)		2.00	2.00

1978

331	1p *A.E.S.* (mail ship 1957–74)			
332	2p *Darwin* (mail ship 1957–73)			
333	3p *Merak-N* (mail ship 1951–52)			
334	4p *Fitzroy* (mail and supply ship 1936–57)			
335	5p *Lafonia* (mail ship 1936–41)			
336	6p *Fleurus* (mail ship 1924–33)			
337	7p *Falkland* (mail ship 1914–34)			
338	8p *Oravia* (mail ship and liner 1900–12)			
339	9p *Memphis* (mail ship 1890–97)			
340	10p *Black Hawk* (mail ship 1873–80)			
341	20p *Foam* (mail ship 1863–72)			
342	25p *Fairy* (mail ship 1857–61)			
343	50p *Amelia* (mail ship 1852–54)			
344	£1 *Nautilus* (mail ship 1846–48)			
345	£3 *Hebe* (mail ship 1842–46)			
		Set of 15	21.00	30.00

1979

370†	25p *Gwendolin* (schooner)		75	1.00

1982

417	5p *Lady Elizabeth* (barque) (shipwreck), 1913			
418	13p *Capricorn* (shipwreck), 1882			
419	15p *Jhelum* (shipwreck), 1870			
420	25p *Snowsquall* (shipwreck), 1864			
421	26p *St. Mary* (shipwreck), 1890			
		Set of 5	2.40	3.75

425†	34p H.M.S. *Beagle* (Darwin), 1831		85	95

Nos. 335 and 342 overprinted **1st PARTICIPATION COMMONWEALTH GAMES 1982**

431	5p *Lafonia*			
432	25p *Fairy*			
		Set of 2	75	1.40

1983

442†	10p *Lenita* (Swedish barque)		60	60
444†	20p H.M.S. *Invincible* (battle cruiser), 1914		90	90

455†	13p *Canberra* (liner) and *Norland* (ferry) at San Carlos, 1982		30	50
457†	50p H.M.S. *Hermes* (aircraft carrier), 1982		1.00	1.40

1984

484	6p *Wavertree* (sail merchantman)			
485	17p *Bjerk* (whale catcher) at Port Stanley quay, c. 1910			
486	22p *Oravia* (liner)			
487	52p *Cunard Countess* (liner)			
		Set of 4	3.25	2.25

488	22p 19th-century sailing ship		55	65

1985

501†	7p *Merchant Providence* (freighter)		50	30

510	7p H.M.S. *Jason* (frigate), 1765			
511	22p H.M.S. *Dolphin* (frigate) (Byron) and H.M.S. *Tamar* (sloop), 1765			
512	27p H.M.S. *Beagle* (Darwin), 1831			
513	54p H.M.S. *Philomel* (brig), 1842			
		Set of 4	3.50	3.00

1986

527	10p *Great Britain* (steam/sail) crossing Atlantic, 1845			
528	24p *Great Britain* beached at Sparrow Cove, 1937			
529	29p *Great Britain* on pontoon, 1970			
530	58p *Great Britain* undergoing restoration, Bristol, 1986			
		Set of 4	3.00	2.50

1987

541†	29p Coasters and accommodation ship, Stanley		1.75	1.25

1988

565†	29p *A.E.S.* (mail ship)		60	60
566†	58p *Charles Cooper* (full-rigged ship)		1.25	1.25

1989

567	1p *Padua* (barque)			
613	2p *Priwall* (barque)			
614	3p *Passat* (barque)			
570	4p *Archibald Russell* (barque)			
571	5p *Pamir* (barque)			
617	6p *Mozart* (barquentine)			
573	7p *Pommern* (barque)			
574	8p *Preussen* (full-rigged ship)			
620	9p *Fennia* (barque)			
576	10p *Cassard* (barque)			
577	20p *Lawhill* (barque)			
578	25p *Garthpool* (barque)			
579	50p *Grace Harwar* (full-rigged ship)			
625	£1 *Criccieth Castle* (full-rigged ship)			
581	£3 *Cutty Sark* (full-rigged ship)			
582	£5 *Flying Cloud* (full-rigged ship)			
		Set of 16	19.00	20.00

593	10p H.M.S. *Invincible* (battle cruiser) and crest		
594	24p *Scharnhorst* (German cruiser) and crest		
595	29p H.M.S. *Ajax* (cruiser) and crest		
596	58p *Admiral Graf Spee* (German pocket battleship) and crest		
		Set of 4	3.00	3.25

1991

642†	62p *Isis* (mail ship), 1891	1.60	1.60

643	14p *Eye of the Wind* (cadet brig)		
644	29p *Soren Larsen* (cadet brigantine)		
645	34p *Santa Maria, Pinta* and *Nina* (Columbus)		
646	68p *Santa Maria* (Columbus)		
		Set of 4	3.50	3.50

664†	68p *Desire* (Davis), 1592	1.60	1.60

1993

MS675	£2 *Queen Elizabeth 2* (liner)	4.00	4.25

FALKLAND ISLANDS DEPENDENCIES

South Atlantic
1944 12 pence = 1 shilling
20 shillings = 1 pound
1971 100 pence = 1 pound

1944

Nos. 155 and 157 of Falkland Islands overprinted **GRAHAM LAND DEPENDENCY OF**

A6†	6d *Discovery II*	9.00	2.25
A7†	9d *William Scoresby*	1.50	1.00

Nos. 155 and 157 of Falkland Islands overprinted **SOUTH GEORGIA DEPENDENCY OF**

B6†	6d *Discovery II*	9.00	2.25
B7†	9d *William Scoresby*	1.50	1.00

Nos. 155 and 157 of Falkland Islands overprinted **SOUTH ORKNEYS DEPENDENCY OF**

C6†	6d *Discovery II*	9.00	2.25
C7†	9d *William Scoresby*	1.50	1.00

Nos. 155 and 157 of Falkland Islands overprinted **SOUTH SHETLANDS DEPENDENCY OF**

D6†	6d *Discovery II*	9.00	2.25
D7†	9d *William Scoresby*	1.50	1.00

1949

As No. 115 of Antigua

G22	2d Paddle-steamer	6.50	2.50

1954

G26	½d *John Biscoe I* (research ship), 1947–52		
G27	1d *Trepassey* (supply ship), 1945–47		
G28	1½d *Wyatt Earp* (Ellsworth), 1934–36		
G29	2d *Eagle* (sealer), 1944–45		
G30	2½d *Penola* (Rymill), 1934–37		
G31	3d *Discovery II* (polar supply vessel), 1929–37		
G32	4d *William Scoresby* (research ship), 1926–46		
G33	6d *Discovery* (Scott), 1925–27		
G34	9d *Endurance* (Shackleton), 1914–16		
G35	1s *Deutschland* (German expedition), 1901–12		
G36	2s *Pourquoi-pas?* (Charcot), 1908–10		
G37	2s6d *Francais* (Charcot), 1903–05		
G38	5s *Scotia* (Bruce), 1902–04		
G39	10s *Antarctic* (Nordenskjold), 1901–03		
G40	£1 *Belgica* (Gerlache), 1897–99		
		Set of 15	£200	80.00

1956

Nos. G27, G30/1 and G33 overprinted **TRANS-ANTARCTIC EXPEDITION 1955-1958**

G41	1d *Trepassey*		
G42	2½d *Penola*		
G43	3d *Discovery II*		
G44	6d *Discovery*		
		Set of 4	1.25	1.10

1980

82†	9p *Louise* (coaling hulk)	30	45
86†	50p *John Biscoe II* (research ship), 1956	1.50	2.00
87†	£1 *Bransfield* (research ship), 1970	2.00	2.75
88†	£3 H.M.S. *Endurance* (ice patrol ship)	5.00	6.50

FAROE ISLANDS

North Atlantic
100 ore = 1 krone

1940

No. 277b of Denmark surcharged **20**

1†	20ore on 15ore Caravel (red)	32.00	10.50

1975

7†	10ore 16th-century sailing ship	10	10
9†	60ore 16th-century sailing ship	95	95
11†	80ore 16th-century sailing ship	35	35
13†	120ore 16th-century sailing ship	50	25

1976

20†	125ore Faroese rowing boat	2.00	1.25

1977

23	100ore Motor fishing boat		
24	125ore *Niels Pauli* (inshore fishing cutter)		
25	160ore Modern seine fishing boat		
26	600ore *Polarfisk* (deep-sea trawler)		
		Set of 4	9.50	6.00

1981

60†	150ore Fishing boats, Torshavn	25	25
61†	200ore Fishing boats, Torshavn	30	30

1983

78	220ore *Arcturus* (cargo liner)		
79	250ore *Laura* (cargo liner)		
80	700ore *Thyra* (cargo liner)		
		Set of 3	2.00	2.00

1983

85	250ore Trawler		
86	280ore Motor fishing boat		
87	500ore Drifter		
88	900ore Deep-sea trawler		
		Set of 4	2.75	2.75

1984

100†	280ore *Westward Ho* (fishing ketch)	50	40

1987

146 300ore *Joannes Patursson* (trawler)
147 550ore *Magnus Heinason* (trawler)
148 800ore *Sjurdarberg* (stern trawler)
          Set of 3 3.25 3.25

150† 300ore Fishing boats, Hestur Island 55 55

1988

162† 5k50 Container ship 95 95

177† 3k50 Wooden toy boat 60 60

1989

181† 200ore Local rowing longboats 30 30

1990

MS195 3k50 *Nyggjaberg* (trawler); 3k50
Sanna (schooner) (third 3k50 design shows
Faroese flag) 1.90 1.90

1991

206† 4k50 Viking longship 80 80

220 200ore *Ruth* (mail ship)
221 370ore *Ritan* (mail ship)
222 550ore *Sigmundur* (mail ship)
223 800ore *Masin* (mail ship)
          Set of 4 3.25 3.25

1992

224 3k70 Viking ship (Leif Eriksson)
225 6k50 *Santa Maria* (Columbus)
          Set of 2 2.10 2.10

FERNANDO POO

Off West Africa
100 centimos = 1 peseta

1929

Nos. 506 and 508 of Spain overprinted **FERNANDO POO**
211† 15c Spanish caravel, Seville 25 25
213† 25c Spanish caravel, Seville 25 25

1960

234† 20c + 5c Whaling canoe 10 10
236† 50c + 20c Whaling canoe 30 10

1962

248 25c *Okume* (Spanish freighter)
249 50c *San Francisco* (Spanish freighter)
250 1p *Okume*
          Set of 3 30 30

252† 35c Liner 35 25

1964

261† 25c 19th-century sail warship 15 10
263† 1p 19th-century sail warship 15 10

264† 25c Canoe 10 10
266† 1p Canoe 10 10

1968

305† 2p50 Spanish frigate (from colonial arms) 15 10

FEZZAN

North Africa
100 centimes = 1 franc

1943

Nos. 54/5 and 59 of Libya surcharged **FEZZAN Occupation**
Francaise *and value*
4† 2f on 30c Roman galley £250 £225
7† 5f on 50c Roman galley 13.00 14.00
8† 10f on 1li Roman galley £750 £650

FIJI

South Pacific
1891 12 pence = 1 shilling
20 shillings = 1 pound
1969 100 cents = 1 dollar

1891

87† 1d Fijian canoe (black) 2.50 3.00
101† 1d Fijian canoe (mauve) 3.50 50
89† 2d Fijian canoe 4.75 80
85† 5d Fijian canoe. 7.00 7.50

1938

249† ½d Outrigger canoe 10 30
252† 1½d Outrigger canoe 60 1.40
257† 3d Outrigger canoe 70 30

1949

As No. 115 *of Antigua*
273† 3d Paddle-steamer 90 1.00

1954

285† 3d *Komowai* (copra freighter) 1.00 20

296† 1½d + ½d Bamboo trading raft 10 30

1963

Overprinted **COMPAC CABLE IN SERVICE DECEMBER 1963**
and illustration of Retriever *(cable ship)*

335 1s *Retriever* (on map design) 25 10

1966

351† 3d H.M.S. *Pandora* (frigate), 1791 ...... 15 10
353† 1s6d H.M.S. *Pandora* 25 20

1967

363† 2s *Oriana* (liner) 40 15

364† 4d H.M.S. *Providence* (sloop) (Bligh),
      1792 .... 10 10
365† 1s *Bounty*'s longboat and canoes, 1789 10 10

1968

377† 9d Bamboo raft 15 15
382† 2s6d Outrigger canoes 1.00 1.00

389† 9d *Vuniwai* (hospital ship) 15 10

1969

As Nos. 377 and 382, but with face values in cents

397† 8c Bamboo raft 10 10
402† 25c Outrigger canoes 1.00 30

412† 8c Racing yacht 10 10

1970

No. 402 overprinted **ROYAL VISIT 1970**

419† 25c Outrigger canoes 20 10

425† 3c H.M.S. *Endeavour* (Cook) 1.00 25
426† 8c *Bounty*'s longboat, 1789 .... 1.00 15
427† 25c Fijian ocean going-canoe 1.00 15

1974

496† 8c *Fijian Princess* (mail ship) 10 10

1977

545 4c Drua canoe
546 15c Tabilai canoe
547 25c Takai canoe
548 40c Camakua canoe
                          Set of 4 80 1.10

1979

571† 40c *Leonidas* (emigrant ship), 1879 .... 40 25

1980

596 6c *Southern Cross* (freighter), 1873
597 20c *Levuka* (freighter), 1910
598 45c *Matua* (inter-island freighter), 1936
599 50c *Oronsay* (liner), 1951
                          Set of 4 80 80

1981

618† 60c *Retriever* (cable ship) 90 90

1982

629† 20c Scout catamaran 50 30

635† 70c *Kiro* (minesweeper) 1.00 1.10

MS646† $1 Royal Yacht *Britannia* (sheet also
        contains two other designs) 2.25 2.75

1983

655† 8c Schooner 10 10

1984

675 8c *Tui Lau* (shipwrecked freighter)
676 40c *Tofua I* (cargo liner)
677 55c *Canberra* (liner)
678 60c *Nedlloyd Madras* (freighter) at wharf,
     Suva
                          Set of 4 3.00 2.25

687† $1 *Fua Kavenga* (container ship) 1.60 1.60

1985

697† 20c Outrigger canoe, Toberua Island 50 30

1988

770 30c Sailboard 70 50

1989

790†	45c Plan of *Bounty's* launch	70	50
793†	$1 *Bounty's* launch at sea	1.40	1.50

1991

827†	54c H.M.S. *Pandora* (frigate), 1791	70	70
829†	75c H.M.S. *Pandora* off Rotuma Island	90	90

1992

846†	$1.40 *Queen Elizabeth 2* (liner) at Suva	1.60	2.00

847	38c *Tabusoro* (inter-island coaster)		
848	54c *Degei II* (inter-island coaster)		
849	$1.40 *Dausoko* (inter-island coaster)		
850	$1.65 *Nivanga* (inter-island coaster)		
	Set of 4	4.00	4.00

852†	86c Yacht	1.00	1.00

FINLAND

Northern Europe
100 pennia = 1 markka

1929

260†	1m *Bore* (freighter)	1.90	3.00

1930

280†	2m + 20p Viking longship	2.00	32.00

1935

307†	2m Viking longship	2.50	1.40

1937

312	1¼m + 15p *Thorborg* (warship), 1772	
313	2m + 20p *Lodbrok* (warship), 1771	
314	3½m + 35p *Styrbjorn* (warship), 1789	
	Set of 3	14.00 10.50

1938

327†	1¼m Postal sledge-boat, 1700	90	2.50

1942

370†	100m *Ilmatar* and *Rigulus* (freighters)	1.90	10

1946

420	8m Sailing ship	30	30

424	8m Rowing boats, Tammisaari	20	30

1949

482	15m 18th-century sailing ship, Kristiinankaupunki	1.75	2.25

483	5m *Salmetar* (lake steamer), Lappeenranta	90	70

1955

542	25m *Ilma* (barque), 1863	1.75	1.75

1956

553a†	5m Rowing boat	25	10
557b†	100m *Ilmatar* and *Rigulus* (as No. 370 but "FINLAND" without scroll, "100" upright and "mk" omitted)	27.00	10

1961

624	30m *Pommern* (barque)	2.75	1.40

1963

660†	5p Rowing boat	15	10
670†	1m *Ilmatar* and *Rigulus*	50	10
674†	1m75 River launch	1.00	10

1964

694†	25p + 4p Red Cross hospital ship	1.40	1.10

1968

747	40p *Ivalo* (container ship)	90	15

1971

780†	30p + 6p Tug and log raft	90	90

787	50p "Lightning" class yachts	1.25	25

1972

795	50p *Suomen Joutsen* (cadet ship)	1.25	25

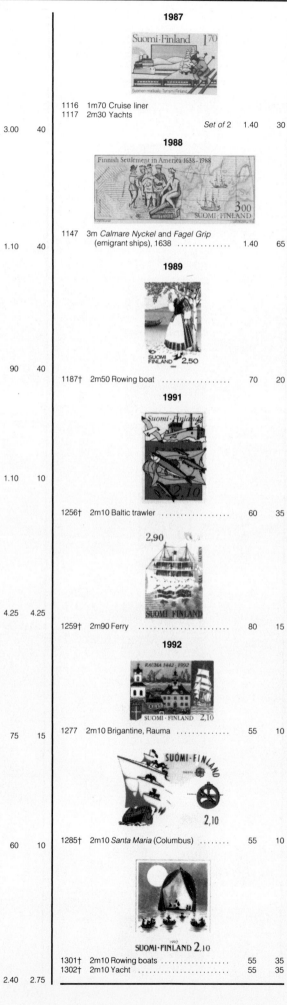

832†   60p Rowing boat, Heinavesi 3.00   40

1975

880   70p *Niilo Saarinen* (lifeboat) and sinking ship 1.10   40

1977

917   90p Ice-breaker and freighter 90   40

1978

931   1m Freighter at wharf 1.10   10

1981

992   1m10 *Furst Menschikoff* (paddle-steamer), 1842 .... 4.25   4.25

993†   1m10 Rowing to church in local longboats 75   15

1983

1040†   1m30 Tourist canoe, River Kitajoki 60   10

1986

MS1107   1m60 *Aura* (paddle-steamer), 1858; 1m60 *Alexander* (steamer), 1858; 2m20 *Nicolai* (steamer), 1858; 2m20 *Express II* (ice-breaker), 1877 .... 2.40   2.75

1987

1116   1m70 Cruise liner
1117   2m30 Yachts
                                    Set of 2   1.40   30

1988

1147   3m *Calmare Nyckel* and *Fagel Grip* (emigrant ships), 1638 .... 1.40   65

1989

1187†   2m50 Rowing boat 70   20

1991

1256†   2m10 Baltic trawler 60   35

1259†   2m90 Ferry 80   15

1992

1277   2m10 Brigantine, Rauma 55   10

1285†   2m10 *Santa Maria* (Columbus) 55   10

1301†   2m10 Rowing boats 55   35
1302†   2m10 Yacht 55   35

1919 100 centesimi = 1 corona
1920 100 centesimi = 1 lira

1919

75†   45c + 5li 13th-century Venetian war galley   2.00   2.50
76†   60c + 5li 13th-century Venetian war galley   2.00   2.50
77†   80c + 5li 13th-century Venetian war galley   2.00   2.50
78†   1cor + 5li 13th-century Venetian war galley 2.00   2.50

Nos. 75/8 surcharged **Valore globale** *and value*
123†   45c on 45 + 5li 13th-century Venetian war galley 20   25
110†   60c on 60c + 5li 13th-century Venetian war galley 20   25
111†   80c on 80c + 5li 13th-century Venetian war galley 25   30
112†   1cor on 1cor + 5li 13th-century Venetian war galley 25   30

1921

Nos. 75/8 overprinted **24 – IV – 1921 Costituente Fiumana** *and* **L** *over the "C" on No. 185*
182†   45c + 5li 13th-century Venetian war galley 1.10   1.60
183†   60c + 5li 13th-century Venetian war galley 1.40   1.90
184†   80c + 5li 13th-century Venetian war galley 2.00   2.75
185†   1li on 1cor + 5li 13th-century Venetian war galley 2.50   3.75

1922

Nos. 75/8 overprinted **24 – IV – 1921 Costituente Fiumana 1922** *and* **L** *over the "C" on No. 197*
194†   45c + 5li 13th-century Venetian war galley 25   70
195†   60c + 5li 13th-century Venetian war galley 25   70
196†   80c + 5li 13th-century Venetian war galley 25   70
197†   1li on 1cor + 5li 13th-century Venetian war galley 25   55

1923

201†   5c Medieval ship 30   35
202†   10c Medieval ship 30   35
203†   15c Medieval ship 30   35

1924

Nos. 201/3 overprinted **REGNO D'ITALIA** *and arms*
213†   5c Medieval ship 20   1.40
214†   10c Medieval ship 20   1.40
215†   15c Medieval ship 20   1.40

Nos. 201/3 overprinted **ANNESSIONE ALL'ITALIA 22 Febb 1924** *and arms*
225†   5c Medieval ship 20   95
226†   10c Medieval ship 20   95
227†   15c Medieval ship 20   95

NEWSPAPER STAMPS

1920

N145   1c Mail steamer 15   35

POSTAGE DUE STAMPS

Nos. 110/12 and 123 surcharged **Segnatasse** and value

D188†	20c on 45c 13th-century Venetian war galley	30	70
D183†	30c on 1cor 13th-century Venetian war galley	30	40
D184†	40c on 80c 13th-century Venetian war galley	25	35
D185†	50c on 60c 13th-century Venetian war galley	25	35
D189†	60c on 45c 13th-century Venetian war galley	30	70
D190†	80c on 45c 13th-century Venetian war galley	30	70

FRANCE

Western Europe
100 centimes = 1 franc

1918

378	15c + 5c Charles Roux (hospital ship)	£100	45.00

1927

458	90c Paris (liner)		
459	1f50 Paris		
	Set of 2	3.25	1.40

1929

| 474b† | 10f Fishing boats, La Rochelle | 65.00 | 5.50 |

1934

521	75c Grande Hermine and Petite Hermine (Cartier), 1534		
522	1f50 Grande Hermine and Petite Hermine		
	Set of 2	55.00	3.25

1935

| 526 | 1f50 Normandie (liner) | 12.00 | 1.00 |

1937

| 585 | 50c + 20c Fishing boats, Constantinople | 1.75 | 3.00 |

1938

| 601† | 20f Grand Banks fishing barquentine, St. Malo | 32.00 | 14.50 |

1939

| 637 | 90c "Dunkerque" class battleship | 50 | 30 |

1940

No. 601 surcharged

| 688† | 10f on 20f Grand Banks fishing barquentine, St. Malo | 1.10 | 1.10 |

1941

| 707 | 1f + 1f on 70c Pasteur (liner) | 25 | 25 |
| 738† | 10f + 10f Medieval ship | 2.00 | 2.00 |

1942

739	2f50 + 7f50 L'Astrolabe and La Boussole (La Perouse), 1788	1.25	1.25
744	1f50 + 8f50 Liner and sampan	75	75
748	1f50 + 8f50 14th-century ship of Jean de Vienne	70	70

1946

| 965 | 2f + 3f Emile Bertin (cruiser) and Lorraine (battleship) | 30 | 30 |

1947

| 1011† | 6f Tug and barges, Paris | 70 | 70 |

1954

| 1204 | 15f Landing craft, Normandy, 1944 | 1.40 | 60 |
| 1251 | 30f Jules Verne's fictional submarine Nautilus | 6.25 | 5.00 |

1955

| 1261 | 30f La Capricieuse (sail warship), 1855 | 5.00 | 3.75 |
| 1263† | 8f Fishing boats, Marseilles | 35 | 15 |

1956

| 1281† | 15f La Frigorifique (early refrigerated freighter) | 70 | 45 |
| 1305 | 30f Rhine barges, Strasbourg | 3.50 | 5.00 |

1957

| 1322 | 12f + 3f 18th-century felucca | 1.40 | 1.10 |
| 1344† | 12f Freighters, Brest | 55 | 35 |

1958

1386†   15f Nautical jousting in rowing boats 1.00   60

1959

1428†   15f + 5f Medieval ships 1.10   1.10

1960

1475   20c + 5c *Ampere* (cable ship) 1.00   1.00

1499f†   30c Medieval ship   30   15

1961

1543†   30c Yachts, Arcachon   20   15

1962

1557   30c *France* (liner)   50   30

1566   95c Freighter, Dunkirk 1.00   30

1963

1595   30c *Archimede* (bathyscaphe)   25   20

1965

1675   25c + 10c *La Guienne* (steam packet),
1860   60   60

1685†   60c Yacht, Aix-les-Bains   50   20
1687†   95c Punt, Vendee 5.00   30

1692   30c *Le Taureau* (warship), 1665   20   20

1966

1722   60c Norman ships, 1066   30   30

1967

1759†   95c *Cap Nord* (trawler), Boulogne 1.25   50

1968

1799   25c *Velox* (freighter)   20   20

1969

1818†   1f15 Yachts, La Trinite-sur-Mer 1.10   35

1835†   45c Landing craft, Normandy, 1944   60   40
1837†   45c Landing craft, Provence, 1944   85   40

1849   70c *Le Redoutable* (submarine)   30   20

1970

1855   70c *Firecrest* (yacht)   55   30

1856   45c Police patrol boat 1.40   40

1883†   50c Fishing boat, Martinique   30   10

1896†   45c Siege of La Rochelle, 1628   65   30

1971

1912   80c Bathysphere   40   25

1920   80c *Antoinette* (barque)   90   60

1972

1947†   2f River barges 3.00   90

1948 90c Antarctic exploration ship, 1772 .... 1.00 1.00

1955† 50c + 10c 18th-century French warship 1.00 1.00

1967 90c *Cote d'Emeraude* (Grand Banks fishing barquentine) 70 40

1973

1993† 50c + 10c 18th-century French warships 80 70

1998† 90c Tanker, Le Havre 70 20

2011 90c *France II* (barque) 80 30

1974

2040 90c Shipwreck and modern lifeboat 45 25

1975

2095 1f40 Tanker, St. Nazaire 60 25

2100 90c *La Melpomene* (cadet ship) 90 35

1976

2122 1f *Duguay Trouin VIII* (cruiser), 1926, and *Duguay Trouin IX* (destroyer), 1976 .... 50 25

2139 1f20 Olympic yacht 45 25

2149 1f45 *Duchesse Anne* (cadet ship) 60 30

1977

2152† 2f10 Canal barge 80 35

2161 50c Container ships and bunker, Dunkirk 25 15

2181 1f40 Breton fishing boats 80 25

1978

2247† 1f40 Gas tanker 55 20
2248† 1f70 Ancient Norman ship 1.00 40

1979

2303 1f50 *Durance* (transport), 1882 .... 50 20

1980

2375 2f50 Rochambeau's fleet, Rhode Island, 1780 .... 1.25 40

1981

2436 1f40 *Borda* (warship), 1831 .... 55 20

1982

2503 1f60 Fishing boats, St. Pierre et Miquelon 65 15

2532† 4f Felucca 1.75 55

2553 3f25 La Salle's ships, 1682 .... 1.00 40

1984

2623   2f *Grande Hermine* (Cartier), 1534 65   10

1985

2686   2f50 19th-century lifeboat, Lake Geneva   75   20

1988

2834†   2f Fishing boat, Ship Museum,
         Douarnenez 50   10

1990

2974†   2f30 *Lucie* (canal barge) 60   10

2984   2f30 *La Poste* (yacht) 90   20

1991

3049   2f50+60c Fishing boats, tug and barges,
         Toulon 80   80

1992

3076†   3f40 Caravel 80   20

3080†   4f 18th-century ship of the line and
         yacht 95   25

1993

3112   2f50 *La Poste* (yacht) 55   15

3116   2f50 Yacht 55   15

FRENCH EQUATORIAL AFRICA

Central Africa
100 centimes = 1 franc

1936

Nos. 127/31 of Gabon overprinted **AFRIQUE EQUATORIALE FRANÇAISE**

17†	1c Log raft	15	30
18†	2c Log raft	15	25
19†	4c Log raft	40	60
20†	5c Log raft	40	55
21†	10c Log raft	40	40

1937

As Nos. 110/11 of Cameroun

27†	20c Liner	1.25	1.25
28†	30c Sailing ships	1.25	1.10

1938

97	65c *La Malouine* (warship), 1838	
98	1f *La Malouine*	
99	1f75 *La Malouine*	
100	2f *La Malouine*	

Set of 4   3.00   2.75

1947

248†	5f Fishing pirogue	35	45
249†	6f Fishing pirogue	30	40
250†	10f Fishing pirogue	35	45

1953

273†	50f Log raft	1.00	35
274†	100f Sailing canoe	4.00	40

1954

As No. 264 of Cameroun

277	15f Landing craft, Normandy, 1944	3.25	4.00

FRENCH GUIANA

South America
100 centimes = 1 franc

1929

126†	30c Native canoe shooting rapids, River Maroni (green)	30	45
127†	30c Native canoe shooting rapids, River Maroni (brown & green)	15	25
128†	35c Native canoe shooting rapids, River Maroni	35	45
129†	40c Native canoe shooting rapids, River Maroni	25	30
130†	45c Native canoe shooting rapids, River Maroni (brown & green)	45	55
131†	45c Native canoe shooting rapids, River Maroni (green & olive)	25	30
132†	50c Native canoe shooting rapids, River Maroni	20	30
133†	55c Native canoe shooting rapids, River Maroni	65	75
134†	60c Native canoe shooting rapids, River Maroni	25	30
135†	65c Native canoe shooting rapids, River Maroni	45	60
136†	70c Native canoe shooting rapids, River Maroni	55	70
137†	75c Native canoe shooting rapids, River Maroni	75	90
138†	80c Native canoe shooting rapids, River Maroni	30	40
139†	90c Native canoe shooting rapids, River Maroni (red)	45	50
140†	90c Native canoe shooting rapids, River Maroni (brown & mauve)	60	60
141†	1f Native canoe shooting rapids, River Maroni (brown & mauve)	45	50
142†	1f Native canoe shooting rapids, River Maroni (red)	1.00	1.25
143†	1f Native canoe shooting rapids, River Maroni (blue & black)	35	45

1931

As No. 109 of Cameroun

163†	1f50 *Leconte de Lisle* (liner)	2.25	2.50

1935

172†	40c D'Estrees' fleet, Cayenne, 1676	2.50	2.75
173†	50c D'Estrees' fleet, Cayenne, 1676	5.75	4.00
174†	1f50 D'Estrees' fleet, Cayenne, 1676	2.50	2.75

1937

As Nos. 110/11 of Cameroun

178†	20c Liner	45	60
179†	30c Sailing ships	45	60
MS183a†	3f Sailing ships	3.75	5.00

1947

230†	2f Pirogue	30	40
231†	2f50 Pirogue	35	40
232†	3f Pirogue	40	50

FRENCH GUINEA

West Africa
100 centimes = 1 franc

1931

As No. 109 of Cameroun

122†	1f50 *Leconte de Lisle* (liner)	1.90	2.00

1937

As Nos. 110/11 of Cameroun

123†	20c Liner	50	90
124†	30c Sailing ships	50	90

FRENCH INDIAN SETTLEMENTS

East coast of Indian sub-continent
24 caches = 1 fanon
8 fanons = 1 rupee

1931

As No. 109 of Cameroun

111†	1f12 *Leconte de Lisle* (liner)	1.75	1.75

1937

As Nos. 110/11 of Cameroun

112†	8c Liner	65	95
113†	12c Sailing ships	75	95

1941

Nos. 112/13 overprinted **FRANCE LIBRE**

154†	8c Liner	3.75	3.75
157†	12c Sailing ships	2.50	2.50

1942

Nos. 112/13 overprinted **FRANCE LIBRE** *and Cross of Lorraine*

189†	8c Liner	4.00	3.75
190†	12c Sailing ships	3.75	3.75

1954

As No. 264 of Cameroun

287	1f Landing craft, Normandy, 1944	3.25	3.50

FRENCH MOROCCO

North-west Africa
100 centimes = 1 franc

1933

179†	45c Local rowing boat, Rabat	20	35
180†	50c Local rowing boat, Rabat	50	10
181†	65c Local rowing boat, Rabat	10	10

1938

No. 181 surcharged **O.S.E. + 65 c**

207†	65c + 65c Local rowing boat, Rabat	2.00	4.00

1939

No. 180 surcharged **40c**

213	40c on 50c Local rowing boat, Rabat	1.75	60

224†	50c Xebec, Sale (red)	55	75
293†	50c Xebec, Sale (green)	10	10
226†	60c Xebec, Sale (blue)	50	75
227†	60c Xebec, Sale (brown)	20	10
232†	90c Xebec, Sale	15	25
237†	1f50 Xebec, Sale (pink)	10	15
297†	1f50 Xebec, Sale (red)	10	10

1940

No. 181 surcharged **35c**

258	35c on 65c Local rowing boat, Rabat	1.00	1.00

1942

No. 232 surcharged **Enfants de France au Maroc +4f**

260†	90c + 4f Xebec, Sale	2.00	3.00

1947

345†	9f + 16f Freighter at quay	1.00	1.50

1948

351	6f + 9f *Dunkerque* (battleship)	50	1.00

1954

436	15f Schooner and destroyer		
437	30f Schooner and destroyer		
		Set of 2 2.00	2.25

FRENCH POLYNESIA

South Pacific
100 centimes = 1 franc

1958

16†	200f Fishing pirogues at night, Moorea	32.00	18.00

1964

38†	2f Outrigger canoe, Tuamotu	55	45
43†	23f Outrigger canoes, Moorea (air)	6.00	2.75

1966

56	10f Pirogue	
57	11f Schooner	
58	12f Fishing launch	
59	14f Pirogues	
60	19f Early schooner	
61	22f *Oiseau des Iles II* (coaster)	
	Set of 6 17.00	9.00

1967

72†	21f Pirogue-racing	6.00	3.50

1968

81†	40f Ship's stern and Tahitian canoe, 1767	6.00	4.00

1971

130†	10f Outboard motor boat	9.00	3.50

137†	15f Yacht	4.00	2.75

1972

153	28f *Meherio* (landing craft) and other shipping in Papeete harbour	8.50	5.50

158	16f *Kon Tiki* (replica of balsa raft)	5.50	3.50

1974

182†	6f Fishing canoe	75	55
184†	15f *Regina Maris* (schooner)	2.25	90

1976

212	24f Battle of the Saints, 782		
213	31f Battle of the Chesapeake, 1781		
	Set of 2	8.50	4.50

218	90f *Firecrest* (yacht)	10.00	7.50

227	25f Marquesas pirogue		
228	30f Raiatea pirogue		
229	75f Tahiti pirogue		
230	100f Tuamotu pirogue		
	Set of 4	13.50	8.50

1977

262	20f Cutter		
263	50f *Tiare Taporo* (schooner)		
264	85f Barque		
265	120f Full-rigged ship		
	Set of 4	14.50	7.50

1978

266	33f H.M.S. *Discovery* (Cook)		
267	39f H.M.S. *Resolution* (Cook)		
	Set of 2	5.50	3.50

284	15f *Tahiti* (inter-island ship)		
285	30f *Monowai* (liner)		
286	75f *Tahitien* (inter-island ship)		
287	100f *Mariposa* (cargo liner)		
	Set of 4	10.50	6.00

1979

Nos. 266/7 overprinted **"1779 – 1979" BICENTAIRE DE LA MORT DE**

290	33f H.M.S. *Discovery*		
291	39f H.M.S. *Resolution*		
	Set of 2	4.50	2.50

Inscribed "DELRIEU" at foot

297†	4f Outboard motor boat, Raiatea	45	10
298†	5f Outrigger canoe, Motu	45	20

1981

349	200f Racing pirogue	5.00	3.50

356†	40f H.M.S. *Resolution* (Cook) and H.M.S. *Adventure* in Matavai Bay	85	60
359†	120f 18th-century ships off Pointe Venus	2.75	1.75

1982

373	90f "Hobie Cat 16" class catamaran	2.00	1.50

1983

392	600f Pirogue	11.00	8.50

409†	40f Beached schooner, Moorea	1.00	60

1985

458	130f 19th-century French warship, Papeete	3.00	2.00
MS459	240f 19th-century French warship, Papeete	6.00	6.00

1986

As Nos. 297/8, but inscribed "CARTOR" at foot

470a†	4f Outboard motor boat, Raiatea	10	10
471†	5f Outrigger canoe, Motu	10	10

476	300f Game fishing boat	5.50	3.50

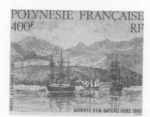

484	400f Sailing ships in harbour, 1880	7.50	4.50

490	46f Building pirogue		
491	50f Building pirogue		
	Set of 2	1.60	1.00

1987

523†	115f *St. Pierre* (fishing boat), Tuamotu Archipelago	2.25	1.40

1988

528† 11f Raft and outrigger canoes, Raiatea ... 30 ... 20

533† 54f Outrigger canoe .... 90 ... 65

548† 80f *Duff* (full-rigged missionary ship) .... 1.40 ... 90
549† 90f Canoes .... 1.60 ... 1.00

1989

565 100f H.M.S. *Bounty* and launch (Bligh) .... 1.75 ... 1.25
MS566 200f H.M.S. *Bounty* and launch (Bligh) 3.50 ... 3.50

578† 82f Outrigger canoe .... 1.40 ... 85

1991

611† 84f Sandwich Islands pirogue race ...... 1.50 ... 85

621† 25f Fishing canoes .... 45 ... 25
623† 62f Fishing canoe .... 1.00 ... 60

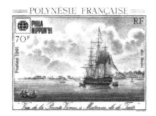

625† 70f Full-rigged ship, Tahiti .... 1.25 ... 75

1992

635† 5f Yachts .... 15 ... 10

642† 130f Ship's boat, 1492 .... 2.25 ... 1.40

649† 22f Model outrigger canoes .... 45 ... 25

652 78f Whaling ship .... 1.50 ... 85

653 40f Raft, Gambier islands
654 65f Pirogues off Tahiti
Set of 2 ... 1.75 ... 1.25

1993

673† 84f Fishing launch .... 95 ... 65

1993

O668† 100f Schooners *Orohena* and *Moana*
(on Oceanic Settlements stamp No. 215) .... 1.25 ... 95

FRENCH SOMALI COAST

East Africa
100 centimes= 1 franc

1931
As No. 109 *of Cameroun*
236† 1f50 *Leconte de Lisle* (liner) .... 3.00 ... 3.25

1937
As Nos. 110/11 *of Cameroun*
237† 20c Liner .... 50 ... 75
238† 30c Sailing ships .... 50 ... 80

1954
As No. 264 *of Cameroun*
428 15f Landing craft, Normandy, 1944 ...... 4.50 ... 5.00

1956

431 15f Freighter at wharf .... 1.40 ... 1.00

1962

453 100f *Forbin* (steam warship), 1862 ...... 3.75 ... 2.40

1964

476 15f Houri (dhow)
477 25f Sambuk (dhow)

478 50f Building sambuks (air)
479 85f Zaruk (dhow)
480 300f Ziema (dhow)
Set of 5 ... 20.00 ... 11.00

FRENCH SOUTHERN AND ANTARCTIC TERRITORIES

Antarctica and nearby Islands
100 centimes = 1 franc

1960

23 25f *Dauphine* (Kerguelen-Tremarec), 1772 ... 27.00 ... 22.00

1962

| 24 | 25f *Pourquoi Pas?* (Charcot), 1936 | ...... | 23.00 | 18.00 |

1968

| 44 | 30f *L' Astrolabe* and *Zelee* (Dumont d'Urville), 1840 | .... | £110 | 80.00 |

1972

78	100f *Mascarin* and *Marquis de Castries* (Dufresne), 1772
79	250f Kerguelen's ships, 1772
		Set of 2	£100	65.00

| 82 | 100f *Gallieni* (Antarctic supply ship) | ...... | 24.00 | 21.00 |

85	120f *Mascarin* (Dufresne), 1772
86	145f *L'Astrolabe* (Dumont d'Urville), 1840
87	150f *Roland* (Kerguelen-Tremarec), 1774
88	185f *Vitoria* (Del Cano), 1522
		Set of 4	27.00	20.00

1974

93	100f *Francais* (Charcot), 1903–05
94	200f *Pourquois Pas?* (Charcot), 1908–10
		Set of 2	12.50	8.00

1975

| 95 | 75f *Sapmer* (modern mail ship) | .... | 8.00 | 7.00 |

104	1f90 *La Curieuse* (topsail schooner)
105	2f70 *Commandant Charcot* (ice patrol ship)
106	4f *Marion Dufresne* (Antarctic supply ship)
		Set of 3	17.00	12.00

1976

| 109 | 3f50 H.M.S. *Discovery* and H.M.S. *Resolution* (Cook), Kerguelen | .... | 12.00 | 9.00 |

1977

| 118† | 1f20 *Magga Dan* (Antarctic supply ship) | 3.00 | 3.00 |
| 119† | 1f40 *Thala Dan* (Antarctic supply ship) | 3.00 | 3.00 |

1979

133	40c *Forbin* (destroyer)
134	50f *Jeanne d'Arc* (helicopter carrier)
		Set of 2	3.50	3.00

| 135 | 2f70 H.M.S. *Challenger* (survey ship), 1872–76 | .... | 2.50 | 1.75 |

1980

136	1f10 *Doudart de Lagree* (frigate)
137	1f50 *Commandant Bourdais* (frigate)
		Set of 2	2.50	2.25

| 142† | 4f *Vitoria* (Del Cano), 1522 | .... | 2.75 | 2.00 |

| 145 | 1f90 *La Recherche* and *L'Esperance* (D'Entrecasteaux), Amsterdam Island, 1792 | .... | 2.50 | 2.25 |

| 146 | 2f70 H.M.S. *Terror* (bomb ketch) (Ross), Kerguelen, 1840 | .... | 1.75 | 1.75 |

155	3f50 *Saint Marcouf* (Antarctic supply ship)
156	7f30 *Norsel* (Antarctic supply ship)
		Set of 2	4.75	3.75

1981

| 166 | 8f40 *Antares* (dispatch vessel), 1916–36 | 2.75 | 2.50 |

1982

| 168 | 5f *Commandant Charcot* (ice patrol ship) | 2.75 | 2.50 |

1983

| 169 | 55c *Le Gros Ventre* (lighter) | .... | 1.25 | 1.10 |

| 175 | 2f30 *Austral* (trawler) | .... | 1.75 | 1.60 |

181   5f *Lady Franklin* (Antarctic supply ship) ..   5.50   5.50

1984

189   2f60 H.M.S. *Erebus* (bomb ketch) (Ross),
1842 ....   1.50   1.50

194   11f30 *Albatros* (patrol boat) 5.00   5.00

195   9f *Gauss* (survey barquentine), 1901–03   5.50   5.50

1985

200   1f80 Research vessel
201   5f20 Research vessel
                           Set of 2   4.50   4.50

204   12f80 *La Novara*, (frigate), St. Paul, 1857   7.50   7.50

GIBBONS STAMP MONTHLY
— finest and most informative magazine for all
collectors. Obtainable from your newsagent or by
postal subscription — details on request.

206   2f *Kerguelen's ships*, 1772
207   12f80 *Kerguelen's ships*, 1772
                           Set of 2   5.50   5.50

1986

212   2f10 *Var A 608* (patrol boat)
213   3f *Polarbjorn* (Antarctic supply ship)
                           Set of 2   2.75   2.75

214   2f10 *Pourquoi Pas?* (Charcot)
215   14f *Pourquoi Pas?* (Charcot)
                           Set of 2   6.00   6.00

1987

227   3f20 *Eure* (sail despatch vessel) 1.40   1.40

228   14f60 *J. B. Charcot* (schooner) 6.00   5.50

229   16f80 Research vessel and drilling ship   6.00   5.50

230   16f80 Research vessel 6.00   5.50

1988

237   3f50 *Le Gros Ventre* (French sail frigate)
238   4f90 *Jules Verne* (Antarctic supply ship)
239   5f *La Fortune* (French sail warship)
                           Set of 3   3.75   3.00

1989

250   2f20 *La Curieuse* (topsail schooner), 1913
251   15f50 *La Curieuse* (supply ship), 1989
                           Set of 2   5.50   5.50

256   5f 18th-century French ship of the line 4.00   2.75

1990

267   15f50 *L'Astrolabe* (D'Urville), 1840 ......   3.00   3.00

268   2f20 *L'Astrolabe* (fishery control vessel),
1988
269   15f50 *L'Astrolabe*, (D'Urville)
                           Set of 2   5.50   5.50

1991

275   3f20 *L'Aventure* (landing craft) 1.00   1.00

278   20f Research vessel 5.75   5.75

1992

287	2f20 Yacht	75	75

292	14f *Tottan* (supply ship), 1951	4.00	4.00

293	22f Columbus's fleet	7.00	7.00

295	25f40 Research ship	7.50	7.50

1993

308	2f20 *Marion Dufresne* (Antarctic supply ship)	50	35

315	3f70 *Italo Marsano* (freighter)	80	50

317	22f *L'Astrolabe* (fishery control vessel), 1991	4.75	3.00

FRENCH SUDAN

West Africa
100 centimes = 1 franc

1931

162†	1f25 Pirogue (purple & mauve)	. . . .	1.25	30
163†	1f25 Pirogue (red)		40	50
164†	1f40 Pirogue		50	60
165†	1f50 Pirogue		50	50
166†	1f60 Pirogue		60	60
167†	1f75 Pirogue (blue & brown)		60	50
168†	1f75 Pirogue (blue)		45	50
169†	2f Pirogue		40	35
170†	2f25 Pirogue		50	50
171†	2f50 Pirogue		60	60
172†	3f Pirogue		40	25
173†	5f Pirogue		85	60
174†	10f Pirogue		1.25	1.25
175†	20f Pirogue		1.75	1.75

As No. 109 of Cameroun

189†	1f50 *Leconte de Lisle* (liner)	1.10	1.10

1937

As Nos. 110/11 of Cameroun

190†	20c Liner	65	70
191†	30c Sailing ships	65	70

1941

Nos. 165 *and* 169 *surcharged* **SECOURS NATIONAL** *and value*

215†	+2f on 1f50 Pirogue	3.75	3.75
216†	+3f on 2f Pirogue	3.75	3.75

FRENCH TERRITORY OF THE AFARS AND THE ISSAS

East Africa
100 centimes = 1 franc

1970

550†	48f Speedboats	2.25	1.50
552†	55f Yacht	2.25	1.50

556	48f *Goubet* (car ferry)	2.00	1.50

1973

584†	30f Freighters in port	5.50	3.25

FRENCH WEST AFRICA

West Africa
100 centimes = 1 franc

1947

36†	40c Canoe	10	25

1951

74†	25f Sailing canoe	85	25

1954

As No. 264 of Cameroun

81	15f Landing craft, Normandy, 1944	2.50	3.00

1955

84	15f Freighter at wharf	85	40

1958

99†	20f Liner and freighters, Dakar	85	60
102†	50f *L'Arachide* (freighter)	1.00	60

FUJEIRA

Arabia
100 dirhams = 1 riyal

1968

32†	25np Yacht	20	10

Appendix

The following have either been issued in excess of postal needs or have not been made available to the public in reasonable quantities at face value. Miniature sheets, imperforate stamps etc. are excluded from this section.

1968

Historical Ships. Postage 15, 25, 50, 75d, 1r; Air 2, 3, 4, 5r

1971

Olympic Games, Munich. Sports. 12d Yacht
Olympic Games, Munich. Venues. 35d Yacht

GABON

West Africa
100 centimes = 1 franc

1931

As No. 109 *of Cameroun*
126† 1f50 *Leconte de Lisle* (liner) 2.25 2.50

1932

127† 1c Log raft 15 25
128† 2c Log raft 20 30
129† 4c Log raft 20 30
130† 5c Log raft 20 30
131† 10c Log raft 20 30
132† 15c Log raft 50 60
133† 20c Log raft 50 65
134† 25c Log raft 35 45

1965

230 25f 16th-century galleon
231 50f 17th-century merchantman
232 85f 18th-century frigate
233 100f 19th-century brig
Set of 4 7.75 3.00

1966

267† 85f *Roger Butin* (oil rig) 2.00 75

274 30f Launches 60 30

1967

311 30f *Belgrano* and *Jean Guiton*
(19th-century steam packets)
312 30f *Ango* and *Lucie Delmas* (modern mail
carriers)
Set of 2 1.40 80

1968

323 30f Tanker, Port Gentil 55 25

335 30f *Junon* (19th-century sail/steam
warship) 65 30

1969

346 50f Log raft (on stamp No. 134) 1.50 1.50

372† 50f Oil rig 65 30

377 30f Mail pirogue, Adoumas 55 30

1972

443 60f Gondolas
444 70f Gondolas
445 140f Gondolas
Set of 3 4.25 2.00

1974

517† 40f Yachts 60 30

521† 30f Pirogue, River Ogooue 30 20

1976

578† 100f Ships of the Boston Tea Party, 1773 90 50

No. 578 *overprinted* **4 JUILLET 1976**
583† 100f Ships of the Boston Tea Party, 1773 90 50

1978

650† 50f Container ships, Owendo Port 45 15

1979

691† 100f Olympic yachts 60 35

698 500f H.M.S. *Resolution* and H.M.S.
Discovery (Cook) 4.50 2.25

1982

805 75f *Leonce Veilvieux* (freighter)
806 100f *Correze* (container ship)
807 200f Oil tanker
Set of 3 2.40 1.50

1983

838† 300f Sailboard 2.00 1.00

848 125f *Ville de Rouen* (container ship) 90 45

863† 125f Pirogue, River Ogooue 75 45

1985

923 185f *La Mpassa* (freighter) 1.50 70

1986

938 100f De Brazza in canoe, 1886 . . . . 75 45

947 250f *L'Abanga* (container ship) 2.25 1.50

948 500f River pirogues 3.50 2.00

1991

1076 500f Sailing ships in Marseille Harbour . . . 2.40 1.25

1094† 175f Fishing canoe 85 45

1992

1130 500f Fleet of Columbus 2.40 1.25

GAMBIA

West Africa
1949 12 pence = 1 shilling
20 shillings = 1 pound
1971 100 bututs = 1 dalasy

1949

As No. 115 of Antigua

167† 3d Paddle-steamer 70 30

1953

172† 1d Sailing cutter 40 15
174† 2½d Barra canoe 45 70
175† 3d *Lady Wright* (river steamer) 35 10
179† 1s3d Sailing cutter 7.00 30
180† 2s Barra canoe 3.50 2.50
184† 10s *Lady Wright* (river steamer) 9.00 6.50

1969

259† 2d *Westfalen* (aircraft tender) 40 15

1971

285† 25b Dugout canoe 25 15
286† 37b Dugout canoe 35 50

1978

396† 1d25 Local rowing longboat 35 45

404 8b *Lady Wright* (river steamer)
405 25b *Lady Chilel Jawara* (river vessel)
406 1d *Lady Chilel Jawara*
Set of 3 1.60 1.25

1980

436 10b *Vampire* (steam launch)
437 25b *Lady Denham* (river steamer)
438 50b *Mansa Kila Ba* (river steamer)
439 1d *Prince of Wales* (river steamer)
Set of 4 1.00 85

441 8b Ancient Phoenician trading vessel
442 67b Ancient Egyptian sea-going galley
443 75b Portuguese caravel
444 1d Spanish galleon
Set of 4 1.00 1.00

1983

494 1b Canoes
495 2b River ferry
496 3b Dredger
497 4b *Sir Dawda* (harbour launch)
498 5b Cargo liner
499 10b *Lady Dale* (launch)
500 20b *Shonga* (container ship)
501 30b Large sailing canoe
502 40b *Lady Wright* (river steamer)
503 50b Container ship
504 75b Fishing boats
505 1d Tug and groundnut barges
506 1d25 Groundnut canoe
507 2d50 *Banjul* (car ferry)
508 5d *Bintang Bolong* (freighter)
509 10d *Lady Chilel Jawara* (river vessel)
Set of 16 12.50 13.00

514† 10b Local ferry boat 10 10

1984

MS533† 5d Olympic yachts 2.00 2.25

550† 85b Bulk carrier 60 40
551† 90b *Dagomba* (freighter) on fire 60 55
552† 1d25 19th-century British sail frigate 1.10 85

Nos. 507/8 overprinted **19th UPU CONGRESS HAMBURG**
553 2d50 *Banjul*
554 5d *Bintang Bolong*
Set of 2 1.00 1.10

560† 85b *Westfalen* (aircraft tender) 1.40 1.25

1985
No. **MS**533 *overprinted* **GOLD MEDAL STAR CLASS U.S.A.**
MS606† 5d Olympic yachts 1.75 1.90

1986

615† 60b Fishing boat, Fotoba, Guinea 30 30

1987

700 20b *America* (yacht), 1851
701 1b *Courageous* (yacht), 1974
702 2b *Volunteer* (yacht), 1887
703 10b *Intrepid* (yacht), 1967
Set of 4 2.50 2.50
MS704 12b *Australia II* (yacht), 1983 .... 2.25 2.40

706† 2b U.S.S. *Nashville* (assault transport)
and launch 10 10
707† 3b U.S.S. *Nashville* and schooner 10 10
708† 5b *Queen Elizabeth 2* (liner) and U.S.S.
John F. Kennedy (aircraft carrier) 10 10

1988
No. 703 overprinted **Praga '88**
777† 10d *Intrepid* (yacht), 1967 .... 1.60 1.75

790† 10d English and Spanish galleons,
Spanish Armada, 1588 .... 2.75 2.75
791† 12d *Titanic* (liner) 3.25 3.25

814† 12d *Sovereign of the Seas* (liner) 1988 2.25 2.25
MS815† Two sheets (a) 15d U.S.S. *Nautilus*
(first nuclear-powered submarine), 1954; (b)
15d *Nautilus* (Fulton's submarine), early
1800's
Price for 2 sheets 4.75 5.50

825† 50b Portuguese caravel 40 40
829† 2d Vasco da Gama and galleon 1.25 1.25
832† 12d Portuguese caravel 3.25 3.25
MS833† Two sheets (a) 15d Spanish galleon
off Gambia; (b) 15d Galleon at anchor off
Gambia
Price for 2 sheets 4.75 5.00

1990

1042† 50b Sailing canoe 10 10
1044† 1d. Canoes on beach 15 20
1046† 2d Canoe fishing for shrimps 30 35

1076† 12d "Tornado" class catamaran 1.75 1.90

1991

1184† 50b Raft 10 10
1189† 7d Outrigger canoe 1.00 1.10

1246† 1d25 Fishing boats on beach,
Scheveningen 20 25

1992

1286† 1d Fishing canoe 15 20
1287† 15d Canoes on beach 2.25 2.40
MS1288† Two sheets (a) 20d *Lady Chilel
Jawara* (river vessel); (b) 20d River ferry being
loaded
Price for 2 sheets 6.00 6.25

1291† 1d50 *Santa Maria* (Columbus) 25 30
MS1293 18d Rowing boat 2.75 3.00

1312† 1d25 "Soling" class yacht 20 25
1315† 15d Galleon 2.25 2.40

1330 20b *Joven Antonia* (launch), River
Gambia
1331 50b *Dresden* (paddle-steamer), River
Elbe
1332 75b *Medway Queen* (paddle- steamer),
River Medway
1333 1d *Lady Wright* (river steamer), River
Gambia
1334 1d25 *Devin* (paddle-steamer), River
Vltava
1335 1d50 *Lady Chilel Jawara* (river vessel),
River Gambia
1336 5d *Robert Fulton* (paddle-steamer), River
Hudson
1337 10d *Coonawarra* (paddle-steamer), River
Murray
1338 12d *Nakusp* (sternwheel steamer), River
Columbia
1339 15d *Lucy Ashton* (paddle-steamer), Firth
of Clyde
Set of 10 6.50 7.00
MS1340 Two sheets (a) 20d *City of Cairo*
(paddle-steamer), River Mississippi; (b) 20d
Rudesheim (paddle-steamer), River Rhine
Set for 2 sheets 6.00 6.25

1341† 2d U.S.S. *Pennsylvania* (battleship) 30 35
1343† 2d U.S.S. *Ward* (destroyer) sinking
Japanese midget submarine, Pearl
Harbor 30 35
1350† 2d Japanese aircraft carrier under air
attack, Battle of Midway, 1942 ...... 30 35

1358†   3d Sailboard   45   50

1993

1414   5d *Santa Maria* (Columbus)
1415   12d Columbus's fleet
                              Set of 2   2.50   2.75
MS1416   18d Bow of caravel 2.75   3.00

1424   10d *Enterprise* (yacht), 1930   ....   1.50   1.60

GERMAN EAST AFRICA

East Africa
1901 64 pesa = 100 heller = 1 rupee
1905 100 heller = 1 rupee

1901

As No. K7/19 of Cameroun, but inscribed
"DEUTSCH-OSTAFRIKA". Face values in pesa and rupees
15   2p *Hohenzollern* (German Imperial yacht)
16   3p *Hohenzollern*
17   5p *Hohenzollern*
18   10p *Hohenzollern*
19   15p *Hohenzollern*
20   20p *Hohenzollern*
21   25p *Hohenzollern*
22   40   *Hohenzollern*
23   1r *Hohenzollern*
24   2r *Hohenzollern*
44   3r *Hohenzollern*
                       Set of 11   95.00   £400

1905

As Nos. 15/44, but face values in heller
34   2½h *Hohenzollern* (German Imperial yacht)
35   4h *Hohenzollern*
36   7½h *Hohenzollern*
37   15h *Hohenzollern*
38   20h *Hohenzollern*
39   30h *Hohenzollern*
32   45h *Hohenzollern*
33   60h *Hohenzollern*
                        Set of 8   38.00   £150

GERMAN NEW GUINEA

Australasia
100 pfennig = 1 mark

1901

As Nos. K7/19 of Cameroun, but inscribed "DEUTSCH-
NEU-GUINEA"
7   3pf *Hohenzollern* (German Imperial yacht)
8   5pf *Hohenzollern*
9   10pf *Hohenzollern*
10   20pf *Hohenzollern*
11   25pf *Hohenzollern*
12   30pf *Hohenzollern*
13   40pf *Hohenzollern*
14   50pf *Hohenzollern*
15   80pf *Hohenzollern*
16   1m *Hohenzollern*
17   2m *Hohenzollern*
18   3m *Hohenzollern*
19   5m *Hohenzollern*
                        Set of 13   £130   £550

GERMAN SOUTH WEST AFRICA

Southern Africa
100 pfennig = 1 mark

1900

As Nos. K7/19 of Cameroun, but inscribed "DEUTSCH-
SUDWESTAFRIKA"
24   3pf *Hohenzollern* (German Imperial yacht)
25   5pf *Hohenzollern*
26   10pf *Hohenzollern*
27   20pf *Hollenzollern*
15   25pf *Hohenzollern*
16   30pf *Hohenzollern*
17   40pf *Hohenzollern*
18   50pf *Hohenzollern*
19   80pf *Hohenzollern*
29   1m *Hohenzollern*
30   2m *Hohenzollern*
22   3m *Hohenzollern*
32   5m *Hohenzollern*
                        Set of 13   £210   £250

GERMANY

Central Europe, divided after the Second World War into
Federal Republic (West Germany), West Berlin and Democratic
Republic (East Germany). Reunited 1990
100 pfennige = 1 reichsmark

1937

639   3pf + 2pf *Bremen* (lifeboat), 1931
640   4pf + 3pf *Elbe I* (lightship)
641   5pf + 3pf Fishing smacks
642   6pf + 4pf *Wilhelm Gustloff* (liner)
643   8pf + 4pf *Padua* (barque)
644   12pf + 6pf *Tannenberg* (liner)
645   15pf + 10pf *Schwerin* (train ferry)
646   25pf + 15pf *Hamburg* (liner)
647   40pf + 35pf *Europa* (liner), 1928
                        Set of 9   23.00   15.00

1939

No. 206 of Danzig surcharged **2 Reichsmark Deutsches Reich**
717†   2rm on 2 g Freighters and tugs on River
         Mottlau 16.00   40.00

1943

819†   3pf + 2pf U-Boat Type V11A
         (submarine)   40   50
823†   8pf + 7pf Pontoon   50   60
830†   50pf + 50pf Motor torpedo-boat 1.00   1.90

1944

861†   3pf + 2pf Landing craft   30   35
869†   16pf + 10pf Motor torpedo-boat   30   70

Allied Occupation—French Zone

BADEN

1947

FB2†   3pf Yachts   10   10
FB5†   15pf Yachts (violet)   10   10
FB9†   45pf Yachts   10   20

1948

Design as Nos. FB2, etc, but new value and colour changed
FB15†   6pf Yachts   25   15
FB18†   15pf Yachts (blue)   50   35

Design as Nos. FB2, etc, but "PF" omitted
FB30†   5pf Yachts   85   70
FB31†   6pf Yachts 22.00   12.00

Federal Republic

100 pfennige = 1 deutschmark

1952

1078   20pf *Senator Schaffer* (trawler) 14.00   4.25

1957

1183   15pf *Bayernstein* (freighter) 1.00   1.25

1964

1331†   20pf *Lichtenfels* (liner), Hamburg   15   15
1332†   20pf *Kronprinz Harald* (ferry), Kiel   15   15

1965

1395†   70pf *Bremen* (liner) and *Hammonia*
         (19th-century steamship)   25   15

1399   20pf *Theodor Heuss* (rescue vessel)   10   10

1970

1528   20pf Liner in Kiel Canal   15   10

1972

1622†   25pf + 10pf Olympic yacht   60   75

1641† 30pf *Wappen von Hamburg* (liner), Heligoland 30 15

1973

1655 40pf Container ship, Hamburg
1656 40pf *Loreley* (Rhine steamer), Rudesheim
Set of 2 1.00 30

1974

1680† 30pf Barge, Saarbrucken 35 15
1682† 40pf Freighters, Bremen 45 15

1975

1746† 70pf Tanker under construction 55 10
1754† 200pf Marine drilling platform 1.50 15

1977

1819 30pf + 15pf *Wappen von Hamburg*, 1731
1820 40pf + 20pf *Preussen* (full-rigged sailing ship), 1902
1821 50pf + 25pf *Bremen* (liner), 1929
1822 70pf + 35pf *Sturmfels* (container ship), 1972
Set of 4 4.25 4.75

1982

1996 60pf Racing yachts 70 25

1983

2030 80pf *Concord* (emigrant ship), 1683 .... 1.40 25

1984

2071 80pf Merchant ship, 1784 .... 1.00 20

1987

2177† 80pf + 40pf Racing yachts 1.25 1.25

1988

2262 80pf Hydrofoil, Bonn 85 30

1989

2273 60pf *Tsurumi Maru* (tanker), tug, fireboat and *Rickmer Rickmers* (full-rigged ship), Hamburg 90 25

1991

2414 100pf Freighters 85 25

2421 100pf Punt 85 25

1992

2444 60pf *Gorch Fock* (cadet barque) and tug, Kiel 65 20

2456† 60pf Columbus's fleet (woodcut) 65 20

1993

2502† 170pf + 80pf Olympic yachts, Kiel 2.00 2.00

West Berlin
100 pfennige = 1 deutschmark

1955

B123 10pf *Berlin* (liner)
B124 25pf *Berlin*
Set of 2 6.50 3.50

1962

B214† 10pf Barges on River Spree 10 10
B220† 60pf Barges on River Spree 35 50

1975

B467 30pf *Prinzess Charlotte* (pleasure boat)
B468 40pf *Siegfried* (pleasure boat)
B469 50pf *Sperber* (pleasure boat)
B470 60pf *Vaterland* (pleasure boat)
B471 70pf *Moby Dick* (pleasure boat)
Set of 5 2.50 2.75

As Nos. 1746 and 1754 of West Germany, but additionally inscribed "BERLIN"
B484† 70pf Tanker under construction 60 15
B490† 200pf Marine drilling platform 1.50 30

1976

B512† 30pf Yacht 30 15

1977

B527 30pf + 15pf Bremen kogge, 1380
B528 40pf + 20pf *Helena Sloman* (steamship), 1850
B529 50pf + 25pf *Cap Polonio* (liner), 1914
B530 70pf + 35pf *Widar* (bulk carrier), 1971
Set of 4 2.50 2.75

Democratic Republic
100 pfennige = 1 mark

1953

E118† 24pf Sailing barge, River Oder 1.25 1.00

E318† 50pf Launching a ship 15 40
E135† 60pf Launching a ship (design in dots) 8.00 2.00
E173† 60pf Launching a ship (design in lines) 12.00 65

1954
No. E173 *surcharged* **50**
E196† 50pf on 60pf Launching a ship 1.25 1.00

1956

E275† 20pf Sailing dinghy 20 15

1957

E295† 20pf *Frieden* (freighter) 25 10

1958

E371 10pf *Freundschaft* (freighter)
E372 20pf Liner and freighters
E373 25pf *Frieden* (freighter)
Set of 3 1.25 1.00

1959

E463† 70pf Shipbuilding 20 15

1960

E482† 25pf Olympic yacht 15 10

No. E371 *overprinted* **Inbetriebnahme des Hochsee-hafens 1. Mai 1960**
E494 10pf *Freundschaft* 25 10

E501 5pf Model and plan of *Fritz Heckert* (liner)
E502 10pf + 5pf *Fritz Heckert* under construction
E503 20pf + 10pf *Fritz Heckert* at sea
E504 25pf *Fritz Heckert* and *Aurora* (Russian cruiser)
Set of 4 4.25 4.00

E537† 20pf *Sassnitz* (train ferry) 15 10

1961

E552† 10pf Trawler 10 10
E554† 25pf *Robert Koch* (trawler) 10 10

1962

E618† 25pf *Ernst Thalmann* (destroyer) 15 15

E639† 25pf *Frieden* (freighter) 2.50 2.00

1963

E678† 25pf Topsail schooner 1.75 1.60

1964

E777† 10pf + 5pf *Freundschaft* (freighter) (on stamp No. E371) 10 10

1967

E1027 10pf *Friedrich der Grosse* (battleship), 1914–18
E1028 15pf *Prinzregent Luitpold* (battleship), 1914–18
E1029 20pf *Seydlitz* (battle cruiser), 1914–18
Set of 3 65 55

E1035† 40pf *Aurora* (Russian cruiser) 2.00 1.75

1968

E1070† 15pf Deep sea trawler 60 30

E1105† 20pf Kogge, Rostock 10 10

1969

E1252† 25pf Fishing boats 1.00 1.25

1970

E1311† 25pf River police patrol boat 1.25 55

1971

E1375† 15pf *Takraf* (dredger) 15 10

E1413 10pf *Ivan Franko* (liner)
E1414 15pf "Type 17" freighter
E1415 20pf *Rostock* (freighter), 1966
E1416 25pf *Junge Welt* (fish-factory ship)
E1417 40pf *Hansel* (container ship)
E1418 50pf *Akademik Kurchatov* (research ship)
Set of 6 2.50 1.60

1972

E1495† 35pf *Wilhelm Pieck* (brigantine) 15 10

E1508† 15pf Sea rescue launch 25 25

1973

E1544† 80pf Freighter (29 x 24 *mm*) 1.00 10
E2208† 80pf Freighter (22 x 18 *mm*) 1.10 35

1974

E1700† 10pf 19th-century paddle-steamer and modern freighter 10 10

1976

E1835† 25pf *Prometey* (deep sea trawler) 30 15

1977

E1973† 35pf River Elbe passenger steamer, 1837 .... 2.40 2.00

E1974† 10pf *Aurora* (Russian cruiser) 20 20

E1995† 50pf Fire-fighting tug 2.50 2.00

1978

E2044† 70pf *Boltenhagen* (container ship) 1.90 1.90

1979

E2119† 35pf H.M.S. *Resolution* (Cook) 25 15

E2121 20pf *Radebeul* (container ship) 30 10

E2139 20pf *Rostock* (train ferry), 1977
E2140 35pf *Rugen* (train ferry)
Set of 2 1.25 1.25

1980

MSE2250† 1m Olympic yachts 1.60 1.60

1981

E2361 10pf Tug
E2362 20pf Tug and barges
E2363 25pf Diesel-electric paddle-ferry, River Elbe
E2364 35pf Ice-breaker, River Oder
E2365 50pf *Schonewalde* (motor barge)
E2366 85pf Dredger
Set of 6 3.50 3.00

1982

E2417 5pf *Frieden* (freighter)
E2418 10pf *Fichtelberg* (roll-on roll-off freighter)
E2419 15pf *Brocken* (heavy cargo carrier)
E2420 20pf *Weimar* (container ship)
E2421 25pf *Vorwarts* (freighter)
E2422 30pf *Berlin* (container ship)
Set of 6 2.50 2.10

E2434† 5pf 17th-century ships in storm 10 10

1983

E2488† 10pf Tanker 15 10
E2489† 20pf Container ship 20 10

1986

E2714† 50pf *Atlantik 488* (factory trawler) 45 35

E2739† 50pf Barges, Magdeburg 65 65

E2762† 50pf Train ferry 65 65

1987

E2823 10pf Longboat 15 10

1988

E2899 5pf *Adolph Friedrich* (brig)
E2900 10pf *Gartenlaube* (barque)
E2901 70pf *Auguste Mathilde* (brig)
E2902 1m20 *Hoffnung* (brig)
Set of 4 2.75 2.75

1989

E2970† 50pf 15th-century fishing boat 45 45

GHANA

West Africa
1957 12 pence = 1 shilling
20 shillings = 1 pound
1965 100 pesewas = 1 cedi
1967 100 new pesewas = 1 new cedi
1972 100 pesewas = 1 cedi

1957

No. 163 of Gold Coast overprinted **GHANA INDEPENDENCE 6th MARCH, 1957**

180†	5s Surfboats	50	10

182	2½d Viking ship		
183	1s3d Galleon		
184	5s Volta River (freighter)		
	Set of 3	2.25	3.75

1965

424†	60p Shama (trawler)	2.00	2.50

1967

469†	10np Shiqma (freighter) and tug, Tema	15	10

476†	12½np 15th-century British galleon	1.00	1.00
477†	20np 15th-century Portuguese galleon ..	1.40	2.00
478†	25np 15th-century Spanish galleon	1.75	2.50

1969

No. 469 overprinted **NEW CONSTITUTION 1969**

550†	10np Shiqma (freighter) and tug, Tema	20	40

1976

756†	30np Scout yachts	85	75

No. 756 overprinted **'INTERPHIL' 76 BICENTENNIAL EXHIBITION**

769†	30np Scout yachts	35	50

1978

838†	60p Fishing canoe	65	60

1981

955†	2c Royal Yacht Britannia	1.25	1.50
954†	3c Royal Yacht Britannia	1.00	1.40
950†	4c Royal Yacht Britannia	80	1.10

1982

993†	80p Sea scout sailing dinghy	1.25	70

1983

1050†	2c30 Cable ship	45	45

1984

Nos. 950 and 954 surcharged **C20 C20**

1068†	20c on 3c Royal Yacht Britannia	6.00	6.00
1069†	20c on 4c Royal Yacht Britannia	6.00	6.00

1988

1230†	5c Dredger and barges	30	15

1238†	5c Fishing boat	15	10

No. 469 surcharged

1247†	50c on 10np Shiqma (freighter) and tug, Tema	25	25

1989

Nos. 950 and 954 surcharged

1300†	300c on 3c Royal Yacht Britannia	1.25	1.40
1301†	500c on 4c Royal Yacht Britannia	2.25	2.50

No. 1050 surcharged

1304†	200c on 2c30 Cable ship	90	95

GIBRALTAR

South-west Europe
1931 12 pence = 1 shilling
20 shillings = 1 pound
1971 100 pence = 1 pound

1931

110	1d Liner and battleship		
111	1½d Liner and battleship		
112	2d Liner and battleship		
113	3d Liner and battleship		
	Set of 4	8.25	7.00

1938

As Nos. 110/11, but with portrait of King George VI

122b†	1d Liner and battleship	40	55
123†	1½d Liner and battleship (red)	35.00	75
123b†	1½d Liner and battleship (violet)	20	85

1949

As No. 115 of Antigua

137†	3d Paddle-steamer	2.00	85

1953

147†	1½d Tunny fishing boat	90	75
149†	2½d Sailing yachts	2.00	60
150†	3d Saturnia (liner)	2.00	10
151†	4d Freighters at coaling wharf	2.25	1.50

1954

As No. 150, but inscribed "ROYAL VISIT 1954"

159†	3d Saturnia	15	20

1967

200	½d H.M.S. Victory (Nelson)	
201	1d Arab (early steamer)	
202	2d H.M.S. Carmania (merchant cruiser)	
203	2½d Mons Calpe (ferry)	
204	3d Canberra (liner)	
205	4d H.M.S. Hood (battle cruiser)	
205a	5d Mirror (cable ship)	
206	6d Xebec (sailing vessel)	
207	7d Amerigo Vespucci (Italian cadet ship)	
208	9d Raffaello (liner)	
209	1s Royal Katherine (galleon), 1696	
210	2s H.M.S. Ark Royal (Second World War aircraft carrier)	
211	5s H.M.S. Dreadnought (nuclear submarine)	
212	10s Neuralia (liner)	
213	£1 Mary Celeste (sail merchantman)	
	Set of 15	35.00 35.00

1974

338†	20p King George V (Second World War battleship)	50	50

1980

438†	9p H.M.S. *Victory* (Nelson)	25	25
440†	40p H.M.S. *Victory* after Trafalgar	80	1.00

1982

475	½p Crest of H.M.S. *Opossum* (frigate)		
476	15½p Crest of H.M.S. *Norfolk* (cruiser)		
477	17p Crest of H.M.S. *Fearless* (destroyer)		
478	60p Crest of H.M.S. *Rooke* (shore base)		
	Set of 4	2.10	2.40

1983

487†	4p Yachts in marina	10	10

493	4p Crest of H.M.S. *Faulknor* (destroyer)		
494	14p Crest of H.M.S. *Renown* (battle cruiser)		
495	17p Crest of H.M.S. *Ark Royal* (aircraft carrier)		
496	60p Crest of H.M.S. *Sheffield* (cruiser)		
	Set of 4	2.75	2.10

1984

510	20p Crest of H.M.S. *Active* (destroyer)		
511	21p Crest of H.M.S. *Foxhound* (destroyer)		
512	26p Crest of H.M.S. *Valiant* (battleship)		
513	29p Crest of H.M.S. *Hood* (battle cruiser)		
	Set of 4	4.25	4.25

1985

522	4p Crest of H.M.S. *Duncan* (destroyer)		
523	9p Crest of H.M.S. *Fury* (destroyer)		
524	21p Crest of H.M.S. *Firedrake* (destroyer)		
525	80p Crest of H.M.S. *Malaya* (battleship)		
	Set of 4	4.25	5.00

1986

541	22p Crest of H.M.S. *Lightning* (destroyer)		
542	29p Crest of H.M.S. *Hermione* (cruiser)		
543	32p Crest of H.M.S. *Laforey* (destroyer)		
544	44p Crest of H.M.S. *Nelson* (battleship)		
	Set of 4	6.00	6.00

1987

563†	22p Yachts in marina	1.25	50

565	18p Crest of H.M.S. *Wishart* (destroyer)		
566	22p Crest of H.M.S. *Charybdis* (cruiser)		
567	32p Crest of H.M.S. *Antelope* (destroyer)		
568	44p Crest of H.M.S. *Eagle* (aircraft carrier)		
	Set of 4	6.50	7.00

1988

588†	22p *Canberra* (liner)	1.25	1.75
589†	22p *Gibline I* (ferry)	1.25	1.75

592	18p Crest of H.M.S. *Clyde* (submarine)		
593	22p Crest of H.M.S. *Foresight* (destroyer)		
594	32p Crest of H.M.S. *Severn* (submarine)		
595	44p Crest of H.M.S. *Rodney* (battleship)		
	Set of 4	5.00	5.75

600†	19p *Zebu* (brigantine)	55	60
602†	32p *Sir Walter Raleigh* (expedition ship)	85	1.25
MS603†	44p *Sir Walter Raleigh* (sheet also contains 22p design)	3.50	3.00

1989

616	22p Crest of H.M.S. *Blankney* (destroyer)		
617	25p Crest of H.M.S. *Deptford* (sloop)		
618	32p Crest of H.M.S. *Exmoor* (destroyer)		
619	44p Crest of H.M.S. *Stork* (sloop)		
	Set of 4	3.75	4.75

1990

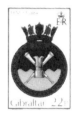

638	22p Crest of H.M.S. *Calpe* (destroyer)		
639	25p Crest of H.M.S. *Gallant* (destroyer)		
640	32p Crest of H.M.S. *Wrestler* (destroyer)		
641	44p Crest of H.M.S. *Greyhound* (destroyer)		
	Set of 4	4.00	4.25

642†	22p Yacht marina (model)	75	75

1991

651	4p Crest of H.M.S. *Hesperus* (destroyer)		
652	21p Crest of H.M.S. *Forester* (destroyer)		
653	22p Crest of H.M.S. *Furious* (aircraft carrier)		
654	62p Crest of H.M.S. *Scylla* (cruiser)		
	Set of 4	4.00	4.00

660†	22p Fishing boats on beach	55	50
663†	42p Schooner at Waterport Wharf	1.40	1.60

1992

669†	24p *Santa Maria* (Columbus)	70	75
670†	24p *Nina*	70	75
671†	34p *Pinta*	90	1.00

673†	4p Yachts	15	10
674†	20p H.M.S. *Arrow* (frigate)	50	55

1993

MS694	24p H.M.S. *Hood* (battle cruiser); 24p H.M.S. *Ark Royal* (aircraft carrier); 24p H.M.A.S. *Waterhen* (destroyer); U.S.S. *Gleaves* (destroyer)	1.90 2.00

GILBERT AND ELLICE ISLANDS

Pacific Ocean
1939 12 pence = 1 shilling
20 shillings = 1 pound
1966 100 cents = 1 dollar

1939

45†	1½d Canoe	30	90
46†	2d Canoe and canoe-house	20	1.00
49†	5d Ellice Islands canoe	2.25	90
51†	1s *Triona* (freighter), 1931	2.50	1.25
52†	2s *Nimanoa* (colonial schooner)	13.00	6.50
53†	2s6d Gilbert Islands canoe	15.00	12.00

1949

As No. 115 *of Antigua*

60†	2d Paddle-steamer	1.25	65

1956

As Nos. 45/6, 49, 51/3, *but with portrait of Queen Elizabeth II*

66†	2d Canoe and canoe-house	90	1.00
69†	5d Ellice Islands canoe	6.00	1.50
71†	1s *Triona*	55	50
72†	2s *Nimanoa*	7.00	4.00
73†	2s6d Gilbert Islands canoe	8.50	5.50
75†	10s Canoe (as stamp No. 45)	21.00	14.00

1960

76†	2d *Triona II* (freighter), 1943	70	25

1967

132†	3c H.M.S. *Royalist* (screw corvette), 1892	30	20

1970

167†	10c *John Williams III* (missionary sailing ship)	20	10
169†	35c *John Williams VII* (missionary motor ship)	30	20

172†	35c Sailing canoes	20	20

1971

174†	2c Fishing canoe	15	20
177†	5c Gilbertese canoe	35	15
184†	35c Fishing canoes at night	2.00	50

192†	35c Outrigger canoe	25	20

1972

197†	10c South Pacific canoe types	15	10

1973

218†	10c Outrigger canoe	10	10

1974

227	3c "Te Mataaua" canoe crest	
228	10c "Te-Nimta-wawa" canoe crest	
229	35c "Tara-Tara-Venei-Na" canoe crest	
230	50c "Te Bou-uoua" canoe crest	
	Set of 4 75 65	

232†	4c "Te Koroba" canoe	10	10
233†	10c *Kiakia* (sailing ship)	10	10

1975

259†	35c Fishing canoes	25	45

GILBERT ISLANDS

Pacific Ocean
100 cents = 1 dollar

1976

Nos. 174, 177 *and* 184 *of Gilbert and Ellice Islands overprinted*
THE GILBERT ISLANDS

4†	2c Fishing canoe	50	75
13†	5c Gilbertese canoe	50	50
20†	35c Fishing canoes at night	2.00	1.75

23†	1c *Teraaka* (training ship)	20	15
24†	3c *Tautunu* (inter-island freighter)	30	20
37†	$1 *Tabakea* (lagoon ferry)	2.00	2.50

1977

48†	8c Outrigger canoe	15	10
49†	20c Royal Yacht *Britannia*	45	35

51 5c H.M.S. *Dolphin* (Byron), 1765
52 15c *Betsey* (American full-rigged ship), 1798
53 20c *Vostok* (Bellingshausen), 1820
54 35c U.S.S. *Vincennes* (sail frigate), 1838–42

Set of 4 7.00 12.00

55† 8c H.M.S. *Resolution* and H.M.S. *Discovery* (Cook) 55 10
58† 40c H.M.S. *Resolution* and ship's boat, Christmas Island 1.75 65

63† 40c Scout outrigger canoe 50 55

1979

80† 10c H.M.S. *Endeavour* (Cook) 25 15

GOLD COAST

West Africa
12 pence = 1 shilling
20 shillings = 1 pound

1948

145† 5s Surfboats 15.00 2.25

1949

As No. 115 of Antigua
150† 2½d Paddle-steamer 1.00 1.50

1952

As No. 145, but with portrait of Queen Elizabeth II
163† 5s Surfboats 15.00 2.50

GREAT BRITAIN

Western Europe
1951 12 pence = 1 shilling
20 shillings = 1 pound
1971 100 pence = 1 pound

1951

509† 2s6d H.M.S. *Victory* (Nelson) 8.00 75
510† 5s Yacht and Thames sailing barge, Dover 30.00 1.50

1963

639† 2½d *J. G. Graves of Sheffield* (lifeboat) 10 10
640† 4d 19th-century lifeboat 40 30

1964

659† 3d Tanker under Forth Road Bridge 15 10

1966

703† 1s3d "SRN6" hovercraft 30 40

711† 6d Norman ship, 1066 .... 10 10

1967

715† 9d Freighter at quay 15 15

751 1s9d *Gipsy Moth IV* (Chichester) 25 25

1968

770† 1s9d H.M.S. *Endeavour* (Cook) 25 25

1969

778 5d *Queen Elizabeth 2* (liner)
779 9d *Elizabeth Jonas* (Elizabethan galleon)
780 9d *Earl of Balcares* (East Indiaman)
781 9d *Cutty Sark* (clipper)
782 1s *Great Britain* (steam/sail), 1843
783 1s *Mauretania I* (liner), 1906

Set of 6 1.60 90

1970

822† 1s6d *Mayflower* (Pilgrim Fathers), 1620 30 30

1972

902† 7½p Wreck of brig *President* 50 50

1974

954† 3½p *Peninsular* (packet steamer), 1888 10 10

1975

980 7p Sailing dinghies
981 8p Racing yachts
982 10p Cruising yachts
983 12p Multi-hulled yachts

Set of 4 1.00 1.00

1978

1050† 9p North Sea oil rig 25 20

1979

1103† 15p River Thames police launch 50 40

1981

1166† 14p *Linsey II* (cockle dredger) 35 35

1982

1187 15½p *Mary Rose* (Henry VIII)
1188 19½p *Triumph* (Blake)
1189 24p H.M.S. *Victory* (Nelson)
1190 26p H.M.S. *Dreadnought* (battleship) (Fisher)
1191 29p H.M.S. *Warspite* (battleship) (Cunningham)

Set of 5   2.50   2.50

1204† 19½p 18th-century galleons 50 60

1983

1217† 28p *Iolair* (oilfield emergency support vessel) 1.10 1.25

1985

1286 17p Lifeboat
1287 22p Trawler
1288 31p Liner
1289 34p Yacht

Set of 4   3.00   3.00

1986

1308† 17p North Sea oil rig 45 45

1987

1367† 18p Rowing boat 50 50
1368† 22p *Great Eastern* (paddle-steamer), 1858 .... 65 65

1988

1393† 26p *Queen Elizabeth* (liner) 80 80

1396† 18p Sailing clipper 60 60

1400 18p Spanish galeasse off the Lizard, 1588
1401 18p English fleet leaving Plymouth, 1588
1402 18p Engagement off Isle of Wight, 1588
1403 18p Attack of English fire-ships, Calais, 1588
1404 18p Armada in storm, North Sea, 1588

Set of 5   2.75   2.75

1405† 19p Rowing boat 50 50

1410† £1 Fishing boats, Carrickfergus 2.25 60

1989

1425† 19p Yachts 2.75 2.25

1987

1439† 35p Toy yacht 1.25 1.25

1443† 35p Canal barge, Pontcysyillte Viaduct (vert design) 1.10 1.10
MS1444† 35p Canal barge, Pontcysyillte Viaduct (horiz design) (sheet also contains three other designs) 6.00 6.00

1992

As No. 1410, but Queen's head in silhouette.
1611 £1 Fishing boats, Carrickfergus 1.50 1.50

1617† 24p *Santa Maria* (Columbus) 65 65
1618† 39p *Kaisei* (Japanese cadet brigantine) 1.10 1.10

1627† 33p Pirate ship 80 80

1993

1775 24p *Midland Maid* and other narrow boats, Grand Junction Canal
1776 28p *Yorkshire Lass* and other Humber keels, Stainforth and Keadby Canal
1777 33p. *Valley Princess* and other horse-drawn barges, Brecknock and Abergavenny Canal
1778 39p *Pride of Scotland* (steam barge) and fishing boats, Crinan Canal

Set of 4   1.75   2.00

GREECE

South-east Europe
100 lepta = drachma

1923

ΕΠΑΝΑΣΤΑΣΙΣ
1922
ΛΕΠΤΑ 10

No. 31 of Crete surcharged

374†	50lep on 1d Warships, Suda Bay,1898	2.00	2.00

1927

410†	5lep Freighter in Corinth Canal	35	10
415†	50lep Freighter in Corinth Canal	1.40	10
416†	80lep Freighter in Corinth Canal	1.25	30
419†	3d *Averoff* (cruiser)	9.25	15

428†	4d Battle of Navarino, 1827	8.00	55

1933

475†	50d *Averoff* (cruiser)	60.00	2.00

1946

646†	50d Second World War convoy	40	10
647†	100d *Helle* (cruiser)	20	10
652†	2000d *Hyacinth* (torpedo-boat) and *Perla* (submarine)	8.75	1.40

1947

68†	450d Greek frigate, 1824	75	10
673†	800d Greek frigate, 1824	1.25	20

1954

723†	4000d Ancient Greek war galley	6.50	30

1955

As No. 723, but face value in revalued currency

741†	4d Ancient Greek war galley	40.00	35

1958

778	50lep *Michael Carras* (tanker)	
779	1d *Queen Frederika* (liner)	
780	1d50 Full-rigged sailing ship, 1821	
781	2d Byzantine galley	
782	3d50 6th-century B.C. galley	
783	5d *Argo* (5th-century B.C.)	
	Set of 6	11.00 7.00

784†	10d *Achilleus* (liner) and other shipping, Piraeus	5.50	15
785†	15d Coasters, Salonika	1.40	20
786†	20d Fishing boats, Patras	5.50	15
787†	25d Fishing boats, Hermoupolis	1.40	25
789†	50d Shipping, Kavalla	2.50	25

1960

827	2d50 Brig in storm		
828	4d50 Brig in calm waters		
	Set of 2	1.75	75

1961

849	2d50 *Nirefs* (Olympic yacht)	50	25

852†	50lep Yachts, Hydra	20	10

1964

958†	6d Corfu war galley	40	35

1967

1052	20lep *Lonchi* (destroyer)		
1053	1d *Eugene Eugenides* (cadet ship)		
1054	2d50 Longboat		
1055	3d *Averoff* (cruiser)		
1056	6d *Australis* (liner)		
	Set of 5	95	65

1969

1101	1d Yachts	15	10

1112	80lep 19th-century brig and steamship		
1113	2d *Olympic Garland* (tanker)		
1114	2d50 *Themistocles* and *Karteria* (warships), 1821		
1115	4d50 *Velos* (destroyer)		
1116	6d Battle of Salamis, 480 B.C.		
	Set of 5	3.25	1.25

1971

1168	20lep *Leonidas* (warship), 1821		
1169	1d *Pericles* (warship), 1821		
1170	1d50 *Terpsichore* (warship), 1821		
1171	2d50 *Karteria* (warship), 1821		
1172	3d Battle of Samos		
1173	6d Battle of Yeronda		
	Set of 6	3.00	1.25

1976

1348†	30d Fishing boat, Lemnos	20	15

1977

1387†	4d H.M.S. *Genoa* (ship of the line) Battle of Navarino, 1827	20	10

1393†	4d Ancient galley, sailing ships and modern liner	10	10

1398†	1d50 Topsail schooner, Kalamata	15	10

1978

1411† 5d *Maximilianos* (passenger steamer) 20 10

1440 50lep Destroyer
1441 1d *Andromeda* (motor torpedo-boat)
1442 2d50 *Papanicolis* (submarine)
1443 4d *Psara* (cruiser)
1444 5d *Madonna of Hydra* (armed sailing caique)
1445 7d Byzantine dromon
1446 50d Athenian trireme

Set of 7 2.25 1.25

1980

1539† 20d Harbour tug 55 20

1981

1556† 12d Oil rig 50 10

1983

1609 11d Figurehead from Tsamados's *Ares* (brig)
1610 15d Figurehead from Miaoulis's *Ares* (full-rigged ship)
1611 18d Figurehead of topsail schooner from Sphakia
1612 25d Figurehead from *Spetses* (full-rigged ship)
1613 40d Figurehead from *Epameinondas* (brig)
1614 50d Figurehead from *Carteria* (steamer)

Set of 6 3.75 2.00

1620† 18d Outboard motor boat 40 20
1621† 27d Sailboard 55 30

1646† 32d Ancient galley 60 10

1988

1795† 2d Barque and rowing boat, Mytilene Harbour 10 10
1801† 10d Fishing boats, Rhodes 10 10

1990

1852† 15d Fishing boats, Chios 10 10
1860† 100d Schooner, Nauplion 70 10

1863† 20d Yacht 15 10

1992

1901 90d *Santa Maria* (Columbus)
1902 340d Galleon, Chios

Set of 2 3.00 1.50

CHARITY TAX STAMPS

1937

ΠΡΟΝΟΙΑ

No. 415 surcharged
500† 50lep Freighter in Corinth Canal 40 10

1941

Κ.Π.
λεπτῶν
50

No. 410 surcharged
C561 50lep on 5lep Freighter in Corinth Canal 15 15

1942

ΦΥΜ· Τ.Τ.Τ.
10 ⚌ ΔΡ.

No. 410 surcharged
C591† 10d on 5lep Freighter in Corinth Canal 10 10

GREENLAND
North Atlantic
100 ore = 1 krone

1945

15† 2k Eskimo kayak 50.00 35.00

No. 15 overprinted **DANMARK BEFRIET 5 MAJ 1945**
24† 2k Eskimo kayak 55.00 40.00

1950

33† 50ore *Gustav Holm* (polar ship) 40.00 18.00
34† 1k *Gustav Holm* 18.00 1.75
35† 2k *Gustav Holm* 8.00 1.75
36† 5k *Gustav Holm* 4.00 1.00

1958

No. 33 surcharged **30 + 10** *and Cross of Lorraine*
40 30 + 10ore on 50ore *Gustav Holm* (polar ship) 3.00 1.75

1971

77† 50ore Mail kayak 25 20
78† 70ore Umiak (women's boat) 50 25
81† 1k *Kununguak* (coaster) and *Dlik* (tug) 70 60
82† 1k30 *Sokongen* (schooner) 40 40
83† 1k50 *Karen* (sailing longboat) 40 40

1972

85 60ore + 10ore *Dannebrog* (Danish royal yacht) 1.25 1.50

1974

91† 1k *Carl Egede* (trawler) and kayaks 65 45

1982

134 2k70 Kayak 50 50

135 2k + 40ore Eric the Red's ship, 900 .... 1.50 1.50

136† 2k Whaleboat 40 40

1983

142† 4k50 16th-century ship 75 85

1985

152 2k80 *Hvalfisken* (brig) 1.00 1.00

GRENADA

West Indies
1898 12 pence = 1 shilling
20 shillings = 1 pound
1949 100 cents = 1 dollar

1898

56 2½d Flagship of Columbus, 1498 .... 11.00 5.00

1906

77	½d Flagship of Columbus, 1498		
78	1d Flagship of Columbus, 1498		
79	2d Flagship of Columbus, 1498		
80	2½d Flagship of Columbus, 1498		
84	3d Flagship of Columbus, 1498		
85	6d Flagship of Columbus, 1498		
86	1s Flagship of Columbus, 1498		
87	2s Flagship of Columbus, 1498		
88	5s Flagship of Columbus, 1498		
83	10s Flagship of Columbus, 1498		

Set of 10 £140 £200

1934

136†	1d Flagship of Columbus, 1498	....	70	1.25
138†	2d Flagship of Columbus, 1498	....	80	40
140†	3d Flagship of Columbus, 1498	....	35	1.00
141†	6d Flagship of Columbus, 1498	....	70	1.10
142†	1s Flagship of Columbus, 1498	....	80	2.50
143†	2s6d Flagship of Columbus, 1498	....	6.50	16.00
144†	5s Flagship of Columbus, 1498	....	32.00	38.00

1938

As Nos. 136, 138 *and* 140/4, *but with portrait of King George VI or similar vert design with royal cyphers*

154†	1d Flagship of Columbus, 1498	....	30	20
156†	2d Flagship of Columbus, 1498	....	30	30
158b†	3d Flagship of Columbus, 1498	....	30	1.10
159†	6d Flagship of Columbus, 1498	....	45	30
160†	1s Flagship of Columbus, 1498	....	40	30
161†	2s Flagship of Columbus, 1498	....	8.00	1.25
162†	5s Flagship of Columbus, 1498	....	2.25	1.50
163b†	10s Flagship of Columbus, 1498	......	48.00	9.00

1949

As No. 115 of Antigua

169† 6c Paddle-steamer 25 30

1951

181†	25c Flagship of Columbus, 1498	....	2.25	50
182†	50c Flagship of Columbus, 1498	....	4.00	40
183†	$1.50 Flagship of Columbus, 1498	....	7.50	3.25
184†	$2.50 Flagship of Columbus, 1498	......	4.75	4.00

1953

As Nos. 181/4, *but with royal cypher of Queen Elizabeth II*

201†	25c Flagship of Columbus, 1498	....	75	20
202†	50c Flagship of Columbus, 1498	....	4.50	40
203†	$1.50 Flagship of Columbus, 1498	......	8.50	7.00
204†	$2.50 Flagship of Columbus, 1498	......	13.00	3.75

1961

209†	8c Flagship of Columbus, 1498	....	30	15
210†	25c *Solent I* (paddle-steamer)	....	30	15

1966

243† $1 Flagship of Columbus, 1498 .... 3.00 1.25

1967

No. 243 *overprinted* **expo67 MONTREAL CANADA** *and emblem*

260† $1 Flagship of Columbus, 1498 .... 30 20

1967

No. 243 *overprinted* **ASSOCIATED STATEHOOD**

274† $1 Flagship of Columbus, 1498 .... 70 60

1968

289†	10c Fishing boat, Antibes	....	10	10
292†	25c Fishing boat, Antibes	....	15	10

No. 243 surcharged **CHILDREN NEED MILK 1c. + 3 cts.**

298† 1c + 3c on $1 Flagship of Columbus, 1498 .... 10 40

1971 ACCORDING TO MICHEL

317a† 75c Yacht, St. George's 8.50 7.00

1970

368† 25c Pirate ketches 50 10

387† 25c Thames river tug 10 10

400†	15c Ship's boats and sinking freighter, Dunkirk, 1940		60	25
402†	50c Landing craft, Normandy, 1944	....	1.25	90

409†	15c *Britannia* (mail paddle-steamer), 1840	....	20	10
410†	25c *Queen Elizabeth 2* (liner)	....	25	10

1971

455† 1c U.S.S. *Iwo Jima* (aircraft carrier) 10 10

1972

522† ½c Olympic yachts 10 10

530	8c Flagship of Columbus, 1498	10	10
531	$1 Flagship of Columbus, 1498	45	55

1973

552†	25c Class II racing yacht	35	15
553†	35c Yachts in St. George's harbour	40	15
554†	60c *Bloodhound* (yacht)	55	55

565†	½c Racing yachts	10	10
566†	1c Cruising yacht	10	10
567†	2c Open-deck sloops	10	10
568†	35c *Mermaid* (sloop)	35	20
571†	$1 Boat-building	90	80
MS572†	$2 Racing yachts	1.25	1.75

1974

No. 317a overprinted **INDEPENDENCE 7TH FEB. 1974**

603†	75c Yacht, St. Georges	2.00	1.25

629†	1c *Caesar* (snow), 1839	10	10
634†	35c *Queen Elizabeth 2* (liner)	75	25

1975

649†	½c Yachts	10	10
650†	1c Racing yachts	10	10
651†	2c Harbour ferry	10	10
652†	3c Fishing boats	10	10
653†	5c *Victoria* (liner)	10	10
658†	15c Fishing boat	10	10
666†	$3 Sailing dinghy	1.25	2.00

699†	10c *Bonhomme Richard* (American frigate) and H.M.S. *Serapis* (frigate), 1779	10	10

714†	1c Scout sailing dinghy	10	10
MS720†	$1 Scouts building raft	90	30

MS744†	$1 Sailing dinghies	1.00	40

1976

771†	2c *Southward* (liner)	10	10
772†	35c Game fishing launch	65	20
MS776†	$2 Sailing dinghies	1.50	2.50

791†	$3 Rowing boat with canon, 1776	3.00	3.00

833	½c *Geestland* (freighter)		
834	1c *Federal Palm* (freighter)		
835	2c H.M.S. *Blake* (cruiser), 1961		
836	25c *Vistafjord* (liner)		
837	75c *Canberra* (liner)		
838	$1 *Regina* (liner)		
839	$5 *Arandora Star* (liner)		
	Set of 7	7.00	7.00
MS840	$2 *Santa Maria* (Columbus)	2.00	3.25

854†	$1 Freighter and tankers	80	1.00

1977

868†	1c Speedboats	10	10
871†	35c Sailing dinghies	25	20
873†	$2 Game fishing launch	1.40	2.25
MS874†	$3 Racing yachts	1.50	2.75

880†	2c Scout sailing dinghies	10	10

1978

973†	$3 H.M.S. *Resolution* (Cook)	4.00	4.00

1980

Nos. 651/2 and 666 overprinted **PEOPLE'S REVOLUTION 13 MARCH 1979**

1040†	2c Harbour ferry	10	10
1041†	3c Fishing boats	10	10
1052†	$3 Sailing dinghy	2.00	3.25

MS1059†	$4 Olympic yacht	80	1.40

1081	½c Carib canoes		
1082	1c Boat building		
1083	2c Fishing boat		
1084	4c *Santa Maria* (Columbus)		
1085	5c West Indiaman barque, *c.* 1840		
1086	6c *Orinoco* (mail paddle-steamer)		
1087	10c Schooner		
1088	12c Trimaran		
1089	15c *Petite Amie* (cruising yacht)		
1090	20c Fishing pirogue		
1091	25c Police launch		
1092	30c Speedboat		
1093	40c *Seimstrand* (freighter)		
1094	50c *Ariadne* (cadet schooner)		
1095	90c *Geestide* (freighter)		
1096	$1 *Cunard Countess* (liner)		
1097	$3 Rum-runner (pleasure launch)		
1098	$5 *Statendam* (liner)		
1099	$10 Coastguard patrol boat		
	Set of 19	29.00	21.00

1981

1116†	40c Crawfish boat	20	20
1117†	90c *Cunard Countess* (liner)	50	50

1166†	90c *Queen Elizabeth 2* (liner) (on stamp No. 410)	75	50
1167†	$4 *Solent* (paddle-steamer) (on stamp No. 210)	2.25	2.00

1983

1245†	$3 Boat building	1.40	1.40

1246† 30c Freighter   15   15

1984

1342 40c Freighter
1343 70c *Queen Elizabeth 2* (liner)
1344 90c Sailing sloops
1345 $4 *Amerikanis* (liner)
                                    Set of 4   9.50   8.50
MS1346 $5 16th-century Spanish galleon 7.00   6.00

1358† $4 *Australia II* (yacht) 4.50   5.00

1985

1404† $1.10 Sailboards   85   85
1405† $4 Sailboards 2.50   3.00

1447† $4 Royal Yacht *Britannia* 3.50   4.25

1987

1611 10c *Columbia* (yacht), 1958
1612 60c *Resolute* (yacht), 1920
1613 $1.10 *Endeavour* (yacht), 1934
1614 $4 *Rainbow* (yacht), 1934
                                    Set of 4   2.75   3.25
MS1615 $5 *Weatherly* (yacht), 1962 . . . .   2.25   3.00

1616† 10c Flagship of Columbus, 1498   15   15
1617† 30c *Santa Maria*, *Pinta* and *Nina*   20   15
1621† $1.10 Spanish caravel   50   60
1622† $2 Carib sailing raft   90   1.25

1626† 15c *Monitor* and *Merrimack* (ironclad
         warships), 1862   30   30
1628† 50c *Sirius* (paddle-steamer), 1838   45   45
1630† 70c U.S.S. *Enterprise* (aircraft carrier),
         1960   50   50
1632† $1.50 U.S.S. *Holland I* (submarine),
         1900 . . . .   1.25   1.25
1633† $2 *Oceanic I* (liner), 1871 . . . .   1.75   1.75

1647† 60c Statue of Liberty and small boats   40   40
1652† $4 *Queen Elizabeth 2* (liner) 2.50   2.75

1988
Nos. 1632/3 *overprinted* **"INDEPENDENCE 40"** (*No.* 1752) *or* **"FINLANDIA '88"** (*No.* 1753).
1752† $1.50 U.S.S. *Holland I* (submarine),
         1900   60   75
1753† $2 *Oceanic I* (liner), 1871   80   1.00

1760 $2 *Santa Maria de Guia* (Columbus),
       1498   80   1.00

1811† 15c Yacht, Lake Constance, 1901   15   15
1812† 25c *George Washington Curtis* (balloon
         barge), 1862   20   20
1819† $4 *Bremen* (liner) 2.00   2.00

1989

1981† 75c + 5c Fishing boat and diving bell   35   40
MS1984 $5 + 5c 17th-century warships 2.10   2.25

1985† 10c Japanese fishing boats, Edo Bay   10   10
1987† 60c Japanese fishing boats, Edo Bay   25   30

2017 25c Xebec
2018 75c Lugger
2019 $1 Full-rigged ship
2020 $4 Ketch
                                    Set of 4   3.25   3.50

1990

2079† $3 Container ship, Hamburg 1.25   1.40
MS2081† Two sheets (a) $6 13th-century
   ships in Hamburg harbour (other sheet shows
   aircraft)
                          Price for 2 sheets   5.25   5.50

2111† 45c Landing craft, Guadalcanal, 1942   20   25
2116† $2 Air attack on Japanese troop convoy,
         Battle of the Bismarck Sea, 1943   85   90
2117† $3 American aircraft carriers, 1941 . . . .   1.25   1.40
2118† $4 Landing craft, Salerno, 1943 . . . .   1.75   1.90
MS2119† $6 *U-30* (German submarine), 1939   2.50   2.75

2140† 75c "Flying Dutchman" class yachts   30   35

1991

2222 5c *Sv. Pyotr* (Bering), 1728–29
2223 10c *La Boudeuse* (Bougainville),
       1766–69
2224 25c Polynesian canoe
2225 50c *Todos los Santos* (Mendana),
       1567–69
2226 $1 H.M.S. *Beagle* (Darwin), 1831–35
2227 $2 H.M.S. *Endeavour* (Cook), 1768–71
2228 $4 *Eendracht* (Schouten), 1615–17
2229 $5 *Heemskerk* (Tasman), 1642–44
                                    Set of 8   5.25   5.50
MS2230 Two sheets (a) $6 *Santa Maria*
   (Columbus) sinking; (b) $6 Bow of *Santa Maria*
                          Price for 2 sheets   5.25   5.50

1992

2366† 5c Sailboard 10 10

MS2379† Two sheets (a) $6 Yacht at anchor
(other sheet shows village on hillside)
                    Price for 2 sheets 5.25 5.50

OFFICIAL STAMPS

1982
Nos. 1085/97 and 1099 overprinted **P.R.G.**

O1†	5c West Indiaman barque, *c. 1840*	15	10
O2†	6c *Orinoco* (paddle-steamer)	15	10
O3†	10c Schooner	15	10
O4†	12c Trimaran	15	10
O5†	15c *Petite Amie* (cruising yacht)	20	15
O6†	20c Fishing pirogue	25	15
O7†	25c Police launch	30	20
O8†	30c Speedboat	30	25
O9†	40c *Seimstrand* (freighter)	35	30
O10†	50c *Ariadne* (sail-training schooner)	40	30
O11†	90c *Geestide* (freighter)	70	70
O12†	$1 *Cunard Countess* (liner)	70	70
O13†	$3 Rum-runner (pleasure launch)	2.00	3.25
O14†	$10 Coastguard patrol boat	6.00	11.00

GRENADINES OF GRENADA

West Indies
100 cents = 1 dollar

1974
Design as No. 629 of Grenada inscribed "GRENADA GRENADINES"

25† 8c *Caesar* (snow), 1839 .... 10 10

1975

98†	75c Boarders in rowing boat, Boston Tea Party	65	10
99†	$2 Naval engagement, American War of Independence	1.50	10

As Nos. 649/53, 658 and 666 of Grenada, but inscribed "GRENADA GRENADINES"

111†	½c Yachts	10	20
112†	1c Racing yachts	10	15
113†	2c Harbour ferry	10	15
114†	3c Fishing boats	10	15
115†	5c *Victoria* (liner)	10	15
120†	15c Fishing boat	10	15
128†	$3 Sailing dinghy	1.75	2.25

COLLECT BUTTERFLIES AND OTHER INSECTS ON STAMPS

A Stanley Gibbons thematic catalogue — available at £12.95 (p. + p. £3) from: Stanley Gibbons Publications, 5 Parkside, Christchurch Road, Ringwood, Hants. BH24 3SH.

1976

155	½c Game fishing launch		
156	1c Schooner		
157	2c Racing yachts		
158	18c Boat building		
159	22c Sailing sloops		
160	75c Cruising yacht		
161	$1 Speedboat		
	Set of 7	90	1.50
MS162	$2 Sailing dinghies	70	1.50

176	½c *South Carolina* (American frigate), 1777		
177	1c *Lee* (American schooner), 1775		
178	2c H.M.S. *Roebuck* (frigate), 1774		
179	35c *Andrew Doria* (American brig), 1775		
180	50c *Providence* (American sloop), 1775		
181	$1 *Alfred* (American frigate), 1775		
182	$2 *Confederacy* (American frigate), 1779		
	Set of 7	6.00	8.00
MS183	$3 *Revenge* (American cutter), 1777	2.50	5.50

MS198† $3 Olympic yacht 80 1.60

1977

249† $3 Scout yachts 1.75 3.25

1978

307†	18c H.M.S. *Resolution* (Cook)	45	10
MS311†	$4 H.M.S. *Resolution*	2.50	3.25

1979

333† $1 *Britanis* (cargo liner) 50 35

1980
Nos. 120 and 128 overprinted **PEOPLE'S REVOLUTION 13 MARCH 1979**

366†	15c Fishing boat	10	10
374†	$3 Sailing dinghy	1.60	1.60

No. 333 overprinted **LONDON 1980**

393† $1 *Britanis* (cargo liner) 75 50

1981

426† 10c H.M.S. *Temeraire* (ship of the line) and paddle-tug 10 10

1982

480† $2.50 *Queen Elizabeth 2* (liner) and sailing clipper 2.25 90

484† 90c Scout sailing dinghies 65 30

1984

581† $4 Olympic yachts 1.75 1.90

609	30c *Geeststar* (freighter)		
610	60c *Daphne* (liner)		
611	$1.10 *Southwind* (schooner)		
612	$4 *Oceanic* (liner)		
	Set of 4	8.00	6.50
MS613	$5 Pirate ship	3.50	4.00

1985

657† $1.10 Sailing dinghy 1.25 90

668† $4 Guide sailing dinghy 2.50 2.25

710† $4 Royal Yacht *Britannia* 3.75   3.75

1986

733†   70c Rowing boats, Central Park, New
         York, 1894 35   40
734† $4 Rowing boats, Central Park, New
         York, 1986 .... 2.00   2.10

805   50c + 20c Olympic yacht 60   70

1987

859   25c *Defender* (yacht), 1895
860   45c *Galatea* (yacht), 1886
861   70c *Azzurra* (yacht), 1981
862   $4 *Australia II* (yacht), 1983
                              Set of 4   3.25   2.50
MS863 $5 *Columbia* and *Shamrock* (yachts),
         1899 .... 5.00   5.50

866†   50c *Santa Maria* (Columbus) 45   45
867†   60c Spanish galleon 50   50
871† $3 Spanish galley 1.90   1.90
MS872†   Two sheets. (a) $5 Carib canoes; (b)
         $5 *Santa Maria*
                         Price for 2 sheets   7.50   8.50

873†   10c "SR-NI" (hovercraft), 1959 15   15
876†   50c *Hunley* (Confederate submarine),
         1864 45   45
881† $2 *Great Britain* (steam/sail), 1843 ...... 1.50   1.50

899†   70c Small boat flotilla 55   55
902† $2 Modern frigate 1.40   1.40

1988

943†   70c Scout canoe 35   40

967†   30c U.S. Navy airship over convoy, 1944   15   15

1038† $6 *Australia II* (yacht) 3.00   3.50

1989

Grenada Grenadines   20c

1098†   20c Japanese fishing boats 10   10
1104† $4 Japanese fishing boats, Lake Biwa   1.75   1.90
MS1105†   Two sheets (b) $5 Japanese fishing
         boats, Miya (other sheet shows bridge)
                         Price for 2 sheets   4.25   4.50

1146†   2c River boat, Paris 10   10

1196†   1c Rowing boat 10   10

1990

1245†   45c Landing craft, Aleutian Islands,
         1943 20   25

MS1298†   Two sheets (a) $6 Sailboards (other
         sheet shows decathlon)
                         Price for 2 sheets   5.25   5.50

1991

1366†   15c *Vitoria* (Magellan), 1519–21 10   10
1367†   20c *Golden Hind* (Drake), 1577–80   10   10
1368†   50c H.M.S. *Resolution* (Cook), 1768–71   20   25
MS1374†   Two sheets (a) $6 Bow of *Pinta*; (b)
         $6 Fleet of Columbus
                         Price for 2 sheets   5.25   5.50

GRENADA GRENADINES $6

MS1415†   Three sheets (a) $6 Sand barges
         (two other sheets show different Van Gogh
         paintings)
                         Price for 3 sheets   7.75   8.00

1992

MS1473†   Two sheets (b) $6 Yachts, St.
         George's (other sheet shows inland scene)
                         Price for 2 sheets   5.25   5.50

MS1484†   Two sheets (a) $15 "Finn" class
         sailing dinghies (other sheet shows baseball)
                         Price for 2 sheets   13.00   13.50

GRENADINES OF ST. VINCENT

West Indies
100 cents = 1 dollar

1974

34	5c Boat building		
31	30c Careening, Port Elizabeth		
32	35c Yachts, Admiralty Bay		
33	$1 Fishing boat race		
		Set of 4	50 60

1975

68†	45c Schooner, Petit St. Vincent	15	10
69†	$1 Sailing dinghies	50	30

1976

74†	5c Yachts at anchor, Union Island	10	10
77†	$1 Mail schooner, Union Island	25	20

1977

91†	45c Cruising yacht, Mayreau	10	10
92†	$1 Yachts, Mayreau	25	15

101†	35c Sailing dinghies and motor boat	10	10
102†	45c Cruising yacht and sailing dinghies	10	15
103†	$1 Sailing dinghies	30	40

107†	35c Cruising yacht, Canouan	10	10
108†	45c Mail schooner, Canouan	10	10

1979

145	5c Racing yachts		
146	40c Racing yachts		
147	50c Racing yachts		
148	$2 Racing yachts		
		Set of 4	1.10 75

1980

172†	50c Racing yacht	10	10

No. 172 surcharged **HURRICANE RELIEF 50c**

176†	50c + 50c Racing yacht	20	30

1981

187†	$1.50 Fishing boats, Bequia	40	40
188†	$2 Friendship Rose (cruising yacht)	55	55

195†	50c Royal Yacht *Mary*	15	15
197†	$3 Royal Yacht *Alexandra*	30	30
199†	$3.50 Royal Yacht *Britannia*	35	35

1982

208	1c H.M.S. *Experiment* (frigate)		
209	3c *Lady Nelson* (cargo liner)		
210	5c *Daisy* (brig)		
211	6c Carib canoe		
212	10c *Hairoun Star* (freighter)		
213	15c *Jupiter* (liner)		
214	20c *Christina* (steam yacht)		
215	25c *Orinoco* (mail paddle-steamer)		
216	30c H.M.S. *Lively* (frigate)		
217	50c *Alabama* (Confederate warship)		
218	60c *Denmark* (freighter)		
219	75c *Santa Maria* (Columbus)		
220	$1 *Baffin* (research vessel)		
221	$2 *Queen Elizabeth 2* (liner)		
222	$3 Royal Yacht *Britannia*		
223	$5 *Geeststar* (freighter)		
224	$10 *Grenadines Star* (ferry)		
		Set of 17	10.00 10.00

1983

243†	60c Yachts, Union Island	15	15
245†	$2 Fishing boats	55	55

246†	45c 18th-century British warship	15	15
247†	60c 18th-century American warship	15	15

256†	60c *Mary Rose* and Henry VIII	25	25
263†	$2.50 *Mary Rose*	35	35

1985

386†	35c Sailboards	20	25
389†	$3 Game fishing launch	1.50	1.60

Nos. 199 and 222 overprinted or surcharged **CARIBBEAN ROYAL VISIT 1985**

424†	$1.50 on $3.50 Royal Yacht *Britannia*	3.00	3.00
426†	$3 Royal Yacht *Britannia*	5.50	5.00

1986

467†	$3 Model sailing dinghy	1.60	1.60

1988

547	50c *Australia IV* (yacht)		
548	65c *Crusader II* (yacht)		
549	75c *New Zealand II* (yacht)		
550	$2 *Italia* (yacht)		
551	$4 *White Crusader* (yacht)		
552	$5 *Stars and Stripes* (yacht)		
		Set of 6	8.00 8.00
MS553	$1 *Champosa V* (yacht)	90	1.25

554	5c Seine fishing boats		
555	50c *Friendship Rose* (cruising yacht)		
556	75c Fishing boats racing		
557	$3.50 Yachts racing		
		Set of 4	1.90 2.00
MS558	$8 Yachts and fishing boats, Port Elizabeth, Bequia	3.75	4.50

564†	15c *Sv. Pyotr* (Bering)	10	10
565†	75c Bering's ships in the ice	30	35

566† $1 *Ma-Robert* (Livingstone's steam
launch) 45 50
569† $3.50 Canoe (Burton and Speke), Lake
Victoria 1.50 1.60
MS572† Two sheets (a) $5 Galleon at anchor;
(b) $5 *Santa Maria* (Columbus)
Price for 2 sheets 4.25 4.50

1989

593† 3c Tourist boat, New Delhi 10 10
598† $5 Canoe, Cape Comorin 2.10 2.25

1990

657† 10c *Wilhelm Heidkamp* (German
destroyer) and *Saphir* (freighter)
sinking, Battle of Narvik, 1940 .... 10 10
659† 20c American aircraft carrier under air
attack, Battle of Midway, 1942 .... 10 10
662† 65c German submarine and Atlantic
convoy, 1943 .... 30 35
666† $6 Japanese battleships under air attack,
Leyte Gulf, 1944 .... 2.50 2.75

1991

738† 35c Fishing boats, Saintes-Maries 15 20

781† $1 Japanese submarine carrying midget
submarine 45 50
782† $1 *Akagi* (Japanese aircraft carrier) 45 50
784† $1 Japanese aircraft attacking American
battleships, Pearl Harbor 45 50
787† $1 U.S.S. *West Virginia* and U.S.S.
Tennessee (battleships) ablaze 45 50
788† $1 U.S.S. *Arizona* (battleship) sinking 45 50
789† $1 U.S.S. *New Orleans* (cruiser) 45 50

1992

810† 45c Schooner at anchor, Mayreau 20 25
812† $4 Yacht and launches at anchor 1.75 1.90

STANLEY GIBBONS STAMP COLLECTING SERIES

Introductory booklets on *How to Start, How to Identify Stamps* and *Collecting by Theme*. A series of well illustrated guides at a low price. Write for details.

815† 40c Caravel on Mississippi 15 10
817† $4 Rowing boat on Rio Grande 1.75 1.90

825† 45c *Santa Maria* and *Nina* (Columbus) in
Acul Bay, Haiti 20 25
826† 55c *Santa Maria* 20 25
827† $2 Columbus's fleet 85 90
828† $4 Wreck of *Santa Maria* 1.75 1.90
829† $5 *Pinta* and *Nina* 2.25 2.40
MS830† Two sheets (a) $6 Caravels and
ship's boat, (b) $6 *Santa Maria* in storm
Price for 2 sheets 5.25 5.50

870 $1 Columbus's ships anchored off beach
871 $2 Columbus's fleet approaching island
Set of 2 1.25 1.40

881† $2 "Tornado" class catamaran 85 90

898 10c *Nina* (Columbus) in Baracoa Harbour
899 $1 Columbus's fleet
Set of 2 50 55

916 $1 *America III* and *Il Moro* (yachts) 45 50

OFFICIAL STAMPS

1982
Nos. 195, 197 and 199 overprinted **OFFICIAL**
O1 50c Royal Yacht *Mary* 15 15
O3 $3 Royal Yacht *Alexandra* 35 35
O5 $3.50 Royal Yacht *Britannia* 50 50

APPENDIX
The following stamps have either been issued in excess of postal needs, or have not been made available to the public in reasonable quantities at face value. Miniature sheets, imperforate stamps etc., are excluded from this section.

Bequia
1984
Grenadines of St. Vincent 1982 Ships definitives (Nos. 208/24) overprinted **BEQUIA.** 1, 3, 5, 6, 10, 15, 20, 25, 30, 50, 60, 75c, $1, $2, $3, $5, $10

1985
Leaders of the World. Warships of the Second World War. Two designs for each value, the first showing technical drawings and the second the ship at sea. 15, 50c, $1, $1.50, each x 2

Union Island
1984
Grenadines of St. Vincent 1982 Ships definitives (Nos. 208/24) overprinted **UNION ISLAND.** 1, 3, 5, 6, 10, 15, 20, 25, 30, 50, 60, 75c, $1, $2, $3, $5, $10

GUADELOUPE

West Indies
100 centimes = 1 franc

1928

128† 1f Fishing boats, Pointe-a-Pitre (blue and
red) 2.75 1.75
129† 1f Fishing boats, Pointe-a-Pitre (orange
and red) 75 75
130† 1f Fishing boats, Pointe-a-Pitre (brown
and blue) 30 45
131† 1f05 Fishing boats, Pointe-a-Pitre 70 80
132† 1f10 Fishing boats, Pointe-a-Pitre 1.75 1.90
133† 1f25 Fishing boats, Pointe-a-Pitre (brown
and blue) 35 50
134† 1f25 Fishing boats, Pointe-a-Pitre (red) 45 60
135† 1f40 Fishing boats, Pointe-a-Pitre 45 60
136† 1f50 Fishing boats, Pointe-a-Pitre 20 25
137† 1f60 Fishing boats, Pointe-a-Pitre 40 60
138† 1f75 Fishing boats, Pointe-a-Pitre (brown
and mauve) 2.25 1.75
139† 1f75 Fishing boats, Pointe-a-Pitre (blue) 3.50 3.00
140† 2f Fishing boats, Pointe-a-Pitre 25 25
141† 2f25 Fishing boats, Pointe-a-Pitre 45 55
142† 2f50 Fishing boats, Pointe-a-Pitre 60 75
143† 3f Fishing boats, Pointe-a-Pitre 25 30
144† 5f Fishing boats, Pointe-a-Pitre 40 40
145† 10f Fishing boats, Pointe-a-Pitre 50 60
146† 20f Fishing boats, Pointe-a-Pitre 65 65

1931
As No. 109 of Cameroun
150† 1f50 *Leconte de Lisle* (liner) 2.50 2.50

1937
As Nos. 110/11 of Cameroun
157† 20c Liner 65 70
158† 30c Sailing ships 65 65
MS162a† 3f Sailing ships 5.00 6.50

1947

211† 10c Brigantine and fishing boat 15 25
212† 30c Brigantine and fishing boat 15 25
213† 50c Brigantine and fishing boat 15 30
230† 200f Fishing boats 6.25 4.75

GUATEMALA

Central America
100 antavos de quetzal = 1 quetzal

1935

291 10c *Agamemnon* (freighter) 4.25 3.25

299†	3c Liner, Puerto Barrios	40	20
315†	30c Freighters, Puerto Barrios (green)	5.00	3.50
315a†	30c Freighters, Puerto Barrios (red)	1.50	20

1956

591	30c Freighter, Champerico	1.50	1.00

1959

623	6c *Quezaltenango* (freighter) and caravel of 1532	60	15

1971

No. 623 overprinted **FERIA INTERNACIONAL "INTERFER—71"**
30 Oct. al 21 Nov.

916	6c *Quezaltenango* (freighter) and caravel of 1532	20	15

1984

1251†	4c Lighter	20	10
1255†	25c Freighter	1.10	30

1992

1325	40c *Pinta* (Columbus)		
1326	60c *Santa Maria* (Columbus)		
	Set of 2	45	20

GUERNSEY

Western Europe
1969 12 pence = 1 shilling
20 shillings = 1 pound
1971 100 pence = 1 pound

1969

27†	10s Fishing boats, Alderney	25.00	28.00
28a†	£1 Yachts, St. Peter Port	2.00	2.00

1970

33†	4d H.M.S *L103*, (landing craft)	35	50
34†	5d British warships off Guernsey, 1945 ..	35	50

1971

As No. 27 but currency changed

58†	50p Fishing boats, Alderney	2.00	3.25

1972

67	2p *Earl of Chesterfield* (sailing packet), 1794		
68	2½p *Dasher* (paddle packet), 1827		
69	7½p *Ibex* (packet steamer), 1891		
70	9p *Alberta* (packet steamer), 1900		
	Set of 4	1.00	85

1973

80	2½p *St. Julien* (mail packet), 1925		
81	3p *Isle of Guernsey* (mail packet), 1930		
82	7½p *St. Patrick* (mail packet), 1947		
83	9p *Sarnia* (mail packet), 1961		
	Set of 4	1.60	1.50

1974

94	2½p *John Lockett* (lifeboat), 1875		
95	3p *Arthur Lionel* (lifeboat), 1912		
96	8p *Euphrosyne Kendal* (lifeboat), 1954		
97	10p *Arun* (lifeboat), 1972		
	Set of 4	1.00	1.00

1977

159†	11p *Flying Christine II* (marine ambulance)	40	35

1978

164†	13p Sailing ships, St. Peter Port, 1830	50	50

1980

223†	13½p Fishing boats, *c.* 1850	40	30

1981

230†	12p Yacht	45	45

240†	8p Sark launch	20	20
242†	18p Hydrofoil	60	60
243†	22p Herm catamaran	75	75
244†	25p *Sea Trent* (Alderney coaster)	85	85

1982

249†	8p Sailing ships off Jethou	20	20

254†	13p Norman ships, 1066	45	45
255†	20p H.M.S. *Crescent* (frigate), 1793	55	55

1983

268†	8p Sailing dinghies	25	25

274†	13p *Earl Goodwin* (ferry), St Peter Port	35	35
275†	20p Sailing ships, St. Peter Port, 1680 ..	75	75

282 9p *Star of the West* (brigantine), 1869
283 13p *Star of the West*
284 26p *Star of the West*
285 28p *Star of the West*
286 31p *Star of the West*
　　　　　　　　　　　　　　　　Set of 5 3.25 3.25

1984

295† 31p Yacht, Castle Cornet 1.10 1.10

297† 2p Dinghies 10 10
300† 5p *Royal Odyssey* (liner) 10 10
304† 9p *Pen-Ar-Roz* and *M.J.C.* (fishing
　　　　boats 20 25
309† 15p Yachts 30 35
310c† 26p Trawler 50 55
313† 50p Yachts and motor cruisers 1.00 1.10

331† 34p Alderney mail boat, 1812 .... 1.10 1.10

1986

360 9p H.M.S. *Victory* (ship of the line), H.M.S.
　　　　Rose (sloop) and *Wanta Litet*, (Swedish
　　　　sloop), 1809
361 14p H.M.S. *Orion* (ship of the line) at
　　　　Battle of the Nile, 1798
362 29p H.M.S. *Orion* engaging *Santissima
　　　　Trinidad* (Spanish ship of the line) at
　　　　Battle of St Vincent, 1797
363 31p H.M.S. *Crescent* (frigate) and
　　　　Reunion (French frigate), 1793
364 34p H.M.S. *Russell* (ship of the line)
　　　　engaging *Ville de Paris* (French ship of
　　　　the line) at Battle of the Saints, 1782
　　　　　　　　　　　　　　　　Set of 5 5.00 5.00

1987
As No. 309, but smaller, 17 × 21 mm
399† 15p Yachts 45 45

1988

415 11p *Golden Spur* (full-rigged ship) off St.
　　　　Sampson
416 15p *Golden Spur* and junk, Hong Kong
417 29p *Golden Spur*, Macao
418 31p *Golden Spur* in China tea race
419 34p *Golden Spur*, 1872
　　　　　　　　　　　　　　Set of 5 1.25 1.25

420† 16p Lihou Island mail-carrying rowing
　　　　boat 55 55
421† 16p Lihou Island mail-carrying rowing
　　　　boat 55 55
Nos. 420/1 form a composite design

429† 16p Powerboats 60 60
430† 30p Powerboats 1.10 1.10
431† 32p Powerboats and hydrofoil 1.10 1.10

1989

463 12p *Ibex* (ferry)
464 18p *Great Western* (paddle-ferry)
465 20p *St. Julien* (ferry)
466 34p *Roebuck* (ferry)
467 37p *Antelope* (ferry)
　　　　　　　　　　　　　Set of 5 3.75 3.75

1990

490† 14p Mail paddle-steamer, 1840 .... 45 45

497† 20p Anson's squadron leaving
　　　　Portsmouth, 1740 .... 60 60
498† 29p Fleet at St. Catherine's Island, Brazil 90 90
499† 34p H.M.S. *Tryal* (sloop) 95 95
500† 37p H.M.S. *Centurion* (ship of the line) at
　　　　Juan Fernandez 1.00 1.00

1991

522† 26p *Sarnia* (ferry), 1961 .... 75 75

COLLECT RAILWAYS ON STAMPS
Second revised edition of this Stanley Gibbons
thematic catalogue. Now available at £9.50
(p. + p. £3) from: Stanley Gibbons Publications,
5 Parkside, Christchurch Road, Ringwood, Hants
BH24 3SH.

524 15p "GP 14" sailing dinghy
525 21p Yachts, Guernsey Regatta
526 26p Yachts, Lombard Channel Islands
　　　　Challenge Race
527 31p Yachts, Rolex Swan Regatta
528 37p Gaff-rigged yacht
　　　　　　　　　　　　Set of 5 3.50 3.50

1992

558† 28p *Santa Maria* (Columbus) 55 60

583† 16p Building Roman ship 30 35
585† 28p Roman ship at sea 55 60
586† 33p Roman ship under attack 65 70

1993

612† 24p Parliamentary warships attacking
　　　　Castle Cornet, 1643–51 .... 50 55

POSTAGE DUE STAMPS

1977

D18 ½p Motor launches
D19 1p Motor launches
D20 2p Motor launches
D21 3p Motor launches
D22 4p Motor launches
D23 5p Motor launches
D24 6p Motor launches
D25 8p Motor launches
D26 10p Motor launches
D27 14p Motor launches
D28 15p Motor launches
D29 16p Motor launches
　　　　　　　　　　　Set of 12 2.10 2.10

1982

D33† 4p Brig at quay, 1892 .... 10 10
D40† 50p Brig at quay, 1892 .... 1.00 1.10

Alderney

1983

A5†	11p Yachts	20	25
A12†	18p *Royalist* (training ship) in Old Harbour	35	40
A12b†	21p Fishing boats, Braye Harbour	40	45
A12e†	28p *Louis Marchesi of Round Table* (lifeboat)	55	60

1987

A32	11p Wreck of *Liverpool* (full-rigged ship), 1902	
A33	15p Wreck of *Petit Raymond* (schooner), 1906	
A34	29p Wreck of *Maina* (yacht), 1910	
A35	31p Wreck of *Burton* (steamer), 1911	
A36	34p Wreck of *Point Law* (oil tanker), 1975	
	Set of 5 18.00 16.00	

1990

A42	14p H.M.S. *Alderney* (bomb ketch), 1738	
A43	20p H.M.S. *Alderney* (frigate), 1742	
A44	29p H.M.S. *Alderney* (sloop), 1755	
A45	34p H.M.S. *Alderney* (submarine), 1945	
A46	37p H.M.S. *Alderney* (patrol vessel), 1979	
	Set of 6 4.00 4.00	

1991

A47†	21p Wreck of H.M.S. *Victory*, 1744	50	50
A48†	26p Rowing boat	60	60
A51†	50p *Patricia* (Trinity House vessel)	1.40	1.40

1992

A52	23p Two French warships on fire, Battle of La Hogue, 1692	
A53	28p Burning ships	
A54	33p French warship sinking	
A55	50p Battle of La Hogue	
	Set of 4 2.40 2.50	

GUINEA

West Africa
1959 100 centimes = 1 franc
1973 100 caury = 1 syli
1986 100 centimes = 1 franc

1959

201†	1f Local fishing boats	10	10
202†	2f Local fishing boats	10	10
203†	3f Local fishing boats	10	10
204†	5f Dhow	15	15
205†	10f Pirogue	15	10

1974

843†	4s Bulk carrier loading bauxite	50	15

861†	10s Liner	1.25	60
MS862†	Two sheets. (a) 10s Pirogue (other sheet shows space satellite)		
	Price for 2 sheets	10.00	10.00

1982

1049†	7s River craft	95	35

1984

1136†	5s Congo river steamer and canoe	60	20

1985

1152†	10s "Flying Dutchman" class yacht	95	40

1172†	10s Fleet of Columbus	1.25	40

1217	10s *Pinta* (Columbus)	
1218	20s *Santa Maria* (Columbus)	
1219	30s *Nina* (Columbus) (air)	
1220	40s *Santa Maria* (Columbus)	
	Set of 4 9.75 3.25	
MS1221	50s *Nina* (Columbus) 3.75 4.00	

1986

Nos. 1217/MS1221 *surcharged*

1242†	5f on 10s *Pinta*	15	10
1243†	35f on 20s *Santa Maria*	25	15
1244†	70f on 30s *Nina* (air)	55	20
1245†	200f on 40s *Santa Maria*	1.50	65
MS1246†	500f on 50s *Nina*	2.40	2.50

1989

MS1387†	750f Sailing dinghy	3.00	75

1396†	100f Fishing canoe	40	10

1991

1436†	100f *Bismarck* (German battleship)	40	10
1437†	150f U.S.S *Yorktown* (aircraft carrier), 1942	55	15
1438†	200f American torpedo boat and D.U.K.W.S., Guadalcanal	75	20
1441†	450f *Yamato* (Japanese battleship) (air)	1.75	45

GUINEA-BISSAU

West Africa
100 centavos = 1 peso

1976

482† 2p *Agamemnon* laying Atlantic cable,
1876 .... 15 10

1981

676 3p50 Viking ship (Eric the Red)
677 5p *Sao Gabriel* (Vasco da Gama)
678 6p *Victoria* (Magellan)
679 30p *Emerillon* (Cartier)
680 35p *Golden Hind* (Drake) (air)
681 40p H.M.S. *Endeavour* (Cook)
          Set of 6 7.50 4.00
MS682 50p *Santa Maria* (Columbus) 4.00 3.25

1982

701† 35p Scout canoes 2.25 90

1983

MS775 50p Portuguese caravel 3.00 3.25

779† 5p Cable ship 40 10
781† 20p Sinking steamship 1.10 40

1984

845† 15p Olympic yachts 50 15
MS850† 100p Sailboard 5.00 5.50

1985

933† 80p Red Cross rescue boat 1.40 55

950 8p *Santa Maria* (Columbus)
951 15p 16th-century Dutch carrack
952 20p *Mayflower* (Pilgrim Fathers)
953 30p *St Louis* (French galleon)
954 35p *Royal Sovereign* (galleon), 1660
955 45p *Soleil Royal* (17th-century French
        warship)
956 80p 18th-century British naval brig
          Set of 7 4.75 1.60

1987

992† 50p *Santa Maria* (Columbus) 2.00 60
993† 50p Galley, Seville, 1492 .... 2.00 60
995† 50p Shipping, Seville, 1492 .... 2.00 60
MS996† 150p 15th-century galleon, Lisbon .. 2.50 1.25

1988

1013† 5p Yacht 10 10

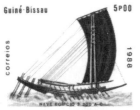

1052 5p Egyptian ship, 3300 B.C.
1053 10p Ship of Sahu Re, 2500 B.C.
1054 50p Ship of Hatshepshut, 1500 B.C.
1055 200p Ship of Rameses III, 1200 B.C.
1056 300p Greek trireme, 480 B.C.
1057 500p Etruscan bireme, 600 B.C.
1058 800p 12th-century Venetian galley
          Set of 7 3.50 1.60

1992

1240 750p Canoe
1241 800p Pirogue
1242 1000p Pirogue
1243 1300p Skiff
          Set of 4 1.25 55

GUYANA

South America
100 cents = 1 dollar

1966

No. 344 *of British Guiana overprinted* **GUYANA**
INDEPENDENCE 1966
406† $2 Gold dredger 1.50 75

1969

502† 30c Building *Independence* (World's first
aluminium ship) 20 10

1974

606† 8c *Sandbach* (on British Guiana stamp
No. 78) 20 10
608† 40c *Sandbach* (on British Guiana stamp
No. 78) 30 20

1983

1071 $4.80 *Sandbach* (sail merchantman) 4.50 5.50

1127 30c *Kurupukari* (river vessel)
1128 60c *Makouria* (river vessel)
1129 120c *Powis* (river vessel)
1130 130c *Pomeroon* (river vessel)
1131 150c *Lukanani* (river vessel)
          Set of 5 2.50 2.40

1985

1550†150c *Den Arendt* (slave ship), 1627
　(lilac backgrourd) 60 55
See also No. 2555

1986

1744†320c *Sandbach* (on British Guiana
　stamp No. 253) 75 60

1987

No. 1744 overprinted **CAPEX '87**
2185†320c *Sandbach* (on British Guiana
　stamp No. 253) 40 45

As No. 1744 in miniature sheet surcharged **THE PASSING OF HALLEY'S COMET: PROPHESY OF THE ARRIVAL OF HERNANCORTES 1519. V CENTENARY OF THE LANDING OF CHRISTOPHER COLUMBUS IN THE AMERICAS $20.00.**
MS2224 $20 on $6.40 *Sandbach* (on British
Guiana stamp No. 253) 5.00 5.25

1988

As No. 1550, but background colour changed.
2555 150c *Den Arendt* (slave ship), 1627 (blue
　background) 20 25

1989

Nos. 1744 and 2185 surcharged **TEN DOLLARS $10.00**
2586†$10 on 320c *Sandbach* (on British
　Guiana stamp No. 253) (No. 1744) 1.25 1.40
2588†$10 on 320c *Sandbach* (on British
　Guiana stamp No. 253) (No. 2185) 1.10 1.40

1990

2695†$15.30 Dutch mail schooner 15 20
2696†$15.30 *Monarch* (paddle-steamer), 1830 15 20
2697†$15.30 *Hindoostan* (paddle-steamer),
　1842 .... 15 20
2698†$15.30 *Chusan I* (screw steamer), 1860 15 20
2699†$15.30 *Madagascar* (sail
　merchantman), 1853 .... 15 20
2700†$15.30 *Orinoco* (mail paddle-steamer),
　1855 .... 15 20
2701†$15.30 *Orpheus* (sailing packet) 15 20
2721†$17.80 Rowing boat 20 25
2722†$17.80 *Arctic* (paddle-steamer), 1850 .... 20 25

EXPRESS LETTER STAMPS

1986

As No. 1744 in miniature sheet surcharged **EXPRESS $20.00**
E3†　$20 on $6.40 *Sandbach* (on British
　Guiana stamp No. 253) 4.50 4.50

1987

No. E3 additionally overprinted with small Maltese Cross
E5　$20 on $6.40 *Sandbach* (on British Guiana
　stamp No. 253) 4.00 4.00

No. 1744 in horizontal pair imperforate between with further 320c value surcharged **EXPRESS FORTY DOLLARS** *and star*
E10　$40 on $6.40 *Sandbach* (on British
　Guiana stamp No. 253) 8.00 8.00

1989

Nos. 1744 and 2185, each in horizontal pair imperforate between with further 320c value, surcharged **EXPRESS FORTY DOLLARS** *without star*
E14　$40 on $6.40 *Sandbach* (on British
　Guiana stamp No. 253) (No. 1744)
E15　$40 on $6.40 *Sandbach* (on British
　Guiana stamp (No. 253) (No. 2185)
　　　　　　　　　　　　Set of 2 3.00 3.50

GWALIOR

Indian sub-continent
12 pies = 1 anna
16 annas = 1 rupee

1938

No. 256 of India overprinted **GWALIOR** *in English and Hindi*
111†　6a *Strathnaver* (liner) 2.25 4.25

HAITI

West Indies
100 centimes = 1 gourde

1943

358　3c *Crete-a-Pierrot* (gunboat), 1902
359　5c *Crete-a-Pierrot*
360　10c *Crete-a-Pierrot*
361　25c *Crete-a-Pierrot*
362　50c *Crete-a-Pierrot*
363　5g *Crete-a-Pierrot*
364　60c *Crete-a-Pierrot* (air)
365　1g25 *Crete-a-Pierrot*
　　　　　　　Set of 8 14.00 7.00

1950

443†　30c Fleet of Columbus 2.25 55

1956

541†　50c Liner 70 15
543†　75c Liner 85 45

1961

764†　20c Pirate ships attacking galleon 30 10
765†　50c Galleon 60 20
766†　20c Pirate ships attacking galleon (air,
　　inscr "AVION") 30 10
767†　50c Galleon (inscr "AVION") 60 20

No. 543 overprinted **Dr. F. Duvalier President 22 Mai 1961**
775†　75c Liner 35 30

1965

929　10c *Likala* (freighter)
930　50c *Likala* (freighter)
931　50c *Likala* (freighter) (air)
932　1g50 *likala* (freighter)
　　　　　　　Set of 4 1.75 70

1978

1383†　5g Olympic yachts 1.40 1.10

1982

1453　25c Freighter in port
1454　50c Freighter in port
1455　1g Freighter in port
1456　1g25 Freighter in port
1457　2g Freighter in port
1458　5g Freighter in port
　　　　　　　Set of 6 4.00 2.00

Nos. 1453 and 1455/7 overprinted **1957 - 1982 25 ANS DE REVOLUTION**
1459　25c Freighter in port
1460　1g Freighter in port
1461　1g25 Freighter in port
1462　2g Freighter in port
　　　　　　　Set of 4 1.40 1.25

1983

1465†　25c Fishing boats 25 10
1467†　75c Fishing boats (air) 65 20
1469†　1g25 Fishing boats 90 30

1986

No. 1467 surcharged **G.O.25**
1549†　25c on 75c Fishing boats 10 10

HAWAII

South Pacific
100 cents = 1 dollar

1894

81　12c *Arawa* (early steamer) 9.00 9.00

HONDURAS

Central America
1931 100 centavos = 1 peso
1933 100 centavos = 1 lempira

1931

321†	5c Steamer on Lake Yojoa	. . . .	55	10

No. 321 *overprinted* **T. S. de C**

330†	5c Steamer on Lake Yojoa	. . . .	50	25

1972

808†	1le Fishing boat, Trujillo Bay	. . . .	1.75	90

1976

890†	5c Continental Navy warships, 1776	. . . .	30	15

1986

1052†	85c Yacht	. . . .	1.50	60

1988

MS1084	3le 18th-century Spanish mail packet	2.25	1.40

1990

1117†	20c *Santa Maria* (Columbus)	. . . .	20	10

HONG KONG

South-east coast of China
100 cents = 1 dollar

1941

164†	4c *Empress of Japan* (liner) and junk	. . . .	2.25	1.00
168†	$1 *Falcon* (sailing clipper)	. . . .	10.00	4.25

1949

As No. 115 *of Antigua*

174†	20c Paddle-steamer	. . . .	4.75	60

1968

247	10c *Iberia* (liner)		
248	20c Pleasure launch		
249	40c Car ferry		
250	50c Passenger ferry		
251	$1 Sampan		
252	$1.30 Junk		
		Set of 6 17.00	8.00

1972

278	$1 Junk	. . . .	2.00	1.50

1975

332†	$1 Dragon boat	. . . .	1.50	2.00

1977

365†	60c Ferry boat	. . . .	1.00	1.50
367†	$2 Junk and sampan	. . . .	1.25	2.50

ALBUM LISTS

Write for our latest list of albums and accessories.
This will be sent on request.

1982

407	20c Junks, Victoria harbour, 1855			
408	$1 Junks at West Point, 1847			
409	$1.30 Junks			
410	$2 *Queen Elizabeth 2* (liner)			
		Set of 4	1.75	2.25

1983

439†	$1 *Liverpool Bay* (container ship)	. . . . . .	60	90

445†	$5 *Jumbo* (floating restaurant)	. . . .	3.00	4.25

1984

454	40c 19th-century sail frigate			
455	$1 Topsail schooner			
456	$1.30 Sailing clipper			
457	$5 19th-century sail frigate			
		Set of 4	3.00	6.00

1985

488	40c Dragon boat prow			
489	$1 Dragon boat drummer and rowers			
490	$1.30 Dragon boat rowers			
491	$5 Dragon boat stern			
		Set of 4	1.90	3.50

1986

519†	$1.70 Container ship	. . . .	70	85

521	50c Fishing sampan			
522	$1 Stern trawler			
523	$1.70 Fishing junk			
524	$5 Junk trawler			
		Set of 4	2.75	4.00

1987

535† $1.30 Boat dwellings, Kowloon, 1838 .... 50 35

613† $10 Junk and container ship, Victoria 1.75 2.00

1988

577† 50c Ferry and yachts 30 10

1990

648† $1.40 *Jumbo* (floating restaurant) 50 20

657† $5 Junk and container ship 1.10 1.40

1991

669† $1.70 Harbour ferry 40 50
672† $5 Jetfoil 1.25 1.75

1992

691† 80c Launch from Royal Yacht *Britannia*
and ferries 15 15

1993

742† $1.80 Freighters at anchor, 1963 .... 30 35
744† $5 Coastal tanker, 1992 .... 80 85

HUNGARY

Central Europe
1926 100 filler = 1 pengo
1946 100 filler = 1 forint

1926

471† 32f Danube steamer 3.25 15
472† 40f Danube steamer 5.00 15

1928

502 30f Danube steamer
503 32f Danube steamer
504 40f Danube steamer
505 46f Danube steamer
506 50f Danube steamer
Set of 5 9.25 65

1941

705† 20f River steamer, Straits of Kazan 15 10
707† 40f River steamer, Straits of Kazan 45 15

1947

988† 20fi Paddle-steamer, Esztergom 15 10

993† 3fo *Falcone* (racing yacht) 2.75 25

1948

1028† 2fi *Santa Maria* (Columbus) 20 15
1029† 4fi *Clermont* (first commercial
paddle-steamer) and *Queen Mary*
(liner) 20 15
1034† 12fi *Fram* (Amundsen) 60 30

1949

1078 50fi Paddle-steamer 5.00 5.00

1950

1092† 3fo Freighter 2.50 20

1136† 1fo60 Freighter 75 10

1953

1287† 1fo Sailing dinghies, Lake Balaton 35 15

1955

1447† 2fo *Beke* (freighter) 1.75 65

1958

1547† 2fo Paddle-steamer, tug and barges,
Budapest 50 10

1959

1553† 20fi Oceanographic research ship 55 10

1569† 2fo *Kisfaludy* (Lake Balaton steamer) .. 70 15

1590†	30fi Kek Madar (yacht)	20	10
1594†	2fo Beloiannis (Lake Balaton steamer)	75	15
1596†	70fi Tihany (water bus) (air)	20	10
1598†	1fo70 Saturnus (yacht)	70	30

1960

| 1683† | 10fi Greek galley | 10 | 10 |

1961

| 1757† | 2fo + 1fo Racing yachts | 65 | 60 |

1963

| 1899† | 10fi Snow White (Danube steamer) | 10 | 10 |

1921	20fi Lake passenger launch		
1922	40fi Beloiannis (lake steamer)		
1923	60fi Yacht		
	Set of 3	1.75	40

1964

2026†	60fi Paddle-steamer, Budapest	30	10
2027†	1fo River steamer, Budapest	55	10
2028†	1fo50 Paddle-steamer, Budapest	75	15
2029†	2fo River freighter, Budapest	1.00	25
2030†	2fo50 Paddle-tug and barges, Budapest	2.00	1.00
MS2030a†	10fo Sirali I (hydrofoil)	4.50	5.00

1965

| 2103 | 1fo + 50fi Flood rescue boat | 1.00 | 1.00 |
| MS2104 | 10fo + 5fo Flood rescue boat | 2.75 | 3.50 |

1966

| 2182 | 1fo Johann Baptist (paddle-tug) | 50 | 15 |
| 2183 | 2fo Rakoczi (passenger vessel) | 90 | 35 |

1967

2275	30fi Ferenc Deak (Danube paddle-steamer)		
2276	60fi Rcvfulop (river bus)		
2277	1fo Hunyadi (Danube passenger vessel)		
2278	1fo50 Szekszard (tug)		
2279	1fo70 Miscolc (tug)		
2280	2fo Tihany (freighter)		
2281	2fo50 Sirali I (hydrofoil)		
	Set of 7	21.00	7.00

1968

2365†	20fi Lake Balaton steamer	15	10
2365a†	40fi Lake Balaton steamer	15	10
2367†	1fo Yachts	20	10

1972

| 2719† | 1fo 19th-century river steamer | 30 | 10 |
| 2720† | 1fo Hydrofoil | 30 | 10 |

| 2743† | 4fo River steamer, Esztergom | 80 | 10 |

1973

| 2806† | 4fo Paddle-steamer, tug and barges, Budapest (on stamp No. 1547) | 95 | 35 |

1975

| 2937† | 80fi Canoe | 20 | 10 |
| 2938† | 1fo20 Freighter | 30 | 10 |

| MS2983 | 2fo + 1fo Galley, Visegrad, 1480 (sheet also contains three other designs) | 8.00 | 9.00 |

1977

| MS3160 | 2fo × 11 Various Danube ships | 12.00 | 12.00 |

1978

| MS3197 | Two sheets. (a) 2fo × 4 Viking longship (Leif Eriksson); Santa Maria (Columbus); Sao Gabriel (Vasco da Gama); Vitoria (Magellan). (b) 2fo × 4 Golden Hind (Drake); Discoverie (Hudson); H.M.S. Resolution (Cook); Roosevelt (Peary) | | |
| | Set of 2 sheets | 6.50 | 6.50 |

1979

| 3263 | 3fo Calypso (Cousteau) | 65 | 15 |

1980

3305†	3fo Galley, Rhodes	55	15
3306†	4fo Pharaonic ship, Alexandria	75	20
3307†	5fo Nile river boat, Egypt	1.75	60

| 3350† | 40fi Harbour steamer, New York | 15 | 10 |

1981

3367†	2fo *Malygin* (icebreaker)	45	10

3399   1fo *Franz I* (Danube paddle-steamer), 1830, and *Ferenc Deak* (on stamp No. 2275)
3400   1fo *Arpad* (paddle-steamer), 1834, and *Revfulop* (on stamp No. 2276)
3401   2fo *Szechenyi* (paddle-steamer), 1855, and *Hunyadi* (on stamp No. 2277)
3402   2fo *Grof Szechenyi Istvan* (paddle-steamer), 1896, and *Szekszard* (on stamp No. 2278)
3403   4fo *Zsofia* (paddle-steamer), 1914, and *Miscolc* (on stamp No. 2279)
3404   6fo *Felszabadulas* (paddle-steamer), 1917, and *Tihany* (on stamp No. 2280)
3405   8fo *Rakoczi* (passenger vessel), 1964, and *Sirali I* (on stamp No. 2281)

	Set of 7	5.00	4.50
MS3406	20fo *Solyom* (hydrofoil) and *Hunyadi* (on stamp No. 2277)	5.00	5.00

1983

3516†	4fo + 2fo Danube houseboats	1.25	1.25

3532†	1fo Yacht, Zanka	30	10

1984

3577†	2fo Danube river boat	40	20
3578†	4fo River tanker	60	30
3581†	8fo Tug and barges	1.25	50

1985

3608†	1fo Danube river steamer	20	10
3609†	1fo Danube passenger launch	20	10
3610†	2fo Hydrofoil	40	15
3611†	2fo River launch	40	15
3612†	4fo River launch	70	30
3613†	6fo River launch	95	50

1986

3707	2fo *Vasa* (Swedish warship), 1628	2.00	1.50

1987

3777†	5fo Cabin cruisers, Toronto	1.25	1.00

3783†	2fo H.M.S. *Resolution* (Cook)	60	30
3787†	4fo *Terra Nova* (Scott)	90	45

1988

3845   2fo *Santa Maria* (Columbus)
3846   2fo *Mayflower*, (Pilgrim Fathers), 1620
3847   2fo *Sovereign of the Seas*, 1637
3848   4fo *Jylland* (steam warship), 1860
3849   6fo *St. Jupat* (yacht), 1985

	Set of 5	4.50	2.25

1991

4063   7fo *Matthew* (Cabot)
4064   12fo Galleon (Amerigo Vespucci)
4065   12fo Galleon and caravel (Cortes)
4066   15fo *Vitoria* (Magellan)
4067   20fo Galleons (Pizzaro)

	Set of 5	4.75	2.25

1992

4086†	10fo Caravels	75	30
4087†	10fo *Santa Maria* (Columbus)	75	30
4088†	15fo Caravel	1.25	55

ICELAND

North Atlantic
100 aurar = 1 krona

1930

159†	5a Viking longship	1.50	4.25
161†	10a Viking longship	6.00	8.00

175†	20a Icelandic fishing boat	20.00	40.00

1933

201†	10a + 10a Shipwreck and breeches-buoy	1.60	3.25
203†	35a + 25a Shipwreck and breeches-buoy	1.60	3.25

1939

239†	35a Viking longship	2.75	5.25

1940

No. 239 overprinted **1940**

258†	35a Viking longship	8.75	18.00

1949

291†	75a + 25a Freighter and ship's lifeboat	90	1.10

1950

297†	10a *Ingolfur Arnarson* (trawler)	20	10
299†	25a *Ingolfur Arnarson*	30	10
304†	1k25 *Ingolfur Arnarson*	15.00	10
305†	1k50 *Ingolfur Arnarson*	13.00	10

1953

No. 304 surcharged **Hollandshjalp 1953 +25**

318†	1k25 + 25a *Ingolfur Amarson*	1.60	3.50

1961

384 2k50 *Gullfoss* (cargo liner)
385 4k50 *Gullfoss*

| | | Set of 2 | 70 | 20 |

1963

401 5k *Huni* (herring trawler)
402 7k50 *Huni*

| | | Set of 2 | 1.10 | 40 |

1964

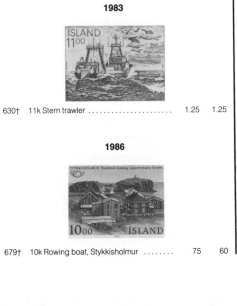

408 10k *Gullfoss* (cargo liner) 1.25 1.00

1973

506† 20k *Esja* (mail steamer) 10 10

1978

567 60k Wreck of *Sargon* (trawler) and
     breeches-buoy 30 15

1983

630† 11k Stern trawler 1.25 1.25

1986

679† 10k Rowing boat, Stykkisholmur 75 60

684† 12k *La Reine Hortense* (French warship),
      Reykjavik, 1856 . . . . 70 40

1987

692 50k *Svanur* (19th-century ketch) 3.00 1.75

MS706 30k Schooner, Djupivogur, 1836 . . . . . . 2.00 2.00

1988

725† 24k Trawler 90 90

1989

730† 21k Toy yachts 40 40

MS736 30k Whaling ship floating barrels at
       whales; 30k Ship harpooning whale; 30k
       16th-century ship encircled by sea serpent . . 2.00 2.00

1990

MS760 40k 16th-century sailing ship and map
       of Denmark; 40k 16th-century sailing ship and
       map of Baltic; 40k 16th-century sailing ship
       and map of Gotland 2.50 2.50

1991

MS771 50k 16th-century ship and map of
       Western Iceland; 50k Two 16th-century ships
       and map of Central Iceland (sheet also
       contains one other 50k design) 3.25 3.25

777 30k *Soloven* (mail brigantine)
778 30k *Arcturus* (cargo liner)
779 30k *Gullfoss I* (cargo liner)
780 30k *Esja II* (cargo liner)

| | | Set of 4 | 2.75 | 2.75 |

1992

785 55k Viking ship (Leif Eriksson)
786 55k *Santa Maria* (Columbus)

| | | Set of 2 | 3.25 | 3.00 |

789† 35k Trawler 85 75

OFFICIAL STAMPS
1930

Nos. 159 *and* 161 *overprinted* **Pjonustumerki**
O175† 5a Viking longship 8.50 26.00
O177† 10a Viking longship 8.50 26.00

IFNI

North-west Africa
100 centimos = 1 peseta

1959

149† 50c + 10c Moroccan fishing boats 15 10

1961

182† 25c + 10c Freighter at wharf 10 10
184† 1p + 10c Freighter at wharf 15 10

1967

227 1p50 Bulk carrier and floating crane 20 10

INDIA

Southern Asia
1937 12 pies = 1 anna
16 annas = 1 rupee
1957 10 naye paisa = 1 rupee
1964 100 paisa = 1 rupee

1937

256†   6a *Strathnaver* (liner) 8.50   40

1954

350†   4a Liner 2.00   15

1965

498   15p *Jalausha* (freighter)   30   30

518†   2r Kashmiri boat, Lake Dal 2.00   10

1966

527   15p *Mysore* (cruiser)   40   30

1968

577   20p *Nilgiri* (frigate)   70   40

1969

591   20p 19th-century sail warships   20   20

599   20p *Ajanta* (bulk carrier)   60   30

1970

622   20p Dredger and pilot vessel   40   30

1972

663   20p Liner   30   30

1977

844   25p *Loyalty* (liner)   40   40

862   3r *Ranchi* (liner) at wharf, Bombay 2.00   2.50

1978

876   1r Kashmiri boat, Lake Dal 1.50   1.25

1981

1029   35p *Taragiri* (frigate) 1.25   85

1982

1049   1r *Sagar Samrat* (oil rig)   30   30

1065   2r Yachts   25   30

1983

1085   2r H.M.S. *Beagle* (Charles Darwin) 1.00   1.50

1984

1115†   1r *Vikrant* (aircraft carrier)   30   50
1116†   1r *Vela* (submarine)   30   50
1117†   1r *Kashin* (destroyer)   30   50

1986

1181   2r50 Landing craft and patrol boat, Bombay Naval Dockyard 1.75   1.75

1184   2r *Vikrant* (aircraft carrier) 2.25   2.25

1987

1227   6r50 *Trishna* (yacht), 1985 ....   2.75   2.00

1989

1365   6r50 Indian Navy task force 1.25   1.00

1990

1433†   6r 18th-century shipping on the Ganges   45   50

1992

1500†	4r Surfboards	20	25
1501†	5r Inflatable dinghy	45	50

INDIAN FORCES IN INDO-CHINA

South-east Asia
100 paisa = 1 rupee

1968

No. 518 of India overprinted **ICC** *in English and Devanagari*

N57	2r Kashmiri boat, Lake Dal	1.00	4.50

INDO-CHINA

South-east Asia
100 cents = 1 piastre

1931

As No. 109 of Cameroun

162†	10c on 1f50 *Leconte de Lisle* (liner)	2.50	1.40

163†	1/10c Junk	15	25
164†	1/5c Junk	15	20
165†	2/5c Junk	15	30
166†	½c Junk	20	25
167†	4/5c Junk	20	30
168†	1c Junk	20	15
169†	2c Junk	25	15

OFFICIAL STAMPS

1933

Nos. 168/9 overprinted **SERVICE**

O197†	1c Junk	50	30
O198†	2c Junk	50	35

INDONESIA

South-east Asia
100 sen = 1 rupiah

1961

852†	10s Ambonese boat	20	10

1963

981†	25r Yachts	15	10

1964

999†	1r75 *Hadji Agus Salim* (freighter)	15	10
1001†	2r50 Buginese sailing boat	15	10
1006†	15r *Sam Ratulangi* (freighter)	25	10

1019	20r *Sandjaja* and *Siliwanghi* (destroyers)		
1020	30r *Nanggala* (submarine)		
1021	40r *Matjan Tutul* (torpedo-boat)		
	Set of 3	75	30

1965

No. 1006 overprinted **'65 Sen**

1075†	(15)s on 15r *Sam Ratulangi* (freighter)	25	10

1966

1121†	1r50 Madurese sailing boat	30	10
1124†	3r Liner in dry dock	60	15

1968

1210†	7r50 Olympic yachts (face value bottom right)	10	10
1211†	7r50 Olympic yachts (face value top right)	10	10

1973

1346	40r Motor torpedo-boat, Battle of Arafura	1.40	45

1974

1389†	100r East Indies galley	1.10	60

1975

1398†	130r Tanker	1.00	55
1400†	200r Oil rig	1.75	95

1980

1562	60r Pinisi sailing ship		
1563	125r Schooner		
1564	150r Madurese sailing boat		
	Set of 3	2.00	85
MS1565	300r Schooner	2.00	1.75

MS1578	500r Pinisi sailing ship	3.00	2.75

1984

1736†	110r Hull on slipway	40	20

1985

1772	50r *Tyro* (oceanographic survey ship)		
1773	100r *Tyro*		
1774	275r *Tyro*		
	Set of 3	1.40	75

1796†	350r Sailboards	1.10	65

1798†	140r Tanker	45	20
1800†	350r Oil rig	1.00	65

1986

1814†	75r Pinisi sailing ship	15	10

1988

1873	140r Oil rig		
1874	400r Trawler		
	Set of 2	65	40

1908	350r Cargo liner	40	20

1990

1971†	1000r Freighter and lighthouse	90	40

IRAN

Western Asia
100 dinars = 1 rial

1935

735†	90d *Palang* (gunboat)	4.00	70

1949

905†	50d Freighters, Bandar Shahpur	1.60	30

1954

1053†	10r Ancient Persian galley	60.00	28.00

1969

1583	8r Oil rig	70	15

1970

1613	8r Tankers *Yowa Maru, Bergetun, Beau, Japan Jasmin, Barbara, Isomeria, Esso Newcastle, British Glory, Katrine Maersk,* and one unidentified, Kharg Island	80	30

1974

1917	10r *Palang* (destroyer)	65	20

1986

2355†	10r *Paykan* (missile boat)	30	15

1987

2397	10r Freighter	30	15

2406†	25r Armed launch	60	40

1989

2510†	20r Container ships	45	30

2520†	30r Weather ship	60	35

2564†	10r People's Militia launch with machine gun	30	15

1991

2623†	100r Sinking ship	2.00	1.10

IRAQ

Western Asia
1918 16 annas = 1 rupee
1931 1000 fils = 1 dinar

1918
No. 508 of Turkey surcharged **IRAQ IN BRITISH OCCUPATION 6An.**

8†	6a on 2pi *Hamidiye* (cruiser)	1.25	1.25

1923

42†	1a Gufas, River Tigris	20	10

1963

620†	1f Gufas, River Tigris	20	10
622†	3f Gufas	25	10

1965

672	10f Oil tanker	55	15

1967

760†	10f Freighter loading at Um Qasr	45	20
761†	15f Freighter loading at Um Qasr	75	20

1969

852	15f *Antara* (floating crane)		
853	20f *Al-Walid* (harbour tender)		
854	30f *Al-Rashid* (pilot boat)		
855	35f *Hillah* (dredger)		
856	50f *Al-Fao* (survey ship)		
	Set of 5	3.50	1.25

1971

940†	5f Marsh canoe	20	10

1976

1268†	10f *Rumaila* (tanker)	35	10
1269†	15f *Rumaila*	45	15

1981

1507	50f *Ibn Khaldoon* (freighter)		
1508	120f *Ibn Khaldoon* (freighter)		
	Set of 2	2.75	1.40

1987

1753	50f *Al Alwah* (freighter)		
1754	100f *Khaled Ibn Al Waleed* (container ship)		
1755	150f *Al Alwah*		
1756	250f *Khaled Ibn Al Waleed*		
	Set of 4	3.75	2.25
MS1757	200f *Khaled Ibn Al Waleed* at wharf	1.75	2.00

1763†	40f Missile boat	25	15
1765†	100f Missile boat	65	35

1988

1832†	90f Missile boats	40	20
1834†	150f Missile boats	70	30

1989

MS1886†	250f *Khawla* (container ship)	1.25	75

1892†	100f Marsh Arab punt	45	20

1893	50f Container ship		
1894	100f Container ship		
1895	150f Liner		
	Set of 3	1.50	70

OFFICIAL STAMPS

1920

No. 8 overprinted **ON STATE SERVICE**

O25†	6a on 2pi *Hamidiye* (cruiser)	4.00	2.00

1923

No. 42 overprinted **ON STATE SERVICE** *in English only*

O55†	1a Gufas, River Tigris	50	10

1924

No. 42 overprinted **ON STATE SERVICE** *in English and Arabic*

O67†	1a Gufas, River Tigris	38.00	28.00

OBLIGATORY TAX

No. 620 surcharged

T931†	5f on 1f Gufas, River Tigris	1.75	2.00

IRELAND

Western Europe
1970 12 pence = 1 shilling
20 shillings = 1 pound
1971 100 pence = 1 pound

1970

279	4d 18th-century yachts	15	10

1974

336	5p Daunt Island lightship and Ballycotton lifeboat, 1936	30	30

1976

398	15p Lobster boat	50	50

1979

457†	13p *William Cory* (cable ship), 1866	40	1.10

1981

477†	25p Holland submarine, 1878	45	85

1982

524 22p *St. Patrick* (Galway hooker)
525 22p *Currach*
526 26p *Asgard II* (cadet brigantine)
527 29p "Howth" 17-foot yacht

Set of 4   3.25   4.00

1985

606† 26p 18th-century fishing boats, Cork   60   30

1986

639† 24p Canal barges, Robertstown 1.00   1.00
641† 30p Motor cruiser on Lough Derg 1.50   2.25

642 24p *Severn* (19th-century paddle-
       steamer)
643 28p *Leinster* (modern ferry)

Set of 2   1.60   1.40

1988

696† 24p *Sirius* (paddle-steamer), 1838   75   50

703† 28p *Eithne* (helicopter patrol vessel)   75   85

706† 46p *Duquesa Santa Ana* (Spanish
       Armada galleon), 1588 . . . .   1.50   1.25

1989

732 28p *NCB Ireland* (yacht) 1.00   1.00

1991

819 28p Trawlers in shipyard
820 32p Inshore trawlers
821 44p Lobster fishing boat
822 52p *Veronica* (fish factory ship)

Set of 4   3.50   4.00

1992

835† 44p Yachts 1.10   1.25

837 32p *Mari* (14th-century cog)
838 52p *Ovoca* (trawler)

Set of 2   2.25   2.25

844 32p Fleet of Columbus
845 44p Fleet of Columbus

Set of 2   2.10   2.10

ISLE OF MAN

North-west Europe
100 pence = 1 pound

1973

12† ½p Motor cruisers, Castletown   10   10
18† 3½p Fishing boats, Port St. Mary   15   15
27† 9p *Ben-my-Chree*, *Mona's Queen* and
      Manxman (ferries) in Douglas Bay   30   35
33† £1 Viking longship 3.25   3.25

34 15p Viking longship, 938   80   80

1974

43† 3½p Wreck of *St. George* (paddle-
       steamer), 1830   15   15
44† 8p *Manchester and Salford* (lifeboat),
       1868   60   65
45† 10p *Osman Gabriel* (lifeboat)   60   65

51† 4½p King Edgar's royal barge, *c*. 970   10   10
52† 8p Viking fleet, 974   40   40

1975

62† 10p *William T. Graves* (19th-century
       steamship) 1.00   1.00

70† 12p River steamer on Niger 1.00   1.00

1978

107† 6p H.M.S. *Ben-my-Chree* (seaplane
       tender), 1915   15   15
108† 7p H.M.S. *Vindex* (seaplane tender),
       1915   20   20

123† 16p Ferry passing Douglas Head   75   65
127† £1 Viking longship 2.50   2.50

1979

158 15p *Odin's Raven* (replica Viking ship)   50   50

159† 6p 18th-century frigate 15 15
161† 13p H.M.S. *Spencer* (ship of the line) 50 40

1980

170 7p *Mona's Isle I* (paddle-steamer)
171 8p *Douglas I* (paddle-steamer)
172 11½p H.M.S. *Mona's Queen* (paddle-steamer) sinking U-boat
173 12p H.M.S. *King Orry III* (requisitioned ferry) leading German destroyers, surrender of High Seas Fleet, 1918
174 13p *Ben-my-Chree IV* (ferry)
175 15p *Lady of Man II* (ferry)
Set of 6   1.75   1.60

179 12p *Norge* (Norwegian royal yacht) and sail-training ships 50 50

183† 7p *Robert Quayle* (brig), 1819 .... 20 20

1981

190 8p Luggers, Douglas
191 9p *Wanderer* (lugger) rescuing survivors from *Lusitania* (liner)
192 18p *Nickey* (fishing boat), Port St. Mary
193 20p *Nobby* (fishing boat), Ramsey
194 22p *Sunbeam* and *Zebra* (Nickey fishing boats), Port Erin
Set of 5   2.00   1.75

196† 18p Fishing lugger 55 55

198† 20p 18th-century British warship, Madras 50 50

1982

208† 20p *Tynwald IV* (ferry) passing wreck of *King Orry*, Dunkirk, 1940 .... 60 50

223 12p *Mona I* (paddle-steamer)
224 19½p *Manx Maid II* (ferry)
Set of 2   1.00   1.00

1983

251† 10p *Three Legs of Man III* (trimaran) 30 30

1984

259 10p *Manx King* (full-rigged sailing ship)
260 13p *Hope* (barque)
261 20½p *Rio Grande* (brig)
262 28p *Lady Elizabeth* (barque)
263 31p *Sumatra* (barque)
Set of 5   3.00   3.00
MS264 28p *Lady Elizabeth* (as stamp No. 262), 31p As wreck (on Falkland Islands stamp No. 417) 2.75   2.75

275† 22p *Anna* (full-rigged ship), 1852 ...... 65 65

1986

313 26p Model of Viking longship 95 95

315† 2p Viking longship 25 25

322† 15p *Mayflower* (Pilgrim Fathers) 55 55
323† 31p *Mayflower* (Pilgrim Fathers) 1.10   1.10

1987

334† 2p Brigantine, North Quay, Douglas 10 10
336† 10p 19th-century yachts, Douglas Bay .. 35 35

340 12p Brig, Douglas, 1899
341 26p Fishing boats, Douglas, 1900
342 29p Brigantine, Peel, 1906
343 34p Fishing boats, Peel, 1909
Set of 4   3.25   3.25

1988

368† 5p *Ben-my-Chree* and *Viking* (ferries), Douglas 10 10

381† 13p *Flex Service 3* (cable ship) and cable 50 50
382† 13p *Flex Service 3* 50 50

385 16p *Euterpe* (full-rigged ship), 1863
386 29p *Vixen* (topsail schooner), 1853
387 31p *Ramsey* (full-rigged ship), 1870
388 34p *Star of India* (barque) (ex *Euterpe*), 1976
Set of 4   3.25   3.25

1989

409† 16p H.M.S. *Bounty* and launch 30 35
410† 23p H.M.S. *Bounty* and launch (on stamp No 345 of Pitcairn Islands) 80 85
412† 30p Tahitian canoes and ship's boat 70 70
413† 32p H.M.S *Bounty* at Pitcairn Island 70 75

1990

437†	37p Ferry	1.25	1.25

450†	15p R.A.F. rescue launch	40	40

1991

469	17p *Sir William Hillary* (lifeboat)	
470	21p *Osman Gabriel* (lifeboat)	
471	26p *Ann & James Ritchie* (lifeboat)	
472	31p *The Gough Ritchie* (lifeboat)	
473	37p *John Batstone* (lifeboat)	
	Set of 5	4.00 4.00

475†	17p Fishing boats and trawler	50	50

518	18p *Ship's boat, Delfshaven* (Pilgrim Fathers)	
519	18p *Speedwell Delfshaven,* (Pilgrim Fathers)	
520	28p *Mayflower,* Dartmouth (Pilgrim Fathers)	
521	28p *Speedwell,* Dartmouth (Pilgrim Fathers)	
	Set of 4	1.60 1.75

527	18p *King Orry V* (ferry), Douglas	
528	23p Yachts, Castletown	
529	37p Fishing boat, cabin cruisers and yachts, Port St. Mary	
530	40p *Glenfyne* (freighter) and fishing boat, Ramsey	
	Set of 4	2.10 2.25

MS531	18p As No. 527 and £1 *St. Eloi* (ferry)	2.40	2.50

1993

539	1p H.M.S *Amazon* (frigate)	
540	2p *Fingal* (lighthouse tender)	
541	4p *Sir Winston Churchill* (cadet schooner)	
542	5p *Dar Mlodziezy* (full-rigged cadet ship)	
543	20p *Tynwald I* (paddle-steamer), 1846	
544	21p *Ben Veg* (freighter)	
545	22p *Waverley* (paddle-steamer)	
546	23p Royal Yacht *Britannia*	
547	24p *Francis Drake* (ketch)	
548	25p *Royal Viking Sky* (liner)	
549	26p *Lord Nelson* (cadet barque)	
550	27p *Europa* (liner), 1981	
	Set of 12	3.75 4.00

ISRAEL
Western Asia
1955 1000 prutot = 1 pound
1960 100 agorot = 1 pound
1980 100 agorot = 1 shekel

1955

104†	5p Immigrant ship	10	10

1958

143	10p Ancient Hebrew ship	
144	20p *Nirit* (immigration ship), 1948	
145	30p *Shomron* (freighter)	
146	1000p *Zion* (liner)	
	Set of 4	65 60

1963

269	I£1 *Shalom* (liner)	1.25	1.00

1964

286	25a Immigrant ship, 1948	10	10

1967

362	40a *Dolphin* (freighter)	10	10

1969

405	30a Freighters and tug, Elat	
406	60a Freighters, Ashod	
407	I£1 *Theodor Herzl* (liner), Haifa	
	Set of 3	65 65

411†	80a *Elat* (destroyer)	20	20

1970

451	15a "420" class yachts	
452	30a "420" class yachts	
453	80a "420" class yachts	
	Set of 3	50 50

1971

505apa†	80a Sailing dinghy, Elat	15	15
509p†	I£2 Pleasure launches, Coral Island	25	25

1980

MS783	2s 17th-century ships, Haifa; 3s Xebec	1.50	1.60

1983

914†	18s *Reshef* (missile vessel)	35	30

1992

1161†	85a Sailboard	50	40

1168   1s60 Models of Columbus's ships 1.00   75

ITALIAN COLONIES

GENERAL ISSUES
Africa
100 centesimi = 1 lira

1934

75   25li Pirogue 12.00   45.00

ITALIAN EAST AFRICA

East Africa
100 centesimi = 1 lira

1923

44†   5c Ethiopian canoe   10   35
47†   50c Ethiopian canoe   45   85

ITALY

Southern Europe
100 centesimi = 1 lira

1923

157†   30c Ferry boat   90   14.00

1931

312†   50c *Amerigo Vespucci* (cadet ship)   75   15
313†   1li25 *Trento* (cruiser) 3.25   70

1932

360†   1li *Rex* and *Conte di Savoia* (liners) 1.75   90

1934

400†   2li55 + 2li *Brindisi* (cruiser), 1924   45   24.00
402†   25c Lugger, Fiume (air)   20   1.00
404†   75c Lugger, Fiume   20   1.25

436†   50c Naval launch   60   2.25
437†   75c Naval launch   80   2.50

1937

513†   1li25 Roman galleys 1.10   80

1949

723†   20li *Bucentaur* (Venetian state galley) 8.00   20

1952

820   25li Fishing boat, Trieste 1.75   60

827†   60li Motor torpedo boat 3.00   2.50

1957

960   25li 16th-century ship   30   10

1958

970   110li Goats in rowing boat   35   15

1960

1019†   60li *Piemonte* and *Lombardo*,
(Sardinian steam warships), 1860   20   20

1965

1133   30li "Flying Dutchman" class yachts
1134   70li "5.5 S.1" class yachts
1135   50li "Lightning" class yachts   *Set of* 3   65   60

1968

1234†   40li *Andrea Doria* (battleship), *Grillo*
(submarine), *Pullino* (submarine) and
Zeffiro (destroyer)   10   10

1971

1303   25li *Tirrenia* (liner)   15   10

1973

1338   50li Survey ship   15   10

1975

1441   70li *San Rita* (oil rig)   15   10

1977

1525	170li *Ferdinando Primo* (paddle-steamer), 1818		
1526	170li *Carracciolo* (sail corvette), 1869		
1527	170li *Saturnia* (liner), 1927		
1528	170li *Sparviero* (hydrofoil missile boat)		
	Set of 4	90	55

1978

1552	170li *Fortuna* (19th-century brigantine)		
1553	170li *Benedetto Brin* (cruiser), 1901		
1554	170li *Lupo* (frigate), 1976		
1555	170li *Africa* (container ship), 1976		
	Set of 4	1.10	85

1979

1621	170li *Cosmos* (full-rigged ship), 1865		
1622	170li *Dandolo* (cruiser), 1878		
1623	170li *Deledda* (ferry), 1978		
1624	170li *Carlo Fecia di Cossato* (submarine), 1977		
	Set of 4	1.10	55

1980

1634†	170li *Vitoria* (Magellan)	30	10

1691	200li *Gabbiano* (corvette), 1942		
1692	200li *Audace* (destroyer), 1971		
1693	200li *Italia* (barque), 1903		
1694	200li *Castoro Sei* (pipe-layer)		
	Set of 4	1.75	55

1981

1728†	200li *Amerigo Vespucci* (cadet ship)	35	10

1990

2089†	600li Fishing boats, Castellammare del Golfo	75	30

1991

2120†	750li Columbus's fleet	1.25	40

1992

2152†	500li Columbus's fleet	75	25
2154†	500li Ship's boat, 1492	75	25

MS2158	Six sheets (c) 900li Fleet of Columbus (sheet contains two other designs); (e) 600li *Santa Maria* (sheet contains two other designs) (other sheets show different Columbus scenes)		
	Price for 6 sheets	30.00	25.00

2171†	600li Departure of Columbus's fleet from Palos	80	25
2174†	1200li Fleet of Columbus off San Salvador	1.60	70

1993

2204	3200li 18th-century sailing barges	3.25	1.25

IVORY COAST

West Africa
100 centimes = 1 franc

1913

43	1c River canoe		
44	2c River canoe		
45	4c River canoe		
46	5c River canoe (green)		
61	5c River canoe (brown and chocolate)		
47	10c River canoe (red and orange)		
62	10c River canoe (green)		
63	10c River canoe (red on blue)		
48	15c River canoe		
49	20c River canoe		
50	25c River canoe (blue)		
64	25c River canoe (violet and black)		
51	30c River canoe (brown and chocolate)		
65	30c River canoe (red and orange)		
66	30c River canoe (red and blue)		
67	30c River canoe (green)		
52	35c River canoe		
53	40c River canoe		
54	45c River canoe (brown and orange)		
68	45c River canoe (purple and red)		
55	50c River canoe (lilac and black)		
69	50c River canoe (blue)		
70	50c River canoe (blue and green)		
71	60c River canoe		
72	65c River canoe		
56	75c River canoe (red and brown)		
73	75c River canoe (blue)		
74	85c River canoe		
75	90c River canoe		
57	1f River canoe (black and yellow)		
76	1f10 River canoe		
77	1f50 River canoe		
78	1f75 River canoe		
58	2f River canoe		
79	3f River canoe		
59	5f River canoe (brown and blue)		
	Set of 36	45.00	45.00

1915

No. 47 surcharged **+5c**

60	10c + 5c River canoe (red and orange)	40	65

1922

Nos. 48, 56, 68, 73, 75 and further colour of 75c surcharged

80	50c on 45c River canoe (purple and red)		
81	50c on 75c River canoe (blue)		
82	50c on 90c River canoe		
83	60c on 75c River canoe (violet on red)		
84	65c on 15c River canoe		
85	85c on 75c River canoe (red and brown)		
	Set of 6	4.50	4.50

1924

Nos. 58, 59 and other values from 1913 issue with colours changed surcharged

86	25c on 2f River canoe		
87	25c on 5f River canoe (brown and blue)		
88	90c on 75c River canoe (red)		
89	1f25 on 1f River canoe (blue)		
90	1f50 on 1f River canoe (blue)		
91	3f on 5f River canoe (green and red)		
92	10f on 5f River canoe (mauve and red)		
93	20f on 5f River canoe (red and green)		
	Set of 8	16.00	20.00

1931

As No. 109 of Cameroun

97†	1f50 *Leconte de Lisle* (liner)	3.00	3.50

1937

As Nos. 110/11 of Cameroun

155†	20c Liner	35	60
156†	30c Sailing ships	35	60

1965

257	30f River steamer, 1900	35	30

1967

286 30f Mail launch, 1937 . . . . 90 60

1968

297† 500 Pirogues, Tiegba 7.50 3.00

303† 30f *Piave* (freighter) at flour mill 55 25

1969

317† 200f River canoe (on stamp No. 59) 4.00 4.00

319 30f *Ville de Maranhao* (mail steamer), 1889 . . . . 60 25

327† 30f Game fishing launch 45 20

1970

337† 50f Freighters under construction 70 25

1972

397 200f Pirogues, Bletankoro 2.50 85

1976

479† 100f *Ranger* (John Paul Jones), 1777 . . . . 90 35
481† 150f 18th-century French warships leaving Newport 1.40 55

1977

515 65f *Yamoussoukro* (container ship) 60 20

1978

556† 60f *Astragale* (oil exploration ship) 85 20

1980

662 60f *Sotra* (ferry) 45 20

1982

721† 80f Scout dinghy 60 40
722† 100f Scout yacht 70 50
723† 150f Scout dinghy 90 65
MS725† 500f Scout yacht 2.50 2.75

1984

816 100f Container ship
817 125f Cargo liner
818 350f *Queen Mary* (liner)
819 500f *France* (liner)
Set of 4 5.00 4.50

1985

835 100f *Adjame* (river steamer) 75 40

865† 250f Container ship 2.00 1.25

1986

899 125f *Stephan* (cable ship), 1910 . . . . 1.00 55

1987

944 155f "Soling" class yachts
945 195f Sailboards
946 250f "470" class yachts
947 550f Sailboard
Set of 4 6.25 2.25
MS948 650f "470" class yachts 3.25 2.50

1990

1006 155f *Afrique* (steam packet) 1.50 75

1991

1041 50f *Europe* (steam packet)
1042 550f *Asie* (steam packet)
Set of 2 3.25 1.40

JAMAICA

West Indies
1919 12 pence = 1 shilling
20 shillings = 1 pound
1969 100 cents = 1 dollar

1919

82a†	2½d Troopship, 1919	90	90
96a†	3d Fleet of Columbus, 1494	40	15
98a†	6d H.M.S. *Cumberland* (ship of the line) and other sailing ships, Port Royal, 1853	6.50	60

1938

126†	3d *Highland Monarch* (liner) (blue & green)	40	50
126a†	3d *Highland Monarch* (green & blue) ..	1.50	85
126b†	3d *Highland Monarch* (green & red)	90	20

1949

As No. 115 of Antigua

146†	2d Paddle-steamer	45	1.00

1955

155†	2d 18th-century warship, Port Royal	20	10

1956

169†	1s6d Raft, Rio Grande	30	10

1960

178†	2d *City of Berlin* (liner), 1860	45	10

1962

198†	6d Sailing dinghies	10	10

1964

225†	9d *Gypsum Duchess* (bulk carrier) loading gypsum	45	10
229a†	3s Game fishing boat	35	65
230†	5s *Sea Diver* (diving vessel)	1.10	60

1969

Nos. 225 *and* 229/30 *surcharged* **C-DAY 8th SEPTEMBER 1969** *and new value*

285†	8c on 9d *Gypsum Duchess* (bulk carrier) loading gypsum	10	10
289†	30c on 3s Game fishing boat	1.50	2.00
290†	50c on 5s *Sea Diver* (diving vessel)	1.25	2.00

1970

As Nos. 225 *and* 229/30, *but with face values in cents*

312†	8c *Gypsum Duchess* (bulk carrier) loading gypsum	20	10
316†	30c Game fishing boat	1.25	1.50
317†	50c *Sea Diver* (diving vessel)	1.25	2.75

320†	3c *Dacia* (cable ship), 1870	15	10

1971

332†	3c 18th-century ships, Port Royal	35	10
334†	30c Pirate schooner attacking merchantman	1.25	1.25

1972

356†	50c River raft	60	40

No. 356 *overprinted* **TENTH ANNIVERSARY INDEPENDENCE 1962-1972**

361†	50c River raft	40	1.25

1974

380	5c *Mary* (sailing packet), 1808–15		
381	10c *Queensbury* (sailing packet), 1814–27		
382	15c *Sheldrake* (sailing packet), 1829–34		
383	50c *Thames I* (steam packet), 1842		
	Set of 4	2.40	2.50

1979

474†	75c Game fishing boat	30	30
476†	$2 Yachts and cruise liner	50	35

1981

527†	$2 *Highland Monarch* (liner)	1.75	1.40

1983

579	15c Cargo ship at wharf		
580	20c *Veendam* (liner)		
581	45c Container ship		
582	$1 Tanker		
	Set of 4	5.50	4.25

586†	20c Yacht	15	15

1984

596†	25c Freighters	65	15

1987

701†	$5 *Alene* (liner), 1887	2.50	3.00

1989

752†	$5 Ships of Columbus in port	1.75	2.00

1990

774   25c Ships of Columbus and chart of first
        voyage, 1492
775   45c Ships of Columbus and chart of
        second voyage, 1493
776   $5 Ships of Columbus and chart of third
        voyage, 1498
777   $10 Ships of Columbus and chart of fourth
        voyage, 1502
                              Set of 4   2.75   3.00

1991

802†   50c Canoes threatening Columbus's
         ships   15   10
803† $1.10 Ship's boat   20   15
804† $1.40 Carib canoes   20   15

1992

813†   50c Ships wrecked in flooded street, Port
         Royal, 1692   10   10

JAPAN

Eastern Asia
100 sen = 1 yen

1921

206   1½s Katori and Kashima (warships), 1921
207   3s Katori and Kashima
208   4s Katori and Kashima
209   10s Katori and Kashima
                          Set of 4   £100   65.00

1935

276†   1½s Hiyei (cruiser) 2.00   1.60
278†   6s Hiyei 12.00   7.50

1937

313†   ½s Goshuin-sen (16th-century trading
         ship) 1.50   70

1942

393†   2s Shipbuilding   80   45

410†   5s + 2s Attack on Pearl Harbour, 1941   2.25   3.25

1948

MS477   2y × 2 Sampans, Seto Inland Sea
          (green border and inscriptions) 10.00   6.00
MS478   2y × 2 Sampans, Seto Inland Sea
          (blue border and inscriptions) 12.00   10.00
MS479   2y × 2 Sampans, Seto Inland Sea
          (turquoise border and inscriptions) 12.00   10.00

1949

519   2y Koan Maru (ferry)
520   5y Koan Maru
                              Set of 2   7.50   2.75

522   10y Sampans, Seto Inland Sea (scarlet)
523   10y Sampans, Seto Inland Sea (carmine)
524   10y Sampans, Seto Inland Sea (claret)
                              Set of 3   90.00   55.00

552†   8y Yacht 4.00   1.50

1956

762   10y Nissyo Maru (freighter) 1.50   60

1957

766   10y Soya (Antarctic research vessel) 2.25   75

1958

777   10y Powhattan (paddle-steamer), 1858,
        and modern liner   30   10

782   10y Kasato Maru (emigrant ship), 1908 ..   40   10

1959

810   30y Junks, Kuwana 9.00   1.40

1960

825†   10y Kanrin Maru (barque), 1860 ....   1.75   30

1962

897   10y Sampan, Suigo   80   20

1963

935†   5y + 5y Olympic yachts   75   25

1965

1006   10y Meiji Maru (cadet ship)   70   10

1017   10y Fuji (Antarctic research vessel) 1.00   15

1967

1090 50y *Sumoto Maru* (liner), Kobe 75 10

1968

1112 15y *Sakura Maru* (liner) 15 10

1141 15y *Shohei Maru* (sail warship), 1868 . . . . 15 10

1969

1164 15y *Mutsu* (nuclear-powered freighter) . . 20 10

1165 15y *KDD Maru* (cable ship) 15 10

1971

1277 7y "Treasure" ship
1278 10y "Treasure" ship
  Set of 2 60 15

1972

1309 20y 19th-century sailing ships,
  Yokohama 55 10

1975

1406 20y *Kentoshisen* (7th-9th centuries) (red)
1407 20y *Kenminsen* (7th-9th centuries)
  (brown)
  Set of 2 80 30

1409 20y *Goshuin-sen* (16th-century trading
  ship) (green)
1410 20y *Tenchi-maru* (state barge), 1630
  (blue)
  Set of 2 80 30

1976

1420 50y *Sengoku-bune* (fishing boat) (blue)
1421 50y *Shohei Maru* (sail warship) (mauve)
  Set of 2 1.00 30

1423 50y *Taisei Maru* (cadet ship) (black)
1424 50y *Tenyo Maru* (liner) (brown)
  Set of 2 1.25 30

1428 50y *Asama Maru* (liner) (green)
1429 50y *Kinai Maru* (cargo liner) (brown)
  Set of 2 1.25 30

1431 50y *Kamakura Maru* (container ship)
  (blue)
1432 50y *Nissei Maru* (oil tanker) (violet)
  Set of 2 1.25 30

1437 50y *KDD Maru* (cable ship) 60 10

1979

1535 50y Customs launch 70 10

1980

1556† 50y Fishing boats 50 20

1569 50y *Nippon Maru I* (cadet ship), 1930 75 20

1982

1682 60y 16th-century Portuguese galleon 70 10

1983

1721 60y *Shirase* (Antarctic research ship) 2.00 35

1986

1846 60y *Nippon Maru II* (cadet ship), 1984 1.40 35

1988

1937† 60y Tanker to right of Seto Great Bridge 80 30
1938† 60y Tanker to left of Seto Great Bridge 80 30
1939† 60y Freighter beneath Seto Great
  Bridge 80 30

1945† 60y Sampan, River Mogami 80 15

1989

1998 62y 17th-century Dutch East Indiamen
  entering Nagasaki 80 15

JAPANESE OCCUPATION OF BURMA

South-east Asia
12 pies = 1 anna
16 annas = 1 rupee

1942

No. O23 of Burma overprinted
J44   80a Sailing craft on River Irrawaddy 60.00

JAPANESE OCCUPATION OF CHINA

Eastern Asia
100 cents = 1 dollar (yuan)

NORTH CHINA

1945

206† $20 River boat, Tientsin 45   65

JAPANESE OCCUPATION OF MALAYA

South-east Asia
100 cents = 1 dollar

1943

J300†   4c Tin-dredger 15   15

JAPANESE OCCUPATION OF NORTH BORNEO

South-east Asia
100 cents = 1 dollar

1942

大日本帝国郵便

No. 313 of North Borneo overprinted
J11†   25c Malay prau £140   £225

1944

大日本
帝国郵便

北ボルネオ

No. 313 of North Borneo overprinted
J30†   25c Malay prau 9.50   22.00

JAPANESE OCCUPATION OF THE PHILIPPINES

South-east Asia
100 centavos = 1 peso

1943

Nos. 566 and 569 of Philippine Islands surcharged with native characters, **1-23-43** *and value*
J13   2c on 8c Filipino prau
J14   5c on 1p Filipino prau

Set of 2   75   75

J21†   12c Morro vinta (sailing canoe)   70   70
J22†   16c Morro vinta (sailing canoe)   10   10
J27†   2p Morro vinta (sailing canoe) 1.40   1.25
J28†   5p Morro vinta (sailing canoe) 4.75   4.00

J29   2c Japanese battleship
J30   5c Japanese battleship

Set of 2   40   40

No. J21 surcharged **BAHA 1943 +21**
J36†   12c + 21c Morro vinta (sailing canoe) ..   15   15

1944

Nos. 567/8 of Philippine Islands surcharged **REPUBLIKA NG PILIPINAS 5-7-44** *and value*
J43   5c on 20c Filipino prau
J44   12c on 60c Filipino prau

Set of 2   1.40   1.40

OFFICIAL STAMPS

No. 569 of Philippine Islands overprinted **REPUBLIKA NG PILIPINAS (K. P.)**
JO47   1p Filipino prau   85   90

JERSEY

North-west Europe
1969 12 pence = 1 shilling
20 shillings = 1 pound
1970 100 pence = 1 pound

1969

15†   ½d Sailing dinghies, Elizabeth Castle   10   60

1970

37†   1s9d *Vega* (Red Cross supply ship) 3.00   2.50

As No. 15, but face value in new currency
42†   ½p Sailing dinghies, Elizabeth Castle   10   10

1971

66†   2½p 18th-century English warships   20   20

1974

110†   20p *Aquila* (paddle-steamer), 1874   70   60

115   3½p *Catherine* and *Mary* (royal yachts)
116   5½p 18th-century French warship
117   8p 18th-century Dutch vessel
118   25p H.M.S. *Britannia* (ship of the line) at Battle of La Hogue, 1692

Set of 4   1.00   1.00

1976

144†   10p Yachts in Gorey Harbour   25   25
147†   13p Cabin cruisers and yachts in Bonne Nuit Harbour   35   35
150†   20p Yachts   50   50

160†   5p Ship's boat, 1584   10   10
162†   11p H.M.S. *Phoenix*, H.M.S. *Rose* and H.M.S. *Rainbow* (frigates), Long Island, 1776   40   35

165†   7p Sampan, River Yangtze   15   15

1977

175†   5p *Santa Anna* (carrack), 1530   10   10

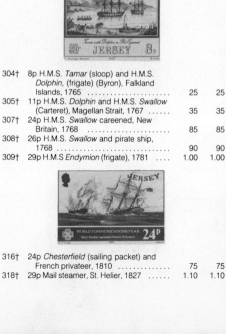

179† 7p Paddle-steamer, 1846 .... 20 20

1978

192† 10½p *Century* (brigantine) 25 25

197 6p Mail cutter, 1778–1827
198 8p *Flamer* (packet steamer), 1831–37
199 10½p *Diana* (packet steamer), 1877–90
200 11p *Ibex* (packet steamer), 1891–1925
201 13p *Caesarea* (packet steamer), 1960–75

Set of 5 1.25 1.25

1980

238† 7p *Eye of the Wind* (cadet brigantine) 20 20
239† 9p Inflatable dinghy 25 25
241† 14p *Discovery* (Scott) 35 35
243† 17½p *Eye of the Wind* 45 45

1981

277† 18p Medieval ship and monks 50 50
278† 18p Medieval ship and whale 50 50

1983

304† 8p H.M.S. *Tamar* (sloop) and H.M.S.
Dolphin, (frigate) (Byron), Falkland
Islands, 1765 .... 25 25
305† 11p H.M.S. *Dolphin* and H.M.S. *Swallow*
(Carteret), Magellan Strait, 1767 .. 35 35
307† 24p H.M.S. *Swallow* careened, New
Britain, 1768 .... 85 85
308† 26p H.M.S. *Swallow* and pirate ship,
1768 .... 90 90
309† 29p H.M.S *Endymion* (frigate), 1781 .... 1.00 1.00

316† 24p *Chesterfield* (sailing packet) and
French privateer, 1810 .... 75 75
318† 29p Mail steamer, St. Helier, 1827 ...... 1.10 1.10

1984

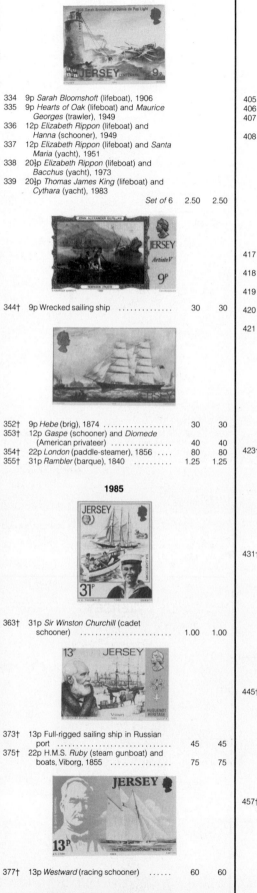

334 9p *Sarah Bloomshoft* (lifeboat), 1906
335 9p *Hearts of Oak* (lifeboat) and *Maurice
Georges* (trawler), 1949
336 12p *Elizabeth Rippon* (lifeboat) and
Hanna (schooner), 1949
337 12p *Elizabeth Rippon* (lifeboat) and *Santa
Maria* (yacht), 1951
338 20½p *Elizabeth Rippon* (lifeboat) and
Bacchus (yacht), 1973
339 20½p *Thomas James King* (lifeboat) and
Cythara (yacht), 1983

Set of 6 2.50 2.50

344† 9p Wrecked sailing ship 30 30

352† 9p *Hebe* (brig), 1874 .... 30 30
353† 12p *Gaspe* (schooner) and *Diomede*
(American privateer) 40 40
354† 22p *London* (paddle-steamer), 1856 .... 80 80
355† 31p *Rambler* (barque), 1840 .... 1.25 1.25

1985

363† 31p *Sir Winston Churchill* (cadet
schooner) 1.00 1.00

373† 13p Full-rigged sailing ship in Russian
port 45 45
375† 22p H.M.S. *Ruby* (steam gunboat) and
boats, Viborg, 1855 .... 75 75

377† 13p *Westward* (racing schooner) 60 60

GIBBONS STAMP MONTHLY
— finest and most informative magazine for all
collectors. Obtainable from your newsagent or by
postal subscription — details on request.

1987

405 10p *Westward* (racing schooner)
406 14p Racing yacht
407 31p *Westward* and *Britannia* (Royal racing
yacht), 1935
408 34p *Westward* fitting out

Set of 4 3.00 3.00

417 11p H.M.S. *Racehorse* and H.M.S.
Carcass (bomb ketches) in Arctic, 1773
418 15p H.M.S. *Alarm* (galley) on fire, Rhode
Island, 1778
419 29p H.M.S. *Arethusa* (frigate) wrecked,
1779
420 31p H.M.S. *Rattlesnake* (sloop) beached,
1782
421 34p Fishing boats and Mont Orgueil, 1792

Set of 5 3.75 3.75

423† 15p Norman ship, 1030 .... 45 45

431† 31p Fishing boat, St. Helier 1.10 1.10

1988

445† 22p Hydrofoil 90 90

457† 34p *Zebu* (brigantine) 1.10 1.10

1989

473† 13p Yacht marina, St. Helier 25 30
475† 15p Yachts, Rozel 30 35
476† 16p Cabin cruisers, St. Aubin 30 35
487† 27p Fishing boat and yachts, St.
Brelade's Bay 55 60

500 £1 Royal Yacht *Britannia* in Elizabeth
Harbour 2.00 2.10

504† 30p Fishing boat, Mont Orgueil, 1795 1.10 1.00
505† 32p Ship's boat, 1796 . . . . 1.10 1.00

507 13p *St. Helier* (ferry)
508 17p *Caesarea II* (ferry)
509 27p *Reindeer* (ferry)
510 32p *Ibex* racing *Frederica* (ferries)
511 35p *Lynx* (ferry)
Set of 5 4.00 4.00

512† 13p Fishing boats, Gorey 50 50
516† 35p Fishing boats, Mont Orgueil 1.25 1.25

1990

522† 24p Yacht 65 65

1991

543† 37p H.M.S. *Surly* (cutter) attacking
French enemy convoy 1.00 1.00

565† 20p Pirate ship 55 55

1992

573† 16p Royal Navy sloop, junks and
sampans, Shanghai, 1860 . . . . 30 35
574† 16p Junk, 1862 . . . . 30 35
575† 22p Junks, 1874 . . . . 45 50

579 16p *Tickler* (brigantine)
580 22p *Hebe* (brig)
581 50p *Gemini* (barque)
582 57p *Percy Douglas* (full-rigged ship)
Set of 4 2.50 2.75

584 22p *Santa Maria*, Columbus
585 28p *Santa Maria*, Columbus
586 39p *Santa Maria*, Columbus
Set of 3 1.60 1.75

1993

606† (-) Surfboard 45 50

POSTAGE DUE STAMPS

1982

D34† 2p Small craft, St. Aubin 10 10
D38† 6p Sailing dinghies, St. Catherine 10 15
D39† 7p Cabin cruisers and rowing boats,
Gorey 15 20
D42† 10p Ferry, St. Helier 20 25
D44† 30p Cruising yachts, La Collette 60 65
D46† £1 Motor cruisers and yacht, St. Helier 2.00 2.10

JIND

Indian sub-continent
12 pies = 1 anna
16 annas = 1 rupee

1937

No. 256 of India overprinted **JIND STATE**
118 6a *Strathnaver* (liner) 1.00 8.50

JOHORE

South-east Asia
100 cents = 1 dollar

1944

As No. 115 of Antigua
149† 15c Paddle-steamer 50 1.00

1960

161† 20c Malay fishing prau 15 10

JORDAN

Middle East
1949 1000 milliemes = 1 pound
1950 1000 fils = 1 dinar

1949

285† 1m Liner 10 25
286† 4m Liner 15 40
287† 10m Liner 15 30
288† 20m Liner 30 50

1962

512 15f *Rida* (freighter), Aqaba
513 35f *Rida*
Set of 2 85 25

1964

624† 35f Scout sailing dinghy 2.50 95

1967

798† 2f Fishing canoes, Lake Patzcuaro,
Mexico 10 10

1976

1136† 60f Freighter, Aqaba 1.00 55

1984

1410† 25f Naval patrol boat 50 15

1985

1458† 60f Sailing dinghies, Aqaba 1.00 65

JORDANIAN OCCUPATION OF PALESTINE

Middle East
1000 milliemes = 1 pound

1949
Nos. 285/8 of Jordan overprinted **PALESTINE** *in English and Arabic*

P30† 1m Liner 15 40
P31† 4m Liner 20 50
P32† 10m Liner 25 65
P33† 20m Liner 35 90

KAMPUCHEA

South-east Asia
100 cents = 1 riel

1983

490† 3r Bulk carrier 2.50 60

1985

655 10c River launch, 1942
656 40c River launch, 1948
657 80c Tug, 1913
658 1r Dredger
659 1r20 Tug
660 2r River freighter
661 2r50 River tanker
                                Set of 7   5.50   2.00

1986

734 20c English kogge of Richard II's reign
735 50c Kogge
736 80c Knarr

---

737 1r Galley
738 1r50 Norman ship
739 2r Mediterranean usciere
740 3r French kogge
                                Set of 7   4.50   1.40

1988

891 20c *Emerald Seas* (liner)
892 50c Car ferry
893 80c Freighter
894 1r *Kosmonavt Yury Gagarin* (research ship)
895 1r50 Tanker
896 2r Hydrofoil
897 3r Hovercraft
                                Set of 7   1.60   65
MS898 6r Hydrofoil 1.10   45

KEDAH

South-east Asia
100 cents = 1 dollar

1949
As No. 115 *of Antigua*
73† 15c Paddle-steamer 50 1.25

1957

98† 20c Malay fishing prau 30 45

1959

110† 20c Malay fishing prau 20 10

KELANTAN

South-east Asia
100 cents = 1 dollar

1949
As No. 115 *of Antigua*
58† 15c Paddle-steamer 50 90

1957

90† 20c Malay fishing prau 30 30

1961

102† 20c Malay fishing prau 60 30

KENYA

East Africa
100 cents = 1 shilling

1963

6† 40c Fishing boats 15 20
13† 10s *Europa* (liner, 1952) and *Tintagel Castle* (freighter) alongside quay 7.00 2.00

1980

170† 3s Speedboat, Mombasa 40 75

1981

209† 5s Royal Yacht *Britannia* 40 35

1983

252† 70c Container barge and tugs 70 10
254† 3s50 Container barge loading 2.00 2.00

279† 10s Customs patrol boat 1.75 2.00

282† 3s50 Modern mail steamer 1.60 1.75

284† 70c Freighters at quay, Kilindini 75 10
286† 3s50 Freighters, Mombasa 2.00 1.75

1986

388† 7s Container ship 2.75 2.75

394 1s Mashua dhow
395 3s Mtepe dhow
396 5s Dau La Mwao dhow
397 10s Jahazi dhow
Set of 4 6.50 6.00
MS398 25s Lamu dhow 4.00 4.50

1988

459† 4s H.M.S. *Sirius* (frigate), 1788 .... 55 55

1989

492† 3s40 Dhow and Vasco da Gama Pillar,
Malindi 35 35
494† 5s50 Dhows, Mombasa 60 70

KENYA, UGANDA AND TANGANYIKA

East Africa
100 cents = 1 shilling

1935

111† 5c Dhow, Lake Victoria 40 20
116† 50c Dhow, Lake Victoria 75 10

1938

As Nos. 111 and 116, but with portrait of King George VI
132† 5c Dhow, Lake Victoria (black and
green) 70 10
133† 5c Dhow, Lake Victoria (brown and
orange) 35 1.75
140† 25c Dhow, Lake Victoria 1.25 90
144e† 50c Dhow, Lake Victoria 3.25 45

1941
No. 115 of South Africa surcharged **5c. KENYA TANGANYIKA UGANDA**. *Alternate stamps inscribed in English or Afrikaans*
151† 5c on 1d *Dromedaris* (Van Riebeeck) 60 1.50

1949
As No. 115 of Antigua
160† 30c Paddle-steamer 40 35

1966

226† 2s50 Game fishing launch 1.75 1.75

1969

256 30c *Umoja* (train ferry)
257 50c *Harambee* (lake freighter)
258 1s30 *Victoria* (lake ferry)
259 2s50 *St. Michael* (car ferry)
Set of 4 1.60 1.90

263† 2s50 Freighters at wharf 20 40

KHOR FAKKAN

Arabian peninsula
100 naye paise = 1 rupee

Appendix
The following have either been issued in excess of postal needs, or have not been made available to the public in reasonable quantities at face value. Miniature sheets, imperforate stamps etc, are excluded from this section.

1965
New York World's Fair. No. 81 of Sharjah overprinted **KHOR FAKKAN** in English and Arabic. Air 20np Oil rig
I.T.U. Centenary. As No. 166 of Sharjah. 1np Monarch (cable ship)

KIAUTSCHOU

China
1901 100 pfennige = 1 mark
1905 100 cents = 1 dollar

1901
As Nos. K7/19 of Cameroun, but inscribed "KIAUTSCHOU"
11 3pf *Hohenzollern* (German Imperial yacht)
12 5pf *Hohenzollern*
13 10pf *Hohenzollern*
14 20pf *Hohenzollern*
15 25pf *Hohenzollern*
16 30pf *Hohenzollern*
17 40pf *Hohenzollern*
18 50pf *Hohenzollern*
19 80pf *Hohenzollern*
20 1m *Hohenzollern*
21 2m *Hohenzollern*
22 3m *Hohenzollern*
23 5m *Hohenzollern*
Set of 13 £800 £1400

1905
As Nos. 11/23, but face values in Chinese currency
34 1c *Hohenzollern* (German Imperial yacht)
35 2c *Hohenzollern*
36 4c *Hohenzollern*
37 10c *Hohenzollern*
38 20c *Hohenzollern*
39 40c *Hohenzollern*
40 ½dol *Hohenzollern*
41 1dol *Hohenzollern*
42 1½dol *Hohenzollern*
43 2½dol *Hohenzollern*
Set of 10 50.00 £700

KIRIBATI

Pacific Ocean
100 cents = 1 dollar

1979

86† 1c *Teraaka* (training ship) 10 10
87† 3c *Tautunu* (inter-island freighter) 10 10
98† $1 *Tabakea* (lagoon ferry) 70 75

101† 20c Gilbert Islands canoe (on Gilbert and
Ellice Islands stamp No. 73) 15 20

1980

112† 12c *Teraaka* (training ship) 10 10

1981

148† $1 H.M.S. *Resolution* (Cook) 90 75

149† 12c Royal Yacht *Katherine* 15 15
151† 50c Royal Yacht *Osborne* 45 45
153† $2 Royal Yacht *Britannia* 75 1.00

161† 50c *Nei Manganibuka* (tuna-fishing boat) 50 50

1982

190† 25c Scouts repairing dinghy 30 30

194† 25c Outrigger canoe 20 20

1983

199† 50c Container ship off Betio 25 25

201† 12c Outrigger canoe 20 20

209† 50c Lighter and launches, Betio 65 55

214† $1 U.S.S. *Tarawa* (aircraft carrier) 1.25 1.10

215† 12c *Betsey* (American full-rigged sealer), 1798 .... 50 15

1984

219 12c *Riki* (tug)
220 35c *Nei Nimanoa* (ferry)
221 50c *Nei Tebaa* (ferry)
222 $1 *Nei Momi* (inter-island ship)
Set of 4 2.75 2.00

225† 30c *Nouamake* (game fishing boat) 50 30

1985

250† 40c *Moanaraoi* (freighter) 2.00 2.25

1986

259† 40c Whaling ship, 1844 .... 1.75 1.75
260† 55c *Vostok* (Bellingshausen), 1820 ...... 2.00 2.00

267† $1.50 *Australia II* (yacht), 1983 .... 1.25 1.50

1987

268† 30c *Moamoa* (freighter) 1.50 1.50

1988

290† $1 18th-century Australian brig 1.25 1.25
MS292† $2 *Logistic Ace* (container ship) 1.90 2.50

1989

295 15c *Hound* (brigantine), 1835
296 30c *Phantom* (brig), 1854
297 40c H.M.S. *Alacrity* (schooner), 1873
298 $1 *Charles W. Morgan* (whaling ship), 1851
Set of 4 4.25 4.00

315† 75c *Mataburo* (inter-island freighter) 2.00 2.25

1990

325† $1 *Teraaka* (training ship) (on Gilbert Island stamp No. 23) 1.75 2.00

343 15c *Herald* (whaling ship), 1851
344 50c *Belle* (barque), 1849
345 60c *Supply* (schooner), 1851
346 75c *Triton* (whaling ship), 1848
Set of 4 2.40 2.40
MS347 $2 *Charlotte* (convict transport), 1789 4.00 4.50

1992

378† 30c Sailing canoe 40 45
379† 50c Fishing boat 60 65

389† 75c Lifeboat training 90 90

391† 50c Fishing canoes at night 70 70
393† 75c *Papuan Chief* (container ship) 90 90

OFFICIAL STAMPS

1981

Nos. 86/7 and 98 overprinted **O.K.G.S.**

O1† 1c *Teraaka* (training ship) 10 10
O2† 3c *Tautunu* (inter-island freighter) 10 10
O13† $1 *Tabakea* (lagoon ferry) 1.00 1.00

KOREA

Eastern Asia

South Korea

1946 100 cheun = 1 won
1955 100 weun = 1 hwan
1962 100 chon = 1 won

1946

92† 50w 16th-century "turtle" ship 30.00 8.50

1952

196 1200w Freighter
197 1800w Freighters
198 4200w Freighters
Set of 3 2.75 65

1953

As Nos. 196/8 but face values in hwan
210 12h Freighters
211 18h Freighters
212 42h Freighters
Set of 3 3.75 95

1955

256   20h 16th-century "turtle" ship 3.00   1.50

1957

301   40h Freighters
302   205h Freighters
Set of 2   2.50   80

1959

336   40h Marine landing-craft   70   25

1961

404   40h Destroyer 1.25   30

1962

433   2w 16th-century 20-oared "turtle" ship
434   4w 16th-century 16-oared "turtle" ship
Set of 2   2.75   1.50

449   4w Trawler 1.00   25

1964

509†   40w Freighter 1.75   35

528†   4w Trawlers 1.25   25

1965

593†   4w *Korea* (freighter) 1.00   25

1969

782   7w 16th-century "turtle" ship   75   25

1971

947†   10w Punt 2.00   45

1973

1057†   10w Excursion launch passing under
Namhae Bridge   40   10

1974

1103   10w Container ships, Inchon   40   10

1977

1272†   20w Tanker   40   10

1311   20w Freighter   35   10

1978

1333   20w Freighter   25   10

1334   20w Destroyer   30   10

1980

1459   30w Cable ship   30   10

1981

1465   30w *Korea Sun* (tanker)
1466   90w *Asia Yukho* (freighter)
Set of 2   1.25   30

1470   30w *Saturn* (bulk carrier)
1471   90w *Hanjin Seoul* (container ship)
Set of 2   1.25   30

1482   40w *Chung Ryong No. 3* (tug)
1483   100w *Soo Gong No. 71* (trawler)
Set of 2   1.40   30

1484   40w *Aldebaran* (log carrier)
1485   100w *Hyundai No. 1* (car carrier)
Set of 2   1.40   30

1501   40w *Stolt Hawk* (chemical carrier)
1502   100w Passenger ferry
Set of 2   1.40   30

1982

1537†   60w Battle of Hansan, 1592   50   10

1983

1553　60w Container ship .... 50　15

1984

1618　70w Container ship .... 65　15

1986

1740†　30w Excursion launch, River Han ...... 40　10
1741†　60w Excursion launch, River Han ...... 40　10

1988

1826†　80w + 20w Olympic yachts .... 35　20

1854†　80w Rowing boat .... 30　10

1992

1990　100w Warship of 1542 attacking
　　　　settlement .... 15　10

North Korea
100 cheun = 1 won

1959

N209†　10ch *Chungnyon-ho* (freighter) ...... 2.25　60

1961

N328†　10ch Trawler .... 1.00　20

1962

N367†　10ch Trawler .... 75　15

1963

N445†　40ch Trawlers .... 1.75　40

N448†　10ch Motor torpedo-boat .... 85　10

1964

N506　5ch Whale-catcher
N507　5ch Trawler
N508　10ch Trawler
N509　10ch Trawler
　　　　　　　　　　　　　　　Set of 4　2.25　55

N535†　10ch *Tobolsk* (passenger ship) ...... 1.00　20

1965

N638　10ch Whale-catcher
N639　10ch Fishing fleet service vessel
　　　　　　　　　　　　　　　Set of 2　2.25　35

GIBBONS STAMP MONTHLY
— finest and most informative magazine for all
collectors. Obtainable from your newsagent or by
postal subscription — details on request.

N667　2ch "Finn" class yachts
N668　10ch "5.5m" class yacht
N669　10ch "Dragon" class yacht
N670　40ch "Star" class yachts
　　　　　　　　　　　　　　　Set of 4　3.50　1.25

1967

N802　10ch *Chollima* (freighter) .... 60　10

1968

N852†　5ch *September 2* (dredger) .... 30　10

1969

N939　10ch *Taesungsan* (freighter) .... 60　10

1971

N1021†　10ch Freighter .... 55　10

N1041†　5ch *Ponghwasan* (refrigerated
　　　　　freighter) .... 90　15

1972

N1086†　5ch Dredger .... 35　10

N1112†　10ch Freighter .... 40　10

1974

N1225† 10ch Whale-catcher and factory ship 50 10

N1324 2ch *Chilbosan* (fish factory ship)
N1325 5ch *Paekdusan* (trawler support ship) and trawler
N1326 10ch *Moranbong* (freighter)
N1327 20ch Whale-catcher
N1328 30ch Trawlers
N1329 40ch Stern trawler
Set of 6 3.75 1.40

1976

N1496† 40ch Cable-laying barge 1.75 20

N1555† 25ch Junk 70 20

1977

N1623† 2ch River launch 60 15
N1625† 30ch Freighters 90 30

1978

N1699 15ch Modern mail steamer 65 15

N1718 2ch *Mangyongbong* (freighter)
N1719 5ch *Hyoksin* (freighter)
N1720 10ch *Chongchongang* (gas carrier)
N1721 30ch *Sonbong* (tanker)
N1722 50ch *Taedonggang* (freighter) (air)
Set of 5 3.75 1.25

1979

N1863† 20ch Olympic yachts 60 15

N1907† 20ch Model Viking ship 1.00 20
N1911† 30ch Model speedboat 1.50 30
MSN1915† Four sheets (c) 80ch Model liner (other 80ch sheets show different toys)
Price for 4 sheets 16.00 4.50

1980

N1958† 10ch Red Cross ship 1.00 25
N1961† 10ch Hospital ship 2.50 60

N1966† 40ch *Calypso* (Cousteau) 2.25 55
MSN1967† 70ch H.M.S. *Resolution* (Cook) 4.75 75

N1995† 10ch 16th-century "turtle" ship 75 25

N2016 10ch *Malygin* (ice-breaker) (on Russia stamp No. 584)
N2017 20ch *Malygin* (on Russia stamp No. 585)
N2018 30ch *Malygin* (on Russia stamp No. 586)
Set of 3 4.50 1.25
MSN2019 50ch *Malygin* (on Russia stamp No. 587) 5.75 2.50

1983

N2312 20ch *Colourful Cow* (kogge), 1402
N2313 20ch "Turtle" ship, 1592
N2314 35ch *Great Harry* (warship), 1555
N2315 35ch "Turtle" ship
N2316 50ch *Eagle of Lubeck* (galleon), 1567
N2317 50ch *Merkur* (full-rigged sailing ship), 1847
N2318 80ch *Herzogin Elisabeth* (cadet ship)
Set of 7 13.00 4.25
MSN2319 80ch *Cristoforo Colombo* (cadet ship) 5.00 3.50

N2334 40ch *Gorch Fock* (German cadet barque) and *Mangyongbong* (on stamp No. N1718) 3.00 1.25

N2351† 40ch Freighter 3.75 1.10

1984

MSN2406 80ch *Gorch Fock* (German cadet barque) and "turtle" ship (on stamp No. N2313) 4.50 3.50

N2418　5ch Trawler
N2419　10ch Trawler
N2420　40ch Game fishing launch
　　　　　　　　　Set of 3　3.00　1.25

N2438　10ch Pongdaesan (container ship)
N2439　20ch Ryongnamsan (container ship)
N2440　30ch Rungrado (container ship)
　　　　　　　　　Set of 3　3.25　90
MSN2441　80ch Kumgangsan (container ship)　4.75　1.50

N2458　20ch Arktika (Russian ice-breaker)
N2459　30ch Ermak (Russian ice-breaker)
　　　　　　　　　Set of 2　3.00　85
MSN2460　80ch Lenin (Russian ice-breaker)　..　4.75　1.50

1985

N2481　10ch Ferry
N2482　20ch Liner
N2483　30ch Freighter
N2484　40ch Tanker
　　　　　　　　　Set of 4　5.00　1.40

1986

N2614　10ch Express II (ice-breaker)　.........　90　20

N2634†　10ch Oil tanker and barrage　........　30　10

1987

N2661　20ch Gorch Foch (German cadet barque)
N2662　30ch Tovarishch (Russian cadet barque)
N2663　50ch Belle Poule (cadet schooner) (air)
N2664　50ch Sagres II (Portuguese cadet barque)
N2665　1wn Koryo period merchantman
N2666　1wn Dar Mlodziezy (Polish cadet full-rigged ship)
　　　　　　　　　Set of 6　9.75　3.00

N2700†　40ch Grande Hermine (Cartier) and ice-breaker　.....................　1.75　40

N2728†　60ch Danmark (Danish cadet full-rigged ship)　.................　1.75　40

1988

N2754　10ch Santa Maria (Columbus)
N2755　20ch Pinta
N2756　30ch Nina
　　　　　　　　　Set of 3　1.40　55

N2765†　40ch Urho (ice-breaker)　............　1.00　25

MSN2796†　80ch H.M.S. Resolution (Cook)　....　2.25　70

N2797　10ch 5-28 (floating crane)
N2798　20ch Hwanggumsan (freighter)
N2799　30ch Changjasan Chongnyon-ho (freighter)
N2800　40ch Samjiyon (liner)
　　　　　　　　　Set of 4　2.25　80

1989

N2898†　5ch Freighter　.....................　10　10

N2928　30ch Vitoria (Magellan)　.............　75　20

1990

N2942†　40ch Tourist launch, Pyongyang　......　75　25

N2961†　10ch Submarine　....................　20　10

1991

N3057†　40ch Antarctic research ship　........　75　25

1992

N3175†	10ch Yacht	10	10
N3176†	20ch Sailboard	15	10
N3177†	30ch Sailing dinghy	20	10
N3178†	40ch Sailing dinghy	25	10
N3179†	50ch Yacht	30	10

Appendix

The following stamps have either been issued in excess of postal needs or have not been made available to the public in reasonable quantities at face value. Miniature sheets, imperforate stamps etc. are excluded from this section.

1984

European Royal History. 10ch x 6, various historical scenes 1571–1844

KOUANG TCHEOU (KWANGCHOW)

South China
100 cents = 1 piastre

1937

Nos. 163/9 of Indo-China overprinted **KOUANG-TCHEOU**

98†	1/10c Junk	15	30
99†	1/5c Junk	20	30
100†	2/5c Junk	15	30
101†	½c Junk	15	25
102†	4/5c Junk	30	30
103†	1c Junk	20	30
104|	2c Junk	20	30

KUWAIT

Arabian Peninsula
1939 12 pies = 1 anna
16 annas = 1 rupee
1957 100 naye paise = 1 rupee
1961 1000 fils = 1 dinar

1939

No. 256 of India overprinted **KUWAIT**

44†	6a *Strathnaver* (liner)	22.00	6.50

1951

Nos. 509/10 of Great Britain surcharged **KUWAIT** *and value*

90†	2r on 2s6d H.M.S. *Victory* (Nelson)	12.00	4.25
91†	5r on 5s Yacht and Thames sailing barge, Dover	15.00	5.00

1958

137†	40np Dhow	45	10
141†	2r Dhow	2.50	25

1961

153†	25f Tankers	60	10
154†	30f Dhow	1.25	10
156†	40f Dhow	1.25	15
158†	75f Dhow	2.50	60
160†	100f Tankers	2.00	10
161†	250f Dhow	7.00	1.50

1964

244	8f Dhow		
245	15f Dhow		
246	20f Dhow		
247	30f Dhow		
	Set of 4	1.25	55

248	8f Dhow		
249	20f Dhow		
250	30f Dhow		
251	45f Dhow		
	Set of 4	1.25	55

1966

324	20f *British Fusilier* (tanker)		
325	45f *British Fusilier*		
	Set of 2	2.00	80

330	4f Dhow		
331	25f Dhow		
	Set of 2	1.75	75

1969

453	20f *Al Sabahiah* (freighter)		
454	45f *Al Sabahiah*		
	Set of 2	2.75	1.25

1970

480	8f Shoue (dhow)		
481	10f Sambuk (dhow)		
482	15f Baggala (dhow)		
483	20f Battela (dhow)		
484	25f Bum (dhow)		
485	45f Baggala (dhow)		
486	50f Dhow-building		
	Set of 7	6.00	1.75

ALBUM LISTS

Write for our latest list of albums and accessories.
This will be sent on request.

513	20f *Medora* (tanker)		
514	45f *Medora*		
	Set of 2	3.00	95

1972

555	5f Fishing boat		
556	10f Fishing boat		
557	20f Fishing boat		
	Set of 3	1.75	50

1978

761†	5f Dhows	15	10
764†	5f Dhows	15	10

1981

894	30f Tanker		
895	80f Tanker		
	Set of 2	3.00	1.50

1982

939	30f Container ship		
940	80f Freighter		
	Set of 2	2.50	1.25

1983

1009	15f Dhow		
1010	30f Dhow		
1011	80f Dhow		
	Set of 3	3.00	1.25

1985

1088　30f Dhow
1089　80f Dhow
　　　　　　　　　　Set of 2　4.50　1.40

1986

1109　20f *Al Mirqab* (container ship)
1110　70f *Al Mubarakiah* (container ship)
　　　　　　　　　　Set of 2　3.75　1.75

1987

1139　25f Container ship
1140　50f Container ship
1141　150f Container ship
　　　　　　　　　　Set of 3　2.50　1.25

1989

1207　50f Dhow
1208　100f Dhow
1209　200f Dhow
　　　　　　　　　　Set of 3　2.50　90

LABUAN

Off North coast of Borneo
100 cents = 1 dollar

1894

As No. 74 of North Borneo, with colours changed, overprinted
LABUAN
69†　8c Malay prau ....　7.00　19.00

1896

No. 69 further overprinted **1846 JUBILEE 1896**
88†　8c Malay prau ....　21.00　11.00

1897

As No. 102b of North Borneo, with colours changed, overprinted
LABUAN
94a†　8c Malay prau ....　13.00　10.00

1899

No. 94a surcharged **4 CENTS**
104a†　4c on 8c Malay prau ....　15.00　25.00

1904

No. 94a surcharged **4 cents**
129†　4c on 8c Malay prau ....　16.00　28.00

POSTAGE DUE STAMPS

1901

No. 94a overprinted **POSTAGE DUE**
D6†　8c Malay prau ....　27.00　55.00

LAOS

South-east Asia
1951 100 cents = 1 piastre
1955 100 cents = 1 kip

1951

1†　10c Pirogue, River Mekong ....　10　10
2†　20c Pirogue, River Mekong ....　10　10
3†　30c Pirogue, River Mekong ....　65　55

1965

176†　25k Pirogue race ....　45　30

1967

202†　60k + 15k Pirogue on flooded airport ....　1.10　1.10

1971

315†　70k Pirogue building ....　45　30

1974

395†　25k Car ferry, River Mekong ....　45　20
397†　250k House boat, River Mekong (air) ....　2.00　1.25

1979

475†　5k River pirogues ....　15　10
478†　500k River pirogues ....　2.25　1.25

COLLECT CHESS ON STAMPS

A Stanley Gibbons thematic catalogue — available at £5 (p. + p. £3) from: Stanley Gibbons Publications, 5 Parkside, Christchurch Road, Ringwood, Hants. BH24 3SH.

1982

559　50c River raft
560　60c River sampan
561　1k River house boat
562　2k River passenger steamer
563　3k River ferry
564　8k Self-propelled barge
　　　　　　　　　　Set of 6　3.00　1.40

1983

MS667　10k Pirogues and sampan, River
　　　　Tachin ....　2.40　1.60

674　1k *Vitoria* (Magellan)
675　2k *Grande Hermine* (Cartier)
676　3k *Santa Maria* (Columbus)
677　4k *El Ray* (Cabral)
678　5k H.M.S. *Resolution* (Cook)
679　6k *Pourquoi Pas?* (Charcot) (inscr
　　　　"CABOT" in error)
　　　　　　　　　　Set of 6　7.00　3.00

1984

795†　1k River house boat ....　45　10

1985

852†　1k *Pinta* (Columbus) ....　30　15
853†　2k *Nina* (Columbus) ....　35　15
854†　3k *Santa Maria* (Columbus) ....　45　15

1987

981　50c Schooner
982　1k Schooner
983　2k Full-rigged ship
984　3k Early screw-steamer

985	4k Early screw-steamer		
986	5k Early paddle-steamer		
987	6k River paddle-steamer		
	Set of 7	1.40	35
MS988	10k *Matthew* (Cabot), 1497 (on Canada stamp No. 412)	70	30

1988

| 1099† | 20k Red Cross pirogue .... | 10 | 10 |
| 1102† | 100k Sampan .... | 20 | 10 |

1989

| 1117† | 1k Gunboat .... | 10 | 10 |

| 1191† | 100k Spanish galleon .... | 30 | 10 |

1991

| 1234† | 330k Olympic yachts .... | 60 | 20 |

POSTAGE DUE STAMPS

1952

| D28† | 10p Sampans .... | 80 | 80 |

Appendix
The following stamps have either been issued in excess of postal needs or have not been available to the public in reasonable quantities at face value. Miniature sheets, imperforate stamps etc, are excluded from this section.

1975
Centenary of Universal Postal Union. 10k Junk and modern liner

---

COLLECT BUTTERFLIES AND OTHER INSECTS ON STAMPS
A Stanley Gibbons thematic catalogue — available at £12.95 (p. + p. £3) from: Stanley Gibbons Publications, 5 Parkside, Christchurch Road, Ringwood, Hants. BH24 3SH.

LATVIA
Eastern Europe
1928 100 santimi (centimes) = 1 lat
1991 100 kopeks = 1 rouble

1925

| 119† | 6-12s Freighters, Libau .... | 1.75 | 4.00 |

1928

| 162† | 50s Tug and freighters, Riga .... | 2.00 | 2.00 |

1991
Nos. 6073 and 6077 of Russia surcharged

328†	100k on 7k Liner	20	20
329†	300k on 2k Sailing packet	65	65
330†	500k on 2k Sailing packet	1.10	1.10
331†	1000k on 2k Sailing packet	2.25	2.25

LEBANON
Middle East
100 centimes = 1 piastre

1930

167†	1p Fishing boat, Saida (green)	50	25
167a†	1p Fishing boat, Saida (purple)	50	25
174†	6p Fishing boats, Tyre	1.10	95

1947

355†	50p Phoenician galley	2.75	75
356†	75p Phoenician galley	3.50	1.25
357†	100p Phoenician galley	5.00	2.50

1961

| 694† | 70p Tourist punt .... | 1.00 | 70 |

713†	5p Fishing boats, Tyre	20	10
714†	10p Fishing boats, Tyre	20	10
715†	15p Fishing boats, Tyre	30	10
716†	20p Fishing boats, Tyre	30	10
717†	30p Fishing boats, Tyre	40	10

1962
As No. 713, but with larger figures of value

| 733† | 5p Fishing boats, Tyre .... | 35 | 10 |

1966

| 938† | 15p Phoenician sailing ship .... | 25 | 10 |

| 942† | 5p Rowing boat .... | 15 | 10 |

1967

| 962† | 20p Fishing boat, Sidon .... | 30 | 10 |

| 980† | 20p Tourist punt, Jeita .... | 35 | 15 |

1968

| 1013† | 17p50 Feluccas, Beirut .... | 15 | 15 |

1969

| 1060† | 30p Yacht .... | 30 | 30 |
| 1061† | 40p Racing yacht .... | 50 | 50 |

1971

| 1108† | 70p *Tarablous* (naval patrol boat) ...... | 1.25 | 45 |

1973

1155† 25p Phoenician galley 15 20

1975

1226† 35p Phoenician galley 45 35

1983

1284† 200p Phoenician galley 1.40 65

POSTAGE DUE STAMPS

1931

D192† 1p Phoenician galley 50 50

LEEWARD ISLANDS

West Indies
12 pence = 1 shilling
20 shillings = 1 pound

1949

As No. 115 of Antigua
120† 3d Paddle-steamer 40 40

LESOTHO

Southern Africa
100 lisente = 1 maloti

1986

742† 35s Rowing boat 55 30

1987

779† 4m Sailboard 3.50 3.75

781 9s Fleet of Columbus, 1492
782 15s Fleet of Columbus, 1492
783 35s Caravel, 1492
784 5m Fleet of Columbus, 1492

Set of 4 4.00 4.25
MS785 4m *Santa Maria* (Columbus) 3.25 3.50

1988

812† 3s Rowing boat 10 10

1989

872† 1m Japanese sampan 40 45
873† 3m20 Japanese houseboat 1.25 1.40
874† 5m Japanese raft 2.00 2.10

1991

999† 30s Sailing dinghy, Kamakura Beach 15 20

1992

MS1098† 5m Red Indian canoe 2.25 2.40

LIBERIA

West Africa
100 cents = 1 dollar

1886

29† 32c *Alligator* (first settlers' ship), 1822 .... 12.00 12.00

1909

252† 5c *Lark* (gunboat) 1.75 35
259† 50c Canoe 2.75 60

1913

Nos 252 and 259 surcharged
323† 2c on 5c *Lark* 2.25 3.50
283† 10c on 50c Canoe (surch **1914 10
        CENTS**) 9.00 9.00
301† 10c on 50c Canoe (surch **10** and
        ornaments) 6.50 6.00

1918

351† 5c *Alligator* (first settlers' ship), 1822 .... 45 10

1921

404† 10c *Alligator* (first settlers' ship), 1822 .. 80 10
408† 30c Canoe 1.00 15
409† 50c Kru canoe 1.00 25
413† $5 Canoe 23.00 1.50

Nos. 404, 408/9 and 413 overprinted **1921**
418† 10c *Alligator* 5.50 50
422† 30c Canoe 3.50 50
423† 50c Kru canoe 3.00 70
427† $5 Canoe 23.00 3.50

1923

466 1c *Alligator* (first settlers' ship), 1822
467 2c *Alligator*
468 5c *Alligator*
469 10c *Alligator*
470 $5 *Alligator*

Set of 5 48.00 3.25

1936

No. 351 surcharged **1936 3 1936 3**
537† 3c on 5c *Alligator* 30 45

No. O364 surcharged **1936 3 1936 3** *with star*
548† 3c on 5c *Alligator* 25 50

1940

575† 3c Immigrant ships, 1839 .... 50 15

1941

No. 575 overprinted **POSTAGE STAMP CENTENNIAL 1840-1940 ROWLAND HILL** with portrait of Rowland Hill (No. 581 additionally overprinted **AIR MAIL** with airplane)

578†	3c Immigrant ships, 1839	1.75	1.75
581†	3c Immigrant ships, 1839 (air)	1.40	1.40

No. 575 surcharged **RED CROSS TWO CENTS** with Red Cross (No. 587 additionally overprinted **AIR MAIL** with airplane)

584†	3c Immigrant ships, 1839	1.40	1.40
587†	3c Immigrant ships, 1839 (air)	1.40	1.40

1949

704†	3c Alligator (first settlers' ship), 1822	1.00	1.50
707†	50c Alligator	3.25	3.25

1953

730†	25c African Glen (freighter), Monrovia (purple)	75	30

1954

As No. 730, but colour changed and inscribed "COMMEMORATING PRESIDENTIAL VISIT U.S.A.—1954"

751†	25c African Glen (blue)	80	20

1960

833†	10c Pirogue	40	75

1969

1001†	20c Yachts, Argenteuil	50	20

1971

1062†	20c Inflatable dinghy	45	15

MS1073†	30c Olympic yachts, Kiel (sheet contains one other design)	1.25	1.25

1972

1099†	3c Elizabeth (emigrant ship), at Providence Island, 1822	50	50
1101†	20c Elizabeth (emigrant ship), at Providence Island, 1822	1.50	55
MS1103†	50c Elizabeth crossing the Atlantic	3.25	2.25

1125	3c H.M.S. Ajax (ship of the line) and figurehead, 1809		
1126	5c H.M.S. Hogue (screw ship of the line) and figurehead, 1848		
1127	7c H.M.S. Ariadne (frigate) and figurehead, 1816		
1128	15c H.M.S. Royal Adelaide (ship of the line) and figurehead, 1828		
1129	25c H.M.S. Rinaldo (screw sloop) and figurehead, 1860		
1130	25c H.M.S. Nymphe (screw sloop), 1888		
	Set of 6	5.50	2.75
MS1131	50c H.M.S. Victory (ship of the line), 1765	3.75	3.00

1974

1187†	2c Thomas Coutts (full-rigged sailing ship), 1817, and Aureol (liner), 1974	20	10
1188†	3c Modern liner	30	10

1221†	15c "Liberty" ship, 1944	55	15

1975

1238†	50c Santa Maria (Columbus) (and on U.S.A. stamp No. 236)	2.00	55
MS1239†	75c Mayflower (Pilgrim Fathers) (and on U.S.A. stamp No. 556) (air)	3.00	1.75

1240†	1c Canoes, Lambarene	10	10

1976

1273†	25c Olympic yachts	65	35

1280†	25c Dominia (cable ship), 1926	1.00	30

1284†	1c Canoe, River Mano	10	10
1287b†	17c Game fishing launch	35	10
1289†	55c Game fishing launch	1.40	35

1979

1382†	25c John Penn (paddle-steamer), 1860	75	25

1388	5c World Peace (tanker)		
1389	$1 World Peace		
	Set of 2	2.50	1.75

1431†	35c Indian canoe	80	45

1981

As Nos. 1284 and 1289, but smaller, 33 × 20mm

1504a†	1c Canoe, River Mano	10	10
1509a†	80c Game fishing launch	2.50	1.50

1984

1588†	31c Bulk carrier, Buchanan	1.25	75

1987

1659† 15c *Sir Winston Churchill* (cadet schooner), New York 35 20
1660† 15c *Bay Queen* (harbour ferry), New York 35 20
1662† 15c Tug and schooner 35 20
1670† 60c Yachts and cabin cruisers 1.25 75

1988

1701† $1 Yacht 1.50 1.00

1710† 45c *Chevron Antwerp* (tanker) 70 40
1711† $1 *Lakonia* (liner) on fire, 1963 .... 1.50 1.00

1989

1728† 10c U.S.S. *Okinawa* (helicopter carrier) 30 10

OFFICIAL STAMPS

1909
As Nos. 252 and 259, but colours changed, overprinted **OS**
O264† 5c *Lark* (gunboat) 1.00 15
O271† 50c Canoe 2.25 40

1915
Nos. O264 and O271 surcharged with new value
O326† 2c on 5c *Lark* (gunboat) 2.50 3.00
O314† 10c on 50c Canoe 6.50 7.50

1918
As No. 351, but with colour changed, overprinted **OS**
O364† 5c *Alligator* 45 10

1921
As Nos. 404, 408/9 and 413, but colours changed, overprinted **OS**
O432† 10c *Alligator* 1.25 15
O436† 30c Canoe 1.40 15
O437† 50c Kru canoe 1.50 25
O441† $5 Canoe 17.00 1.75

Nos. O432, O436/7 and O441 overprinted **1921**
O446† 10c *Alligator* 1.75 25
O450† 30c Canoe 1.75 30
O451† 50c Kru canoe 3.50 40
O455† $5 Canoe 16.00 3.00

REGISTRATION STAMPS

Each inscribed with the name of a different town

1919

R388 10c *Quail* (patrol boat) (Buchanan)
R389 10c *Quail* (Grenville)
R390 10c *Quail* (Harper)
R391 10c *Quail* (Monrovia)
R392 10c *Quail* (Robertsport)
Set of 5 4.00 25.00

1923

R499 10c Sailing skiff (Buchanan)
R500 10c Lighter (Grenville)
R501 10c Full-rigged sailing ship (Harper)
R502 10c *George Washington* (liner) (Monrovia)
R503 10c Canoe (Robertsport)
Set of 5 38.00 2.50

LIBYA

North Africa
1912 100 centesimi = 1 lira
1961 1000 milliemes = 1 pound
1982 1000 dirhams = 1 dinar

1921

54† 30c Roman galley 10 35
55† 50c Roman galley 10 10
30† 55c Roman galley 1.90 5.00
59† 1li25 Roman galley 10 10

1961

263 15m *Esso Canterbury* (tanker)
264 50m *Esso Canterbury*
265 100m *Esso Canterbury*
Set of 3 2.50 90

1967

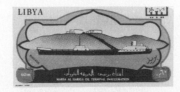

392 60m *British Confidence* (tanker) 85 30

1968

416 10m Tanker
417 60m Tanker
Set of 2 75 30

1969

Face values in white
444 5m Destroyer
445 10m Destroyer
446 15m Destroyer
447 25m Destroyer
448 45m Destroyer
449 60m Destroyer
Set of 6 3.75 2.00

1970
As Nos. 444/9 but face values in black
457 5m Destroyer
458 10m Destroyer
459 15m Destroyer
460 25m Destroyer
461 45m Destroyer
462 60m Destroyer
Set of 6 3.75 2.00

1978

828† 30dh Frigate 40 15

1980

994† 20dh Italian landings at El Hani, 1911 .... 35 15
995† 35dh Italian landings at El Hani, 1911 .... 60 25

1014† 25dh Liner 45 15

1982

1227†	30dh Modern naval vessels	50	25
MS1231†	200dh Modern naval vessels	3.00	3.00

1983

1303	100dh Phoenician galley		
1304	100dh Ancient Greek galley		
1305	100dh Ancient Egyptian ship		
1306	100dh Roman sailing ship		
1307	100dh Viking longship		
1308	100dh Libyan xebec		
	Set of 6	4.25	3.00

1353†	100dh Sailboard	65	45

1984

1432†	25dh Sailboards	20	10
1433†	25dh Sailing dinghy (orange and red sails)	20	10
1434†	25dh Sailing dinghy (mauve sails)	20	10
1437†	25dh Rowing boat	20	10
1438†	25dh Motor boat	20	10

1552†	100dh Sailboards	70	40

1573†	25dh Liner at quay	30	10

1985

1713†	50dh Burning of U.S.S. *Philadelphia*, 1804	60	20
1715†	100dh Felucca	1.25	45

1986

1873†	50d American aircraft carrier	40	25
1874†	100d Capture of U.S.S. *Philadelphia* (frigate), 1801	1.00	50

1989

1983†	150dh U.S.S. *Philadelphia* exploding, 1804	1.00	55

1988†	100dh Ships' boats	55	25

1991

2036†	400dh Naval transport and ship's boat	2.50	95

LIECHTENSTEIN

Central Europe
100 rappen = 1 franc

1928

82†	20r + 10r Pontoon	17.00	21.00

LITHUANIA

Eastern Europe
100 centu = 1 litas

1923

219†	1li Paddle-tug and freighter, Memel	3.00	3.00

LOURENCO MARQUES

East Africa
100 centavos = 1 escudo

1913

Nos. 1/2, 5 and 7 of Portuguese Colonies surcharged **REPUBLICA LOURENCO MARQUES** *and value*

107†	½c on 2½r Departure of Vasco da Gama's fleet	50	45
108†	½c on 5r Vasco da Gama's fleet at Calicut	50	45
111†	5c on 50r *Sao Gabriel* (flagship)	50	45
113†	10c on 100r *Sao Gabriel*	65	45

Nos. 104/5, 108 and 110 of Macao surcharged **REPUBLICA LOURENCO MARQUES** *and value*

115†	½c on ½a Departure of Vasco da Gama's fleet	60	45
116†	½c on 1a Vasco da Gama's fleet at Calicut	60	45
119†	5c on 8a *Sao Gabriel* (flagship)	60	45
121†	10c on 16a *Sao Gabriel*	75	45

Nos. 58/9, 62 and 64 of Timor surcharged **REPUBLICA LOURENCO MARQUES** *and value*

123†	½c on ½a Departure of Vasco da Gama's fleet	60	45
124†	½c on 1a Vasco da Gama's fleet at Calicut	60	45
127†	5c on 8a *Sao Gabriel* (flagship)	60	45
129†	10c on 16a *Sao Gabriel*	75	45

LUXEMBOURG

Western Europe
100 centimes = 1 franc

1964

743	3f Barge, Moselle Canal	30	15

1967

807†	3f Barges, River Moselle	20	15

1971

876†	3f Yachts	40	20

1975

948†	4f River barge, Remich	1.00	20

1988

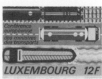

1223†	12f Canal barge	60	35

MACAO

South-east coast of China
1898 78 avos = 1 rupee
1913 100 avos = 1 pataca

1898

As Nos. 378/9, 382 and 384 of Portugal, but inscribed "MACAU"

104†	½a Departure of Vasco da Gama's fleet	1.00	70
105†	1a Vasco da Gama's fleet at Calicut	1.00	70
108†	8a *Sao Gabriel* (flagship)	1.40	1.00
110†	16a *Sao Gabriel*	2.25	1.50

1913

Nos. 104/5, 108 and 110 overprinted **REPUBLICA**

256†	½a Departure of Vasco da Gama's fleet	60	45
257†	1a Vasco da Gama's fleet at Calicut	60	45
260†	8a *Sao Gabriel* (flagship)	95	70
262†	16a *Sao Gabriel*	1.10	80

1934

338	½a Galeasse
339	1a Galeasse
340	2a Galeasse
341	3a Galeasse
342	4a Galeasse
343	5a Galeasse
344	6a Galeasse
345	7a Galeasse
346	8a Galeasse
347	10a Galeasse
348	12a Galeasse
349	14a Galeasse
350	15a Galeasse
351	20a Galeasse
352	30a Galeasse
353	40a Galeasse
354	50a Galeasse
355	1p Galeasse
356	2p Galeasse
357	3p Galeasse
358	5p Galeasse

Set of 21	65.00	30.00

1936

Nos. 340/1, 344/6 and 350 overprinted **Aviao** and Greek characters, 6a also surcharged **5 avos**

359	2a Galeasse
360	3a Galeasse
361	5a on 6a Galeasse
362	7a Galeasse
363	8a Galeasse
364	15a Galeasse

Set of 6	9.75	6.75

1940

Nos. 344/6 and 352/4 surcharged

391†	1a on 6a Galeasse	1.50	1.00
394†	2a on 6a Galeasse	90	80
395†	3a on 6a Galeasse	90	80
396†	5a on 7a Galeasse	90	80
397†	5a on 8a Galeasse	90	80
398†	8a on 30a Galeasse	1.90	1.75
399†	8a on 40a Galeasse	1.90	1.75
400†	8a on 50a Galeasse	1.90	1.75

1951

447†	1p Sampan	4.50	1.25
448†	3p Junk	16.00	3.00
449†	5p Junk	32.00	11.00

1967

504	10a *Vega* (fast patrol boat)		
505	20a *Don Fernando* (sail frigate)		
	Set of 2	2.50	1.50

1975

525	20a Ferry passing under Macao–Taipa Bridge		
526	2p20 Junk and liner at bridge		
	Set of 2	2.25	1.40

1981

542	10a Junk
543	30a Junk
544	1p Junk
545	3p Junk

Set of 4	2.25	1.50

1983

585	4p 16th-century Portuguese galleon		
586	4p 16th-century Portuguese galleon and emblem		
	Set of 2	3.25	2.50

1984

598	20a Hok Lou T'eng (local fishing boat)		
599	60a Tai T'ong (local fishing boat)		
600	2p Tai Mei Chai (local fishing boat)		
601	5p Ch'at Pong T'o (local fishing boat)		
	Set of 4	3.25	2.25

1985

605	1p50 Junk	70	30

617	50a Tou (sailing barge)		
618	70a Veng Seng Lei (motor junk)		
619	1p Tong Heng Long No. 2 (motor junk)		
620	6p Fong Vong San (container ship)		
	Set of 4	4.00	2.25

1986

630	10a Hydrofoil
631	40a *Tejo* (hovercraft)
632	3p *Tercera* (jetfoil)
633	7p50 High speed ferry

Set of 4	5.00	3.75

635†	2p Sampan, Sao Paulo da Monte	90	90
637†	2p Junk, Guia	90	90

1987

645	50a Dragon boat
646	5p Dragon boat figurehead

Set of 2	1.60	90

1989

705†	4p Junk	80	50

1990

717†	7p50 Junk	1.25	1.00

733	50a Galleon
734	1p Galleon
735	3p50 Galleon
736	6p50 Galleon

Set of 4	2.25	1·40

MS737	5p Galleon	90	90

1991

760† 4p20 16th-century ship's boat 85 55

1992

782† 5p Yacht 85 60

POSTAGE DUE STAMPS

1949

Nos. 342, 344, 346/8 and 352/3 surcharged **PORTEADO** *and new value*

D424	1a on 4a Galeasse		
D425	2a on 6a Galeasse		
D426	4a on 8a Galeasse		
D427	5a on 10a Galeasse		
D428	8a on 12a Galeasse		
D429	12a on 30a Galeasse		
D430	20a on 40a Galeasse		

Set of 7 5.00 4.75

MADAGASCAR AND DEPENDENCIES

Indian Ocean off East Africa
100 centimes = 1 franc

1931

As No. 109 of Cameroun
152† 1f50 *Leconte de Lisle* (liner) 1.40 1.00

1937

As Nos. 110/11 of Cameroun
187† 20c Liner 60 75
188† 30c Sailing ships 75 85
MS192a† 3f Liner 4.00 5.50

1954

As No. 264 of Cameroun
330 15f Landing craft, Normandy, 1944 ...... 2.00 1.50

1956

335† 10f Dredger 30 15
336† 15f Pirogue 40 15

MADEIRA

Atlantic Ocean, north-west of Africa
100 centavos = 1 escudo

1898

Nos. 378/9, 382 and 384 of Portugal, but inscribed "MADEIRA"
134† 2½r Departure of Vasco da Gama's fleet 1.25 75
135† 5r Vasco da Gama's fleet at Calicut 1.25 75
138† 50r *Sao Gabriel* (flagship) 3.00 1.75
140† 100r *Sao Gabriel* 3.50 2.75

1980

177† 30e Local fishing boat 80 35

1981

180† 8e50 Portuguese caravel, 1418 .... 25 10

1984

213† 51e Local sailing boat 70 35

1985

221† 60e Coastal ferry 75 40

1986

224 68e50 Tanker 1.25 60

1988

238 80e *Maria Cristina* (mail boat) 75 40

1990

270 32e Tunny boat
271 60e Desert Islands boat
272 70e Maneiro type of fishing boat
273 95e Chavelha type of fishing boat
Set of 4 2.00 95

STANLEY GIBBONS STAMP COLLECTING SERIES

Introductory booklets on *How to Start, How to Identify Stamps* and *Collecting by Theme*. A series of well illustrated guides at a low price. Write for details.

1992

281 38e *Gaviao* (ferry)
282 65e *Independencia* (catamaran ferry)
283 85e *Madeirense* (car ferry)
284 120e *Funchalense* (freighter)
Set of 4 2.75 1.25

MALACCA

South-east Asia
100 cents = 1 dollar

1949

As No. 115 of Antigua
19† 15c Paddle-steamer 45 1.75

1957

45† 20c Malay fishing prau 30 40

1960

As No. 45, but with tree and deer emblem instead of Queen Elizabeth II
56† 20c Malay fishing prau 20 20

MALAGASY REPUBLIC

Indian Ocean off East Africa
100 centimes = 1 franc

1962

42† 50f Pirogue 60 25

51† 15f *Esso Gasikara* (tanker) 35 15

1965

105† 12f Pirogue 30 20
109† 65f *Porthos* (hydrofoil) 1.50 50

1971

205† 5f Outrigger canoe 15 10

1974

272†   300f Scout canoe 2.75   1.50

1975

305   40f *Randolph* (American frigate), 1777
306   50f *Lexington* (American brigantine) and
      H.M.S. *Edward* (sloop), 1776
307   100f *Languedoc* (French ship of the line),
      1778 (air)
308   200f *Bonhomme Richard* (American
      frigate) and H.M.S. *Serapis* (frigate),
      1779
309   300f *Millern* (full-rigged merchantman) and
      Montgomery (American brig)
                          Set of 5   7.00   3.50
MS310   500f *Hanna* (American schooner), 1775   4.50   4.50

336   8f Sailing pirogue
337   45f Malagasy schooner
                          Set of 2   75   40

1976

360†   200f *Emile Baudot* (cable ship) 1.75   70

    Nos. 305/10 overprinted **4 JUILLET 1776—1976**
371   40f *Randolph*
372   50f *Lexington* and H.M.S. *Edward*
373   100f *Languedoc* (air)
374   200f *Bonhomme Richard* and H.M.S.
      Serapis
375   30f *Millern* and *Montgomery*
                          Set of 5   4.75   2.75
MS376   500f *Hanna* 4.00   4.25

1985

554†   20f Fishing boats, Saintes-Maries   20   10

COLLECT FUNGI ON STAMPS
A Stanley Gibbons thematic catalogue — available at £5 (p. + p. £3) from: Stanley Gibbons Publications, 5 Parkside, Christchurch Road, Ringwood, Hants. BH24 3SH.

1987

617   60f *Sarimanok* (replica of early dhow)
618   150f *Sarimanok* (replica of early dhow)
                          Set of 2   1.50   50

642†   60f Fleet of Dias, 1492   20   10
643†   150f Portuguese galleon   45   20
647†   450f *Nina* (Columbus) 1.50   50

659†   10f Ship's boat   15   10

1988

710   20f Russian ship of the line, Black Sea
711   80f *Lesnoie* (Russian ship of the line)
712   80f Dutch ship of the line
713   100f *Orel* (Russian galleon)
714   250f Dutch fleet on exercise
                          Set of 5   1.60   75
MS715   550f Dutch sail warship at anchor 1.10   70

1990

802†   250f Canoe   40   15

808   250f Liner   45   15

MALAWI
Central Africa
1964 12 pence = 1 shilling
20 shillings = 1 pound
1970 100 tambalas = 1 kwacha

1964

219†   4d Fishing pirogue   25   15

1967

277   4d *Ilala I* (lake steamer), 1875
278   9d *Dove* (lake paddle-steamer), 1892
279   1s *Chauncy Maples I* (lake steamer),
      1901
280   3s *Gwendolen* (lake steamer), 1899
                          Set of 4   2.25   1.40

1975

486   3t *Mpasa* (lake vessel)
487   8t *Ilala II* (lake vessel), 1949
488   15t *Chauncy Maples II* (lake vessel)
489   30t *Nkwazi* (lake vessel)
                          Set of 4   1.25   1.00

1977

549†   20t *Ilala II* (lake vessel), 1949   90   30

1983

682†   1k Pirogue 1.10   2.25

1985

727   1k Trawler 3.00   3.25

728   7t *Ufulu* (lake tanker)
729   15t *Chauncy Maples II* (lake vessel)
730   20t *Mtendere* (lake vessel)
731   1k *Ilala II* (lake vessel)
                          Set of 4   6.50   4.25

1988

808† 2k *Seawise University* (liner, previously
Queen Elizabeth) on fire, 1972 .... 2.75 2.25

MALAYAN FEDERATION

South-east Asia
100 cents = 1 dollar

1957

3† 25c Tin dredger 55 10

MALAYSIA

South-east Asia
100 cents = 1 dollar

1974

127† 50c Tin dredger 2.75 3.00

1983

254† 20c *Tenaga Satu* (liquid gas tanker) 80 50

268† 20c Missile boat 75 45

1985

325† 15c Oil rig 20 10

1987

381 40c *Misc* (container ship) 45 45

1990

434† $1 Sailboard and yachts 65 1.25

MALDIVE ISLANDS

Indian Ocean
100 larees = 1 rupee

1950

21 2la Dhow
22 3la Dhow
23 5la Dhow
24 6la Dhow
25 10la Dhow
26 15la Dhow
27 25la Dhow
28 50la Dhow
29 1r Dhow

Set of 9 15.00 22.00

1968

268 50la Punt
269 1r Ancient Greek galley
270 2r Yacht, Argenteuil
271 5r Fishing boats, Les Saintes-Maries

Set of 4 5.50 5.50

298† 10la Local fishing dhow 75 20

1971

368† 1r Inflatable dinghy 50 50

1973

439† 2la Scout rowing boat 10 20
443† 1r Scout rowing boat 2.50 75

1974

477† 3la *Nomad* (weather ship) 10 10
481† 3r *Nomad* 2.25 1.75

508† 2la Paddle-steamer and modern mail
ship 10 10
511† 2r50 Paddle-steamer and modern mail
ship 1.60 1.60

537† 3la H.M.S. *Conqueror* and *H.M.S.*
Thunderer (battleships) 15 30
538† 4la H.M.S. *Indomitable* (aircraft carrier) 15 30
MS543† 10r H.M.S. *Indomitable* (aircraft
carrier) 17.00 17.00

1975

579† 7la Motor cruisers, Mahe 10 10

No. 443 *overprinted* **14th Boy Scout Jamboree July 29—**
August 7, 1975
582† 1r Scout rowing boat 30 30

586 1la Madura prau
587 2la Ganges patela
588 3la Indian palla
589 4la Odhi (dhow)
590 5la Maldivian schooner
591 25la *Cutty Sark* (clipper)
592 1r Maldivian baggala
593 5r *Maldive Courage* (freighter)

Set of 8 4.75 5.00
MS594 10r Maldivian baggala 7.50 10.00

619† 5la Tourist launch and outboard motor
boats 10 10
620† 7la Yachts 10 10
623† 10r Motor cruisers 4.00 5.00

1976

647† 1r *Salernum* (cable ship) 70 55

1977

MS720† 7.50r *Ostfriesland* (German
battleship), 1914 .... 12.00 13.00

721† 6la Boat building 30 15

1978

746 1la Mas odi (fishing boat)
747 2la Battela (dhow)
748 3la Bandu odi (fishing boat)
749 5la *Maldive Trader* (freighter)
750 1r *Fath-hul Baaree* (brigantine)
751 1r25 Mas dhoni (dhow)
752 3r Baggala (dhow)
753 4r Baggala (dhow)
　　　　　　　　　　　　　　Set of 8 3.50 3.50
MS754 1r Battela (dhow), 4r Mas dhoni (dhow) 3.25 3.50

764† 3la H.M.S. *Endeavour* (Cook) 10 15
766† 75la H.M.S. *Resolution* and H.M.S.
　　　 Discovery (Cook) 1.25 1.25
MS769† 5r H.M.S. *Endeavour* 18.00 18.00

785† 1la Fishing boat 10 10
791† 1r25 Dhow at night 50 45
MS794† 3r Fishing boats 3.00 3.50

1981

950† 5la Fishing boat 30 15
951† 15la Fishing boats 45 25

1983

1011† 2r Motor fishing boat 55 55

1025† 6r Fishing dhows 1.50 1.50

1984

1047† 15la 10how 10 10
1049† 2r Sailboard 40 40
1051† 6r Fishing launch 1.25 1.25
1052† 8r Game fishing launch 1.50 1.50

1985

1091† 2r Coastguard cutter 90 55

1108 3la Mas odi (fishing boat)
1109 5la Battela (dhow)
1110 10la Addu odi (dhow)
1111 2r60 Modern dhoni (fishing boat)
1112 2r70 Mas dhoni (fishing boat)
1113 3r Batheli dhoni (fishing boat)
1114 5r *Inter I* (inter-island ferry)
1115 10r Dhoni-style yacht
　　　　　　　　　　　　　　Set of 8 3.25 3.50

1116† 6r Sailboards 1.10 1.40

1986

1213† 2r Boat building 40 45
MS1216† 15r Diving bell 2.75 3.50

1987

1245 15la *Intrepid* (yacht), 1970
1246 1r *France II* (yacht), 1974
1247 2r *Gretel* (yacht), 1962
1248 12r *Volunteer* (yacht), 1887
　　　　　　　　　　　　　　Set of 4 2.40 3.00

1988

MS1296† 15r Fishing dhow 1.75 2.25

1989

1319† 50la Japanese sampan, Lake
　　　 Kawaguchi 10 10
1321† 2r Japanese sampans and fishing boats 20 25
1323† 6r Japanese fishing boat 65 70
1325† 12r Japanese ferry, River Sumida ... 1.25 1.40
MS1326† Two sheets. (b) 18r Japanese
sampans (other sheet shows landscape)
　　　　　　　　　　　　Price for 2 sheets 4.00 4.25

1357† 10r H.M.S. *Bounty* (Bligh) 1.60 1.60
1358† 12r Tugs and barges, Hamburg 1.75 1.75

1990

1410† 2r50 Landing craft, D-Day, 1944 .... 30 35
1411† 3r50 Transports and landing craft,
　　　 Norway, 1940 .... 40 45
1415† 12r Landing craft, Sicily, 1943 .... 1.40 1.50
MS1416† 18r Liberty ship, Atlantic convoy . 2.10 2.25

1991

1490 3r50 Maldive dhoni
1491 7r *Maldive Trader* (freighter)
　　　　　　　　　　　　　　Set of 2 1.10 1.25

1574†	3r50 American aircraft carrier and Admiral King	40	45
1576†	3r50 American aircraft carrier and Admiral Halsey	40	45
1577†	3r50 American aircraft carrier and Admiral Mitscher	40	45

1992

1583†	6r Landing craft, D-Day, 1944	70	75

MS1630†	Two sheets 18r Dhow (other sheet shows beach scene)		
	Price for 2 sheets	4.00	4.25

1652†	3r50 Coastguard patrol boats	40	45

MALI

West Africa
100 centimes = 1 franc

1966

125†	3f Fishing pirogue	15	15
127†	20f Fishing pirogue	35	15
128†	25f Fishing pirogue	50	20
130†	85f Fishing pirogue	1.25	50

1970

262†	100f Scout canoes	90	35

1971

271†	200f America's Cup yacht	2.00	60

288	100f Santa Maria (Columbus), 1492		
289	150f Mayflower (Pilgrim Fathers), 1620		
290	200f Potemkin (Russian battleship), 1905		
291	250 Normandie (French liner), 1935		
	Set of 4	5.25	2.25

1972

312†	130f Gondolas, Venice	70	35
313†	270f Gondolas, Venice	1.40	60

1974

439†	80f Full-rigged sailing ship and modern liner	55	25

No. 439 surcharged **9 OCTOBRE 1974 250F**

463†	250f on 80f Full-rigged sailing ship and modern liner	1.40	80

1975

503†	370f Battle of the Chesapeake, 1781	1.90	95

1976

535†	400f 18th-century warships	3.50	85

554	200f Freighter	1.10	45

563	160f Muscat fishing boat		
564	180f Cochin-China junk		
565	190f Ruytingen (Dunkirk lightship)		
566	200f Nile felucca		
	Set of 4	2.50	1.25

1978

622†	300f Captain Cook's ship	1.75	70

1979

723	300f H.M.S. Resolution (Cook), Kerguelen, 1776		
724	480f H.M.S. Resolution (Cook), Hawaii, 1778		
	Set of 2	3.75	1.90

1980

752†	300f Racing yachts	1.00	50

782†	420f French fleet, Rhode Island, 1780	1.50	75

No. 752 overprinted **FINN RECHARDT (Fin.) MAYRHOFER (Autr.) BALACHOV (Urss)**

792†	300f Racing yacht	1.00	55

808†	120f Freighter	1.40	45

1981

862	180f Fleet of Columbus, 1492 (also on U.S.A. stamp No. 238)		
863	200f Nina (also Santa Maria on Spain stamp No. 593)		
864	260f Pinta (also Santa Maria on Spain stamp No. 597)		
865	30f Santa Maria (also on U.S.A. stamp No. 237)		
	Set of 4	4.50	1.90

1982

947	200f Sailboard
948	270f Sailboard
949	300f Sailboard
	Set of 3	3.00	1.40

1983

| 956† | 300f Sailboards .... | 1.10 | 55 |

| 968† | 700f Container ship .... | 4.50 | 2.50 |

| 981 | 240f Liner .... | 1.25 | 50 |

1984

| **MS**1003† | 700f Olympic yacht .... | 1.90 | 2.25 |

No. 981 surcharged **120F**

| 1006† | 120f on 240f Liner .... | 1.10 | 50 |

No. **MS**1003 *surcharged* **350F VOILE 470 1. ESPAGNE 2. ETATS-UNIS 3. FRANCE**

| **MS**1050† | 350f on 700f Olympic yacht .... | 1.00 | 1.25 |

MALTA

Mediterranean
1899 12 pence = 1 shilling
20 shillings = 1 pound
1972 10 mils = 1 cent
100 cents = 1 pound

1899

57†	4½d Gozo fishing boat (brown)	17.00	5.50
58†	4½d Gozo fishing boat (orange)	3.00	3.25
59†	5d Galley of Knights of St. John (red)	20.00	3.75
60†	5d Galley of Knights of St. John (green)	3.00	3.25
35†	10s Roman shipwreck (inscr "POSTAGE")	75.00	60.00

1914

As No. 35, but inscribed "POSTAGE REVENUE"

| 104† | 10s Roman shipwreck .... | £300 | £475 |

1922

No. 104 overprinted **SELF-GOVERNMENT**

| 121† | 10s Roman shipwreck .... | £100 | £150 |

1926

| 166† | 1s Local felucca .... | 4.25 | 2.25 |
| 169† | 2s6d Gozo fishing boat .... | 10.00 | 29.00 |

1928

Nos. 166 and 169 overprinted **POSTAGE AND REVENUE**

| 186† | 1s Local felucca .... | 2.25 | 2.00 |
| 189† | 2s6d Gozo fishing boat .... | 13.00 | 23.00 |

1930

As Nos. 166 and 169, but inscribed "POSTAGE AND REVENUE"

| 203† | 1s Local felucca .... | 4.00 | 8.00 |
| 206† | 2s6d Gozo fishing boat .... | 13.00 | 38.00 |

1949

As No. 115 of Antigua

| 252† | 3d Paddle-steamer .... | 1.75 | 40 |

1958

| 290† | 3d German E-boats (motor torpedo-boats), 1941 .... | 10 | 10 |

1965

| 337† | 4½d Galleys of Knights of St. John ...... | 40 | 40 |

| 354† | 6d Turkish fleet, 1565 .... | 50 | 10 |

1966

| 363† | 3d H.M.S. *Marlborough* (battleship) .... | 15 | 10 |
| 365† | 1s6d H.M.S. *Marlborough* (battleship) | 35 | 40 |

1973

489†	8m Freighter at wharf	10	10
490†	1c Fishing boats	10	10
494†	4c Yachts	15	10
496†	7c5m Luzzu regatta	25	10
500b†	£2 Luzzu	9.00	11.00

1974

| 528† | 5c *Washington* (paddle-steamer) and *Royal Viking Star* (liner) .... | 30 | 10 |

1976

| 560† | 5c Olympic yachts .... | 20 | 10 |

1977

| 585† | 20c Canal barge .... | 35 | 80 |

1979

| 619† | 2c Maltese luzzu and aircraft carrier .... | 10 | 10 |
| 622† | 8c Maltese luzzu and aircraft carrier .... | 30 | 40 |

| 625† | 7c Speronara (fishing boat) .... | 15 | 10 |

1981

669†	2c Building a galleon	15	10
672†	6c Trawler	30	25
676†	12c Modern shipyard	40	45
681†	£1 *Dwejra* (freighter) and container ship	3.50	4.25

1982

686 3c Shipyard
687 8c Fishing boats under construction
688 13c *Chenna Selvan* (tanker under
      construction)
689 27c Shipyard
                              Set of 4   2.00   2.00

701 3c *Ta' Salvo Serafino* (oared brigantine),
      1531
702 8c *La Madonna del Rosaria* (tartane),
      1740
703 12c *San Paola* (xebec), 1743
704 20c *Ta' Pietro Saliba* (xprunara), 1798
                              Set of 4   3.50   1.60

1983

710† 15c Sailboard   50   65

725 2c *Strangier* (full-rigged sailing ship), 1813
726 12c *Tigre* (topsail schooner), 1839
727 13c *La Speranza* (brig), 1844
728 20c *Wignacourt* (barque), 1844
                              Set of 4   3.35   3.00

1985

772 3c *Scotia* (paddle-steamer), 1844
773 7c *Tagliaferro* (screw steamer), 1882
774 15c *Gleneagles* (screw steamer), 1885
775 23c *L'Isle Adam* (screw steamer), 1886
                              Set of 4   4.75   5.25

1986

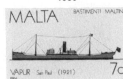

792 7c *San Paul* (freighter), 1921
793 10c *Knight of Malta* (mail steamer), 1930
794 12c *Valetta City* (freighter), 1948
795 20c *Saver* (freighter), 1959
                              Set of 4   6.75   6.75

1987

809 2c *Medina* (freighter), 1969
810 11c *Rabat* (container ship), 1974
811 13c *Ghawdex* (passenger ferry), 1979
812 20c *Pinto* (car ferry), 1987
                              Set of 4   5.00   6.00

1988

827† 10c Harbour ferry 1.00   75

1990

887 10c Roman shipwreck (on stamp No. 35)   60   70

1991

908† 4c Luzzu at Spinola Palace   15   20
910† 10c Sailboards, Mellieha Bay   35   40
911† 12c Fishing boat, Wied iz-Zurrieq   40   45
912† 14c Fishing boats and luzzu, Mgarr   50   55
913† 20c Yachts   70   75
914† 50c Ferry, Gozo Channel 1.75   1.90

1992

919† 10c Columbus's fleet   55   55

923† 50c *Ohio* (tanker) 2.50   2.75

COLLECT CHESS ON STAMPS
A Stanley Gibbons thematic catalogue — available at £5 (p. + p. £3) from: Stanley Gibbons Publications, 5 Parkside, Christchurch Road, Ringwood, Hants. BH24 3SH.

MANAMA

Arabian peninsula
100 dirhams = 1 riyal

1967
Nos. 140 and 148 of Ajman overprinted **MANAMA** *in English and Arabic*
5†   15d *Yankee* (sail training and cruise ship)   10   10
13† 10r *Brasil* (liner) 6.50   6.50

Appendix

The following stamps have either been issued in excess of postal needs, or have not been made available to the public in reasonable quantities at face value. Miniature sheets, imperforate stamps etc. are excluded from this section.

1966
New currency surcharges. No. 35 of Ajman surcharged **Manama 3 Riyals** *in English and Arabic. 3r on 3r Sailing yacht.*

1971
18th and 19th-century Ships Paintings. Postage 15, 20, 25, 30, 50d; Air 60d, 1, 2r.

MARIANA ISLANDS

Pacific Ocean
100 pfennig = 1 mark

1901
As Nos. K7/19 of Cameroun, but inscribed "MARIANEN"
13 3pf *Hohenzollern* (German Imperial yacht)
14 5pf *Hohenzollern*
15 10pf *Hohenzollern*
16 20pf *Hohenzollern*
17 25pf *Hohenzollern*
18 30pf *Hohenzollern*
19 40pf *Hohenzollern*
20 50pf *Hohenzollern*
21 80pf *Hohenzollern*
22 1m *Hohenzollern*
23 2m *Hohenzollern*
24 3m *Hohenzollern*
25 5m *Hohenzollern*
                              Set of 13   £140   £750

MARSHALL ISLANDS

North Pacific
1901 100 pfennig = 1 mark
1984 100 cents = 1 dollar

1901
As Nos. K7/19 of Cameroun, but inscribed "MARSHALL INSELN"
G11 3pf *Hohenzollern* (German Imperial
      yacht)
G12 5pf *Hohenzollern*
G13 10pf *Hohenzollern*
G14 20pf *Hohenzollern*
G15 25pf *Hohenzollern*
G16 30pf *Hohenzollern*
G17 40pf *Hohenzollern*
G18 50pf *Hohenzollern*
G19 80pf *Hohenzollern*
G20 1m *Hohenzollern*
G21 2m *Hohenzollern*
G22 3m *Hohenzollern*
G23 5m *Hohenzollern*
                              Set of 13   £120   £800

1984

22† 40c *Hohenzollern* (on stamp No. G11)   70   50
24† 40c *Hohenzollern* (on stamp No. G23)   70   50

33 20c Sailing canoe
34 20c *U.N. Sec-General* (container ship)
35 20c Aircraft carrier
36 20c Freighter
                              Set of 4   1.25   90

1985

58 14c *Morning Star I* (missionary brigantine), 1856
59 22c Launch of *Morning Star I*
60 33c *Morning Star I* leaving Honolulu
61 44c *Morning Star I* entering Ebon lagoon
Set of 4   1.75   1.40

66† 22c Satellite communications ship   65   45

1986

80† 22c Outrigger canoe   40   20
81† 22c Amphibious dukw and U.S.S. *Sumner* (landing ship)   45   30
82† 22c *L.S.T. 1108* (tank landing ship)   45   30
MS84† 44c U.S.S. *Saratoga* (aircraft carrier)   1.60   1.60

1987

107 22c *James T. Arnold* (whaling ship), 1854
108 22c *General Scott* (whaling ship), 1859
109 22c *Charles W. Morgan* (whaling ship), 1865
110 22c *Lucretia* (whaling ship), 1884
Set of 4   1.75   1.25

118† 44c *Itasca* (U.S. coastguard cutter), 1937   80   65
120† 44c *Koshu* (Japanese patrol boat), 1937   80   65

1988

176† 25c *Casco* (schooner) off San Francisco, 1888   35   25
177† 25c *Casco* in the Marquesas   35   25
178† 25c *Equator* (schooner)   35   25
179† 25c Chieftain's canoe, Majuro   35   25
181† 25c *Janet Nicoll* (inter-island steamer) ..   35   25
183† 25c Samoan canoe, Apia   35   25

185 25c *Vitoria* (Magellan)
186 25c *Charlotte* and *Scarborough* (British transports), 1788
187 25c U.S.S. *Flying Fish* (schooner) and U.S.S. *Peacock* (sloop), 1841
188 25c *Planet* (German auxiliary schooner), 1909
Set of 4   1.50   1·25

1989

201† 25c Satellite recovery vessel   30   20

206† 45c Japanese fishing boats   55   45

230† 25c *Bussard* (German cruiser)   30   20
232† 25c *L.S.T. 119* (floating post office)   30   20
233† 25c Mailboat, Mili Island   30   20
235† 25c Outrigger canoe   30   20
236† 45c *Morning Star V* (missionary ship), 1905   55   45
238† 45c *Prinz Eitel Freiderich* (German auxiliary cruiser), 1914   55   45
239† 45c *Scharnhorst* (German cruiser), 1914   55   45

MARTINIQUE

West Indies
100 centimes = 1 franc

1931
As No. 109 of Cameroun
133† 1f50 *Leconte de Lisle* (liner) 2.25   2.25

1937
As Nos. 110/11 of Cameroun
180† 20c Liner   85   95
181† 30c Sailing ships   85   95
MS185a† 3f Liner 3.75   5.25

1947

234† 60c Local fishing boats   25   35
235† 1f Local fishing boats   25   35
236† 1f50 Local fishing boats   25   35

MAURITANIA

West Africa
1931 100 centimes = 1 franc
1973 5 khoum = 1 ouguiya (um)

1931
As No. 109 of Cameroun
70† 1f50 *Leconte de Lisle* (liner) 2.50   2.50

1937
As Nos. 110/11 of Cameroun
71† 20c Liner   60   75
72† 30c Sailing ships   60   80

1960

139† 15f Fishing boat   40   15

1963

164† 200f Bulk carrier, Port-Etienne 4.50   1.75

1965

223† 10f Freighters and lighters, Nouakchott   15   10

1966

250 500f Raft from the *Medusa*, 1816 ....   9.00   6.50

1969

348† 15f Fishing boats, Nouadhibou   25   15

1972

398 45f 18th-century sailing ships, Venice
399 100f Gondolas, Venice
400 250f Gondolas, Venice
Set of 3   4.50   2.10

416   35f Freighter 30   20

1975

478   60u Canoe, River Ogowe 2.50   1.50

1979

614   12u *Sirius* (paddle-steamer)
615   14u *Great Republic* (paddle-steamer)
616   55u *Mauretania I* (liner)
617   60u *Stirling Castle* (liner)
         Set of 4   5.00   1.75

1981

708†   81um Battle of the Chesapeake, 1781 .. 2.25   1.50

709   19um *Pinta* (Columbus)
710   55um *Santa Maria* (Columbus)
         Set of 2   3.75   1.50

1982

720†   19um Scout rowing boat   90   35
721†   22um Scout rowing boat 1.00   40
722†   92um Scout yacht 3.00   1.25

1984

790†   18um Building fishing boat   85   55

810   14um Sail boards
811   18um "Finn" class yachts
812   19um "470" class yachts
813   44um "Soling" class yacht
         Set of 4   3.75   1.25
MS814   100um "Flying Dutchman" class yachts   . 2.75   3.00

1987

859†   2um *Santa Maria* (Columbus)   10   10
860†   22um *Nina* (Columbus)   65   30
861†   35um *Pinta* (Columbus) 1 10   50

1989

917   24um Container ship in port 1.25   65

1991

969†   60um Container ship in dock 2.00   85

MAURITIUS

Indian Ocean
100 cents = 1 rupee

1949
As No. 115 *of Antigua*
273†   20c Paddle-steamer   60   70

1950

277†   2c Local rowing boat   15   10

1953
As No. 277, *but with portrait of Queen Elizabeth II*
293†   2c Local rowing boat   10   10

1970

423†   2r50 *Heros* (settlers' ship), 1783   50   70

1971

429†   60c Sailing dinghies   45   10

1972

459†   15c Pirate dhow   55   10
461†   1r *L'Hirondelle* (pirate brig) 1.00   15
462†   2r50 18th-century British frigate 4.00   6.50

1974

470   60c Capture of the *Kent* (East Indiaman),
         1800   50   70

1976

501   10c *Pierre Loti* (packet steamer), 1953
502   15c *Secunder* (mail ship), 1907
503   50c *Hindoostan* (paddle-steamer), 1842
504   60c *St. Geran* (French sailing packet),
         1740
505   2r50 *Maen* (Dutch merchantman), 1638
         Set of 5   3.25   4.50

1978

538†   90c Battle of Grand Port, 1810   55   55

1980

592   25c *Emirne* (French steam packet)
593   1r *Boissevain* (cargo liner)
594   2r *La Boudeuse* (Bougainville)
595   5r *Sea Breeze* (English clipper)
         Set of 4   1.40   1.00

1982

642† 10r H.M.S. *Beagle* (Darwin) 1.40 2.50

1983

656† 10r Freighters, Port Louis 70 1.50

666† 1r Fishing boat 55 15

1984

682 25c Wreck of *Tayaeb* (freighter)
683 1r *Taher* (freighter)
684 5r *Triton* (East Indiaman)
685 10r *Astor* (modern liner)
　　　　　　　　　　　　　Set of 4 4.25 5.50

694† 10r Indian immigrant ship, 1834 .... 2.75 3.25

1985

707† 10r Sailboards 3.00 4.00

715† 10r Sailing canoe, Coin de Mire Island 3.25 3.50

1987

768† 1r50 Racing yachts 60 40
770† 5r *Svanen* (cadet barquentine) 1.75 2.00

MEMEL

LITHUANIAN OCCUPATION

Eastern Europe
1920 100 pfennig = 1 mark
1923 100 centi = 1 litas

1923

28† 40m Liner, Memel 2.50 10.00
29† 50m Liner, Memel 2.50 10.00
30† 80m Liner, Memel 2.50 10.00
31† 100m Liner, Memel 2.50 10.00

Nos. 28/31 surcharged with new value
70† 15c on 40m Liner, Memel 3.25 12.00
71† 30c on 50m Liner, Memel 2.50 6.50
72† 30c on 80m Liner, Memel 3.25 10.00
73† 30c on 100m Liner, Memel 2.50 6.50

Nos. 29 and 31 surcharged with new value and bars
87† 15c on 50m Liner, Memel £225 £450
88† 25c on 100m Liner, Memel £110 £225

MEXICO

Central America
100 centavos = 1 peso

1940

662† 20c 17th-century pirate galleon 70 35

1950

1012a† 5p 17th-century galleon 1.10 60

1964

1086† 80c 16th-century Spanish galleon 1.40 25

1968

1165† 80c Olympic yachts 30 10

1972

1253 40c *Zaragoza* (cadet sail corvette) 30 10

1975

1331 80c *Acali* (trans-Atlantic balsa raft) 30 10

1977

1416 1p60 *Rio Yaqui* (freighter) 40 10

1978

1428† 4p30 Oil rig 35 10

1979

MS1535 10p 16th-century Spanish galleon 1.40 1.10

1983

1669 16p *Nauticas Mexico* (container ship) .. 80 20

1987

1851   150p *Santa Maria* (Columbus)   30   15

1853†   150p Fishing canoes, Michoacan   15   10

1988

1871†   300p Tanker   20   10

1888   500p Container ship   35   10

1991

1994   700p Caravel
1995   700p Caravel
                     Set of 2   75   35

2004†   1000p Container ship   40   35
2013†   1000p Stern of container ship   40   25
2023†   1500p Bow of container ship   55   35

1992

MS2077   7000p Ships of Columbus 3.00   2.00

MICRONESIA

Pacific Ocean
100 cents = 1 dollar

1984

14a†   22c *Senyavin* (full-rigged ship) (Lutke) ..   30   15
15a†   36c *Senyavin*   50   20
19† $2 Outrigger canoes, Kosrae 3.00   1.50

25†   28c *Hohenzollern* (on Caroline Islands
        stamp No. 13)   45   30
27†   28c *Hohenzollern* (on Caroline Islands
        stamp No. 25)   65   50

1985

32   22c U.S.S. *Jamestown* (sail warship), 1870
33   33c *L'Astrolabe* (D'Urville), 1826 (air)
34   39c *La Coquille* (Duperrey), 1822
35   44c *Shenandoah* (Confederate warship),
       1865
                     Set of 4   1.50   1.10

1986

54†   44c *Trienza* (cargo liner), 1946   55   45

1988

79†   44c Outrigger canoe   65   55

1990

179   45c *Lyra* (whaling ship), 1826
180   45c *Prudent* (whaling ship), 1827
181   45c *Rhone* (whaling ship), 1851
182   45c *Sussex* (whaling ship), 1843
                     Set of 4   2.00   1.60
MS183 $1 Whaleboat 1.25   90

194†   25c Tourist launch, New York   25   15

197†   45c *Nantaku* (inter-island freighter) and
         mail launch, 1940   50   40

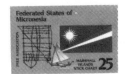

198   25c Outrigger canoe
199   25c U.S.S. *Constitution* (frigate), 1797
200   25c Outrigger canoe
                     Set of 3   95   55

210†   25c Canoe   25   15

1991

221†   29c U.S.S. *Missouri* (battleship), 1991 ..   35   25

1992

253   40c Outrigger canoe
254   50c Outrigger canoe
                     Set of 2   1·40   1.00

MIDDLE CONGO

Central Africa
100 centimes = 1 franc

1931
As No. 109 of Cameroun
68† 1f50 *Leconte de Lisle* (liner) 2.00 1.10

POSTAGE DUE STAMPS

1930

D83† 1f *William Guinet* (river steamer) 6.00 6.00
D84† 2f *William Guinet* 6.50 6.50
D85† 3f *William Guinet* 6.50 6.50

MOLDOVA

South-east Europe
100 kopeks = 1 rouble

1992
No. 5941 of Russia surcharged **MOLDOVA** *and new value*
30† 10r on 3 k *Aurora* (cruiser) 1.25 1.25

50† 1r *Galleon*
51† 6r *Carrack*
52† 6r *Caravel*
  Set of 3 2.10 2.10

MONACO

Southern Europe
100 centimes = 1 franc

1924

102† 2f 18th-century sailing ships, Monaco .. 70 60
103† 3f 18th-century sailing ships, Monaco .. 12.00 6.50
104† 5f 18th-century sailing ships, Monaco .. 5.50 3.75
105† 10f 18th-century sailing ships, Monaco 12.00 10.00

1926
No. 102 surcharged **1f50**
112† 1f50 on 2f 18th-century sailing ships,
  Monaco 2.50 2.25

1933
No. 104 surcharged **1F50** *and airplane*
143 1f50 on 5f 18th-century sailing ships,
  Monaco 22.00 22.00

1939

182† 70c *Hussar* (steam yacht) 35 20
183† 75c *Hussar* (green) 35 20
189† 3f *Hussar* (red) 40 20

1940
As Nos. 183 and 189, with colours changed, and surcharged with Red Cross and **+1**f
221† 75c + 1f *Hussar* (black) 1.90 2.25
225† 3f + 1f *Hussar* (blue) 9.50 7.75

1941
As 1939 issue, but new values
258† 1f20 *Hussar* 15 15
260† 2f *Hussar* 10 10
394† 10f *Hussar* 60 20
268† 15f *Hussar* 20 15
270† 25f *Hussar* (green) 90 60
374† 25f *Hussar* (black) 17.00 8.50

1944

301† 20f + 60f 4th-century fishing boat 2.75 3.25

1948

351† 15f + 25f Yachts including *Margaret* and
  Old Chap 15.00 25.00

1949

375† 2f *Hirondelle I* (Prince Albert I's
  schooner), 1870 .... 25 20
378† 5f *Princess Alice* (Prince Albert's steam
  yacht), 1906 .... 40 40
380† 10f *Hirondelle II* (Prince Albert's steam
  yacht), 1914 .... 80 65
381† 12f Whaleboat 1.25 85

1953

465† 3f Olympic yachts 25 20

475 2f *Princess Alice* (Prince Albert's steam
  yacht)
476 5f *Princess Alice*
477 15f *Princess Alice*
  Set of 3 2.50 1.25

1955

530† 2f *Great Eastern* (paddle-steamer) and
  tanker 10 10
534† 8f Fishing boats, River Orinoco 35 35
538† 30f U.S.S. *Nautilus* (submarine) 4.00 3.25

1956

549† 30f Fleet of Columbus, 1492 .... 2.25 1.75
552† 100f Paddle-steamer, River Mississippi 2.75 2.75

1960

691† 50c *Hirondelle I* (schooner) and *Princess
  Alice* (steam yacht) 1.75 1.00

1962

741† 10c Galeazzi's diving turret 10 10
742† 25c *Trieste* (bathyscaphe) 10 10
745† 85c *Nautilus* (submarine), 1800 .... 65 60
746† 1f Beebe's bathysphere 90 90

1964

787† 1c Steam yachts in Monaco Harbour 10 10

1965

828† 95c *Great Eastern* and *Alsace* (cable
  ships) 65 65

1966

861 1f *Hirondelle I* (schooner) and *Princess Alice* (steam yacht) 1.40 1.00

865 1f *Precontinent III* (underwater research craft) 35 30

1972

1028 1f Battle of Lepanto, 1571 .... 60 40

1037 90c Tanker 50 30

1043† 30c Gondolas, Venice 25 20
1044† 60c Gondolas, Venice 35 25

1974

1116 40c Destroyer 20 10

COLLECT RAILWAYS ON STAMPS
Second revised edition of this Stanley Gibbons thematic catalogue. Now available at £9.50 (p. + p. £3) from: Stanley Gibbons Publications, 5 Parkside, Christchurch Road, Ringwood, Hants BH24 3SH.

1977

1285† 10c *Hirondelle I* (Prince Albert I's schooner) 10 10
1288† 80c Ship's boat 35 25
1290† 1f25 Ship's boat 65 40
1291† 1f40 Ship's boat 1.00 80
1293† 2f50 Ship's boat 2.25 2.00

1298 2f Yachts, Deauville 2.25 2.00

1305† 10c *Princess Alice* (Prince Albert's steam yacht) 10 10
1307† 30c *Princess Alice* 20 20
1312† 1f90 Ship's steam launch in ice 1.50 1.25
1313† 3f *Princess Alice* 2.25 1.60

1978

1343† 80c *Ramoge* (research vessel) 40 25

1979

1396† 1f50 18th-century felucca 80 40

1981

1495 2f50 *Faddey Bellingshausen* (Russian hydrographic research ship) 1.00 80

1530 1f50 17th-century ship in Arctic ice 1.00 55

1982

1599 1f60 Viking longships, Greenland, 982 .. 1.40 65

1600 1f80 Roman war galley 1.10 65

1983

1643 5f *Tazerka* (oil rig) 1.75 1.10

1984

1659† 4f Bathyscaphe (Piccard) 1.40 75

1665† 30c Barge and rowing boat 15 10
1667† 50c Sailing ships in harbour 20 10
1671† 90c Paddle-steamer 25 20
1673† 2f Fishing boats 60 25

1692† 2f Medieval ship 65 40

1738 2f10 *Hirondelle* (Prince Albert I's schooner) and *Denise* (midget submarine) 75 40

MS1749 4f Catamaran; 4f Single-hull yacht; 4f Trimaran 4.00 4.00

1985

1763† 4f Yacht and fishing boats, 1912 ...... 1.50 1.10

1986

1778† 2f20 *Ramoge* (research vessel) 80 40

1987

1824† 5f Sailing dinghies and sail board 1.75 1.10

1988

MS1888 17f "470" class yacht (sheet also contains 3 other sport designs) 5.00 5.00

1889† 6f Steam packet, 1910 .... 2.00 1.40

1898† 4f Roman galleys 1.25 65

1989

1965† 7f Fishing boats, Monaco, 1915 .... 2.00 1.50

1990

1981† 5f 4th-century fishing boat 1.50 75

1993 2f30 Powerboat 1.25 75

1991

2022† 90c Fishing boats, Pont de Fontvielle .. 30 15
2025† 3f Yacht 1.10 80

2040† 3f25 Research vessel 90 60

2062 4f50 4th-century fishing boat
2063 5f50 4th-century fishing boat
                              Set of 2 2.50 2.00

1992

2082 2f50 *Pinta* (Columbus)
2083 3f40 *Santa Maria*
2084 4f *Nina*
                              Set of 3 2.10 1.60

2088† 6f 14th-century fleet of Rainier I 1.50 1.10

2100 4f Projected tourist submarine 1.00 80

2101† 6f Burning fishing boat 1.50 1.10

POSTAGE DUE STAMPS

1953

D480† 2f Brig 10 10
D481† 2f *United States* (liner) 10 10

1960

D698† 1c 18th-century felucca 55 55
D699† 2c *La Palmaria* (paddle-steamer) 15 15
D703† 30c *Charles III* (paddle-steamer), 1866 90 90

MONGOLIA

Central Asia
100 mung = 1 tugrik

1961

228† 25m *Sukhe Bator* (lake steamer) 30 15

1965

356† 5m Marine exploration ship and bathysphere 30 10
362† 20m Antarctic research vessel 2.75 55

1970

MS591 4t American aircraft carrier 3.00 3.00

1971

622† 1t Sukhe Bator (lake steamer) 2.00 70

1973

755† 30m Medieval kogge (on Russia stamp
No. 3194) 30 15

1974

820† 50m Sukhe Bator (lake steamer) 2.00 40

1975

Тээвэр—50
1975—7—15.
No. 622 overprinted
924† 1t Sukhe Bator 3.75 3.75

1976

999† 30m Steamer, Lake Khobsogol 55 15

1977

1066† 30m Kosmonavt Yury Gagarin (research
ship) 60 15

1088† 50m Aurora (Russian cruiser) 60 15

1978

1147 1t Liner 75 20

1979

1214† 1t Hindoostan (paddle-steamer) 1.75 1.00

1980

1317† 40m Bathysphere (Cousteau) 95 30

1981

1367 10m 15th-century B.C. Pharonic ship
1368 20m 9th-century Mediterranean sailing
ship
1369 40m 12th-century Hanse kogge
1370 50m 13th-century Venetian felucca
1371 60m Santa Maria (Columbus)
1372 80m H.M.S. Endeavour (Cook)
1373 1t Poltava (Russian ship of the line)
1374 1t20 19th-century American schooner
Set of 8 6.25 2.75

1394† 50m Malygin (Russian ice-breaker) (on
Russia stamp No. 584) 60 30
1395† 60m Malygin (on Russia stamp No.
585) 1.00 20
1396† 80m Malygin (on Russia stamp No.
586) 1.25 20
1397† 1t20 Malygin (on Russia stamp No.
587) 1.50 65
MS1398† 4t Malygin (on Russia stamp No.
584) 5.00 4.00

1478† 20m Motor fishing boat 35 15

MONTENEGRO

ITALIAN OCCUPATION
100 para = 1 dinar

1941

Montenegro

Црна Гора

17-IV-41-XIX

Nos. 360 *and* 364 *of Yugoslavia overprinted*
15† 50p Yacht 2.50 5.00
19† 5d Yacht 22.00 38.00

MONTSERRAT

West Indies
1949 12 pence = 1 shilling
20 shillings = 1 pound
1951 100 cents = 1 dollar

1949

As No. 115 *of Antigua*
118† 3d Paddle-steamer 30 30

1967

190† 5c Sailing dinghies 10 10

1969

233† 25c Game fishing launch 40 10

1973

315† 60c Carrack (Columbus), 1493 .... 1.50 1.50

1975

346† 70c Carib canoe 25 40

1976

361† $1.10 Antelope (sailing packet), 1786 .. 1.00 1.00

391 15c Esmeralda (Chilean cadet barquentine)
392 40c Raleigh (American frigate), 1776
393 75c H.M.S. Druid (frigate), 1776
394 $1.25 Gloria (Colombian cadet ship)
Set of 4 2.40 1.40

1977

396† 30c Royal Yacht Britannia 15 15

405† 40c Statesman (freighter) 25 15
407† $1.50 Statesman unloading 80 1.00

414† 55c Local dinghies 20 10

1980

460† 40c Marquess of Salisbury (sailing packet), 1817 .... 20 15
462† $1.20 La Plata (liner), 1901 .... 45 45
463† $1.20 Lady Hawkins (packet steamer), 1929 .... 45 45
464† $1.20 Avon I (paddle-steamer), 1843 .... 45 45

482 40c Lady Nelson (cargo liner), 1928
483 55c Chignecto (packet steamer), 1913
484 $1 Solent II (packet steamer), 1878
485 $2 Dee (packet paddle-steamer), 1841
Set of 4 1.60 1.60

1981

510† 90c Royal Yacht Charlotte 25 25
512† $3 Royal Yacht Portsmouth 60 60
514† $4 Royal Yacht Britannia 75 75

519† 50c H.M.S. Dorsetshire (cruiser), 1931 .. 40 30

1983

Nos. 512 and 514 surcharged

582† 70c on $3 Royal Yacht Portsmouth 60 70
584† $1.15 on $4 Royal Yacht Britannia 1.00 1.10

1984

615 55c Tagus II (packet steamer), 1907
616 90c Cobequid (packet steamer), 1913
617 $1.15 Lady Drake (cargo liner), 1942
618 $2 Factor (packet steamer), 1948
Set of 4 3.50 3.50

1985

No. 514 surcharged **CARIBBEAN ROYAL VISIT 1985 $1.60**

655† $1.60 on $4 Royal Yacht Britannia 3.50 3.50

1986

696 90c Antelope (sailing packet) being attacked by L'Atalante (French privateer), 1793
697 $1.15 Montagu (sailing packet), 1810
698 $1.50 Little Catherine (sailing packet) being pursued by L'Etoile (French frigate), 1813
699 $2.30 Hinchinbrook I (sailing packet), 1813
Set of 4 7.50 7.25

710† 70c Sailing dinghy and sailboards 1.00 70

1989

793 90c Morning Prince (schooner), 1942
794 $1.15 Western Sun (inter-island freighter)
795 $1.50 Kim G (inter-island freighter) under construction
796 $3.50 Romaris (ferry), 1942
Set of 4 3.00 3.25

Nos. 795/6 surcharged **Hurricane Hugo Relief Surcharge $2.50**
802 $1.50 + $2.50 Kim G (freighter) under construction
803 $3.50 + $2.50 Romaris (ferry), 1942
Set of 2 4.50 5.00

1990

809 70c Yamato (Japanese battleship)
810 $1.15 U.S.S. Arizona (battleship)
811 $1.50 Bismarck (German battleship)
812 $3.50 H.M.S. Hood (battle cruiser)
Set of 4 3.50 3.50
MS813 $5 Bismarck (German battleship) 3.75 4.25

Nos. 460, 462 and 464 surcharged **Stamp World London 90**, emblem and value
818† 70c on 40c Marquess of Salisbury (sailing packet), 1817 .... 40 40
820† $1 on $1.20 La Plata (liner), 1901 .... 65 65
821† $1.15 on $1.20 Lady Hawkins (packet steamer), 1929 .... 75 75
822† $1.50 on $1.20 Avon I (paddle-steamer), 1843 .... 1.00 1.00

1992

875† $3 Ships of Columbus 1.50 1.75

1993

907† $1 Santa Maria (Columbus) (on coin) 60 60
908† $1.15 Santa Maria (on coin) 75 75

911	$1 Ships of Columbus at anchor		
912	$2 Ships of Columbus at sea		
	Set of 2	1.75	1.75

OFFICIAL STAMPS

1983

Nos. 510, 512 and 514 surcharged **O.H.M.S.** *and value*

O53†	45c on 90c Royal Yacht *Charlotte*	25	30
O55†	75c on $3 Royal Yacht *Portsmouth*	35	35
O57†	$1 on $4 Royal Yacht *Britannia*	50	50

MOROCCO

North-west Africa
1960 100 centimes = 1 franc
1962 100 francs = 1 dirham

1960

90†	45f Olympic yacht	75	35

1966

191	40f *Maroc* (liner)	55	15

1989

772	2d Rowing boat	30	25

MOROCCO AGENCIES

North-west Africa
12 pence = 1 shilling
20 shillings = 1 pound

1951

Nos. 509/10 of Great Britain overprinted **MOROCCO AGENCIES**

99	2s6d H.M.S. *Victory* (Nelson)	9.00	14.00
100	5s Yacht and Thames sailing barge, Dover	11.00	16.00

1951

Nos. 509/10 of Great Britain overprinted **TANGIER**

286†	2s6d H.M.S. *Victory* (Nelson)	3.75	2.75
287†	5s Yacht and Thames sailing barge, Dover	9.50	11.00

MOZAMBIQUE

South-east Africa
1960 100 centavos = 1 escudo
1980 100 centavos = 1 metical

1913

Nos. 1/2, 5 and 7 of Portuguese Colonies surcharged **REPUBLICA MOCAMBIQUE** *and value*

173†	¼c on 2½r Departure of Vasco da Gama's fleet	45	30
174†	½c on 5r Vasco da Gama's fleet at Calicut	40	30
177†	5c on 50r *Sao Gabriel* (flagship)	40	30
179†	10c on 100r *Sao Gabriel*	50	45

Nos. 104/5, 108 and 110 of Macao surcharged **REPUBLICA MOCAMBIQUE** *and value*

181†	¼c on ½a Departure of Vasco da Gama's fleet	60	50
182†	½c on 1a Vasco da Gama's fleet at Calicut	50	50
185†	5c on 8a *Sao Gabriel* (flagship)	1.50	1.25
187†	10c on 16a *Sao Gabriel*	60	50

Nos. 58/9, 62 and 64 of Timor surcharged **REPUBLICA MOCAMBIQUE** *and value*

189†	¼c on ½a Departure of Vasco da Gama's fleet	60	50
190†	½c on 1a Vasco da Gama's fleet at Calicut	60	50
193†	5c on 8a *Sao Gabriel* (flagship)	90	70
195†	10c on 16a *Sao Gabriel*	50	45

1952

468	1e50 Liner	50	30

1953

492	1e Liner (on stamp No. 468)		
493	3e Liner (on stamp No. 468)		
	Set of 2	2.40	60

1957

510	2e50 Freighters in Beira Harbour	40	15

1960

513	5e 15th-century caravel	40	15

1962

537†	15e Speedboat	90	70

1963

549	10c Nef, 1430		
550	20c Caravel, 1436		
551	30c Caravel, 1460		
552	50c *Sao Gabriel* (Vasco da Gama), 1497		
553	1e Don Manuel's nau, 1498		
554	1e50 Galleon, 1530		
555	2e *Flor de la Mar* (nau), 1511		
556	2e50 *Redonda* (caravel), 1519		
557	3e50 Nau, 1520		
558	4e Portuguese Indies galley, 1521		
559	4e50 *Santa Tereza* (galleon), 1639		
560	5e *N. Senhora da Conceicao* (nau), 1716		
561	6e *N. Senhora do Bom Sucesso* (warship), 1764		
562	7e50 Bomb launch, 1788		
563	8e *Lebre* (naval brigantine), 1793		
564	10e *Andorinha* (corvette), 1799		
565	12e50 *Maria Teresa* (naval schooner), 1820		
566	15e *Vasco da Gama* (warship), 1841		
567	20e *Don Fernando II e Gloria* (sail frigate), 1843		
568	30e *Sagres I* (cadet barque), 1924		
	Set of 20	23.00	5.00

1964

571†	15c State barge of Joao V, 1728	10	10
572†	35c State barge of Jose I, 1753	10	10
573†	1e Alfandega barge, 1768	30	10
575†	2e50 *Pinto da Fonseca* (state barge), 1780	20	10
576†	5e State barge of Carlota Joaquina, 1790	25	15
577†	9e State barge of Don Miguel, 1831	45	30

1967

592	3e *Tete* (paddle-gunboat)		
593	10e *Granada* (paddle-gunboat)		
	Set of 2	80	35

1969

600†	50c Nau, 1553	10	10
601†	1e50 14th-century caravels	20	10

1972

617†	4e 16th-century Portuguese galley and dhow	1.25	30

619† 1e Rowing boats 10 10

1973

620 1e Racing yachts
621 1e50 Racing yachts
622 3e Racing yachts

Set of 3 55 35

1975
Nos. 537 and 620/2 overprinted **INDEPENDENCIA 25 JUN 75**

634†	1e Racing yachts	30	25
635†	1e50 Racing yachts	60	50
639†	3e Racing yachts	45	40
644†	15e Speedboat	1.25	1.10

1981

915 50c *Matchedje* (tanker)
916 1m50 *Macuti* (tug)
917 3m *Vega 7* (trawler)
918 5m *Linde* (freighter)
919 7m50 *Pemba* (freighter)
920 12m50 *Rovuma* (dredger)

Set of 6 2.00 1.25

1982

969 1m Caique (sailing boat)
970 2m Machua (sailing boat)
971 4m Calaua (piroque)
972 8m Chitatarro (raft)
973 12m Cangaia (outrigger canoe)
974 16m Chata (punt)

Set of 6 3.00 1.40

1983

996† 20m Olympic yachts 1.00 65

1011† 4m Red Cross inflatable dinghy 20 10

1017† 50c Fishing canoe 10 10

1026† 8m Mail canoe 40 40

1989

1203†	50m Container ship, Quelimane	10	10
1204†	75m Freighter, Pemba	15	10
1206†	250m Container ship, Nacala	65	35
1207†	500m Freighter, Maputo	1.40	70

MOZAMBIQUE COMPANY
South-east Africa
100 centavos = 1 escudo

1918

204†	2½c Dhow, River Buzi	15	15
254†	1e40 Liner, Beira	1.00	40

1920
No. 204 surcharged in words

219†	1½c on 2½c Dhow, River Buzi	90	90
221†	2c on 2½c Dhow, River Buzi	60	50

1937

288†	10c Dhow	10	10
298†	85c *Sao Gabriel* (Vasco da Gama)	20	15
299†	1e Dugout canoe	15	15

1939
Nos. 298/9 overprinted **28–VII–1939 Visita Presidencial**

309†	85c *Sao Gabriel*	60	45
310†	1e Dugout canoe	1.00	60

MUSCAT AND OMAN
Arabia
64 baizas = 1 rupee

1969

106† 20b Tankers, Mina el Fahal 70 35

NABHA
Indian subcontinent
12 pies = 1 anna
16 annas -1 rupee

1938
No. 256 of India overprinted **NABHA STATE**

86† 6a *Strathnaver* (liner) 1.50 7.50

NAMIBIA
Southern Africa
100 cents = 1 rand

1993

614† 60c Cattle on barge 40 40

NAURU
Pacific
1924 12 pence = 1 shilling
20 shillings = 1 pound
1966 100 cents = 1 dollar

1924

26 ½d *Century* (freighter)
27 1d *Century* (freighter)
28 1½d *Century* (freighter)
29 2d *Century* (freighter)
30b 2½d *Century* (freighter)
31a 3d *Century* (freighter)
32 4d *Century* (freighter)
33 5d *Century* (freighter)
34 6d *Century* (freighter)
35 9d *Century* (freighter)
36 1s *Century* (freighter)
37 2s6d *Century* (freighter)
38 5s *Century* (freighter)
39 10s *Century* (freighter)

Set of 14 £180 £275

1935
Nos. 28/30b and 36 overprinted **HIS MAJESTY'S JUBILEE.**
1910 – 1935

40 1½d *Century*
41 2d *Century*
42 2½d *Century*
43 1s *Century*

Set of 4 6.50 9.00

1954

50†	3½d *Trienza* (freighter) loading phosphate	1.50	30
52†	6d Outrigger canoe	70	20

1966

As No. 50, but face value in decimal currency and colour changed

68†	3c *Trienza*	30	40

1968

No. 68 overprinted **REPUBLIC OF NAURU**

82†	3c *Trienza*	15	10

1974

116†	7c *Eigamoiya* (bulk carrier)	1.25	90
120†	35c H.M.S. *Hunter* (frigate), 1798	5.50	2.50
121†	50c H.M.S. *Hunter*	2.50	1.40

1975

131†	15c Freighter and barges	1.25	1.25

133	20c Micronesian outrigger canoe		
134	20c Polynesian double hulled canoe		
135	20c Melanesian outrigger canoe		
136	20c Polynesian outrigger canoe		
	Set of 4	2.75	1.40

1976

151†	10c *Enna G* (cargo liner)	15	10

1977

161†	7c *Anglia* (cable ship)	25	10
163†	20c *Anglia*	35	20

1979

204†	5c *Hohenzollern* (German Imperial yacht) (on Marshall Islands stamp No. G17)	15	10

1980

222†	25c Junks in Hong Kong Harbour	45	15

1981

239†	20c Outrigger canoe	20	15
240†	32c Outboard motor boat	25	20
241†	40c Trawler	30	25

253†	20c *Enna G* (cargo liner)	35	25

1982

267†	5c *Fido* (freighter)	50	10
270†	60c *Eigamoiya* (bulk carrier)	1.50	80
MS271†	$1 *Eigamoiya, Rosie-D* and *Kolle-D* (bulk carriers)	2.00	1.75

1983

288†	15c *Trienza* (freighter), 1946	20	25

1984

295	20c *Ocean Queen* (cargo liner)		
296	25c *Enna G* (cargo liner)		
297	30c *Baron Minto* (bulk carrier)		
298	40c Sinking of *Triadic* (cargo liner), 1940		
	Set of 4	2.00	1.40

305†	5c Modern trawler	20	20

1985

326†	50c Outrigger canoe	1.25	1.50

1988

358†	25c Bulk carrier loading phosphate	80	80
362†	30c *Hohenzollern* (German Imperial yacht) (on Marshall Islands stamp No. G23)	30	35

NEGRI SEMBILAN

South-east Asia
100 cents = 1 dollar

1949

As No. 115 of Antigua

64†	15c Paddle-steamer	45	70

1957

75†	20c Malay fishing prau	20	10

NEPAL

Central Asia
100 paisa = 1 rupee

1970

251†	25p Canoe, Lake Phewa Tal	30	30

NETHERLANDS

North-west Europe
100 cents = 1 gulden

1907

211 ½c 17th-century naval battle
212 1c 17th-century naval battle
213 2½c 17th-century naval battle

Set of 3   9.50   4.25

1924

294† 10c Lifeboat 7.00   2.00

1928

366† 5c + 1c Olympic yacht 2.25   80

1931

395b† 80c *Balorean* and *Christian Huygens*
       (liners) 95.00   3.00

1933

414† 5c + 3c *De Hoop* (hospital ship) 12.00   2.50
415† 6c + 4c Lifeboat 17.00   2.50

1934

441† 12½c Dutch warship, 1634 ....   26.00   2.75

1944

596† 2½c *Nieuw Amsterdam* (liner)   10   10
598† 5c *De Ruyter* (cruiser)   10   10

1949

683† 20c + 5c Yachts 2.50   2.25

1950

717† 10c + 5c *Adelaar, Stormvogel* and *Jan
      Blanken* (tugs) towing bridge sections   5.00   20
718† 20c + 5c *Overijssel* (canal freighter) 14.00   13.00

1953

794† 10c + 5c Dutch tjalk   10   10

1956

831† 2c + 3c Olympic yacht   40   40

1957

843 4c + 3c *Gaasterland* (freighter)
844 6c + 4c Coaster
845 7c + 5c *Willem Barendsz* (whale factory
     ship)
846 10c + 8c *Curacao* (trawler)
847 30c + 8c *Nieuw Amsterdam* (liner)

Set of 5   13.00   8.50

849† 30c *De Zeven Provincien* (De Ruyter) 5.00   1.75

851† 6c + 4c *J. Henry Dunant* (hospital ship)   65   65

1959

877† 4c + 4c Tugs 1.10   1.25
878† 6c + 4c Dredger   90   90

1962

924† 12c + 8c Figurehead 1.50   25

938† 10c Dredger   10   10

1973

1167 25c + 15c *De Zeven Provincien* (De
      Ruyter)
1168 30c + 10c *W.A. Scholten* (early
      steamship)
1169 35c + 15c *Veendam* (liner)
1170 50c + 20c Fishing boat

Set of 4   5.00   5.00

1974

1195† 40c *Suzanna* (lifeboat)   20   10

1975

1214 35c *Stad Middleburg* (schooner)   30   10

1976

1252† 40c Dutch tjalk   25   10

1977

1271† 55c + 20c Remains of Zwammerdam
       Roman ship   30   20

1979

1316†   75c Liner   50   35

1980

1343   80c Motorised canal barge   40   10

1988

1535†   75c Dutch warship, 1688   45   10

1539   75c 17th-century sailing ship   45   10

1989

1552   55c Boier (type of inshore sailing boat)
1553   65c Fishing smack
1554   75c Clipper
          Set of 3   95   25

1990

1579†   65c Construction and wreck of
          Amsterdam (East Indiaman)   40   10

1991

1610†   55c + 30c Rowing boat   50   35

1992

1646†   80c Galleon   60   10

NETHERLANDS ANTILLES

West Indies
100 cents = 1 gulden

1949

306†   6c Spanish galleon, 1499 . . . .   3.50   1.75
308†   15c Spanish galleon, 1499 . . . .   3.75   2.25

1952

339†   15c + 10c Tanker 10.00   4.00
340†   25c + 15c Liner 8.50   3.50

1961

428   20c Andrew Doria (American naval brig),
          1776   70   60

1965

462†   20c Asprella (tanker)   25   15

1967

486   6c Gelderland (cruiser)
487   10c Pioneer (schooner)
488   20c Oscilla (tanker)
489   25c Santa Rosa (liner)
          Set of 4   55   50

1976

626†   40c Andrew Doria (American naval brig),
          1776   70   45

1978

661†   20c + 10c Yacht   15   15

1983

769   70c Pilot gig, 1882
770   85c Pilot boat and modern liner
771   1g Pilot boat
          Set of 3   2.75   2.75

803†   85c + 40c Sailboard 1.50   1.40

805†   45c Motor boat   75   55

807   1g Liner 1.25   1.10

809†   45c Curacao (paddle-steamer)   70   60

1984

862   1g Southward (liner) 1.50   1.25

1987

933†   85c Emerald Seas (liner)   90   60

1989

983 70c *Sun Viking* (liner)
984 155c *Eugenio C* (liner)
Set of 2   2.10   1.75

1990

1017† 100c 19th-century sail warship 1.10   90

1992

1070† 250c *Santa Maria* (Columbus) 2.00   1.60

1072 80c Container ship, Curacao
1073 125c Loading container ship
Set of 2   1.50   1.25

NETHERLANDS INDIES
South-east Asia
100 cents = 1 gulden

1931

325† 5c + 2½c Fishing prau 3.50   3.00

NETHERLANDS NEW GUINEA
South-east Asia
100 cents = 1 gulden

1957

51† 5c + 5c Outrigger canoe 90   85
53† 25c + 10c Outrigger canoe 90   85

NEVIS
West Indies
100 cents = 1 dollar

1980

No. 399 of St. Kitts-Nevis with "St. Christopher" *and* "Anguilla" *obliterated*
42† 30c *Europa* (liner) 20   15

51 5c Nevis lighter
52 30c Local fishing boat
53 55c *Caona* (catamaran)
54 $3 *Polynesia* (cruise schooner)
Set of 4   90   70

1981

58† 5c Fishing boat and coaster, Charlestown   10   10

72† 55c Royal Yacht *Royal Caroline* 20   20
74† $2 Royal Yacht *Royal Sovereign* 40   40
76† $5 Royal Yacht *Britannia* 80   80

1983

103 55c H.M.S. *Boreas* (frigate) (Nelson)
104 $2 H.M.S. *Boreas*
Set of 2   85   85

No. 58 overprinted **INDEPENDENCE 1983**
109B† 5c Fishing boat and coaster, Charlestown 10   10

1985

No. 76 surcharged **CARIBBEAN ROYAL VISIT 1985 $1.50**
345† $1.50 on $5 Royal Yacht *Britannia* 2.25   2.25

1986

381† $2.50 *Santa Maria* and *Pinta* (Columbus) 1.75   1.75
382† $2.50 *Nina* (Columbus) 1.75   1.75

405† $3 Fishing boat on beach 2.50   2.75

444† 25c Schooner and Statue of Liberty 15   15
447† 75c Brigantine and Statue of Liberty 30   30
448† $1 *Libertad* (Argentine full-rigged cadet ship) 35   35

458† 10c Sailing dinghies 10   10

1987

MS470 $5 Replica float of *Hamilton* (frigate), 1788 .... 6.50   6.50

No. 54 overprinted **America's Cup 1987 Winners 'Stars & Stripes'**
471 $3 *Polynesia* (cruise schooner) 1.40   1.75

474† $1 H.M.S. *Boreas* (frigate) (Nelson), 1787 80   80

1988

509† 60c *Cunard Countess* (liner) 45   40
511† $3 *Viking Princess* (cargo liner) on fire, 1966 .... 1.60   1.75

1989

517† 50c Battle of Frigate Bay, 1782 20   25
518† $1.20 Battle of Frigate Bay, 1782 50   55
519† $2 Battle of Frigate Bay, 1782 85   90

1991

MS600† Two sheets (a) $6 Bow of *Santa Maria* (other sheet shows Columbus)

		Price for 2 sheets	5.25	5.50

1992

678†	20c Caravel	15	20
679†	50c Columbus's fleet	20	25
680†	80c *Santa Maria* (Columbus)	35	40
681†	$1.50 *Santa Maria* (Columbus)	65	70

MS684† Two sheets (b) $6 Carib canoe (other sheet shows bird)

		Price for 2 sheets	5.25	5.50

OFFICIAL STAMPS

1980

No. 42 overprinted **OFFICIAL**

O3†	30c *Europa*	15	15

1983

Nos. 72, 74 and 76 surcharged or overprinted **OFFICIAL**

O23†	45c on $2 *Royal Sovereign*	20	25
O25†	55c *Royal Caroline*	20	25
O27†	$1.10 on $5 *Britannia*	45	50

NEW BRUNSWICK

North America
100 cents = 1 dollar

1860

18	12½c *Washington* (paddle-steamer)	50.00	40.00

NEW CALEDONIA

South Pacific
100 centimes = 1 franc

1905

99†	1f *President Felix Faure* (barque) (blue on green)	50	45
123†	1f *President Felix Faure* (blue)	90	95
100†	2f *President Felix Faure*	1.40	1.10
101†	5f *President Felix Faure* (black on orange)	4.00	3.75

1912

Nos. 99, 100/1 and 123, some with colours changed, surcharged in figures

126†	25c on 2f *President Felix Faure*	40	50
127†	25c on 5f *President Felix Faure* (black on orange)	40	50

132†	1f25 on 1f *President Felix Faure* (blue)	30	35
133†	1f50 on 1f *President Felix Faure* (blue on blue)	60	70
134†	3f on 5f *President Felix Faure* (mauve)	60	75
135†	10f on 5f *President Felix Faure* (green)	4.00	4.25
136†	20f on 5f *President Felix Faure* (red on yellow)	8.50	8.50

1928

137†	1c Fishing boat, Pointe des Paletuviers	10	20
138†	2c Fishing boat, Pointe des Paletuviers	10	30
139†	3c Fishing boat, Pointe des Paletuviers	15	25
140†	4c Fishing boat, Pointe des Paletuviers	15	30
141†	5c Fishing boat, Pointe des Paletuviers	15	35
142†	10c Fishing boat, Pointe des Paletuviers	20	25
143†	15c Fishing boat, Pointe des Paletuviers	20	25
144†	20c Fishing boat, Pointe des Paletuviers	20	35
145†	25c Fishing boat, Pointe des Paletuviers	25	30

161	1f *L'Astrolabe* (La Perouse) (red and brown)	3.75	2.00
162	1f *L'Astrolabe* (red)	65	75
163	1f *L'Astrolabe* (green and red)	40	50
164	1f10 *L'Astrolabe*	8.25	7.50
165	1f25 *L'Astrolabe* (green and brown)	55	65
166	1f25 *L'Astrolabe* (red)	40	50
167	1f40 *L'Astrolabe*	40	50
168	1f50 *L'Astrolabe*	35	40
169	1f60 *L'Astrolabe*	65	70
170	1f75 *L'Astrolabe* (orange and blue)	45	45
171	1f75 *L'Astrolabe* (blue)	45	50
172	2f *L'Astrolabe*	40	50
173	2f25 *L'Astrolabe*	45	50
174	2f50 *L'Astrolabe*	65	70
175	3f *L'Astrolabe*	45	50
176	5f *L'Astrolabe*	45	50
177	10f *L'Astrolabe*	80	80
178	20f *L'Astrolabe*	1.40	1.10

1931

As No. 109 of *Cameroun*

182†	1f50 *Leconte de Lisle* (liner)	2.50	2.50

1933

Nos. 137/8, 140/5, 161, 165, 168, 170, 172 and 175/8 overprinted with small aeroplane and **PARIS-NOUMEA Premiere liaison aerienne 5 Avril 1932**

185†	1c Fishing boat, Pointe des Paletuviers	4.75	4.75
186†	2c Fishing boat, Pointe des Paletuviers	4.75	4.75
187†	4c Fishing boat, Pointe des Paletuviers	4.75	4.75
188†	5c Fishing boat, Pointe des Paletuviers	4.75	4.75
189†	10c Fishing boat, Pointe des Paletuviers	4.75	4.75
190†	15c Fishing boat, Pointe des Paletuviers	4.75	4.75
191†	20c Fishing boat, Pointe des Paletuviers	4.75	4.75
192†	25c Fishing boat, Pointe des Paletuviers	4.75	4.75
202†	1f *L'Astrolabe* (La Perouse)	5.25	5.50
203†	1f25 *L'Astrolabe*	5.25	5.50
204†	1f50 *L'Astrolabe*	5.25	5.50
205†	1f75 *L'Astrolabe*	5.00	5.50
206†	2f *L'Astrolabe*	6.25	6.25
207†	3f *L'Astrolabe*	5.75	6.25
208†	5f *L'Astrolabe*	5.75	6.25
209†	10f *L'Astrolabe*	6.00	6.25
210†	20f *L'Astrolabe*	6.00	6.25

1937

As Nos. 110/11 of *Cameroun*

211†	20c Passenger liner	60	80
212†	30c Sailing ships	65	85

1941

Nos. 137/8, 140/5, 162, 165, 167/70 and 172/8 overprinted **France Libre**

232†	1c Fishing boat, Pointe des Paletuviers	12.50	12.50
233†	2c Fishing boat, Pointe des Paletuviers	12.50	12.50
234†	3c Fishing boat, Pointe des Paletuviers	12.50	12.50
235†	4c Fishing boat, Pointe des Paletuviers	12.50	12.50
236†	5c Fishing boat, Pointe des Paletuviers	11.50	12.50
237†	10c Fishing boat, Pointe des Paletuviers	11.50	12.50
238†	15c Fishing boat, Pointe des Paletuviers	12.50	12.50
239†	20c Fishing boat, Pointe des Paletuviers	12.50	12.50
240†	25c Fishing boat, Pointe des Paletuviers	12.50	12.50
254†	1f *L'Astrolabe* (La Perouse)	14.00	14.00

255†	1f25 *L'Astrolabe*	14.00	14.00
256†	1f40 *L'Astrolabe*	14.00	14.00
257†	1f50 *L'Astrolabe*	14.00	14.00
258†	1f60 *L'Astrolabe*	14.00	14.00
259†	1f75 *L'Astrolabe*	14.00	14.00
260†	2f *L'Astrolabe*	14.00	14.00
261†	2f25 *L'Astrolabe*	14.00	14.00
262†	2f50 *L'Astrolabe*	15.00	15.00
263†	3f *L'Astrolabe*	15.00	15.00
264†	5f *L'Astrolabe*	15.00	15.00
265†	10f *L'Astrolabe*	18.00	18.00
266†	20f *L'Astrolabe*	20.00	20.00

1948

312†	1f Outrigger canoe, Porcupine Island	25	35
313†	1f20 Outrigger canoe, Porcupine Island	25	35
314†	1f50 Outrigger canoe, Porcupine Island	25	35
315†	2f Freighter	30	25
316†	2f40 Freighter	40	35
317†	3f Freighter	3.50	1.00
318†	4f Freighter	75	45

1953

331†	1f50 D'Entrecasteaux's ships, 1792	4.25	3.75

1954

As No. 264 of *Cameroun*

335	3f Landing craft, Normandy, 1944	4.00	3.50

1959

345†	2f Outrigger canoes racing	70	40
348†	5f Yachts	1.40	65
357†	200f Pirogue (air)	28.00	13.00

1966

402	30f Shipping, Noumea Harbour, 1866	4.00	2.75

1967

425	25f Ocean racing yachts	4.50	3.00

1968

442	9f Ferry, River Tontouta, c. 1900	1.75	1.00

1969

475   50f Outrigger canoe 4.50   2.75

1970

479   9f *Natal* (packet steamer), 1883 .... 2.00   1.00

1971

483   20f Racing yachts 2.50   1.25

485   16f Ocean racing yachts 3.50   1.75

492   200f Yacht marina, Noumea 14.50   7.75

1973

516   60f *El Kantara* (liner) 5.50   3.00

1974

539†   20f H.M.S. *Endeavour* (Cook) 1.50   80
540†   25f *L'Astrolabe* (La Perouse) 1.50   1.00
542†   30f D'Entrecasteaux's ship, 1792 ...... 2.25   1.40
543†   36f *L'Astrolabe* (Dumont d'Urville) 3.50   2.00

1979

610†   11f Outrigger canoe, Ouvea Island 60   40

613†   49f 19th-century barque and modern
          container ship 1.50   80

618†   75f Shipping, Noumea Harbour, 1854 .. 2.75   1.50

621   16f Catamarans 85   45

1980

630   45f Outrigger canoe 1.40   1.00

638   27f Sailing canoe 80   65

1981

655   29f *Zealandia* (troopship), 1940 .... 1.40   80

659   10f *Constantine* (sail corvette), 1854
660   25f *Le Phoque* (paddle-gunboat), 1853
                              Set of 2   1.60   95

1982

680   44f *Le Cher* (naval transport barque)
681   59f *Kersaint* (sloop), 1902
                              Set of 2   2.25   1.40

1984

725   18f *St Joseph* (freighter)
726   31f *St Antoine* (freighter)
                              Set of 2   1.40   1.00

1985

763   17f Trawler 45   25

1987

802   30f *Challenge France* (yacht)
803   70f *French Kiss* (yacht)
                              Set of 2   2.50   1.50

807   72f Canoe, Isle of Pines
808   90f Canoe, Ouvea
                              Set of 2   3.25   2.00

1988

823   36f *L'Astrolabe* and *La Boussole* (La
          Perouse)   80   45

834 42f Governor Phillip's fleet in Botany Bay, 1788
835 42f *La Boussole, L'Astrolabe* (La Perouse) and H.M.S. *Sirius* (Phillip), 1788
　　　　　　　　　Set of 2　1.60　1.40

852† 54f 18th-century sailing ships .... 1.25　80

1989

864 180f Ferry boat, Ouaieme .... 3.25　1.75

868 350f "Hobie Cat 14" yachts .... 6.00　3.50

871† 130f Rowing boat .... 2.50　1.50

1991

925 200f *Camden* (missionary brig), 1841 .... 3.00　1.75

1992

941 80f *Pinta* (Columbus)
942 80f *Santa Maria*
943 80f *Nina*
　　　　　　　　　Set of 3　3.00　2.75
MS944 110f Viking longship (Eric the Red) (sheet also contains two other 110f designs)　4.50　4.50

951 110f D'Entrecasteaux's ships, 1792 ...... 1.50　90

POSTAGE DUE STAMPS

1906

D102 5c Outrigger canoe
D103 10c Outrigger canoe
D104 15c Outrigger canoe
D105 20c Outrigger canoe
D106 30c Outrigger canoe
D107 50c Outrigger canoe
D108 60c Outrigger canoe
D109 1f Outrigger canoe
　　　　　　　　　Set of 8　4.50　4.50

1926
As No. D109, *but colour changed, surcharged*
D137 2f on 1f Outrigger canoe .... 2.25　2.25
D138 3f on 1f Outrigger canoe .... 2.25　2.25

PARCEL POST STAMPS
1926
Nos. 100, 123 *and as No.* 101, *but colour changed, overprinted* **Colis Postaux** *or surcharged also*
P137 50c on 5f *President Felix Faure* (green on mauve)
P138 1f *President Felix Faure*
P139 2f *President Felix Faure*
　　　　　　　　　Set of 3　2.75　2.75

NEWFOUNDLAND
North Atlantic
100 cents = 1 dollar

1865

29† 13c Schooner .... 75.00　50.00

1887

54† 10c Brigantine .... 48.00　35.00

1897

72† 8c Fishing boats .... 11.00　7.00
73† 10c *Matthew* (Cabot) .... 19.00　2.50
76† 24c Salmon-fishing boat .... 17.00　16.00

1910

98† 4c *Endeavour* (immigrant ship), 1610 .... 8.00　11.00

1928

180† 2c *Caribou* (cargo liner) .... 1.25　10

1931

193† 50c Sailing packet .... 20.00　28.00

1932

282† 8c *Humbet Arm* and *Corner Brook* (freighters) .... 1.00　75
228† 24c *Willemsplein* (freighter) loading ore　60　2.25
219† 25c Sealing fleet .... 1.25　1.75
220† 30c Fishing fleet .... 17.00　24.00
289† 48c Fishing fleet .... 2.50　5.00

1933

231† 10c Canoe .... 4.00　15.00
232† 30c *Beothic* (sealer) .... 24.00　32.00
233† 60c Fishing schooners .... 40.00　60.00

242† 8c Sir Humphrey Gilbert's fleet, 1583 .... 5.00　8.50

1937

265† 24c *Willemplein* (freighter) loading ore .. 2.25　3.50
266† 25c Sealing fleet .... 2.75　1.75
267† 48c Fishing fleet .... 7.00　4.50

1941

275	5c *Maraval* (missionary ship)	15	15

NEW GUINEA

Australasia
12 pence = 1 shilling
20 shillings = 1 pound

1914

Nos. 7/19 of German New Guinea surcharged **G.R.I.** and value in
English currency

16	1d on 3pf *Hohenzollern*	40.00	50.00
17	1d on 5pf *Hohenzollern*	14.00	22.00
3	2d on 10pf *Hohenzollern*	50.00	60.00
4	2d on 20pf *Hohenzollern*	35.00	42.00
5	2½d on 10pf *Hohenzollern*	65.00	£140
6	2½d on 20pf *Hohenzollern*	65.00	£140
22	3d on 25pf *Hohenzollern*	80.00	£100
23	3d on 30pf *Hohenzollern*	70.00	95.00
24	4d on 40pf *Hohenzollern*	85.00	£110
25	5d on 50pf *Hohenzollern*	£120	£150
26	8d on 80pf *Hohenzollern*	£300	£400
12	1s on 1m *Hohenzollern*	£1400	£1900
13	2s on 2m *Hohenzollern*	£1500	£2250
14	3s on 3m *Hohenzollern*	£3000	£3750
15	5s on 5m *Hohenzollern*	£5000	£6000

Nos. 3/4 surcharged **1**

31	1 on 2d on 10pf *Hohenzollern*	£9000	£9000
32	1 on 2d on 20pf *Hohenzollern*	£9000	£9000

Nos. G11/23 of Marshall Islands surcharged **G.R.I.** and value in
English currency

50	1d on 3pf *Hohenzollern*	40.00	55.00
51	1d on 5pf *Hohenzollern*	42.00	50.00
52	2d on 10pf *Hohenzollern*	14.00	22.00
53	2d on 20pf *Hohenzollern*	15.00	25.00
54	3d on 25pf *Hohenzollern*	£250	£325
55	3d on 30pf *Hohenzollern*	£275	£350
56	4d on 40pf *Hohenzollern*	85.00	£120
57	5d on 50pf *Hohenzollern*	£130	£170
58	8d on 80pf *Hohenzollern*	£375	£475
59	1s on 1m *Hohenzollern*	£1600	£2250
60	2s on 2m *Hohenzollern*	£1100	£1600
61	3s on 3m *Hohenzollern*	£2750	£3750
62	5s on 5m *Hohenzollern*	£4750	£6000

1915

Nos. 52/3 surcharged **1**

63	1 on 2d on 10pf *Hohenzollern*	£140	£170
64	1 on 2d on 20pf *Hohenzollern*	£3000	£2000

OFFICIAL STAMPS

1914

Nos. 16/17 overprinted **O.S.**

O1	1d on 3pf *Hohenzollern*	25.00	70.00
O2	1d on 5pf *Hohenzollern*	75.00	£130

NEW HEBRIDES

South Pacific
100 centimes = 1 franc

BRITISH ADMINISTRATION

52	5c Outrigger canoe, Lopevi Islands	
53	10c Outrigger canoe, Lopevi Islands	
54	15c Outrigger canoe, Lopevi Islands	
55	20c Outrigger canoe, Lopevi Islands	
56	25c Outrigger canoe, Lopevi Islands	
57	30c Outrigger canoe, Lopevi Islands	
58	40c Outrigger canoe, Lopevi Islands	
59	50c Outrigger canoe, Lopevi Islands	
60	1f Outrigger canoe, Lopevi Islands	
61	2f Outrigger canoe, Lopevi Islands	
62	5f Outrigger canoe, Lopevi Islands	
63	10f Outrigger canoe, Lopevi Islands	
	Set of 12	£275 £130

1953

68†	5c Outrigger sailing canoes	50	10
69†	10c Outrigger sailing canoes	50	10
70†	15c Outrigger sailing canoes	50	10
71†	20c Outrigger sailing canoes	50	10

1956

80†	5c Portuguese galleon, 1606	10	10
81†	10c Portuguese galleon, 1606	10	10

1957

84†	5c Freighters, Port Vila	40	10
85†	10c Freighters, Port Vila	30	10
86†	15c Freighters, Port Vila	50	20
87†	20c Freighters, Port Vila	40	10

1963

98†	5c Freighter loading manganese	35	30
101†	20c Trawlers	45	10

1967

127†	60c H.M.A.S. *Canberra* (cruiser)	20	15

1968

131†	25c *La Boudeuse* and *L'Etoile*		
	(Bougainville), 1768	15	15
132†	60c Ship's figurehead	15	10

1970

No. 101 surcharged **35**

144	35c on 20c Trawlers	30	30

COLLECT RAILWAYS ON STAMPS

Second revised edition of this Stanley Gibbons
thematic catalogue. Now available at £9.50
(p. + p. £3) from: Stanley Gibbons Publications,
5 Parkside, Christchurch Road, Ringwood, Hants
BH24 3SH.

1973

178	25c Freighters at wharf, Vila		
179	70c Freighters at wharf, Vila		
	Set of 2	60	40

183†	70c Outrigger canoe	20	20

1974

192†	35c H.M.S. *Resolution* (Cook)	1.75	2.00
193†	35c Ship's boat	1.75	2.00
195†	1f15 H.M.S. *Resolution* (Cook)	4.00	4.50

1975

203†	5f Outrigger canoe	2.50	2.50

1977

250†	50f Outrigger canoe, Shepherd Island . .	70	40

1979

271†	10f Outrigger canoe, Lopevi Island, (on		
	stamp No. 52)	10	10

POSTAGE DUE STAMPS

1938

Nos. 52/3, 55, 58 and 60 overprinted **POSTAGE DUE**

D6	5c Outrigger canoe, Lopevi Islands	
D7	10c Outrigger canoe, Lopevi Islands	
D8	20c Outrigger canoe, Lopevi Islands	
D9	40c Outrigger canoe, Lopevi Islands	
D10	1f Outrigger canoe, Lopevi Islands	
	Set of 5 £120 £160	

1953

Nos. 68/9 and 71 overprinted **POSTAGE DUE**

D11†	5c Outrigger sailing canoes	5.00	7.50
D12†	10c Outrigger sailing canoes	1.75	5.00
D13†	20c Outrigger sailing canoes	5.00	12.00

FRENCH ADMINISTRATION

1908

No. 99 of New Caledonia overprinted **NOUVELLES HEBRIDES**

F5†	1f President Felix Faure (barque)	11.50	11.50

1910

No. 99 of New Caledonia overprinted **NOUVELLES HEBRIDES CONDOMINIUM**

F10†	1f President Felix Faure (barque)	13.00	14.00

The following are as issues of the British Administration, but are inscribed "NOUVELLES HEBRIDES"

1938

As Nos. 52/63

F53	5c Outrigger canoe, Lopevi Islands
F54	10c Outrigger canoe, Lopevi Islands
F55	15c Outrigger canoe, Lopevi Islands
F56	20c Outrigger canoe, Lopevi Islands
F57	25c Outrigger canoe, Lopevi Islands
F58	30c Outrigger canoe, Lopevi Islands
F59	40c Outrigger canoe, Lopevi Islands
F60	50c Outrigger canoe, Lopevi Islands
F61	1f Outrigger canoe, Lopevi Islands
F62	2f Outrigger canoe, Lopevi Islands
F63	5f Outrigger canoe, Lopevi Islands
F64	10f Outrigger canoe, Lopevi Islands
	Set of 12 £125 £100

1941

Nos. F53/64 overprinted **France Libre**

F65	5c Outrigger canoe, Lopevi Islands
F66	10c Outrigger canoe, Lopevi Islands
F67	15c Outrigger canoe, Lopevi Islands
F68	20c Outrigger canoe, Lopevi Islands
F69	25c Outrigger canoe, Lopevi Islands
F70	30c Outrigger canoe, Lopevi Islands
F71	40c Outrigger canoe, Lopevi Islands
F72	50c Outrigger canoe, Lopevi Islands
F73	1f Outrigger canoe, Lopevi Islands
F74	2f Outrigger canoe, Lopevi Islands
F75	5f Outrigger canoe, Lopevi Islands
F76	10f Outrigger canoe, Lopevi Islands
	Set of 12 £110 £170

1953

As Nos. 68/71

F81†	5c Outrigger sailing canoes	35	40
F82†	10c Outrigger sailing canoes	55	40
F83†	15c Outrigger sailing canoes	55	45
F84†	20c Outrigger sailing canoes	65	45

1956

As Nos. 80/1

F92†	5c Portuguese galleon, 1606	1.00	80
F93†	10c Portuguese galleon, 1606	1.00	80

1957

As Nos. 84/7

F96†	5c Freighters, Port Vila	70	40
F97†	10c Freighters, Port Vila	70	40
F98†	15c Freighters, Port Vila	1.10	40
F99†	20c Freighters, Port Vila	1.10	40

1963

As No. 98 and 101

F110†	5c Freighter loading manganese	40	30
F114†	20c Trawlers ("RF" at left)	2.25	3.00
F115†	20c Trawlers ("RF" at right)	60	25

1967

As No. 127

F143†	60c H.M.A.S. Canberra (cruiser)	1.10	1.25

1968

As Nos. 131/2

F146†	25c La Boudeuse and L'Etoile (Bougainville), 1768	40	40
F147†	60c Ship's figurehead	90	90

1970

No. F115 surcharged **35**

F159	35c on 20c Trawlers	60	50

1973

As Nos. 178/9

F193	25c Freighters at wharf, Vila		
F194	70c Freighters at wharf, Vila		
	Set of 2	2.25	2.50

As No. 183

F198†	70c Outrigger canoe	1.00	75

1974

As Nos. 192/3 and 195

F207†	35c H.M.S. Resolution (Cook)	4.50	4.00
F208†	35c Ship's boat	4.50	4.00
F210†	1f15 H.M.S. Resolution (Cook)	10.00	8.50

1975

As No. 203

F217†	5f Outrigger canoe	10.00	9.00

1977

As No. 250

F264†	50f Outrigger canoe, Shepherd Island	2.00	75

1979

As No. 271

F285†	10f Outrigger canoe, Lopevi Islands, (on stamp No. F53)	30	35

POSTAGE DUE STAMPS

1938

Nos. F53/4, F56, F59 and F61 overprinted **CHIFFRE TAX**

FD65	5c Outrigger canoe, Lopevi Islands
FD66	10c Outrigger canoe, Lopevi Islands
FD67	20c Outrigger canoe, Lopevi Islands
FD68	40c Outrigger canoe, Lopevi Islands
FD69	1f Outrigger canoe, Lopevi Islands
	Set of 5 £110 £160

1941

Nos. FD65/9 overprinted **France Libre**

FD77	5c Outrigger canoe, Lopevi Islands
FD78	10c Outrigger canoe, Lopevi Islands
FD79	20c Outrigger canoe, Lopevi Islands
FD80	40c Outrigger canoe, Lopevi Islands
FD81	1f Outrigger canoe, Lopevi Islands
	Set of 5 42.00 90.00

1953

Nos. F81/2 and F84 overprinted **TIMBRE-TAXE**

FD92†	5c Outrigger sailing canoes	3.50	8.00
FD93†	10c Outrigger sailing canoes	3.50	8.00
FD94†	20c Outrigger sailing canoes	8.75	14.00

NEW ZEALAND

Australasia
1898 12 pence = 1 shilling
20 shillings = 1 pound
1967 100 cents = 1 dollar

1898

325†	8d Maori war canoe	25.00	5.50

1901

303	1d Duchess (ferry)	3.00	10

1906

370†	½d Te Arawa (Maori canoe)	16.00	23.00
372†	3d H.M.S. Endeavour (Cook)	45.00	55.00
373†	6d H.M.S. Britomart (sloop), 1840	£140	£225

1907

386†	1d Duchess (ferry)	30.00	50

No. 386 differs from No. 303 in the top corner ornaments.

1909

405†	1d Duchess (ferry)	1.25	10

1913

No. 405 overprinted **AUCKLAND EXHIBITION 1913**

413†	1d Duchess (ferry)	16.00	27.00

1936

597†	6d Tamaroa (freighter)	1.25	3.75

1940

614†	1d H.M.S. Endeavour (Cook)	2.75	10
616†	2d Heemskerk (Tasman)	1.50	10
618†	3d Aurora, Helena and Cuba (emigrant ships), 1840	2.50	25
619†	4d Awatea (liner)	12.00	50
620†	5d H.M.S. Britomart (sloop), 1840	5.00	2.25
621†	6d Dunedin (refrigerated full-rigged sailing ship), 1882	12.00	45
624†	9d Gold dredger, 1940	7.00	75

1946

673†	5d H.M.N.Z.S. Achilles (cruiser) and Dominion Monarch (liner)	20	15

1948

692†	1d John Wickliffe and Philip Lang (emigrant ships), 1848	10	10

1951

708 1½d + ½d *Health* (yacht)
709 2d + 1d *Health* (yacht)
Set of 2   20   40

1956

752† 2d 19th-century whaleboat and *Samuel Enderby* (whaling ship), Foveaux Strait   10   10

1957

759† 8d *Dunedin* (refrigerated full-rigged ship), 1882 and *Port Brisbane* (refrigerated freighter),1957   60   65

1959

772† 2d H.M.S. *Endeavour* (Cook) careened   15   10
773† 3d Wool lighter, Wairau, 1857   15   10

1967

870† 7c *Kaiti* (trawler) 1.50   90

1968

886† 28c H.M.N.Z.S. *Achilles* (cruiser) at the River Plate, 1939, and H.M.N.Z.S. *Waikato* (modern frigate)   70   1.40

1969

907† 6c H.M.S. *Endeavour* (Cook) 1.25   2.75

**STANLEY GIBBONS
STAMP COLLECTING SERIES**
Introductory booklets on *How to Start, How to Identify Stamps* and *Collecting by Theme*. A series of well illustrated guides at a low price. Write for details.

1970

930a† 25c Yachts, Hauraki Gulf   70   40

1971

950† 5c *Rainbow II* (yacht)   15   20

1972

981† 8c French frigate, 1772 ....   1.50   1.60

996† 23c Speed boat, Lake Rotomahana 2.25   2.75

1975

1069 4c *Lake Erie* (scow)
1070 5c *Herald* (schooner)
1071 8c *New Zealander* (brigantine)
1072 10c *Jessie Kelly* (schooner)
1073 18c *Tory* (barque)
1074 23c *Rangitiki* (full-rigged clipper)
Set of 6   3.00   2.75

1976

1112† 8c *William Bryan* (emigrant ship), 1876   15   10

1978

1174† 12c Gas drilling rig   20   15
1175† 15c Stern trawler   30   25

1980

1221 25c Small craft, Auckland Harbour
1222 30c Freighters, Wellington Harbour
1223 35c Container ships, Lyttleton
1224 50c *New Zealand Pacific* and *Columbus Australia* (container ships), Port Chalmers
Set of 4   1.50   1.40

1982

1259† 30c *Dunedin* (refrigerated full-rigged ship), 1882, and *New Zealand Pacific* (container ship)   35   40

1276† 45c Surf lifeboat   50   40

1983

1312† 24c Fishing boats   30   10

1984

1332 24c *Mountaineer* (paddle-ferry), Lake Wakatipu
1333 40c *Waikana* (ferry), Otago
1334 58c *Britannia* (paddle-ferry), Wakatipu
1335 70c *Wakatere* (paddle-ferry), Firth of Thames
Set of 4   1.75   1.60

1985

1379 25c H.M.N.Z.S. *Philomel* (cruiser), 1914
1380 45c H.M.N.Z.S. *Achilles* (cruiser), 1936
1381 60c H.M.N.Z.S. *Rotoiti* (frigate), 1949
1382 75c H.M.N.Z.S. *Canterbury* (frigate), 1971
Set of 4   4.50   4.25

1986

1388† 25c *Lady Elizabeth II* (police patrol boat) 35 50

1987

1411† 60c Jet boat 50 50
1414† 85c Sailboard 70 75
1416† $1.30 Inflatable dinghy 1.10 1.25

1417 40c Yacht (Southern Cross Cup)
1418 80c Yacht (Admiral's Cup)
1419 $1.50 Yacht (Kenwood Cup)
1420 $1.30 Yacht (America's Cup)
Set of 4 2.75 3.25

1989

1508† 80c Whaling ship and whaleboat 75 85

1522† 80c Yachts 85 90

1524† 40c Sailboard 40 35
1525† 60c Trawler 60 70
1526† 65c Game fishing launch 65 75
1527† 80c Yachts and rowing boat 80 85
1529† $1.50 *Rotorua* (container ship) and tug 1.50 1.60

1990

1541 40c Maori ocean-going canoe
1542 50c H.M.S. *Endeavour* (Cook), 1769
1543 60c *Tory* (barque), 1839

1544 80c *Crusader* (full-rigged immigrant ship), 1871
1545 $1 *Edwin Fox* (full-rigged immigrant ship), 1873
1546 $1.50 *Arawa* (steamer), 1844
Set of 6 6.25 4.50

1557† $1.80 Yachts, Takapuna Beach 1.60 1.60

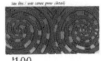

1566† $1 War canoe prow 90 95

1991

1586† 80c H.M.S. *Chatham* (brig), 1791 ...... 70 70

1992

1655 45c *Kiwi Magic* (yacht), 1987
1656 80c *New Zealand II* (yacht), 1988
1657 $1 *America I* (yacht), 1851
1658 $1.50 " America's Cup" Class yacht, 1992
Set of 4 3.00 3.00

1659 45c *Heemskerk* (Tasman)
1660 80c *Zeehan* (Tasman)
1661 $1 *Santa Maria* (Columbus)
1662 $1.50 *Pinta* and *Nina* (Columbus)
Set of 4 3.00 3.00

1706† $1.50 Yachts .... 1·00 1·10

LIFE INSURANCE DEPARTMENT

1947

L43† 1d *Pamir* (barque) 50 30

1967
No. L43 surcharged **1c**
L50† 1c on 1d *Pamir* 2.25 4.25

OFFICIAL STAMPS

1907
No. 303 overprinted **OFFICIAL**
O60c 1d *Duchess* (ferry) 7.50 3.00

1908
No. 386 overprinted **OFFICIAL**
O70 1d *Duchess* (ferry) 60.00 1.75

1910
No. 405 overprinted **OFFICIAL**
O78 1d *Duchess* (ferry) 3.00 10

1940
Nos. 614, 616, 618/19, 621 and 624 overprinted **Official**
O142† 1d H.M.S. *Endeavour* (Cook) 3.25 10
O144† 2d *Heemskerk* (Tasman) 3.25 10
O146† 3d *Aurora, Helena* and *Cuba* (emigrant ships), 1840 .... 7.00 80
O147† 4d *Awatea* (liner) 40.00 2.00
O148† 6d *Dunedin* (refrigerated full-rigged ship), 1882 .... 20.00 2.00
O150† 9d Gold dredger, 1940 .... 8.00 7.00

NICARAGUA

Central America
100 centavos = 1 cordoba

1937

997† 3c Yacht 30 20
998† 5c Packet steamer 30 20

1939

1013† 2c Fishing boats, Lake Managua 15 15
1014† 3c Fishing boats, Lake Managua 15 15
1015† 8c Fishing boats, Lake Managua 15 15
1016† 16c Fishing boats, Lake Managua 25 15
1017† 24c Fishing boats, Lake Managua 25 15
1018† 32c Fishing boats, Lake Managua 35 15
1019† 50c Fishing boats, Lake Managua 40 15

1945

1068† 20c Fleet of Columbus, 1492 .... 40 15
1069† 35c Fleet of Columbus, 1492 .... 70 20
1070† 75c Fleet of Columbus, 1492 .... 1.25 40
1071† 90c Fleet of Columbus, 1492 .... 1.50 60
1072† 1cor Fleet of Columbus, 1492 .... 1.75 45
1073† 2cor50 Fleet of Columbus, 1492 ...... 4.50 2.25

1949

1129† 40c Yachts 1.75 30
1137† 5c Yachts (air) 35 15

1952

1160†	96c Fleet of Columbus	1.00	55
1161†	98c *Santa Maria* (Columbus)	1.00	55
1166†	3cor *Santa Maria* (air)	3.25	1.50
1167†	3cor30 Fleet of Columbus	3.25	1.75

1957

1300†	4c *Honduras* (freighter)	15	10
1301†	5c *Guatemala* (freighter)	15	10
1302†	6c *Guatemala* (freighter)	15	10
1303†	10c *Salvador* (freighter)	20	10
1304†	15c Freighter	30	10
1306†	25c *Managua* (freighter)	30	10
1309†	60c *Costa Rica* (freighter)	55	20
1310†	1cor *Nicarao* (freighter)	75	30
1311†	2cor50 Freighter	1.75	1.00

1960

No. 1166 *overprinted* **X Aniversario Club Filatelico S. J.—C. R.**

1385	3cor *Santa Maria* (Columbus)	1.40	90

1973

1849†	10c Elizabethan galleon	30	10

1974

1911†	10c Landing craft, Normandy, 1944	30	10

1936†	3c Packet steamer (on stamp No. 998)	10	10

1975

2013†	2cor American Presidential barge, 1789	70	30

2017†	2c Scout canoe	10	10

1976

2068†	2cor75 *Bonhomme Richard* and H.M.S. *Serapis*, Battle of Flamborough Head, 1779	1.50	70
2069†	2cor75 U.S.S. *Glenard Phipscomp* (nuclear submarine)	1.50	70

1981

2279†	3cor Container ship	65	30

MS2303	10cor 17th-century frigate	2.50	1.50

1982

2356†	1cor20 *Victoria* (packet steamer)	60	20

2407†	50c *Santa Maria* (Columbus)	50	15
2408†	1cor *Nina* (Columbus)	1.00	30
2409†	1cor50 *Pinta* (Columbus)	1.40	35
2410†	2cor Fleet of Columbus	1.60	55
2411†	2cor50 Fleet of Columbus (air)	1.75	55
MS2414†	10cor *Santa Maria*	4.50	1.75

1983

MS2440†	15cor Olympic yacht	2.25	1.25

2496†	1cor Container ship	45	15

2534†	1cor Sinking liner and ship's lifeboat	45	15

1984

2607	15cor Container ship	4.00	2.10

MS2628	15cor H.M.S. *Discovery* (Cook)	5.00	2.75

1985

2699†	3cor Lifeboat	20	10

1986

2791†	1cor *Pinta* (Columbus)	45	20
2792†	1cor *Santa Maria* and *Nina* (Columbus)	45	20

1987

2904†	15cor Columbus's fleet	65	20

2917†	30cor *Aurora* (Russian cruiser)	35	15

NIGER

West Africa
100 centimes = 1 franc

1926

37†	20c Canoe, River Niger	....	15	30
38†	25c Canoe, River Niger	....	15	30
39†	30c Canoe, River Niger (green)	....	35	55
40†	30c Canoe, River Niger (mauve and yellow)	....	20	40
41†	35c Canoe, River Niger (blue and red on blue)	....	15	30
42†	35c Canoe, River Niger (turquoise)	......	35	50
43†	40c Canoe, River Niger	....	25	40
44†	45c Canoe, River Niger (mauve and yellow)	....	55	70
45†	45c Canoe, River Niger (green)	....	35	55
46†	50c Canoe, River Niger	....	25	30
47†	55c Canoe, River Niger	....	50	70
48†	60c Canoe, River Niger	....	40	65
49†	65c Canoe, River Niger	....	25	45
50†	70c Canoe, River Niger	....	55	70
51†	75c Canoe, River Niger	....	70	90
52†	80c Canoe, River Niger	....	80	95
53†	90c Canoe, River Niger (orange and red)		55	70
54†	90c Canoe, River Niger (green and red)		55	70

1931

As No. 109 of Cameroun

76†	1f50 *Leconte de Lisle* (liner)	....	2.50	2.75

1937

As Nos. 110/11 of Cameroun

77†	20c Liner	....	60	85
78†	30c Sailing ships	....	60	85
MS82a†	3f Liner	....	3.75	5.00

1941

Nos. 46 and 52 surcharged **SECOURS NATIONAL** *and value*

98a†	1f on 50c Canoe, River Niger	....	2.00	2.00
98b†	2f on 80c Canoe, River Niger	....	3.00	3.00

1963

140†	100f Canoe building	....	2.00	1.10

1966

215	50f *France I* (weather ship)	....	1.25	55

1967

257	50f Weather ship	....	1.25	65

1968

281†	45f Pirogue	....	75	35

1972

429†	40f 16th-century galleon	....	1.00	25

1973

515	50f Barges on River Niger			
516	75f *Barban Maza* (tug) and barge			
		Set of 2	1.75	80

1974

534	50f *Elettra* (Marconi's steam yacht)	......	50	30

545†	150f Liner	....	1.50	80

1975

593†	40f River Niger trading canoe	....	50	25

1976

624†	40f Yachts, Lake Constance	....	40	15

630†	100f Freighter	....	90	50

1979

765†	100f Mail canoes	....	60	25

1982

897	65f Scout pirogue			
898	85f Scout inflatable dinghy			
899	130f Scout canoe			
900	200f Scout raft			
		Set of 4	3.75	1.50

903†	65f Fishing pirogue	....	55	30

1984

989	80f *Paris* (early steamer)			
990	120f *Jacques Coeur* (full-rigged ship)			
991	150f *Bosphorus* (full-rigged ship)			
992	300f *Comet* (full-rigged ship)			
		Set of 4	4.50	1.75

997	300f *Rickmer Rickmers* (full-rigged ship)		2.50	1.50

999† 120f Canoes, Ayerou Market 90 60

1985

1053 110f Power boats
1054 150f Power boat
1055 250f Power boat
                  Set of 3   3.25   2.10

1989

1162 100f Tanker
1163 120f Tanker
                  Set of 2   2.75   1.40

1991

1209 85f *Santa Maria* (Columbus)
1210 110f 15th-century Portuguese caravel
1211 200f 16th-century four-masted caravel
1212 250f *Estremadura* (Spanish caravel), 1511
1213 400f *Vija* (Portuguese caravel), 1600 (air)
1214 500f *Pinta*
                Set of 6   11.00   4.25
MS1215 600f *Nina* 3.75   1.90

NIGERIA

West Africa
1936 12 pence = 1 shilling
20 shillings = 1 pound
1973 100 kobo = 1 naira

1936

34† ½d *Apapa* (freighter) at wharf, Apapa 85 85
36† 1½d Tin dredger 40 30
38† 3d Fishing canoes 70 75
45† £1 Canoe 75.00 £120

1949

As No. 115 *of Antigua*
65† 3d Paddle-steamer 35 65

1953

69† ½d 19th-century brigantine and canoes .. 15 30
76† 1s Freighter loading timber 40 10
80† £1 Shipping at Lagos in 19th and 20th centuries 11.00 5.00

1961

105† 2s6d Liner 30 45

1962

125† 2s6d Tanker 30 20

1963

132† 1s3d *Kingsport* (satellite communications ship) 35 20

1970

248† 2d Oil rig 10 10

1973

294† 7k Freighter at timber wharf 30 65
301† 25k Freighter at wharf 85 45

1974

324† 30k Freighter and canoe 1.60 2.50

326† 18k *Mercury* (cable ship) 1.25 60

1988

418† 25k Bulk carrier 10 10

1986

517† 15k Freighter at wharf 10 10

NIUAFO'OU

South Pacific
100 sentiti = 1 pa'anga

1983

26† 1p50 Sailing canoe 3.50 3.75

1985

53† 47s Tongan canoes 75 45
54† 1p50 *Eendracht* (Le Maire), 1616 .... 2.25 2.00
MS55† 1p50 *Eendracht* 1.50 1.75

56 9s *Ysabel* (barquentine), 1902
57 13s *Tofua I* (cargo liner), 1908
58 47s *Mariposa* (cargo liner), 1934
59 1p50 *Matua* (inter-island freighter), 1936
                Set of 4   2.75   2.75

61† 42s Freighter off Niuafo'ou 90 90
63† 1p50 Freighter off Niuafo'ou 2.75 2.75

1986

86†	57s Outrigger canoe	1.10	1.10
87†	1p Freighter	2.00	2.00
88†	2p50 Outrigger canoe	3.50	3.50

1988

MS107	2s Immigrant ship and ship's boat, 1788 (sheet also contains eleven other 42s stamps)	10.00	10.00

1989

MS112	42s H.M.S. *Bounty* and *Bounty's* launch (sheet also contains eleven other 42s stamps)	9.50	10.00

1990

139	42s Inter-island steamer
140	57s Inter-island steamer
141	75s Inter-island steamer
142	2p50 Inter-island steamer

Set of 4   6.50   6.50

143†	15s Canoe	55	55
144†	42s Canoe	1.00	1.00
145†	57s Canoe	1.25	1.25

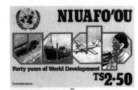

151†	2p50 Freighter	3.25	3.25

ALBUM LISTS

Write for our latest list of albums and accessories.
This will be sent on request.

1991

152†	32s H.M.S. *Bounty* (Bligh)	75	75
154†	57s H.M.S. *Pandora* (frigate), 1791	1.10	1.10
MS155†	2p H.M.S. *Pandora* (Capt. Edwards); 3p H.M.S. *Bounty* (Bligh)	6.50	7.00

1992

MS164	57s Ship's boat, 1492; 57s *Nina*; 57s Bow of *Santa Maria*; 57s Stern of *Santa Maria*; 57s *Pinta* (sheet also contains seven other designs connected to Columbus)	7.50	8.00

165†	42s American battleship ablaze, Pearl Harbor, 1941	60	60
173†	42c U.S.S. *Mississippi* (battleship)	60	60
174†	42s U.S.S. *Enterprise* (aircraft carrier)	60	60

1993

190†	45s *Pangai* (patrol boat)	40	10
194†	2p *Pangai* (patrol boat)	1.75	1.75

NIUE

South Pacific
1902 12 pence = 1 shilling
20 shillings = 1 pound
1967 100 cents = 1 dollar

1902

No. 303 of New Zealand overprinted **NIUE**

1	1d *Duchess* (ferry)	£350	£350

No. 303 of New Zealand surcharged **NIUE. TAHA PENI.**

9†	1d *Duchess* (ferry)	50	65

1917

No. 405 of New Zealand surcharged **NIUE. TAHA PENI.**

21†	1d *Duchess* (ferry)	5.50	5.50

No. 405 of New Zealand overprinted **NIUE.**

24†	1d *Duchess* (ferry)	2.75	3.75

1920

As Nos. 82 and 84 of Cook Islands, but inscribed "NIUE"

39†	1d Schooner	1.75	1.25
47†	4d Local sailing canoe	3.00	8.50

1932

As Nos. 106, 108/9 and 111 of Cook Islands, but additionally inscribed "NIUE"

62†	½d Captain Cook and ship	50	90
64†	2d Double Maori canoe	40	70
92†	2½d Schooner	60	95
67†	6d *Monowai* (liner)	70	65

1935

Nos. 65 and 94 overprinted **SILVER JUBILEE OF KING GEORGE V. 1910 – 1935.**

70†	2½d Schooner	3.25	2.50
71†	6d *Monowai* (liner)	3.25	5.00

1938

As No. 145 of Cook Islands, but additionally inscribed "NIUE"

97†	3s Canoe	9.50	6.00

1950

114†	1d H.M.S. *Resolution* (Cook)	2.25	80
115†	2d Canoes, Alofi	15	15
118†	6d *Maui Pomare* (freighter), Alofi	60	20

1967

Nos. 114/15 and 118 surcharged

126†	1c on 1d H.M.S. *Resolution* (Cook)	80	15
127†	2c on 2d Canoes, Alofi	10	10
130†	5c on 6d *Maui Pomare* (freighter), Alofi	10	10

1970

155†	3c Outrigger canoe	10	10
156†	5c *Tofua II* (cargo liner)	15	10

1972

170†	4c Cargo liner	10	10

1974

183†	3c H.M.S. *Resolution* (Cook)	30	25

1976

205†	50c Outrigger canoe	40	60

1978

236†	16c H.M.S. *Resolution* and canoes, Hawaii, 1778	95	40
238†	30c Hawaiian canoes, 1778	1.40	50
239†	35c Hawaiian canoe, 1778	1.50	55

Design as No. 205 but with silver frame
256† $1.10 Outrigger canoe 1.10   80

1979
As No. 256, but with gold frame and inscribed "AIRMAIL"
267† 50c Outrigger canoe 70   20

288† 35c *Washington* (paddle-steamer) and
U.S.A. stamp 35   25
289† 35c *Washington* (paddle-steamer) and
Rowland Hill 35   25

296† 30c Ship's boat 75   40
297† 35c H.M.S. *Resolution* and H.M.S.
Discovery (Cook), Queen Charlotte's
Sound 85   45

302† 60c American aircraft carrier 40   40

1980
Nos. 288/9, 297 and 302 surcharged **HURRICANE RELIEF Plus
2c** *(over pair for Nos. 314/15)*
314† 35c + 2c *Washington* (paddle-steamer)
and U.S.A. stamp 35   40
315† 35c + 2c *Washington* (paddle-steamer)
and Rowland Hill 35   40
322† 35c + 2c H.M.S. *Resolution* and H.M.S.
Discovery (Cook), Queen Charlotte's
Sound 35   40
326† 60c + 2c American aircraft carrier 60   65

Nos. 288/9 overprinted **ZEAPEX'80 AUCKLAND** *(No. 357) or*
NEW ZEALAND STAMP EXHIBITION *and emblem (No. 358)*
357† 35c *Washington* (paddle-steamer) and
U.S.A. stamp 35   25
358† 35c *Washington* (paddle-steamer) and
Rowland Hill 35   25

370† 30c "Soling" class yachts (yacht with
green sail at left) 20   20
371† 30c "Soling" class yachts (yacht with
red sail at left) 20   20

1983

476† 70c H.M.S. *Resolution* and H.M.S.
Adventure (Cook), 1774 65   70

1987

MS648 Two sheets. 75c Cadet full-rigged ship
and Brooklyn Bridge; 75c *Esmeralda* (Chilean
cadet barquentine); 75c Cadet barque at dusk
(sheets also contain seven other designs)
Set of 2 sheets   4.25   4.75

1992

732† $3 Columbus's fleet 2.50   2.50
733† $5 *Santa Maria* (Columbus) 4.50   4.50

NORFOLK ISLAND
Australasia
100 cents = 1 dollar

1967

77 1c H.M.S. *Resolution* (Cook), 1774
78 2c *La Boussole* and *L'Astrolabe* (La
Perouse), 1788
79 3c H.M.S. *Supply* (brig), 1788
80 4c H.M.S. *Sirius* (frigate), 1790
81 5c *Norfolk* (cutter), 1798
82 7c H.M.S. *Mermaid* (survey cutter), 1825
83 9c *Lady Franklin* (full-rigged ship), 1853
84 10c *Morayshire* (full-rigged transport), 1856
85 15c *Southern Cross* (missionary ship), 1866
86 20c *Pitcairn* (missionary schooner), 1891
87 25c *Black Billy* (Norfolk Island whaleboat),
1895
88 30c *Iris* (cable ship), 1907
89 50c *Resolution* (schooner), 1926
90 $1 *Morinda* (freighter), 1931
Set of 14   12.50   8.00

1969

100 5c 19th-century cutter
101 30c 19th-century cutter
Set of 2   30   20

1970

119† 10c H.M.S. *Endeavour* (Cook) 45   10

1973

129 35c H.M.S. *Resolution* (Cook) in the
Antarctic 3.00   2.25

1974

153† 10c H.M.S. *Resolution* (Cook) 2.50   1.75

1975

163† 10c H.M.S. *Mermaid* (survey cutter),
1825 45   45

170 25c *Resolution* (schooner), 1926
171 45c *Resolution* (schooner), 1926
Set of 2   65   85

1976

172† 18c *Charles W. Morgan* (whaling ship)   30   15

1978

214† 90c H.M.S. *Resolution* and H.M.S.
Discovery (Cook) in Arctic 1.50   80

1979

220† 20c H.M.S. *Resolution* (Cook) 80   30
223† 40c H.M.S. *Resolution* and H.M.S.
Discovery (Cook), Hawaii 90   50

1981

258† 5c *Morayshire* (full-rigged transport), 1856 .... 15 15

1982

287 24c Shipwreck of H.M.S. *Sirius* (frigate), 1790
288 27c Shipwreck of *Diocet* (brigantine), 1873
289 35c Shipwreck of *Friendship* (brigantine), 1835
290 40c Shipwreck of *Mary Hamilton* (barque), 1873
291 55c Shipwreck of *Fairlie* (full-rigged ship), 1840
292 65c Shipwreck of *Warrigal* (brigantine), 1918

Set of 6 4.75 4.25

1983

314† 30c *Chantik* (inshore cable ship) 40 40
315† 45c *Chantik* 55 55
316† 75c *Mercury* (cable ship) 95 95

1984

343† 30c H.M.S. *Resolution* (on stamp No. 153) 30 35

349† 30c Full-rigged sailing ship, 1884 ...... 40 45

1985

356 5c *Fanny Fisher* (19th-century whaling ship)
357 33c *Costa Rica Packet* (19th-century whaling ship)
358 50c *Splendid* (19th-century whaling ship)
359 90c *Onward* (19th-century whaling ship)

Set of 4 3.75 3.00

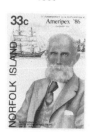

360 15c *Waterwitch* (whaling ship)
361 20c *Canton* (whaling ship)
362 60c *Aladdin* (whaling ship)
363 80c *California* (whaling ship)

Set of 4 3.50 4.00

1986

385† 33c 19th-century whaling ship 60 35

403† 36c Outrigger canoe 65 45

1987

421† 5c Loading First Fleet supply ship, 1787 40 40
422† 55c First Fleet leaving Spithead, 1787 .. 1.40 1.50
423† 55c H.M.S. *Sirius* (frigate), 1787 .... 1.40 1.50

434† 90c *L'Astrolabe* and *La Boussole* (La Perouse) off Norfolk Island, 1788 ...... 1.75 2.00
435† $1 *L'Astrolabe* wrecked in Solomon Islands, 1788 .... 2.25 2.50

1988

436 37c Ship's cutter, 1788
437 $1 First Fleet at Sydney Cove, 1788

Set of 2 3.00 2.75

439† 37c H.M.S. *Supply* (brig), 1788 .... 75 75
441† 70c H.M.S. *Supply*, 1788 .... 1.50 1.50
442† 90c H.M.S. *Supply*, 1788 .... 1.75 1.75

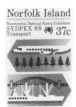

444† 37c Container ship 65 65

451† 63c Sailing dinghies 85 1.00

452† 39c Local longboats 35 40
453† 55c Local longboat 50 55

1989

460† 5c H.M.S. *Bounty* (Bligh) off Tasmania .. 40 30
463† $1.10 H.M.S. *Bounty* and *Bounty's* launch 2.75 2.50
MS464† $1 H.M.S. *Bounty* and *Bounty's* launch (on Pitcairn Islands stamp No. 345) (sheet also contains two other values) 5.00 5.00

472† 75c Rowing boat 1.60 1.60

1990

477† 70c H.M.S. *Bounty* on fire, Pitcairn Island, 1790 .... 1.75 1.75

479†	41c H.M.S. *Sirius* (frigate) striking reef, 1790	1.25 1.25
480†	41c H.M.S. *Sirius* failing to clear bay	1.25 1.25

483	5c Lighters unloading and freighter	
484	10c Lighters unloading and freighter	
485	45c *La Dunkerquoise* (French patrol vessel)	
486	50c *Dimitri Mendeleev* (Russian research vessel)	
487	65c *Pacific Rover* (tanker)	
488	70c *Ile de Lumiere* (freighter)	
489	75c *Norfolk Trader* (freighter)	
490	80c *Roseville* (transport)	
491	90c *Kalia* (container ship)	
492	$1 H.M.S. *Bounty* (replica)	
493	$2 H.M.A.S. *Success* (supply ship)	
494	$5 H.M.A.S. *Whyalla* (patrol vessel)	
	Set of 12	10.00 11.00

1991

512†	43c Model of H.M.S. *Sirius* (transport), 1790	70 50

516	$1 Wreck of H.M.S. *Pandora* (frigate), 1790	
517	$1.20 H.M.S. *Pandora* (frigate)	
	Set of 2	3.25 3.75

524†	$1 Destroyer, 1941	1.75 2.00

1992

526†	$1.05 *Santa Maria* (Columbus)	1.40 1.50

529†	70c H.M.A.S. *Australia* (cruiser)	1.00 1.10
530†	$1.05 U.S.S. *Yorktown* (aircraft carrier)	1.60 1.75

532†	70c Aircraft carrier and destroyer	1.00 1.10
533†	$1.05 Japanese aircraft carrier under attack	1.60 1.75

534†	45c Landing craft, Guadalcanal, 1942	50 45

1993

541†	45c Longboat on beach	50 45

NORTH BORNEO

South-east Asia
100 cents = 1 dollar

1894

74†	8c Malay prau	2.50 8.00

1897

102b†	8c Malay prau	15.00 2.75

1899

No. 102b surcharged **4 CENTS**

114†	4c on 8c Malay prau	13.00 10.00

1901

No. 102b overprinted **BRITISH PROTECTORATE.**

133†	8c Malay prau	2.75 3.00

1904

No. 102b surcharged **4 cents**

148†	4c on 8c Malay prau	11.00 23.00

1939

313†	25c Malay prau	7.00 4.50

1945

No. 313 overprinted **BMA**

330†	25c Malay prau	2.75 75

1947

No. 313 overprinted **GR** *and cypher with bars obliterating* "THE STATE OF" *and* "BRITISH PROTECTORATE"

345†	25c Malay prau	40 30

1949

As No. 115 of Antigua

353†	10c Paddle-steamer	60 30

1950

363†	15c Malay prau, Sandakan	30 40
365†	30c Suluk river canoe	55 10

1954

As Nos. 363 and 365, but with portrait of Queen Elizabeth II

379†	15c Malay prau, Sandakan	25 10
381†	30c Suluk river canoe	40 15

1961

388†	15c Malay prau	25 30

NORTHERN RHODESIA

Central Africa
12 pence = 1 shilling
20 shillings = 1 pound

1949

As No. 115 of Antigua

51†	3d Paddle-steamer	85 1.25

NORWAY

Northern Europe
100 ore = 1 krone

1930

Size 35½ × 21½ mm

223	15ore + 25ore *Bergensfjord* (liner)	
224	20ore + 25ore *Bergensfjord*	
225	30ore + 25ore *Bergensfjord*	
	Set of 3	80.00 90.00

1938

As Nos. 224/5, but reduced to 27½ × 21 mm

349	15ore + 25ore *Bergensfjord* (liner)	
350	20ore + 25ore *Bergensfjord*	
351	30ore + 25ore *Bergensfjord*	
	Set of 3	3.25 5.25

1941

295 15ore + 10ore *Femboring* (fishing boat) 90 3.00

296 10ore + 10ore *Colin Archer* (lifeboat)
297 15ore + 10ore *Colin Archer*
298 20ore + 10ore *Osloskoyta* (lifeboat)
299 30ore + 10ore *Osloskoyta*
  Set of 4 5.00 6.50

327† 30ore Viking fleet 90 1.60

1942

333† 15ore Viking fleet 1.25 1.60

1943

341† 5ore *Sleipner* (destroyer) 10 10
342† 7ore Convoy of merchant ships 20 20
343† 10ore *Sleipner* (destroyer) 10 10
346† 30ore Convoy of merchant ships 85 85

357† 10ore + 10ore Trawlers 70 4.25

1944

360 10ore+ 10ore Sinking of *Baroy* (freighter)
361 15ore + 10ore Sinking of *Sanct Svithun* (cargo liner)
362 20ore + 10ore Sinking of *Irma* (freighter)
  Set of 3 1.90 11.50

1947

386† 15ore 18th-century warship 45 10
388† 30ore *Restaurationen* (emigrant sloop), 1825 .... 1.10 15
389† 40ore *Constitutionen* (paddle-steamer), 1827 .... 1.60 10
391† 50ore *Spes et Fides* (whale catcher) 2.50 15
392† 55ore *Fram* (Amundsen and Nansen) 4.00 20

1953

Design as Nos. 223/5, but reduced to 27½ × 21 mm
442 20ore + 10ore *Bergensfjord*
464 25ore + 10ore *Bergensfjord*
443 30ore + 15ore *Bergensfjord*
465 35ore + 15ore *Bergensfjord*
444 55ore + 25ore *Bergensfjord*
466 65ore + 25ore *Bergensfjord*
  Set of 6 40.00 40.00

1960

501 20ore Viking longship
502 25ore Hanse kogge
503 45ore *Skomvaer* (barque)
504 55ore *Dalfon* (tanker)
505 90ore *Bergensfjord* (liner)
  Set of 5 5.25 4.00

1961

511† 90ore Yacht 70 80

518† 45ore *Fram* (Amundsen), 1911 .... 50 15

1963

551 50ore River mail boat
552 90ore Northern femboring (sailing vessel)
  Set of 2 2.40 2.25

1969

625† 50ore *Princesse Ragnild* (liner) 40 30

1970

649† 100ore Second World War convoy of merchant ships 1.40 1.25

1972

682† 80ore Figurehead of Oseberg viking ship 1.00 50

690 60ore *Maud* (polar ship)
691 80ore *Fram* (Amundsen and Nansen)
692 1k20 *Gjoa* (polar ship)
  Set of 3 2.25 1.40

1974

716† 1k Fishing boat, Hardanger Fjord 40 10

1975

734† 1k Trawlers, Nusfjord 50 20

1977

800 1k *Constitutionen* (paddle-steamer)
801 1k25 *Westeraalen* (freighter)
802 1k30 *Kong Haakon* and *Dronningen* (ferries)
803 1k80 *Nordstjernen* and *Harald Jarl* (ferries)
  Set of 4 2.40 1.90

804† 1k25 Trawler 20 10

1979

844† 1k50 Rowing boat, Skjernoysund 20 10

850† 10k Statfjord "A" (drilling platform) 1.90 35

1980

MS862 1k25 *Bergen* (paddle-steamer) (sheet contains three other designs) 7.00 7.00

1981

879† 2k20 *Christian Radich* (cadet ship) 50 40

880 1k10 *Skibladner* (lake paddle-steamer)
881 1k30 *Victoria* (lake ferry)
882 1k50 *Faemund II* (lake ferry)
883 2k30 *Storegut* (train ferry)
                      Set of 4 90 65

1983

913† 3k50 Cruise liner 35 25

922 2k Northern femboring (sailing vessel)
923 3k Northern jekt (sailing vessel)
                      Set of 2 95 60

1984

931† 3k50 Rowing boat 85 50

1985

MS960 2k + 1k *Neptuno Nordraug* (oil rig);
2k + 1k Statfjord "C" (oil platform);
Treasure Scout (drilling platform) and *Odin
Viking* (supply ship) (sheet contains one other
design) 1.75 2.00

965† 2k50 *Berghavn* (dredger) 35 10

1986

983 2k50 Cabin cruisers, Moss
984 4k Fishing boats, Alesund
                      Set of 2 1.25 70

1988

1039† 4k60 Pontoons 75 35

1045 2k90 *Prinds Gustav* (paddle-steamer)
1046 3k80 Trawler
                      Set of 2 1.10 40

1989

1055 3k Fishing boats, Vardo
1056 4k Fishing boats, Hammerfest
                      Set of 2 1.10 45

1990

1074 3k20 Second World War convoy
1075 4k H.M.S. *Coventry*, H.M.S.
     Southampton and H.M.S. *Cairo*
     (cruisers), Narvik, 1940
                      Set of 2 1.10 45

1991

1087 5k Plan and elevation of container ship 90 45

1090 3k20 17th-century shipping
1091 5k50 Yachts
                      Set of 2 1.60 75

1094 3k20 *Skomvaer III* (lifeboat)
1095 27k *Colin Archer* (lifeboat)
                      Set of 2 5.25 2.50

1992

1144 3k30 *Restaurationen* (emigrant sloop)
1145 4k20 *Stavangerfjord* (liner)
                      Set of 2 1.50 50

1993

1160 4k Kayak
1161 4k50 Raft
                      Set of 2 1.60 1.00

NYASALAND

Central Africa
12 pence = 1 shilling
20 shillings = 1 pound

1945

144† ½d Canoe, Lake Nyasa 10 10
151† 9d Canoe, Lake Nyasa 75 2.25

1949

As No. 115 of Antigua
164† 3d Paddle-steamer 1.00 50

1953

As Nos. 144 and 151, but with portrait of Queen Elizabeth II
173a† ½d Canoe, Lake Nyasa 10 55
181† 9d Canoe, Lake Nyasa 70 2.25

1964

203† 4d Fishing pirogue 20 20

NYASSA COMPANY

South-east Africa
1911 1000 reis = 1 milreis
1912 100 centavos = 1 escudo

1911

Overprinted **REPUBLICA**

62†	300r *Sao Gabriel* (Vasco da Gama)	1.25	90
63†	400r *Sao Gabriel*	1.40	1.00
64†	500r *Sao Gabriel*	1.75	1.40

1921

Nos. 62/4 surcharged in figures and words

87†	1½c on 300r *Sao Gabriel*	80	80
90†	3c on 400r *Sao Gabriel*	80	80
94†	12c on 500r *Sao Gabriel*	80	80

105†	7½c *Sao Gabriel*	55	40
106†	8c *Sao Gabriel*	55	40
107†	10c *Sao Gabriel*	55	40
108†	15c *Sao Gabriel*	55	40
109†	20c *Sao Gabriel*	65	50
114†	2e Dhow	2.00	1.25
115†	5e Dhow	1.60	1.10

POSTAGE DUE STAMPS

1924

D136†	5c *Sao Gabriel*	1.75	1.25
D137†	6c *Sao Gabriel*	1.75	1.25
D138†	10c *Sao Gabriel*	1.75	1.25

OCEANIC SETTLEMENTS

East Pacific Ocean
100 centimes = 1 franc

1931

As No. 109 of Cameroun

82†	1f50 *Leconte de Lisle* (liner)	3.50	3.50

1934

83†	1c Fishing canoe	15	30
84†	2c Fishing canoe	15	30
85†	3c Fishing canoe	15	30
86†	4c Fishing canoe	15	30
87†	5c Fishing canoe	35	45
88†	10c Fishing canoe	15	30
89†	15c Fishing canoe	25	35
90†	20c Fishing canoe	15	30

1937

As Nos. 110/11 of Cameroun

121†	20c Liner	1.10	1.10
122†	30c Sailing ships	1.10	1.10

1942

147†	5c Polynesian travelling canoe	15	30
148†	10c Polynesian travelling canoe	15	30
149†	25c Polynesian travelling canoe	15	30
150†	30c Polynesian travelling canoe	15	25
151†	40c Polynesian travelling canoe	15	30
152†	80c Polynesian travelling canoe	15	30
153†	1f Polynesian travelling canoe	20	25
154†	1f50 Polynesian travelling canoe	25	35
155†	2f Polynesian travelling canoe	25	30
156†	2f50 Polynesian travelling canoe	60	1.10
157†	4f Polynesian travelling canoe	40	55
158†	5f Polynesian travelling canoe	50	70
159†	10f Polynesian travelling canoe	75	85
160†	20f Polynesian travelling canoe	90	90

1945

Nos. 147, 149 and 156 surcharged

169	50c on 5c Polynesian travelling canoe	
170	60c on 5c Polynesian travelling canoe	
171	70c on 5c Polynesian travelling canoe	
172	1f20 on 5c Polynesian travelling canoe	
173	2f40 on 25c Polynesian travelling canoe	
174	3f on 25c Polynesian travelling canoe	
175	4f50 on 25c Polynesian travelling canoe	
176	15f on 2f50 Polynesian travelling canoe	

Set of 8   3.25   4.00

1948

186†	10c Outrigger canoe, Moorea	15	30
187†	30c Outrigger canoe, Moorea	15	30
188†	40c Outrigger canoe, Moorea	15	30
192†	1f Outrigger canoe, Faa	30	40
193†	1f20 Outrigger canoe, Faa	30	40
194†	1f50 Outrigger canoe, Faa	30	40
199†	5f Outrigger canoe, Bora-Bora	75	70
200†	6f Outrigger canoe, Bora-Bora	90	75
202†	10f Outrigger canoe, Bora-Bora	2.75	1.75

1954

As No. 264 of Cameroun

214	3f Landing craft, Normandy, 1944	2.75	2.50

1956

215	3f *Orohena* (schooner) and *Moana* (yacht) in dry dock, Papeete	1.40	1.00

OMAN

Arabia
1000 baizas = 1 rial saidi

1972

158	5b Dhow and British warship, Matrah, 1809	
147	10b Dhow and British warship, Matrah, 1809	
148	20b Dhow and British warship Matrah, 1809	
192	25b Dhow and British warship, Matrah, 1809	
193	30b British warship, Shinas, 1809	
194	40b British warship, Shinas, 1809	
195	50b British warship, Shinas, 1809	
196	75b British warship, Shinas, 1809	
154	100b British warship, Muscat, 1809	
155	¼r British warship, Muscat, 1809	
156	½r British warship, Muscat, 1809	
157	1r British warship, Muscat, 1809	

Set of 12   25.00   12.50

1973

172†	15b Dhow building	40	20
174†	65b Dhow and tanker	2.00	1.25

1979

226†	75b Dhow and modern trawler	1.25	1.10

227†	40b Landing craft	1.75	60

1980

235†	150b Naval patrol boat	1.25	1.00

1981

No. 235 surcharged **POSTAGE 20 BAISA**

241†	20b on 150b Naval patrol boat	50	30

250	50b *Sohar* (replica of medieval dhow), Muscat	50	50
251	100b *Sohar*	1.00	1.00
252	130b *Sohar*	1.25	1.25
253	200b *Sohar*, and 17th-century Portuguese galleons	1.75	1.75

Set of 4   4.00   4.00

256†	400b Missile-armed corvettes	3.25	3.25

1982

257 50b Police launch 1.25 60

1984

298 100b *Al Munassir* (landing craft) 1.00 70

1985

299 100b Helicopter rescue from tanker 2.50 1.25

314 100b Missile-armed corvettes 1.50 80

1986

323 50b *Sultana* (full-rigged sailing ship), 1840
324 100b *Shabab Oman* (cadet barquentine)
　　　　　　　　　　　　　 Set of 2 1.75 1.25

1990

384 200b *Sultana* (full-rigged ship), 1840 .... 85 60

1991

394 100b Missile-armed corvette 50 35

PAHANG

South-east Asia
100 cents = 1 dollar

1949

As No. 115 *of Antigua*
50† 15c Paddle-steamer 35 70

1957

82† 20c Malay fishing prau 20 10

PAKISTAN

Indian Sub-continent
100 paisa = 1 rupee

1954

71† 2r Fishing boats, East Pakistan 2.00 10

1960

120 14a Freighter 15 10

1965

227† 15p *Tughril* (destroyer) 80 10

1968

268† 50p *Tughril* (destroyer) and *Ghazi*
　　　　(submarine) 55 15

1975

383 2r25 African canoe 2.00 2.25

1980

532 1r Dhow 70 70

1983

619 60p "Enterprise" class yacht
620 60p "O.K." class dinghy
　　　　　　　　　　　　 Set of 2 2.00 1.50

1987

707† 5r Landing ship 85 55

1988

750† 10r Yacht 75 75

1989

763 1r "Daphne" class submarine
764 1r "Fleet Snorkel" class submarine
765 1r "Agosta" class submarine
　　　　　　　　　　　　 Set of 3 80 55

772 6r Container ship 1.25 1.50

OFFICIAL STAMPS

1954

No. 71 *overprinted* **SERVICE**
O59† 2r Fishing boats, East Pakistan 2.50 10

PALAU

North Pacific
100 cents = 1 dollar

1983

34	20c *Antelope* (sail merchantman), 1783		
35	20c *Antelope* and Palau canoe		
36	20c *Antelope*		
37	20c *Antelope*		
38	20c *Antelope*		
39	20c *Antelope* and Palau canoe at sea		
40	20c *Antelope* and building *Oroolong* (schooner)		
41	20c *Antelope*		
	Set of 8	3.00	2.10

1984

56	40c *Oroolong* (schooner), 1783		
57	40c *Duff* (full-rigged missionary ship), 1797		
58	40c *Peiho* (expedition steamer), 1908		
59	40c *Albatross* (German gunboat), 1885		
	Set of 4	3.00	2.40

61†	20c Fishing pirogue	35	25

1985

73	22c Borotong (cargo canoe)		
74	22c Kabeki (war canoe)		
75	22c Olechutel (bamboo raft)		
76	22c Kaeb (sailing canoe)		
	Set of 4	1.75	1.40

81	44c German warship, 1885		
82	44c Outrigger canoe		
83	44c *Hohenzollern* (German Imperial yacht) (on Caroline Islands stamp No. 25)		
84	44c *Cormoran* (German cruiser), 1914, and *Hohenzollern* (German Imperial yacht) (on Caroline Islands stamp No. 19)		
	Set of 4	3.00	2.10

94	44c Kaeb (sailing canoe)		
95	44c U.S.S. *Vincennes* (sail frigate), 1835		
96	44c *Scharnhorst* (German cruiser), 1910		
97	44c Tourist cabin cruiser		
	Set of 4	3.25	2.40

1986

103†	14c Olechutel (raft)	90	55
104†	14c Kaebs (sailing canoes)	90	55
106†	14c Inter-island ferry	90	55

143†	44c Kabeki (war canoe)	90	60

153†	22c Abandoned landing craft, Airai	40	30

1987

208†	14c Goshuin-sen (16th century trading ship) (on stamp No. 316 of Japan)	25	20

213	22c Three outrigger canoes		
214	22c Kaeb and bird		
215	22c Holy Family in kaeb		
216	22c Kaeb		
217	22c Two outrigger canoes		
	Set of 5	1.60	1.40

1988

MS236†	25c Kaeb; 25c Spanish "Vizcaya" class cruiser; 25c *Cormoran* (German cruiser); 25c U.S. Trust Territory freighter at Malakal (sheet also contains two other designs)	2.00	2.00

1989

289†	25c American aircraft carrier	30	20

323†	25c Kaebs	30	20
324†	25c Two kaebs	30	20

1990

336†	25c H.M.S. *Victory* (Nelson)	25	20
338†	25c Ships in Rotherhithe docks, 1784	25	20

357†	25c Yacht	30	20
358†	25c Kaebs	30	20

380†	45c *Delphin* (Spanish mail ship), 1890 ..	55	45

388†	45c Rocket-firing landing craft, 1944	55	45
MS391†	$1 U.S.S. *Peleliu* (helicopter carrier)	1·25	90

1991

397†	30c Kaeb	35	25
398†	30c *Hohenzollern* (German Imperial yacht) (on Caroline Islands stamp No. 19)	35	25
400†	30c German copra freighter	35	25
404†	30c Freighter loading phosphate	35	25
406†	30c *Hohenzollern* (on Marshall Islands stamp No. G13)	35	25
407†	30c *Scharnhorst* (German cruiser)	35	25
408†	30c *Emden* (German cruiser)	35	25
411†	30c H.M.A.S. *Sydney* (cruiser)	35	25

Aircraft Carrier *RANGER* (CV61)

464† 20c U.S.S. *Ranger* (aircraft carrier), 1991   25   20
465† 20c *PHM-1* (patrol boat), 1991 25   20
466† 20c U.S.S. *Wisconsin* (battleship), 1991   25   20

491† 29c Fishing boat 40   30

494† 29c *Zuiho Maru* (marine research vessel)   40   30

501† 29c American battleships under attack,
     Pearl Harbor, 1941 40   30
502† 29c U.S.S. *Nevada* (battleship) 40   30
504† 29c *Akagi* (Japanese aircraft carrier)
     under attack 40   30
505† 29c U.S.S. *Wasp* (aircraft carrier) sinking,
     Guadalcanal 40   30
506† 29c American aircraft carriers under
     attack, Battle of Philippine Sea 40   30
507† 29c American landing craft, Saipan ... 40   30
510† 29c American landing craft, Iwo Jima 40   30

1992

525† 29c *Golden Hind* (Drake) 40   30
526† 29c *Santa Maria* (Columbus) 40   30
529† 29c *Vitoria* (Magellan) 40   30

PANAMA

Central America
100 centesimos = 1 balboa

1918

178† 12c *Panama* (cargo liner) at Culebra Cut   17.00   5.50
179† 15c *Panama* at Culebra Cut 10.00   2.75
180† 24c *Cristobal* (cargo liner) in Gatun Lock   24.00   7.50
181† 50c *General George W. Goethals* and
     General W. C. Gorgas (freighters) in
     Balboa docks 25.00   16.00
182† 1b *Nereus* (U.S. Navy collier) in Pedro
     Miguel Lock 35.00   19.00

1929

No. 182 overprinted **CORREO AEREO** *and aeroplane*
239† 1b *Nereus* (U.S. Navy collier) in Pedro
     Miguel Lock 18.00   14.00

1936

281† 50c *Resolute* (liner) in Gaillard Cut 8.00   2.75

1937

No. 281 overprinted **UPU**
297† 50c *Resolute* (liner) in Gaillard Cut 7.00   4.25

No. 182 surcharged **CORREO AEREO 5c**
322† 5c on 1b *Nereus* (U.S. Navy collier) in
     Pedro Miguel Lock 2.50   1.25

1939

358† 1c *Santa Elena* (liner) in Pedro Miguel
     Lock 1.50   1.50
360† 5c *Rangitata* (liner) in Culebra Cut 1.50   20
361† 10c Panama Canal ferry 2.00   50

1955

574† 1b *Ancon I* (cargo liner), 1914 .... 2.75   1.75

1964

878† 10c Yachts 1.50   60
879† 21c Speedboats 2.75   1.50

1970

984† 13c Tanker 70   20

1979

1144 3c *Flavia* (liner) in Panama Canal lock ...
1145 23c Liner
                 Set of 2   60   25

1984

1377 19c Liner in Panama Canal lock 25   25

1985

1399 19c Tanker in Panama Canal lock 70   20

1989

1495 35c *Ancon I* (cargo liner), 1914
1496 60c Tanker
                 Set of 2   1.60   1.25

1992

1539 20c Fleet of Columbus at sea
1540 30c Columbus's ships at anchor in New
     World
                 Set of 2   80   55

APPENDIX

The following stamps have either been issued in excess of postal needs, or have not been available to the public in reasonable quantities, at face value. Miniature sheets, imperforate stamps etc., are excluded from this section.

1965

Peaceful Uses of Atomic Energy. Postage ½c US Navy atomic submarine, 1c *Savannah* (nuclear powered freighter); Air 6c *Lenin* (atomic ice-breaker)

1968

Sailing Ship Paintings. Postage 1, 3, 4c; Air 5, 13c

PAPUA

Australasia
12 pence = 1 shilling
20 shillings = 1 pound

1901

9   ½d Lakatoi (trading canoe)
10   1d Lakatoi
11   2d Lakatoi
12   2½d Lakatoi
5   4d Lakatoi
6   6d Lakatoi
14a   1s Lakatoi
8   2s6d Lakatoi
                 Set of 8   £750   £700

1906

Nos. 9, etc, overprinted **Papua.**

40	½d Lakatoi	
41	1d Lakatoi	
42	2d Lakatoi	
38	2½d Lakatoi	
43	4d Lakatoi	
44	6d Lakatoi	
25	1s Lakatoi	
46	2s6d Lakatoi	

Set of 8 £110 £180

1907

As Nos. 9, etc, but inscribed "PAPUA"

66	½d Lakatoi (black & green)	
100	1d Lakatoi (black & red)	
68	2d Lakatoi (black & purple)	
51a	2½d Lakatoi (black & blue)	
52	4d Lakatoi (black & brown)	
80	6d lakatoi (black & green)	
54	1s Lakatoi (black & orange)	
83	2s6d Lakatoi (black & brown)	

Set of 8 80.00 £100

1911

As Nos. 66, etc, but colours changed

84a	½d Lakatoi (green)	
85	1d Lakatoi (red)	
86	2d Lakatoi (mauve)	
87	2½d Lakatoi (blue)	
88	4d Lakatoi (olive)	
89	6d Lakatoi (brown)	
90	1s Lakatoi (yellow)	
91	2s6d Lakatoi (red)	

Set of 8 45.00 70.00

1917

Nos. 84a, 86/9 and 91 surcharged **ONE PENNY**

93	1d on ½d Lakatoi	
94	1d on 2d Lakatoi	
95	1d on 2½d Lakatoi	
96	1d on 4d Lakatoi	
97	1d on 6d Lakatoi	
98	1d on 2s6d Lakatoi	

Set of 6 22.00 40.00

1919

As Nos. 66, etc, but colours changed and additional values

99	½d Lakatoi (green & olive)	
101	1½d Lakatoi	
102	2d Lakatoi (brown & purple)	
102a	2d Lakatoi (brown & red)	
103	2½d Lakatoi (green & blue)	
104	3d Lakatoi	
105	4d Lakatoi (brown & orange)	
106	5d Lakatoi	
107	6d Lakatoi (purple & red)	
127	9d Lakatoi	
108	1s Lakatoi (brown & green)	
128	1s3d Lakatoi	
109a	2s6d Lakatoi (red & pink)	
110	5s Lakatoi	
111	10s Lakatoi	

Set of 15 £250 £375

1929

No. 104 overprinted **AIR MAIL**

114	3d Lakatoi	80	7.00

1930

Nos. 104 and 107/8 overprinted **AIR MAIL** on aeroplane

118	3d Lakatoi	
119	6d Lakatoi	
120	1s Lakatoi	

Set of 3 10.50 27.00

1931

Nos. 101 and 108/10 surcharged in words or figures

122	2d on 1½d Lakatoi	
125	5d on 1s Lakatoi	
126	9d on 2s6d Lakatoi	
123	1s3d on 5d Lakatoi	

Set of 4 10.50 21.00

1932

135†	4d Lakatoi (trading canoe)	3.00	8.50
137†	6d Lakatoi (trading canoe)	4.25	7.00
140†	1s3d Lakatoi (trading canoe)	8.50	20.00

1938

158	2d Katoomba (liner), Port Moresby	
159	3d Katoomba (liner), Port Moresby	
160	5d Katoomba (liner), Port Moresby	
161	8d Katoomba (liner), Port Moresby	
162	1s Katoomba (liner), Port Moresby	

Set of 5 42.00 30.00

1939

163	2d Outrigger canoes	
164	3d Outrigger canoes	
165	5d Outrigger canoes	
166	8d Outrigger canoes	
167	1s Outrigger canoes	
168	1s6d Outrigger canoes	

Set of 6 80.00 45.00

OFFICIAL STAMPS

1931

Nos. 99/102 and 104/9a overprinted **O S**

O55	½d Lakatoi	
O56a	1d Lakatoi	
O57	1½d Lakatoi	
O58	2d Lakatoi	
O59	3d Lakatoi	
O60	4d Lakatoi	
O61	5d Lakatoi	
O62	6d Lakatoi	
O63	9d Lakatoi	
O64	1s Lakatoi	
O65	1s3d Lakatoi	
O66	2s6d Lakatoi	

Set of 12 £120 £275

PAPUA NEW GUINEA

Australasia
1952 12 pence = 1 shilling
20 shillings = 1 pound
1966 100 cents = 1 dollar
1975 100 toea = 1 kina

1952

10†	1s Lakatoi (trading canoe)	2.75	10

1957

No. 10 surcharged **7d**

17†	7d on 1s Lakatoi (trading canoe)	20	10

1963

47†	8d Dedele (freighter)	40	15

1965

72	4d Canoe figurehead	
73	1s3d Canoe figurehead	
74	1s6d Canoe figurehead	
75	4s Canoe figurehead	

Set of 4 3.50 1.10

1967

120†	50c U.S.S. Lexington (aircraft carrier), 1942	50	30

1969

156†	5c "Fireball" class yacht	10	10

1970

170†	10c Masawa canoe	20	15
172†	30c H.M.S. Basilisk (paddle-sloop), 1873	60	20

1971

204†	7c Outrigger canoe	15	10

1972

220†	7c Eureka (schooner), 1922	40	10
222†	20c Gold dredger	1.10	1.25

1973

245†	7c Lakatoi (trading canoe)	30	10
249†	14c Outrigger canoe	45	70
251†	20c Racing canoes, Manus	1.50	40
255†	30c Outrigger canoe	1.25	75
256†	40c Fishing canoes, Madang	1.50	80

PAPUA NEW GUINEA

261† 6c *Hohenzollern* (German Imperial yacht)
(on New Guinea stamp No. G17) 25 35
263† 9c *Lakatoi* (trading canoe) (on Papua
stamp No. 14a) 35 45

1974

277 7c *Lakatoi* (trading canoe), Motu
278 10c *Morobe* (canoe), Tami
279 25c Racing canoe, Aramia
280 30c Buka Island canoe
Set of 4 2.75 3.25

1976

297 7t *Bulolo* (liner)
298 15t *Macdhui* (liner)
299 25t *Malaita* (liner)
300 60t *Montoro* (cargo liner)
Set of 4 2.75 3.25

311† 15t Scout outrigger canoe 50 65

1979

363 14t East New Britain canoe figurehead
364 21t Sepik war canoe figurehead
365 25t Tobriand Island canoe figurehead
366 40t Milne Bay canoe
Set of 4 95 1.10

1981

410† 40t *Aitape* (patrol boat) 70 65

418† 15t Fishing canoe 30 30
420† 60t Fishing canoe 95 85

1982

457† 10t French sail warship, 1882 .... 25 20

1983

467† 50t Freighter at wharf 60 75

1984

487 10t H.M.S. *Nelson* (armoured frigate),
1884
488 10t Yacht, 1984
489 45t Coaster and yacht, 1984
490 45t *Elisabeth* (German warship), 1884
Set of 4 3.00 4.00

1985

509† 40t *Ellengowan* (missionary steamer),
1888 .... 1.25 95

1987

543 1t *La Boudeuse* (De Bougainville), 1768
544 5t *Roebuck* (Dampier), 1700
545 10t H.M.S. *Swallow* (Carteret), 1767
546 15t H.M.S. *Fly* (sloop) (Blackwood), 1845
547 17t H.M.S. *Fly*
548 20t H.M.S. *Rattlesnake* (survey ship)
(Owen Stanley), 1849
549 30t *Vitiaz* (Maclay)
550 35t *San Pedrico* and zabra (Torres), 1606
551 40t *L'Astrolabe* (D'Urville), 1827
552 45t *Neva* (steam launch) (D'Albertis),
1876
553 60t Spanish galleon (Jorge de Meneses),
1526
554 70t *Eendracht* (Schouten and Le Maire),
1616
555 1k H.M.S. *Blanche* (screw sloop)
(Simpson), 1872
556 2k *Merrie England* (screw steamer), 1889
557 3k *Samoa* (German colonial steamer)
Set of 15 12.00 12.50

1988

575 35t Lakatoi (trading canoe) 80 50

1991

656† 40t Missionary schooner and canoe,
1891 .... 80 80

1992

662 21t *Nina* (Columbus)
663 45t *Pinta*
664 60t *Santa Maria*
665 90t Columbus's fleet
Set of 4 4.25 3.75

674† 90t Landing craft 1.40 1.50

PARAGUAY

South America
1931 10 centavos = 1 peso
1944 100 centimos = 1 guarani

1931

397 1p *Paraguay* (gunboat) (red)
398 1p *Paraguay* (blue)
399 2p *Paraguay* (orange)
400 2p *Paraguay* (brown)
401 3p *Paraguay* (green)
402 3p *Paraguay* (blue)
403 3p *Paraguay* (red)
404 6p *Paraguay* (green)
405 6p *Paraguay* (mauve)
406 6p *Paraguay* (blue)
407 10p *Paraguay* (red)
408 10p *Paraguay* (green)
409 10p *Paraguay* (brown)
410 10p *Paraguay* (blue)
411 10p *Paraguay* (pink)
Set of 15 11.00 10.00

412 1p50 *Humaita* (gunboat) (violet)
413 1p50 *Humaita* (blue)
                    Set of 2   80   40

1933

456 10c Fleet of Columbus
457 20c Fleet of Columbus
458 50c Fleet of Columbus
459 1p Fleet of Columbus
460 1p50 Fleet of Columbus
461 2p Fleet of Columbus
462 5p Fleet of Columbus
463 10p Fleet of Columbus
                    Set of 8   7.50   4.00

1944

591† 10c *Tacuary* (paddle-steamer) 1.00 45

595† 1c Freighter, Port Asuncion (air) 15 15
597† 3c *Tacuary* 50 20

1946
As Nos. 591 and 595
640† 1c *Tacuary* 15 15
648† 20c Freighter, Port Asuncion (air) 40 20

1948

678 2c *Paraguari* (freighter)
679 5c *Paraguari*
680 10c *Paraguari*
681 15c *Paraguari*
682 50c *Paraguari*
683 1g *Paraguari*
                  Set of 6   1.60   65

1961

901† 90c Motorised timber barge 10 10
903† 2g Motorised timber barge 10 10
906† 18g15 Motorised timber barge (air) 55 35

1962

1030† 30c *Lago Ypoa* (freighter) 10 10
1031† 90c Freighter 10 10
1032† 1g50 *Olympo* (freighter) 15 10
1033† 2g Freighter 25 15
1034† 4g20 *Rio Apa* (freighter) 35 20

1973

1162 50g *Presidente Stroessner* (liner) 1.00 45

APPENDIX
The following stamps have either been issued in excess of postal needs, or have not been available to the public in reasonable quantities, at face value. Miniature sheets, imperforate stamps, etc. are excluded from this section.

1965
Pres J. Kennedy Commem. 15c American motor torpedo-boat

1968
Mexico Olympic Games. 36g Olympic yacht

1971
Munich Olympic Games. 75c Olympic yachts
150th Death Anniv. of Napoleon. 12g45 Battle of Trafalgar, 1805

1972
Famous Sailing Ships. Postage 10, 15, 20, 25, 30, 50, 75c; Air 12g45, 18g25, 50g
Visit of President of Paraguay to Japan. 10c Paddle-steamer and launch, 1871

1973
"Apollo" Moon Missions and Future Space Projects. 20c American aircraft carrier

1974
Sailing Ships (diamond-shaped designs). 5, 10, 15, 20, 25, 35, 40, 50c
Centenary of U.P.U. Air 20g Full-rigged sailing ship and modern liner

1975
"Expo '75", Okinawa, Japan. 10g Japanese junk
Bicentenary of American Revolution. Ship Paintings. 5, 10, 15, 20, 25, 35, 40, 50c
Bicentenary of American Revolution (2nd issue). 40g Battle of Flamborough Head, 1779

1976
Ship Paintings (sailing ships and first oil tanker). Postage 1, 2, 3, 4, 5g; Air 10, 15, 20g
German Ship Paintings. (1st series). Postage 1, 2, 3, 4, 5g; Air 10, 15, 20g
Bicentenary of American Revolution (4th series). 4g *Savannah* (paddle-steamer)

1977
German Ship Paintings (2nd series). Postage 1, 2, 3, 4, 5g; Air 10, 15, 20g

1978
Paintings and Stamp Exhibition Emblems. 3g Schooner

1979
Famous Sailing Ships (1st series). Postage 3, 4, 5, 6, 7, 8, 20g; Air 10, 25g

1980
Famous Sailings Ships (2nd series). Postage 3, 4, 5, 6, 7, 8, 20g; Air 10, 25g

1981
Wedding of Prince of Wales. Historic British Ships. Postage 25, 50c, 1, 2, 3, 4, 5g; Air 5, 10, 30g

1983
Aircraft carriers. 25, 50c, 1, 2, 3, 4, 5g
25th Anniv. of International Maritime Organization (sailing ships). 5, 10, 30g

1984
19th U.P.U. Congress Stamp Exhibition, Hamburg. Sailing Ships. 25, 50c, 1, 2, 3, 4, 5g

1985
"Mophla 85" Stamp Exhibition, Hamburg. 1984 U.P.U. Congress Stamp Exhibition stamp overprinted. 5g
International Youth Year. American River Steamers. 25c, 2, 3g
Government Achievements. 75g (tanker)
Explorers and their Ships. 5, 10, 30g

1986
"Ameripex '86" International Stamp Exhibition, Chicago. Stamps of Spain and U.S.A. showing Columbus. 5, 10, 30g
Centenary of Statue of Liberty. Liners. 25, 50c, 1, 2, 3, 4, 5g

1987
12th Spanish American Stamp and Coin Exhibition, Madrid, and 500th Anniversary of Discovery of America by Columbus. 1983 I.M.O. stamp overprinted. 10g
500th Anniversary of Discovery of America by Columbus. Sailing Ships. 1, 2, 3, 5, 60g
Spanish Ships. 1, 2, 3, 4, 60g

PATIALA
Indian Sub-continent
12 pies = 1 anna
16 annas = 1 rupee

1937
No. 256 of India overprinted **PATIALA STATE**
89† 6a *Strathnaver* (liner) 11.00 16.00

PENANG
South-east Asia
100 cents = 1 dollar

1949
As No. 115 of Antigua
24† 15c Paddle-steamer 35 40

1957

50† 20c Malay fishing prau 20 30

1960
As No. 50, but with crest in place of Queen Elizabeth II
61† 20c Malay fishing prau 20 10

PENRHYN ISLAND
South Pacific
1920 12 pence = 1 shilling
20 shillings = 1 pound
1973 100 cents = 1 dollar

1920
As No. 82 of Cook Islands, but inscribed "PENRHYN"
39† 1d Schooner 2.00 4.75

1981

166 1c *Amatasi* (canoe)
167 1c *Ndrua* (canoe)
168 1c *Waka* (canoe)
169 1c *Tongiaki* (canoe)
170 3c *Va'a Teu'ua* (canoe
171 3c *Vitoria* (Del Cano)
172 3c *Golden Hind* (Drake)
173 3c *La Boudeuse* (Bougainville)

174	4c H.M.S. *Bounty* (Bligh)		
175	4c *L'Astrolabe* (Dumont D'Urville)		
176	4c *Star of India* (full-rigged ship), 1861		
177	4c *Great Republic* (clipper), 1853		
178	6c *Balcutha* (clipper), 1886		
179	6c *Coonatto* (clipper), 1863		
180	6c *Antiope* (clipper), 1866		
181	6c *Taeping* (clipper), 1863		
182	10c *Preussen* (full-rigged ship), 1902		
183	10c *Pamir* (barque), 1921		
184	10c *Cap Hornier* (full-rigged ship), 1910		
185	10c *Patriarch* (clipper), 1869		
186	15c *Amatasi*		
187	15c *Ndrua*		
188	15c *Waka*		
189	15c *Tongiaki*		
190	20c *Va'a Teu'ua*		
191	20c *Vitoria*		
192	20c *Golden Hind*		
193	20c *La Boudeuse*		
194	30c *H.M.S. Bounty*		
195	30c *L'Astrolabe*		
196	30c *Star of India*		
197	30c *Great Republic*		
198	50c *Balcutha*		
199	50c *Coonatto*		
200	50c *Antiope*		
201	50c *Taeping*		
202	$1 *Preussen*		
203	$1 *Pamir*		
204	$1 *Cap Hornier*		
205	$1 *Patriarch*		
206	$2 *Cutty Sark* (clipper), 1869		
207	$4 *Mermerus* (clipper), 1872		
208	$6 H.M.S. *Resolution* and H.M.S. *Discovery* (Cook)		
	Set of 43	48.00	38.00

1983

290†	8c 19th-century whaling ship	85	40
292†	35c 19th-century whaleboat	1.75	1.00
293†	60c 19th-century whaling ship	2.75	1.40

295†	36c *Mercury* (cable ship)	40	35
297†	60c *Mercury*	70	60
MS298	36c + 3c *Mercury*, 60c + 3c *Mercury* (sheet contains one other design)	1.50	1.60

Nos. 182/5, 190/7 and 206 surcharged
299†	18c on 10c *Preussen*	20	20
300†	18c on 10c *Pamir*	20	20
301†	18c on 10c *Cap Hornier*	20	20
302†	18c on 10c *Patriarch*	20	20
303†	36c on 20c *Va'a Teu'ua*	35	35
304†	36c on 20c *Vitoria*	35	35
305†	36c on 20c *La Boudeuse*	35	35
307†	36c on 30c *H.M.S. Bounty*	35	35
308†	36c on 30c *L'Astrolabe*	35	35
309†	36c on 30c *Star of India*	35	35
310†	36c on 30c *Great Republic*	35	35
311†	$1.20 on $2 *Cutty Sark*	1.40	1.40

No. 208 surcharged **$5.60**
319†	$5.60 on $6 H.M.S. *Resolution* and H.M.S. *Discovery*	15.00	6.50

GIBBONS STAMP MONTHLY

— finest and most informative magazine for all collectors. Obtainable from your newsagent or by postal subscription — details on request.

1984

337	2c *Waka*		
338	4c *Amatasi*		
339	5c *Ndrua*		
340	8c *Tongiaki*		
341	10c *Vitoria*		
342	18c *Golden Hind*		
343	20c *La Boudeuse*		
344	30c *H.M.S. Bounty*		
345	36c *L'Astrolabe*		
346	48c *Great Republic*		
347	50c *Star of India*		
348	50c *Coonatto*		
349	72c *Antiope*		
350	80c *Balcutha*		
351	96c *Cap Hornier*		
352	$1.20 *Pamir*		
353	$3 *Mermerus*		
354	$5 *Cutty Sark*		
355	$9.60 H.M.S. *Resolution* and H.M.S. *Discovery*		
	Set of 19	13.50	14.50

360†	60c *Golden Hind* (Drake) (on stamp No. 172)	50	75
MS362	96c *Golden Hind* (Drake) (on stamp No. 172) (sheet also contains another 96c value)	1.75	2.00

1991

No. 208 overprinted **COMMEMORATING 65th BIRTHDAY OF H.M. QUEEN ELIZABETH II**
456	$6 H.M.S. *Resolution* and *H.M.S. Discovery* (Cook)	5.50	6.00

1992

466	$1.15 Marquesan twin-hulled canoe		
467	$1.75 Raratonga canoe		
468	$1.95 Manihiki twin-hulled canoe		
	Set of 3	2.75	3.00

Nos. 466/8 overprinted **ROYAL VISIT**
469	$1.15 Marquesan twin-hulled canoe		
470	$1.75 Raratonga canoe		
471	$1.95 Manihiki twin-hulled canoe		
	Set of 3	2.75	3.00

477	$1.15 *Nina* (Columbus)		
478	$1.35 *Pinta*		
479	$1.75 *Santa Maria*		
	Set of 3	2.40	2.75

1985

Nos. 206/8, 337/47 and 349/55 overprinted **O.H.M.S.** or surcharged also
O18†	2c *Waka*	10	10
O19†	4c *Amatasi*	10	10
O20†	5c *Ndrua*	10	10
O21†	8c *Tongiaki*	10	10
O22†	10c *Vitoria*	10	10
O23†	18c *Golden Hind*	10	10
O24†	20c *La Boudeuse*	10	15
O25†	30c *H.M.S. Bounty*	20	25
O26†	40c on 36c *L'Astrolabe*	25	30
O27†	50c *Star of India*	35	40
O28†	55c on 48c *Great Republic*	35	40
O29†	75c on 72c *Antiope*	50	55
O30†	75c on 96c *Cap Hornier*	50	55
O31†	80c *Balcutha*	55	60
O32†	$1.20 *Pamir*	80	85
O33†	$2 *Cutty Sark*	1.25	1.40
O34†	$3 *Mermerus*	2.00	2.10
O35†	$4 *Mermerus*	2.75	3.00
O36†	$5 *Cutty Sark*	3.25	3.50
O37†	$6 H.M.S. *Resolution* and H.M.S. *Discovery*	4.00	4.25
O38†	$9.60 H.M.S. *Resolution* and H.M.S. *Discovery*	6.25	6.50

PERAK

South-east Asia
100 cents = 1 dollar

1949

As No. 115 of Antigua
125†	15c Paddle-steamer	45	35

1957

157†	20c Malay fishing prau	20	10

PERLIS

South-east Asia
100 cents = 1 dollar

1949

As No. 115 of Antigua
4†	15c Paddle-steamer	50	2.00

1957

36†	20c Malay fishing prau	20	60

PERU

South America
1936 100 centavos = 1 peso
1985 100 centimos = 1 inti

1936

567†	2c *San Cristobal* (caravel), 1527	90	20
571†	15c *Reina del Pacifico* (liner) in Callao docks	1.40	25
574†	1s *Sacramento* (gunboat), 1821	18.00	1.60

625† 15c *Inca* (mail steamer), Lake Titicaca
(blue) 70 15

1943

681† 25c *San Pedro* (Orellana) and Amazon
canoe 1.40 35
687† 1s *San Pedro* and Amazon canoe 3.25 70

1952

775† 5c Tuna fishing boat 15 10
784† 40c *Maranon* (river gunboat) (green) (air) 30 10

1953

793† 1s25 *Santa Maria*, *Pinta* and *Nina*
(Columbus) 1.40 30
795† 2s20 *Santa Maria*, *Pinta* and *Nina*
(Columbus) 3.25 55

1957

800† 1s25 *La Victorieuse* (French 19th-century
steam frigate) 1.25 35

803† 10c *Peru* (paddle-steamer) (on Pacific
Steam Navigation local stamp of 1857) 10 10
804† 15c *Peru* (paddle-steamer) (on Pacific
Steam Navigation local stamp of 1857) 10 10

1961

847 50c *Amazonas* (cadet sailing ship)
848 80c *Amazonas* (cadet sailing ship)
849 1s *Amazonas* (cadet sailing ship)
Set of 3 1.00 35

1963

As No. 784 but colour changed
923† 40c *Maranon* (river gunboat) (orange) .. 30 10

1969

987 2s50 *Kon Tiki* (replica of balsa raft)
988 3s *Kon Tiki* (air)
989 4s *Kon Tiki*
990 5s50 *Kon Tiki*
991 6s50 *Kon Tiki*
Set of 5 1.40 70

1005 50s *Huascar* (ironclad warship), 1879 .. 3.50 1.75

1971

1100† 7s50 *Sacramento* (naval schooner),
1821 .... 1.00 30

1973

1198† 50s Reed boats 2.75 1.00

1216† 1s50 *Ilo* (freighter) 40 15
1217† 2s50 Trawler 60 15

1977

1341 14s Tanker 1.25 30

1979

1440† 14s Battle of Iquique, 1879 .... 20 10
1442† 25s *Union* (steam corvette), 1879 ...... 40 15
1443† 25s Battle of Angamos, 1879 .... 40 15
1446† 100s *Huascar* (ironclad warship), 1877 1.40 60

1980

No. 1440 surcharged **25**
1473† 25s on 14s Battle of Iquique, 1879 ...... 30 15

1983

1558 150s *Almirante Grau* (cruiser), 1907
1559 350s *Ferre* (submarine), 1913
Set of 2 1.75 75

1984

1577 250s Container ship at wharf
1578 300s Container ship
Set of 2 1.00 45

1593† 600s Battle of Angamos, 1879 .... 70 30
1595† 600s Battle of Iquique, 1879 .... 70 30

1597 250s *Almirante Guise* (destroyer), 1934
1598 400s *America* (river gunboat), 1905
Set of 2 80 35

1986

1636 3i50 Reed canoe 55 20

1641 1i50 *Casma (R-1)* (submarine), 1926
1642 2i50 *Abtao* (submarine), 1954
Set of 2 1.25 40

1652 1i *Gamarra* (brigantine)
1653 1i *Manco Capac* (ironclad warship)
Set of 2   1.00   35

1987

1668 1i *Peru* (paddle-steamer) (on Pacific
Steam Navigation local stamps of
1857)   10   10

1988

1688 7i *Humboldt* (Antarctic supply vessel) . .   70   20

1989

Unissued stamp surcharged **230**
1703 230i on 300s Spanish galleon   40   15

1712 600i Galleons   95   20

1990

Unissued stamps surcharged
1744 110000i on 200i Tank landing ship
1745 230000i on 400i *Morona* (hospital ship)
Set of 2   1.50   85

ALBUM LISTS
Write for our latest list of albums and accessories.
This will be sent on request.

1750 250000i *Peru* (paddle-steamer) (on
Pacific Steam Navigation 1r local
stamp of 1857) and container ship
1751 350000i *Peru* (paddle-steamer) (on
Pacific Steam Navigation 2r local
stamp of 1857) and container ship
Set of 2   3.00   1.50

1755 600000i Yachts 2.50   1.40

POSTAGE DUE STAMPS

1874

D32† 5c *Adriatic* (paddle-steamer)   15   15
D33† 10c *Adriatic*   15   15
D34† 20c *Adriatic*   30   30
D35† 50c *Adriatic* 7.50   3.00

1881
Nos. D32/5 *overprinted* **UNION POSTAL UNIVERSAL LIMA
PLATA** *in oval*
D48† 5c *Adriatic* 5.50   5.00
D49† 10c *Adriatic* 5.50   5.50
D50† 20c *Adriatic* 21.00   17.00
D51† 50c *Adriatic* 45.00   42.00

Nos. D32/5 *overprinted* **LIMA CORREOS** *in double-lined circle*
D53† 5c *Adriatic* 5.50   5.00
D54† 10c *Adriatic* 6.75   5.50
D55† 20c *Adriatic* 21.00   17.00
D56† 50c *Adriatic* 65.00   55.00

1883
Nos. D48/51 *additionally overprinted* **PERU** *within triangle*
D250† 5c *Adriatic* 6.25   5.75
D253† 10c *Adriatic* 6.25   5.75
D256† 20c *Adriatic* £375   £375
D257† 50c *Adriatic* 45.00   35.00

1884
Nos. D32/5 *overprinted* **PERU** *in triangle*
D262† 5c *Adriatic*   20   20
D267† 10c *Adriatic*   25   25
D269† 20c *Adriatic*   85   35
D271† 50c *Adriatic* 2.50   75

1896
Nos. D32/4 *overprinted* **DEFICIT**
D349† 5c *Adriatic*   15   15
D350† 10c *Adriatic*   45   15
D351† 20c *Adriatic*   55   20

1902
No. D34 *surcharged* **DEFICIT** *and value in words*
D363 1c on 20c *Adriatic*
D364 5c on 20c *Adriatic*
Set of 2   1.75   1.40

PHILIPPINES
South-east Asia
1932 100 centavos = 1 peso
1962 100 sentimos = 1 piso

1932

426† 12c Freighters at pier, Manila   60   50

1935

470 2p U.S.S. *Olympia* (cruiser) and *Reina
Cristina* (Spanish cruiser), Manila Bay,
1898 . . . .   4.00   1.25

1936
No. 470 *overprinted* **COMMONWEALTH**
535† 2p U.S.S. *Olympia* (cruiser) and *Reina
Cristina* (Spanish cruiser), Manila Bay,
1898 . . . .   4.00   75

1941

566 8c Filipino vinta
567 20c Filipino vinta
568 60c Filipino vinta
569 1p Filipino vinta
Set of 4   3.75   2.25

1954

774 5c Filipino vinta
775 18c Filipino vinta
776 50c Filipino vinta (air)
Set of 3   3.75   1.75

1960

848 6c Filipino vinta, Manila Bay
849 25c Filipino vinta, Manila Bay
Set of 2   50   40

1963

946† 20s Outrigger canoe   35   30

950   6s 16th-century Spanish galleon
951   30s 16th-century Spanish galleon
                              Set of 2   60   30

1965

1003† 70s 16th-century Spanish galleon   90   40

1967

1051   4s River launches
1052   20s River launches
1053   50s River launches
                              Set of 3   75   45

1054   70s Outrigger canoes   70   50

1969

No. 1051 overprinted **PHILATELIC WEEK NOV. 24-30. 1968**
1099   4s River launches   15   10

No. 946 surcharged **1969 PHILATELIC WEEK 10s KOREO**
1135† 10s on 20s Outrigger canoe   25   10

1970

1167† 10s Outrigger tourist canoe   10   10

1971

1193† 20s Outrigger canoe, Mindanao   15   10

1196† 10s Filipino vinta, Fort Del Pilar   10   10

1208   10s 16th-century Spanish galleon
1209   75s 16th-century Spanish galleon
                              Set of 2   75   40

1972

No. 950 surcharged **1972 PHILATELIC WEEK TEN 10s**
1275† 10s on 6s 16th-century Spanish galleon   10   10

1975

1352   15s Malayan prau   10   10

1382   1p50 Full-rigged sailing ship and junks,
       Manila, 1875 ....   1.25   35

1977

1437   1p30 Mercury (cable ship)   55   25

1978

1461† 5p Filipino vinta 2.75   2.00
MS1462† 7p50 Filipino vinta, 7p50 Schooner
       (sheet contains two other designs) 35.00   35.00

1472   1p40 Mercury (cable ship)   65   25

1979

1502   30s Oil rig
1503   45s Oil rig
                              Set of 2   50   20

1532   30s Bagong Lakas (patrol boat)
1533   45s Bagong Lakas (patrol boat)
                              Set of 2   60   20

1980

1606   30s Filipino vinta
1607   2p30 Filipino vinta
                              Set of 2   1.50   90

1984

MS1822† 7p50 16th-century Spanish galleon
       (sheet contains three other designs) 4.00   4.00

Stamp from No. **MS**1822 surcharged **420TH PHIL-MEXICAN FRIEND-SHIP 8.3.84 20**
1832   7p20 on 7p50 16th-century Spanish
       galleon   85   40

1836† 7p20 Sailboards   75   35
MS1839† 6p Sailboards (sheet contains three
       other designs) 3.00   3.00

1850   60s Caracao (canoes)
1851   1p20 Junk
1852   6p Spanish galleon
1853   7p20 Casco (Filipino cargo prau)
1854   8p40 Early paddle-steamer
1855   20p Modern liner
                              Set of 6   4.25   2.00

1985

1908   1p20 Spanish galleon, 1565
1909   3p60 Spanish galleon, 1565
                              Set of 2   55   20

1987

2046† 1p Shipwrecked 16th-century Spanish
       galleon 10   10

1988

2093† 4p Yachts 25   15

1989

2156† 6p25 Vinta regatta, Iloilo Paraw 30   15

2177† 1p Water carnival pagoda float 30   15

2188 1p Liner 10   10

1991

2311† 4p Refugee boat 20   10

PITCAIRN ISLANDS

South Pacific
1940 12 pence = 1 shilling
20 shillings = 1 pound
1968 100 cents = 1 dollar

1940

4†   2d H.M.S. *Bounty* (Bligh) 1.75   1.40
6†   6d H.M.S. *Bounty* 5.00   2.25

1949

As No. 115 of Antigua
14† 3d Paddle-steamer 8.50   4.00

1957

26† 1s Model of H.M.S. *Bounty* 1.00   40
28† 2s6d Pitcairn whaleboat 12.00   6.50

1961

31† 1s *Mary Ann* (brigantine), 1859 60   25

1964

36† ½d Pitcairn longboat 10   30
37† 1d H.M.S. *Bounty* 30   30
38† 2d Pitcairn longboat 30   30

1967

64   ½d Mangarevan canoe, *c.* 1325
65   1d *San Pedro y Pablo* (Quiros), 1606
66   8d *San Pedro y Pablo* and *Los Tres Reyes*
     (Quiros), 1606
67   1s H.M.S. *Swallow* (Carteret), 1767
68   1s 6d *Hercules* (East Indiaman), 1819
                              Set of 5   85   35

Nos. 36/8 surcharged with Bounty *anchor and value*
69† ½c on ½d Pitcairn longboat 10   10
70† 1c on 1d H.M.S. *Bounty* 30   30
71† 2c on 2d Pitcairn longboat 25   30

82† 1c Launch from H.M.S. *Bounty* 10   10
83† 8c Launch from H.M.S. *Bounty* 25   10

1969

97†   4c H.M.S. *Bounty* (plans) 30   15
100† 8c Pitcairn longboat 35   20

1972

124 4c Pitcairn longboat
125 20c Pitcairn longboat
                              Set of 2   1.00   1.50

1974

154† 35c Pitcairn longboat and mail steamer   50   60

1975

157 4c H.M.S. *Seringapatam* (frigate), 1830
158 10c *Pitcairn* (missionary schooner), 1890
159 18c *Athenic* (liner), 1901
160 50c *Gothic* (liner), 1948
                              Set of 4   3.50   5.00

1976

168† 10c H.M.S. *Bounty* 50   80
170† 50c *Mayflower* (Pilgrim Fathers), 1620 .. 1.00   1.50

1977

175† 2c Building a longboat 30   5
176† 5c Pitcairn longboats 35   5
183† $1 Royal Yacht *Britannia* 65   1.1

1978

191† 20c R.F.A. *Sir Geraint* (landing ship) and
landing craft 40   50

1980

MS205 35c Pitcairn longboats (sheet contains
three other designs) 1.00   1.50

1981

216† 9c *Morayshire* (full-rigged transport),
1856 15   20
218† 70c *Morayshire* 45   65

1983

234† 6c Freighter 10   10
236† 70c Fishing punt 80   1.10

238† 6c *Topaz* (American sealer), 1808 20   15
239† 20c *Topaz* and canoe 30   30

1984

MS263 50c Aluminium longboat, $2 Wooden
longboat 2.00   2.25

1985

273 50c *ACT 6* (container ship)
274 50c *Columbus Louisiana* (container ship)
275 50c *Essi Gina* (tanker)
276 50c *Stolt Spirit* (tanker)
Set of 4   3.50   4.50

1986

293† 20c *Pitcairn* (missionary schooner), 1890   1.00   1.00
295† $2 Pitcairn longboat 3.25   3.25

1987

296 50c *Samoan Reefer* (freighter)
297 50c *Brussel* (container ship)
298 50c *Australian Exporter* (container ship)
299 50c *Taupo* (cargo liner)
Set of 4   4.50   5.50

1988

MS314 $3 H.M.S. *Bounty* (full-size replica) 2.10   2.25

315 5c H.M.S. *Swallow* (Carteret), 1767
316 10c H.M.S. *Pandora* (frigate), 1791
317 15c H.M.S. *Briton* and H.M.S. *Tagus*
(frigates), 1814
318 20c H.M.S. *Blossom* (survey ship), 1825
319 30c *Lucy Anne* (barque), 1831
320 35c *Charles Doggett* (whaling brig), 1831
321 40c H.M.S. *Fly* (sloop), 1838
322 60c *Camden* (missionary brig), 1840
323 90c H.M.S. *Virago* (paddle-sloop), 1853
324 $1.20 *Rakaia* (screw-steamer), 1867
325 $1.80 H.M.S. *Sappho* (screw-sloop), 1882
326 $5 H.M.S. *Champion* (corvette), 1893
Set of 12   6.50   7.25

1989

335† 20c H.M.S. *Bounty* (Bligh) loading stores,
Deptford 40   30
336† 20c H.M.S. *Bounty* leaving Spithead   40   30
337† 20c H.M.S. *Bounty* at Cape Horn   40   30
338† 20c H.M.S. *Bounty* at anchor, Tasmania   40   30
339† 20c Ship's boat, Tahiti 40   30

341† 90c H.M.S. *Bounty* leaving Tahiti 1.40   1.10
344† 90c Launch alongside H.M.S. *Bounty* 1.40   1.10
345† 90c H.M.S. *Bounty* and Bligh in *Bounty's*
launch 1.40   1.10
346† 90c H.M.S. *Bounty* and floating breadfruit   1.40   1.10

350† $1.05 U.S.S. *Breton* (aircraft carrier),
1969 .... 1.10   1.10

1990

357† 40c Ship's boat, Pitcairn   50   40
358† 40c H.M.S. *Bounty* off Pitcairn   50   40
359† 40c H.M.S. *Bounty* and ship's boat,
Pitcairn 50   40
360† 40c H.M.S. *Bounty* on fire   50   40

383† $1.05 H.M.S. *Bounty* and Royal Yacht
Britannia (on stamp No. 183) 1.00   1.00
384† $1.30 H.M.S. *Briton* and H.M.S. *Tagus*
(frigates) (on stamp No. 317) 1.40   1.40

1991

389† 80c Longboat 1.00   1.10
393† 80c Model of H.M.S. *Bounty* 1.00   1.10

395 15c *Europa* (liner), 1981
396 80c *Royal Viking Star* (liner)
397 $1.30 *World Discoverer* (liner)
398 $1.80 *Sagafjord* (liner)
Set of 4   3.75   3.75

1992

418 20c *Te Manu* (ketch)
419 $1 *Te Manu*
420 $1.50 *Te Manu*
421 $1.80 *Te Manu*
Set of 4   3.50   3.50

422†	20c H.M.S. *Resolution* (Cook)	15	15
424†	$1.50 *Bounty's* launch	1.40	1.40
425†	$1.80 Battle of Copenhagen, 1797	1.60	1.60

1993

426	15c H.M.S. *Chichester* (frigate)		
427	20c H.M.S. *Jaguar* (frigate)		
428	$1.80 H.M.S. *Andrew* (submarine)		
429	$3 H.M.S. *Warrior* (aircraft carrier)		
	Set of 4	3.00	3.25

POLAND

Eastern Europe
100 groszy = 1 zloty

1925

247†	20g Galleon	3.00	10
251†	45g Galleon	10.00	40

1935

318†	10g *Batory* (liner)	75	10
315†	15g *Pilsudski* (liner)	3.25	10

1941

485†	1z50 *Orzel* (submarine)	6.00	5.00

1943

486†	5g U-boat under attack	85	85
487†	10g Second World War convoy	60	90

1944

No. 485 surcharged **MONTE CASSINO 18.V.1944 Zt1 Gr20**

497†	1z20 on 1z50 *Orzel*	10.00	13.00

1945

526†	50g + 2z H.M.S. *Dragon* (cruiser) (loaned to Polish Navy, 1943–44)	8.50	6.50
527†	1z + 3z *Dar Pomorza* (full-rigged cadet ship)	4.50	6.50

534	1z + 9z *Schleswig-Holstein* (German battleship), Westerplatte, 1939	20.00	24.00

1948

619	6z *Oliwa* under construction		
620	15z Freighter at wharf		
621	35z *General M. Zaruski* (cadet ketch)		
	Set of 3	7.00	6.50

1949

653	30z Liner	1.75	1.60

1952

738†	55g Tug and freighters	40	25

762	30g + 15g Yachts		
763	45g + 15g *Dar Pomorza* (full-rigged cadet ship)		
764	90g Freighter under construction		
	Set of 3	4.00	1.60

783	5g Shipbuilding yard, Gdansk		
784	15g Shipbuilding yard, Gdansk		
	Set of 2	30	20

1953

814	80c *Dalmor* (trawler)		
815	1z35 *Czech* (freighter) at wharf		
	Set of 2	3.50	3.00

1954

883†	1z55 *Soldek* (freighter) at wharf	3.25	55

1956

962	5g *Kilinski* (freighter)		
963	10g Tug and barges		
964	20g *Pokoj* (freighter)		
965	45gf *Marceli Nowatka* (freighter) in shipyard		
966	60g *Fryderyk Chopin* (freighter) and *Radunia* (trawler)		
	Set of 5	1.75	70

1957

1040c†	50z *Batory* (liner)	7.00	1.60

1043	60g *Torrens* (full-rigged sailing ship), 1884		
1044	2z50 *Torrens*		
	Set of 2	1.40	20

1958

1067†	3z40 Kogge	35	20

1959

1080†	40g Yacht	35	10

1100† 6z40 Barges and fishing boats 2.75 1.00

1960

1190† 95g *Czarny Orzel* (17th-century
warship) 30 10
1192† 1z15 Galleon 30 10
1194† 1z50 Hanseatic kogge 30 10
1195† 1z55 17th-century sailing barge 30 10

1961

1231 60g *Leskov* (trawler support ship)
1232 1z55 *Severodvinsk* (depot ship)
1233 2z50 *Rambutan* (coaster)
1234 3z40 *Krynica* (freighter)
1235 4z *B54* (freighter)
1236 5z60 *Bavsk* (tanker)
                                    Set of 6   7.75   2.75

1245† 2z50 Tug and floating crane 30 15

1962

1311† 1z55 Shipyard, Gdansk 20 10

1343 60g *Aurora* (Russian cruiser) 30 10

1963

Coloured backgrounds
1370 5g 15th-century B.C. Egyptian galley
1371 10g 15th-century B.C. Phoenician
merchantman
1372 20g 5th-century B.C. Greek trireme
1373 30g 3rd-century B.C. Roman
merchantman
1374 40g *Mora* (Norman ship), 1066
1375 60g 14th-century Hanse kogge
1376 1z 16th-century hulk
1377 1z15 15th-century carrack
                                    Set of 8   2.00   70

1412† 40g *Blyskawica* (destroyer) 15 10
1417† 2z50 Amphibious troop carrier 40 10

1964

*As No. 1370/7, but without coloured backgrounds, and some new
designs*
1451 5g 15th-century B.C. Egyptian galley
1452 10g 15th-century B.C. Phoenician
merchantman
1453 20g 5th-century B.C. Greek trireme
1454 30g 3rd-century Roman merchantman
1455 40g 9th-century Viking longship
1456 60g 14th-century Hanse kogge
1457 1z 16th-century hulk
1458 1z15 15th-century carrack
1459 1z35 *Santa Maria* (Columbus)
1460 1z50 *Ark Royal* (English galleon), 1587
1461 1z55 *Wodnik* (17th-century Polish
warship)
1462 2z 17th-century Dutch fleute
1463 2z10 18th-century ship of the line
1464 2z50 19th-century sail frigate
1465 3z *Flying Cloud* (clipper)
1466 3z40 *Dar Pomorza* (full-rigged cadet
ship)
                                    Set of 16   5.50   1.40

1501† 60g Shipbuilding yard, Gdansk 10 10

1526† 60g Pontoon 15 10

1965

1566 30g "Dragon" class yachts
1567 40g "5.5m" class yachts
1568 50g "Finn" class yachts
1569 60g "V" class yachts
1570 1z35 "Cadet" class yachts
1571 4z "Star" class yachts
1572 5z60 "Flying Dutchman" class yachts
1573 6z50 "Amethyst" class yachts
                                    Set of 8   4.75   1.90
MS1573a 15z "Finn" class yachts 2.00 1.25

1966

1631 60g Freighter 15 10

1633† 60g Freighter 15 10

1686† 40g Yacht 10 10
1687† 60g Yacht, Warsaw 10 10
1692† 2z *Batory* (liner) 45 10

1967

1774† 60g *Aurora* (Russian cruiser) 30 10

1968

1860† 60g *Blyskawica* (destroyer) 30 10

1969

1898† 1z35 Cruising yacht 30 10
1899† 1z50 Trawler 30 10

1904 60g *Opty* (yacht) 30 10

1970

2010 40g *Piorun* (destroyer)
2011 60g *Orzel* (submarine)
2012 2z50 H.M.S. *Garland* (destroyer) (loaned
to Polish Navy 1940–46)
                                    Set of 3   1.50   50

1971

2030 40g *Dar Pomorza* (full-rigged cadet ship)
2031 60g *Stefan Batory* (liner)
2032 1z15 *Perkun* (ice-breaker)
2033 1z35 *R-1* (lifeboat)
2034 1z50 *Ziemia Szczecinska* (bulk carrier)
2035 2z50 *Beskidy* (tanker)
2036 5z *Hel* (fast freighter)
2037 8z50 *Gryf* (ferry)
                                    Set of 8   4.50   1.25

2110† 60g *Manifest Lipcowy* (container ship) and ship under construction 10 10

1973

2263† 1z50 Missile boat 30 10

2268† 1z50 *Lucy Margaret* (schooner) 30 10
2271† 2z70 Drzewiecki's submarine, 1877 .... 35 15

1974

2304 1z 16th-century galleon
2305 1z50 *Dal* (sloop), 1934
2306 2z70 *Opty* (yacht), 1969
2307 4z *Dar Pomorza* (full-rigged cadet ship), 1972
2308 4z90 *Polonez* (yacht), 1973
Set of 5 2.25 80

1975

2388 1z *Mary and Margaret* (emigrant ship), 1608 .... 20 10

2463 1z *Zawrat* (tanker)
2464 1z *Gryf* (ferry)
2465 1z50 *General Bem* (container ship)
2466 1z50 *Stefan Batory* (liner)
2467 2z *Ziemia Szczecinska* (bulk carrier)
2468 4z20 Bulk carrier
2469 6z90 Hydrofoil and river boat
2470 8z40 Bulk carrier and tanker
Set of 8 4.25 1.10

1979

2619 1z *Ksiaze Ksawery* (river paddle-steamer), 1830
2620 1z50 *General Swierczewski* (river paddle-steamer), 1914
2621 4z50 *Zubr* (river tug), 1960
2622 6z *Syrena* (passenger launch), 1959
Set of 4 2.25 45

1980

2685 2z *Lwow* (cadet ship)
2686 2z50 *Antoni Garnuszewski* (cadet freighter)
2687 6z *Zenit* (cadet ship)
2688 6z50 *Jan Turleski* (cadet ship)
2689 6z90 *Horyzont* (cadet ship)
2690 8z40 *Dar Pomorza* (full-rigged cadet ship)
Set of 6 3.25 85

1981

2765† 2z Model of *Atlas 2* (tug) 30 10

1982

2846† 12z Log rafts, River Vistula 15 10
2848† 25z 16th-century merchant ships, Danzig 25 10

1983

2866† 30z Sail fishing boat 1.10 45

2890 6z Medieval ships 30 15

COLLECT BIRDS ON STAMPS
Third revised edition of this Stanley Gibbons thematic catalogue. Now available at £15.95 (p. + p. £3) from: Stanley Gibbons Publications, 5 Parkside, Christchurch Road, Ringwood, Hants BH24 3SH.

1984

2938† 6z Vistula river craft 25 10
2939† 25z Punts 1.00 35

1985

3000 5z *Iskra* (cadet ship) 40 10

1986

3042 10z *Wilanow* (ferry)
3043 10z *Wawel* (ferry)
3044 15z *Pomerania* (ferry)
3045 25z *Rogalin* (ferry)
Set of 4 2.75 1.10

3047 5z *Kopernik* (Antarctic research vessel)
3048 40z *Professor Siedlecki* (Antarctic research vessel)
Set of 2 4.00 1.10

3055† 10z Sailboards 50 10

1987

3089 5z *Antoni Garnuszewski* (cadet freighter)
3090 5z *Zulawy* (supply ship)
3091 10z *Pogoria* (cadet brigantine)
3092 10z *Gedania* (yacht)
3093 30z *Dziunia* (research vessel)
3094 40z *Kapitan Ledochowski* (research vessel)
Set of 6 2.75 1.10

1988

3197 10z *Blysk* (fire boat)
3198 15z *Plomien* (fire boat)
3199 15z *Zar* (fire boat)
3200 20z *Strazak 11* (fire boat)
3201 20z *Strazak 4* (fire boat)
3202 45z *Strazak 25* (fire boat)

Set of 6   2.00   80

1990

3278† 100z Yachts   10   10

1991

3357 2000z *Piorun* (destroyer) attacking
Bismarck (German battleship), 1941 ..   35   15

1992

3404† 3000z *Santa Maria* (Columbus)   45   15

POLISH POST IN DANZIG

Eastern Europe
100 groszy = 1 zloty

1936

No. 315 of Poland overprinted **PORT GDANSK**
R30 15g *Pilsudski* (liner) 3.25   5.00

PORTUGAL

South-west Europe
1894 100 reis = 1 milreis
1912 100 centavos = 1 escudo

1894

314†	5r Caravel	1.25	1.00
315†	10r Caravel	1.75	1.00
316†	15r Caravel	2.75	1.50
317†	20r Caravel	3.00	1.50
318†	25r Caravel	2.50	1.00
319†	50r Caravel	6.00	2.00
320†	75r Caravel	12.00	4.00
321†	80r Caravel	15.00	4.50
322†	100r Caravel	9.00	2.50

1898

378†	2½r Departure of Vasco da Gama's fleet	60	25
379†	5r Vasco da Gama's fleet at Calicut	60	25
382†	50r *Sao Gabriel* (flagship)	4.50	1.50
384†	100r *Sao Gabriel*	15.00	5.00

1911

Nos. 378/9, 382 and 384 overprinted **REPUBLICA** *or surcharged also*

441†	2½r Departure of Vasco da Gama's fleet	20	15
444†	15r on 5r Vasco da Gama's fleet at Calicut	1.10	20
447†	50r *Sao Gabriel* (flagship)	2.00	1.75
450†	100r *Sao Gabriel*	2.50	1.50

Nos. 134/5, 138 and 140 of Madeira overprinted **REPUBLICA** *or surcharged also*

455†	2½r Departure of Vasco da Gama's fleet	1.50	70
456†	15r on 5r Vasco da Gama's fleet at Calicut	1.50	1.00
458†	50r *Sao Gabriel* (flagship)	4.50	3.50
461†	100r *Sao Gabriel*	12.00	4.25

1923

578	1c Portuguese galleon, 1500	
579	2c Portuguese galleon, 1500	
580	3c Portuguese galleon, 1500	
581	4c Portuguese galleon, 1500	
582	5c Portuguese galleon, 1500	
583	10c Portuguese galleon, 1500	
584	15c Portuguese galleon, 1500	
585	20c Portuguese galleon, 1500	
586	25c Portuguese galleon, 1500	
587	30c Portuguese galleon, 1500	
588	40c Portuguese galleon, 1500	
589	50c Portuguese galleon, 1500	
590	75c Portuguese galleon, 1500	
591	1e Portuguese galleon, 1500	
592	1e50 Portuguese galleon, 1500	
593	2e Portuguese galleon, 1500	

Set of 16   4.75   4.50

1941

937† 40c Fishing boat, Aveiro   15   10

1943

942	5c Caravel
943	10c Caravel
944	15c Caravel
945	20c Caravel
946	30c Caravel
947	35c Caravel
948	50c Caravel
948a	80c Caravel
949	1e Caravel (red)
949a	1e Caravel (lilac)
949b	1e20 Caravel
949c	1e50 Caravel
950	1e75 Caravel
950a	1e80 Caravel
951	2e Caravel (red)
951a	2e Caravel (blue)
952	2e50 Caravel
953	3e50 Caravel

953a	4e Caravel
954	5e Caravel
954a	6e Caravel
954b	7e50 Caravel
955	10e Caravel
956	15e Caravel
957	20e Caravel
958	50e Caravel

Set of 26   £180   7.50

1958

1156 1e Liner
1157 4e50 Liner

Set of 2   1.50   70

1960

1179† 2e50 15th-century caravel   55   25
1182† 8e 15th-century barketta   35   50

1961

1191 1e Barkettas
1192 4e30 Barkettas

Set of 2   3.00   2.50

1964

1243 1e Sail/steam ship, 1864
1244 2e50 Sail/steam ship, 1864
1245 3e50 Sail/steam ship, 1864

Set of 3   1.40   85

1966

1294† 1e *France* (French liner)   30   10
1295† 2e50 *France* 1.00   30

1967

1322†	1e Lisnave shipyard, Lisbon	....	10	10
1324†	3e50 Lisnave shipyard, Lisbon	....	45	20

1969

1355†	6e50 Cabral's fleet, 1500	....	1.25	80

1377†	4e Vasco da Gama's fleet, 1497	......	1.00	40

1970

1399†	1e *Great Eastern* (cable ship)	....	15	10
1400†	2e50 *Great Eastern*	....	80	25

1405	3e50 Wine barge, Oporto	....	60	10

1972

1480†	4e50 Olympic yachts	....	55	40

1974

1538†	3e30 Sailing packet and modern liner		30	10

1977

1673	2e Poviero (fishing boat)			
1674	3e Rowing boat, Mar			
1675	4e Rowing boat, Nazare			
1676	7e Caicque, Algarve			
1677	10e Tunny fishing boat, Xavega			
1678	15e Buarcos fishing boat			
		Set of 6	2.50	1.10

1978

1689†	5e Trawler and tunny fishing boats, Xavega		15	10
1703†	100e Tanker and shipyard	....	1.75	55

1725	5e Trawler			
1726	9e Trawler			
1727	12e50 Trawler			
1728	15e Trawler			
		Set of 4	1.40	95

1980

1794†	60e Vasco da Gama's ships, 1499	....	1.00	75

1804†	10e 16th-century sea battle	....	35	25

1809†	19e50 Fishing boats, River Aveiro	......	60	40

1811	6e50 Caravel			
1812	8e Nau			
1813	16e Galleon			
1814	19e50 Early paddle-steamer			
		Set of 4	1.25	90

1981

1824	8e Fragata, River Tejo			
1825	8e50 Rabelo, River Douro			
1826	10e Moliceiro, River Aveiro			
1827	16e Barco, River Lima			
1828	19e50 Carocho, River Minho			
1829	20e Varino, River Tejo			
		Set of 6	2.50	1.00

1982

1849†	8e50 15th-century caravel	....	30	10

1870†	19e Shipyard	....	55	50

1873†	27e *Sagres I* (cadet barque)	....	1.00	40
1875†	50e "470" class yachts	....	1.75	85

1983

1906	10e Tug and container ship	....	45	15

1908	12e50 *Vasco da Gama* (frigate), 1782			
1909	25e *Estefania* (steam corvette), 1845			
1910	30e *Adamastor* (cruiser), 1900			
1911	37e50 *Joao Belo* (frigate), 1983			
		Set of 4	2.50	1.25

1918†	25e 16th-century caravel		65	35

1987

2068† 57e Fishing boats, Espinho 75 45

2083 25e Dias's fleet leaving Lisbon, 1487
2084 25e Dias's fleet off Africa
Set of 2 70 40

1988

2099† 27e Dias's ships in storm, 1488 .... 30 10

MS2118† 200e Yacht 1.75 1.75

1989

2127† 55e Caravel 60 20

MS2142† 250e Ferry, River Tagus 2.25 2.25

1990

2202 32e 15th-century barketta
2203 60e 15th-century caravel-built fishing boat
2204 70e 15th-century nau
2205 95e 15th-century caravel
Set of 4 2.25 1.10

1991

2233 35e 16th-century caravel
2234 75e Port view of 16th-century nau
2235 80e Stern view of 16th-century nau
2236 110e 16th-century galleon
Set of 4 1.75 1.25

2244† 110e 15th-century caravel 1.10 45

2256† 110e Sailing dinghies 1.10 45

1992

2280† 38e Ship's boat, 1542 .... 45 15

2290† 120e Freighter, Leixoes Docks 1.10 55

1993

2317† 65e Trawlers 60 30

PORTUGUESE COLONIES IN AFRICA

100 reis = 1 milreis

1898

As Nos. 378/9, 382 and 384 of Portugal, but inscribed "AFRICA"

1† 2½r Departure of Vasco da Gama's fleet 40 30
2† 5r Vasco da Gama's fleet at Calicut 40 30
5† 50r *Sao Gabriel* (flagship) 40 40
7† 100r *Sao Gabriel* 1.50 1.00

PORTUGUESE CONGO

South-west Africa
100 centavos = 1 escudo

1913

Surcharged **REPUBLICA CONGO** *and value*

(a) On Nos. 1/2, 5 and 7 of Portuguese Colonies in Africa

95† ¼c on 2½r Departure of Vasco da Gama's fleet 50 45
96† ½c on 5r Vasco da Gama's fleet at Calicut 50 45
99† 5c on 50r *Sao Gabriel* (flagship) 50 45
101† 10c on 100r *Sao Gabriel* 50 45

(b) On Nos. 104/5, 108 and 110 of Macao

103† ¼c on ½a Departure of Vasco da Gama's fleet 60 50
104† ½c on 1a Vasco da Gama's fleet at Calicut 60 50
107† 5c on 8a *Sao Gabriel* (flagship) 60 50
109† 10c on 16a *Sao Gabriel* 85 65

(c) On Nos. 58/9, 62 and 64 of Timor

111† ¼c on ½a Departure of Vasco da Gama's fleet 70 60
112† ½c on 1a Vasco da Gama's fleet at Calicut 70 60
115† 5c on 8a *Sao Gabriel* (flagship) 70 60
117† 10c on 16a *Sao Gabriel* 90 60

PORTUGUESE GUINEA

West Africa
100 centavos = 1 escudo

1913

Surcharged **REPUBLICA GUINE** *and value*

(a) On Nos. 1/2, 5 and 7 of Portuguese Colonies in Africa

138† ¼c on 2½r Departure of Vasco da Gama's fleet 70 70
139† ½c on 5r Vasco da Gama's fleet at Calicut 70 70
142† 5c on 50r *Sao Gabriel* (flagship) 70 70
144† 10c on 100r *Sao Gabriel* 70 50

(b) On Nos. 104/5, 108 and 110 of Macao

146† ¼c on ½a Departure of Vasco da Gama's fleet 80 70
147† ½c on 1a Vasco da Gama's fleet at Calicut 80 70
150† 5c on 8a *Sao Gabriel* (flagship) 80 70
152† 10c on 16a *Sao Gabriel* 1.25 1.10

(c) On Nos. 58/9, 62 and 64 of Timor

154† ¼c on ½a Departure of Vasco da Gama's fleet 80 70
155† ½c on 1a Vasco da Gama's fleet at Calicut 80 70
158† 5c on 8a *Sao Gabriel* (flagship) 80 70
160† 10c on 16a *Sao Gabriel* 1.25 1.00

1967

376 50c *Republica* (cruiser)
377 1e *Guadiana* (destroyer)
Set of 2 55 30

PORTUGUESE INDIA

Indian Sub-continent
12 reis = 1 tanga
16 tangas = 1 rupia

1898

As Nos. 378/9, 383 and 384 of Portugal, but inscribed "INDIA"

275† 1½r Departure of Vasco da Gama's fleet 35 25
276† 4½r Vasco da Gama's fleet at Calicut 35 25
279† 1t *Sao Gabriel* (flagship) 75 55
281† 4t *Sao Gabriel* 1.00 75

1913

Nos. 275/6, 279 and 281 overprinted **REPUBLICA**

389† 1½r Departure of Vasco da Gama's fleet 25 15
390† 4½r Vasco da Gama's fleet at Calicut 25 25
393† 1t *Sao Gabriel* (flagship) 40 20
395† 4t *Sao Gabriel* 50 20

1925

493	6r *Sao Gabriel* (Vasco da Gama)		
494	1t *Sao Gabriel*		
	Set of 2	4.00	2.50

1933

504	1r Portuguese galeasse	
505	2r Portuguese galeasse	
506	4r Portuguese galeasse	
507	6r Portuguese galeasse	
508	8r Portuguese galeasse	
509	1t Portuguese galeasse	
510	1½t Portuguese galeasse	
511	2t Portuguese galeasse	
512	2½t Portuguese galeasse	
513	3t Portuguese galeasse	
514	5t Portuguese galeasse	
515	1rp Portuguese galeasse	
516	2rp Portuguese galeasse	
517	3rp Portuguese galeasse	
518	5rp Portuguese galeasse	
	Set of 15	30.00 20.00

1942

Nos. 508 and 510/18 surcharged

549	1r on 8r Portuguese galeasse	
546	1r on 5t Portuguese galeasse	
550	2r on 8r Portuguese galeasse	
547	3r on 1½t Portuguese galeasse	
551	3r on 2t Portuguese galeasse	
552	3r on 3rp Portuguese galeasse	
553	6r on 2½t Portuguese galeasse	
554	6r on 3t Portuguese galeasse	
542	1t on 1½t Portuguese galeasse	
548	1t on 2t Portuguese galeasse	
543	1t on 1rp Portuguese galeasse	
544	1t on 2rp Portuguese galeasse	
545	1t on 5rp Portuguese galeasse	
	Set of 13	11.00 10.00

POSTAGE DUE STAMPS

1943

Nos. 512/14 surcharged **Porteado** *and new value*

D549	3r on 2½t Portuguese galeasse	
D550	6r on 3t Portuguese galeasse	
D551	1t on 5t Portuguese galeasse	
	Set of 3	85 85

PUERTO RICO

West Indies
100 centavos = 1 peso

1893

110	3c Ship's boat, 1493	....	£100	28.00

QATAR

Arabia
1961 100 naye paise = 1 rupee
1966 100 dirhams = 1 riyal

1961

33†	75np Dhow	....	60	60

1964

No. 33 overprinted **1964**, *Olympic Rings and Arabic inscription*

39†	75np Dhow	....	2.50	1.75

No. 33 overprinted **John F. Kennedy 1917 – 1963** *in English and Arabic*

44†	75np Dhow	....	2.50	1.75

1966

No. 33 surcharged **Dirham**

147†	75d on 75np Dhow	....	1.50	45

1967

222	1d Norman ship, 1066	
223	2d *Santa Maria* (Columbus)	
224	3d *Sao Gabriel* (Vasco da Gama)	
225	75d *Vitoria* (Magellan)	
226	1r *Golden Hind* (Drake)	
227	2r *Gipsy Moth IV* (Chichester)	
	Set of 6	9.00 4.00

1968

231†	60d Rowing boat	....	1.25	55

244†	35d Dhow	....	1.00	20
246†	60d *Ahmed* (tanker)	....	2.25	30

1969

276†	1d *Ross Rayyan* (trawler)	....	10	10

288†	1d *Sivella* (tanker)	....	10	10
290†	3d *Sea Shell* (oil rig) and *Shell Dolphin* (supply vessel)	....	10	10
293†	3r Tankers from 1890 to 1968	....	6.00	2.25

294†	1d Dhow building	....	10	10

306†	2r Inflatable dinghy	....	3.75	2.00

1970

308†	2d *Oriental Empress* (liner)	....	10	10

333†	3d Japanese fishing boat	....	10	10

1971

345†	3d Felucca	....	10	10

356†	2d *Ariel* (cable ship)	....	10	10

1972

426†	5d *Sea Shell* (oil rig)	10	10
429†	3r *Sea Shell*	7.50	3.50

1973

471†	2d Weather ship	10	10

1974

503†	10d *Hindoostan* (paddle-steamer) and *Iberia* (liner)	35	10

532†	35d Yachts	45	15
533†	55d Fishing boat	75	20

1975

539†	55d Pipe-laying barge	85	20

1976

592	10d Dhow at anchor		
593	35d Dhows at anchor		
594	80d Dhows at anchor		
595	1r25 Dhow at anchor		
596	1r50 Dhow under construction		
597	2r Dhow under construction		
	Set of 6	6.25	2.75

599†	10d Olympic yacht	15	10

618†	1r25 *Dana* (oil rig)	1.25	65

1982

745	20d Container ship		
746	2r35 Container ship		
	Set of 2	2.75	1.90

1984

765†	15d Dhow	10	10
766†	40d Dhow	25	15
767†	50d Dhow	25	15

1986

798	1r50 *Qatari ibn al-Fuja'a* (container ship)		
799	4r *Al-Wajda* (container ship)		
	Set of 2	3.25	2.25

1990

849†	50d Dhow	20	15

1992

894†	1r50 Fishing boats	55	45

QUELIMANE

East Africa
100 centavos = 1 escudo

1913

Surcharged **REPUBLICA QUELIMANE** *and value*

(a) On Nos. 1/2, 5 and 7 of Portuguese Colonies in Africa

1†	¼c on 2½r Departure of Vasco da Gama's fleet	40	30
2†	¼c on 5r Vasco da Gama's fleet at Calicut	40	30
5†	5c on 50r *Sao Gabriel* (flagship)	40	30
7†	10c on 100r *Sao Gabriel*	45	35

(b) On Nos. 104/5, 108 and 110 of Macao

9†	¼c on ½a Departure of Vasco da Gama's fleet	40	30
10†	¼c on 1a Vasco da Gama's fleet at Calicut	40	30
13†	5c on 8a *Sao Gabriel* (flagship)	40	30
15†	10c on 16a *Sao Gabriel*	45	35

(c) On Nos. 58/9, 62 and 64 of Timor

17†	¼c on ½a Departure of Vasco da Gama's fleet	40	30
18†	¼c on 1a Vasco da Gama's fleet at Calicut	40	30
21†	5c on 8a *Sao Gabriel* (flagship)	40	30
23†	10c on 16a *Sao Gabriel*	40	35

RAS AL KHAIMA

Arabia
100 dirhams = 1 riyal

1964

6†	1r Dhow	1.50	45
7†	2r Dhow	2.50	1.25
8†	5r Dhow	5.50	3.00

1965

Nos. 6/8 overprinted **OLYMPIC TOKYO 1964** *in English and Arabic with Olympic rings*

15	1r Dhow		
16	2r Dhow		
17	5r Dhow		
	Set of 3	3.50	3.00

Nos. 6/8 overprinted **ABRAHAM LINCOLN 1809-1865** *in English and Arabic*

18	1r Dhow		
19	2r Dhow		
20	5r Dhow		
	Set of 3	3.50	3.00

Nos. 6/8 overprinted **FRANKLIN D. ROOSEVELT 1882-1945** *in English and Arabic*

21	1r Dhow		
22	2r Dhow		
23	5r Dhow		
	Set of 3	3.50	3.00

1966

Nos. 6/8 surcharged in dirhams or riyals

64b†	5d on 5r Dhow	15	10
65†	1r on 1r Dhow	75	30
66†	2r on 2r Dhow	1.50	1.25
67†	5r on 5r Dhow	3.50	2.25

Appendix

The following stamps have either been issued in excess of postal needs, or have not been made available to the public in reasonable quantities at face value. Miniature sheets, imperforate stamps etc., are excluded from this section.

1967

European Paintings. 2r Fishing boats, Les Saines-Maries
Summer Olympics Preparation, Mexico 1968. 40d Mexican fishing boats.

1969

Famous Men. 20d Dhow

1971

13th World Jamboree, Japan. 60d Scout rowing boat

REDONDA

West Indies
100 cents = 1 dollar

Appendix

The following stamps were issued in anticipation of commercial and tourist development, philatelic mail being handled by a bureau in Antigua. Since the island is at present uninhabited we do not list these items in full. It is understood that such stamps are valid for the payment of postage in Antigua. Miniature sheets, imperforate stamps etc, are excluded from this section.

1980

Olympic Medal Winners, Lake Placid and Moscow. 25c Olympic yacht

1982

Boy Scout Anniversaries. 8c Scout sailing dinghy

REUNION

Indian Ocean
100 centimes = 1 franc

1907

73†	1f Brigantine, St. Pierre (blue & brown)	40	45
110†	1f Brigantine, St. Pierre (blue)	50	65
111†	1f Brigantine, St. Pierre (lilac & brown) ..	50	50
112†	1f10 Brigantine, St. Pierre	55	60
113†	1f50 Brigantine, St. Pierre	6.00	4.50
74†	2f Brigantine, St. Pierre	2.25	1.60
114†	3f Brigantine, St. Pierre	6.25	4.75
75†	5f Brigantine, St. Pierre (brown & pink)	3.50	3.00

1917

Nos. 75 (some with colours changed) and 110 surcharged

124†	25c on 5f Brigantine, St. Pierre	40	60
125†	1f25 on 1f Brigantine, St. Pierre	35	45
126†	1f50 on 1f Brigantine, St. Pierre	35	35
127†	3f on 5f Brigantine, St. Pierre (blue & red)	1.25	1.25
128†	10f on 5f Brigantine, St. Pierre (red & green)	8.75	7.25
129†	20f on 5f Brigantine, St. Pierre (pink & brown)	11.00	9.00

1931

As No. 109 of Cameroun

133†	1f50 *Leconte de Lisle* (liner)	2.00	2.00

1937

As Nos. 110/11 of Cameroun

175†	20c Liner	85	95
176†	30c Sailing ships	95	1.10
MS180a†	3f Liner	3.75	5.00

1943

No. 75 overprinted **France Libre**

197†	5f Brigantine, St. Pierre	27.00	27.00

1947

300†	15f *Ville de Strasbourg* (liner)	1.75	1.90
301†	20f *Ville de Strasbourg*	2.25	2.25
302†	25f *Ville de Strasbourg*	2.75	2.75

1949

No. 1263 of France surcharged **3F CFA**

370†	3f on 8f Fishing boats, Marseille	80	80

1965

As No. 1692 of France but additionally inscribed "CFA"

439	15f *Le Taureau* (warship), 1665	45	30

1971

No. 1920 of France surcharged **40F CFA**

467	40f on 80c *Antoinette* (barque)	1.10	90

1972

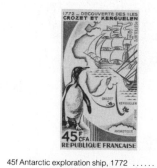

479	45f Antarctic exploration ship, 1772	1.75	1.50

1973

No. 2011 of France surcharged **45F CFA**

488	45f on 90c *France II* (barque)	1.25	1.00

1974

No. 2040 of France surcharged **45 FCFA**

500	45f on 90c Shipwreck and modern lifeboat	1.10	90

RHODESIA

Central Africa
100 cents = 1 dollar

1970

443b†	6c *Seaflight* (hydrofoil)	4.00	3.00
445†	10c Yachts, Lake McIlwaine	60	10

RHODESIA AND NYASALAND

Central Africa
12 pence = 1 shilling
20 shillings = 1 pound

1959

23†	4d Pirogue, Lake Bangweulu	90	10
26†	1s3d *Ilala II* (lake vessel)	1.75	10

ROSS DEPENDENCY

Antarctica
1957 12 pence = 1 shilling
20 shillings = 1 pound
1968 100 cents = 1 dollar

1957

1†	3d H.M.S. *Erebus* (Ross), 1839	2.50	75

1968

As No. 1, but with face value in decimal currency

5†	2c H.M.S. *Erebus*	8.00	4.75

1972

12a†	8c H.M.N.Z.S. *Endeavour* (supply ship), 1962	40	90

RUANDA-URUNDI

Central Africa
100 centimes = 1 franc

1916

No. 74 of Belgian Congo overprinted **RUANDA.** (*No. 5*) *or* **URUNDI.** (*No. 12*)

5†	40c Native canoe		15.00
12†	40c Native canoe		15.00

No. 74 of Belgian Congo overprinted **EST AFRICAIN ALLEMAND OCCUPATION BELGE. DUITSCH OOST AFRIKA BELGISCHE BEZETTING.**

19†	40c Native canoe	5.00	4.00

1918

Nos. 82 and 86 of Belgian Congo overprinted **A. O.**

27†	40c + 40c Native canoe	25	25
31†	10f + 10f *Deliverance* (stern wheel paddle-steamer)	50.00	60.00

1922

No.19 surcharged **.25c.**

34a†	25c on 40c Native canoe	2.00	90

1925

No. 141 of Belgian Congo overprinted **RUANDA-URUNDI**

61†	25c + 25c Native canoe	20	30

RUMANIA

South-east Europe
100 bani = 1 leu

1913

629†	10b Gunboat, River Danube	55	15

1931

1205	6le *Mircea* (cadet ship), 1882	
1206	10le *Lascar Catargiu and Mihail Kogalniceaunu* (monitors)	
1207	16le *Ardeal* (monitor)	
1208	20le *Regele Ferdinand* (destroyer)	
	Set of 4	35.00 12.50

1936

1343	1le + 1le *Delfinul* (submarine)	
1344	3le + 2le *Mircea* (cadet ship), 1882	
1345	6le + 3le *Transylvania* (liner)	
	Set of 3	15.00 10.00

1947

1899†	15le *Transylvania* (liner)	1.00	20
1901†	32le *Transylvania* (liner), Constantza	4.75	2.25

1948

Nos. 1899 *and* 1901 *overprinted* **R·P·R·**

1940†	15le *Transylvania* (liner)	2.00	40
1942†	32le *Transylvania* (liner), Constantza	8.50	3.75

1971†	8le + 8le Destroyer	1.50	1.50

1991	2le + 2le Yachts	
1992	5le + 5le *Mircea* (cadet ship), 1882	
1993	8le + 8le *Romana Mare* (Danube river steamer)	
1994	10le + 10le *Transylvania* (liner)	
	Set of 4	6.25 6.25

2006†	100le Liner	4.00	3.25

2007†	1le + 1le Freighter at wharf	60	60

1951

2135†	50le Liner	5.00	3.50

1952

Nos. 2006 *and* 2135 *surcharged with revalued currency*

2159†	3b on 100le Liner	4.00	3.00
2217†	1le on 50le Liner	8.50	4.50

1954

2338	55b Destroyer	1.75	20

1957

2528	1le75 *Stalingrad* (destroyer)	1.75	20

1958

2597†	55b *Belgica* (Gerlache expedition), 1897	3.25	40

2602†	1le75 Destroyer	70	20

1959

2680	1le75 *Lenin* (Russian atomic ice-breaker)	2.50	30

1960

2770†	35b *Transylvania* (liner) and figurehead of *Luceafrul* (cadet yacht)	40	10
2774†	1le60 Yacht, Eforie	1.50	20

1961

2841	20b *Galati* (freighter)	
2842	40b *Oltenita* (Danube passenger vessel)	
2843	55b *Tomis* (hydrofoil)	
2844	1le *Arad* (freighter)	
2845	1le55 *N.Cristea* (tug)	
2846	1le75 *Dobrogea* (freighter)	
	Set of 6	5.50 80

1962

2922†	1le Yachts (blue & red)	1.00	15
2923†	1le20 Power boats (blue & purple)	1.25	15
2924†	1le55 Yacht (blue & orange)	1.50	15

As Nos. 2922/4, *but imperforate and colours changed*

2930†	1le Yachts (blue & brown)	1.10	60
2931†	1le20 Power boats (blue & violet)	1.25	75
2932†	1le55 Yacht (blue & red)	1.40	85

2948	10b Fishing punts	10	10
2955	3le25 Fishing punts	1.60	20

1963

3034†	1le35 *Oltenita* (Danube passenger vessel)	1.75	30

1967

Size 23 × 29 *mm*

3527†	3le25 *Transylvania* (liner)	1.75	10

3689†	60b Medieval ship	35	10

1970

3746†	55b Freighter	45	10

1971

3802†	1le Fishing punt and tourist launch	45	10

3837†	35b 17th-century Dutch jacht	15	10
3838†	60b Fishing boats	25	10
3839†	1le75 Sailing craft in storm	65	20
3840†	3le Fishing boats, Braila	1.40	40
MS3841†	5le Fishing boats, Venice	4.50	4.50

As No. 3527, but smaller, 17 × 23 mm

3852†   3le25 *Transylvania* (liner) 1.50   10

3881†   40b Magellan and ships, 1521 40   10

1972

3910   1le35 Danube tug and barge
3911   1le75 Danube tourist launch
3912   2le75 Danube freighter
                    Set of 3   4.00   80

3952†   20b Gondolas, Venice 10   10

1974

4042   1le35 *Impingator* (tug) and barges, River
          Danube
4043   1le45 *Dimbovita* (freighter)
4044   1le50 *Muntenia* (Danube passenger
          vessel)
4045   1le55 *Mircea* (cadet barque), 1938
4046   1le75 *Transylvania* (liner)
4047   2le20 *Oltul* (bulk carrier)
4048   3le65 *Mures* (trawler)
4049   4le70 *Arges* (tanker)
                    Set of 8   4.00   50

4075†   20b Postal motor boat 10   10

1977

4346†   55b *Carpati* (Danube passenger vessel)   30   10
4347†   1le *Mircesti* (Danube passenger vessel)   40   10
4348†   1le50 *Oltenita* (Danube passenger
          vessel) 60   15
4349†   2le15 Hydrofoil 65   25
4350†   3le *Herculani* (Danube passenger
          vessel) 80   30
4351†   3le40 *Muntenia* (Danube passenger
          vessel) 95   35

1979

4476   55b *Galati* (freighter)
4477   1le *Bucuresti* (freighter)
4478   1le50 *Resita* (bulk carrier)
4479   2le15 *Tomis* (bulk carrier)
4480   3le40 *Dacia* (tanker)
4481   4le80 *Independenta* (tanker)
                    Set of 6   2.00   80

1981

4620   55b *Stefan cel Mare* (Danube paddle-
          steamer)
4621   1le Danube Commission steam launch
4622   1le50 *Tudor Vladimirescu* (Danube
          paddle-steamer)
4623   2le15 *Sulina* (dredger)
4624   3le40 *Republica Populara Romana*
          (Danube paddle-steamer)
4625   4le80 Freighter
                    Set of 6   3.00   1.25
MS4626   10le *Moldova* (tourist ship) 3.50   3.50

1982

4722†   5le Sailing dinghy, Neptun 1.00   40

1983

MS4792   Two sheets. 3le *Pizarro* (Humboldt),
1799 (sheets also contain seven other
designs)
              Price for 2 sheets   9.50   9.50

1984

MS4846   Two sheets. 3le Danube barge, 3le
Barges, Innsbruck, 3le *Royal Daffodil*
(pleasure steamer), London (sheets also
contain five other designs).
              Price for 2 sheets   9.75   9.75

1985

4932†   2le Danube barges 70   25
4933†   3le *Dacia* (motorised barge) 90   25
4934†   4le Tug and barges 1.25   35

5007†   1le50 *Calypso* (Cousteau) 60   15
5012†   5le Polar supply ship (Byrd) 2.00   55

1986

5060†   2le *Belgica* (polar barque) 75   15
5063†   5le *Sinoe* and *Tirnava* (fishery research
          vessels) 1.50   45

1988

MS5179   Two sheets 3le *Santa Maria*
(Columbus) (sheets also contain seven other
designs)
              Price for 2 sheets   4.50   3.50

1989

5228†   5le Lifeguard rowing boat 1.10   25

5230†   1le50 Pusher tug and barge 20   10
5233†   4le Mangalia–Constantza ferry 95   15
5234†   5le *Gloria* (oil drilling platform) 1.10   25

5246†   2le Rowing boat 30   10

1991

5391† 10le Junk 10 10

1992

MS5438 35le *Santa Maria*; 35le *Nina*; 35le
Pinta; 35le *Santa Maria* and island 60 60

5442† 10le *Filipino vinta* 10 10

5466† 6le *Santa Maria* (Columbus) 10 10
5467† 10le *Nina* 10 10
5468† 25le *Pinta* 10 10
MS5470 100le *Santa Maria* 20 10

RUSSIA

Eastern Europe and Northern Asia
100 kopeks = 1 rouble

1922

286† (20r + 5r) Freighter 40 2.00

1928

530† 14k *Aurora* (cruiser), 1917 .... 2.25 50

1930

576† 3k *Potemkin* (battleship), 1905 .... 1.75 50

1931

584 30k *Malygin* (ice-breaker)
585 35k *Malygin*
586 1r *Malygin*
587 2r *Malygin*
                 Set of 4 85.00 48.00

1932

588 50k *Sibiriakov* (ice-breaker)
589 1r *Sibiriakov*
                 Set of 2 70.00 35.00

1933

626† 20k Koryak kayak 6.00 1.60

1934

647† 80k *Ob* (ice-breaker) 13.00 3.50

1935

678† 1k *Chelyuskin* (ice-breaker) 4.00 1.00

1938

787† 10k *Murman* (ice-breaker) 4.00 50
788† 20k *Murman* 4.00 70

829† 80k *Marat* (battleship) 5.00 1.25

1940

898† 15k *Iosif Stalin* (ice-breaker) 2.25 40
899† 30k *Georgy Sedov* (ice-breaker) 3.00 70

1941

945a† 20k Passenger launches, Moscow–
Volga Canal 1.75 70

973† 30k Galley on the Volga 2.75 70
975† 1r Galley on the Volga 8.00 2.50

1943

1018 30k *Sv. Pyotr* (Bering), 1741
1019 60k *Sv. Pyotr* (Bering), 1741
1020 1r *Sv. Pyotr* (Bering), 1741
1021 2r *Sv. Pyotr* (Bering), 1741
                 Set of 4 15.00 2.00

1946

1220† 15k Liner 1.25 40

1947

1237† 20k *Senyavin* (full-rigged ship) (Lutke),
1862 (brown) 2.00 50
1238† 20k *Senyavin* (blue) 2.00 50

1273† 50k Tourist launch, Moscow 1.25 30

1295† 60k *Moskovich* (river launch) 1.75 55

1948

1346† 30k Battleship, 1918 .... 1.25 35

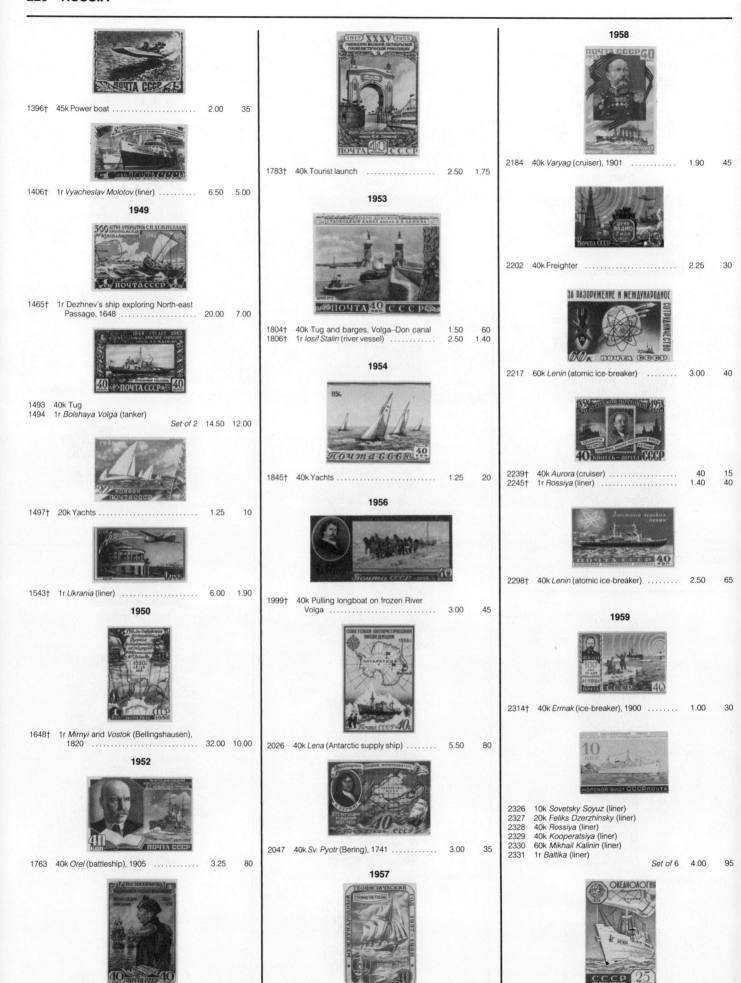

1396†	45k Power boat	2.00	35
1406†	1r *Vyacheslav Molotov* (liner)	6.50	5.00

1949

1465†	1r Dezhnev's ship exploring North-east Passage, 1648	20.00	7.00
1493	40k Tug		
1494	1r *Bolshaya Volga* (tanker)		
	Set of 2	14.50	12.00
1497†	20k Yachts	1.25	10
1543†	1r *Ukrania* (liner)	6.00	1.90

1950

1648†	1r *Mirnyi* and *Vostok* (Bellingshausen), 1820	32.00	10.00

1952

1763	40k *Orel* (battleship), 1905	3.25	80
1774	40k *Rotislav* (ship of the line), 1853	2.75	1.25

1783†	40k Tourist launch	2.50	1.75

1953

1804†	40k Tug and barges, Volga–Don canal	1.50	60
1806†	1r *Iosif Stalin* (river vessel)	2.50	1.40

1954

1845†	40k Yachts	1.25	20

1956

1999†	40k Pulling longboat on frozen River Volga	3.00	45
2026	40k *Lena* (Antarctic supply ship)	5.50	80
2047	40k *Sv. Pyotr* (Bering), 1741	3.00	35

1957

2095b†	40k *Zarya* (research schooner)	2.50	40

1958

2184	40k *Varyag* (cruiser), 1901	1.90	45
2202	40k Freighter	2.25	30
2217	60k *Lenin* (atomic ice-breaker)	3.00	40
2239†	40k *Aurora* (cruiser)	40	15
2245†	1r *Rossiya* (liner)	1.40	40
2298†	40k *Lenin* (atomic ice-breaker)	2.50	65

1959

2314†	40k *Ermak* (ice-breaker), 1900	1.00	30
2326	10k *Sovetsky Soyuz* (liner)		
2327	20k *Feliks Dzerzhinsky* (liner)		
2328	40k *Rossiya* (liner)		
2329	40k *Kooperatsiya* (liner)		
2330	60k *Mikhail Kalinin* (liner)		
2331	1r *Baltika* (liner)		
	Set of 6	4.00	95
2372†	25k *Vityaz* (oceanographic survey ship)	1.25	15

1960

2489	25k *Karl Marx* (river vessel)		
2490	40k *Lenin* (river vessel)		
2491	60k *Raketa* (hydrofoil)		
	Set of 3	2.00	45

1961

2570	6k *Lenin* (atomic ice-breaker)	90	30

2621†	10k *Lenin* (atomic ice-breaker) (on stamp No. 2298)	1.10	45

2658	6k *Fram* (Nansen)	1.75	15

1962

2665†	6k *K-3* (submarine), 1942	1.00	20

2738	4k Liner	30	10

2773†	4k Ice-breaker and hydrofoil	55	20

1963

2880†	6k Freighter	60	15

2894†	3k *Ob* (Antarctic supply ship)	2.00	30
2897†	12k *Sovetskaya Ukraina* (whale factory ship) and whale catcher	4.00	50

2913	4k *Aurora* (cruiser) (orange, black & red)		
2914	4k *Aurora* (cruiser) (pink, black & red)		
	Set of 2	80	40

1964

3040	6k *Havel* (German freighter)	45	15

1965

3194†	2k Medieval kogge	20	10
3196†	6k Modern mail boat	60	15

3199†	4k *Taimyr* and *Vaigach* (ice-breakers), 1915	90	15
3200†	4k *Lenin* (atomic ice-breaker)	90	15
3202†	10k *Vostok* and *Mirnyi* (Bellingshausen), 1820	1.75	35

1966

3251†	10k *Ob* (Antarctic supply ship), 1956 ..	2.50	50

3271†	10k Barge in canal lock	65	20
3272†	12k *Aleksandr Pushkin* (liner)	1.00	20
3273†	16k *Aleksandr Puskin* (liner) (silhouette)	1.00	25

3319†	4k Cruise ships, River Volga	30	10

3334†	6k Trawler	30	10

3370†	1k *Sv. Pyotr* (Bering)	40	10
3372†	4k *Ilich* (liner) and freighter	65	10

1967

3390	6k *Cheryashevsky* (fish factory ship)		
3391	6k Refrigerated trawler		
3392	6k Crab-canning ship		
3393	6k Trawler		
3394	6k Seine-fishing boat, Black Sea		
	Set of 5	2.00	70

3506†	4k Liner	20	10

3509†	4k Brig, 1840	25	10

1968

3572†	6k Liner	20	10

COLLECT CHESS ON STAMPS

A Stanley Gibbons thematic catalogue — available at £5 (p. + p. £3) from: Stanley Gibbons Publications, 5 Parkside, Christchurch Road, Ringwood, Hants. BH24 3SH.

3577† 6k Yachts 30 10

3600 6k *Ivan Franko* (liner) 25 10

1969

3678† 4k Tourist launch 15 10

3773† 4k Speed boat 15 10

1970

3788† 4k *Vostok* and *Mirnyi* (Bellingshausen),
1820 .... 2.00 25

3843 3k *Aurora* (cruiser)
3844 4k *Groznyi* (missile cruiser)
3845 10k *Oktyabrskaya Revolyutsiya* (cruiser)
3846 12k *Varyag* (missile cruiser)
3847 20k *Leninsky Komsomol* (nuclear
submarine)
Set of 5 3.25 85

3899 10k *Jolly George* (freighter) 35 15

1971

3965 16k Hydrofoil 50 20

3974 4k Tourist ship, Gorky 15 10

3996† 3k Tourist launch, Pskov 15 10

4016 1k Peter the Great's Imperial barge,
1723
4017 4k *Orel* (galleon), 1668
4018 10k *Poltava* (ship of the line), 1712
4019 12k *Ingermanland* (ship of the line), 1715
4020 16k *Vladimir* (steam frigate), 1848
Set of 5 3.00 90

1972

4087† 6k Cruiser 25 15

4117 2k *Pyotr Veliky* (battleship), 1872
4118 3k *Varyag* (cruiser), 1899
4119 4k *Potemkin* (battleship), 1900
4120 6k *Ochakov* (cruiser), 1902
4121 10k *Amur* (minelayer), 1907
Set of 5 2.40 60

1973

4171 16k *Mikhail Lermontov* (liner) 70 30

4172 4k Ice-breaker 55 10

4209 3k *Kirov* (cruiser)
4210 4k *Oktyabrskaya Revolyutsiya*
(battleship)
4211 6k *Krasnogvardeets* (submarine)
4212 10k *Soobrazitelnyi* (destroyer)
4213 16k *Krasnyi Kavkaz* (cruiser)
Set of 5 2.25 80

1974

4264† 4k Battle of Chesme, 1770 .... 15 10
4266† 10k Brig, 1868 .... 35 15

4303 3k Minesweeper
4304 4k Landing ship
4305 6k Helicopter carrier
4306 16k *Otvazhny* (destroyer)
Set of 4 1.60 55

4311† 6k Yachts 20 15
4313† 16k Fishing boats 65 30

4328 6k Viking longship 20 10

4341   4k *Aleksandr Pushkin* (liner), freighter
         and tanker 30   10

1976

4598   4k *Pailot* (ice-breaker)
4599   6k *Ermak* (ice-breaker)
4600   10k *Fedor Litke* (ice-breaker)
4601   16k *Vladimir Ilich* (ice-breaker)
4602   20k *Krasin* (ice-breaker)
                              Set of 5   3.50   95

1977

4611   4k *Sv. Foka* (polar vessel) 1.10   20

4654   4k *Aleksandr Sibiryakov* (ice-breaker)
4655   6k *Georgy Sedov* (ice-breaker)
4656   10k *Sadko* (ice-breaker)
4657   12k *Dezhnev* (ice-breaker)
4658   14k *Sibir* (ice-breaker)
4659   16k *Lena* (Antarctic supply ship)
4660   20k *Amguema* (ice-breaker)
                              Set of 7   4.00   1.25

MS4683 50k *Arktika* (atomic ice-breaker) 10.00   5.00

4704†   4k *Aurora* (cruiser)   15   10

4716†   4k Liner   15   10

1978

4779†   32k *Vladimir Komorov* (research vessel)   95   35

4814   6k *Tsarevich*, *Bogatyr* and two other
         Russian warships, 1908   20   10

MS4818 30k Hydrofoil   65   40

4820   4k + 2k "Star" class yacht
4821   6k + 3k "Soling" class yacht
4822   10k + 5k "470" class yacht
4823   16k + 6k "Finn" class yacht
4824   20k + 10k "Flying Dutchman" class
         yacht
                              Set of 5   2.40   1.00
MS4825 50k + 25k "Tornado" class
         catamaran 5.00   3.00

4827   6k Black Sea ferry   15   10

COLLECT FUNGI ON STAMPS
A Stanley Gibbons thematic catalogue — available at £5 (p. + p. £3) from: Stanley Gibbons Publications, 5 Parkside, Christchurch Road, Ringwood, Hants. BH24 3SH.

4843   4k *Vasily Pronchishchev* (ice-breaker)
4844   6k *Kapitan Belousov* (ice-breaker)
4845   10k *Moskva* (ice-breaker)
4846   12k *Admiral Makarov* (ice-breaker)
4847   16k *Lenin* (atomic ice-breaker)
4848   20k *Arktika* (atomic ice-breaker)
                              Set of 6   2.40   85

1979

4879   15k Satellite communication ship   30   15

4948   1k *Vulkanolog* (research ship)
4949   2k *Professor Bogorov* (research ship)
4950   4k *Ernst Krenkel* (research ship)
4951   6k *Kosmonavt Vladislav Volkov* (research
         ship)
4952   10k *Kosmonavt Yury Gagarin* (research
         ship)
4953   15k *Akademik Kurchatov* (research ship)
                              Set of 6   1.90   85

1980

5053   2k *Ayu-dag* (research vessel)
5054   3k *Valerian Uryvaev* (research vessel)
5055   4k *Mikhail Somov* (research vessel)
5056   6k *Akademik Sergei Korolev* (research
         vessel)
5057   10k *Otto Schmidt* (research vessel)
5058   15k *Akademik Mstislav Keldysh*
         (research vessel)
                              Set of 6   1.50   70

5067†   2r Atomic ice-breaker 5.50   2.00

1981

5085†   15k Antarctic supply ship 2.25   40

5099 15k Freighter 40 20

5101 4k Liner 10 10

5119 4k Freighters 10 10

✓ 5143 4k *Lenin* (river vessel)
✓ 5144 6k *Kosmonavt Gagarin* (river tourist ship)
✓ 5145 15k *Valerian Kuibyshev* (river tourist ship)
✓ 5146 32k *Baltysky* (river tanker)
                    Set of 4 2.25 85

5147 15k *Malygin* (ice-breaker) 65 15

5151† 4k Container ship 15 10

5167 4k *Tovarishch* (four-masted cadet barque)
5168 6k *Vega* (cadet barquentine)
5169 10k *Kodor* (cadet schooner)
5170 15k *Tovarishch* (three-masted cadet barque)
5171 20k *Kruzenshtern* (four-masted cadet barque)
5172 32k *Sedov* (four-masted cadet barque)
                    Set of 6 2.75 1.10

STANLEY GIBBONS STAMP COLLECTING SERIES

Introductory booklets on *How to Start, How to Identify Stamps* and *Collecting by Theme.* A series of well illustrated guides at a low price. Write for details.

1982

5270 4k *S-56* (submarine)
5271 6k *Gremyashchy* (minelayer)
5272 15k *Gafel* (minesweeper)
5273 20k *Krasnyi Krym* (cruiser)
5274 45k *Sevastopol* (battleship)
                    Set of 5 3.50 1.50

5293† 6k Freighter 40 15
5296† 6k Full-rigged ship 40 15

1983

5323 4k Hydrofoil, River Don 15 10

5330 5k 18th-century warship and modern missile cruiser 40 15

5341 4k Coastal trawlers
5342 6k Refrigerated trawler
5343 10k *Pulkovsky Meridian* (deep-sea trawler)
5344 15k Refrigerated freighter
5345 20k *50 let SSR* (factory ship)
                    Set of 5 2.25 1.00

1984

5429† 6k *Chelyuskin* (ice-breaker), 1934 ...... 25 10
5430† 15k *Chelyuskin* sinking 60 25

5447 5k Freighter 15 10

5455 10k Liner 35 15

1985

5563 5k *Potemkin* (battleship), 1905 .... 20 10

5600 5k *Aurora* (cruiser), 1917 .... 20 10

1986

5673† 15k Oceanographic research vessel 55 30

5690 15k *Mukran* (train ferry) 75 25

5693 5k *Vladivostok* (ice-breaker)
5694 10k *Mikhail Somov* (research vessel)
                    Set of 2 75 30
MS5695 50k *Mikhail Somov* 2.00 1.60

15.III—26.VII.1985
Дрейф во льдах Антарктики

No. 5055 overprinted

5696 4k *Mikhail Somov* 20 10

1987

5758 5k *Maksim Gorky* (river tourist ship)
5759 10k *Aleksandr Pushkin* (river tourist ship)
5760 30k *Sovetsky Soyuz* (river tourist ship)
                    Set of 3 1.50 65

5788† 10k 16th and 18th-century sailing
packets 35 15

5824 4k *Trisvyatitelya* (ship of the line)
(Spiridov), 1770
5825 5k *Sv. Pavel* (ship of the line) (Ushakov),
1799
5826 10k Battle of Afon (Senyavin), 1807
5827 25k *Azov* (ship of the line) (Lazarev),
1827
5828 30k *Imperatritsa Maria* (ship of the line)
(Nakhimov), 1853
Set of 5 2.25 1.00

1988

5839 15k Sail frigate 45 25

5859 5k Yacht, Sochi 20 10

5927 20k *Sibir* (ice-breaker) 60 30

6073† 2k Sailing packet 10 10
5941† 3k *Aurora* (cruiser) 10 10
6077† 7k Liner 15 10
6084† 30k Antarctic research vessel 65 35

1989

MS6025 50k Battle of Hango Head, 1714 ...... 1.25 75

6026 5k Container ship 20 10

6055† 20k Red Indian canoe 50 25

6091 5k *Pervaz Bati* (steam warship) and V. A.
Kornilov
6092 10k *Parizh* (ship of the line) and V. I.
Istomin
6093 15k *Baikal* (brig) and G. I. Nevelskoi
6094 20k Iron-clad squadron and G. I. Butakov
6095 30k *Pyotr Veliky* and *Vitze Admiral
Popov* (battleships) and A. A. Popov
6096 35k Torpedo-boats attacking *Intibah*
(Turkish warship) and *Veliky Khyaz
Konstantin* (battleship) and S. O.
Makarov
Set of 6 2.25 1.25

1990

6120† 10k Paddle-steamer 15 10

6195 5k *Sever 2* (research submarine)
6196 10k *Tinro 2* (research submarine)
6197 15k *Argus* (research submarine)
6198 25k *Paisis* (research submarine)
6199 35k *Mir* (research submarine)
Set of 5 1.75 1.00

1991

6222† 10k Fishing boats, Sorrento 25 15
6223† 10k Rowing boats on River Tiber 25 15

6229† 20k Coasters on dried-out bed of Aral
Sea 45 25

6234 20k Russian exploration ship and kayaks,
Kodiak, 1784
6235 30k Russian full-rigged ship, Sitka, 1804
6236 30k Scow, Fort Ross, 1812
Set of 3 1.90 1.00

6237 10k Liner 20 10

6273† 5k Ice-breaker 10 10

6275† 30k *Sv. Pyotr* (Bering) 60 30

6279† 10k *Santa Maria* (Columbus) 20 10

1992

MS6353 3r *Santa Maria* (Columbus) 65 35

6365† 55k Red Indian canoe 10 10

RUSSIAN POST OFFICES IN TURKEY

South-east Europe and Asia Minor
1865 100 kopeks = 1 rouble
1900 40 paras = 1 piastre

1865

4 2k Early steamship £600 £400
5 20k Early steamship £800 £450

6	2k Early steamship	20.00	35.00
7	20k Early steamship	35.00	42.00

1909

57	5pa on 1k Liner, 1907		
58	10pa on 2k Liner, 1907		
59	20pa on 4k Liner, 1907		
60	1pi on 10k Liner, 1907		
61	5pi on 50k Liner, 1907		
62	7pi on 70k Liner, 1907		
63	10pi on 1r Liner, 1907		
64	35pi on 3r50 Liner, 1907		
65	70pi on 7r Liner, 1907		
	Set of 9	35.00	95.00

RWANDA

Central Africa
100 centimes = 1 franc

1969

187†	1f Nile felucca	10	10
191†	15f Nile felucca	60	50

331†	80c Shipbuilding, Ostend	10	10

1970

MS344	100f 16th-century naval battle, Bay of Naples	2.50	2.25

1972

495†	18f Olympic yachts	35	30

1973

No. **MS**344 *cut down and overprinted* **NAPLES 1973**

MS573	100f 16th-century naval battle, Bay of Naples	2.00	1.90

1974

602†	20c *Elettra* (Marconi's steam yacht)	20	10
603†	30c *Carlo Alberto* (cruiser)	20	10
MS608†	50f *Elettra*	1.50	1.25

1976

MS735†	100f *Bonhomme Richard* (Jones), Battle of Flamborough Head, 1779	2.50	2.25

743†	20c Olympic yachts	10	10

1977

816†	1f *Goliath* (cable paddle-steamer)	10	10
818†	18f *Kingsport* (satellite communications ship)	65	40
MS822†	Two sheets. 60f 17th-century Dutch warship (other sheet shows a non-maritime subject)		
	Set of 2 sheets	2.50	2.00

1978

856†	18f Scouts in canoe	35	35

1979

948†	20c Native canoe (on Ruanda-Urundi stamp No. 5)	10	10
950†	50c *Deliverance* (stern wheel paddle-steamer) (on Ruanda-Urundi stamp No. 31)	10	10

1981

1062†	15f Tanker	30	25

1984

1187†	30c Liner	15	10

1201†	200f Freighter	3.00	1.60

1203†	30c Sailboards	15	10

1985

1225†	30c Pirogue	15	10

1988

1330†	10f Refugees in rowing boat	15	10

RYUKYU ISLANDS

Northern Pacific
1948 100 sen = 1 yen
1958 100 cents = 1 dollar

1948

4†	30s Junk	3.25	2.00
6†	50s Junk	3.50	2.50

1953

40†	6y American fleet, Naha, 1853	1.00	2.40

1961

106	3c Junk and liner	1.75	1.25

1969

221†	3c Canoe race	50	40

SAAR

Western Europe
1921 100 pfennige = 1 mark
1921 100 centimes = 1 franc

1921

56†	25pf Tug and barges	35	25

No. 56 surcharged

71†	5c on 25 pf Tug and barges	15	30

1922

As No. 56, but larger

92†	50c Tug and barges	75	10

1952

318†	3f Temporary bridge on barges, Gersweiler	15	10
327†	18f Temporary bridge on barges, Gersweiler	2.75	3.25

1955

No. 327 overprinted **VOLKSBEFRAGUNG 1955**

360†	18f Temporary bridge on barges, Gersweiler	15	40

OFFICIAL STAMPS

1922

No. 92 overprinted **DIENSTMARKE**

O106†	50c Tug and barges	70	15

ST. HELENA

South Atlantic
1922 12 pence = 1 shilling
20 shillings = 1 pound
1971 100 pence = 1 pound

1922

97	½d *London* (East Indiaman), 1659	
98	1d *London*	
99	1½d *London*	
100	2d *London*	
101	3d *London*	
92	4d *London*	
103	5d *London*	
104	6d *London*	
105	8d *London*	
106	1s *London*	
107	1s6d *London*	
108	2s *London*	
109	2s6d *London*	
110	5s *London*	
111	7s6d *London*	
112	10s *London*	
113	15s *London*	
96	£1 *London*	

Set of 18	£1500	£2000

1934

123†	10s *London* (East Indiaman), 1659	£200	£250

1938

131	½d *London* (East Indiaman), 1659	
132	1d *London* (green)	
132a	1d *London* (orange)	
149	1d *London* (black & green)	
133	1½d *London* (red)	
150	1½d *London* (black & red)	
134	2d *London* (orange)	
151	2d *London* (black & red)	
135	3d *London* (blue)	
135a	3d *London* (grey)	
135b	4d *London*	
136	6d *London*	
136a	8d *London*	
137	1s *London*	
138	2s6d *London*	
139	5s *London*	
140	10s *London*	

Set of 17	£130	55.00

1949

As No. 115 of Antigua

146†	4d Paddle-steamer	1.50	90

1953

153†	½d *London* (East Indiaman), 1659	30	30

1959

170†	6d *London* (East Indiaman), 1659	30	35

1967

212	1s *London* (East Indiaman), 1659	
213	2s6d *London*	

Set of 2	30	30

215†	3d *Charles* (East Indiaman), 1667	15	10
216†	6d Ship's boat, 1667	15	10

1968

240†	£1 *John Dutton* (lifeboat)	10.00	15.00

1969

241	4d *Perseverance* (brig), 1819	
242	8d *Phoebe* (screw steamer) (inscr "DANE" in error), 1857	
243	1s9d *Llandovery Castle* (liner), 1925	
244	2s3d *Good Hope Castle* (cargo liner), 1969	

Set of 4	1.25	1.00

1973

297	1½p *Westminster* and *Claudine* (East Indiamen), 1849	
298	4p *True Briton* (East Indiaman), 1790	
299	6p *General Goddard* (East Indiaman) in action against *Alblasserdam* (Dutch East Indiaman), 1795	
300	22½p *Kent* (East Indiaman) on fire, 1825	

Set of 4	3.00	3.25

1974

301†	5p Freighters	25	25

1975

307† 5p H.M.S. *Resolution* (Cook) 50   50

1976

317† 8p *London* (East Indiaman) (on stamp
        No. 98) 25   30
318† 25p *Good Hope Castle* (cargo liner) 40   45

330† £1 British warships, 1815 .... 1.50   3.00
331† £2 British warships, 1821 .... 3.50   5.50

1977

332† 8p Local longboat, 1947 20   35

1978

341† 3p 17th-century Dutch East Indiaman 15   15
346† 20p 17th-century Dutch East Indiaman 60   70

1979

347† 3p H.M.S. *Discovery* (Cook) 20   15

1980

359† 8p Ship's boat, 1880 25   25

362† 5p 17th-century East Indiaman 15   15

1982

396† 29p H.M.S. *Beagle* (Darwin) 95   1.25

1984

433† 59p *London* (East Indiaman) (on stamp
        No.123) 1.10   2.00

436 11p H.M.S. *Invincible* (aircraft carrier)
437 60p H.M.S. *Herald* (survey ship)
                         Set of 2 1.50   1.65

438† 10p *St. Helena* (schooner), 1814 20   20
441† 50p *Papanui* (freighter), 1898 .... 1.00   1.00

1986

485† 65p *Unity* (Halley), 1676 .... 1.40   1.40

488 1p H.M.S. *Erebus* (Ross)
489 3p H.M.S. *Beagle* (Fitzroy)
490 5p *Nadezhda* (Von Kruenstern)
491 9p H.M.S. *Resolution* (Bligh)
492 10p *Rurik* (Von Kotzebue)
493 12p H.M.S. *Swallow* (Carteret)
494 15p *Desire* (Cavendish)
495 20p *La Boudeuse* (De Bougainville)
496 25p *Senyavin* (Lutke)
497 40p *La Coquille* (Duperrey)
498 60p H.M.S. *Dolphin* (Byron)
499 £1 H.M.S. *Endeavour* (Cook)
500 £2 *L'Astrolabe* (Dumont d'Urville)
                         Set of 13 9.00   10.00

1987

501 9p H.M.S. *Repulse* (battle cruiser), 1925
502 13p H.M.S. *Vanguard* (battleship), 1941
503 38p Royal Yacht *Britannia*, 1957
504 45p H.M.S. *Herald* (survey ship), 1984
                         Set of 4 3.75   3.75

1988

519 9p *Defence* (Dampier), 1691
520 13p H.M.S. *Resolution* (Cook), 1775
521 45p H.M.S. *Providence* (sloop) (Bligh),
        1792
522 60p H.M.S. *Beagle* (Darwin), 1836
                         Set of 4 9.00   7.50

528† 20p *Edinburgh Castle* (liner) 40   45
529† 45p *Bosun Bird* (freighter) 90   95
530† 60p *Spangereid* (full-rigged ship) on fire,
        1920 .... 1.25   1.40

1990

572† 13p *Dane* (mail ship), 1857 40   40
573† 20p *St. Helena I* (mail ship) 65   65
574† 38p Launch of *St. Helena II* (mail ship) . 1.10   1.10
MS576† £1 *St. Helena II* 3.00   3.50

582† 13p Napoleon's funeral barge, St.
        Helena, 1840 40   40
583† 20p French Squadron, St. Helena, 1840   70   70
584† 38p *Belle Poule* (sail frigate) and
        Normandie (paddle-steamer) 1.25   1.25

1992

603	15p *Eye of the Wind* (cadet brig)		
604	25p *Soren Larsen* (cadet brigantine)		
605	35p *Santa Maria*, *Pinta* and *Nina* (Columbus)		
606	50p *Santa Maria*		
	Set of 4	3.75	3.75

612	13p H.M.S. *Ledbury* (minesweeper)		
613	20p H.M.S. *Brecon* (minesweeper)		
614	38p *St. Helena I* (mail ship) off South Georgia		
615	45p Naval launch		
	Set of 4	3.00	3.00
MS616	13p + 3p H.M.S. *Ledbury*; 20p + 4p H.M.S. *Brecon*; 38p + 8p *St. Helena I*; 45p + 9p Naval launch	3.00	4.00

623†	38p H.M.S. *Providence* (sloop) (Bligh)	1.00	1.00

ST. KITTS

West Indies
100 cents = 1 dollar

1980

No. 399 of St. Kitts-Nevis overprinted **St. Kitts**

34†	30c *Europa* (liner)	15	15

42	4c H.M.S. *Vanguard* (ship of the line), 1762		
43	10c H.M.S. *Boreas* (frigate), 1787		
44	30c H.M.S. *Druid* (frigate), 1827		
45	55c H.M.S. *Winchester* (frigate), 1831		
46	$1.50 *Philosopher* (full-rigged merchantman), 1857		
47	$2 *Contractor* (cargo liner), 1930		
	Set of 6	1.25	90

1981

75†	55c Royal Yacht *Saudadoes*	15	15
77†	$2.50 Royal Yacht *Royal George*	35	35
79†	$4 Royal Yacht *Britannia*	50	50

1982

92†	15c Naval action off St. Kitts, 1782	10	10

1983

108	55c *Stella Oceanis* (liner)		
109	$2 *Queen Elizabeth 2* (liner)		
	Set of 2	70	50

1985

172†	$3 *Polynesia* (cruise schooner)	1.75	2.00

173	40c *Tropic Jade* (container ship)		
174	$1.20 *Atlantic Clipper* (schooner)		
175	$2 *Mandalay* (schooner)		
176	$2 *Cunard Countess* (liner)		
	Set of 4	6.00	5.50

182†	40c *Golden Hind* (Drake)	75	35

1986

217†	$1.50 *Isere* (French screw warship), 1885	1.50	1.50

1989

283†	$2 Inflatable dinghy	95	1.25

291†	15c *Santa Mariagallante* (Columbus), 1493	45	20

1990

312	10c *Romney* (freighter)		
313	15c *Baralt* (freighter)		
314	20c *Wear* (mail steamer)		
315	25c *Sunmount* (freighter)		
316	40c *Inanda* (cargo liner)		
317	50c *Alcoa Partner* (freighter)		
318	60c *Dominica* (freighter)		
319	80c *C.G.M. Provence* (container ship)		
320	$1 *Director* (freighter)		
321	$1.20 Barque		
322	$2 *Chignecto* (packet steamer)		
323	$3 *Berbice* (mail steamer)		
324	$5 *Vamos* (freighter)		
325	$10 *Federal Maple* (freighter)		
	Set of 14	9.75	11.00

1992

ST KITTS $1

359	$1 Columbus's fleet		
360	$2 Columbus's fleet		
	Set of 2	2.00	2.00

OFFICIAL STAMPS

1980

No. 34 overprinted **OFFICIAL**

O3	30c *Europa* (liner)	10	10

1983

Nos. 75, 77 and 79 overprinted **OFFICIAL** *or surcharged also*

O23†	45c on $2.50 Royal Yacht *Royal George*	25	25
O25†	55c Royal Yacht *Saudadoes*	30	30
O27†	$1.10 on $4 Royal Yacht *Britannia*	60	70

ST. KITTS-NEVIS

West Indies
1923 12 pence = 1 shilling
20 shillings = 1 pound
1951 100 cents = 1 dollar

1923

48	½d Merchantman, 1623		
49	1d Merchantman, 1623		
50	1½d Merchantman, 1623		
51	2d Merchantman, 1623		
52	2½d Merchantman, 1623		
53	3d Merchantman, 1623		
54	6d Merchantman, 1623		
55	1s Merchantman, 1623		
56	2s Merchantman, 1623		
57	2s6d Merchantman, 1623		
59	5s Merchantman, 1623		
58	10s Merchantman, 1623		
60	£1 Merchantman, 1623		
	Set of 13	£1000	£1700

1949

As No. 115 of Antigua

83†	3d Paddle-steamer	40	30

1963

138† 20c Boat building 20 10

1968

188 25c *Jamaica Producer* (freighter)
189 50c *Jamaica Producer*
                            Set of 2 30 20

1970

207†	1c English two-decker warship, 1650		30	10
210†	4c 16th-century Portuguese caravels		20	10
211†	5c Fireships, 1669		30	10
212†	6c 16th-century pirate carrack		30	10
213†	10c 17th-century smugglers' ship		30	10
218†	60c 17th-century Dutch flute		2.25	70
221†	$5 16th-century sea battle		2.50	4.25

1973

261† $2.50 *Concepcion* (Sir Thomas Warner),
     1623 .... 80 1.10

No. 261 overprinted **VISIT OF H. R. H. THE PRINCE OF WALES**
1973

268† $2.50 *Concepcion* 45 50

285† 4c Schooner and launch 20 10

1978

399† 30c *Europa* (liner) 60 45

ST. LUCIA
West Indies
1938 12 pence = 1 shilling
20 shillings = 1 pound
1949 100 cents = 1 dollar

1938

137† 5s *Lady Hawkins* (packet steamer)
     loading bananas 11.00 5.00

1949

As No. 115 of Antigua
161† 6c Paddle-steamer 35 25

1960

188 8c *Santa Maria* (Columbus)
189 10c *Santa Maria* (Columbus)
190 25c *Santa Maria* (Columbus)
                            Set of 3 75 60

1964

204† 12c Fishing boats 15 10
207† 35c Schooners, Castries 1.25 10
208† 50c Fishing boat 1.10 10

1967

Nos. 204 and 207/8 overprinted **STATEHOOD 1st MARCH 1967**
234† 12c Fishing boats 20 10
237† 35c Schooners, Castries 50 35
238† 50c Fishing boat 50 55

1970

279† 5c Liner and freighter, Castries 15 10
284† 25c Yacht 40 10

1971

315† 25c 18th-century shipping 20 20

1972

335 5c Barque (on local stamp of St. Lucia
    Steam Conveyance Co Ltd)
336 10c Barque (on local stamp of St. Lucia
    Steam Conveyance Co Ltd)
337 35c Barque (on local stamp of St. Lucia
    Steam Conveyance Co Ltd)
338 50c Barque (on local stamp of St. Lucia
    Steam Conveyance Co Ltd)
                         Set of 4 1.60 1.00

1973

352 15c H.M.S. *St. Lucia* (brig), 1803
353 35c H.M.S. *Prince of Wales* (ship of the
    line), 1765
354 50c *Oliph Blossom* (merchantman), 1605
355 $1 H.M.S. *Rose* (frigate), 1757
                         Set of 4 1.00 70

1976

406 ½c *Hanna* (American schooner), 1775
407 1c *Prince of Orange* (British sailing
    packet), 1777
408 2c H.M.S. *Edward* (sloop), 1776
409 5c *Millern* (British full-rigged
    merchantman), 1777
410 15c *Surprise* (American lugger), 1777
411 35c H.M.S. *Serapis* (frigate) 1779
412 50c *Randolph* (American frigate), 1777
413 $1 *Alliance* (American frigate), 1778
                         Set of 8 5.00 1.75

434 10c Crest of H.M.S. *Ceres* (sloop)
435 20c Crest of H.M.S. *Pelican* (frigate)
436 40c Crest of H.M.S. *Ganges* (ship of the
    line)
437 $2 Crest of H.M.S. *Ariadne* (frigate)
                         Set of 4 3.00 2.00

1977

452† 20c Scout sailing dinghy 20 15
454† $1 Scout motor boat 75 1.10
MS455† $2.50 Scout motor boat 1.50 2.50

1978

480†   50c Defence of St. Lucia, 1778   40   15

1980

540†	20c Refrigerated freighter	35	10
542†	30c *Charles* (pilot boat)	40	20
544†	75c *Cunard Countess* (liner)	65	75
546†	$2 Cargo liner	1.25	1.50
548†	$10 *Queen Elizabeth 2* (liner)	5.50	6.50

MS558† $5 Schooner by moonlight 1.50   1.75

No. 540 surcharged **1980 HURRICANE $1.50 RELIEF**

565† $1.50 on 20c Refrigerated freighter   30   40

1982

617†   35c Battle of the Saints, 1782   80   15

1983

634†   30c Cruising yacht   15   10

641†   10c *Cunard Countess* (liner)   15   10

1984

675†	35c Elizabethan galleon	20	20
677†	60c Battle of Trafalgar, 1805, and royal crest	30	30
678†	60c Battle of Trafalgar, 1805, and King George III	30	30
681†	$2.50 Defeat of Spanish Armada, 1588	75	75
682†	$2.50 Defeat of Spanish Armada, 1588, and Queen Elizabeth I	75	75

1986

MS885† $7 Royal Yacht *Britannia* 4.00   4.50

1987

948†   80c *Mauretania I* (liner)   75   55

1988

1006†   80c *Lady Nelson* (hospital ship), 1942   1.10   90

1989

1016† $2.50 Liner 1.00   1.10

1029† $3.50 *La Felicite* (French corvette), 1792 ....   4.00   4.50

1991

1060	50c *Vistafjord* (liner)
1061	80c *Windstar* (schooner)
1062	$1 *Unicorn* (brig)
1063	$2.50 Game-fishing launch

                Set of 4   4.00   4.00

MS1064 $5 *Vistafjord* (liner), *Fyodor Dostoevsky* (liner) and *Sun Viking* (liner) in Castries Harbour 3.25   3.50

COLLECT RAILWAYS ON STAMPS

Second revised edition of this Stanley Gibbons thematic catalogue. Now available at £9.50 (p. + p. £3) from: Stanley Gibbons Publications, 5 Parkside, Christchurch Road, Ringwood, Hants BH24 3SH.

1992

1073	60c Schooner-rigged yacht
1074	80c Bermuda and yawl-rigged yachts

                Set of 2   1.25   1.25

1075	$1 Columbus's fleet
1076	$2 Columbus's fleet

                Set of 2   2.00   2.00

1077	15c Amerindian canoes
1078	40c Ships of Juan de la Cosa, 1499
1079	50c Columbus's fleet, 1502
1080	$5 Wrecked galleon

                Set of 4   3.25   3.25

OFFICIAL STAMPS

1983

Nos. 540, 542, 544, 546 and 548 overprinted **OFFICIAL**

O4†	20c Refrigerated freighter	30	20
O6†	30c Pilot boat	40	25
O8†	75c *Cunard Countess* (liner)	75	50
O10†	$2 Cargo liner	1.75	1.75
O12†	$10 *Queen Elizabeth 2* (liner)	6.50	7.50

ST. PIERRE & MIQUELON

North Atlantic
100 centimes = 1 franc

1909

93†	1f Fishing brigantine	2.00	1.40
121†	1f10 Fishing brigantine	2.00	2.00
122†	1f50 Fishing brigantine	6.25	6.25
94†	2f Fishing brigantine	2.00	1.50
123†	3f Fishing brigantine	6.00	6.25
95†	5f Fishing brigantine	6.25	4.25

1924

Nos. 93/5, some with colours changed, surcharged in figures and bars

125†	25c on 2f Fishing brigantine	30	40
126†	25c on 5f Fishing brigantine	30	40
130†	1f25 on 1f Fishing brigantine	1.25	1.50
131†	1f50 on 1f Fishing brigantine	2.00	2.00
132†	3f on 5f Fishing brigantine	1.60	1.75
133†	10f on 5f Fishing brigantine	10.00	10.50
134†	20f on 5f Fishing brigantine	15.00	15.00

1931

As No. 109 of Cameroun

138†   1f50 *Leconte de Lisle* (liner) 1.75   1.75

1932

141†	4c Jacques Coeur (trawler)	25	40
142†	5c Jacques Coeur	25	40
147†	30c Jacques Coeur	70	70
148†	40c Jacques Coeur	70	70
151†	65c Jacques Coeur	95	1.00
154†	1f Jacques Coeur	70	70
157†	1f75 Jacques Coeur	1.25	1.25
158†	2f Jacques Coeur	5.25	5.50
161†	10f Jacques Coeur	42.00	42.00

1934

No. 157 overprinted **JACQUES CARTIER 1534 · 1934**

166†	1f75 Jacques Coeur (trawler)	2.75	2.75

1937

As Nos. 110/11 of Cameroun

168†	20c Liner	1.10	1.10
169†	30c Sailing ships	1.10	1.10

1941

Nos. 141/2, 148, 151, 154 and 157/8 overprinted **FRANCE LIBRE F. N. F. L.** *or surcharged also*

248†	4c Jacques Coeur (trawler)	35.00	35.00
249†	5c Jacques Coeur	£600	£600
250†	40c Jacques Coeur	10.50	10.50
253†	65c Jacques Coeur	24.00	24.00
254†	1f Jacques Coeur	£250	£250
255†	1f75 Jacques Coeur	8.25	8.25
256†	2f Jacques Coeur	11.00	11.00
258†	5f on 1f75 Jacques Coeur	9.75	9.75

1942

322	5c Fishing schooner	
323	10c Fishing schooner	
324	25c Fishing schooner	
325	30c Fishing schooner	
326	40c Fishing schooner	
327	60c Fishing schooner	
328	1f Fishing schooner	
329	1f50 Fishing schooner	
330	2f Fishing schooner	
331	2f50 Fishing schooner	
332	4f Fishing schooner	
333	5f Fishing schooner	
334	10f Fishing schooner	
335	20f Fishing schooner	

Set of 14 4.50 5.75

1945

Nos. 322, 324 and 331 surcharged

346	50c on 5c Fishing schooner	
347	70c on 5c Fishing schooner	
348	80c on 5c Fishing schooner	
349	1f20 on 5c Fishing schooner	
350	2f40 on 25c Fishing schooner	
351	3f on 25c Fishing schooner	
352	4f50 on 25c Fishing schooner	
353	15f on 2f50 Fishing schooner	

Set of 8 3.25 4.00

1947

374†	5f Colonel Pleven (trawler)	80	80
375†	6f Colonel Pleven	80	80
377†	10f Colonel Pleven	1.10	95
382†	50f 16th-century galleon (air)	3.25	2.50
383†	100f Fishing schooner	4.75	3.75
384†	200f Snow-bound fishing schooner	8.75	4.75

1954

As No. 264 of Cameroun

398	15f Landing craft, Normandy, 1944	4.50	4.75

1955

399†	30c Trawler	25	35
401†	50c Trawler	20	35
404†	3f Trawler	40	40
405†	4f Fishing dinghies	50	50
406†	10f Fishing dinghies	75	70
409†	40f Trawler	1.60	1.60

1956

413	15f Galantry (trawler)	1.25	90

1962

420	500f Surcouf (Free French submarine)	£100	70.00

1963

426	30f Fishing schooner	6.00	3.50

427	200f Garonne (French warship), 1763	15.00	8.00

1966

440	100f Revanche (immigrant ship), 1816	10.00	4.50

1967

442	25f Trawlers and fishing dinghies	
443	100f Richelieu (French cruiser)	

Set of 2 50.00 30.00

444	48f Trawler	5.00	2.75

1968

451†	6f French warship, 1791	3.50	2.00
452†	15f Belle Poule (sail frigate) and Cassard (survey ship), 1841	4.50	3.00
453†	25f Provence (French battleship)	7.00	4.50

1969

465	34f L'Estoile (French merchantman), 1690	
466	40f La Jolie (French merchantman), 1750	
467	48f La Juste (full-rigged ship), 1860	
468	200f L'Esperance (expedition ship), 1600	

Set of 4 55.00 25.00

1970

487†	48f Narrando (trawler)	8.50	4.00

488	25f 18th-century French warships	
489	50f Grande Hermine (Cartier), 1534	
490	60f 17th-century French galleons	

Set of 3 25.00 14.00

1971

491	30f St. Francis of Assisi (fisheries patrol vessel), 1900	
492	35f St. Jehanne (fisheries patrol vessel), 1920	
493	40f L'Aventure (fisheries patrol frigate), 1950	
494	80f Commandant Bourdais (frigate), 1970	

Set of 4 85.00 40.00

495	22f H.M.S. Aconite (corvette) (on loan to Free French, 1941–47)	
496	25f H.M.S. Alyssum (corvette) (on loan to Free French, 1941–42 as Alysse)	
497	50f H.M.S. Mimosa (corvette) (on loan to Free French, 1941–42)	

Set of 3 40.00 30.00

1973

513† 1f60 18th-century French warships 5.00 2.75
515† 4f 17th-century French warships 11.00 5.50

523 10f Freighter 35.00 20.00

1974

524 1f60 Weather ship 9.50 5.00

533† 20c Fishing schooner 4.00 2.25

1976

550 1f20 *Croix de Lorraine* (stern trawler)
551 1f40 *Geolette* (stern trawler)
Set of 2 15.00 9.00

1986

568 2f50 Yacht and motor cruiser 1.50 90

1987

591 2f50 Schooner on slipway 90 60

594 3f *La Normande* (trawler) 2.25 1.60

1988

604 2f50 *Nellie J. Banks* (smuggling schooner) 1.50 90

605 3f *Le Marmouset* (stern trawler) 1.40 90

1989

MS615 5f Brigantine, 1789 (sheet also contains
3 other 5f stamps) 8.25 8.25

616 2f20 Fishing boats
617 13f70 Sailboard and yacht
Set of 2 6.00 4.25

618 3f *Le Malabar* (ocean-going tug) 1.00 60

1990

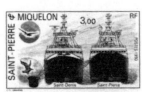

649 2f50 Red Indian canoe 80 45

650 3f *Saint Denis* and *Saint Pierre* (trawlers) 90 60

652† 14f50 Freighter and trawlers alongside
fish factory 4.00 2.40

654† 2f30 Trawler 70 45

1991

673 3f *Cryos* (stern trawler) 90 60

1992

679 1f50 Boat-building tools and stern of ship
680 1f80 Boat-building tools and stern of ship
Set of 2 1.00 70

1993

691 2f50 Free French corvette 60 40

692 5f Wreck of *L'Hortense* 1.25 75

STANLEY GIBBONS STAMP COLLECTING SERIES

Introductory booklets on *How to Start, How to Identify Stamps* and *Collecting by Theme*. A series of well illustrated guides at a low price. Write for details.

POSTAGE DUE STAMPS

1973

D516	2c Sinking fishing boat		
D517	10c Sinking fishing boat		
D518	20c Sinking fishing boat		
D519	30c Sinking fishing boat		
D520	1f Sinking fishing boat		
	Set of 5	9.50	9.50

ST. THOMAS AND PRINCE ISLANDS

In Atlantic off West Africa
1913 100 centavos = 1 escudo
1977 100 centimes = 1 dobra

1913

Surcharged **REPUBLICA S. TOME E PRINCIPE** *and new value*

(a) On Nos. 1/2, 5 and 7 of Portuguese Colonies in Africa

203†	½c on 2½r Departure of Vasco da Gama's fleet	50	40
204†	½c on 5r Vasco da Gama's fleet at Calicut	50	40
207†	5c on 50r *Sao Gabriel* (flagship)	50	40
209†	10c on 100r *Sao Gabriel*	50	40

(b) On Nos. 104/5, 108 and 110 of Macao

211†	½c on ½a Departure of Vasco da Gama's fleet	70	50
212†	½c on 1a Vasco da Gama's fleet at Calicut	70	50
215†	5c on 8a *Sao Gabriel* (flagship)	80	60
217†	10c on 16a *Sao Gabriel*	80	60

(c) On Nos. 58/9, 62 and 64 of Timor

219†	½c on ½a Departure of Vasco da Gama's fleet	70	50
220†	½c on 1a Vasco da Gama's fleet at Calicut	70	50
223†	5c on 8a *Sao Gabriel* (flagship)	90	70
225†	10c on 16a *Sao Gabriel*	80	60

1962

437†	2e Sailing dinghy	40	20

1967

453†	1e50 *Vasco da Gama* (19th-century steam corvette)	45	30

1969

458	2e50 Vasco da Gama's fleet, 1469	15	15

1972

467	20e 16th-century caravel	3.50	1.00

469	2e50 *Gladiolus* (Portuguese cruiser), 1922	30	15

1975

475	1e50 Sailing canoes		
476	4e Sailing canoes		
477	7e50 Sailing canoes		
478	20e Sailing canoes		
479	50e Sailing canoes		
	Set of 5	3.25	2.00

Appendix

The following stamps have either been issued in excess of postal needs or have not been available to the public in reasonable quantities at face value. Miniature sheets, imperforate stamps etc., are excluded from this section.

1979

15th and 16th-century Sailing Ships. 50c, 1, 3, 5, 8, 25d

ST. VINCENT

West Indies
100 cents = 1 dollar

1949

As No. 115 of Antigua

179†	6c Paddle-steamer	30	40

1965

226†	4c H.M.S. *Providence* (sloop) (Bligh), 1793	10	10

231†	1c Boat building (inscr "BEQUIA")	10	60
231a†	1c Boat building (inscr "BEQUIA")	10	10
239†	12c *Antilles* (liner), 1952	30	10

COLLECT BIRDS ON STAMPS

Third revised edition of this Stanley Gibbons thematic catalogue. Now available at £15.95 (p. + p. £3) from: Stanley Gibbons Publications, 5 Parkside, Christchurch Road, Ringwood, Hants BH24 3SH.

1971

330†	1c Careening fishing schooner	10	10
333†	15c Careening fishing schooner	10	10

1972

349†	30c H.M.S. *Arethusa* (frigate), 1807	40	10
350†	$1 H.M.S. *Blake* (ship of the line), 1808	1.40	70

1973

355†	12c Fleet of Columbus, 1492	45	20
357†	50c *Santa Maria* (Columbus)	1.50	1.10

1974

387	15c *Istra* (liner)		
388	20c *Oceanic* (liner)		
389	30c *Aleksandr Pushkin* (liner)		
390	$1 *Europa* (liner)		
	Set of 4	1.10	40

1975

450†	70c *Geestide* (freighter)	40	30

455†	$1.25 Yachts	1.25	1.50

1980

654†	$2 Yachts	50	30

1981

656 50c *Ville de Paris* (French ship of the line), 1782
657 60c H.M.S. *Ramillies* (ship of the line), 1782
658 $1.50 H.M.S. *Providence* (sloop) (Bligh), 1793
659 $2 *Dee* (paddle-steamer packet), 1840
Set of 4   2.75   3.25

668† 60c Royal Yacht *Isabella* 15 15
670† $2.50 *Alberta* (royal yacht tender) 30 30
672† $4 Royal Yacht *Britannia* 40 40

1982

706 45c *Geestport* (freighter)
707 60c *Stella Oceanis* (liner)
708 $1.50 *Victoria* (liner)
709 $2 *Queen Elizabeth 2* (liner)
Set of 4   2.00   2.75

1984

760† 35c 18th-century British warship and ship's boat 20 30
762† $1 18th-century British warship 40 60

786† $4 Battle of Jutland, 1916, and royal arms 75 75
787† $4 Battle of Jutland, 1916, and King George V 75 75

1985

No. 672 surcharged **$1.50 CARIBBEAN ROYAL VISIT 1985**
937 $1.50 on $4 Royal Yacht *Britannia* 2.00 2.50

1986

952† 60c *Santa Maria* (Columbus) 30 35
956† $2.75 *Santa Maria* 1.40 1.50

1987

1115† $10 Fishing boats (on $10 currency note) 4.25 4.50

1988

1125† 15c *Santa Maria* (Columbus) 15 15
1126† 75c *Nina* and *Pinta* (Columbus) 50 50
1128† $1.50 *Santa Maria* (Columbus) 90 90
MS1131† $5 *Santa Maria* (Columbus) 4.25 4.75

1132† 10c Sailboard 20 25
1136† $5 Cruising yacht 2.10 2.25

1137 15c *Nuestra Senora del Rosario* (Spanish galleon) and ships of Spanish Armada
1138 75c *Ark Royal* (galleon)
1139 $1.50 English fleet
1140 $2 Dismasted Spanish galleon
1141 $3 English fireships in action at Calais
1142 $5 *Revenge* (English galleon)
Set of 6   4.75   5.25
MS1143 $8 Spanish Armada 3.50 3.75

1989

1189† 40c Noah's Ark 15 20

1221 10c *Ile de France* (liner)
1222 40c *Liberte* (liner)
1223 50c *Mauretania I* (liner), 1906
1224 75c *France* (liner)
1225 $1 *Aquitania* (liner)
1226 $2 *United States* (liner)
1227 $3 *Olympic* (liner)
1228 $4 *Queen Elizabeth* (liner)
Set of 8   6.25   6.00
MS1229 Two sheets (a) $6 *Queen Mary* (liner); (b) $6 *Queen Elizabeth 2* (liner)
Price for 2 sheets   7.00   7.50

1258 30c French schooner
1259 55c French sail corvette
1260 75c French sail frigate
1261 $1 French ship of the line
1262 $3 *Ville de Paris* (French ship of the line)
Set of 5   3.25   3.25

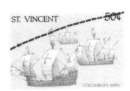

1308† 50c Columbus's fleet 20 25
1317† 50c Caravel and dugout canoe 20 25
1319† 50c Caravel 20 25

MS1506 Two sheets (a) $5 Scout in Indian canoe (other sheet shows colour party)
Price for 2 sheets   5.50   6.00

1990

1512† 5c *Admiral Graf Spee* (German pocket battleship) on fire, 1939 .... 10 10
1515† 25c U.S.S. *Reuben James* (destroyer), 1941 .... 10 15
1518† 55c H.M.S. *King George V* (battleship) engaging *Bismarck* (German battleship), 1941 .... 20 25
1519† 75c American battleships entering Tokyo Bay, 1945 .... 35 40
1521† $6 American aircraft carriers, Battle of Philippine Sea, 1944 .... 2.50 2.75

Nos. 1221/9 overprinted with Rotary International symbol
1564 10c *Ile de France* (liner)
1565 40c *Liberte* (liner)
1566 50c *Mauretania I* (liner), 1906
1567 75c *France* (liner)
1568 $1 *Aquitania* (liner)
1569 $2 *United States* (liner)
1570 $3 *Olympic* (liner)
1571 $4 *Queen Elizabeth* (liner)
Set of 8   4.50   5.00
MS1572 Two sheets (a) $6 *Queen Mary* (liner); (b) $6 *Queen Elizabeth 2* (liner)
Price for 2 sheets   5.25   5.50

1587† 10c Fishing boat 10 10
MS1595† Four sheets (c) $6 Fishing boat (other sheets show different Rubens paintings)
Price for 4 sheets   10.50   11.00

1991

1641†	3c *Santa Maria* (Columbus) (on U.S.A. stamp No. 237)	10	10
1642†	4c Fleet of Columbus (on U.S.A. stamp No. 238)	10	10
1655†	$10 *Santa Maria*, parrot and flower	4.25	4.50
1656†	$10 *Santa Maria* and compass rose	4.25	4.50
MS1657†	Two sheets (a) $6 Ship's fo'c'sle; (b) $6 Figurehead		
	Prices for 2 sheets	5.25	5.50

MS1685†	Two sheets (a) $6 Bow of caravel; (b) $6 Caravel		
	Price for 2 sheets	5.25	5.50

1992

1862†	20c Freighter and yachts	10	10
MS1865†	Two sheets (a) $6 Small craft, Kingstown (other sheet shows beach)	5.25	5.50

OFFICIAL STAMPS

1982

Nos. 668, 670 and 672 overprinted **OFFICIAL**

O1†	60c Royal Yacht *Isabella*	25	25
O3†	$2.50 *Alberta* (royal yacht tender)	50	50
O5†	$4 Royal Yacht *Britannia*	80	80

SAMOA

West Pacific
1901 100 pfennig = 1 mark
1935 12 pence = 1 shilling
20 shillings = 1 pound
1967 100 sene = 1 tala

1901

As Nos. K7/19 of Cameroun, but inscribed "SAMOA"

G7	3pf *Hohenzollern* (German Imperial yacht)	
G8	5pf *Hohenzollern*	
G9	10pf *Hohenzollern*	
G10	20pf *Hohenzollern*	
G11	25pf *Hohenzollern*	
G12	30pf *Hohenzollern*	
G13	40pf *Hohenzollern*	
G14	50pf *Hohenzollern*	
G15	80pf *Hohenzollern*	
G16	1m *Hohenzollern*	
G17	2m *Hohenzollern*	
G18	3m *Hohenzollern*	
G19	5m *Hohenzollern*	
	Set of 13 £140 £750	

1914

Nos. G7/19 surcharged **G.R.I.** *and value in British currency*

101	½d on 3pf *Hohenzollern*	
102	½d on 5pf *Hohenzollern*	
103	1d on 10pf *Hohenzollern*	
104	2½d on 20pf *Hohenzollern*	
105	3d on 25pf *Hohenzollern*	
106	4d on 30pf *Hohenzollern*	
107	5d on 40pf *Hohenzollern*	
108	6d on 50pf *Hohenzollern*	
109	9d on 80pf *Hohenzollern*	
110	1s on 1m *Hohenzollern*	
111	2s on 2m *Hohenzollern*	
112	2s on 2m *Hohenzollern*	
113	3s on 3m *Hohenzollern*	
114	5s on 5m *Hohenzollern*	
	Set of 13 £9000 £8000	

1935

182†	2d Outrigger canoe	2.50	1.75
184†	4d Bonito-fishing canoe	40	15

1952

224†	6d Bonito-fishing canoe	50	10

1962

243†	6d Liner	20	10

1968

309†	25s *La Boudeuse* and *L'Etoile* (Bougainville), 1768	60	25

1969

328†	20s Olympic yacht	10	10

1970

341	5s Wreck of *Adler* (German steam gunboat), Apia, 1889		
342	7s U.S.S. *Nipsic* (steam sloop), Apia, 1889		
343	10s H.M.S. *Calliope* (screw corvette), Apia, 1889		
344	20s Wrecked small craft, Apia, 1889		
	Set of 4	3.25	1.50

347†	20s Canoe	1.75	60

352†	30s H.M.S. *Endeavour* (Cook)	2.75	1.75

1971

MS364	70s Fautasi (large canoe)	85	1.40

1972

378†	1s *Mini Lagoon* (freighter)	10	10

386	2s *Arend, Thienhoven* and *Africaansche Galey* (Roggeveen), 1722		
387	8s *Arend, Thienhoven* and *Africaansche Galey*, 1722		
388	10s Two of Roggeveen's ships and outrigger canoe, 1772		
389	30s Two of Roggeveen's ships and outrigger canoe, 1772		
	Set of 4	2.50	1.60

399b†	$4 Game fishing launch	5.00	7.00

1974

431†	20s *Mariposa* (cargo liner) at wharf, Apia	35	15
433†	50s *Age Unlimited* (raft), 1963	80	1.00

1975

444 1s *Joyita* (inter-island coaster) at Apia,
     1955
445 8s *Joyita* at sea
446 20s Crew leaving *Joyita*
447 22s *Joyita* and crew in life rafts
448 50s *Joyita* drifting

                                    Set of 5   1.90   1.75

1976

461† 20s Sinking of *Bonhomme Richard*
      (American frigate), 1779   60   35

466† 12s Fishing canoe   15   10
467† 22s Fishing canoe   30   10

1977

479† 12s Royal Yacht *Britannia* at Apia   20   10
481† 32s Royal Yacht *Britannia*   50   25

491† 50s *Energy* (schooner), 1877   80   1.00

1978

514† 26s Collier, Whitby, 1766   70   35
515† 50s H.M.S. *Resolution* (Cook) 1.25   1.50

1979

540 12s *Charles W. Morgan* (19th-century
     whaling ship)
541 14s *Lagoda* (19th-century whaling ship)
542 24s *James T. Arnold* (19th-century
     whaling ship)
543 50s *Splendid* (19th-century whaling ship)
                                    Set of 4   2.25   1.10

1980

561 12s *William Hamilton* (19th-century
     whaling ship)
562 14s *California* (19th-century whaling ship)
563 24s *Liverpool II* (19th-century whaling
     ship)
564 50s *Two Brothers* (19th-century whaling
     ship)
                                    Set of 4   2.25   1.10

MS571 $1 *Fautasi* (large canoe) 1.00   1.50

1981

584 12s *Ocean* (19th-century whaling ship)
585 18s *Horatio* (19th-century whaling ship)
586 27s H.M.S. *Calliope* (screw corvette),
     1884
587 32s H.M.S. *Calypso* (screw corvette),
     1883
                                    Set of 4   1.25   90

591† 32s H.M.S. *Alisma* (corvette) and convoy,
      1941   40   30

MS606 $2 Game fishing launch 1.25   1.50

1982

616† 18s *Forum Samoa* (container ship)   30   20

1984

673 32s Liner at wharf, Apia
674 48s U.S.S. *Trenton* (screw frigate), 1889
675 60s *Forum Samoa* (container ship)
676 $1 *Matua* (inter-island freighter)
                                    Set of 4   1.75   1.75

1986

731† 48s U.S.S. *Vincennes* (sail frigate)   30   35
733† 60s U.S.S. *Swan* (patrol boat)   35   40

1987

746† 60s Local longboat race   65   40

767† 80s Canoe   45   50

1988

779† 45s Sailing canoe   25   30

811† 60s Fishing canoe   45   35

1989

822 50s *Eber* (German gunboat), 1889
823 65s *Olga* (German corvette), 1889
824 85s H.M.S. *Calliope* (screw corvette),
     1889
825 $2 U.S.S. *Vandalia* (corvette), 1889
                                    Set of 4   3.75   3.75

1990

840†	18s Pao pao (outrigger canoe)	15	15
841†	55s Fautasi (large canoe)	35	40
843†	$3 *Lady Samoa* (ferry)	1.75	2.00

845†	$3 *Adler* (German steam gunboat), 1889	2.00	2.00

SAN MARINO

Southern Europe
100 centisimi = 1 lira

1942

243†	1li25 Galleon, Arbe	10	10
244†	1li75 Galleon, Arbe	10	10
245†	2li75 Galleon, Arbe	25	30
246†	5li Galleon, Arbe	2.00	3.50

1952

426†	2li Fleet of Columbus	10	15
433†	25li Fleet of Columbus	1.75	70

As No. 426, but colours changed, overprinted **FIERA DI TRIESTE**
1952

439†	2li Fleet of Columbus	10	15

1955

490	100li Yacht	3.25	1.50

1956

As No. 490, but additionally inscribed "1956"
518	100li Yacht	1.75	1.25

1959

592†	200li Fishing boats, Palermo	75	65

1960

623	30li Fishing boat, Riccione		
624	125li Fishing boat, Riccione (air)		
	Set of 2	1.50	1.25

1961

629†	4li 16th-century wildfowl punt	10	10

1962

686†	70li Modern wildfowl punt	20	15

1963

690	1li Egyptian merchant ship, 2000 B.C.	
691	2li 5th-century B.C. Greek trier	
692	3li 1st-century B.C. Roman trireme	
693	4li 10th-century Viking longship	
694	5li *Santa Maria* (Columbus)	
695	10li Carrack, *c.* 1550	
696	30li Galley, *c.* 1600	
697	60li *Sovereign of the Seas* (English galleon), 1637	
698	70li Danish ship of the line, *c.* 1750	
699	115li *Duncan Dunbar* (full-rigged merchantman), 1850	
	Set of 10	3.50 2.75

1970

891	230li 16th-century naval battle, Bay of Naples	30	30

1971

907	20li Gondolas, Venice	
908	180li Gondolas, Venice	
909	200li Gondolas, Venice	
	Set of 3	70 65

1973

960†	200li 17th-century shipping, New York ..	35	35

1980

1144	200li Tugs, London, 1850		
1145	400li H.M.S. *President* (drillship), London		
	Set of 2	70	70

1983

1211†	500li Piccard's bathyscaphe, 1948	1.00	1.00

1215†	400li Fishing boats, Rio de Janeiro, 1845	35	35

1988

1324†	1200li Liner	1.40	1.40

1991

1402†	3000li *Santa Maria*, *Pinta* and *Nina* (Columbus)	4.50	4.50

1992

1417	1500li Columbus's fleet		
1418	2000li Columbus's fleet and map of voyages		
	Set of 2	3.50	3.50

1432	750li Caravel		
1433	850li Caravel		
	Set of 2	1.60	1.60

SARAWAK

South-east Asia
100 cents = 1 dollar

1949
As No. 115 of Antigua

168†	15c Paddle-steamer	1.40	2.25

1955

194†	12c Barong panau (sailing prau)	3.00	55

SAUDI ARABIA

Arabia
1945 110 guerche = 10 riyals
1961 5 halalahs = 1 guerche (piastre)
20 guerche = 1 riyal
1976 100 halalas = 1 riyal

1945

352	½g *Fakhr el Bihar* (Egyptian royal yacht)		
353	3g *Fakhr el Bihar*		
354	5g *Fakhr el Bihar*		
355	10g *Fakhr el Bihar*		
	Set of 4	65.00	32.00

1961

446	3p Freighter at wharf, Dammam		
447	6p Freighter at wharf, Dammam		
448	8p Freighter at wharf, Dammam		
	Set of 3	5.50	1.10

1976

Size 36 × 26 mm

1167	5h Oil rig
1168	10h Oil rig
1169a	15h Oil rig
1170	20h Oil rig
1171	25h Oil rig
1172	30h Oil rig
1173	35h Oil rig
1174	40h Oil rig
1175	45h Oil rig

1176b	50h Oil rig
1177	55h Oil rig
1179	65h Oil rig
1180	1r Oil rig
1181	2r Oil rig

	Set of 14	30.00	4.25

1982
As Nos. 1167/80 but smaller, 25 × 20 mm

1306a	5h Oil rig
1307c	10h Oil rig
1308c	15h Oil rig
1309c	20h Oil rig
1310	25h Oil rig
1315c	50h Oil rig
1318c	65h Oil rig
1325c	1r Oil rig

	Set of 8	2.75	1.40

1983

1355	20h *Bar'zan* (container ship)		
1356	65h *Al Drieya* (container ship)		
	Set of 2	1.60	85

SELANGOR

South-east Asia
100 cents = 1 dollar

1949
As No. 115 of Antigua

112†	15c Paddle-steamer	45	45

1957

123†	20c Malay fishing prau	25	10

1961

135†	20c Malay fishing prau	60	10

SENEGAL

West Africa
100 centimes = 1 franc

1931
As No. 109 of Cameroun

138†	1f50 *Leconte de Lisle* (liner)	1.40	1.40

1935

139†	1c Canoe, Dakar	10	30
140†	2c Canoe, Dakar	10	25
141†	3c Canoe, Dakar	10	25
142†	4c Canoe, Dakar	10	30

143†	5c Canoe, Dakar	10	15
144†	10c Canoe, Dakar	10	20
145†	15c Canoe, Dakar	10	15
146†	20c Canoe, Dakar	10	20
147†	25c Canoe, Dakar	25	15
148†	30c Canoe, Dakar	15	30
150†	40c Canoe, Dakar	15	20
151†	45c Canoe, Dakar	15	30

1937
As Nos. 110/11 of Cameroun

194†	20c Liner	40	60
195†	30c Sailing ships	40	55

1944
Nos. 140 and 145 surcharged

219†	1f50 on 15c Canoe, Dakar	40	30
221†	4f50 on 15c Canoe, Dakar	40	40
222†	5f50 on 2c Canoe, Dakar	85	80
224†	10f on 15c Canoe, Dakar	1.10	1.00

1961

241†	1f Pirogue racing	10	10

1964

276†	5f Titanium sand dredger	15	15
281†	85f Bulk carrier at wharf, Dakar	1.60	1.10

1965

301†	60f *Alsace* (cable ship)	80	50

306	10f Goree sailing pirogue
307	20f Large pirogue, Soumbedioun
308	30f Pirogue, Fadiouth Island
309	45f Pirogue, River Senegal

	Set of 4	1.90	1.10

1966

344†	25f *France* (liner), Dakar	1.00	20

1969

418†	45f Pirogues, Fadiouth Island	75	20

1970

424	500f Sailing pirogue	5.00	2.75

432†	75f Japanese sampan	55	30

1972

484	50f Gondolas, Venice		
485	100f Gondolas, Venice		
	Set of 2	1.75	1.00

506	40f Freighter	50	15

1974

559	100f Packet steamer	1.25	60

1976

582	140f Game fishing launch		
583	200f Yachts		
	Set of 2	3.50	2.25

COLLECT BUTTERFLIES AND OTHER INSECTS ON STAMPS

A Stanley Gibbons thematic catalogue — available at £12.95 (p. + p. £3) from: Stanley Gibbons Publications, 5 Parkside, Christchurch Road, Ringwood, Hants. BH24 3SH.

1977

625†	5f Fishing pirogue	
627†	15f Fishing pirogue	

631†	80f River steamer	45	35

1978

652†	30f Racing canoes, Soumbedioun	20	15
653†	65f Racing canoes, Soumbedioun ...:....	45	25

1985

838†	150f Fishing canoe on beach	1.00	60

1987

890†	145f Canoe, Dakar (on stamp No. 148)	85	50

1989

978†	80f Sailboard	30	25

983†	145f Game fishing launch	1.00	55

1990

1068†	10f Pirogue, Basse-Casamance	10	10
1069†	25f Yachts, Goree	10	10

1991

1113†	180f *Santa Maria* (Columbus)	70	45
1114†	200f *Nina*	80	55
1115†	220f *Pinta*	90	60
1116†	500f Caravels (from woodcuts)	2.00	1.25

SERBIA

100 paras = 1 dinar

GERMAN OCCUPATION

1941

G46†	50p + 1d Paddle-steamer, Smederovo	15	70
G49†	2d + 4d Paddle-steamer, Smederovo	40	2.00

SEYCHELLES

Indian Ocean
100 cents = 1 rupee

1938

137†	6c Fishing pirogue (orange)	4.25	2.50
137ab†	6c Fishing pirogue (green)	40	50
140†	20c Fishing pirogue (blue)	35.00	5.50
140ab†	20c Fishing pirogue (yellow)	85	55
143a†	45c Fishing pirogue	1.00	1.00
146†	1r Fishing pirogue (green)	95.00	48.00
146a†	1r Fishing pirogue (black)	1.50	60
149†	5r Fishing pirogue	4.50	3.00

1949

As No. 115 of Antigua

155†	50c Paddle-steamer	35	40

1952

Design as Nos. 137/49, but full face portrait

161†	15c Fishing pirogue	40	65
163†	20c Fishing pirogue	90	60
166†	45c Fishing pirogue	60	30

1954

Design as Nos. 161, 163, 166 and new value but with portrait of Queen Elizabeth II

177†	15c Fishing pirogue	15	15
179†	20c Fishing pirogue	30	20
182†	45c Fishing pirogue	20	15
183a†	70c Fishing pirogue	1.75	1.25

1957

*No. 182 surcharged **5 cents***

191	5c on 45c Fishing pirogue	10	10

1962

203† 45c Fishing pirogue 3.50 3.25

1967

No. 203 overprinted **UNIVERSAL ADULT SUFFRAGE 1967**
239† 45c Fishing pirogue 10 10

1968

No. 203 surcharged **60 CENTS**
247† 60c on 45c Fishing pirogue 10 10

253† 20c Ship's longboat, 1768 .... 20 10
254† 50c French warships, 1768 .... 25 15
256† 2r25 French warships, 1768 .... 65 50

1969

262† 5c French warship, 1742 .... 10 10
264† 15c *Konigsberg* (German cruiser)
(design shows the second cruiser of
this name, instead of the first) 1.75 25
265† 20c H.M.S. *Belfast* (cruiser), H.M.S.
Rapid (destroyer) and H.M.S. *Reward*
(tug), 1945 .... 30 10
270† 60c 18th-century merchantman under
attack 1.00 1.50
271† 65c 18th-century merchantman under
attack 2.00 3.00
275† 1r50 H.M.S. *Sybille* (frigate) and *Chiffone*
(French frigate), 1801 .... 1.75 2.00

1970

280† 20c French warship, 1770 .... 20 10
281† 50c French warship, 1770 .... 20 10

1971

No. 270 surcharged **65c**
304† 65c on 60c 18th-century merchantman,
under attack 40 75

1972

No. 265 overprinted **ROYAL VISIT 1972**
306† 20c H.M.S. *Belfast* (cruiser), H.M.S.
Rapid (destroyer) and H.M.S *Reward*
(tug), 1945 .... 15 20

316† 15c Pirogue racing 10 10

1975

Nos. 265 and 275 overprinted **VISIT OF Q.E. II** *and silhouette of
liner*
334† 20c H.M.S. *Belfast* (cruiser), H.M.S.
Rapid (destroyer) and H.M.S. *Reward*
(tug), 1945 .... 15 15
337† 1r50 H.M.S. *Sybille* (frigate) and *Chiffone*
(French frigate), 1801 .... 35 60

Nos. 265 and 271 overprinted **INTERNAL SELF-GOVERNMENT
OCTOBER 1975**
338† 20c H.M.S. *Belfast* (cruiser), H.M.S.
Rapid (destroyer) and H.M.S. *Reward*
(tug), 1945 .... 15 15
339† 65c 18th-century merchantman under
attack 25 30

1976

355† 20c English merchantman, 1609 .... 10 10
357† 40c French warship, 1770 .... 15 15

Nos. 265 and 271 overprinted **Independence 1976** *or
surcharged also*
374† 20c H.M.S. *Belfast* (cruiser), H.M.S.
Rapid (destroyer) and H.M.S. *Reward*
(tug), 1945 .... 25 55
382† 25r on 65c 18th-century merchantman
under attack 11.00 16.00

1977

402 1r50 *Aurora* (Russian cruiser), 1917 .... 35 30

1980

476† 5r Olympic yachts 60 40

480† 3r Cruise liner and pirogue 50 50
481† 5r *La Belle Coralline* (tourist launch) 70 75

485† 5r Fishing pirogue 55 55

1981

495 40c *Sao Gabriel* (Vasco da Gama), 1497
496 2r25 *Caravel* (Mascarenhas), 1505
497 3r50 H.M.S. *Beagle* (Darwin), 1831
498 5r *Queen Elizabeth 2* (liner), 1968
Set of 4 2.50 2.75

505† 1r50 Royal Yacht *Victoria and Albert I* 20 25
507† 5r Royal Yacht *Cleveland* 60 60
509† 10r Royal Yacht *Britannia* 1.00 1.50

1983

Nos. 505, 507 and 509 surcharged
573† 50c on 1r50 Royal Yacht *Victoria and
Albert I* 15 15
575† 2r25 on 5r Royal Yacht *Cleveland* 45 50
577† 3r75 on 10r Royal Yacht *Britannia* 75 80

1984

582† 10r Model pirogue 2.00 3.00

584† 2r Cargo liner, 1930's 55 55
585† 3r *Sun Viking* (cruise liner) 80 80
586† 10r R.F.A *Ennerdale II* (tanker) 2.25 2.75

599† 3r Yacht 80 75

1985

611† 3r Sailboards 1.50 95

622† 10r Sailboards 2.40 2.40

1986

644† 50c Inter-island sailing ferry 50 10

1987

680† 2r Trawler 45 50

1988

683† 1r Sailboard 20 25
684† 2r Speedboat and yachts 45 50
685† 3r Yacht 70 75

702† 2r Cinq Juin (travelling post office) 1.25 55
703† 3r Queen Elizabeth 2 (liner) 1.75 80

707† 3r Andromanche (patrol boat) 1.75 1.60

1989

752† 2r Liberty (hospital ship), 1914–18 ...... 95 85

765† 3r Variola (fishing boat) 1.40 1.00
766† 10r Deneb (fishing boat) 4.00 4.50

1992

812† 3r Shipping in Victoria harbour 1.10 1.10

SHARJAH

Arabia
1964 100 naye paise = 1 rupee
1966 100 dirhams = 1 riyal

1964

81† 20np Mr. Gus (oil rig) 30 15

1965

115† 5np Medieval ship 10 10
116† 5np Savannah (nuclear-powered
freighter) 10 10

166† 1np Monarch IV (cable ship) 10 10
170† 5np Monarch IV 10 10

Appendix

The following stamps have either been issued in excess of postal needs or have not been available to the public in reasonable quantities at face value. Miniature sheets, imperforate stamps etc., are excluded from this section.

1967
Famous Paintings. 5d 18th-century sea battle

1969
"Apollo 8" Moon Mission. Postage 5d; Air 4r American aircraft carrier

Post Day. Famous Sailing Ships. Postage 5d × 8; Air 90d × 8

"Apollo 12" Moon Mission. Overprinted on Post Day. Famous Sailing Ships issue. 5d × 8

1970
5th Anniversary of Ruler's Accession. Postage 5d; Air 35, 40, 60d Freighter at wharf

1971
Safe Return of "Apollo 13". Overprinted on 1969 "Apollo 8" issue. 4r American aircraft carrier

1972
Olympic Games, Munich. 15d Yacht
Munich Olympic Medal Winners. 5r Yacht
13th World Jamboree. Postage 2d; Air 35d Chinese junk

SIERRA LEONE

West Africa
1933 12 pence = 1 shilling
20 shillings = 1 pound
1964 100 cents = 1 leone

1933

174† 5d Bullom sailing canoe 6.50 16.00
175† 6d Dugout canoe 6.50 8.00

1949

As No. 115 of Antigua
206† 3d Paddle-steamer 35 90

1956

217† 1s Bullom sailing canoe 80 10

1961

239† 1s3d Royal Yacht Britannia 1.75 30

1963

No. 239 overprinted **1853–1959–1963 Oldest Postage Stamp Newest G.P.O. in West Africa AIRMAIL**
280† 1s3d Royal Yacht Britannia 1.00 55

1969

479 1c Ore carrier
480 2c Ore carrier
481 3½c Ore carrier
482 10c Ore carrier
483 18½c Ore carrier
484 50c Ore carrier

485 7½c Ore carrier (air)
486 9½c Ore carrier
487 15c Ore carrier
488 25c Ore carrier
489 1le Ore carrier
490 2le Ore carrier

Set of 12 5.00 7.00

1980

640 6c Maria (packet schooner), 1884
641 31c Tarquah (steam packet), 1902
642 50c Aureol (liner), 1951
643 1le Africa Palm (container ship), 1974

Set of 4 1.10 1.75

654† 50c Speedboat 40 40

1981

667† 1le Navy patrol boat 2.50 1.25

686† 6c Freighter 10 10

1983

751† 10c Mail canoe, River Mano 10 10
753† 1le British sailing packet, c. 1805 ...... 55 65

1984

820 2c Portuguese caravel
821 5c *Merlin* (British galleon)
822 10c *Golden Hind* (Drake)
823 15c *Mordaunt* (British galleon)
824 20c *Atlantic* (sail transport)
825 25c H.M.S. *Lapwing* (frigate), 1785
826 30c *Traveller* (brig)
827 40c *Amistad* (schooner)
828 50c H.M.S. *Teazer* (gun vessel), 1868
829 70c *Scotia* (cable ship)
830 1le H.M.S. *Alecto* (paddle-steamer), 1882
831 2le H.M.S. *Blonde* (cruiser), 1889
832 5le H.M.S. *Fox* (cruiser), 1893
833 10le *Accra* (liner)
833c 15le H.M.S. *Favourite* (sloop), 1829
833d 25le H.M.S. *Euryalus* (screw frigate), 1883

Set of 16 38.00 27.00

835† 2le H.M.S. *Euryalus* (screw frigate), 1855 1.25 65

1985

863† 1le25 Langley's aircraft-launching barge,
1903 .... 1.75 1.50

1986

960† 1le Large cargo canoe 10 10
963† 10le Fishing canoe 55 55

Nos. 820, 826/7 and 829 surcharged
964 30le on 2c Portuguese caravel
965 40le on 30c *Traveller* (brig)
966 45le on 40c *Amistad* (schooner)
967 50le on 70c *Scotia* (cable ship)
Set of 4 8.75 9.00

1987

MS1000 60le Early 19th-century British
warship, Freetown 2.50 2.75

1011 1le *U.S.A.* (yacht), 1987
1012 1le50 *New Zealand II* (yacht), 1987
1013 2le50 *French Kiss* (yacht), 1987
1014 10le *Stars and Stripes* (yacht), 1987
1015 15le *Australia II* (yacht), 1983
1016 25le *Freedom* (yacht), 1980
1017 30le *Kookaburra* (yacht), 1987
Set of 7 3.00 3.50
MS1018 50le *Constellation* (yacht), 1964 ...... 2.00 2.50

1077† 5le *Santa Maria* (Columbus) 25 20
1078† 10le *Pinta* (Columbus) 40 35
1079† 45le *Nina* (Columbus) 1.50 1.60

1092† 15le Scout sailing dinghy 55 60

1988

Nos 1016 and 1079 overprinted **INDEPENDENCE 40** *(No. 1131)*
or **Praga 88** *(No. 1133), each with Exhibition symbol*
1131† 25le *Freedom* (yacht), 1980 .... 75 80
1133† 45le *Nina* (Columbus) 1.25 1.40

1151 31e *Aureol* (liner)
1152 10le *Dunkwa* (freighter)
1153 15le *Melampus* (container ship)
1154 30le *Dumbaia* (freighter)
Set of 4 3.75 3.75
MS1155 65le Container ship, Freetown 1.90 2.25

1166† 5le American aircraft carrier 15 20

1172† 20le Hospital ship and sinking warship,
Second World War 1.25 1.25

1989

1321† 25le Japanese ferry, Kawasaki 20 20
1330† 25le Fishing boat, Ejiri 20 20
1335† 25le Ferry, Mistuke 20 20
1344† 25le Fishing boats, Kuwana 20 20

1990

1417† 1le American warships 10 10
1419† 3le Japanese convoy 10 10
MS1427† Two sheets (a) 150le U.S.S. *Hornet*
(aircraft carrier) (other sheet shows B17
aircraft)
Price for 2 sheets 90 95

1436† 200le Trawler 60 65

1440† 9le 15th-century English kogge 10 10
1441† 16le Greek galley 10 10
1444† 70le Gondola 20 25

1991

1636† 250le Fishing boats, Saintes-Maries 75 80

MS1670† Three sheets (c) 450le Burning
American cruiser (from film *Tora, Tora, Tora*)
(other sheets show different film shots)
Price for 3 sheets 3.75 4.00

1728† 250le Scout yacht 75 80

1736† 75le Japanese dive bomber and
American warships, Pearl Harbor 20 25
1737† 75le Japanese air attack on American
warships 20 25
1738† 75le American battleships on fire 20 25
1742† 75le American cruisers under attack 20 25
1746† 75le Anchored American warships 20 25
1747† 75le Japanese aircraft attacking
American warships 20 25

1992

MS1773† Three sheets (b) 700le Gondola,
Venice (other sheets show different countries)
Price for 3 sheets 6.25 6.00

1777† 400le Canoe .... 1.25 1.·40

1828† 200le Sailboard 60 65

1920† 400le Submarine 1.25 1.40

1932 300le Caravel
1933 500le Ship's boat and Columbus's fleet
Set of 2 2.40 2.50

SINGAPORE

South-east Asia
100 cents = 1 dollar

1949

As No. 115 *of Antigua*
34† 15c Paddle-steamer 3.25 1.40

1955

38† 1c Chinese sampan 10 40
39† 2c Malay fishing kolek 60 1.00
40† 4c Twa-kow lighter 45 15
41† 5c Lombok sloop 35 15
42† 6c Trengganu pinas 35 30
43† 8c Palari (schooner) 55 70
44† 10c Timber tongkong 2.25 10
45† 12c Hainan junk 2.25 2.50
46† 20c Cocos-Keeling schooner 1.10 10
48† 30c Tanker 2.00 10
49† 50c *Chusan III* (liner) 1.25 10

1970

143 15c *Neptune Aquamarine* (freighter)
144 30c Container ship
145 75c Tanker under construction
Set of 3 8.50 8.50

1971

151† 20c Sampans and houseboats 55 40
153† 50c Freighters, tugs and sampans 2.75 4.50

165† 10c Sampans, 1843 .... 1.75 1.25
167† 20c Junks, 1848 .... 3.25 3.00
170† $1 Shipping off Singapore, 1861 .... 12.00 15.00

1972

185 15c *Neptune Ruby* (container ship)
186 75c *Maria Rickmers* (barque)
187 $1 Chinese junk
Set of 3 8.50 11.00

1973

196† $1 Sampan and houseboats 3.25 4.25

1975

247† 20c Houseboats 60 70
248† $1 Fishing sampans 2.75 6.00

251† 50c Tanker 1.40 2.25
252† $1 Container ship 2.25 4.50

1976

279†   10c Junk and sampans, *c.* 1905   30   10

1977

302†   10c Freighter   15   10

1978

335   10c *Neptune Spinel* (bulk carrier)
336   35c *Neptune Aries* (tanker)
337   50c *Anro Temasek* (container ship)
338   75c *Neptune Pearl* (container ship)
            Set of 4   1.60   2.75

1980

364   1c Hainan junk
365   5c Full-rigged clipper ship
366   10c Fujian junk
367   15c Golekkan (sailing craft)
368   20c Palari (sailing craft)
369   25c East Indiaman
370   35c Galleon
371   50c Caravel
372   75c Jiangsu trading junk
373   $1 *Kedah* (coaster)
374   $2 *Murex* (tanker)
375   $5 *Chusan* (screw steamer)
376   $10 *Braganza* (paddle-steamer)
            Set of 13   12.00   12.50

1982

431   10c Container ship at berth
432   35c Container ship at berth
433   50c Container ship at berth
434   75c Container ship at berth
            Set of 4   90   1.00

1983

466† $1 Freighter   65   95

1986

535   10c *Vercors* (cable ship)
536   35c *Vercors*
537   50c *Vercors*
538   75c *Vercors*
            Set of 4   1.75   1.75

1987

554†   10c Patrol boat   20   30
MS557†   35c Patrol boat (sheet contains four
   other designs) 1.75   1.50

558†   10c Dragon boats   10   10
559†   50c Fishing punt   45   40

1989

588   10c Container ships
589   30c Liners, tug, container ships and tanker
590   75c Container ships
591   $1 Container ships and tanker
            Set of 4   2.00   1.75

1990

617†   75c Sail warship, 1837   85   70

627†   25c Dragon boats   20   25
631†   50c Chinese New Year boat float   40   45

637†   15c Missile gunboats   30   15

1992

677†   20c Sampans   30   20
679† $1 Sampans   95   1.10
680† $2 Sampans 1.90   2.25

694† $1 Missile corvette 1.25   1.40

697† $1 Dragon boat 1.10   1.10

704† $1 Palari schooner (on currency note) . .   95   95

SLOVAKIA

Central Europe
100 haleru = 1 koruna

1939

No. 362 of Czechoslovakia optd **Slovensky stat 1939**
22†   10k River tug and barge, Bratislava 80.00   90.00

SLOVENIA

South-east Europe
1945 100 centesimi = 1 lira
1992 Tolar

1945

119†   10c Punt, Lake Zirknitz   20   1.50

1992

158† 47t *Santa Maria* (Columbus) 60 60

SOLOMON ISLANDS

West Pacific
1907 12 pence = 1 shilling
20 shillings = 1 pound
1966 100 cents = 1 dollar

1907

1	½d War canoe		
2	1d War canoe		
3	2d War canoe		
4	2½d War canoe		
5	5d War canoe		
6	6d War canoe		
7	1s War canoe		

Set of 7 £225 £275

1908

8	½d War canoe		
9	1d War canoe		
10	2d War canoe		
11	2½d War canoe		
11a	4d War canoe		
12	5d War canoe		
13	6d War canoe		
14	1s War canoe		
15	2s War canoe		
16	2s6d War canoe		
17	5s War canoe		

Set of 11 £150 £225

1939

62†	1½d Malaita canoes	35	90
63†	2d Canoe and canoe house	30	1.00
64†	2½s Roviana canoe	70	65
65†	3d Roviana canoes	30	70
71†	5s Malaita canoe	25.00	8.00

1949

As No. 115 of Antigua
78† 3d Paddle-steamer 1.25 70

1956

82†	½d Ysabel canoe	15	50
83†	1d Roviana canoes	15	15
84†	1½d Malaita canoes	15	40
85†	2d Canoe and canoe house	20	30
86†	2½d Roviana canoe prow	30	45
87†	3d Malaita canoe	25	15
89†	6d *Miena* (trading schooner)	50	25
91†	1s H.M.S. *Swallow* (Carteret), 1767	50	50
94†	5s *Todos los Santos* (Mendana), 1568	12.00	2.00

1965

126† £1 Western canoe figurehead 11.00 5.00

1966

No. 126 surcharged
152† $2 on £1 Western canoe figurehead 5.00 3.00

1968

162†	3c *Todos los Santos* (Mendana), 1568 ..	15	10
164†	35c "King George V" class battleship, 1939–45	30	10
165†	$1 H.M.S. *Curacoa* (corvette), 1893	50	1.10

167†	2c Fishing canoe	10	10
172†	12c Boat building	65	40
179†	$1 *Kylix* (tanker) and *Hollybank* (freighter)	2.50	2.00

1970

192†	14c War canoe (on stamp No. 3)	25	15
193†	18c War canoe (on stamp No. 17)	25	15

1971

201†	3c *La Boussole* (La Perouse), 1787	55	20
203†	12c *Heemskerk* (Tasman), 1643	1.50	45
204†	35c Te Puki outrigger canoe, Santa Cruz	3.00	75

206†	4c Missionary schooner, 1871	10	10
208†	45c Canoe	20	10

1972

215†	4c *La Boudeuse* (Bougainville), 1776	30	10
217†	15c H.M.S. *Swallow* (Carteret), 1707	85	15
218†	45c Malaita canoe	3.75	1.25

1973

236†	4c *La Recherche* (D'Entrecasteaux), 1791	30	15
238†	15c H.M.S. *Alexander* (Shortland), 1788	75	20
239†	35c Tomoko (war canoe)	3.25	1.75

1974

254†	4c *Titus* (freighter)	20	10
256†	15c "Blackbirder" brig (illegal labour ship)	40	15
257†	45c U.S.S. *PT 109* (motor torpedo-boat), 1943	2.00	1.25

1975

272	4c *Walande* (coaster)		
273	9c *Melanesian* (coaster)		
274	15c *Marsina* (container ship)		
275	45c *Himalaya* (liner)		

Set of 4 1.75 1.60

1976

304† 45c Nguzu-nguzu canoe prow 30 25

322†	20c *Amagiri* (Japanese destroyer) ramming U.S.S. *PT 109* (motor torpedo-boat), 1943	60	30

1978

371† 45c Scout canoe 50 70

1979

372† 8c H.M.S. *Discovery* (Cook) 30 10

384† 8c War canoe (on stamp No. 13) 10 10

1980

409 8c H.M.S. *Curacoa* (frigate), 1839, and crest
410 20c H.M.S. *Herald* (survey ship), 1854, and crest
411 35c H.M.S. *Royalist* (screw corvette), 1889, and crest
412 45c H.M.S. *Beagle* (survey schooner), 1878, and crest

Set of 4 1.60 1.00

413 8c *Solomon Fisher* (fishery training vessel)
414 20c *Solomon Hunter* (fishery training vessel)
415 45c *Ufi Na Tasi* (refrigerated fish transport)
416 80c Fishery research vessel

Set of 4 1.10 1.50

417† 45c *Comliebank* (cargo liner) 25 40
420† 45c *Corabank* (container ship) 25 40

1981

430 8c H.M.S. *Mounts Bay* (frigate), 1959, and crest
431 20c H.M.S. *Charbydis* (frigate), 1970, and crest
432 45c H.M.S. *Hydra* (survey ship), 1972, and crest
433 $1 Royal Yacht *Britannia*, 1974, and crest

Set of 4 1.90 1.40

436† 45c *La Princesa* (Maurelle), 1781 . . . . . . 60 65

WHEN YOU BUY AN ALBUM LOOK FOR THE NAME "STANLEY GIBBONS"
It means Quality combined with Value for Money.

450† 45c Outrigger canoe 20 20

1982

MS475 $1 Royal Yacht *Britannia* (sheet also contains two other designs) 1.60 2.50

1983

510† 25c War canoe (on stamp No. 11) 35 30
511† $1 War canoe (on stamp No. 13) 1.25 1.40

1984

519 12c *Olivebank* (barque), 1892
520 15c *Tinhow* (freighter), 1906
521 18c *Oriana* (liner)
522 $1 *Silwyn Range* (container ship)

Set of 4 3.00 3.25

1985

MS542 $1.50 Gondola, Venice 1.40 1.50

545† 45c *Soltai No 7* (trawler) 40 45

547† 12c Outrigger canoe, Titiana 10 10
548† 35c Motorised canoe, Langa 25 30

550† 12c Brownie canoe 40 10

561† $1 *Sir Walter Raleigh* (support ship) and *Zebu* (brigantine) 2.00 1.60

1986

570a 18c *America*, 1851; *Magic*, 1870; *Puritan*, 1885; *Mayflower*, 1886; *Columbia*, 1899; *Columbia*, 1901; *Rainbow*, 1934; *Ranger*, 1937; *Intrepid*, 1967; *Intrepid*, 1970; *Mischief*, 1881; *Madeleine*, 1876; *Vigilant*, 1893; *Defender*, 1895; *Resolute*, 1920; *Enterprise*, 1930; *Weatherly*, 1962; *Constellation*, 1964; *Courageous*, 1977; *Freedom*, 1980; 30c *Columbia*, 1871; *Volunteer*, 1887; *Reliance*, 1903, *Columbia*, 1958; *Courageous*, 1974; *Australia II*, 1983; $1 *America II*, 1987; *South Australia*, 1987; *KA-14*, 1987; *Kookaburra*, 1987; *Eagle*, 1987; *Secret Cove*, 1987; *Courageous III*, 1987; *Crusader*, 1987; *Sail America*, 1987; *French Kiss*, 1987; *Heart of America*, 1987; *St. Francis IX*, 1987; *New Zealand II*, 1987; *Italia*, 1987; *True North*, 1987; *Azzurra*, 1987; *France*, 1987, *Australia III*, 1987 (all yachts, sheet also contains six other stamps) 25.00

1987

MS575 $5 *Stars and Stripes* (yacht), 1987 . . . . 3.25 3.50

1988

617† $1 Canoe 55 60

618†	22c Building fishing boat	15	15
619†	80c War canoe	40	45

622†	22c *Todos los Santos* (Mendana), 1568	35	15

626	35c *Papuan Chief* (container ship)		
627	60c *Nimos* (container ship)		
628	70c *Malaita* (freighter)		
629	$1.30 *Makambo* (inter-island freighter)		
	Set of 4	2.00	1.60

637†	50c *Forthbank* (container ship)	50	30
639†	$2 *Empress of China* (liner), 1911	1.75	1.75

1990

679†	50c War canoe (on stamp No. 1)	40	40

1991

709†	30c Tuna fishing boat	20	20

1992

715†	40c Fishing boats, Honiara harbour	30	30

718†	10c Mendana's galleons in Thousand Ships Bay, 1568	15	10
720†	80c Mendana's ships	70	70
721†	$1 Galleons at anchor, Graciosa Bay	90	90
722†	$5 *Todos los Santos* (Mendana)	3.00	3.25

728	25c *Santa Maria* (Columbus)		
729	80c *Santa Maria*		
730	$1.50 *Santa Maria*		
731	$5 *Santa Maria*		
	Set of 4	4.25	4.50

734†	30c American landing craft, Guadalcanal, 1942	20	20
735†	30c Australian cruiser	20	20
740†	80c U.S.S. *Quincy* (cruiser)	55	55
741†	80c H.M.A.S. *Canberra* (cruiser)	55	55
742†	80c American landing craft, Guadalcanal	55	55
743†	80c *Ryujo* (Japanese aircraft carrier)	55	55
746†	80c Japanese destroyer	55	55
747†	80c *Chockai* (Japanese cruiser)	55	55

1993

770†	$4 American aircraft carrier and local canoe	1.60	1.75

SOMALIA

East Africa
1924 100 besa = 1 rupia
1950 100 centesimi = 1 somalo

1924

No. 157 of Italy surcharged **SOMALIA ITALIANA besa 13**

56†	13b on 30c Ferry boat	25	2.00

1950

244†	30c Pirogue	30	30
245†	45c Pirogue	30	30
246†	65c Pirogue	30	30
247†	70c Pirogue	30	30
248†	90c Pirogue	30	30
249†	1s Pirogue	45	30
250†	1s35 Pirogue	70	70
251†	1s50 Pirogue	85	50
252†	3s Pirogue	7.00	2.25
253†	5s Pirogue	8.00	3.00
254†	10s Pirogue	9.50	2.25

1959

342†	1s20 Ancient Egyptian ships	25	25
343†	2s Freighter, Mogadishu	40	40

1979

632	75c Fishing punt		
633	80c Felucca		
634	2s30 Motor fishing boats		
635	2s50 Trawler		
	Set of 4	2.00	1.25

1983

707†	3s20 Modern warship	50	25

SOMALILAND PROTECTORATE

East Africa
12 pies = 1 anna
16 annas = 1 rupee

1949

As No. 115 *of Antigua*

122†	3a on 30c Paddle-steamer	30	30

SOUTH AFRICA

Southern Africa
1926 12 pence = 1 shilling
20 shillings = 1 pound
1961 100 cents = 1 rand

PRICES. Nos. 115, 106, 127 and O366 were issued inscribed in English or Afrikaans. The prices quoted are for one of each version in a horizontal pair.

1926

115†	1d *Dromedaris* (Van Riebeeck), 1652 (black & red)	35	40

1943

As No. 115 *but redrawn with plain background to centre oval*

106†	1d *Dromedaris* (red)	1.25	2.50

1949

127	1½d *Wanderer* (emigrant ship), 1849	30	30

1952

138†	2d Van Riebeeck's fleet, 1652	20	10

No. 138 overprinted **SADIPU**
142† 2d Van Riebeeck's fleet, 1652 .... 20 50

1961

324† 50c Freighter 4.50 1.25

1962

222 2½c *Chapman* (emigrant ship), 1820
223 12½c *Chapman*
Set of 2 3.00 1.90

1971

305† 2c Ship's boat, 1820 .... 15 10

1973

333† 5c Shipwreck of *De Jonge Thomas*
(Dutch East Indiaman), 1773 .... 40 10
334† 15c Shipwreck of *De Jonge Thomas* 5.50 6.00

1975

379† 5c Dutch East Indiaman, Table Bay 20 10

1976

409 10c Steam packet, 1876 .... 60 85

1978

439 15c Brig, Walvis Bay, 1878 .... 60 40

1980

481† 5c 17th-century Dutch yacht 10 10

1982

506 8c *Maria van Riejbeck* (submarine)
507 15c Missile patrol vessel
508 20c Minesweeper
509 25c Harbour patrol boats
Set of 4 70 1.40

1983

547† 25c Yacht 40 45

1988

633† 40c Caravels (Dias), 1488 .... 90 90

680† 50c *GEO* (midget submarine) 1.00 1.25

696† 18c Gas-drilling rig, Mossel Bay 30 10

1991

740† 27c *Agulhas* (Antarctic research ship) .. 30 10

1992

745† 35c Dutch East Indiaman approaching
Table Bay 25 25
746† 35c Ship's boat 25 25
748† 35c Dutch East Indiaman at anchor 25 25

1993

773† 55c Ore carrier, East London 35 35

794† 45c *Watussi* (German freighter) on fire,
1936 .... 20 20

OFFICIAL STAMPS

No. 115 overprinted **OFFICIAL OFFISIEEL**
O36b† 1d *Dromedaris* (Van Riebeeck), 1652 90 1.75

SOUTH GEORGIA
South Atlantic
1963 12 pence = 1 shilling
20 shillings = 1 pound
1971 100 pence = 1 pound

1963

6† 4d *R-1* (whale-catcher) 3.25 50
9† 9d *R-2* (whale-catcher) 3.75 30

1971
Nos. 6 and 9 surcharged in decimal currency
24† 4p on 4d *R-1* 90 50
26† 6p on 9d *R-2* 1.50 70

1972

32 1½p *Endurance* (Shackleton), 1915
33 5p *James Caird* (whaleboat), 1915
34 10p *James Caird*
35 20p *Quest* (Shackleton), 1921
Set of 4 5.50 3.25

1974

41† 25p H.M.S. *Belfast* (cruiser) 2.00 1.00

1975

44† 8p H.M.S. *Resolution* (Cook) 2.75 1.50

1976

46† 2p *Discovery* (Scott), 1901 .... 1.00 35
47† 8p *William Scoresby* (research ship) 1.40 50
48† 11p *Discovery II* (polar supply vessel) 1.75 55

1977

50†   6p Royal Yacht *Britannia*, 1957 80   30

1979

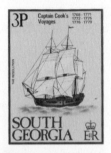

70†   3p H.M.S. *Resolution* (Cook) 1.50   80
71†   6p H.M.S. *Resolution* 1.50   70

SOUTH GEORGIA AND SOUTH SANDWICH ISLANDS

South Atlantic
100 pence = 1 pound

1988

184†   24p *Lindblad Explorer* (liner) 50   55
185†   29p Whale-catchers, Leith Harbour 60   65
186†   58p *Horatio* (tanker) on fire, 1916 ...... 1.10   1.25

1989

193†   29p H.M.S. *Protector* (ice patrol ship) 80   80

1990

197   12p *Brutus* (wreck), Prince Olav Harbour
198   26p *Bayard* (wreck), Ocean Harbour
199   31p *Karrakatta* (wreck), Husvik
200   62p *Louise* (wreck), Grytviken
                          Set of 4   3.50   3.50

1992

219†   29p + 11p *Queen Elizabeth 2* (liner) in
         Cumberland Bay 1.10   1.25
221†   68p + 32p H.M.S. *Endurance* (ice patrol
         ship) 2.75   3.00

SOUTH KOREA

See under Korea

SOUTH VIETNAM

See under Vietnam

SOUTH WEST AFRICA

Southern Africa
1926 12 pence = 1 shilling
20 shillings = 1 pound
1961 100 cents = 1 rand

1926

No. 115 *of South Africa overprinted* **South West Africa.** *or*
Suidwes Africa. *alternately*
46†   1d *Dromedaris* (Van Riebeeck), 1652 .... 1.40   2.50
         The prices quoted are for a horizontal pair, containing one of
each overprint

1927

No. 115 *of South Africa overprinted* **S. W .A.**
59†   1d *Dromedaris* (Van Riebeeck), 1652 .... 1.25   3.25
         No. 59 exists with the basic stamp inscribed in either English or
Afrikaans. The prices quoted are for one of each in a horizontal
pair.

1931

75†   1d Portuguese galleon, Cape Cross 1.25   2.00
         No. 75 exists inscribed in either English or Afrikaans. The prices
quoted are for one of each in a horizontal pair.

1937

96   1½d *Capetown Castle* (liner) 9.50   2.00
         No. 96 exists inscribed in either English or Afrikaans. The prices
quoted are for one of each in a horizontal pair.

1952

No. 138 *of South Africa overprinted* **SWA**
146†   2d Van Riebeeck's fleet, 1652 50   10

1961

177†   3½c Trawler 70   15

1971

As No. 305 of South Africa, but inscribed "SWA"
232†   2c Ship's boat, 1820 .... 3.25   75

1975

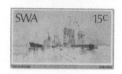

279†   15c Tanker at wharf 55   45
280†   15c Trawler and tug, Walvis Bay 55   45

1982

396†   25c Dias's caravel, 1488 55   40
397†   30c Dias's caravel, 1488 55   45

1983

420†   20c Lobster boat and dinghies 25   30
421†   25c Lobster dinghy 30   35

1984

434†   45c *Elisabeth* and *Leipzig* (German
         steam corvettes), 1884 .... 1.25   1.60

1986

457†   25c Diogo Cao's caravel, 1486 70   35

467†   14c Pirogue, Lake Liambezi 50   15

1987

483   16c Wreck of *Hope* (Dutch whaling
         schooner), 1804
484   30c Wreck of *Tilly* (brig), 1885
485   40c Wreck of *Eduard Bohlen* (steamer),
         1909
486   50c Wreck of *Dunedin Star* (liner), 1942
                          Set of 4   4.00   3.25

1988

488† 30c Caravel (Dias), 1488 .... 70 55

OFFICIAL STAMPS

1927

No. 46 overprinted **OFFICIAL** *or* **OFFISIEEL** *alternately*
O2† 1d *Dromedaris* (Van Riebeeck), 1652 .... 65.00 £150
The price quoted is for a horizontal pair containing one of each overprint.

1929

No. 59 overprinted **OFFICIAL** *or* **OFFISIEEL** *alternately*
O10† 1d *Dromedaris* (Van Riebeeck), 1652 .... 75 11.00
The prices quoted are for a horizontal pair containing one of each overprint.

1938

Nos. 75 and 96 overprinted **OFFICIAL** *or* **OFFISIEEL** *alternately*
O24† 1d *Portuguese galleon, Cape Cross* 1.50 10.00
O20† 1½d *Capetown Castle* (liner) 28.00 26.00
The prices quoted are for horizontal pairs containing one of each overprint.

SOUTHERN CAMEROONS

West Africa
12 pence = 1 shilling
20 shillings = 1 pound

1960

Nos. 69 and 80 of Nigeria overprinted **CAMEROONS U.K.T.T.**
1† ½d 19th-century brigantine and canoes .. 10 20
12† £1 Shipping at Lagos in 19th and 20th
centuries 6.50 1.00

SOUTHERN RHODESIA

Central Africa
12 pence = 1 shilling
20 shillings = 1 pound

1949

As No. 115 of Antigua
68† 2d Paddle-steamer 65 20

SPAIN

South-west Europe
100 centimos = 1 peseta

1929

502† 1c Caravel 20 20
506† 15c Caravel 40 25
508† 25c Caravel 55 35

1930

593† 1c *Santa Maria* (Columbus) 15 10

594† 2c *Santa Maria* (bow view) 15 10
595† 2c *Santa Maria* (stern view) 15 10
596† 5c *Santa Maria* (bow view) 15 10
597† 5c *Santa Maria* (stern view) 15 10
598† 10c *Santa Maria* 1.00 75
599† 15c *Santa Maria* 1.00 75
600† 20c *Santa Maria* 1.00 1.00
601† 25c *Santa Maria, Pinta and Nina* 1.00 1.00
602† 30c Ship's boat, 1492 .... 5.00 5.00
603† 40c *Santa Maria, Pinta and Nina* 4.75 4.00
604† 50c Ship's boat, 1492 .... 5.50 5.00
605† 1p *Santa Maria, Pinta and Nina* 5.50 5.00

651† 4p *Santa Maria* (Columbus) 2.25 3.00

1938

857a 1p *Isaac Peral* (submarine)
857b 2p *Narcisco Monturiol* (submarine)
857c 4p *B-2* (submarine)
857d 6p *Narcisco Monturiol*
857e 10p *B-2*
857f 15p *Isaac Peral*
Set of 6 £400 £425

MS924 2c, 5c (each x 2) *Almirante Cervera*
(cruiser) (sheet contains 16 other stamps) 30.00 22.00

MS937 50c Battle of Lepanto, 1571 .... 10.00 12.00

1940

997† 50c + 5c 15th-century caravel 25 20
1002† 1p40 + 40c 15th-century caravel 25 30

1949

1130† 5c Galleon 10 10
1131† 10c Galleon 10 10
1132† 50c + 10c Galleon 40 30

1955

1234 20c 15th-century caravel
1235 25c 15th-century caravel
1236 50c 15th-century caravel
1237 1p 15th-century caravel
1238 1p10 15th-century caravel
1239 1p40 15th-century caravel
1240 3p 15th-century caravel
1241 4p80 15th-century caravel
1242 5p 15th-century caravel
1243 7p 15th-century caravel
1244 10p 15th-century caravel
Set of 11 4.00 1.25

1956

1254 3p *Ciudad de Toledo* (cargo liner) 6.00 1.75

1961

1420† 2p50 Shipbuilding 30 30

1963

1575† 80c Fleet of Columbus 30 10

1964

1660 15c Medieval ship
1661 25c Carrack
1662 40c *Santa Maria* (Columbus)
1663 50c Galley
1664 70c Galleon
1665 80c Xebec
1666 1p *Santissima Trinidad* (ship of the line), 1769
1667 1p50 *Atrevida* (corvette), 1794
1668 2p *Isabel II* (steam frigate)
1669 2p50 *Numancia* (steam frigate)
1670 3p *Destructor* (destroyer)
1671 5p Isaac Peral's submarine
1672 6p *Baleares* (cruiser)
1673 10p *Juan Sebastian de Elcano* (cadet schooner)
Set of 14 4.25 2.25

1965

1709† 1p Fishing boats, Cudillero 20 10

1967

1847 1p50 Fishing boats, Palma 10 10

1876 1p50 16th-century caravel 15 10

1880† 1p20 *La Princesa* (Maurelle), Nutka 15 10
1884† 6p 18th-century warships and Indian
canoe, Alaska 20 10

1968

1946 6p Olympic yacht 20 10

1971

2114† 5p Battle of Lepanto, 1571 .... 1.50 10

1972

2138† 4p Fishing boats 70 10

2167† 5p Galleon and fishing boats, San Juan,
1625 .... 50 10

1973

2202 2p Trawler 10 10

1974

2240† 15p 18th-century shipyard 75 10

1975

2288† 8p Sailing packet of the West Indian
service 1.10 10

1976

2353† 7p *San Juan Nepomucendo*
(18th-century ship of the line) 1.40 10
2355† 50p *Vitoria* (Del Cano) 1.00 15

2374† 1p Freighter 30 10

2434 12p *Santa Maria* (Columbus) 50 10

1977

2486 15p West Indies sailing packet 70 50

1978

2520† 12p Tanker and oil rig 25 10

2527† 12p 16th-century shipping, Las Palmas 15 10

1979

2573 5p *Roger de Lauria* (destroyer) 40 10

2584 5p English fleet, Tenerife, 1797 .... 30 10

1980

2610† 8p Tankers 10 10

2618 8p Destroyers 30 10

1981

2649 7p 16th-century galleon
2650 12p 16th-century galleon
Set of 2 35 20

1985

2803†   18p *Santissima Trinidad* (ship of the line), 1785   25   10

1987

2900   19p 18th-century warship   40   10

1987

2928   20p *Ictineo* (early submarine)   30   10

MS2930†   12p 14th-century shipping in Coruna harbour, 20p 18th-century sailing packet, Havana, 50p 18th-century sailing packets (sheet contains one other design) 1.75   1.75

1988

2973   50p "Olympic" class yacht   60   10

1990

3079   8p + 5p Caravel
3080   8p + 5p Caravels
3081   20p + 5p Caravel
3082   20p + 5p Galleon
                                Set of 4   1.25   75

1991

3139†   55p *Las Palmas* (Antarctic survey ship)   95   15

1992

3145†   25p + 5p Yachts   35   30

MS3147 17p + 5p Fleet of Columbus (red); 17p + 5p Fleet of Columbus (blue); 17p + 5p Fleet of Columbus (black)   80   65

3157†   17p Tourist launch, Seville   20   10
MS3172   17p + 5p 10th-century shipping, Seville   20   10

3175   17p Columbus's ships, Palos
3176   45p Ships of Columbus
                                Set of 2   70   20

3190   60p Stern of *Santa Maria* (Columbus)   70   10

EXPRESS LETTER STAMPS

1930

As No. 600, *but colour changed, overprinted* **URGENTE**
E608   20c *Santa Maria* (Columbus) 2.00   2.00

SPANISH GUINEA

West Africa
100 centimos = 1 peseta

1925

209   5c Nipa canoe
210   10c Nipa canoe
211   15c Nipa canoe
212   20c Nipa canoe
213   25c Nipa canoe
214   30c Nipa canoe
215   40c Nipa canoe
216   50c Nipa canoe
217   60c Nipa canoe
218   1p Nipa canoe
219   4p Nipa canoe
220   10p Nipa canoe
                                Set of 12   16.00   7.25

1929

Nos. 506 and 508 of Spain overprinted **GUINEA**
235†   15c Caravel   10   10
237†   25c Caravel   10   10

1949

329   4p Pirogue 1.75   50

330   5p *Catalina* (ship of the line) 1.75   50

331†   2c Canoe, San Carlos Bay   20   10
333†   10c Sailing canoe, Fernando Poo   20   10
334†   15c Canoe, River Benito   20   10
335†   25c Canoe, San Carlos Bay   20   10
337†   40c Sailing canoe, Fernando Poo   20   10
338†   45c Canoe, River Benito   20   10
339†   50c Canoe, San Carlos Bay   20   10
341†   90c Sailing canoe, Fernando Poo   20   10
342†   1p Canoe, River Benito 1.50   20
343†   1p35 Canoe, San Carlos Bay 5.00   85
345†   5p Sailing canoe, Fernando Poo 18.00   6.00
346†   10p Canoe, San Carlos Bay 70.00   20.00

1951

353†   1p *Dominie* (liner)   10   10
356†   5p *Dominie* 5.50   2.00

SPANISH MOROCCO

North Africa
100 centimos = 1 peseta

II. SPANISH PROTECTORATE

1929

Nos. 502, 506 and 508 of Spain overprinted **PROTECTORADO MARRUECOS**
138†   1c Caravel   15   10
142†   15c Caravel   10   10
144†   25c Caravel   10   10

1948

317†   10p *Arango* (freighter) at quay 1.75   1.10

1950

361†   10p *Carabo* (fishing boat) 2.00   50

1951

367† 1p + 5p *Hernan Cortes* (brig) 8.00 3.50

1953

394† 35c *Carabo* (fishing boat) 15 10

III. INTERNATIONAL ZONE OF TANGIER

1929
Nos. 506 and 508 of Spain overprinted **TANGER**
29† 15c Caravel 25 10
31† 25c Caravel 25 10

SPANISH SAHARA

West Africa
100 centimos = 1 peseta

1929
Nos. 506 and 508 of Spain overprinted **SAHARA**
27† 15c Caravel 10 15
29† 25c Caravel 10 15

1955

117 10c + 5c Fishing boat
118 25c + 10c Felucca
119 50c Fishing boat
Set of 3 30 30

1966

246 50c Bow of *Rio de Oro* (sailing ship)
247 1p Bow of *Rio de Oro* (sailing ship)
248 1p50 *Fuerta Ventura* (freighter)
Set of 3 30 20

SRI LANKA

Indian Ocean
100 cents = 1 rupee

1983

796† 50c *Lanka Athula* (container ship) 10 10
798† 5r *Lanka Kalyani* (freighter) 25 65
799† 20r *Tammanna* (tanker) 1.10 2.50

1992

1180 1r Container ship 20 20

1219† 1r Fleet of Columbus 10 10
1220† 11r *Santa Maria* and ship's boats 35 40
1221† 13r Wreck of *Santa Maria*, 1492 .... 40 45

SUDAN

North-east Africa
1000 milliemes = 100 piastres = 1 pound

1950

115† 2p Nile felucca 3.50 30
120† 4½p *Gordon Pasha* (Nile mail boat) 2.25 3.00

1951

131† 3p Ambatch reed canoe 1.50 10

1962

195† 10p Nile felucca 30 20

1988

420† 25p Fishing boat 10 10

1990
No. 195 surcharged in Arabic
468 £S1 on 10p Nile felucca 10 10

GIBBONS STAMP MONTHLY
— finest and most informative magazine for all
collectors. Obtainable from your newsagent or by
postal subscription — details on request.

POSTAGE DUE STAMPS

1901

D5 2m *Zafir* (Nile gunboat)
D10 4m *Zafir*
D11 10m *Zafir*
D8 20m *Zafir*
Set of 4 8.00 7.50

1948
Arabic inscription at foot differs from Nos. D5/8
D12 2m *Zafir* (Nile gunboat)
D13 4m *Zafir*
D394 10m *Zafir*
D395 20m *Zafir*
Set of 4 22.00 55.00

OFFICIAL STAMPS

1950
Nos. 115 and 120 overprinted **S.G.**
O59† 2p Nile felucca 9.00 1.50
O64† 4½p *Gordon Pasha* (Nile mail boat) 2.50 8.50

1951
No. 131 overprinted **S.G.**
O75† 3p Ambatch reed canoe 75 10

1962
No. 195 overprinted **S.G.** *in Arabic*
O222† 10p Nile felucca 1.00 20

SURINAM

South America
100 cents = 1 gulden

1936

236† ½c *Johannes van Walbeeck* (Dutch
galleon), 1634 .... 20 25
237† 1c *Johannes van Walbeeck* 30 10
238† 1½c *Johannes van Walbeeck* 45 35
239† 2c *Johannes van Walbeeck* 55 25
240† 2½c *Johannes van Walbeeck* 10 15
241† 3c *Johannes van Walbeeck* 50 35
242† 4c *Johannes van Walbeeck* 55 65
243† 5c *Johannes van Walbeeck* 55 20
244† 6c *Johannes van Walbeeck* 2.25 1.60
245† 7½c *Johannes van Walbeeck* 10 10

1942
Nos. 239, 240 and 245 surcharged with red cross and value
289† 2c + 2c *Johannes van Walbeeck* (Dutch
galleon), 1634 .... 1.00 1.75
291† 2½c + 2c *Johannes van Walbeeck* 1.00 1.75
292† 7½ + 5c *Johannes van Walbeeck* 1.00 1.75

1945
Nos. 237 and 245 surcharged
298† ½c on 1c *Johannes van Walbeeck*
(Dutch galleon), 1634 .... 10 20
299† 1½c on 7½c *Johannes van Walbeeck* 10 20
300† 2½c on 7½c *Johannes van Walbeeck* 1.75 2.25

314† 1½c Canoes 1.00 1.00
317† 3c Canoe, River Surinam 1.00 50

1953

410†	6c Log raft	1.50	1.10
416†	20c Pirogue	45	10

1962

510†   10c Trading canoe 30   30

1965

553†	20c Canoe	20	10
557†	40c *Surinam* (coaster)	35	15

1966

604†   20c Coaster, 1916 25   10

1967

617	10c Dutch galleons, Paramaribo, *c.* 1670
618	20c Dutch galleon, New York, *c.* 1660
619	25c Dutch river boats, Breda, *c.* 1667
	Set of 3 50 50

1971

711†   20c Canoe, Albina, 1846 30   30

1977

884†	5c *Curacao* (paddle-steamer), 1827	15	10
885†	15c Steamship in dock, Hellevoetsluis, 1827	30	15
889†	95c *Stuyvesant* (liner)	1.50	1.50

1986

1290†   110c *Saramacca* (container ship) 2.00   1.10

1991

1490	60c Caravel
1491	110c Caravel
	Set of 2 1.50 1.50

1992

1529   250c Nau, 1492 .... 2.25   2.25

SWAZILAND

Southern Africa
1949 12 pence = 1 shilling
20 shillings = 1 pound
1975 100 cents = 1 lilangeni

1949

As No. 115 *of Antigua*
49†   3d Paddle-steamer 40   50

1981

373†   15c Sailing dinghies 15   10

SWEDEN

Northern Europe
100 ore = 1 krona

1936

191†	20ore *Hiorten* (sailing packet), 1692 (blue)	8.00	2.50
192†	25ore *Constitutionen* (paddle-steamer), 1824 (ultramarine)	5.25	40
198†	60ore *Gripsholm* (liner) (purple)	28.00	50

1938

204†   15ore *Calmare Nyckel* and *Fagel Grip* (emigrant ships), 1638 (brown) 70   10

COLLECT CHESS ON STAMPS

A Stanley Gibbons thematic catalogue — available at £5 (p. + p. £3) from: Stanley Gibbons Publications, 5 Parkside, Christchurch Road, Ringwood, Hants. BH24 3SH.

1944

273†	10ore *Smalands Lejon* (ship of the line), 1634 (violet)	20	10
275†	30ore *Kung Karl* (ship of the line), 1693 (blue)	55	50
276†	40ore Stern of *Amphion* (royal yacht), 1778 (olive)	70	40
277†	90ore *Gustav V* (cruiser), 1918	9.00	1.25

1953

338†   25ore Shipping, Stockholm, 1650 20   10

1957

381a	30ore Shipwrecked trawler
382	1k40 Shipwrecked trawler
	Set of 2 10.00 2.00

1958

395†	15ore Galleon and *Gripsholm II* (liner) ..	20	10
397†	40ore Galleon and *Gripsholm II* (liner) ..	4.25	2.10

1966

As Nos. 273, 204, 191/2 *and* 275/6, *but colours changed and dated "*1966*" at foot*

517	10ore *Smalands Lejon* (ship of the line) (red)
518	15ore *Calmare Nyckel* and *Fagel Grip* (emigrant ships), 1638 (red)
519	20ore *Hiorten* (sailing packet), 1692 (green)
520	25ore *Constitutionen* (paddle-steamer), 1824 (blue)
521	30ore *Kung Karl* (ship of the line), 1693 (red)
522	40ore Stern of *Amphion* (royal yacht), 1778 (red)
	Set of 6 50 1.00

1967

539†	10ore *Svent Skepp* (warship), 1650	15	10
541†	40ore Canal steamer, Dalsland Canal ..	20	10

1969

592†   55ore *Wasa* (ship of the line), 1628 40   20

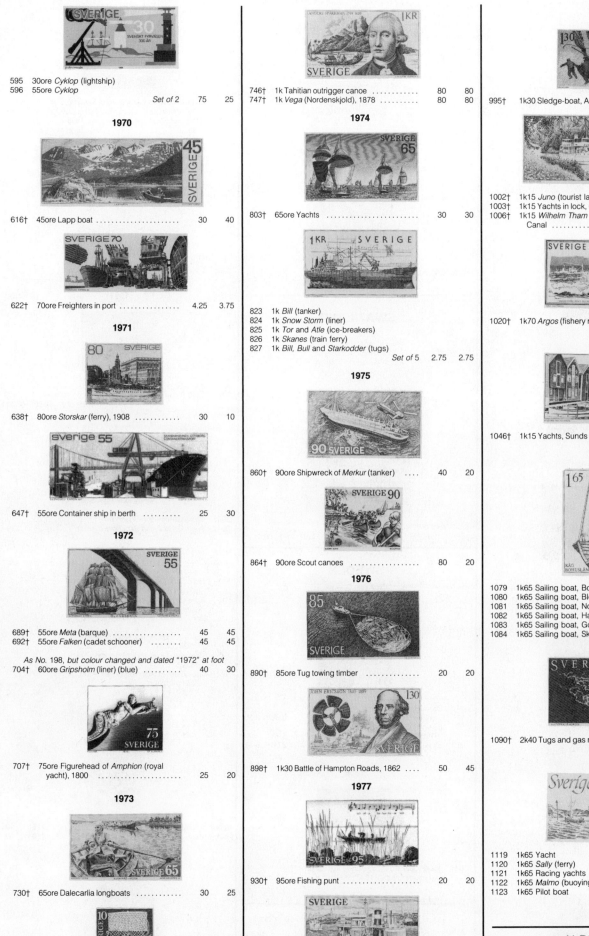

595   30ore *Cyklop* (lightship)
596   55ore *Cyklop*
                                    Set of 2   75   25

1970

616†   45ore Lapp boat 30   40

622†   70ore Freighters in port 4.25   3.75

1971

638†   80ore *Storskar* (ferry), 1908 30   10

647†   55ore Container ship in berth 25   30

1972

689†   55ore *Meta* (barque) 45   45
692†   55ore *Falken* (cadet schooner) 45   45

As No. 198, but colour changed and dated "1972" at foot
704†   60ore *Gripsholm* (liner) (blue) 40   30

707†   75ore Figurehead of *Amphion* (royal
        yacht), 1800 25   20

1973

730†   65ore Dalecarlia longboats 30   25

735†   10ore Viking longship from Larbro Stone   10   10

746†   1k Tahitian outrigger canoe 80   80
747†   1k *Vega* (Nordenskjold), 1878 80   80

1974

803†   65ore Yachts 30   30

823   1k *Bill* (tanker)
824   1k *Snow Storm* (liner)
825   1k *Tor* and *Atle* (ice-breakers)
826   1k *Skanes* (train ferry)
827   1k *Bill, Bull* and *Starkodder* (tugs)
                                    Set of 5   2.75   2.75

1975

860†   90ore Shipwreck of *Merkur* (tanker) 40   20

864†   90ore Scout canoes 80   20

1976

890†   85ore Tug towing timber 20   20

898†   1k30 Battle of Hampton Roads, 1862 50   45

1977

930†   95ore Fishing punt 20   20

939†   1k10 *Djurgarden 6* (ferry) 50   40

1979

995†   1k30 Sledge-boat, Aland 30   10

1002†   1k15 *Juno* (tourist launch), Gota Canal   45   45
1003†   1k15 Yachts in lock, Gota Canal 45   45
1006†   1k15 *Wilhelm Tham* (motor barge), Gota
         Canal 45   45

1020†   1k70 *Argos* (fishery research ship) 35   40

1980

1046†   1k15 Yachts, Sunds Canal 30   30

1981

1079   1k65 Sailing boat, Bohuslan
1080   1k65 Sailing boat, Blekinge
1081   1k65 Sailing boat, Norrbotten
1082   1k65 Sailing boat, Halsingland
1083   1k65 Sailing boat, Gotland
1084   1k65 Sailing boat, Skane
                                    Set of 6   2.10   1.10

1090†   2k40 Tugs and gas rig 50   40

1982

1119   1k65 Yacht
1120   1k65 *Sally* (ferry)
1121   1k65 Racing yachts
1122   1k65 *Malmo* (buoying ship)
1123   1k65 Pilot boat
                                    Set of 5   1.75   65

ALBUM LISTS

Write for our latest list of albums and accessories.
This will be sent on request.

1983

1151†   2k40 Yachts   60   20

1984

1205†   1k90 17th-century fishing boats, Gavle   50   30

1985

1257†   2k *A. F. Chapman* (youth hostel),
Stockholm   60   15

1988

1374   3k10 Fishing skiff, Lake Hjalmaren
1375   3k10 Market boat, Lake Vattern
1376   3k10 Logging boat, River Byske
1377   3k10 Rowing boat, Lake Asnon
1378   3k10 Ice boat, Lake Vanern
1379   3k10 Church longboat, Lake Lockne
       Set of 6   3.25   1.60

1380†   3k60 *Calmare Nyckel* and *Fagel Grip*
(emigrant ships), 1638   70   65

1390†   2k Garlanded longboat   40   15
1394†   2k *Norrskar* (tourist launch)   40   15

1989

1443†   2k10 Sailing dinghy   50   15

1465†   3k30 *Oden* (ice research ship)   75   30
1466†   3k30 *Antarctic* (Nordenskjold), 1901   75   30

1990

1486†   2k50 Yacht, Angso   60   20

1496†   2k50 Viking longships   60   20
1500†   2k50 Stern of Viking roundship   60   20
1501†   2k50 Bow of Viking roundship   60   20

1513   2k50 Bow of *Wasa* (17th-century
warship)
1514   4k60 Stern of *Wasa*
       Set of 2   1.50   60

1529†   2k50 Barque   60   20

1538†   4k70 Schooner 1.00   40

COLLECT BIRDS ON STAMPS
Third revised edition of this Stanley Gibbons thematic catalogue. Now available at £15.95 (p. + p. £3) from: Stanley Gibbons Publications, 5 Parkside, Christchurch Road, Ringwood, Hants BH24 3SH.

1992

1628   4k50 *Sprengtporten* (frigate), 1785
1629   4k50 *Superb* (brig), 1855
1630   4k50 *Big T* (yacht)
       Set of 3   2.40   1.25

SWITZERLAND
Central Europe
100 centimes = 1 franc

1942

428†   10c + 10c Medieval fishing boat, Lake
Geneva   30   40

1945

MS446a   3f + 7f Lifeboat £190   £200

1949

518†   40c Rhine barge, Basel 3.00   10

1959

597†   5c Rhine ferry   25   10

1978

MS952   20c *La Suisse* (lake steamer), 1900;
20c *Il Verbano* (lake paddle-steamer), 1826;
40c *Gotthard* (lake steamer), 1970; 40c *Ville
de Neuchatel* (lake steamer), 1972; 40c
Romanshorn (lake steamer), 1958; 40c *Le
Winkelried* (lake paddle-steamer), 1871; 70c
Loetschberg (lake paddle-steamer), 1914; 80c
Waedenswil (lake steamer), 1895 ....   9.00   9.00

1985

1078† 70c *Sauvetage* (lifeboat) 70 60

1986

1108† 45c *Stadt Luzern* (paddle-steamer),
c 1830 .... 40 20

1991

1237† 80c Fishing boat, Melchsee 75 15

1992

1241† 50c *Santa Maria* (Columbus) 45 15

PRO JUVENTUTE CHARITY STAMPS

1929

J48† 5c Fishing boat, Lake Lugano 15 60

OFFICIAL STAMPS

1950
No. 518 overprinted **Officiel**
O529 40c Rhine barge, Basel 5.00 2.50

INTERNATIONAL ORGANIZATION SITUATED IN SWITZERLAND

B. International Labour Office

1950
No. 518 overprinted **BUREAU INTERNATIONAL DU TRAVAIL**
LB87† 40c Rhine barge, Basel 7.00 5.50

C. International Education Office

1950
No. 518 overprinted **BUREAU INTERNATIONAL D'EDUCATION**
LE36† 40c Rhine barge, Basel 5.50 7.00

D. World Health Organization

1950
No. 518 overprinted **ORGANISATION MONDIALE DE LA SANTE**
LH13† 40c Rhine barge, Basel 2.75 1.50

E. International Refugees Organization

1950
No. 518 overprinted **ORGANISATION INTERNATIONALE POUR LES REFUGIES**
LR5† 40c Rhine barge, Basel 16.00 10.00

H. United Nations

1950
No. 518 overprinted **NATIONS UNIES OFFICE EUROPEEN**
LU8† 40c Rhine barge, Basel 4.00 3.75

SYRIA
Middle East
100 centimes = 1 piastre

1925

177† 0p50 Ancient Phoenician ships 25 15
180† 1p25 Fishing boats, Latakia 70 50

1926
Nos. 177 and 180 surcharged **Secours aux Refugies Afft,** *in English and Arabic, and new value*
197† 0p25 on 0p50 Ancient Phoenician ships 1.00 1.00
200† 0p50 on 1p25 Fishing boats, Latakia 1.00 1.00

No. 180 surcharged in English and Arabic figures
223† 2p on 1p25 Fishing boats, Latakia 25 10
218† 12p on 1p25 Fishing boats, Latakia 20 10
220† 20p on 1p25 Fishing boats, Latakia 30 15

1929
Nos. 177 and 180 overprinted with airplane or surcharged also in English and Arabic figures
225† 0p50 Ancient Phoenician ships 30 20
227† 2p on 1p25 Fishing boats, Latakia 70 70

No. 177 overprinted **EXPOSITION INDUSTRIELLE DAMAS 1929** *in English and Arabic. No. 237 is additionally overprinted with airplane*
230† 0p50 Ancient Phoenician ships 1.40 1.40
237† 0p50 Ancient Phoenician ships (air) 1.00 1.00

1950

497 2p50 Freighters in Latakia Harbour
498 10p Freighters in Latakia Harbour (turquoise)
526 10p Freighters in Latakia Harbour (blue)
499 15p Freighters in Latakia Harbour
500 25p Freighters in Latakia Harbour
Set of 5 8.00 70

1956

599† 35p Phoenician galley 55 55

1957

623† 25p *Latakia* (freighter) at quay 25 15
627† 70p *Latakia* (freighter) at quay 90 50

628 12½p Freighter
629 17½p Freighter (air)
630 40p Freighter
Set of 3 1.25 70

1968

987 12½p Tankers
988 17½p Tankers
Set of 2 75 30

1980

1484 50p Frigate 70 25

1987

1673 330p Phoenician galley 2.00 1.50

TANZANIA
East Africa
100 cents = 1 shilling

1965

136† 1s *Ouwerkerk* (freighter), Dar-es-Salaam 50 10
138† 2s50 Fishing boat, Mafia Island 2.75 90

1978

247† 10s Canoes, Mafia Island 80 90

1984

MS399 15s *Mapinduzi* (ferry) 1.50 3.00

1987

MS534† 20s Container ship 50 50

1990

717† 13s *Trieste* (bathyscaph) 10 10
718† 50s *Nina* (Columbus) 20 25
719† 60s *Pinta* 25 30
720† 75s *Santa Maria* 30 35
MS724† Two sheets (a) 350s Caravels (other
sheet shows spacecraft)
Price for 2 sheets 2.75 3.00

739† 9s Fishing canoe 10 10

799 9s Canoe
800 13s Sailing canoe
801 25s Dhow
802 100s Freighter
Set of 4 65 70
MS803 40s Mashua dhow 15 20

1991

823† 50s *Reichstag* (German mail steamer),
1890 .... 20 25
824† 75s Dhows, Zanzibar 30 35

865† 160s Yacht 60 65

887† 5s "Soling" class yachts 10 10
894† 300s Power boat 1.10 1.25

1992

1316† 75s H.M.S. *Repulse* (battle cruiser)
 under attack, 1941 .... 30 35
1317† 75s H.M.S. *Prince of Wales* (battleship)
 under attack, 1941 .... 30 35
1319† 75s H.M.S. *Hermes* (aircraft carrier)
 sinking, 1942 .... 30 35
1322† 75s Japanese landing craft 30 35
1323† 75s *Haguro* (Japanese cruiser) 30 35

1329† 15s Scouts in rowing boats 10 10

OFFICIAL STAMPS

1965

No. 136 overprinted **OFFICIAL**
O154† 1s *Ouwerkerk* (freighter), Dar-es-
Salamm 30 20

TETE

East Africa
100 centavos = 1 escudo

1913

Surcharged **REPUBLICA TETE** *and value*

(a) On Nos. 1/2, 5 and 7 of Portuguese Colonies in Africa
1† ¼c on 2½r Departure of Vasco da Gama's
 fleet 40 30
2† ½c on 5r Vasco da Gama's fleet at Calicut 40 30
5† 5c on 50r *Sao Gabriel* (flagship) 40 30
7† 10c on 100r *Sao Gabriel* 45 40

(b) On Nos. 104/5, 108 and 110 of Macao
9† ¼c on ½a Departure of Vasco da Gama's
 fleet 40 30
10† ¼c on 1a Vasco da Gama's fleet at
 Calicut 40 30
13† 5c on 8a *Sao Gabriel* (flagship) 40 30
15† 10c on 16a *Sao Gabriel* 45 40

(c) On Nos. 58/9, 62 and 64 of Timor
17† ¼c on ½a Departure of Vasco da Gama's
 fleet 40 30
18† ¼c on 1a Vasco da Gama's fleet at
 Calicut 40 30
21† 5c on 8a *Sao Gabriel* (flagship) 40 30
23† 10c on 16a *Sao Gabriel* 45 40

THAILAND

South-east Asia
100 satangs = 1 baht

1967

582 2b *Sri Suphanahong* (royal barge) 70 15

1971

679 4b Market boats, Wat Sai 90 15

1975

868 75s *Sukrip Khrong Maung* (ceremonial
 barge)
869 1b *Anekchat Phulbong* (royal barge)
870 2b *Anantana Karot* (royal barge)
871 2b75 *Krabi Ram Ron Rap* (ceremonial
 barge)
872 3b *Asura Wayuphak* (ceremonial barge)
873 4b *Asura Paksi* (ceremonial barge)
874 5b *Sri Suphanahong* (royal barge)
875 6b *Phali Rang Thamip* (ceremonial barge)
Set of 8 7.00 3.50

1976

901† 4b Post canoe, 1950 .... 60 25

1979

1002 2b *Makutrajakumarn* (frigate)
1003 3b *Tapi* (frigate)
1004 5b *Prabparapak* (missile craft)
1005 6b *T 91* (patrol boat)
Set of 4 3.00 1.50

1983

1136	1b25 Junks	10	10

1147†	1b25 Cable ship	40	15

1153†	2b Cable ship	60	15

1984

1165	1b25 *Makutrajakumam* (frigate)	20	10

1987

1278	2b Container ship	15	10
1298	2b *Sri Suphanahong* (royal barge)	15	10

1989

1395†	2b Market boats	20	10

1420	2b Container ship	20	10
1431	2b Container ship	20	10

1990

1494†	2b + 1b Sailboards	20	15

1992

1570†	2b Oil rig	10	10
1589†	2b Stylized container ships	10	10

TIMOR
Australasia
1898 100 avos = 1 pataca
1960 100 centavos = 1 escudo

1898
Designs as Nos. 378/9, 382 and 384 of Portugal, but inscribed "TIMOR" and with face values in avos

58†	½a Departure of Vasco da Gama's fleet	90	60
59†	1a Vasco da Gama's fleet at Calicut	90	60
62†	8a *Sao Gabriel* (flagship)	1.25	75
64†	16a *Sao Gabriel*	1.75	1.50

1913
Nos. 58/9, 62 and 64 overprinted **REPUBLICA**

169†	½a Departure of Vasco da Gama's fleet	30	20
170†	1a Vasco da Gama's fleet at Calicut	30	20
173†	8a *Sao Gabriel* (flagship)	50	30
175†	16a *Sao Gabriel*	60	50

1935

232	½a Portuguese galeasse
233	1a Portuguese galeasse
234	2a Portuguese galeasse
235	3a Portuguese galeasse
236	4a Portuguese galeasse
237	5a Portuguese galeasse
238	6a Portuguese galeasse
239	7a Portuguese galeasse
240	8a Portuguese galeasse
241	10a Portuguese galeasse
242	12a Portuguese galeasse
243	14a Portuguese galeasse
244	15a Portuguese galeasse
245	20a Portuguese galeasse
246	30a Portuguese galeasse
247	40a Portuguese galeasse
248	50a Portuguese galeasse
249	1p Portuguese galeasse
250	2p Portuguese galeasse
251	3p Portuguese galeasse
252	5p Portuguese galeasse

Set of 21 45.00 22.00

1961

369†	50c Model of outrigger canoe	15	15

1967

387†	10c *Patria* (gunboat)	15	15

1969

399	4e50 *Almirante Gago Coutinho* (frigate)	1.75	70

1972

415	1e Portuguese galleon, 1572	15	15

TOGO

West Africa
1900 100 pfennig = 1 mark
1914 12 pence = 1 shilling
20 shillings = 1 pound
1914 100 centimes = 1 franc

GERMAN COLONY

1900

As Nos. K7/19 of Cameroon, but inscribed "TOGO"

G7	3pf *Hohenzollern* (German Imperial yacht)	
G21	5pf *Hohenzollern*	
G9	10pf *Hohenzollern*	
G10	20pf *Hohenzollern*	
G11	25pf *Hohenzollern*	
G12	30pf *Hohenzollern*	
G13	40pf *Hohenzollern*	
G14	50pf *Hohenzollern*	
G15	80pf *Hohenzollern*	
G16	1m *Hohenzollern*	
G17	2m *Hohenzollern*	
G18	3m *Hohenzollern*	
G19	5m *Hohenzollern*	
	Set of 13 £140 £750

ANGLO-FRENCH OCCUPATION

1914

Nos. G7/19 overprinted **TOGO Anglo-French Occupation**

H1	3pf *Hohenzollern* (German Imperial yacht)	£110	95.00
H2	5pf *Hohenzollern*	£100	90.00
H3	10pf *Hohenzollern*	£120	£100
H4	20pf *Hohenzollern*	28.00	26.00
H5	25pf *Hohenzollern*	28.00	23.00
H6	30pf *Hohenzollern*	30.00	35.00
H7	40pf *Hohenzollern*	£225	£250
H8	50pf *Hohenzollern*	£9000	£7000
H9	80pf *Hohenzollern*	£225	£275
H10	1m *Hohenzollern*	£5000	£2500
H11	2m *Hohenzollern*	£7500	£8000
H25	3m *Hohenzollern*	—	£30000
H26	5m *Hohenzollern*	—	£30000

Nos. H1/2 surcharged in words

H27	½d on 3pf *Hohenzollern* (German Imperial yacht)	
H28	1d on 5pf *Hohenzollern*	
	Set of 2 30.00 30.00

Nos. G7, G21, G10/13 and G15 overprinted **TOGO Occupation franco-anglaise** *or surcharged also in figures*

1	05 on 3pf *Hohenzollern* (German Imperial yacht)	
2	10 on 5pf *Hohenzollern*	
3	20pf *Hohenzollern*	
4	25pf *Hohenzollern*	
5	30pf *Hohenzollern*	
6	40pf *Hohenzollern*	
7	80pf *Hohenzollern*	
	Set of 7 £950 £850

FRENCH ADMINISTRATION

1931

As No. 109 of Cameroun

102†	1f50 *Leconte de Lisle* (liner)	3.25	3.25

1937

As Nos. 110/11 of Cameroun

103†	20c Liner	1.00	1.25
104†	30c Sailing ships	1.00	1.40

1940

131†	20c Fishing canoes	10	25
132†	25c Fishing canoes	10	20
133†	30c Fishing canoes	15	20
134†	40c Fishing canoes	20	30
135†	45c Fishing canoes	10	30
136†	50c Fishing canoes	20	40
137†	60c Fishing canoes	25	30

1941

No. 136 surcharged **SECOURS + 1 fr. NATIONAL**

151†	1f on 50c Fishing canoe	2.00	2.00

1954

As No. 264 of Cameroun

188	15f Landing craft, Normandy, 1944	2.50	2.75

INDEPENDENT REPUBLIC

1961

287†	20f Motor launch	20	15

1963

320†	50c Paddle-steamer and *Hohenzollern* (German Imperial yacht) (on stamp Nos. G9 and G18)	10	10

1964

376†	85f *Panama Maru* (bulk carrier) loading phosphate	1.25	50

1967

493	5f Fishing boat		
494	10f Fishing boat		
495	15f Fishing boat		
496	25f Galleon		
497	30f Fishing boat		
498	45f Fishing boat (air)		
499	90f Fishing boat		
	Set of 7 3.25 1.75

553†	5f *Hohenzollern* (German Imperial yacht) (on stamp No. G9)	15	10
559†	90f *Hohenzollern* (on stamp No. G9) (air)	90	50

1968

588	5f Viking longship and Portuguese galleon		
589	10f *Clermont* (first commercial paddle-steamer) and *Athlone Castle* (liner)		
590	20f Freighters, Lome		
591	30f Viking longship and Portuguese galleon		
592	45f *Clermont* and *Athlone Castle*		
593	90f *Savannah* (nuclear-powered freighter)		
	Set of 6 3.00 1.25

1969

635	50f Paddle-steamer and *Hohenzollern* (German Imperial yacht) (on stamp No. G16)	80	80

1973

940†	100f Scout canoe	70	40

963†	90f Early steam packet and modern liner	75	40

1974

998†	30f Freighter	25	15
1000†	90f Fishing canoe	55	35
1001†	100f Sailing canoe	70	35

1008†	30f Fishing canoe	25	15
1009†	40f Fishing canoe	25	20

1047†	30f H.M.S. *Loch Fada* (frigate)	45	15
1049†	100f H.M.S. *Loch Fada* (air)	1.00	55

1975

No. 940 overprinted **14eme JAMBOREE MONDIAL DES ECLAIREURS**

1107†	100f Scout canoe	55	30

1976

1119†	35f H.M.S. *Phoenix*, H.M.S. *Roebuck* and H.M.S. *Tartar* (frigates) in Hudson, 1776	30	20

1126†   25f Cable ship 20   15

1147†   70f Olympic yachts 40   25

1977
No. 1147 overprinted **CHAMPIONS OLYMPIQUES YACHTING–FLYING DUTCHMAN REPUBLIQUE FEDERALE ALLEMAGNE**
1176†   70f Olympic yachts 40   30

1242   60f French warships, 1824 45   20

1245   50f *Aurora* (Russian cruiser), 1917 40   20

1978

1276†   25f Trawlers, Lome 30   15
1277†   60f Tankers under construction, Lome
              (air) 55   20
1278†   100f Freighters, Lome 80   30

1324†   60f *Slieve Roe* (full-rigged ship) 65   25

1979

1335†   25f H.M.S. *Endeavour* (Cook) 50   15
1336†   50f H.M.S. *Endeavour* careened 80   35
1337†   60f *Freelove* (Whitby collier) (Cook) (air)   75   35
1338†   70f H.M.S. *Resolution* (Cook) 1.25   45
1340†   200f H.M.S. *Endeavour* (sail plan) 2.50   1.10

1382†   30f Olympic yachts 15   15

1980

1444†   40f Market canoes 15   15

1982

1579†   130f Scout canoe 80   50

1593†   90f *Hohenzollern* (German Imperial
              yacht) (on stamp No. G19) 40   40

1984

1671†   35f Pirogue, Baguida, 1884 15   10
1678†   45f *Hohenzollern* (German Imperial
              yacht) (on stamp No. G19) 15   15
1683†   45f *Hohenzollern* (on stamp No. G9)   15   15
1684†   70f *Hohenzollern* (on stamp Nos. G10
              and G17) 25   20
1698†   120f *Hohenzollern* (on stamp No. G21)   40   35
1700†   270f *Mowe* (German gunboat), 1884 ..   95   90
1701†   270f *Sophie* (German sail corvette),
              1884 95   90

ALBUM LISTS
Write for our latest list of albums and accessories.
This will be sent on request.

1988

2018†   120f Canoes on beach 45   40

TOKELAU
South Pacific
1970 100 cents = 1 dollar
1982 100 sene or cents = 1 tola or dollar

1970

22   5c H.M.S. *Dolphin* (Byron), 1765
23   10c H.M.S. *Pandora* (frigate), 1791
24   25c *General Jackson* (American whaling
         ship), 1835
                              Set of 3   5.75   1.25

1971

31†   20c Outrigger canoe 1.25   2.00

1976

49†   1c Canoe building 20   50

1978

65   8c Canoe racing
66   12c Canoe racing
67   15c Canoe racing
68   30c Canoe racing
                              Set of 4   1.10   1.10

1980

75†   30c Canoe 20   25
76†   50c Canoe 25   35

1982

85	5s Fishing canoe		
86	18s Fishing canoe		
87	23s Fishing canoe		
88	34s Fishing canoe		
89	63s Fishing canoe		
90	75s Fishing canoe		
	Set of 6	2.25	1.50

1983

91†	5s Outrigger canoe	10	10
92†	18s Wooden whaleboat	15	15
93†	23s Aluminium motor whaleboat	15	20
94†	34s *Alia* (fishing catamaran)	25	25
95†	63s *Frysna* (freighter)	35	40

1984

107†	48s Freighter and motorised whaleboat loading copra	40	45

1988

154	50c Small boat flotilla, Sydney Harbour		
155	50c Liners and *Juan Sebastian de Elcano* (Spanish cadet schooner) at re-enactment of First Fleet, 1988		
156	50c Small boats and Sydney Opera House		
157	50c Small boats and Harbour Bridge		
158	50c Small boats and Sydney waterfront		
	Set of 5	4.50	4.50

163†	60c Outrigger canoe	40	45

165†	5c Outrigger canoe	10	10
167†	40c Canoe	35	35

1989

171†	50c Launching outrigger canoe	85	85
172†	50c Outrigger canoe	85	85
173†	50c Fishing punt and sailing canoe	85	85
174†	50c Canoe on beach	85	85
175†	50c Loading canoe	85	85

1990

187†	50c Two men building canoe	85	85
188†	50c Three men building canoe	85	85

1992

193†	40c *Santa Maria* (Columbus)	75	30
195†	$1.20 Fleet of Columbus	80	85
196†	$1.80 *Santa Maria* at anchor in New World	1.25	1.40

TONGA

South Pacific
1897 12 pence = 1 shilling
20 shillings = 1 pound
1967 100 seniti = 1 pa'anga

1897

51a†	2s Yacht, Haapai	18.00	21.00

1923

No. 51 surcharged **TWO PENCE PENI-E-UA**

68a†	2d on 2s Yacht, Haapai	4.25	4.50

1949

As No. 115 of Antigua

89†	3d Paddle-steamer	40	1.25

1951

98†	3d H.M.N.Z.S. *Bellona* (cruiser)	50	70

1953

103†	2d *Hifofua* and *Aoniu* (ketches)	50	10
104†	3d Outrigger canoe	20	10
106†	4d Freighter at wharf	45	10
109†	8d *Matua* (inter-island freighter)	50	40
111†	2s Outrigger canoe	60	60
112†	5s H.M.S. *Bounty* and launch (Bligh)	14.00	5.50

1961

116†	2d Whaling ship and whaleboat	20	10
118†	5d *Aoniu II* (inter-island freighter)	25	10

1962

Nos. 104, 109 and 112 overprinted **1862 TAU'ATAINA EMANCIPATION 1962** *or surcharged also*

124†	8d *Matua* (inter-island freighter)	40	30
126†	2s on 3d Outrigger canoe	40	65
127†	5s H.M.S. *Bounty* and launch	1.50	1.10

1966

Nos. 116 and 118 surcharged **1866–1966 TUPOU COLLEGE & SECONDARY EDUCATION** *and value, with Nos. 168, 171/2 additionally overprinted* **AIRMAIL** *and* **CENTENARY**

164†	6d on 2d Whaling ship and whaleboat	10	10
165†	1s2d on 2d Whaling ship and whaleboat	10	10
166†	2s on 2d Whaling ship and whaleboat	15	10
167†	3s on 2d Whaling ship and whaleboat	15	15
168†	5d *Aoniu II* (inter-island freighter) (air)	10	10
171†	2s9d on 2d Whaling ship and whaleboat	15	15
172†	3s6d on 5d *Aoniu II*	15	15

1967

Nos. 103/4, 106, 109, 111/12 and 167 surcharged in new currency

186†	2s on 4d Freighter at wharf	10	10
230†	3s on 3d Outrigger canoe	10	10
232†	5s on 2d *Hifofua* and *Aoniu* (ketches)	10	10
190†	6s on 8d *Matua* (inter-island freighter)	10	10
235†	8s on 8d *Matua* (inter-island freighter)	10	10
193†	9s on 3d Outrigger canoe	15	15
238†	20s on 5s H.M.S. *Bounty* and launch	40	40
196†	21s on 3s on 3d Whaling ship and whaleboat	25	35
198†	30s on 2s Outrigger canoe (surch **Seniti**)	1.25	1.75
199†	30s on 2s Outrigger canoe (surch **SENITI**)	1.50	2.00
201†	60s on 2d *Hifofua* and *Aoniu* (ketches)	1.25	1.75
239†	2p on 2s Outrigger canoe	1.50	1.50

As Nos. 103/4, 106, 111/12, but imperforate, surcharged **The Friendly Islands welcome the United States Peace Corps S**

217†	2s on 2d *Hifofua* and *Aoniu* (ketches)	10	10
218†	3s on 3d Outrigger canoe	10	10
219†	4s on 4d Freighter at wharf	10	10
222†	20s on 2s Outrigger canoe	15	15
223†	50s on 5s H.M.S. *Bounty* and launch	30	35

As Nos. 103/4, 106, 109 and 111/12, but imperforate, surcharged **Friendly Islands Field and Track Trials South Pacific Games Port Moresby 1969** *and value*

259†	15s on 2s Outrigger canoe	15	15
260†	25s on 2d *Hifofua* and *Aoniu* (ketches)	15	15
264†	7s on 4d Freighter at wharf (air)	10	10
265†	8s on 8d *Matua* (inter-island freighter)	10	10
267†	11s on 3d Outrigger canoe	10	10
269†	38s on 5s H.M.S. *Bounty* and launch	20	20

1969

As No. 109, but imperforate, 165/6 and 171/2 surcharged in new currency

271†	1s on 1s2d on 2d Whaling ship and whaleboat	1.25	85
272†	1s on 2s on 2d Whaling ship and whaleboat	1.25	85
276†	4s on 8d *Matua* (inter-island freighter)	70	50
277†	1s on 2s9d on 2d Whaling ship and whaleboat (air)	1.25	85
278†	1s on 3s6d on 5d *Aoniu II* (inter-island freighter)	1.25	85

1971

As Nos. 106, 109 and 111, but imperforate, surcharged **PHILATOKYO '71**, emblem and value (Nos. 355/6, 359, 361) or **HONOURING JAPANESE POSTAL CENTENARY 1871–1971 T$1·00 AIRMAIL** (No. 364)

355†	3s on 8d *Matua* (inter-island freighter) ..	10	10
356†	7s on 4d Freighter at wharf	10	10
359†	75s on 2s Outrigger canoe	85	85
361†	10s on 4d Freighter at wharf (air)	10	10
364†	1p on 2s Outrigger canoe	1.00	1.00

1972

393	2s *Olovaha* (inter-island freighter)		
394	10s *Olovaha*		
395	17s *Olovaha*		
396	21s *Olovaha*		
397	60s *Olovaha*		
398	9s *Niuvakai* (inter-island freighter) (air)		
399	12s *Niuvakai*		
400	14s *Niuvakai*		
401	75s *Niuvakai*		
402	90s *Niuvakai*		
	Set of 10	11.00	6.50

No. 398 surcharged **7S NOVEMBER 1972 INAUGURAL Internal Airmail Nuku'alofa — Vava'u**

428	7s on 9s *Niuvakai* (inter-island freighter)	1.40	2.25

1973

449†	5s Scout outrigger canoe	20	10
450†	7s Scout outrigger canoe	30	15
451†	15s Scout outrigger canoe	95	40
452†	21s Scout outrigger canoe	1.25	50
453†	50s Scout outrigger canoe	4.50	2.00

464†	9s H.M.S. *Resolution* (Cook)	60	25
465†	14s H.M.S. *Resolution*	1.00	30
466†	29s H.M.S. *Resolution*	3.50	1.50
467†	38s H.M.S. *Resolution*	4.00	1.75
468†	75s H.M.S. *Resolution*	7.50	3.00

1974

508	5s H.M.S. *Resolution* (Cook)		
509	10s H.M.S. *Resolution*		
510	25s H.M.S. *Resolution*		
511	50s H.M.S. *Resolution*		
512	75s H.M.S. *Resolution*		
513	9s *James Cook* (bulk carrier) (air)		
514	14s *James Cook*		
515	17s *James Cook*		
516	60s *James Cook*		
517	90s *James Cook*		
	Set of 10	19.00	11.00

1976

583†	9s *Triton* (missionary brigantine)	30	25
584†	12s *Triton*	35	30
585†	14s *Triton*	40	35
586†	17s *Triton*	50	40
587†	38s *Triton*	1.25	1.00

1977

618†	10s H.M.S. *Resolution* (Cook)	1.75	75
619†	17s H.M.S. *Resolution*	2.25	1.10
620†	25s H.M.S. *Resolution*	3.75	2.00
621†	30s H.M.S. *Resolution*	3.75	2.25
622†	40s H.M.S. *Resolution*	4.50	3.00

1978

No. 583 surcharged **17s**

646†	17s on 9s *Triton* (missionary brigantine)	1.00	1.60

WHEN YOU BUY AN ALBUM LOOK FOR THE NAME "STANLEY GIBBONS"
It means Quality combined with Value for Money.

1980

746†	15s *L'Aventure* (French warship), 1855	20	25
747†	17s *L'Aventure*	25	30
748†	22s *L'Aventure*	35	40
749†	31s *L'Aventure*	40	45
750†	39s *L'Aventure*	55	60

Nos. 584/5 surcharged in figures only

774†	29s on 14s *Triton* (missionary brigantine)	80	80
779†	47s on 12s *Triton*	1.40	1.40

1981

793†	9s *La Princesa* (Maurelle), 1781	30	20
795†	47s *La Princesa*	2.00	1.25
796†	1p *La Princesa*	4.50	3.00

802†	1p *Port au Prince* (full-rigged ship), 1806	1.50	75

1982

813†	9s *Olovaha II* (inter-island freighter)	10	10
814†	13s *Olovaha II*	15	15

817†	13s Mail canoe, Niuafo'ou	15	15
818†	32s Mail canoe and freighter	25	25
819†	47s Mail canoe and freighter	35	35

Nos. 817/19 overprinted **Christmas Greetings 1982**

831†	13s Mail canoe, Niuafo'ou		
832†	32s Mail canoe and freighter		
833†	47s Mail canoe and freighter		
	Set of 3	80	90

1983

834†	29s H.M.S *Resolution* (Cook) and *Canberra* (liner)	1.00	80
835†	32s H.M.S *Resolution* and *Canberra*	1.10	90
MS838†	2p50 *Canberra*	3.50	4.00

841†	47s Trawler	50	50

857	29s Yacht, Vava'u		
858	32s Yacht in cave		
859	1p50 Yacht at sunset		
860	2p50 Yacht at sea		
	Set of 4	2.25	2.75

1984

861	32s *Zeehan* (Tasman)		
862	47s H.M.S. *Dolphin* (Wallis), 1767		
863	90s H.M.S. *Bounty* (Bligh)		
864	1p50 H.M.S. *Resolution* (Cook)		
	Set of 4	7.50	7.50

1985

896	32s *Eendracht* (Schouten), 1616		
897	47s *Hoorn* (Le Maire), 1616		
898	90s H.M.S. *Bounty* (Bligh)		
899	1p50 *La Princesa* (Maurelle), 1781		
	Set of 4	9.00	7.00

905	29s *Port au Prince* (full-rigged ship), 1806		
906	32s *Port au Prince* under attack		
907	47s 19th-century Tongan double canoe		
908	1p50 Outrigger canoe		
909	2p50 *Cuffnells* (full-rigged ship), 1810		
	Set of 5	4.25	4.50

ALBUM LISTS
Write for our latest list of albums and accessories.
This will be sent on request.

1986

MS955 50s H.M.S. *Resolution* (Cook) (on stamp No. 464); 50s *Olovaha II* (inter-island freighter (on stamp No. 814) (sheet also contains six other designs) 6.50 7.00

959†	2p Outrigger canoe	3.25	3.50

1987

962†	32s *L'Astrolabe* (D'Urville), 1837	1.40	1.10
964†	1p *L'Astrolabe*	3.25	3.00
965†	2p50 *L'Astrolabe* aground	6.00	6.00

MS971	32s, 42s, 57s, 1p50 Racing canoes	2.10	2.50

The component stamps of No. **MS**971 were also available separately.

1988

982†	57s Outrigger canoe	60	65

985†	32s *Olovaha II* (inter-island freighter)	30	35

MS989 42s Emigrant ship, Sydney (sheet also contains eleven other 42s values) .... 7·50 8·00

991†	75s Yachting	70	75

1018†	42s H.M.S. *Resolution* (Cook)	60	50
1019†	57s *Santa Maria* (Columbus)	75	70

1989

1033†	42s H.M.S. *Bounty* (Bligh)	1.00	90
1034†	57s H.M.S. *Bounty* and *Bounty's* launch	1.50	1.40
MS1035†	2p H.M.S. *Bounty*; 3p *Bounty's* launch	6.00	7.00

1061†	57s Outrigger canoe	80	80

MS1063 57s Early screw steamer; 57s *Queen Mary* (liner) (sheet also contains ten other 57s designs) 8.50 9.00

1990

1078	32s Ocean-going canoe		
1079	42s Ocean-going canoe		
1080	1p20 Ocean-going canoe		
1081	3p Ocean-going canoe		
	Set of 4	8.50	9.00

As No. 985, *but inscribed* "Silver Jubilee" *instead of* "70th Birthday"

1082†	32s *Olovaha II* (inter-island freighter) ..	40	30

1109† 57s Yacht 90 90

1991

MS1129 1p Yacht at dawn; 1p Yacht in
morning; 1p Yacht at midday; 1p Yacht in
evening; 1p Yacht at night 6.75 7.00

1131† 57s Yacht 70 55

1142† 42s Sinking coaster 65 65
1144† 42s Patrol boat 65 65

1149† 57s Longboat 70 55
1150† 1p Outrigger canoe 1.40 1.40
1151† 2p Stern of fautasi (large canoe) 2.50 2.75
1152† 2p Bow of fautasi 2.50 2.75

1157† 42s Pangai (patrol boat) 50 50
1160† 57s Neiafu (patrol boat) 70 70
1161† 2p Savea (patrol boat) 2.25 2.50

1992

MS1164 57s Model of Santa Maria (Columbus)
(sheet contains eleven other 57s stamps) 8.00 8.50

1165† 42s U.S.S. Arizona (battleship) under
attack, Pearl Harbor, 1941 .... 50 50
1173† 42s Battleship Row, Pearl Harbor 50 50
1174† 42s Japanese aircraft carrier 50 50

MS1196† 45s Twin-hulled canoe (sheet also
contains three other designs) 4.25 4.50

1993

1215† 1p50 Sailboard 1.25 1.40

1242† 60s Heemskerk and Zeehan (Tasman)
at sea 50 55
1243† 80s Heemskerk and Zeehan at anchor
with Tongan canoes 70 75
1244† 3p50 Zeehan and ship's boats 3.00 3.25

OFFICIAL STAMPS

1962
Nos. 112, 116 *and* 118 *overprinted* **OFFICIAL AIR MAIL 1862
TAU'ATAINA EMANCIPATION 1962**
O11† 2d Whaling ship 11.00 6.00
O12† 5d Aoniu II (inter-island freighter) 12.00 6.50
O14† 5s H.M.S. Bounty and launch (Bligh) 90.00 55.00

1967
No. 112 *surcharged* **OFFICIAL AIRMAIL ONE PA'ANGA**
O21 1p on 5s H.M.S. Bounty and launch
(Bligh) 1.75 2.25

1970
As No. 112, *but imperforate, surcharged* **OFFICIAL
Commonwealth Member JUNE 1970 AIRMAIL** *and value*
O42 50s on 5s H.M.S. Bounty and launch
(Bligh)
O43 90s on 5s H.M.S. Bounty and launch
O44 1p50 on 5s H.M.S. Bounty and launch
Set of 3 3.00 2.50

As No. 112, *but imperforate, surcharged* **Centenary British Red
Cross 1870–1970 OFFICIAL AIRMAIL**, *red cross and value*
O56† 80s on 5s H.M.S. Bounty and launch
(Bligh) 3.25 3.25
O57† 90s on 5s H.M.S. Bounty and launch 3.25 3.25

1972

O76 20s Aoniu (inter-island freighter)
O77 50s Aoniu
O78 1p20 Aoniu
Set of 3 6.50 4.50

1973
No. 396 *surcharged* **TONGA 1973 ESTABLISHMENT BANK OF
TONGA OFFICIAL AIRMAIL** *and value*
O100 40s on 21s Olovaha (inter-island
freighter)
O101 85s on 21s Olovaha
O102 1p25 on 21s Olovaha
Set of 3 4.50 2.50

O106 25s James Cook (bulk carrier)
O107 80s James Cook
O108 1p30 James Cook
Set of 3 19.00 8.50

1983
Nos. 834/5 *overprinted* **OFFICIAL**
O217† 29s H.M.S. Resolution (Cook) and
Canberra (liner) 2.75 2.75
O218† 32s H.M.S. Resolution and Canberra .. 3.50 3.50

TRANSKEI
Southern Africa
100 cents = 1 rand

1986

181† 20c Umzimvubu (coaster) 30 15

1988

221† 16c Grosvenor (East Indiaman), 1782 .. 20 10

TRENGGANU

South-east Asia
100 cents = 1 dollar

1949
As No. 115 of Antigua
64† 15c Paddle-steamer 55 1.60

1957

95† 20c Malay fishing prau 20 30

TRIESTE

Southern Europe

Zone A. Allied Military Government
100 centesimi = 1 lira

1952
No. 820 of Italy overprinted **AMG FTT**
239 25li Fishing boat, Trieste 35 25

No. 827 of Italy overprinted **AMG FTT**
246† 60li Motor torpedo boat 35 45

Zone B. Yugoslav Military Government
100 paras = 1 dinar

1952

B58† 28d Yachts 45 25

1954
No. 675 of Yugoslavia, with colour changed, overprinted **STT VUJNA**
B108† 1d River steamer 10 10

TRINIDAD AND TOBAGO

West Indies
100 cents = 1 dollar

1949
As No. 115 of Antigua
262† 6c Paddle-steamer 30 35

1966

314† 8c Royal Yacht *Britannia* 1.25 70

1970

385† 40c Brigantine, San Fernando, 1860 .... 45 15

1972

413 5c *Lady McLeod* (paddle-steamer), 1847, and on local stamp
414 10c *Lady McLeod*, 1847, (on local stamp)
415 30c *Lady McLeod*, 1847, (on local stamp)
Set of 3 1.00 55

1974

454 40c *Hummingbird I* (ketch), 1960
455 50c *Hummingbird II* (ketch), 1969
Set of 2 1.00 50

1976

479† 5c Fleet of Columbus, 1498 .... 80 10
488† 35c Longboat on beach 85 10

1979

541† 45c Oil rig 30 30

1980

558† $1.50 H.M.S. *Bacchante* (screw corvette), 1880 .... 1.00 1.60

No. 479 overprinted **1844—1980 POPULATION CENSUS 12th MAY 1980**
560† 5c Fleet of Columbus, 1498 .... 15 20

1981

586† 55c Sinking tanker and yacht 45 30

STANLEY GIBBONS STAMP COLLECTING SERIES
Introductory booklets on *How to Start, How to Identify Stamps* and *Collecting by Theme*. A series of well illustrated guides at a low price. Write for details.

1982

607† $1 Yacht and speedboat 55 55

1984

658† $1.50 Yachts 70 80

661† 35c Slave schooner 75 20

1985

676 30c *Lady Nelson* (cargo liner), 1928
677 95c *Lady Drake* (cargo liner), 1928
678 $1.50 *Federal Palm* (freighter), 1961
679 $2 *Federal Maple* (freighter), 1961
Set of 4 5.50 5.50

1988

735† $1.50 Naval patrol boat 2.00 1.50

751† $1.55 Freighter and container ship alongside steel works 1.25 1.00
752† $2 *Atlantic Empress* (tanker) on fire, 1979 .... 1.75 1.25

754† $1 19th-century sailing ship (on Tobago emblem) 75 50
755† $1.80 19th-century British warships (on Trinidad emblem) 1.00 90

1991

803†	40c Second World War convoy	20	10
804†	80c German U-boat under air attack	35	35
806†	$2.25 H.M.S. *Wye* (frigate), 1943	1.00	1.40

TRIPOLITANIA

North Africa
100 centisimi = 1 lira

ITALIAN COLONY

1927

36†	20c + 05c Freighter, Tripoli	1.50	2.50
37†	25c + 05c Freighter, Tripoli	1.50	2.50

BRITISH ADMINISTRATION

1951

Nos. 509/10 of Great Britain surcharged **B.A. TRIPOLITANIA** *and value in* **M.A.L.**

T32†	60li on 2s6d H.M.S. *Victory* (Nelson)	3.50	13.00
T33†	120li on 5s Yacht and Thames sailing barge, Dover	7.50	16.00

TRISTAN DA CUNHA

South Atlantic
1952 12 pence = 1 shilling
20 shillings = 1 pound
1971 100 pence = 1 pound

1952

Nos. 131, 135a/40 and 149/51 of St. Helena overprinted **TRISTAN DA CUNHA**

1	½d *London* (East Indiaman), 1659	
2	1d *London*, 1659	
3	1½d *London*, 1659	
4	2d *London*, 1659	
5	3d *London*, 1659	
6	4d *London*, 1659	
7	6d *London*, 1659	
8	8d *London*, 1659	
9	1s *London*, 1659	
10	2s6d *London*, 1659	
11	5s *London*, 1659	
12	10s *London*, 1659	

Set of 12 95.00 £100

1954

19†	3d Tristan longboat	80	20

1965

72†	1d Tristao da Cunha's caravel, 1506	30	15
73†	1½d *Heemstede* (Dutch East Indiaman), 1643	30	15
74†	2d *Edward* (American whaling ship), 1864	30	15

75†	3d *Shenandoah* (Confederate warship), 1862	30	15
75a†	4d H.M.S. *Challenger* (survey ship), 1873	5.50	4.00
76† ·	4½d H.M.S. *Galatea* (screw frigate), 1867	30	15
77†	6d H.M.S. *Cilicia* (transport), 1942	30	15
78†	7d Royal Yacht *Britannia*	30	20
79†	10d H.M.S. *Leopard* (frigate)	30	20
80†	1s *Tjisadane* (liner)	30	20
81†	1s6d *Tristania* (crayfish trawler)	2.50	2.00
82†	2s6d *Boissevain* (cargo liner)	2.75	2.50
83†	5s *Bornholm* (liner)	4.00	3.50
84a†	10s *R.S.A.* (research vessel)	17.00	11.00

1966

93	3d H.M.S. *Falmouth* (frigate), 1816	
94	6d H.M.S. *Falmouth*	
95	1s6d H.M.S. *Falmouth*	
96	2s6d H.M.S. *Falmouth*	

Set of 4 80 45

1967

No. 76 surcharged **4d**

108	4d on 4½d H.M.S. *Galatea* (screw frigate), 1867	10	10

1969

121	4d 18th-century frigate	
122	1s Full-rigged sailing ship	
123	1s6d Barque	
124	2s6d Full-rigged clipper	

Set of 4 1.60 80

125†	4d 19th-century full-rigged ship	10	10

1970

133†	4d Tristan longboat	20	10
135†	1s6d Tristan longboat	35	25

1971

Nos. 72/4, 75a, 77/83 and 84a surcharged in decimal currency

137	½p on 1d Tristao da Cunha's caravel, 1506	
138	1p on 2d *Edward* (American whaling ship), 1864	
139	1½p on 4d H.M.S. *Challenger* (steam survey ship), 1873	
140	2½p on 6d H.M.S. *Cilicia* (transport), 1942	
141	3p on 7d Royal Yacht *Britannia*	
142	4p on 10d H.M.S. *Leopard* (frigate)	
143	5p on 1s *Tjisadane* (liner)	
144	7½p on 1s6d *Tristania* (crayfish trawler)	
145	12½p on 2s6d *Boissevain* (cargo liner)	
146	15p on 1½d *Heemstede* (Dutch East Indiaman), 1643	
147	25p on 5s *Bornholm* (liner)	
148	50p on 10s *R.S.A.* (research vessel)	

Set of 12 18.00 21.00

1971 (right column)

149†	1½p *Quest* (Shackleton), 1921	90	30
152†	12½p Tristan longboat	1.40	45

153	1½p H.M.S. *Victory* (Nelson) at Trafalgar, 1805		
154	2½p *Emily of Stonington* (American schooner), 1836		
155	4p *Italia* (Italian barque) (incorrectly shown as brig), 1892		
156	7½p H.M.S. *Falmouth* (frigate), 1816		
157	12½p 19th-century American whaling ship		

Set of 5 2.00 2.40

1972

170†	2½p Tristan longboat	15	10
173†	12½p Longboat under sail	30	20

1973

178†	5p H.M.S. *Challenger* (survey ship), 1873	30	25
179†	7½p H.M.S. *Challenger*'s steam pinnace, 1873	30	30

1976

204†	5p *London* (East Indiaman) (on stamp No. 1)	15	20
206†	25p *Tristania II* (crayfish trawler)	40	50

1977

212†	10p Royal Yacht *Britannia*	25	30

215 5p H.M.S. *Eskimo* (frigate), 1970
216 10p H.M.S. *Naiad* (frigate), 1968
217 15p H.M.S. *Jaguar* (frigate), 1964
218 20p H.M.S. *London* (destroyer), 1964
　　　　　　　　　　　　Set of 4 1.25 75

1978

235 10p Tristan longboats 20 25

250 5p R.F.A. *Orangeleaf* (tanker)
251 10p R.F.A. *Tarbatness* (store carrier)
252 20p R.F.A. *Tidereach* (tanker)
253 25p R.F.A. *Reliant* (store carrier)
　　　　　　　　　　　　Set of 4 1.10 65

1979

259 5p Tristan longboat
260 10p *Queen Mary* (liner)
261 15p *Queen Elizabeth* (liner)
262 20p *Queen Elizabeth 2* (liner)
　　　　　　　　　　　　Set of 4 95 1.10
MS263 25p *Queen Elizabeth 2* (liner) 1.00 2.25

264† 5p *London* (East Indiaman) (on stamp
　　　No. 12) 15 15

1980

277† 5p *Tristania II* (crayfish trawler) 15 15
278† 10p Tristan longboat 15 15

283† 5p *Golden Hind* (Drake) 20 10

1982

323 5p *Marcella* (barque)
324 15p *Eliza Adams* (full-rigged ship)
325 30p *Corinthian* (American whaling ship)
326 50p *Samuel and Thomas* (American
　　　whaling ship)
　　　　　　　　　　　　Set of 4 2.00 2.50

1983

341 5p *Islander* (barque)
342 20p *Roscoe* (full-rigged ship)
343 35p *Columbia* (whaling ship)
344 50p *Emeline* (schooner)
　　　　　　　　　　　　Set of 4 1.90 1.75

350† 3p *Tristao da Cunha's* caravel, 1506 . . . . 40 30
351† 4p *Heemstede* (Dutch East Indiaman),
　　　1643 . . . . 40 30
353† 10p H.M.S. *Falmouth* (frigate), 1816 . . . . 45 40
357† 25p *John and Elizabeth* (American
　　　whaling ship) 85 75
359† £1 Tristan longboat 2.50 2.50
360† £2 H.M.S. *Leopard* (frigate), 1961 . . . . . . 3.75 4.00

1984

365 10p *London* (East Indiaman) (on stamp
　　　No. 7)
366 15p *London* (on stamp No. 9)
367 25p *London* (on stamp No. 10)
368 60p *London* (on stamp No. 12)
　　　　　　　　　　　　Set of 4 1.40 1.40

1985

386† 10p Shipwreck of H.M.S. *Julia* (sloop),
　　　1817 . . . . 60 70
388† 35p Shipwreck of *Glenhuntley* (barque),
　　　1898 . . . . 1.40 1.60

397† 25p H.M.S. *Falmouth* (frigate), 1816 . . . . 1.10 1.25

399† 10p Lifeboat and *West Riding* (barque),
　　　1885 . . . . 35 60

1986

405† 50p H.M.S. *Paramour* (pink), 1694 . . . . . . 1.40 1.75

411† 9p Ship's boat and wreck of *Allanshaw*
　　　(barque), 1893 . . . . 30 35
413† 40p Figurehead 1.10 1.40

1987

427† 17p Wreck of *Henry A. Paull*
　　　(barquentine), 1879 . . . . 45 45

437† 50p *Thorshammer* (whale factory ship) 2.25 2.25

1988

451† 50 Model longboat 1.10 1.10

455† 50p 19th-century whaling ships 1.10 1.10

458† 25p *Tristania II* (crayfish trawler) 55 55
459† 35p *St. Helena I* (mail ship) 80 80
460† 50p *Kobenhavn* (cadet barque) 1.25 1.25

467† 20p Schooner, 1824 .... 40 45

1989

483† 20p Whaling ship 60 60

1990

500† 10p *Dunnottar Castle* (liner), 1942 ...... 35 35
501† 15p *St. Helena I* (mail ship) 50 50
502† 35p Launch of *St. Helena II* (mail ship) 1.00 1.00
MS504† £1 *St. Helena II* 2.50 3.00

1991

505 10p H.M.S. *Pyramus* (frigate), 1829
506 25p H.M.S. *Penguin* (sloop), 1815
507 35p H.M.S. *Thalia* (screw corvette), 1886
508 50p H.M.S. *Sidon* (paddle frigate), 1858
Set of 4 3.25 3.25

509 10p H.M.S. *Milford* (sloop), 1938
510 25p H.M.S. *Dublin* (cruiser), 1923
511 35p H.M.S. *Yarmouth* (cruiser), 1919
512 50p H.M.S. *Carlisle* (cruiser), 1937
Set of 4 3.25 3.25

MS513 £1 *Royal Viking Sun* (liner) 3.00 3.50

514† 10p H.M.S. *Galatea* (screw frigate), 1867 50 50
516† 30p Royal Yacht *Britannia* 1.00 1.00

1992

522 10p *Eye of the Wind* (cadet brig)
523 15p *Soren Larsen* (cadet brigantine)
524 35p *Columbus's fleet*
525 60p *Santa Maria* (Columbus)
Set of 4 4.00 4.00

527† 20p Tristan longboat under sail 60 60

535 10p *Italia* (barque) leaving Greenock, 1892
536 45p *Italia* in mid-Atlantic
537 65p *Italia* ashore on Stony Beach
Set of 3 3.25 3.25
MS538 £1 *Italia* becalmed 3.00 3.25

TRUCIAL STATES

Arabian peninsula
100 naye paise = 1 rupee

1961

8† 1r Dhow 3.00 50
9† 2r Dhow 3.00 6.50
10† 5r Dhow 4.50 11.00
11† 10r Dhow 12.00 20.00

TUNISIA

North Africa
1906 100 centimes = 1 franc
1959 1000 milliemes = 1 dinar

1906

41† 1f Carthaginian galley (brown & red) 65 35
111† 1f Carthaginian galley (blue) 25 25
42† 2f Carthaginian galley (green & brown) 2.75 80
112† 2f Carthaginian galley (red & green on red) 35 45
43† 5f Carthaginian galley (blue & violet) 6.75 3.00
113† 5f Carthaginian galley (green & lilac) 55 75

1916
As Nos. 41 etc, but colours changed, surcharged **10c** *and red cross*
57† 10c on 1f Carthaginian galley (green & red) 2.50 2.50
58† 10c on 2f Carthaginian galley (blue & brown) 60.00 60.00
59† 10c on 5f Carthaginian galley (red & violet) 70.00 65.00

1918
As Nos. 41, etc, but colours changed, surcharged **15c.** *and red cross*
66† 15c on 1f Carthaginian galley (violet & red) 11.50 13.50
67† 15c on 2f Carthaginian galley (red & brown) 45.00 50.00
68† 15c on 5f Carthaginian galley (black & violet) £100 £100

1923
As Nos. 41, etc, but colours changed, surcharged **AFFt 25c** *below medal*
97† 25c on 1f Carthaginian galley (mauve & lake) 2.25 2.75
98† 25c on 2f Carthaginian galley (red & blue) 9.00 10.50
99† 25c on 5f Carthaginian galley (brown & green) 32.00 45.00

1927
Nos. 111/13 overprinted **Poste Aerienne** *and aeroplane or surcharged also*
148† 1f Carthaginian galley (blue) 40 50
150† 1f75 on 5f Carthaginian galley (green & lilac) 1.50 1.90
151† 2f Carthaginian galley (red & green on red) 1.60 1.50

1947
No. 965 of France surcharged **TUNISIE 10 + 15**
300 10f + 15f on 2f + 3f *Emile Bertin* (cruiser) and *Lorraine* (battleship) 60 70

1959

503† 200m Fishing boats, Sfax 4.00 1.90

1982

997 150m Oil rig and drilling vessel 60 30

1983

1040   80m French frigate, 1963   30   15

1986

1108†   160m Phoenician ship, 800 B.C.   50   20

1991

1206   450m Yachts in marina, Montazah
Tabarka   55   30

TURKEY

South-east Europe and Asia Minor
1914 40 paras = 1 piastre or grush
1929 40 paras = 1 kurus
100 kurus = 1 lira

1914

508†   2pi Hamidiye (cruiser) 1.00   30

No. 508 overprinted

530†   2pi Hamidiye (cruiser) 3.00   75

1940

1272†   10k Early paddle-steamer and modern
mail launch 1.50   65

1941

1274   30p Etrusk (freighter), Izmir   20   10

1281†   3k Barbarossa's corsair fleet, *c.* 1540   20   10
1282†   6k Barbarossa's corsair fleet, *c.* 1540   35   20
1283†   10k Barbarossa's corsair fleet, *c.* 1540   45   25
1284†   12k Barbarossa's corsair fleet, *c.* 1540   1.00   30

1946

1353   9k U.S.S. *Missouri* (battleship)
1354   10k U.S.S. *Missouri*
1355   27½k U.S.S. *Missouri*
                                      Set of 3   1.75   55

1949

1409†   5k Galley   25   10
1410†   10k Mahmudiye (ship of the line)   60   10
1411†   15k Hamidiye (cruiser)   65   10
1412†   20k Sakarya (submarine)   70   20
1413†   30k Yavuz (battle cruiser) 1.25   40

1951

1457†   15k Providence (liner) and Hora (tug)   55   15
1458†   20k Iskendrun (liner)   55   15

1464†   60k Halas (ferry) 1.60   70

1953

1506†   10k 15th-century naval battle between
Turks and Byzantines   20   10
1507†   12k 15th-century galleys   25   10

1955

1558†   30k Nusret (minelayer), 1915   50   20

1958

1753†   5k Freighters and fishing boats, Trabzon   10   10

1959

1854†   5k Karadeniz (liner)   20   10

1965

2128   50k Savarona (naval training ship)
2129   60k Piri Reis (submarine)
2130   100k Alpaslan (destroyer)
2131   130k Gelibolu (destroyer)
2132   220k Gemlik (destroyer)
                                      Set of 5   4.00   2.00

1968

2244   50k Kismet (ketch)   45   15

1969

2280†   60k Bandirma (cargo liner), 1919   50   15

1970

2350†   250k Fishing boats   70   25

1971

2388†   110k Orhan Atliman (train ferry), Lake
Van 1.60   20

1973

2451   5k Nusret II (minelayer), 1971 .
2452   25k Istanbul (destroyer)
2453   100k Simsek (motor torpedo-boat)
2454   250k Nuvid-i-Futuh (cadet brig)
                                      Set of 4   2.50   80

2473 75k Freighter
2474 90k Freighter
2475 100k Freighter
2476 250k Freighter
2477 325k Freighter
2478 475k Freighter
         Set of 6 3.00 40

1977

2573 400k *Hora* (oil exploration ship) 85 25

1982

2782 30li Tanker 35 15

1986

2929 20li *Abdulhamit* (submarine) 15 10

1988

2989† 200li Liner 30 10

3002† 200li Container ship, Bosphorus 25 10

1989

3045 150li *Sahilbent* (paddle-steamer)
3046 300li *Ragbet* (paddle-steamer)
3047 600li *Tari* (freighter)
3048 1000li *Guzelhisar* (ferry)
         Set of 4 2.75 70

1990

3078† 1000li + 100li Liner, Istanbul 55 20

3086 1000li *Ertugrul* (frigate), 1890 .... 75 15

1986

3090† 700li Fishing boats, Saintes Maries 30 10

3099† 200li Liner 10 10

1991

3116 500li Cable ship 20 10

1992

3143 1500li Immigrant caravel, 1492 .... 20 10

OBLIGATORY TAX STAMPS

1944

T1349 2½k Hospital ship 25 10

TURKS AND CAICOS ISLANDS

West Indies
1900 12 pence = 1 shilling
   20 shillings = 1 pound
1969 100 cents = 1 dollar

1900

110 ½d 19th-century full-rigged ship
102 1d 19th-century full-rigged ship
103 2d 19th-century full-rigged ship
104a 2½d 19th-century full-rigged ship
112 3d 19th-century full-rigged ship
105 4d 19th-century full-rigged ship
106 6d 19th-century full-rigged ship
107 1s 19th-century full-rigged ship
108 2s 19th-century full-rigged ship
109 3s 19th-century full-rigged ship
       Set of 10 £100 £150

1948

210† ½d 19th-century full-rigged ship 15 15
211† 2d 19th-century full-rigged ship 30 15
212† 3d Freighter 35 15

1949

As No. 115 *of Antigua*
218† 3d Paddle-steamer 50 50

1950

223† 1½d Caicos sloop 20 55
225† 2½d Caicos sloop 20 50
232† 5s Caicos sloop 7.00 3.75
233† 10s 19th-century full-rigged ship 14.00 13.00

1955

235† 5d *Kirksons* (coaster) 30 30

1957

244† 6d Caicos sloop 1.00 30
248† 2s *Uakon* (Caicos sloop) 3.25 2.25
250† 10s 19th-century full-rigged ship 9.00 8.00

1966

268† 1d British frigate, 1766 .... 10 10
269† 8d Merchant ships, 1766 .... 10 10

1967

275† 1½d Boat building 10 10
278† 4d Caicos sloop 30 10
285† 5s Caicos sloops and trawler 1.25 2.00

1969

Nos. 275, 278 *and* 285 *surcharged in decimal currency*
301† 4c on 4d Caicos sloop 10 10
304† 8c on 1½d Boat building 10 10
309† 50c on 5s Caicos sloops and trawler 1.00 45

1971

As Nos. 275, 278 *and* 285, *but face values in decimal currency*
336† 4c Caicos sloop 50 10
339† 8c Boat building 50 10
344† 80c Caicos sloops and trawler 2.50 2.00

351† 2c Pirate sloop 10 10

1972

368 1c Fleet of Columbus, 1492
369 8c *Revenge* (English galleon), 1591
370 10c 17th-century English merchantman
371 30c Spanish caravel
                    Set of 4   1.40   75

1973

396 2c Bermuda sloop
397 5c H.M.S. *Blanche* (screw sloop), 1867
398 8c *Grand Turk* (American privateer) and
      Hinchinbrook II (British sailing packet),
      1813
399 10c H.M.S. *Endymion* (frigate), 1790
400 15c *Medina* (paddle-steamer)
401 20c H.M.S. *Daring* (brig), 1804
                    Set of 6   1.60   1.75

1974

427† 12c Caicos sloop 20 10

430† 12c Second World War convoy 15 15

1976

446 6c American schooner, 1776
447 20c British ship of the line, 1776
448 25c *Grand Turk* (American privateer),
      1778
449 55c British ketch, 1776
                    Set of 4   2.25   95

1978

490† 20c Caicos sloop 35 55
491† 25c Motor cruiser 40 65
492† 55c *Jamaica Planter* (freighter) 85 1.60

1979

545† 6c *Medina* (paddle-steamer) 10 10
547† 45c *Orinoco I* (mail paddle-steamer) 25 25
548† 75c *Shannon* (screw steamer) 40 40
549† $1 *Trent I* (paddle-steamer) 55 55
550† $2 19th-century full-rigged ship (on
      stamp No. 102) 90 90

557† 15c Roman galley 20 20
560† 25c Paddle-steamer 30 30

1980

612† $1 Lobster trawler 1.00 80

1981

630 6c Yachts
631 15c Yachts and trimaran
632 35c Speedboats
633 $1 Caicos sloops
                    Set of 4   90   80

1983

738† 65c Yacht........................... 85 90

769 4c Arawak dug-out canoe
770 5c *Santa Maria* (Columbus)
771 8c 18th-century Spanish galleon and
      British warship
772 10c Bermuda sloop

773 20c *Grand Turk* (American privateer)
774 25c H.M.S. *Boreas* (frigate), 1784
775 30c H.M.S. *Endymion* (frigate), 1790
776 35c *Caesar* (barque)
777 50c *Grapeshot* (American schooner)
778 65c H.M.S. *Invincible* (battle cruiser),
      1907
779 95c H.M.S. *Magicienne* (cruiser), 1888
780 $1.10 H.M.S. *Durban* (cruiser), 1919
781 $2 *Sentinel* (cable ship)
782 $3 H.M.S. *Minerva* (frigate), 1964
783 $5 Caicos sloop
                    Set of 15   27.00   28.00

1985

841† 65c *Isere* (French screw warship), 1885 2.25 1.50

844 20c H.M.S. *Royal George* (ship of the
      line), 1782
845 30c H.M.S. *Victory* (ship of the line)
      (Nelson), 1805
846 65c H.M.S. *Albion* (ship of the line), 1802
847 95c H.M.S. *Indefatigable* (battle cruiser),
      1916
                    Set of 4   10.00   8.50

850† 35c *Grand Turk* (Mississippi river
      steamer) 1.25 55

1987

902 8c H.M.S. *Victoria* (ship of the line), 1855
903 35c *Victoria* (paddle-steamer)
904 55c Royal Yacht *Victoria and Albert I*,
      1843
905 95c Royal Yacht *Victoria and Albert II*,
      1854
                    Set of 4   6.75   6.50
MS906 $2 *Victoria* (barque) 4.50 5.00

1988

912 4c *Santa Maria* (Columbus)
913 25c Ship's boat
914 70c *Santa Maria*
915 95c *Santa Maria*
                    Set of 4   5.25   5.00
MS916 $2 *Santa Maria, Pinta* and *Nina* 3.50 4.25

918† 35c *Santa Maria* (Columbus) 55 55

Nos 772, 774 and 781 overprinted **40TH WEDDING ANNIVERSARY H.M. QUEEN ELIZABETH II H.R.H. THE DUKE OF EDINBURGH**

922	10c Bermuda sloop		
923	25c H.M.S. *Boreas* (frigate), 1784		
924	$2 *Sentinel* (cable ship)		
	Set of 3	3.75	3.75

926†	30c Yachts	35	40

930†	8c Game fishing boat	30	15
932†	70c Game fishing boat	1.75	1.75

1989

950†	$1 Carib canoe	1.50	1.50

1991

1072†	5c *Discoverie* (Hudson), 1611	10	10
1074†	15c *Gjoa* (Amundsen), 1906	15	20
1075†	50c U.S.S. *Nautilus* (submarine), 1958	60	65
1076†	75c *Terra Nova* (Scott), 1911	85	90
1079†	$1.50 H.M.S. *Resolution* (Cook), 1772–75	1.75	1.90
MS1080†	Two sheets (a) $2 *Santa Maria* (Columbus); (b) $2 *Nina*		
	Price for 2 sheets	4.75	5.00

1992

1149†	50c Fishing boats, Grand Turk	60	65
1151†	80c Motor boats	95	1.00
MS1153†	Two sheets (a) $2 Fishing boat on foreshore (other sheet shows beach)		
	Price for 2 sheets	4.75	5.00

1166†	10c *Nina* (Columbus)	10	10
1167†	15c *Santa Maria* leaving Palos	15	20
1169†	25c Ships of Columbus	30	35
1170†	30c *Pinta*	35	40
1171†	35c Ship's boat	40	45
1173†	65c *Santa Maria*	75	80
MS1176†	Two sheets (a) $2 Ships of Columbus on coins (other sheet shows different coins)		
	Price for 2 sheets	4.75	5.00

TUVALU

Pacific Ocean
100 cents = 1 dollar

1976

3†	35c Canoes of Gilbert and Ellice Islands	75	1.50

Nos. 174, 177 and 184 of Gilbert and Ellice Islands overprinted **TUVALU**

20†	2c Fishing canoe	80	40
5†	5c Gilbertese canoe	80	60
25†	35c Fishing canoes at night	1.75	1.00

41†	50c Fishing canoe	75	30
69†	$5 *Nivanga* (inter-island coaster)	6.50	4.00

1977

51†	35c Ceremonial canoe	70	40

74†	20c Scout canoe	30	25

80†	35c H.M.S. *Beagle* (Darwin), 1831	40	20

1978

85	8c *Laweduna* (inter-island coaster)		
86	20c *Wallacia* (tug)		
87	30c *Cenpac Rounder* (freighter)		
88	40c *Pacific Explorer* (freighter)		
	Set of 4	65	65

1979

123†	8c H.M.S. *Resolution* (Cook), 1779	30	20
124†	30c H.M.S. *Resolution* (Cook), 1779	40	25
126†	$1 H.M.S. *Resolution* (Cook), 1779	50	35

133†	$1 Canoes of Gilbert and Ellice Islands (on stamp No. 3)	50	30

1981

162	10c *Elizabeth* (brig), 1809		
163	25c *Rebecca* (brigantine), 1919		
164	35c *Independence II* (whaling ship), 1821		
165	40c H.M.S. *Basilisk* (paddle-sloop), 1872		
166	45c H.M.S. *Royalist* (screw corvette), 1890		
167	50c *Olivebank* (barque), 1920		
	Set of 6	1.75	2.00

168†	10c Royal Yacht *Carolina*	10	15
170†	45c Royal Yacht *Victoria and Albert III*	15	15
172†	$2 Royal Yacht *Britannia*	50	50

1982

181†	25c Motor launch	25	2.
182†	35c Motor launch	35	35
183†	45c Freighter	40	4

No. 170 surcharged **TONGA CYCLONE RELIEF 1982 +20c**

187†	45c + 20c Royal Yacht *Victoria and Albert III*	30	5

1983

213†	20c *Te Tautai* (trawler)	15	15
216†	50c *Morning Star* (container ship)	40	40

222†	35c Outrigger canoe	40	45

1984

235	10c *Titus* (freighter), 1897		
236	20c *Malaita* (freighter), 1905		
237	25c *Aymeric* (freighter), 1906		
238	35c *Anshun* (freighter), 1965		
239	45c *Beaverbank* (freighter), 1970		
240	50c *Benjamin Bowring* (freighter), 1981		
	Set of 6	1.40	1.40

1986

377	15c *Messenger of Peace* (missionary schooner)		
378	40c *John Wesley* (missionary brig)		
379	50c *Duff* (full-rigged ship missionary)		
380	60c *Triton* (missionary brigantine)		
	Set of 4	1.25	1.40

1987

442	15c *Southern Cross IV* (missionary steamer)		
443	40c *John Williams VI* (missionary steamer)		
444	50c *John Williams IV* (missionary steamer)		
445	60c *Southern Cross* (missionary steamer)		
	Set of 4	3.75	3.75

494†	60c H.M.S. *Endeavour* (Cook)	80	80

1988

523†	20c H.M.S. *Endeavour* (Cook)	55	55
524†	40c Stern of H.M.S. *Endeavour*	80	80
525†	50c H.M.S. *Endeavour* at Tahiti	90	90
527†	80c H.M.S. *Resolution* and Hawaiian canoe	1.25	1.25
MS529†	$2.50 H.M.S. *Resolution* in Antarctic	4.50	4.50

538†	80c Yacht	75	80

1989

MS563	$1.50 *Nivaga II* (inter-island ship)	2.75	3.00

1990

578	15c Camouflaged Japanese freighter, 1940		
579	30c U.S.S. *Unimack* (seaplane tender)		
580	40c *Amagiri* (Japanese destroyer)		
581	50c U.S.S. *Platte* (attack transport)		
582	60c Japanese "Shumushu" class escort		
583	90c U.S.S. *Independence* (aircraft carrier)		
	Set of 6	5.25	5.25

592†	$1.20 *Te Tautai* (trawler)	1.90	1.90

1991

613	40c U.S.S. *Tennessee* (battleship)		
614	50c *Haguro* (Japanese cruiser)		
615	60c H.M.N.Z.S. *Achilles* (cruiser)		
616	$1.50 U.S.S. *North Carolina* (battleship)		
	Set of 4	5.00	5.25

1992

625	40c Cargo liner		
626	50c Freighter and barges		
627	60c Freighter		
628	$1.50 H.M.S. *Royalist* (cruiser), 1915		
	Set of 4	3.50	3.75

660†	40c Outrigger canoes	35	40
661†	50c Fishing canoes	45	50
662†	60c Canoe on beach	50	55

UBANGI-SHARI

Central Africa
100 centimes = 1 franc

1931

As No. 109 of Cameroun
106†	1f50 *Leconte de Lisle* (liner)	3.50	3.75

UGANDA

East Africa
100 cents = 1 shilling

1986

530	50s *Gloria* (Colombian cadet ship)		
531	100s *Mircea* (Rumanian cadet barque)		
532	140s *Sagres II* (Portuguese cadet barque)		
533	2500s *Gazela Primiero* (wrongly inscribed "Primero") (American cadet ship)		
	Set of 4	8.00	8.00

1987

574†	35s U.S.S. *Pennsylvania* (battleship) (first aircraft take-off and landing from ship), 1911	1.25	1.25

603†	35s Scout canoe, Lake Victoria	70	75

1989

765†	150s Pharaonic ship of 600 B.C.	85	85
766†	250s 15th-century caravel	1.00	1.00
767†	300s *Lady Alice* (Stanley's sectional boat)	1.25	1.25
MS768†	Two sheets.. (a) 500s *Ma-Robert* (Livingstone's steam launch) (other sheet shows map)		
	Price for 2 sheets	5.00	5.50

775†	250s *Wappen von Hamburg* and *Leopoldus Primus* (galleons)	1.50	1.50

1990

811†	200s Landing craft, Philippines, 1944	20	25
812†	300s Japanese aircraft carrier under attack, Coral Sea, 1942	30	35
814†	500s American battleship in action, 1942	50	55

1992

1051†	200s U.S.S. *Vestal* (transport) under attack, Pearl Harbor, 1941	20	25
1053†	200s U.S.S. *Arizona* (battleship) on fire	20	25
1054†	200s U.S.S. *Nevada* (battleship) passing burning ships	20	25
1056†	200s *Hiryu* (Japanese aircraft carrier) under attack, Battle of Midway, 1942	20	25
1059†	200s American aircraft carrier, Battle of Midway	20	25
1060†	200s U.S.S. *Yorktown* (aircraft carrier) torpedoed, Battle of Midway	20	25

1113†	200s *Nina* (Columbus)	20	25
1114†	600s *Pinta*	65	70

UNITED ARAB EMIRATES

Arabian peninsula
100 fils = 1 dirham

1973

10†	3d Motor barge, Ras al Khaima	5.00	1.75

1975

32†	50f *Al Ittiad* (offshore oil drilling platform)	1.40	35
34†	125f Marine oil production platform	2.50	1.50

1984

177†	1d Dhow	1.10	95

1986

201	2d Container ship		
202	3d Container ship		
	Set of 2	4.00	2.75

214†	50f Dhow	40	20
215†	1d Dhow	85	50

1987

228†	50f Oil rig	40	30
231†	2d Tanker	1.90	1.90

1988

255†	50f Dhow	30	30

257†	1d Container ship	60	60
258†	175f "Ro-Ro" ferry and small craft	1.00	1.00
259†	2d Container ship	1.40	1.40

1989

271†	3d *Bombala* (freighter)	1.25	1.25

280	1d Dhow		
281	3d Dhow		
	Set of 2	1.75	1.75

1990

308	50f Dhows and oil rig		
309	1d Dhows and oil rig		
	Set of 2	70	70

321†	50f Oil rig	20	15

1991

353†	175f Motor launches	65	65
354†	2d Container ship and tug, Jebel Ali Port	70	70

1992

377	50f Container ships, Zayed Port, Abu Dhabi		
378	1d Container ships		
379	175f Loading container ship		
380	2d Container ship and map		
	Set of 4	1.75	1.75

381† 50f Yacht 20 20

1993

406† 1d Fishing launch 35 35
407† 2d Yacht 70 70

410† 250f Fishing boat 90 90

UNITED NATIONS
A. New York Headquarters
100 cents = 1 dollar

1964

127 5c Freighter and liner
128 11c Freighter and liner
                              Set of 2 50 40

1975

263 10c Bulk carrier
264 26c Bulk carrier
                              Set of 2 40 30

1990

581 25c Shipping in port 60 15

1992

619 29c Yachts and fishing launch
620 29c Liner
                              Set of 2 80 40

B. Geneva Headquarters
100 centimes = 1 franc

1975
As Nos. 263/4 but inscribed in French
G46 60c Bulk carrier
G47 70c Bulk carrier
                              Set of 2 1.60 1.60

1990

G182 1f50 Shipping in port 1.25 1.25

G188† 90c Liner 70 70

C. Vienna Headquarters
100 groschen = 1 schilling

1990

V96 12s Shipping in port 1.75 1.75

UNITED STATES OF AMERICA
North America
100 cents = 1 dollar

1869

119† 12c *Adriatic* (paddle-steamer) £475 55.00

1893

237† 3c *Santa Maria* (Columbus) 35.00 10.00
238† 4c Fleet of Columbus 50.00 4.00

1898

299† $2 *Grey Eagle* and *St. Paul* (Mississippi
        paddle-steamers) £1800 £600

1901

300† 1c *City of Alpena* (Great Lakes steamer) 13.00 2.75
304† 8c *Carrington* (freighter) in Sault Sainte
        Marie canal lock £100 50.00
305† 10c *St. Paul* (liner) and *Fred A. Lee* (tug) £150 24.00

1909

379 2c *Clermont* (Fulton's first commercial
      paddle-steamer), 1807, and *Half Moon*
      (Hudson), 1609 .... 11.00 3.25

1920

556† 1c *Mayflower* (Pilgrim Fathers), 1620 .... 3.75 2.00

1922

698† 20c *W. F. Babcock* (brig) and *Charles
        Nelson* (steamer), San Francisco 4.75 10

1924

618† 1c *Nieu Nederland* (emigrant ship), 1642 3.25 3.00

624 2c *Restaurationen* (emigrant sloop), 1825
625 5c *Raven* (replica Viking longship)
                              Set of 2 22.00 18.00

1929

682 2c *H. D. Williams* (paddle-steamer) 30 30

1934

735 3c *Ark* and *Dove* (emigrant ships), 1634 20 15

1936

786† 1c Battle of Flamborough Head, 1779 .. 15 10
787† 2c U.S.S. *United States* (frigate), 1812 .. 15 10
788† 3c U.S.S. *Hartford* (steam frigate), 1862 25 10

1938

846 3c *Calmare Nyckel* (emigrant ship), 1638   15   10

1939

853 3c *Andrea F. Luckenbach* (freighter) in Panama Canal 25   10

1944

920 3c *Savannah* (paddle-steamer), 1819 10   10

1945

933 3c *Arthur Middleton* (supply ship) and U.S. Coastguard landing craft 10   10

1946

936 3c "Liberty" type freighter 10   10

944 3c Liner 15   10

1947

A949† 15c Tug, New York 20   10

948 3c U.S.S. *Constitution* (frigate), 1797 15   10

1948

953 3c Sinking of *Dorchester* (liner), 1943 10   10

1949

981 3c *Het Vergulde Vsanker* (sailing barge)   10   10

1950

991 3c Mississippi river steamer, 1850 10   10

994 3c *Oregon* (paddle-steamer), 1850 10   10

1952

1007 3c French warship, 1777 10   10

1953

1018 5c U.S.S. *Susquehanna* and U.S.S. *Mississippi* (paddle-steamers), Tokyo Bay, 1853 15   15

1024 3c Dutch galleon, New York, 1653 10   10

1954

1065 3c Keel boat 10   10

1955

1071 3c *Altadoc* (Great Lakes freighter) 15   10

1957

1090 3c *Pathfinder*, *Explorer* and *Surveyor* (coastguard vessels) 10   10

1093 3c U.S.S. *Forrestal* (aircraft carrier) 15   10

1097 3c *Virginia of Sagadahock* (Maine shallop), 1607 10   10

1959

1127 4c U.S.S. *Nautilus* (submarine) 10   10

1962

1196 4c Mississippi sternwheel steamer 10   10

1210 4c Yachts 10   10

1965

1252 5c Fulton and *Clermont* (first commercial paddle-steamer), 1807 10   10

1967

1305 5c Canal barge 10   10

1968

1341 6c Indian canoe, 1668 15   10

1343 6c River tanker 15   10

1969

1361   6c Rowing boat, 1869   15   10

1970

HAIDA CEREMONIAL CANOE

1379†   6c Haida ceremonial canoe   20   10

GREAT NORTHWEST
1820 FORT SNELLING 1970

1405   6c Keel boat, 1820   15   10

1416   6c *Mayflower* (Pilgrim Fathers), 1620   20   10

1971

HISTORIC PRESERVATION

1444†   8c *Charles W. Morgan* (whaling ship)   ..   20   10

1973

THE BOSTON TEA PARTY

1501   8c English merchantman, Boston, 1773
1502   8c English merchantman, Boston, 1773
1503   8c Rowing boats, Boston, 1773
1504   8c Rowing boat, Boston, 1773
            Set of 4   55   35

1978

1710†   13c H.M.S. *Resolution* and H.M.S.
            Discovery (Cook) at Hawaii, 1778   15   10

1981

1915†   18c Battle of Virginia Capes, 1781   35   10

1983

2028   20c *Concord* (emigrant ship), 1683   40   10

1984

2077   20c Eastern Polynesian canoe   50   10

2090   20c *Elizabeth* (English galleon), 1584   35   10

1985

2163a†   10c Canal barge, 1880s   15   10
2169†   14c Iceboat, 1880s   20   10
2170†   15c Tug, 1900s   25   10

2202†   22c Indian canoe   35   10

1986

2224†   22c *Advance* (polar brig), 1853   45   10

2235†   22c Ship's figurehead   45   10

1988

2330   22c *Charles W. Morgan* (whaling ship)   30   10

2339   22c *Clarence Crockett* (yacht)   30   10

2345   44c *Calmare Nyckel* and *Fagel Grip*
            (emigrant ships), 1638   60   20

2370†   25c *Hero* (sloop) (Palmer)   35   10
2371†   25c Antarctic exploration ship, Wilkes
            Expedition, 1838   35   10

1989

2388   25c Red Indian canoe, Reflection Lake,
            Washington   30   10

2389   25c *Experiment* (paddle-steamer), 1788
2390   25c *Phoenix* (paddle-steamer), 1809
2391   25c *New Orleans* (paddle-steamer), 1812
2392   25c *Washington* (paddle-steamer), 1816
2393   25c *Walk in the Water* (paddle-steamer),
            1818
            Set of 5   1.50   25

2419   25c *Chesapeake* (Mississippi river
            steamer)   30   10

1990

2504†   5c Red Indian canoe   10   10

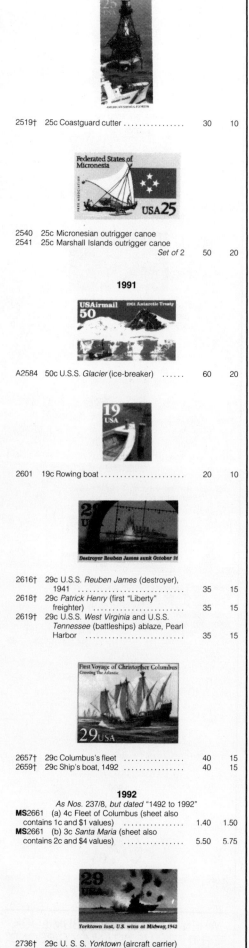

2519† 25c Coastguard cutter 30 10

2540 25c Micronesian outrigger canoe
2541 25c Marshall Islands outrigger canoe
Set of 2 50 20

1991

A2584 50c U.S.S. *Glacier* (ice-breaker) 60 20

2601 19c Rowing boat 20 10

2616† 29c U.S.S. *Reuben James* (destroyer),
1941 .... 35 15
2618† 29c *Patrick Henry* (first "Liberty"
freighter) 35 15
2619† 29c U.S.S. *West Virginia* and U.S.S.
Tennessee (battleships) ablaze, Pearl
Harbor 35 15

2657† 29c Columbus's fleet 40 15
2659† 29c Ship's boat, 1492 .... 40 15

1992
As Nos. 237/8, but dated "1492 to 1992"
MS2661 (a) 4c Fleet of Columbus (sheet also
contains 1c and $1 values) 1.40 1.50
MS2661 (b) 3c *Santa Maria* (sheet also
contains 2c and $4 values) 5.50 5.75

2736† 29c U. S. S. *Yorktown* (aircraft carrier)
on fire, Battle of Midway, 1942 ...... 40 15
2738† 29c Landing craft, Guadalcanal, 1942 .. 40 15

2750 29c Spanish galleon, California, 1542 .... 40 15

2760† 29c Toy steamer 40 15

PARCEL POST STAMPS
1912

P428† 10c *Kronprinz Wilhelm* (liner) 32.00 1.40

UPPER VOLTA
West Africa
100 centimes = 1 franc

1931
As No. 109 of Cameroun
66† 1f50 Liner 2.75 4.25

1970

299† 15f Medieval German kogge 30 15

1971

353 40f Outboard motor boat 50 20

1972

362† 150f Gondolas 1.40 85

382 40f Freighter 30 20

389 200f Olympic yacht 1.25 80

1973
No. 353 surcharged **O. M. S. 25e Anniversaire 45F**
401 45f on 40f Outboard motor boat 50 30

1976

417† 200f H.M.S. *Victory* (ship of the line) at
Battle of St. Vincent, 1797 .... 1.60 60

1978

487† 65f H.M.S. *Endeavour* (Cook) 1.00 40
490† 350f H.M.S. *Resolution* (Cook) 3.50 2.25

1983

663† 45f Canoe 20 10

673† 50f Fishing canoe 20 10

675 90f "Soling" class yacht
676 120f "Type 470" yacht
677 300f Sailboard
678 400f Sailboard
Set of 4 2.75 2.50

1984

710† 450f *Trieste* (Piccard's bathyscaphe) 1.60 1.40

734 20f *Maiden Queen* (full-rigged ship)
735 60f *Scawfell* (full-rigged ship)
736 120f *Harbinger* (full-rigged ship)
737 400f *True Briton* (East Indiaman)
Set of 4 3.00 1.90

Appendix

The following stamps have either been issued in excess of postal needs, or have not been available to the public in reasonable quantities at face value. Miniature sheets, imperforate stamps etc., are excluded from this section.

1974
Centenary of U.P.U. 40f Liner
Centenary of Berne Convention (1974). Centenary of U.P.U. issue optd **100e ANNIVERSAIRE DE L'UNION POSTAL UNIVERSELLE 9 OCTOBER 1974.** 40f Liner

1975
Birth Centenary of Sir Winston Churchill 125f Convoy
Expo'75 Exhibition, Okinawa. Modern Japanese ships. Postage 15, 25, 45, 50, 60 f, Air 150f

1976
Olympic Games, Montreal (1st issue) Pre-olympic year (1975). 50f Yachts
Zeppelin Airships. 40f Yachts

URUGUAY
South America
1000 milesimos = 100 centesimos = 1 peso

1895

158† 20c *Elbe* (early steamer) (black & green) 6.00 55

1897
As No. 158, but colour changed
188† 20c *Elbe* (early steamer) (black & mauve) 5.00 40

1908

279 1c *Montevideo* (cruiser) and *Diez-y-Ocho de Julio* (cadet ship)
280 2c *Montevideo* and *Diez-y-Ocho de Julio*
281 5c *Montevideo* and *Diez-y-Ocho de Julio*
Set of 3 3.00 2.50

1909

282 2c *Montevideo* (cruiser)
283 5c *Montevideo*
Set of 2 3.00 1.60

1919

349 5m Shipping, Montevideo
350 1c Shipping, Montevideo
351 2c Shipping, Montevideo
352 4c Shipping, Montevideo
353 5c Shipping, Montevideo
354 8c Shipping, Montevideo
355 20c Shipping, Montevideo
356 23c Shipping, Montevideo
357 50c Shipping, Montevideo
358 1p Shipping, Montevideo
Set of 10 20.00 6.00

1930

647† 20c Shipping, Montevideo, 1830 .... 1.40 70
649† 50c Shipping, Montevideo, 1930 .... 3.75 1.75

1945

913 8c *La Eolo* (full-rigged ship) 1.75 35

1963

1231† 90c *Alferez Campora* (ketch), 1960 .... 20 10
1232† 1p40 *Alferez Campora* 30 25

1968

1381† 12p *Suarez* (screw gunboat) 35 15
1385† 20p *Isabel* (privateer), 1818 (air) 65 15

1974

1582 200p Naval vessel in dry-dock 40 30

1979

1723 10p Caravel 1.75 85

1982

1807 3p *Capitan Miranda* (cadet schooner) .. 75 20

1983

1815† 3p *Santa Maria* (Columbus) 1.50 30

1984

1831 4p50 Tanker 50 15

1988

1940 30p *Capitan Miranda* (cadet schooner) 50 20

COLLECT BIRDS ON STAMPS
Third revised edition of this Stanley Gibbons thematic catalogue. Now available at £15.95 (p. + p. £3) from: Stanley Gibbons Publications, 5 Parkside, Christchurch Road, Ringwood, Hants BH24 3SH.

1989

1954	90p *Santa Maria* (Columbus)		
1955	115p *Santa Maria*		
	Set of 2	70	40

1991

2040	1510p Yacht	75	40

OFFICIAL STAMPS

1895

No. 158 overprinted **OFICIAL**

O173†	20c *Elbe* (early steamer) (black and green)	1.25	60

1897

No. 188 overprinted **OFICIAL**

O205†	20c *Elbe* (early steamer) (black and mauve)	5.50	2.00

PARCEL POST STAMPS

1974

P1558†	300p Paddle-steamer	75	50

VANUATU

South Pacific
1980 100 centimes = 1 franc
1981 Vatus

1980

295E†	50f Outrigger canoe, Shepherd Island (inscribed in English)	65	70
295F†	50f Outrigger canoe, Shepherd Island (inscribed in French)	1.00	70

1983

362†	20v *Oriana* (liner) and outrigger canoe	20	15

368†	25v Fishing boats off Dover, 1785	30	30

1984

382†	20v *Induna* (container ship)	30	35
384†	45v *Brahman Express* (container ship) ..	65	70

390	25v *Makambo* (inter-island freighter)		
391	45v *Rockton* (inter-island freighter)		
392	100v *Waroonga* (inter-island freighter)		
	Set of 3	3.50	3.75

1985

411†	35v *Mala* (patrol boat)	45	50
412†	45v Japanese trawlers	65	70

428†	100v Sailboard	1.40	1.25

434†	45v *President Coolidge* (liner) leaving San Francisco	65	60
435†	55v *President Coolidge* as troopship, 1942	75	70

1988

496	20v *Tambo* (freighter)		
497	45v *Induna* (freighter)		
498	55v *Morinda* (freighter)		
499	65v *Marsina* (freighter)		
	Set of 4	1.75	2.00

As No. 428, but with additional Australian "Expo 88" symbol

MS501	100v Sailboard (sheet contains one other design)	2.25	1.90

508†	55v *Shirrabank* (freighter)	75	65
509†	65v *Adela* (ferry)	85	75
510†	145v *General Slocum* (excursion paddle-steamer) on fire, New York, 1904	2.00	1.75

1990

544†	100v Sailing packet	2.00	2.00

1992

595†	80v U.S.S. *Hornet* (aircraft carrier)	1.40	1.40
MS596†	200v Freighters in Port Vila, 1942	3.25	3.50

VATICAN CITY

Southern Europe
100 centesimi = 1 lira

1972

575†	50li Galleons, Venice, 1581	15	15
576†	50li Galleons, Venice, 1581	15	15
577†	50li Galleons, Venice, 1581	15	15
578†	50li Galleons, Venice, 1581	15	15

1987

893†	4000li Pacific Islands canoe and sampans	8.00	8.00

VENDA

Southern Africa
100 cents = 1 rand

1992

242†	1r05 Egyptian ship, 1600 B.C.	45	45

VENEZIA GIULIA AND ISTRIA

Southern Europe
100 centesimi = 1 lira

YUGOSLAV MILITARY GOVERNMENT

1945

62	4li Istrian fishing boat (blue)	10	10
79	4li Istrian fishing boat (red)	10	10
101	6li Istrian fishing boat	20	15

VENEZUELA

South America
100 centimos = 1 bolivar

1926

394	10c Paddle-steamer	1.10	55

1937

464†	10c Sailing barges, River Orinoco	80	25

488†	70c Liner, La Guaira	2.25	80
489†	1b80 Liner, La Guaira	4.00	1.50

No. 464 overprinted **RESELLADO 1937–1938**

492†	10c Sailing barges, River Orinoco	1.40	65

1941
No. 464 overprinted **HABILITADO 1940**

648†	10c Sailing barges, River Orinoco	1.25	35

1943
No. 464 overprinted **Resellado 1943**

659†	10c Sailing barges, River Orinoco	5.00	3.50

1948

Size 37½ × 22½ mm (Nos. 780/90) or 22½ × 37½ mm (Nos. 791/806). Inscribed "AMERICAN BANK NOTE COMPANY" at foot

780	5c *Republica de Venezuela* (freighter)
781	7½c *Republica de Venezuela*
782	10c *Republica de Venezuela*
783	15c *Republica de Venezuela*
784	20c *Republica de Venezuela*
785	25c *Republica de Venezuela*
786	30c *Republica de Venezuela*
787	37½c *Republica de Venezuela*
788	40c *Republica de Venezuela*
789	50c *Republica de Venezuela*
790	1b *Republica de Venezuela*
791	5c *Republica de Venezuela* (air)
792	10c *Republica de Venezuela*
793	15c *Republica de Venezuela*
794	20c *Republica de Venezuela*
795	25c *Republica de Venezuela*
796	30c *Republica de Venezuela*
797	45c *Republica de Venezuela*
798	50c *Republica de Venezuela*
799	70c *Republica de Venezuela*
800	75c *Republica de Venezuela*
801	90c *Republica de Venezuela*
802	1b *Republica de Venezuela*
803	2b *Republica de Venezuela*
804	3b *Republica de Venezuela*
805	4b *Republica de Venezuela*
806	5b *Republica de Venezuela*

Set of 27 55.00 20.00

1949

820	5c *Santa Maria* (Columbus)
821	10c *Santa Maria*
822	20c *Santa Maria*
823	1b *Santa Maria*
824	5c *Santa Maria* (air)
825	10c *Santa Maria*
826	15c *Santa Maria*
827	25c *Santa Maria*
828	30c *Santa Maria*
829	1b *Santa Maria*

Set of 10 38.00 9.00

1951
Nos. 781 and 787 surcharged **RESELLADO** *and value*

884	5c on 7½c *Republica de Venezuela* (freighter)
885	10c on 37½c *Republica de Venezuela*

Set of 2 70 30

As Nos. 780/2 and 791/3 but size 38 × 23½ mm (Nos. 1012/14) or 23½ × 38 mm (Nos. 1015/17). Inscribed "COURVOISIER S.A." at foot

1012	5c *Republica de Venezuela* (freighter)
1013	10c *Republica de Venezuela*
1014	15c *Republica de Venezuela*
1015	5c *Republica de Venezuela* (air)
1016	10c *Republica de Venezuela*
1017	15c *Republica de Venezuela*

Set of 6 7.00 55

1953

1185	5c Paddle-steamer on arms of Delta Amacuro

1186	10c Paddle-steamer on arms of Delta Amacuro
1187	15c Paddle-steamer on arms of Delta Amacuro
1188	20c Paddle-steamer on arms of Delta Amacuro
1189	40c Paddle-steamer on arms of Delta Amacuro
1190	45c Paddle-steamer on arms of Delta Amacuro
1191	3b Paddle-steamer on arms of Delta Amacuro
1192	5c Paddle-steamer on arms of Delta Amacuro (air) (inscribed "CORREO AEREO")
1193	10c Paddle-steamer on arms of Delta Amacuro
1194	15c Paddle-steamer on arms of Delta Amacuro
1195	25c Paddle-steamer on arms of Delta Amacuro
1196	30c Paddle-steamer on arms of Delta Amacuro
1197	50c Paddle-steamer on arms of Delta Amacuro
1198	60c Paddle-steamer on arms of Delta Amacuro
1199	1b Paddle-steamer on arms of Delta Amacuro
1200	2b Paddle-steamer on arms of Delta Amacuro

Set of 16 19.00 10.00

1963

1789†	30c *Shell Charaima* (tanker), Lake Maracaibo	55	15
1790†	35c *Shell Charaima*, Lake Maracaibo ..	65	20
1791†	80c *Shell Charaima*, Lake Maracaibo ..	1.25	40

1965
Nos. 1791, 804 and 805 surcharged **RESELLADO VALOR** *and value*

1852†	60c on 80c *Shell Charaima* (tanker), Lake Maracaibo	85	35
1860†	10c on 3b *Republica de Venezuela* (freighter) (air)	15	10
1861†	10c on 4b *Republica de Venezuela*	70	35

1966

1933	60c 19th-century sailing packet	1.50	50

1968

2039†	5b Olympic yacht	3.75	1.40

1973

2228†	1b Battle of Maracaibo, 1823	60	40
2229†	2b Battle of Maracaibo, 1823	1.10	60

1974

2278†	50c Liner and sailing packet	40	20

1980

2437†	1b50 *Mariscal Sucre* (frigate)	1.00	40
2438†	1b50 *Picua* (submarine)	1.00	40
2440†	1b50 *Simon Bolivar* (cadet barque)	1.00	40

1985

2561†	3b Support vessel and oil rig	80	30

1987

2672†	6b Sailing dinghy	55	20
2675†	6b50 Motor boat marina	55	20
2677†	6b50 Rowing boats	55	20

2691†	2b Bulk carrier	20	10

2704†	4b *Zulia* (freighter)	50	20
2705†	4b *Guarico* (freighter)	50	20
2706†	5b *Cerro Bolivar* (bulk carrier)	55	20

2710†	2b National Guard patrol boat	30	15
2719†	4b National Guard patrol boat	60	20

1988

2757†	6b Fishing boat	35	15

1991

2954†	12b Santa Maria	20	10

2962†	12b Caravel	20	10

VIETNAM

South-east Asia

South Vietnam

100 cents = 1 piastre

1955

S5	70c Refugee raft	
S6	80c Refugee raft	
S7	10p Refugee raft	
S8	20p Refugee raft	
S9	35p Refugee raft (inscribed "CHEIN-DICH-HUYNE-DE")	
S10	100p Refugee raft	
	Set of 6 30.00 20.00	

1956

No. S9 with inscription obliterated by bar

S26	35p Refugee raft	4.50	3.25

1964

S229†	1p50 Junks, Phan Thiet	30	15

1968

S318†	80c Junk	10	10

1971

S383	3p Warships	
S384	40p Warships	
	Set of 2 1.40 60	

1972

S397†	40p Trawler	15	10

1974

S455	5p Sampan	
S456	10p Sampan	
	Set of 2 35 20	

National Front for the Liberation of South Vietnam

100 xu = 1 dong

1964

NLF8	30x Sinking of U.S.S. *Card* (destroyer)	2.50	1.50

North Vietnam

100 xu = 1 dong

1961

N187	5x Freighter loading at Haiphong	
N188	12x Freighter loading at Haiphong	
	Set of 2 5.00 1.40	

1963

N265†	12x Trawler	2.75	1.10

1964

N315 12x Sampans 65 30

N327† 5x Naval longboat 60 20

N340† 12x Patrol boat and junks 65 25

1967

N491† 20x Aurora (Russian cruiser), 1917 .... 60 35

N498† 12x Fast patrol boat 50 20

1969

N567† 12x Log raft 30 15
N568† 12x Tug and log rafts 30 15

Socialist Republic of Vietnam

100 xu = 1 dong

1977

183† 1d Aurora (Russian cruiser), 1917 ...... 50 35

338† 1d Olympic yachts 65 35

1982

511† 30x Aurora (Russian cruiser), 1917 ...... 20 15

1983

531 30x Sampan
532 50x Junk
533 1d Houseboats
534 3d Junk
535 5d Sampan
536 10d Sampan

Set of 6 3.50 1.60

540† 3d Balloon over sailing ships in harbour 55 25

1984

714† 50x Junks 20 10
717† 50x Junks 20 10
719† 1d Junk 30 15
721† 3d Junk 80 30
722† 5d Junk 1.10 40
723† 8d Junks 1.40 55

1985

811† 5d Barge, Haiphong 15 10

856† 2d Freighter 10 10

864† 1d Oil rig 10 10

1986

988 1d Greek bireme
989 1d Viking longship
990 2d Medieval kogge
991 3d Greek cargo galley
992 3d Phoenician war galley
993 5d Ancient Mediterranean cargo ship
994 5d Roman trireme

Set of 7 1.25 30

1987

1056† 3d Three canoes 10 10
1057† 3d Canoe 10 10

1078† 10d Junks, Hai Phong 20 10

1132† 20d Aurora (Russian cruiser) 40 20

1157† 30d Loading freighter 55 20

1988

1170† 10d Junk, Spratley Islands 30 15

1173 80d Vietnamese fleet, 1288
1174 200d Battle of Bach Dang River, 1288
Set of 2 2.50 75

1175 1000d Oil rig 6.25 1.75

1989

1292† 100d Oil rig 20 10

1299 10d Fishing junk, Quang-Nam
1300 10d Fishing junk, Quang-Tri
1301 20d Fishing junk, Thua-Thien
1302 20d Fishing junk, Da-Nang
1303 30d Fishing junk, Quang-Tri (different)
1304 30d Fishing junk, Da-Nang (different)
1305 50d Fishing junk, Hue
Set of 7 4.50 1.25

1372† 50d *Santa Maria, Pinta* and *Nina*
(Columbus) 10 10

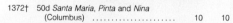
1990

1403 100d 8th-9th-century Viking longship
1404 500d 15th-century caravel
1405 1000d 15th-century carrack
1406 1000d 14th-15th-century carrack
1407 1000d 17th-century frigate
1408 2000d 16th-century galleon and pinnance
1409 3000d 16th-century galleon
Set of 7 2.75 1.25
MS1410 4200d Ancient Egyptian Nile galley .. 2.00 2.00

1490 100d *Pyotr Emtsov* (container ship)
1491 300d Mexican Lines container ship
1492 500d Liner
1493 1000d *Ben Nevis* (tanker)
1494 2000d "RoRo" ferry
1495 3000d Sealink train ferry
Set of 6 2.25 95

1496† 100d Freighter 10 10

1500† 1000d Satellite communications ship .. 35 15

WALLIS AND FUTUNA ISLANDS

South Pacific
100 centimes = 1 franc

1920

Nos. 99/101 and additional value of New Caledonia overprinted
ILES WALLIS et FUTUNA
15† 1f *President Felix Faure* (barque) (blue on
green) 2.00 2.00
28† 1f10 *President Felix Faure* 1.60 1.75
16† 2f *President Felix Faure* 3.25 3.25
17† 5f *President Felix Faure* (black on orange) 5.50 5.50

1922

As Nos. 15/17, some with colours changed, surcharged in figures
33† 25c on 2f *President Felix Faure* 50 60
34† 25c on 5f *President Felix Faure* 50 60
38† 1f25 on 1f *President Felix Faure* 50 50
39† 1f50 on 1f *President Felix Faure* (blue) 1.75 1.75
40† 3f on 5f *President Felix Faure* (mauve) 3.50 3.50
41† 10f on 5f *President Felix Faure* (brown on
mauve) 14.00 14.00
42† 20f on 5f *President Felix Faure* (red on
yellow) 20.00 20.00

1930

Nos. 137/45 and 161/70 of New Caledonia overprinted **ILES
WALLIS et FUTUNA**
43† 1c Fishing boat, Pointe des Paletuviers .. 20 30
44† 2c Fishing boat, Pointe des Paletuviers .. 30 35
45† 3c Fishing boat, Pointe des Paletuviers .. 35 40
46† 4c Fishing boat, Pointe des Paletuviers .. 30 35

47† 5c Fishing boat, Pointe des Paletuviers .. 35 25
48† 10c Fishing boat, Pointe des Paletuviers 30 40
49† 15c Fishing boat, Pointe des Paletuviers 30 40
50† 20c Fishing boat, Pointe des Paletuviers 35 45
51† 25c Fishing boat, Pointe des Paletuviers 50 60
67† 1f *L'Astrolabe* (La Perouse) (red & brown) 2.00 2.00
68† 1f *L'Astrolabe* (red) 85 80
69† 1f *L'Astrolabe* (green & red) 35 80
70† 1f10 *L'Astrolabe* 15.00 15.00
71† 1f25 *L'Astrolabe* (green & brown) .. 1.10 1.25
72† 1f25 *L'Astrolabe* (red) 45 55
73† 1f40 *L'Astrolabe* 60 60
74† 1f50 *L'Astrolabe* 45 55
75† 1f60 *L'Astrolabe* 65 65
76† 1f75 *L'Astrolabe* (red & blue) 6.25 6.25
77† 1f75 *L'Astrolabe* (blue) 1.25 1.25
78† 2f *L'Astrolabe* 80 80
79† 2f25 *L'Astrolabe* 65 65
80† 2f50 *L'Astrolabe* 65 65
81† 3f *L'Astrolabe* 80 80
82† 5f *L'Astrolabe* 80 80
83† 10f *L'Astrolabe* 1.50 1.50
84† 20f *L'Astrolabe* 2.25 2.25

1931

As No. 109 of Cameroun
88† 1f50 *Leconte de Lisle* (liner) 3.00 3.00

1941

Nos. 43/51, 68, 71, 74, 77/8 and 80/4 further overprinted **France
Libre**
96† 1c Fishing boat, Pointe des Paletuviers 70 70
97† 2c Fishing boat, Pointe des Paletuviers 70 70
97a† 3c Fishing boat, Pointe des Paletuviers 60.00 60.00
98† 4c Fishing boat, Pointe des Paletuviers 70 70
99† 5c Fishing boat, Pointe des Paletuviers 70 70
100† 10c Fishing boat, Pointe des Paletuviers 70 70
101† 15c Fishing boat, Pointe des Paletuviers 70 70
102† 20c Fishing boat, Pointe des Paletuviers 1.40 1.40
103† 25c Fishing boat, Pointe des Paletuviers 1.40 1.40
116† 1f *L'Astrolabe* (La Perouse) 1.40 1.40
117† 1f25 *L'Astrolabe* 1.40 1.40
118† 1f50 *L'Astrolabe* 70 70
119† 1f75 *L'Astrolabe* 70 70
120† 2f *L'Astrolabe* 1.40 1.40
121† 2f50 *L'Astrolabe* £110 £110
122† 3f *L'Astrolabe* 70 70
123† 5f *L'Astrolabe* 2.75 2.75
124† 10f *L'Astrolabe* 35.00 35.00
125† 20f *L'Astrolabe* 55.00 55.00

1954

As No. 264 of Cameroun
160† 3f Landing craft, Normandy, 1944 ...... 4.25 4.50

1955

168a† 27f Freighter at wharf 3.50 2.00
169† 33f *Stella Matutina* (full-rigged ship) 5.50 5.00

1965

186 11f *Reine Amelia* (inter-island ferry) 5.00 4.00

1967

195 12f H.M.S. *Dolphin* (frigate) (Wallis), 1767 5.00 3.50

1969

199†	1f Outrigger canoe	80	80
203†	50f Fishing canoe	5.00	3.50

1971

No. 169 surcharged

208†	21f on 33f 19th-century full-rigged ship	3.50	2.75

1972

217†	14f Model pirogue	4.00	2.25
219†	18f Racing pirogue	4.50	3.50
220†	200f Racing pirogues (air)	25.00	14.00

1973

221	22f *La Boussole* (La Perouse), 1788	
222	28f H.M.S. *Dolphin* (frigate) (Wallis), 1767	
223	40f *L'Astrolabe* (D'Urville), 1828	
224	72f *La Boudeuse* (Bougainville), 1768	
	Set of 4	16.00	10.00

1976

255†	47f Battle of Virginia Capes, 1781	3.00	2.25

1977

No. 255 *overprinted* **JAMES COOK Bicentenaire de la decouverte des Iles Hawaii 1778–1978**

277†	47f Battle of Virginia Capes, 1781	4.50	2.75

1978

287	150f *Triomphant* (destroyer)	
288	200f *Cap des Palmes* and *Chevreuil* (patrol boats)	
289	280f *Savorgnan de Brazza* (destroyer)	
	Set of 3	28.00	19.00

1979

308†	68f *Moana II* (inter-island freighter)	1.75	1.40

310†	10f Bonito fishing boat	40	30

317†	52f Model outrigger canoe	1.50	95

323†	70f *President Felix Faure* (on stamp No. 15)	1.75	1.10

332	130f H.M.S. *Resolution* (Cook), Hawaii, 1779	4.00	2.75

1980

Design as No. 308

350†	3f *Moana II* (inter-island freighter)	15	15

1981

380	66f Battle of Virginia Capes, 1781	
381	74f Battle of Virginia Capes, 1781	
	Set of 2	3.25	2.10

386	60f *La Dieppoise* (patrol boat)	
387	85f *Protet* (frigate)	
	Set of 2	3.25	2.50

1982

391	300f Fishing boats	6.50	4.50

395†	140f *L'Astrolabe* (on stamp No. 67)	2.50	1.75

1983

419	270f Sailboard	5.50	3.25

1984

437	67f *Commandant Bory* (frigate)	1.50	1.00

1985

471	350f Sailing canoe	6.00	3.25

473	51f *Jacques Cartier* (landing ship)	1.00	65

ALBUM LISTS

Write for our latest list of albums and accessories. This will be sent on request.

1986

488† 8f *Eendracht* (Schouten), 1616 .... 20 15
489† 9f *Hoorn* (Le Maire), 1616 .... 20 15

494 6f *La Lorientaise* (patrol boat)
495 7f *Commandant Blaison* (frigate)
496 120f *Balny* (frigate)
Set of 3   2.25   1.60

1987

516 135f Piccard's bathyscaphe, 1948 ...... 2.50 1.60

526 260f French frigate, 1838 .... 4.75 3.00

1988

530 70f *L'Astrolabe* and *La Boussole* (La Perouse), 1788 .... 1.40 90

537† 60f Sailboard 1.25 1.00

541 400f Outrigger canoes 7.25 4.50

1989

542 26f *Amiral Charner* (French frigate) 75 45

553 23f Canoe on beach 75 60

1990

563 40f *Moana II* (inter-island freighter)
564 50f *Moana III* (container ship)
Set of 2   2.00   1.40

567 46f Outrigger canoe 1.25 65

1991

570 52f *La Glorieuse* (French patrol boat) 1.50 85

578 42f *La Moqueuse* (French patrol boat) 1.25 65

1992

595 35f *President Felix Faure* (barque) (on New Caledonia stamp No. 100) 45 30

598 200f Columbus's fleet 2.75 2.10

608 70f Pirogues 90 55

614 20f *La Garonne* (supply vessel) 25 15

617 130f Modern frigate and canoes 1.75 1.25

POSTAGE DUE STAMPS

1920

Nos. D102/9 *of New Caledonia overprinted* **ILES WALLIS et FUTUNA**

D18 5c Outrigger canoe
D19 10c Outrigger canoe
D20 15c Outrigger canoe
D21 20c Outrigger canoe
D22 30c Outrigger canoe
D23 50c Outrigger canoe
D24 60c Outrigger canoe
D25 1f Outrigger canoe
Set of 8   6.50   7.50

1927

No. D109 *of New Caledonia but colours changed, surcharged in figures*
D43 2f on 1f Outrigger canoe
D44 3f on 1f Outrigger canoe
Set of 2   13.00   14.00

YEMEN

Arabia
40 bogaches = 1 imadi

1952

90 30b Dhow
91 30b Dhow (air)
Set of 2   15.00   18.00

1961

138 4b Freighter
139 6b Freighter
140 16b Freighter

Set of 3 3.00 2.75

REPUBLIC ISSUES

1963

Nos. 139/40 overprinted **Y. A. R. 27. 9. 1962** *in English and Arabic*
217† 6b Freighter 1.25 1.25
218† 16b Freighter 2.00 2.00

1964

267† ½b Liner and freighter, Hodeida 25 20

270† 16b Liner and freighter, Hodeida (air) 1.75 1.25

1966

Nos. 267 *and* 270 *overprinted* **1965 SANA'A** *in English and Arabic*
427† ½b Liner and freighter, Hodeida 20 15

430† 16b Liner and freighter, Hodeida (air) 2.50 2.00

444† ½b American aircraft carrier 15 15

446† 8b American aircraft carrier (air) 95 75

Nos. 444 *and* 446 *overprinted* **GEMINI IX CERNAN-STAFFORD JUNE 3-1966** *in English and Arabic*
453† ½b American aircraft carrier 15 15

455† 8b American aircraft carrier (air) 1.40 1.00

Appendix

The following stamps have either been issued in excess of postal needs, or have not been made available to the public in reasonable quantities at face value. Miniature sheets, imperforate stamps etc., are excluded from this section.

1971

Pres. Gamal Nasser of Egypt Commemoration. 2b Freighter in Suez Canal

ROYALIST ISSUES

1967

R336† ½b Fishing boats, Lake Patzcuaro, Mexico 10 10

R342† 20b Fishing boats, Lake Patzcuaro, Mexico (air) 2.00 60

Appendix

The following stamps have either been issued in excess of postal needs or have not been made available to the public in reasonable quantities at face value. Miniature sheets, imperforate stamps etc., are excluded from this section.

1967

Visit of Queen of Sheba to Solomon. 6b Galley

YEMEN PEOPLE'S DEMOCRATIC REPUBLIC

Arabia
1000 fils = 1 dinar

1972

105 25f Dhow building
106 80f Dhow at sea

Set of 2 2.00 1.10

1979

MS229 250f Dhow (on stamp No. 12 of Aden) 1.25 1.25

1980

237 110f *Dido* (screw steamer)
238 180f *Anglia* (screw steamer)
239 250f *India* (screw steamer)

Set of 3 2.75 2.50

1983

289† 50f Postal barge 50 35

305 50f *Europa* (liner)
306 100f *World Discoverer* (liner)

Set of 2 2.50 1.40

MS307 Two sheets. (a) 20f *Kruzenshtern* (Russian cadet barque); 40f *Grossherzogin Elisabeth* (German cadet schooner); 60f *Sedov* (Russian cadet barque); 80f *Dar Pomorza* (Polish cadet full-rigged ship); (b) 200f *Gorch Fock* (German cadet barque)

Set of 2 sheets 10.00 10.00

1988

408 75f Freighters and dhows, Old Harbour, Aden
409 500f Container ships and bulk carrier, New Harbour, Aden

Set of 2 2.50 1.75

YUGOSLAVIA

South-east Europe
100 paras = 1 dinar

1939

406 50p + 50p *Jadran* (cadet barquentine)
407 1d + 50p *King Alexander* (liner)
408 1d50 + 1d *Triglav* (freighter)
409 2d + 1d50 *Dubrovnik* (destroyer)

Set of 4 5.00 4.00

1948

582 2d *Krajina* (former Royal yacht)
583 3d *Krajina* (former Royal yacht)
584 5d *Krajina* (former Royal yacht)
585 10d *Krajina* (former Royal yacht)

Set of 4 17.00 17.00

1950

665 2d 16th-century galleon
666 3d Partisan patrol boat
667 5d Freighter
668 10d *Zagreb* (freighter)
669 12d Yachts
670 20d *Golesnica* (torpedo boat)

Set of 6 7.50 2.75

1951

675† 1d Paddle-steamer, River Danube 15 10

1958

892† 5d Shipbuilding (brown) 15 10
983† 5d Shipbuilding (orange) 30 10

1960

| 952† | 55d Olympic yachts | 35 | 10 |

1966

As No. 983, but value expressed as "0.05"

| 1194† | 5p Shipbuilding | 10 | 10 |

| 1224 | 30p Yachts | 20 | 10 |

1969

1378	50p *Eber* (barque)		
1379	1d25 *Tare* (barque)		
1380	1d50 *Sela* (brigantine)		
1381	2d50 16th-century galleon, Dubrovnik		
1382	3d25 *Madre Mimbelli* (sail frigate)		
1383	5d 16th-century caravel		
	Set of 6	2.50	1.50

1972

| 1512† | 6d50 Olympic yachts | 60 | 55 |

1973

| 1547† | 2d50 18th-century shipping, Kotor | 15 | 10 |
| 1549† | 5d 19th-century fishing boats, Split | 30 | 15 |

1979

| 1887 | 4d90 Rowing | 30 | 10 |

1910	4d90 *Deligrad* (Danube paddle-steamer)		
1911	10d *Serbia* (Danube paddle-steamer)		
	Set of 2	2.25	1.50

1981

2001	8d *Karlovac* (tug) pushing barges, River Danube		
2002	13d Paddle-steamer towed by railway locomotive, Sip Canal		
	Set of 2	1.75	95

1982

| 2017† | 15d *Splendido* (Austrian sail frigate) | 80 | 25 |

| 2035† | 8d80 Armed tug, 1942 | 50 | 15 |
| 2036† | 15d *Rade Koncar* (missile gunboat) | 90 | 30 |

1983

| 2067 | 8d80 Freighters | 35 | 15 |

1985

2225	8d Yacht (aerial view)		
2226	10d Sailboard		
2227	50d Yacht at sunset		
2228	70d Yacht near coast		
	Set of 4	1.40	80

1986

| 2278† | 200d Freighter | 10 | 10 |

2307	50d "Flying Dutchman" class yachts		
2308	80d "Flying Dutchman" class yachts		
	Set of 2	60	40
MS2309	100d "Flying Dutchman" class yachts	45	45

1987

| 2397† | 200d Fire-fighting tug | 20 | 10 |

| 2417 | 80d Tug in canal, Titov Vrbas | 15 | 10 |

1988

| 2446† | 1200d Container ship | 40 | 25 |

1988

| 2469† | 1000d Shipping on the Danube | 30 | 15 |

1989

2539	1000d Ancient Greek galleys		
2540	1000d Roman warships		
2541	1000d 13th-century crusader nefs		
2542	1000d 16th-century Dubrovnik navas		
2543	1000d 17th-century French warships		
2544	1000d 18th-century ships of the line		
	Set of 6	70	40

1990

| 2596† | 2d Freighter | 20 | 10 |

1991

2703	7d50 Danube river steamer		
2704	15d Danube river steamer		
	Set of 2	2.10	75

2730† 10d River freighters 50 30

1992

2785 150d *Titanic* (liner) sinking, 1912 .... 8.00 4.75

2786 150d Fishing boat, Seville 8.00 4.75

ZAIRE

Central Africa
100 sengi = 1 kuba
100 kuba = 1 zaire

1980

MS1012 10z 18th-century fishing boats, Naples 5.00 5.00

1044† 75k Canoes, Stanley's expedition, 1879 45 20

1982

1091† 1k River launch 10 10

1984

1180† 10k River ferry 10 10

1985

1258† 7z *Kokolo* (pusher-tug) 30 10
1260† 15z *Luebo* (pusher-tug) 55 20

1986

1267† 7z *Deliverance* (stern wheel paddle-
steamer) (on Belgian Congo stamp
No. 79) 10 10

1990
No. 1044 *surch* **300Z.**
1355† 300z on 75k Canoes, Stanley's
expedition, 1879 .... 10 10

ZAMBIA

Central Africa
1964 12 pence = 1 shilling
20 shillings = 1 pound
1968 100 ngwee = 1 kwacha

1964

101† 1s Night fishing boat, Mpulungu 15 10

1970

159† 25n Nalikwanda ceremonial canoe 70 1.00

1978

276† 18n Police motorised canoe 40 55

1987

504† 1k25 Inflatable raft, River Zambezi 30 25

1988

543† 2k50 Fishing canoe 60 50

1992

689† 35k Fishing canoe 65 65

ZANZIBAR

Indian Ocean
1908 100 cents = 1 rupee
1936 100 cents = 1 shilling

1908

239† 10r Dhow 65.00 £120
240† 20r Dhow £160 £275
241† 30r Dhow £250 £400
242† 40r Dhow £400
243† 50r Dhow £350
244† 100r Dhow £650
245† 200r Dhow £950

1913

290† 1r Sailing canoe 1.75 1.60
291† 2r Sailing canoe 2.50 4.75
292† 3r Sailing canoe 4.00 6.50
293† 4r Sailing canoe 10.00 23.00
294† 5r Sailing canoe 13.00 45.00
295† 10r Dhow 45.00 £110
296† 20r Dhow £100 £225
260b† 30r Dhow £110 £225
260c† 40r Dhow £225 £375
260d† 50r Dhow £225 £375
260e† 100r Dhow £300
260f† 200r Dhow £600

1936
As Nos. 290/5, *but with face values in shillings*
318† 1s Sailing canoe 45 10
319† 2s Sailing canoe 55 40
320† 5s Sailing canoe 2.50 3.50
321† 7s50 Sailing canoe 8.50 8.50
322† 10s Dhow 5.00 6.00

1944

327 10c *Shah Alam* (Sultan's dhow)
328 20c *Shah Alam*
329 50c *Shah Alam*
330 1s *Shah Alam*
Set of 4 70 1.75

1949

As No. 115 of Antigua

336† 30c Paddle-steamer 1.40 60

1957

360† 15c *Ummoja Wema* (dhow) 10 40
361† 20c Sultan's barge 10 10
363† 30c *Ummoja Wema* (dhow) 15 10
368† 1s25 *Ummoja Wema* (dhow) 70 10

1961

As Nos. 360/8, but with portrait of Sultan Seyyid Sir Abdulla bin Khalifa

375† 15c *Ummoja Wema* (dhow) 20 60
376† 20c Sultan's barge 15 10
378† 30c *Ummoja Wema* (dhow) 60 10
383† 1s25 *Ummoja Wema* (dhow) 80 35

1964

Nos. 375/83 overprinted **JAMHURI 1964**

416† 15c *Ummoja Wema* (dhow) 10 10
417† 20c Sultan's barge 10 10
419† 30c *Ummoja Wema* (dhow) 10 10
424† 1s25 *Ummoja Wema* (dhow) 50 10

1966

456† 20c Freighter 10 10
458† 1s30 Freighter 10 10

ZIL ELWANNYEN SESEL

Indian Ocean
100 cents = 1 rupee

1980

17† 1r50 *Cinq Juin* (travelling post office) 30 15

1981

23† 40c Royal Yacht *Royal Escape* 10 10
25† 5r Royal Yacht *Victoria and Albert II* 40 40
27† 10r Royal Yacht *Britannia* 85 85

1982

35 1r75 *Cinq Juin* (travelling post office)
36 2r10 *Junon* (fisheries protection launch)
37 5r *Diamond M. Dragon* (drilling ship)
                 Set of 3 1.60 90

38 40c *Paulette* (inter-island ferry)
39 1r75 *Janette* (inter-island ferry)
40 2r75 *Lady Esme* (inter-island ferry)
41 3r50 *Cinq Juin* (travelling post office)
                 Set of 4 1.50 1.10

1983

Nos. 23, 25 and 27 surcharged

73† 30c on 40c Royal Yacht *Royal Escape* 25 25
75† 2r on 5r Royal Yacht *Victoria and Albert II* 70 70
77† 3r on 10r Royal Yacht *Britannia* 85 55

1984

83† 50c Game fishing launch 15 15
86† 10r Game fishing launch 2.00 2.50

93† 3r Sailing canoe 75 80

1985

125 50c Phoenician trading ship, 600 B.C.
126 2r H.M.S. *Sealark* (survey ship), 1908
127 10r *Sao Gabriel* (Vasco da Gama), 1502
                 Set of 3 4.75 3.50

1988

186† 2r *Retriever* (cable ship) 90 70
187† 3r *Chantel* (fishing boat) 1.50 1.25
188† 5r *Torrey Canyon* (tanker) aground,
     Cornwall, 1967 .... 2.00 1.60

1989

MS197† 10r Ship's boat 4.00 4.50

202† 1r Fishing canoe on beach 50 50
203† 2r Fishing canoe 80 80

1991

236 1r50 *St. Abbs* (full-rigged ship), 1860
237 3r *Norden* (barque), 1862
238 3r50 *Clan Mackay* (freighter), 1984
239 10r *Glenlyon* (freighter), 1905
                 Set of 4 4.75 4.75

Index Section

This section is arranged in two parts, indexed by ship name or by type.

I. By Individual Ship Name

Ottawa, H.M.C.S. (frigate)
British Virgin Islands 310
Otto Schmidt (research vessel)
Russia 5057
Otvazhny (destroyer)
Russia 4306
Ouwerkerk (freighter)
Tanzania 136 O15
Overijssel (canal freighter)
Netherlands 718
Ovoca (trawler)
Ireland 838

P

Pacific Explorer (freighter)
Tuvalu 88
Pacific Guardian (cable ship)
British Virgin Islands 620 **MS**623
Pacific Rover (tanker)
Norfolk Island 487
Padua (barque)
Falkland Islands 567
Germany 643
Paekdusan (trawler support ship)
Korea (North Korea) N1325
Pahlawan (patrol boat)
Brunei 180
Pailot (ice-breaker)
Russia 4598
Paisis (research submarine)
Russia 6198
Palang (destroyer)
Iran 1917
Palang (gunboat)
Iran 735
Pallas, H.M.S. (frigate)
Bermuda 523
Pamir (barque)
Aland Islands 34
Falkland Islands 571
New Zealand L43 L50
Penrhyn Island 183 203 300 352 O32
Panama (cargo liner)
Canal Zone 59/60
Panama 178/9
Panama (liner)
Canal Zone 160
Panama (paddle steamer)
Canal Zone 198
Panama Maru (bulk carrier)
Togo 376
Pandora, H.M.S. (frigate)
Fiji 351 353 827 829
Niuafo'ou 154/5
Norfolk Island 516/17
Pitcairn Islands 316
Tokelau 23
Pangai (patrol boat)
Niuafo'ou 190 194
Tonga 1157
Panulirus II (research vessel)
Bermuda 358
Papanicolis (submarine)
Greece 1442
Papanui (freighter)
St. Helena 441
Papuan Chief (container ship)
Kiribati 393
Solomon Islands 626
Paraguari (freighter)
Paraguay 678/83
Paraguay (gunboat)
Paraguay 397/411
Paramour, H.M.S. (pink)
Tristan da Cunha 405
Parana (sail/steam corvette)
Argentine 1891
Parati (gunboat)
Brazil 1340
Pargo (tunny fishing boat)
Cuba 2487
Paris (early steamer)
Niger 989
Paris (liner)
France 458/9
Parizh (ship of the line)
Russia 6092
Passat (barque)
Falkland Islands 614
Passport (paddle-steamer)
Canada 852
Pasteur (liner)
France 707
Pathfinder (coastguard vessel)
United States of America 1090
Pathfinder (tug)
Antigua 285
Barbuda 121
Patience (pinnace)
Bermuda 276 278
Patoka, U.S.S. (airship tender)
Bermuda 468

Patria (gunboat)
Timor 387
Patriarch (clipper)
Penrhyn Island 185 205 302
Patricia (Trinity House vessel)
Guernsey (Alderney) A51
Patrick Henry (freighter)
United States of America 2618
Patrol (cable ship)
Cocos (Keeling) Islands 131
Paulette (inter-island ferry)
Zil Elwannyen Sesel 38
Paykan (missile boat)
Iran 2355
Peacock, U.S.S. (sloop)
Marshall Islands 187
Pegasus, H.M.S. (frigate)
Antigua 275
Barbuda 108
Peiho (expedition steamer)
Palau 58
Peleliu, U.S.S. (helicopter carrier)
Palau **MS**391
Pelican, H.M.S. (frigate)
Antigua 330
Barbuda 118
St. Lucia 435
Pelican, H.M.S. (sloop)
Ascension 151
Pemba (freighter)
Mozambique 919
Pen-Ar-Roz (fishing boat)
Guernsey 304
Penelope, H.M.S. (armoured corvette)
Ascension 422
Penelope, H.M.S. (frigate)
Ascension 130 538
Penguin H.M.S. (sloop)
Tristan da Cunha 506
Peninsular (packet steamer)
Great Britain 954
Pennsylvania, U.S.S. (battleship)
Gambia 1341
Uganda 574
Penola (Rymill)
Australian Antarctic Territory 38
British Antarctic Territory 78a 139
Falkland Islands Dependencies G30 G42
Penzance, H.M.S. (sloop)
Ascension 168
Percy Douglas (full-rigged ship)
Jersey 582
Pereire (steamer)
Central African Republic 1013
Pericles (warship)
Greece 1169
Perkun (ice-breaker)
Poland 2032
Perla (submarine)
Greece 652
Pernambuco (destroyer)
Brazil 1281
Perseverance (brig)
St. Helena 241
Peru (paddle-steamer)
Chile 572/3
Peru 803/4 1668 1750/1
Peruvian, H.M.S. (sloop)
Ascension 195
Pervaz Bati (steam warship)
Russia 6091
Peter von Danzig (sailing ship, 1472)
Danzig 280
Peter von Danzig (yacht, 1936)
Danzig 276
Petimata ot RMS (freighter)
Bulgaria 2936
Petite Amie (cruising yacht)
Grenada 1089
Petite Hermine (Cartier)
British Virgin Islands 796
Canada 195
France 521/2
Petit Raymond (schooner)
Guernsey (Alderney) A33
Phantom (brig)
Kiribati 296
Pheasant, H.M.S. (sloop)
Ascension 414
Philadelphia, U.S.S. (sail frigate)
Libya 1713 1874 1983
Philip Lang (emigrant ship)
New Zealand 692
Philomel, H.M.S. (brig)
Falkland Islands 513
Philomel, H.M.N.Z.S. (cruiser)
New Zealand 1379
Philosopher (full-rigged merchantman)
Barbados 752
St. Kitts 46
PHM 1 (patrol boat)
Palau 465
Phoebe (screw steamer)
St. Helena 242

Phoenix, H.M.S. (frigate, 1776)
Jersey 162
Togo 1119
Phoenix (paddle-steamer)
United States of America 2390
Phoenix, H.M.S. (sloop, 1850)
Ascension 149
Piave (freighter)
Ivory Coast 303
Pickering (brig)
British Indian Ocean Territory 116
Picua (submarine)
Venezuela 2438
Pie X (river vessel)
Central African Republic 180
Piemonte (steam warship)
Italy 1019
Pierre Loti (packet steamer)
Mauritius 501
Pigot (sailing ship)
Christmas Island 40
Pilot (sail troopship)
Ciskei 82
Piloto Pardo (Antarctic supply ship)
Chile 1288
Pilsudski (liner)
Poland 315
Polish Post in Danzig R30
Pingouin (gunboat)
Djibouti 103 111
Pinta (Columbus)
Andorra F459/60
Anguilla 160 162/3 902 904/5
Argentine 1867
Ascension 576
Bahamas **MS**874 909 933
Bolivia 1142 1244 1251
Brazil 2528
British Virgin Islands 819
Burkina Faso 856 1035
Burundi 1535/6
Caicos Islands 21 56
Cape Verde Islands 696
Chile 1215 1409/10
Colombia 857
Comoro Islands 654
Congo (Brazzaville) 1227
Cook Islands 1302/3
Cuba 2857 3052 3383 3565 3664 3720
3748 3773/4
Cyprus 819/20
Cyprus (Turkish Cypriot Posts) **MS**334
Djibouti 978
Dominica **MS**1128
Dominican Republic **MS**1546
Ecuador 2119
El Salvador 2121
Equatorial Guinea 149
Falkland Islands 645
French Southern & Antarctic Territories 293
Gabon 1130
Gambia 1415
Germany (Federal Republic) 2456
Gibraltar 671
Grenada 1617
Grenadines of Grenada **MS**1374
Grenadines of St. Vincent 827 829 870/1
899
Guatemala 1325
Guinea 1217 1242
Ireland 844/5
Israel 1168
Italy 2120 2152 **MS**2158 2171 2174
Jamaica 752 774 802
Korea (North Korea) N2755
Laos 852
Lesotho 781/2 784
Malta 919
Mauritania 709 861
Mexico **MS**2077
Monaco 2082
Montserrat 875 911/12
Nevis 381 679
New Caledonia 941
New Zealand 1662
Nicaragua 2409 2791 2904
Niger 1214
Niuafo'ou **MS**164
Niue 732
Panama 1539/40
Papua New Guinea 663 665
Penrhyn Island 478
Peru 793 795
Rumania **MS**5438 5468
St. Helena 605
St. Kitts 359/60
St. Lucia 1075/6
St. Vincent 1126 1308 1642
San Marino 1402 1417/18
Senegal 1115
Sierra Leone 1078 1933
Spain 601 603 605 **MS**3147 3175/6
Sri Lanka 1219
Tanzania 719
Tokelau 195

Tristan da Cunha 524
Turks and Caicos Islands **MS**916
1169/70 **MS**1176
Uganda 1114
United States of America 2657 **MS**2661
Vietnam 1372
Wallis and Futuna Islands 598
Pinto (car ferry)
Malta 812
Pinto da Fonseca (state barge)
Mozambique 575
Pioneer (schooner)
Netherlands Antilles 487
Pionyr (trawler)
Czechoslovakia 2970
Piorun (destroyer)
Poland 2010 3357
Pitcairn (missionary schooner)
Norfolk Island 86
Pitcairn Islands 158 293
Piyale Pasha (tug)
Cyprus (Turkish Cypriot Posts) 228
Pizarro (Humboldt)
Rumania **MS**4792
Planet (auxiliary schooner)
Marshall Islands 188
Platte, U.S.S. (attack transport)
Tuvalu 581
Plomien (fire boat)
Poland 3198
Pobeda (ship of the line)
Bulgaria 3377
Pogoria (cadet ship)
Poland 3091
Point Law (oil tanker)
Guernsey (Alderney) A36
Pokoj (freighter)
Poland 964
Polarbjorn (Antarctic supply ship)
French Southern & Antarctic Territories 213
Polarfisk (deep-sea trawler)
Faroe Islands 26
Polonez (yacht)
Poland 2308
Poltava (ship of the line)
Mongolia 1373
Russia 4018
Polynesia (cruise schooner)
Nevis 54 471
St. Kitts 172
Polys (tanker)
Cyprus 621
Pomerania (ferry)
Poland 3044
Pomeroon (river vessel)
Guyana 130
Pommern (barque)
Aland Islands 16
Falkland Islands 573
Finland 624
Pongdaesan (container ship)
Korea (North Korea) N2438
Ponghwasan (refrigerated freighter)
Korea (North Korea) N1041
Port au Prince (full-rigged ship)
Tonga 802 905/6
Port Brisbane (refrigerated freighter)
New Zealand 759
Porthos (hydrofoil)
Malagasy Republic 109
Portland (brig)
Australia 1140
Portsmouth (royal yacht)
Montserrat 512 582 O55
Potemkin (battleship)
Mali 290
Russia 576 4119 5563
Pourquoi-pas? (Charcot)
British Antarctic Territory 74
Falkland Island Dependencies G36
French Southern & Antarctic Territories 24
94 214/15
Laos 679
Powhattan (paddle-steamer)
Japan 777
Powis (river vessel)
Guyana 1129
Prabparapak (missile craft)
Thailand 1004
Praha Liben (dredger)
Czechoslovakia 1136
Precontinent III (underwater research craft)
Monaco 865
President (brig)
Great Britain 902
President, H.M.S. (drill ship)
San Marino 1145
President Coolidge (liner)
Vanuatu 434/5
Presidente Allende (ore carrier)
Cuba 2323
Presidente Peron (liner)
Argentine 829
Presidente Sarmiento (cadet ship)
Argentine 670 795 1404

II. By Ship Type

Entries are arranged under the following headings:

Ancient Craft
Cable Ships
Cadet Sailing Ships
Canoes—Indigenous Types
Cargo and Cargo/Passenger Vessels
Catamarans and Trimarans
Coastguard, Customs and Police Patrol Boats
Dredgers
Exploration, Survey and Research Vessels
Ferries
Figureheads
Fishing Boats—Commercial
Fishing Boats—Indigenous
Fishing Boats—Sport
General Shipping Scenes
Hospital and Missionary Ships
Hovercraft and Hydrofoils
Ice-breakers
Lifeboats and Shipwrecks
Lightships and Weather Ships
Liners and Passenger Ships
Local Craft
Merchant Sail and Sail/Steam Ships

Naval Battles
Naval Crests
Oil Rigs and Support Craft
Paddle-steamers
Pirate Ships and Privateers
Polar Vessels
River, Lake and Inland Waterway Craft
Royal or State Yachts and Ceremonial
  Barges
Schooners and Small Commercial Sailing
  Vessels
Ship and Boat Building
Ships' Boats and Longboats
Speedboats, Motorboats and Launches
Tankers
Tugs
Warships—Modern
  A. Aircraft Carriers
  B. Battleships
  C. Cruisers
  D. Destroyers, Frigates and Corvettes
  E. Exploration and Survey Ships
  F. Gunboats and Patrol Craft
  G. Submarines
  H. Support and Miscellaneous Vessels
Warships—Sail and Sail/Steam
Whaling Ships
Yachts and Sailboards

ANCIENT CRAFT
Aden 71/2
Aegean Islands 18 27 57 169
  170 193 215 225
Afghanistan 1137/43 **MS**1144
Aitutaki 647 649
Albania 969 2424/6
Algeria 371 807/8
Antigua 1503/10
Argentine 1719 1724
Bahamas 845
Barbuda 1285/92
Belarus 3
Belgium 1589/92
Benin 968
Bhutan 918 920
Brazil 2290 230
Bulgaria 1828 2435/40 2864/9
  MS3151
Canada 1209
Ceylon 438
China (Taiwan) 512/3
Colombia 422/5 1697
Comoro Islands 194
Congo 633
Croatia 151 169
Cuba 422/4 478 1978 1980 **MS**3119
Cyprus 286 586 706/9 826
Cyrenaica 103 105
Dahomey 204
Danzig 44/53
Denmark 277b 277d 278a 278b 279
  279ab 280a 281 282 282b 319a 320
  321 520 618 P252/4 P303/7
Dominican Republic 89 90 125/30
  443 447 1273 1543
Egypt 138/43 771 1226 1309 1518 1852
Egyptian Occupation of Palestine 142
Estonia 11/14
Faroe Islands 206 224
Fernando Poo 211 213
Fezzan 4 7 8
Finland 280
Fiume 75/8 110/12 123 182/5 194/7
  201/3 213/15 225/7 D183/5 D188/90
France 738 1428 1499 1772 2248 2532
  2834
French Morocco 224/7 232 237 260 297
Gambia 441/4
Germany (West Berlin) B527
Germany (Democratic Republic) E1105
Ghana 182/3 476/8
Greece 723 741 781/3 958 1393 1445/6
  1646
Guernsey 254 585/6
Guinea-Bissau **MS**775 951 1052/8
Hungary 1683 **MS**2983 3305/7
Iceland 159 161 239 258 O175 O177
Indonesia 1389
Ireland 837
Iran 1053
Isle of Man 33/4 52 127 158 313 315
Israel 143
Italy 513 723
Japan 316 1277/8 1406/7 1682
Jersey 277/8 423
Kampuchea 734/40
Korea (South Korea) 92 256 433/4 782
Korea (North Korea) N1407 N1907
  N2312/13 N2315
Lebanon 355/7 938 1115 1226 1284 D192
Libya 30 54/5 59 1303/8
Maldive Islands 269
Malta 33 59 60 337 887
Monaco 1599 1600 1692 1898

Mongolia 755 1367/70
Mozambique 513 549 550/7 559 600
Netherlands 1271
Norway 327 333 501 502
Palau 208
Poland 247 251 1067 1192 1194 1105
  1370/7 1478 1451/5 2304 2848 2890
Portugal 578/93 1919
Portuguese India 504/18 542/54 D549/51
Qatar 222
Rumania 3689
Russia 973 975 3194 4328
St. Vincent 1189
San Marino 243/6 690/3 695/6
Sharjah 115
Sierra Leone 964 1441
Somalia 342
Spain 997 1002 1234/44 1660/1 1663/5
  1876 **MS**3172
Sweden 347/56 735 1496 1500/1
Switzerland 428
Togo 588 591
Tunisia 41/3 57/9 66/8 97/9 111/13 148
  150/1 1108
Turkey 1409 1506 1507
Turks and Caicos Islands 557
Uganda 765
United States of America 625
Upper Volta 299
Vatican City 575/8
Venda 242
Vietnam 984/90 1403/10
Yugoslavia 665 2539/42
Zil Elwannyen Sesel 125

CABLE SHIPS
Ascension 249 250 252 475
Barbados 441
Bermuda 208 211 568 619 621 623
British Virgin Islands 217 219 615/23
Canada 1244
Cocos (Keeling) Islands 29 129/31
Cyprus 449
Djibouti **MS**905
Fiji 335 618
France 1475
Ghana 1050 1304
Gibraltar 205a
Great Britain 1368
Guinea-Bissau 482
Ireland 457
Isle of Man 381/2
Ivory Coast 899
Jamaica 320
Japan 1165 1437
Korea (South Korea) 1459
Korea (North Korea) N1496
Liberia 1280
Malagasy Republic 360
Maldive Islands 647
Monaco 828
Nauru 161 163
Nigeria 326
Norfolk Island 88 314/16
Penrhyn Island 295 297/8
Philippines 1437 1472
Portugal 1399 1400
Qatar 356
Rwanda 816
Senegal 301
Sharjah 166 170
Sierra Leone 829 967
Singapore 535/8
Thailand 1147 1153
Togo 1126
Turkey 3116
Turks and Caicos Islands 781 924
Zil Elwannyen Sesel 186

CADET SAILING SHIPS
Ajman 140
Aland Islands 54
Anguilla 145/6 690/95
Antigua 911
Argentine 670 795 1211 1224 1404
Ascension 574/5
Australia 1333
Barbuda 791
Bermuda 361/5 532
Bhutan 678 681
Brazil 847 1423 1995/6
British Virgin Islands 275/6
Canada 1119
Chile 697 752 756 760 1158 1246
Cocos (Keeling) Islands 58 61
Colombia 1723
Danish West Indies 57/9
Denmark 621
Dominica 1303
Falkland Islands 643/4
Finland 795
France 2100 2149
Germany (Federal Republic) 2444
Gibraltar 207
Greece 1053

Grenada 1094 O10
Guernsey (Alderney) A12
Ireland 526
Isle of Man 541/2 549
Italy 312 1728
Japan 1006 1423 1569 1618 1846
Jersey 238 243 363
Korea (North Korea) N2318/19 N2334
  MS2404 N2661/4 N2666 N2728
Liberia 1659
Manama 5
Mauritius 770
Mexico 1253
Montserrat 391 394
Mozambique 568
Nevis 444 447/8
Niue **MS**648
Norway 879
Oman 324
Peru 847/9
Poland 527 621 763 1466 2030 2307
  2685/90 3000 3089 3091
Portugal 1873
Rumania 1205 1344 1992 2770 4045
Russia 5167/72
St. Helena 603/4
Solomon Islands 561
Spain 1673
Sweden 692
Tokelau 155
Tristan da Cunha 460 522/3
Turkey 2454
Uganda 530/3
Uruguay 279/81 1807 1940
Venezuela 2440
Yemen People's Democratic Republic
  MS307
Yugoslavia 406

CANOES (INDIGENOUS TYPES)
Aitutaki 632/41
Aland Islands 49
Angola 998 1001
Antigua 269 427
Bahamas 873 935
Bangladesh 200 362 446
Barbuda 116 217
Belgian Congo 27 50 64 74 82 89 91 103
  112 193 319/20
Benin 727 753 806 D721
Botswana 432 717 720
Brazil 1594 **MS**1858 2044 2063 2499 2540
British Honduras 157
British Indian Ocean Territory 7 32/3
British Virgin Islands 240
Brunei 337
Cameroun 402 601 620 644 679 704
Canada 477 491 724 1232 1287 1315/18
  1380 1431 1433 1445 O45
Central African Empire 491 464 581
Central African Republic 395 432
Ceylon 426 459
Chad 222 410 578/9 594/5 D77/9
Cocos (Keeling) Islands 114 121 126
Colombia 1708
Comoro Islands 42 44 91/3 419 476/7
Congo (Brazzaville) 463 467 469 552/3 662
  966 1131 1215 D23
Congo (Kinshasa) 460/3 507/10
Cook Islands 108 145 155 437 439/43 1311
  1315
Cuba 3456
Czechoslovakia 1584
Dahomey 133/8 144 162 172 183 280 341
  396 499 547 D308
Dominica 164 168 170 216 220 222 655
  828 1221
Dominican Republic 1781
Ecuador 1044/5b 1047/a
El Salvador 1308 1799
Equatorial Guinea 72/3
Ethiopia 373a/4 394 420 499 809 811 1186
Fernando Poo 234 236 264 266
Fiji 85 87 89 101 249 252 257 382 402 419
  427 545/8 697
French Equatorial Africa 248/50 274
French Guiana 126/43 230/2
French Polynesia 16 38 43 56 59 72 81 182
  227/30 298 349 392 471 490/1 528 533
  549 578 611 621 623 649 654
French Sudan 162/75 215/16
French West Africa 36 74
Gabon 377 521 863 948
Gambia 174 180 285/6 494 501 506 1042
  1044 1046 1189 1286/7
Gilbert and Ellice Islands 45/6 49 53 66 69
  73 75 172 174 177 184 192 197 218
  227/30 232 259
Gilbert Islands 4 13 20 48 63
Grenada 1081 O6
Grenadines of Grenada **MS**872 943
Grenadines of St. Vincent 211 598
Guinea 205 **MS**862
Guinea-Bissau 701 1240/3
Hungary 2937

Italian Colonies (general issue) 75
Italian East Africa 44 47
Ivory Coast 43/93 297 317 397
Jamaica 802 804
Japanese Occupation of North Borneo
  J11 J30
Japanese Occupation of Philippines
  J13/14 J21/2 J27/8 J36 J43/4 JO47
Jordan 798
Kiribati 101 194 201 378 391
Laos 1/3 176 202 315 475 478 **MS**667 1099
Lesotho **MS**1098
Liberia 259 408/9 413 422/3 427 833
  1240 1284 1431 1504 O271 O314
  O436/7 O441 O450/1 O455 R503
Madagascar 336
Malagasy Republic 42 105 205 272 336 802
Malawi 219 682
Mali 125 127/8 130 262
Marshall Islands 33 80 179 183 235
Mauritania 478
Mexico 1853
Micronesia 19 79 198 200 210 253/4
Montserrat 1026
Mozambique 1017 1026
Mozambique Company 299 310
Nauru 52 133/6 239 326
Nepal 251
Netherlands New Guinea 51 53
New Caledonia 312/18 345 357 475
  610 630 638 807/8 D102/9 D137/8
Newfoundland 231
New Hebrides 52/63 68/71 183 203 250
  271 D6/13 F53/76 F81/4 F198 F217
  F264 F285 FD65/69 FD77/81 FD92/94
New Zealand 325 370 1541 1566
Nicaragua 2017
Niger 37/54 98a/b 140 281 593 765
  897 899 903 999
Nigeria 38 45
Niuafo'ou 26 53 86 88 143/5
Niue 47 64 97 115 127 155 205
  238/9 256 267
Norfolk Island 403
North Borneo 365 381
Norway 1160
Nyasaland 144 151 173a 181 203
Oceanic Settlements 83/90 147/60
  169/76 186/8 192/4 199 200 202
Pakistan 383
Palau 73/6 82 94 103/4 143 213/7 **MS**236
Papua 5/6 8/12 14a 25 38 40/4 46 51a
  52 54/66 68 80 83/91 93/111 114
  118/20 122/3 125/8 135 137 140
  163/8 O55/66
Papua New Guinea 10 17 170 204 245 249
  251 255/6 263 277/80 311 418 420 575
Penrhyn Island 166/70 186/90 303
  337/40 466/71 O18/21
Peru 681 687
Philippines 946 1054 1135 1167 1193 1850
Pitcairn Islands 64
Rhodesia and Nyasaland 23
Ruanda-Urundi 5 12 19 27 34a 61
Russia 6055 6365
Rwanda 856 948 1225
Ryukyu Islands 221
St. Lucia 1077
St. Pierre et Miquelon 649
St. Thomas and Prince Islands 475/9
St. Vincent 1317 **MS**1506
Samoa 182 184 224 347 **MS**364 466/7
  MS571 779 811 840/1
Senegal 139/51 219 221/2 224 241 306/9
  418 424 625 627 652/3 838 890 1068
Seychelles 137 137b 140 140a 143 146
  146a 149 161 163 166 177 179 182
  183a 191 203 239 247 316 485 582
Sierra Leone 174/5 217 751 960 963 1777
Singapore 559
Solomon Islands 1/17 62/5 71 82/7 167
  192/3 204 208 218 239 371 384 450
  510/11 547/8 550 617 619 679
Somalia 244/54
South West Africa 467
Spain 1884
Spanish Guinea 209/20 329 331 333/5
  337/9 341/3 345/6
Spanish Sahara 118
Sudan 131 O75
Surinam 314 317 416 510 553 711
Sweden 746 864
Tanzania 247 739 799 800
Thailand 901
Timor 369
Togo 940 1000/1 1008/9 1107 1444
  1579 1671 2018
Tokelau 31 49 65/8 75/6 85/91 163
  165 167 171/5
Tonga 104 111 126 193 198/9 216
  222 230 239 259 267 359 364 449/53
  817/19 831/3 907 **MS**971 1061 1078/81
  1150/2 **MS**1196
Turks and Caicos Islands 769 950
Tuvalu 3 5 41 51 74 133 222 660/2

Surinam 617/9
Sweden 273 275 517 521 539 592 1513/14 1628
Togo 1119 1242 1700
Trinidad and Tobago 558 755
Tripolitania T32
Tristan da Cunha 75 75a 93/6 108 121 139 153 156 351 353 397 405 505/8
Turkey 1410 3086
Turks and Caicos Islands 369 397 401 446/8 774/5 844/6 902 923
United States of America 786/8 948 1007 1018
Upper Volta 417
Yugoslavia 2543/4

WHALING SHIPS
Australia 359 402
Australian Antarctic Territory 41
British Antarctic Territory 95
Equatorial Guinea 72
Falkland Islands 129 485
Falkland Islands Dependencies G29
Fernando Poo 234 236
French Polynesia 652
Iceland **MS**736
Kiribati 259 298 343 346
Korea (North Korea) N506 N638 N1225 N1327
Marshall Islands 107/10
Micronesia 179/83
Netherlands 845
Newfoundland 219 232 266
New Zealand 752 1508
Norfolk Island 87 172 356/63 385
Norway 391
Penrhyn Island 290 292
Pitcairn Islands 28 320
Russia 2897
Samoa 540/3 561/4
South Georgia 6 9 26 59 185
Tonga 116 164/7 171 196 271/2 277 O11
Tristan da Cunha 74 138 157 325 357 437 455 483 514
Tuvalu 164
United States of America 1444 2330

YACHTS & SAILBOARDS
Aitutaki 191 196
Ajman 32 35 49
Albania 848
Angola 705 950 958
Anguilla 32/3 517 883 890/6
Antigua 218 283 345/6 430/1 504 524 576/8 **MS**580 715 832 944 1011 1072/5 **MS**1076 1190/3 **MS**1194 **MS**1524 1605 1611
Argentine 1116 1226 1649 2075 2134
Aruba 87
Australia 833/6 1036 1046/9 1174 1334 1365/6
Austria 777 932 1687

Bahamas 188 211 238 245 248 254 264 274 279 296 301 316 319 322 335 385 480 499 806/7 **MS**943
Bahrain 95
Barbados 429 866 907
Barbuda 30 95 119 220/1 403/5 **MS**407 723 840 920 936/9 **MS**940 1066/70 **MS**1333
Belgium 2082 2650 2689 **MS**2690 2938
Belize 985/8 1115
Bermuda 98 101 106 138 183 220/3 461/4 481 640
Bhutan **MS**929
Brazil 1587 1761/4 2471
British Honduras 343
British Indian Ocean Territory 114
British Virgin Islands 191 208 237 289 533/6 543/7 592 680 684 686 702/6 757 **MS**760
Bulgaria 1298 2018/19 2282/7 2410 2655
Canada 1314
Cayman Islands 176 208 410/11 600 673
Central African Republic 784 949 1092
Chad 251 **MS**577
Chile 476
China (People's Republic) 3279
Christmas Island 77 171/2 174 215
Cocos (Keeling) Islands 159
Colombia 1290
Comoro Islands 510/13 **MS**514 694/5 729/30
Congo 908/11 974/7 1180/1 1183
Cook Islands 277
Cuba 954 1028e 1340 2262 3542 3586 3645/6 3738 3741
Cyprus 180 195 655 685
Cyprus (Turkish Cypriot Posts) 50
Czechoslovakia 1318 1409
Danzig 276
Denmark 534 760
Djibouti 854 874 884 969
Dominica 329/30 581 1052/6 1090 1381
Dominican Republic 756 772 1545 1617 1649 1777
Eritrea E31
Fiji 412 629 770 852
Finland 787 1117 1302
France 1543 1685 1818 1855 2139 2984 3080 3112 3116
French Polynesia 218 635
French Southern & Antarctic Territories 287
French Territory of the Afars and the Issas 552
Gabon 517 691 838
Gambia **MS**533 **MS**606 700/3 **MS**704 777 1358 1424
Germany FB2 FB5 FB9 FB15 FB18 FB30/1
Germany (Federal Republic) 1622 1996 2177 2502
Germany (West Berlin) B512
Germany (Democratic Republic) E275 E482
Ghana 756 769 993
Gibraltar 149 487 642 673
Great Britain 510 751 980/2 1289 1425 1439
Greece 849 852 1101 1621 1863
Grenada 317a 522 552/4 565/7 **MS**572 603 649/50 666 714 **MS**744 **MS**776 **MS**874

880 1052 **MS**1059 1089 1344 1358 1404/5 1611/12 1614 **MS**1615 1811 2140 2366 **MS**2379 O5
Grenadines of Grenada 111/12 128 157 160 **MS**162 **MS**198 249 374 484 581 657 668 805 859/62 **MS**863 1038 **MS**1298 **MS**1473 **MS**1484
Grenadines of St. Vincent 32 69 74 91/2 101/3 107 145/8 172 176 188 243 386 467 547/52 **MS**553 555 557 **MS**558 812 881 916 1116
Guernsey 230 268 295 297 309 313 524/8
Guernsey (Alderney) A5
Guinea 1152 **MS**1387
Guinea-Bissau 845 **MS**850 1013
Haiti 1383
Honduras 1052
Hong Kong 577
Hungary 993 1287 1590 1598 1757 1923 2367 3532 3849
Iceland 730
India 1065 1227 1500/1
Indonesia 981 1121 1201 1211 1796
Ireland 527 732 835
Isle of Man 528/9 549
Israel 451/3 1161
Italy 1133/5
Ivory Coast 721/3 **MS**725 944/7 **MS**948
Jamaica 198 476 586
Japan 552 935
Jersey 15 42 144 147 150 239 337/9 377 405/8 473 475 487 522 606 D38 D44 D46
Jordan 624 1458
Kiribati 267
Korea (South Korea) 1826
Korea (North Korea) N667/70 N1863 N3175/9
Kuwait 91
Laos 1234
Lebanon 1060/1
Lesotho 999
Liberia 1001 1062 **MS**1073 1273 1701 R499
Libya 1353 1432/4 1552
Luxembourg 876
Macao 782
Malaysia 434
Maldive Islands 270 620 1049 1115/6 1245/8
Mali 271 752 792 947/9 956 **MS**1003 **MS**1050
Malta 494 496 560 710 910 913
Mauritania 722 810/13 **MS**814
Mauritius 429 707 768
Mexico 1165
Monaco 182/3 189 221 225 258 260 268 270 351 374 394 465 787 1298 **MS**1749 1763 1824 **MS**1888 2025
Montenegro 15 19
Montserrat 190 414 710
Morocco 90
Morocco Agencies 100 287
Mozambique 620/2 634/5 639 996
Netherlands 366 683 831
Netherlands Antilles 661 805
Nevis 458

New Caledonia 348 425 483 485 492 802/3 868
New Zealand 708/9 930a 950 1417/20 1522 1524 1527 1557 1655/8 1706
Nicaragua 997 1129 1137 **MS**2440
Niger 624
Niue 370/1
Norfolk Island 451
Norway 511 1091
Oceanic Settlements 215
Pakistan 619/20 750
Palau 357
Panama 878
Papua New Guinea 156 488
Peru 1755
Philippines 1836 **MS**1839 2093
Poland 762 1080 1566/73 **MS**1573a 1686/7 1898 1904 2305/6 2308 3055 3092 3278
Portugal 1480 1875 **MS**2118 2256
Qatar 227 532 599
Rhodesia 445
Rumania 1991 2774 2922 2924 2930 2932
Russia 1497 1845 3577 4311 4820/4 5859
Rwanda 495 743 1203
St. Kitts 283
St. Lucia 284 452 634 1073/4
St. Pierre et Miquelon 617
St. Thomas and Prince Islands 437
St. Vincent 455 654 1032/6 1862
Samoa 328
San Marino 490 518
Senegal 583 978 1069
Seychelles 476 599 611 622 683/5
Sierra Leone 1011/17 **MS**1018 1092 1728 1828
Solomon Islands 570a **MS**575
South Africa 481 547
Spain 1946 2973 3145
Swaziland 373
Sweden 803 1003 1046 1121 1151 1443 1486 1630
Tanzania 865 887
Thailand 1494
Togo 1147 1176 1382
Tonga 51 68 857/60 991 1109 **MS**1129 1131 1215
Trieste B58
Trinidad and Tobago 454/5 586 607 658
Tripolitania T33
Tunisia 1206
Turkey 2244
Turks and Caicos Islands 630/1 738 926
Tuvalu 538
United Arab Emirates 381 407
United Nations 619
United States of America 1210 2339
Upper Volta 389 675/8
Uruguay 1231/2 2040
Vanuatu 428 **MS**501
Venezuela 2039 2672
Vietnam 338
Wallis and Futuna Islands 419 537
Yugoslavia 669 952 1224 1512 2225/8 2307/8 **MS**2309

IMPORTANT MESSAGE TO THEMATIC STAMP COLLECTORS!

You know how important it is to have the very latest Stanley Gibbons Thematic Catalogues with their listings of all new issues, up to date information on earlier stamps and of course prices accurately set by experts with their finger on the pulse of the current international stamp market.

If you would like us to notify you of the next edition all you have to do is complete the form below and post it to:

**The Advance Information Service,
Stanley Gibbons Publications Ltd.,
5 Parkside, Christchurch Road,
Ringwood, Hampshire BH24 3SH.**

For similar information on other SG thematic catalogues please indicate title of interest on the form.

ADVANCE INFORMATION WITHOUT OBLIGATION

To: The Advance Information Service,
    Stanley Gibbons Publications
    5 Parkside, Christchurch Road,
    Ringwood, Hampshire BH24 3SH.

Please notify me of publication dates of new editions

of ....

Name: ....

Address: ....

....

....